# The Roots of Morality

# The Roots of MORALITY

*Maxine Sheets-Johnstone*

THE PENNSYLVANIA STATE UNIVERSITY PRESS
UNIVERSITY PARK, PENNSYLVANIA

Library of Congress Cataloging-in-Publication Data

Sheets-Johnstone, Maxine.
 The roots of morality / Maxine Sheets-Johnstone.
    p. cm.
 Includes bibliographical references and index.
 ISBN 978-0-271-03393-8 (pbk : alk. paper)
 1. Ethics, Evolutionary.
 I. Title.

BJ1311.S44  2008
171'.2—dc22
2008020798

Copyright © 2008 The Pennsylvania State University
All rights reserved
Printed in the United States of America
Published by The Pennsylvania State University Press,
University Park, PA 16802–1003

The Pennsylvania State University Press is a member of the Association of American University Presses.

It is the policy of The Pennsylvania State University Press to use acid-free paper. This book is printed on Natures Natural, containing 50% post-consumer waste, and meets the minimum requirements of American National Standard for Information Sciences—Permanence of Paper for Printed Library Material, ANSI Z39.48–1992.

*To Albertini*
*for his abiding love and wisdom*

# Contents

Prologue
Human Nature and Human Morality:
The Challenge of Grounding the Moral Sense                         1

I.    Introduction                                                   1
II.   The Foundations Laid by Hume in His Moral
      Philosophy                                                     3
III.  On the Origin of Sympathy and Selfishness: An Initial
      Determination                                                  6
IV.  Unevenly Valorized Binary Oppositions: A Question of
      Life and Death                                                 8
V.    Hume's Affective Polarity Revisited                           13
VI.  The Culture/Nature Opposition                                 15
      From the Perspective of Mythology and
      Religion                                                      16
      From the Perspective of Patriarchal Symbolism                 19
      From the Perspective of Practices in Present-
      Day Western Science                                           21
      From the Perspective of the Cultural Practice of
      War                                                           22
VII.  Conclusion                                                    28
Notes                                                              30

## PART I

CHAPTER 1   Size, Power, and Death: Constituents in
the Making of Human Morality                                       35

I.    Introduction                                                  35
II.   Size and Power                                                36
III.  Cultural Translations of Biological Facts                       40
IV.  Cultural Transformations and Evolutionary Ethics                 42
V.    Immortality Ideologies                                        46
VI.  Implications                                                    53
Notes                                                              55

CHAPTER 2  Death and Immortality Ideologies in
            Western Philosophy                          63
  I.   Introduction                                      63
  II.  Descartes                                         65
         On the Purpose of the *Meditations* as Specified
           in the Synopsis                               65
         Mind as Immaterial Substance                    66
         Mind and the Question of Time                   68
  III. Heidegger and Immortality Ideologies              70
  IV.  Psychological Underpinnings of Immortality
         Ideologies                                      73
  V.   Derrida's Immortality Reading of Husserl and
         Derrida's Own Immortality Ideology              78
  VI.  The Double: A Further Sign of Derrida's Immortality
         Ideology                                        81
  VII. The Last Word and the Ultimate Mortal Question    86
  Notes                                                  88

CHAPTER 3  *Real* Male-Male Competition                  93
  I.   Introduction                                      93
  II.  On Natural and Sexual Selection                   95
  III. Darwin's Seminal Insights into Male-Male
         Competition and Their Total Neglect in Current
         Research                                        97
  IV.  Exemplifications                                 102
  V.   Evolutionary Considerations                      105
  VI.  A Methodological Imperative and A Closing Apologue 109
  VII. An Afterword                                     109
  Notes                                                 123

CHAPTER 4  On the Pan-Cultural Origins of Evil         127
  I.    Introduction                                    127
  II.   The Banality of Evil                            129
  III.  Affective Elaborations of the Banality of Evil  133
  IV.   Toward Pan-Cultural Understandings of the Banality
          of Evil                                       137
  V.    Beginning Evolutionary Considerations           139
  VI.   Clarifications Along Motivational Lines         143
  VII.  Killing, Death, Fear: Elementary Facts of Human Life 146
  VIII. Warriors and the Heroic Honing of Males         151
  IX.   A Finer Analysis of Motivation                  157
  X.    Broader Socio-Political Understandings of the Heroic

|  | Honing of Males: A Return to Evolutionary Considerations | 161 |
|---|---|---|
| XI. | Classic Studies: An Afterword on History and Science | 173 |
| Notes | | 185 |

## PART II

### CHAPTER 5   Empathy — 193

| I. | Introduction | 193 |
|---|---|---|
| II. | Early Clues and Husserl's Archival Texts | 194 |
| III. | Affect Attunement and the Qualitative Nature of Movement | 200 |
| IV. | Emotions and Movement | 203 |
| V. | Spontaneity | 208 |
| VI. | The Kinetic Foundations of "Knowing Other Minds" | 212 |
| VII. | Responsivity | 215 |
| VIII. | Deepened Understanding of Empathy | 225 |
| IX. | A Postscript on Origins, History, and Methodology | 228 |
| Notes | | 234 |

### CHAPTER 6   Child's Play: A Multidisciplinary Perspective — 241

| I. | Introduction | 242 |
|---|---|---|
| II. | Rough and Tumble Play | 243 |
| III. | Locomotor-Rotational Play | 249 |
| IV. | Play and Laughter | 253 |
| V. | Morality and Child's Play | 256 |
| Notes | | 260 |

### CHAPTER 7   On the Nature of Trust — 265

| I. | Introduction | 265 |
|---|---|---|
| II. | Learning to Trust: Uncovering Affective and Existential Realities | 266 |
| III. | A Critical Examination of Luhmann's Thesis of a "Readiness to Trust" | 272 |
| IV. | Affective Experience, Human Freedom, and Uncertainty: Deepened Understandings of Trust | 275 |
| Notes | | 281 |

### CHAPTER 8   The Rationality of Caring: Forging a Genuine Evolutionary Ethics — 285

| I. | Introduction | 286 |
|---|---|---|
| II. | Transfers of Sense: The Ground of Caring | 288 |

|      |                                                                                                                              |     |
| ---- | ---------------------------------------------------------------------------------------------------------------------------- | --- |
| III. | Comsigns: The Evolutionary Basis of Intercorporeal Life                                                                      | 295 |
| IV.  | The Rationality of Caring: Laying the Groundwork                                                                             | 300 |
| V.   | The Living Import of the "Metaphysically Significant": The Experience of Interconnectedness                                  | 310 |
| VI.  | The Living Import of the Metaphysically Significant: Interconnectedness, the Principle of Not Harming, and "Difference Removed" | 324 |
| VII. | A Closer Look at the First Moral Principle and the Challenge of Human Existence                                              | 330 |
|      | Notes                                                                                                                        | 336 |

Epilogue
Re-Naturing the De-Natured Species:
An Interdisciplinary Perspective                                                                                                  341

|       |                                                      |     |
| ----- | ---------------------------------------------------- | --- |
| I.    | Introduction                                         | 341 |
| II.   | Endangered Species                                   | 343 |
| III.  | Ontogeny and Natural Signs                           | 349 |
| IV.   | Aggressive Complexities in the Socialization of Fear | 367 |
| V.    | Acquisitive Complexities in the Socialization of Fear| 379 |
| VI.   | On Psychological Ignorance                           | 385 |
| VII.  | A Moral Education                                    | 393 |
| VIII. | Concluding Thought                                   | 406 |
|       | Notes                                                | 409 |

|                |     |
| -------------- | --- |
| References     | 412 |
| Index of Names | 436 |
| Index of Terms | 442 |

# Prologue

## Human Nature and Human Morality:
## The Challenge of Grounding the Moral Sense

> The "man without a shadow" is statistically the commonest human type, one who imagines he actually *is* only what he cares to know about himself. Unfortunately neither the so-called religious man nor the man of scientific pretensions forms any exception to this rule.... [V]ast numbers of people ... apply their scientific scrupulosity only to external objects, never to their own psychic condition. Yet the psychic facts are as much in need of objective scrutiny and acknowledgment.
> —CARL G. JUNG, *On the Nature of the Psyche*

> We have to keep finding out what it means to be human.
> —GLEN A. LOVE, *Practical Ecocriticism*

I. INTRODUCTION

This book elucidates an understanding of morality grounded in the nature of human nature. Its guiding thesis is that a bona fide ethics rests on bona fide understandings of what it is to be human, and in consequence, on bona fide explorations of human experience, of the phylogenetic and ontogenetic heritages of humans, of the human psyche, and of elemental facets of human existence. In carrying out these explorations, it articulates a morality that emanates from within rather than from without. That is, it proceeds not from a consideration of rules, duties, rights, moral judgments, moral status, moral agency, current ethical issues in Western society and in the world at large, and so on, but from an examination of fundamental realities of human nature. It thereby articulates understandings of human morality grounded in pan-cultural aspects of human existence—war, trust, and the concept of death, for example. In a word, it articulates a foundationalist morality, each successive chapter offering an in-depth analysis of an essential element of the whole. Chapters in Part I offer an in-depth analysis of what is classically considered the dark side of human nature; those in Part II offer in-depth analyses of what is classically considered the positive side. Given a nature basically conflicted by opposing dispositions, an interdisciplinary therapeutic is called for. It is set forth in the form of a moral education and justified in detail in the Epilogue.

An ethics formulated on the foundation of anything other than human nature, hence on anything other than an identification of pan-cultural human realities, lacks solid empirical moorings. It easily loses itself in isolated hypotheticals, reductionist scenarios, or theoretical abstractions—in the prisoner's dilemma, selfish genes, dedicated brain modules, evolutionary altruism, or psychological egoism, for example—or it easily becomes itself an ethical system over and above the ethics it formulates. In the latter instance, specifying how we ought to conceive ethics and how we ought to behave in light of that conception ties us to a particular theoretical system of thought and to a correlative set of prescriptions to guide our actions. For example, it prescribes an ethics conceived as a system of duties requiring us to behave according to "categorical imperatives"; or an ethics conceived as a compilation of rules requiring us to behave in ways that secure equal justice for all; or an ethics conceived on the basis of utility, which requires us to conduct ourselves in ways that produce happiness for the greatest number of individuals; or an ethics conceived on the basis of care, which requires us to behave in ways that show a solicitous concern for the welfare of others.

Hume, Rousseau, and Hobbes—and to some extent, Bentham and Mill—are notable in dissenting from this theoretical-prescriptive approach to morality. Each philosopher spelled out an understanding of morality rooted in what he saw as the nature of human nature. Hume saw humans as naturally sympathetic toward one another but at the same time powerfully driven by a self-interest mitigated to a degree by a *"limited generosity"* (Hume [1739] 1888, 586); Rousseau saw humans as naturally—in a "state of nature"—compassionate toward one another, joined together in a basic positive mutual accord that is negatively transformed by culture; Hobbes saw humans as aggressively self-interested and destructive of one another, and thus needing the rule of law to keep them civil. Each of these views is strongly empirical in the sense that, whether acknowledged as such or not, it is based on evidence from both personal and social experience. Were each view cast in phenomenological perspective, it would be seen as offering a *profile* of human nature, i.e., just as an object offers multiple possible profiles to a phenomenological observer, so also does human nature. The views are thus not speculative, but neither are they radically empirical; they are rooted neither in a rigorous phenomenological methodology or phenomenologically informed psychology, nor in an evolutionarily and developmentally resonant pan-human perspective. The challenge, in effect, is to discover the nature of the human condition on the basis of which just such profiles emerge—or in other words, the challenge is to discover the roots of human morality.

## II. THE FOUNDATIONS LAID BY HUME IN HIS MORAL PHILOSOPHY

What is distinctive about Hume's analysis of "moral subjects" is his attempt to ground "the moral sense" in human nature and his discovery that that nature harbors dichotomous tendencies. As indicated above, Hume finds that humans are naturally both sympathetically attuned to each other and acquisitive. While "kind affection" ([1739] 1888, e.g., 482) toward others is not universal—"there is no such passion in human minds, as the love of mankind, merely as such, independent of personal qualities, of services, or of relation to ourself" (481)—sympathetic feelings nonetheless link us with others, notably with our family and friends, but also with strangers with whose plights we sympathize. On the other hand, our *"natural temper"* (486) also disposes us toward a selfish possessiveness that is "insatiable, perpetual, universal, and directly destructive of society" (492).

Though Hume clearly minimizes the selfish nature of humans in comparison with sympathy—"it is rare to meet with one ... in whom all the kind affections, taken together, do not over-balance all the selfish" (487)—his basic insight into the opposing tendencies of human nature stands. The basic insight, however, commonly goes unnoticed, his moral philosophy being customarily discussed in terms of its emphasis on sentiment over reason and its arguments against there being any universal principles determining the rightness or wrongness of an action. The oversight results in a less than full appreciation of his moral philosophy. From a methodological viewpoint, it has the effect of skipping over his keen empirical insights into human nature and his quasi-biological concerns with origins. However skipped over, his conception of humans as *by nature* conflicted by two opposing sentiments is of considerable interest; his conception of the origin of human society as a solution to the deficits of that nature is equally so. That his treatise is *A Treatise of*

*Human Nature* shows that he considers human nature to be part of the natural world. It is thus not surprising but provocative and even edifying that he begins his inquiry into the origin of justice and property with the observation, "Of all the animals, with which this globe is peopled, there is none towards whom nature seems, at first sight, to have exercis'd more cruelty than towards man, in the numberless wants and necessities, with which she has loaded him, and in the slender means, which she affords to the relieving these necessities" (484). His subsequent comparison of the way in which necessities and abilities are conjunctive in other animals rather than disjunctive as in humans, and his observation, "'Tis by society alone he [man] is able to supply his defects, and raise himself up to an equality with his fellow-creatures" (485) is moreover compelling and equally provocative. Further still, his identification of three specific "inconveniences"—the force of a single individual, the ability of a single individual, and the relationship of an individual's force and ability to his sense of security—warrants serious attention. In particular, when Hume writes, "By society all his [man's] infirmities are compensated" and "'Tis by [the] additional *force, ability,* and *security* [that society provides through common labor] . . . that society becomes advantageous" (485), he is identifying the elemental motivations of humans to come together to form societies and specifying the fundamental positive value of society. He is, in effect, elucidating both the fundamental nature of human nature and the social consequences of that nature.

Hume's subsequent observations concerning selfishness take on added significance precisely in view of the dangers posed by society. "[O]ur *outward circumstances*," Hume writes—i.e., *our membership in society itself*—put us at risk: "such possessions as we have acquir'd by our industry and good fortune" become "expos'd to the violence of others" (487). His point is that our naturally opposing sentiments—our inherent "contrariety of passions"—would by itself pose little problem. It is only in virtue of living in a far larger setting, among others who are neither family members nor friends, that humans are at risk. The risk traces back to both the basically deficient nature of humans and to their "limited generosity," i.e., their natural possessiveness and cupidity. Though Hume does not put the matter in these terms, it is clear that when he writes of the *instability* of possessions—what one has may be taken by others—and of *scarcity*—there is an insufficient quantity of goods for all—he is affirming that human desire outruns itself: humans continually want *more*. "[T]he love of gain," he says, is insatiable (492). Not only this but "the larger our possessions are, the more ability we have of gratifying all our appetites" (492). Hence the pursuit of *more* is self-propelling. The theme of *more* is indeed of quintessential significance in human morality. We will find it surfacing again in the following section and in a later section as well as in chapters of Part I, and will examine it in existential detail in a section of the Epilogue.

Hume's analysis of human nature is consistently rich in insights and correlatively rich in its methodological rationale. As the subtitle of his *Treatise* specifies, his attempt is to provide an analysis of "moral subjects" on the basis of "a cautious observation of human life," which means collecting and comparing observations, and regarding them as "experimental" evidence (xxiii). The aim of his analysis is to provide a "solid foundation" for the science of man, one grounded in "experience and observation," and in turn a "solid foundation" for all other sciences (xx). Given his aim and methodological program, it is hardly surprising that his *Treatise* has a quasi-phenomenological tone: its dual aims coincide with Husserl's later phenomenological ones. Not only this, but if feelings of sympathy and selfishness are indeed part of our *natural temper*, then it should be possible to specify the natural conditions of their possibility, the natural ground on which they arise—what in evolutionary and developmental as well as phenomenological terms would be described as their origin. Hume's experiential-observational findings concerning human nature might thus be taken as clues to the phenomenology of feelings underlying human morality—or perhaps better, the fundamental moral tension underlying human social behavior. The clues would open a phenomenological path leading to an elucidation of the distinctive origins of sympathy and selfishness. Being of the nature of human nature, the identified origins would be natural, and being natural, would be pan-cultural. To follow through on the clues would mean to ask two questions: what experiences are the generative source of sympathy? what experiences are the generative source of possessiveness and cupidity? In light of his central concern with human nature, his recognition of human nature as the starting point for understanding human morality, and his subsequent insights into the nature of human morality, the clues Hume offers are particularly compelling. The possibility of grounding his findings in a more detailed phenomenology of human morality is inviting. Accordingly, we will turn to the two questions and in an initial way lay out the terrain to be covered in this book.

## III. ON THE ORIGIN OF SYMPATHY AND SELFISHNESS: AN INITIAL DETERMINATION

Human existence begins with birth and ends with death. These thoroughly individual events anchor incontrovertible realities of every human life. However differently treated, attended, explained, managed, valued, mythologized, or memorialized in any given society, birth and death are pan-cultural events. Oddly enough in view of their pan-cultural nature, they are events to which each human has a peculiar relationship. Though birth is individually experienced and may be remembered by others, it is not remembered by the birthed individual; though dying may be individually experienced and death may be remembered by others, neither dying nor death are remembered by the dead individual. There are, in effect, no first-person experiences to be consulted with regard to either birth or death. What as adults one knows of either is a matter of what one learns in the course of living. This fact poses a problem for phenomenology since there is no direct, first-person evidential ground to which to return.[1] The problem may be initially circumvented by a reliance on studies of human nature, and in particular, studies that highlight fundamental human affective dispositions. Hume's study, being what might be called a composite rather than one-sided picture of human nature, is obviously of moment in this respect. In contrast to the strongly positive picture of human nature painted by Rousseau and the strongly negative one painted by Hobbes, Hume suggests that "kind affection" and "possessiveness" exist along an affective gradient; that is, sympathy and selfishness are polar affective opposites that in broad moral terms define the two fundamental ways in which humans actively relate to one another. Put in the context of birth and death, the import of these natural affective dispositions is magnified. To sketch out the expanded significance in a beginning way, let us first briefly consider what we have learned from others and thus know second-hand of birth and death, then broaden that knowledge by putting it in preliminary evolutionary and ontogenetical perspectives, and in turn suggest how it may be deepened phenomenologically by probing along elusive experiential borders to reach the roots of human morality.

It is commonplace to remark that human infants are helpless, and that they are so for a relatively long period of time. Unlike many mammals—rodents, ungulates, cetacea, for example—human infants do not begin life by crawling or walking, or if in water, by swimming about on their own. Moreover unlike other primate infants, they do not cling to the fur on their mothers' ventral side, hanging on by themselves while their mothers move about. They are, in effect, neither capable of getting around on their own nor capable of supporting their own weight. Being capable of neither, human infants are quite incapable of sustaining themselves by themselves. They must be cared for and nurtured by others; they are totally dependent creatures. Thus, all humans, not only those living today but those living across past millennia, are and were alive because at birth they were cared for and nurtured—however minimally, however sufferably. That they live or lived is indisputable testimony to the ministerings of others. Hume would likely judge feelings of *sympathy* (based on resemblance and contiguity, as we shall presently see) to undergird and to have undergirded the ministerings. Darwin would likely agree with Hume in basic ways (though differentiating sharply between feelings of sympathy and of love [Darwin [1871] 1981, 1:81]).[2] Indeed, concordances in the writings of the two men indicate that Darwin read Hume closely, as is apparent in his discussion of sympathy as a constituent of "the moral sense," for example, where he in fact cites Hume (1:85; see also Sheets-Johnstone 1996, 122). Moreover observations of Hume are prescient of those of Darwin: for example, "A man naturally loves his children better than his nephews, his nephews better than his cousins, his cousins better than strangers, where every thing else is equal" (Hume 1739, 483–84). Psychiatrist Daniel Stern would likely judge *affect attunement* to undergird and to have undergirded the caring and ministerings in that affect attunement is a more fundamental relational form of affectivity than sympathy (Stern 1985). The focal emphasis nevertheless remains on a feeling accord between infant and parent. A detailed, phenomenologically anchored analysis would specify *empathy*, and spell out its provenience in ontogenetical relationships such as those described by Stern. In the process, it would show how empathy, being fundamentally a social transfer of sense, translates naturally into a basic moral character; that is, how it is first and foremost generated from, and anchored in social affective bodily experiences, how it is carried over and exemplified in the phenomenon of child's play, and how it is sustained by trust. This phenomenologically anchored analysis in fact constitutes chapters in Part II.

Humans, like all living creatures, are helpless in an altogether different sense in the face of death. They are helpless not in the sense of lacking self-sufficiency among others, but helpless in the sense of lacking existential autonomy over their own lives. They are helpless to change their fate, helpless *not* to leave the world, helpless to outstrip their own mortality. The reality of death is in fact a uniquely human reality (see Sheets-Johnstone 1990, chap. 8). Noticing a lapse in the physiognomic animateness of another and feelings of loss are certainly documented aspects of nonhuman animal life, as are also feelings of grief (e.g., Goodall 1971), but the concept of death is non-existent in nonhuman animal worlds. Humans alone know that they lead a punctuated existence, that their life, like the lives of all creatures, is on the line. They know that once their time has come, i.e., once death is imminent, there will be no more time: there is no generosity on the side of death. From a Humean perspective, whatever security they might amass in the form of possessions or find in the form of fame (see Hume [1789] 1888, 316–24), it cannot protect them from death. All the same, the security *more* buys is or can be soothing, even lulling—whether a matter of possessions, fame, political power, economic killings, territory, or even children. *More* is a palliative to the no-moreness of death, a temporal fortress of sorts. Cupidity thus becomes a cultivated human affection by which one's own inevitable no-moreness is psychically tempered. Living amidst plenty diminishes thoughts—and fears—of death. How it does so, how size and power are constituents in the making of human morality, how immortality ideologies are constructed to preserve one beyond the nothingness of death, how male-male competition is a culturally elaborated built-in of human morality, especially as played out politically and economically, and how self-interest and self-aggrandizements are tied to knowledge and fear of death, are each basic themes of Part I.

## IV. UNEVENLY VALORIZED BINARY OPPOSITIONS: A QUESTION OF LIFE AND DEATH

The originating relationship sketched above between sympathy/selfishness and birth/death can be put in pan-cultural human perspective. It can indeed be validated by a detailed examination of a fundamental form of human thinking, namely, thinking along the lines of binary oppositions, *unevenly valorized* binary oppositions. In that examination, the replacement of the opposition *birth and death* by the opposition *life and death* is neither inadvertent nor arbitrary. The latter opposition is the more common binary mode by which adults conceive death, most probably because thoughts of death propel adults toward thoughts of life, not thoughts of birth—at least in Western society. Birth, after all, is something far back in the past, while death, being not yet but ominously personalized in its hoverings at the fringe of existence, is something antithetical not to a distant past event but to one's own present life.

No polarity is as starkly powerful and as unevenly valorized as the polarity life/death. The polarity is unmentioned in typical Western listings of binary oppositions such as, sacred/profane, tame/wild, even/odd, mind/body, right/left, light/dark, male/female, reason/emotion (e.g., Hertz 1973; Needham 1973, 1987; see also Allen 1991 for the Pythagorean Table of Opposites). That it goes unmentioned is puzzling, all the more so given that the distinction between the animate and the inanimate is a primary distinction made by young infants (Spitz 1983).[3] Though one might speculate as to why it goes unmentioned—perhaps it is too broad an opposition or too simple an opposition—a strongly empirical explanatory thesis readily suggests itself. To begin with, the polarity is more properly characterized as concealed rather than unmentioned, concealed precisely because it is so powerful; the difference between life and death is a foundational and ultimate difference in comparison with which all other polarities pale. Reckoning with death in the course of life through conceptually tempered, unevenly valorized oppositions is, accordingly, far easier than reckoning with death itself. Such indirect reckoning is in line with psychiatrist Otto Rank's observation that humans need illusions in order to live and with cultural anthropologist Ernest Becker's elaboration of Rank's observation (Rank 1936; Becker 1973; see also this text, Chapters 1 and 2). Unevenly valorized binary oppositions articulated by cultures allow life to emerge and be experienced as consistently victorious over death—exactly as with the sacred over the profane, the even over the odd, the (heroic and strong) male over the (timid and weak) female, the right over the left, and so on. The challenge is thus to bring the concealed to light, showing how the polarity is in actuality the conceptual spawning ground and driving force of fundamental unevenly valorized binary oppositions. Prior to meeting that challenge, it will be instructive to consider an exemplary constructionist text that denies the validity of any natural categories, that thus straightforwardly rejects the notion that binary oppositions are rooted in nature, and in effect, that would reject the notion of a foundational human polarity. In short, the notion of a foundational polarity—

and with it, pan-cultural binary oppositions—would be readily disputed by social constructionist and postmodernist thinkers. This being so, an example of their reasoning needs to be set forth and critically examined.

In his critical inquiry into binary oppositions, well-known Oxford social anthropologist Rodney Needham questions the origin of binary oppositions, wondering in particular whether they are reflections of actual physical facts or whether they are products of the human mind. What is at stake is precisely the *naturalness* of binary oppositions: are they naturally generated by worldly phenomena or the result of a mental disposition?[4] Classical philosopher G. E. R. Lloyd and philosopher/anthropologist Robert Hertz both single out light/dark, male/female, and right/left as fundamental natural oppositions (Lloyd 1966; Hertz 1973). What Needham tries to show is the waywardness of their judgment and the judgment of others like them: nature is invented by humans in their interpretation of the world. In his book *Counterpoints*, Needham attempts to validate this claim by analyzing each of the three fundamental so-called 'natural' oppositions in turn, showing that each is a social construction. A brief summary of his three arguments follows.

Needham correlates the opposition light/dark with the opposition day/night, and proceeds to show that the opposition is an abstraction rather than a fact of experience. He does this by appeal to a photometer and to an imaginary photometric measurement of daylight over a period of several days. The measurement, he states, would show that there is no decisive moment separating day from night; hence, the opposition light and dark is an abstraction. He opens his investigation of the binary opposition male/female by acknowledging a genetic distinction, but says that "from a cultural point of view we can ignore chromosomes" (Needham 1987, 210). He proceeds to replace the opposition male/female with the opposition man/woman. On this basis, he affirms that man/woman are "cultural ideals," not natural "physical realit[ies]" (210), and that the opposition male/female is hence an arbitrary division. He cites as evidence the fact that there is "an immense array of physical types," and that in consequence, a classification in terms of visible genitalia is impossible. He cites as examples quail and hyena, whose genitalia are not easily distinguishable as male and female, and points out that shamans can take on "all the signs of femininity," and that a Nuer woman can "acquire the status of a man" (211). In his investigation of right/left, Needham argues that the idea of hands, sides, or directions as naturally opposed right/left pairings is mistaken. The putative right/left pairing is either language-dependent, a "cultural partition" (214) rather than a fact of experience, or it is contingent on "cultural definitions" (216) rather than being a natural phenomenon. More specifically, he finds that hands must first be named in order to form a pair, that the distinction between sides is "a cultural partition of what is physically an entity with a continuous surface" (214), and that since "on neither side is there a straight base line to which the lateral direction would be at right angles," there is no natural right/left direction (216).

Needham's arguments and the examples he adduces in support of his claim are instructive. His appeal to measuring devices, language, natural and cultural exceptions, mathematics, and the like, betrays experience. In fact, it ignores not only a deep and rigorous examination of bodily experiences but fails to acknowledge evolutionary matters of fact. What results are thoroughly exteriorized, objectified understandings of the oppositions in question, understandings that, at certain points, show themselves to be conceptually parasitic on the very opposition they are attempting to discredit. When one turns attention instead to actual experience, one finds what may readily be called *natural* oppositions: one finds eyes that open and shut, and thus light and dark; one finds distinctive visible differences not only between penises and vaginas, but between rams and ewes, roosters and hens, lions and lionesses, and so on, and thus males and females, distinctive individual animals who are not only differentially capable of generating new life, but who, together, are the sole progenitors of future generations of the same species, and who themselves are living testimony to past generations of the same species; one finds a laterally anchored gait in walking with its laterally anchored arm swings and foot impacts, and thus right and left virtually throughout the moving body, to say nothing of the predominant opposed binariness evident in the very structure of a human body: two nostrils, two breasts, two knees, two arms, and so on, one on the right and one on the left. Needham's claim aside, one finds further a body that moves in binarily coordinated ways, not only in walking, jumping, and the like, but in threading, hammering, and so on, acts in which one hand holds while the other hand moves.[5] In brief, one finds binary oppositions embedded in bodily experiences.

Fundamental human concepts are modelled on bodily experience: not only light and dark, male and female, right and left, but concepts such as inside and outside, up and down, front and back, movement and stillness, life and death.⁶ The body is a semantic template: human thinking follows in fundamental ways the experiential lines of the body (Sheets-Johnstone 1990). The relationship should not be surprising. As with other animals in the animal kingdom, how humans move and think is quintessentially tied to the animate form they are. Fundamental binary oppositions—like fundamental analogies such as that between stone tools and teeth—are natural products of thinking along the experiential lines of the body. They have their source in human nature, in the cultural universal that is the human body. Indeed, they are pan-cultural phenomena because the human body is a pan-cultural phenomenon—*the* cultural universal *par excellence*.

In sum, Needham may well find that binary oppositions are products of the human mind, but being products of the human mind does not thereby make them social constructions. On the contrary, products of the human mind are in the most fundamental sense pan-cultural products of pan-cultural human bodies (Sheets-Johnstone 1990). However elaborated theologically, philosophically, literarily, psychologically, or anthropologically, the foundational reality of the opposition life/death is hardly a social construction.

While it might appear one thing to trace fundamental binary oppositions back to their source in nature and quite another to show the provenience of unevenly valorized binary oppositions, the latter endeavor follows naturally enough from the former. When one asks how unevenly valorized binary oppositions come to arise pan-culturally, and in consequence, when one begins to examine the nature of their positive and negative "functional tones" (to borrow a descriptive term from von Uexküll 1957), one is readily led to an appreciation of the underlying psychology of the valorizations and of the powerful import of the concept of death. Light is valued over dark, male over female, right over left, mind over body, reason over emotion, sacred over profane, and so on: all follow the hierarchical valuation paradigmatic of the classic polarity: life/death. Connotations solidify the connection beyond the fact that one member of the dyad is consistently conceived to be the more advantageous, admirable, favored, or estimable member. That member connotatively symbolizes something good, propitious, truthful, sound, or genuine.⁷ The lesser or negative member, in contrast, has an ominous character: left symbolizes something sinister; dark symbolizes something funereal or grim; female symbolizes something unknown and foreboding; body symbolizes something vulnerable; emotion symbolizes something irrational and uncontrollable; profane symbolizes something worldly and vulgar, hence raw and uncultivated. In effect, fundamental pan-cultural binary oppositions not only structurally mirror the *Ur* polarity life/death; they give muted voice to the fear of death. In indirectly acknowledging the classical human polarity life/death, the unevenly valorized pairings at the same time give muffled voice to the dreaded reality of death.

V. HUME'S AFFECTIVE POLARITY REVISITED

The foregoing examination of unevenly valorized binary oppositions may be conceptually coupled with the earlier discussion of Hume's bivalent description of human nature. In theory, sympathy is the superior value. In social practice, however, it is not infrequently the lesser one, as business dealings, career manoeuverings, highway behaviors, and so on, indicate. Yet a striking exception is evident *with respect to one's infancy and early childhood,* at least to the degree that one was fed, bathed, clothed, housed, carried about, and so on: one was cared for and nurtured by others. However minimal the sympathy and however less than consistently comforting its expression, as noted earlier, one prospered through the efforts of others; one progressively grew and reached the age at which one could get about on one's own and care for oneself. Though Hume does not speak at any length of infancy and early childhood in his *Treatise,* what he finds basic to sympathy applies equally, and in notable ways, to the affective accord underlying early nurturing treatment of infants by parents:

> [N]ature has preserv'd a great resemblance among all human creatures. . . . However the parts may differ in shape or size, their structure and composition are in general the same. There is a very remarkable resemblance, which preserves itself amidst all their variety; and this resemblance must very much contribute to make us enter into the sentiments of others, and embrace them with facility and pleasure. . . . The stronger the relation is betwixt ourselves and any object, the more easily does the imagination make the transition [from ourselves to other].
> (Hume [1739] 1888, 318)

Insofar as what is close to us touches us, and in a figurative as well as literal sense, Hume names contiguity as well as resemblance a condition of sympathy, contiguity not only in the sense of family, but of acquaintances, neighbors, fellow citizens, "those of the same trade, profession, and even name [as ours]" (352). Indeed, "to feel . . . sympathy in its full perfection," he affirms, "we must be assisted by the relations of resemblance and contiguity" (320; see also 351–57). The affective accord generating infant care is clearly motivated by both conditions. The presence of both conditions in fact helps to explain not only the naturalness of human care-giving behavior but the naturalness of care-giving behavior among all who nurture their young, i.e., mammals generally, and many species of birds.

In a broader sense, however, sympathy is tied to culture as well as nature since whatever the culture, it is dependent on basically like-minded as well as resemblant and contiguously related people. It is furthermore dependent on cooperative as against selfish people whose self-interest exceeds that of a concern for the culture at large. As Hume points out when he speaks of the "inconveniences" posed by one's limitations to provide totally for oneself with comfort and security, individuals depend on others in their culture in myriad ways. He later opines, however, that "each person loves himself better than any other single person" (487). Thus, as we have seen, a "contrariety of passions" may arise. "Sentiments must touch the heart, to make them controul our passions" (586), Hume writes, and of course, selfish feelings can "touch the heart" as well as sympathetic ones, in turn, controlling or dispelling any disposition one might have toward the latter feelings. Moreover selfish feelings too can eventuate in acts that promote life—specifically, one's own life—by providing not only material abundance but axiological and ideological security. From this perspective, being exposed to the violence of others extends to more than just the taking of possessions, wealth, land, and the like. It extends to *the taking of life itself*, and this because insofar as the beliefs and values of another are foreign to one's own, they threaten the validity of one's own. Hence, to exterminate the other is to exterminate beliefs and values that call the very meaning of one's life into question. Axiological and ideational resemblance and contiguity thus become as significant as physical resemblance and contiguity. As sympathy is tied in this broader sense to resemblance and contiguity, so selfishness is tied in this broader sense to what is not resemblant and contiguous but at variance, alien, and thereby threatening, a theme we will examine in detail in the immediate chapters that follow. The point here is that sympathy and selfishness play out both culturally and interculturally. Given the human condition of dependence on others and the tight social cohesion facilitated by like-minded people, culture is necessarily a constituent of human morality, in fact a fundamental moral domain and variable in itself. It warrants attention, specifically in its customary opposition to nature.

VI. THE CULTURE/NATURE OPPOSITION

When Hobbes writes that life is "solitary, poor, nasty, brutish, and short" (Hobbes [1651] 1930, 253), he is in essence describing how an individual is at the mercy of both others and death, and in turn how society must provide laws to curb the natural disposition of others to harm, to kill, and to impoverish. In just such terms, he recognizes a nature/culture opposition. When Rousseau writes that man is naturally compassionate, he is describing, in contrast, how an individual is by nature a socially affable creature, and in turn how natural affability is corrupted by society. He too recognizes a nature/culture opposition, but one in which nature is beneficent and culture is pernicious.

The unevenly valorized foundational polarity of life and death affords an altogether different perspective on the opposition, and this because, being foundational, the polarity is not an aspect of the opposition but axiologically and ideationally undergirds it, in part precisely along the lines implicit in Hobbes's characterization of human life as "solitary" and "short." In particular, the prominencing of culture is a prominencing of what lasts, or what is thought and felt to last, and what lasts, or is thought and felt to last, has power and enduring meaning. We experience the power and enduring meaning of culture regularly in the fact that buildings outlive flowers; coastal sands shift and change while great art and great sages endure beyond their age. Culture is stable and known, a secure stronghold against Nature, which in great measure is unpredictable and volatile, causing devastation and famine, suffering and havoc. The opposition culture/nature is from this vantage point of a piece with other pan-cultural binary oppositions with their hidden ties to life and death. In fact, that the opposition 'nature/culture' was not mentioned in earlier discussions might be considered odd. The opposition itself, however, is what is odd. Cultures specify and elaborate binary oppositions as conceptually distinct polarities at the same time that they implicitly identify themselves as the entitled member of a polarity. In a word, culture privileges and sanctifies itself from within with respect to nature. As with other pan-cultural binary oppositions in which connotations of the greater member point toward something esteemed and those of the lesser member toward something dangerous or untoward, so also with culture/nature. Associated with unpredictability and destruction, nature is readily and regularly positioned alongside dark, wild, body, female, left, profane, and so on, and similarly linked with death.

Yet one might well wonder: what could be more appropriate than a linkage of nature with harbingers, reminders, or forebodings of death since death is the very handiwork of Nature? Indeed, while it is said that the Lord giveth and taketh away, it is Nature that everywhere giveth and taketh away, conclusively and absolutely, with no promise of *more*. On these grounds, it is reasonable to conclude that, while *natural oppositions* abound—life/death, light/dark, male/female, right/left, animate/inanimate, up/down, and so on—*unevenly valorized oppositions* originate with Culture in its recognition of the death-giving power of Nature. Death authorizes cultures to perform miracles that take the sting of nothingness away, along with the impotency of humans to escape the sting, let alone control or predict it. The conclusion is in essence a restatement—arrived at from a different perspective—of Rank's thesis that humans need illusions in order to live. Unevenly valorized binary oppositions preserve illusions by concealing the spectre of death and muffling the thought of nothingness. In one way and another, they support immortality ideologies.

The relationship of the progenitive culture/nature opposition to illusions is significant and can be more precisely elucidated from a variety of vantage points: it can be considered from the perspective of mythology and religion, of patriarchal symbolism, of practices within present-day Western science, and of the centuries-old cultural practice of war. Consideration of each perspective will provide substantive evidence of the diverse ways in which cultures promote and sustain illusions in the form of life-over-death ideologies and in so doing, provide the thematic backbone of the chapters of Part I that follow.

## From the Perspective of Mythology and Religion

Anthropologist Edmund Leach states not only that "Binary oppositions are intrinsic to the process of human thought" (Leach 1967, 3), but that

"Religion everywhere is preoccupied with . . . life and death . . . and seeks to deny the binary link between the two words" (3). Religion does this, he says, "by creating the mystical idea of 'another world,' a land of the dead where life is perpetual" (3). In his analysis of the binary structure of the Bible as myth, he observes that some events and narratives are redundant—man is created not once but twice, for example, and there are four gospels telling the same story (1–2). He states that redundancy is the source of uncertainty, hence the source of multiple meanings, and that the possibility of multiple meanings "explains what is surely the most striking of all religious phenomena—the passionate adherence to sectarian belief" by which "members of each particular Christian sect are able to convince themselves that they alone possess the secret of revealed truth" (3).

Leach clearly links religion with mythology, yet however tenuous and blurred the dividing line between them, mythologies and religions are differently oriented. Mythologies tend to be more attentive to life; religions, as Leach himself and other anthropologists attest, are more attentive to death. This difference is implicitly affirmed in an observation of cultural anthropologist Bronislaw Malinowski, whose field-based sociopsychological interpretations of cultural practices, however contested by more purely sociological-minded researchers, are both well respected and well known. Malinowski observed that "Of all sources of religion, the supreme and final crisis of life—death—is of the greatest importance" (Malinowski 1948, 29).[8] One cannot say the same of mythologies; they are not so focused. They are, on the whole, earlier human creations that explain the world in terms of gods who run both the cosmos and the natural world of humans, and that recount the adventures and challenges of heroes who grapple with the vicissitudes of human life and who are exemplars of how humans should act. As psychologist Jordan Peterson demonstrates in his penetrating analysis of the meaning of myths, myths show humans how to navigate in everyday life between the safe territory of the known and the unsafe territory of the unknown (Peterson 1999). Religions are later creations that also explain the world, but they are less tethered to symbolizing the challenges of human life than they are to setting forth behavioral rules and ritual practices to be observed in the glorification of a single God or Savior, or of a pantheon of Gods symbolizing various aspects of a single divinity, and to specifying what humans must do to win redemption, namely, honor the divine and have faith or belief in the redeeming power of the divine. Resurrection, eternal life, or reincarnation is the reward.[9]

Given a stronger concern with the life-world, it is not surprising that, in contrast with religions, mythologies are often intimately bound to nature. Indigenous myths, for example, are regularly anchored to nature—to rain and its presence or absence, to the sea and its power to afford a safe or unsafe crossing, to harvests and the degree of their bounty, to the phenomenon of pregnancy and childbirth, and so on. Neither is it surprising that rituals enacted in conjunction with mythological beliefs are temporally sensitive observances[10]—the planting of crops, the advent of a hunt, the passage from one stage of life to another, as in puberty, menstruation, and marriage. Characteristically, such mythologies are temporally bound to the natural facts of life of a people rather than to a projected life they will have in a hereafter. If one lives one's life well within the mythological framework of the culture's traditions, the afterworld will take care of itself. Mythologies are furthermore intimately bound with nature in a second sense. In their recountings of the interactions of gods, they commonly recognize a fluid boundary between gods and animals, the former readily transforming themselves into the latter.[11] Moreover such mythologies pattern the behavior of gods after the behavior of humans: the gods engage in love-chase affairs (Graves 1960, e.g., 1:207); they are sold into slavery (2:162); they quarrel, marry, do battle, and end their feud by coming to an agreement (1:237–38); and so on. In short, nature—the natural world, animal nature, and human nature—figures centrally in mythologies. One might say that natural phenomena are their point of departure; death is certainly included, but not centrally as with religion.

Religions closely related to nature might be interpreted as having mythological ties. Hinduism, for example, recognizes all forms of life—hence nature—as sacred. Stories in which gods transform themselves into animals, the veneration of the cow as sacred Mother (Neumann 1963, e.g., 47, 128), and so on, are testimony to the ways in which such religions may be seen as permeated with mythological elements. The major Western religions of Christianity, Judaism, and Islam, in contrast, categorically distance themselves from nature. On the one hand, their basic lack of interest in such elemental human concerns as the planting and care of crops, and more generally, in the diversity and complexity of flora and fauna of the natural world, suggests that nature is of comparatively small consequence: what matters is "man," his faith in and obedience to God, and his salvation or afterlife. On the other hand, their strong affirmation that nature can and should be transcended leaves no doubt as to the standing of nature. One does not *have* to accept the inevitable; one can be resurrected and have life everlasting by affirming one's faith in God and following the path He has laid out. In effect, one surmounts nature. Faith is thus to these religions as nature is to mythologies. A faith-based religious cosmology, in turn, is substantively unlike a natural cosmology: a natural cosmology—like Nature itself—does not promise *more*.

## From the Perspective of Patriarchal Symbolism

Patriarchal symbolism promises more by what might be called priapic totemism: the phallus is a never-ending sign of life (for more on the cultural exaltation of the phallus, see Sheets-Johnstone 1994b). As Jungian analyst and former Episcopalian minister Eugene Monick writes, "[B]idden or unbidden, phallos makes males feel alive" (Monick 1987, 83–84). Sociologist George Bataille's fancifully erotic linkage of sexuality and death echoes Monick's more sober and insightful analysis.[12] Consumed by thoughts of the aftermath of sex, and linking it with death, Bataille asks, "How can I fully *live* the 'little death' if not as a foretaste of the final death?" (Bataille 1989, 20). Freud's essay on fire and water testifies to Bataille's anxiety, but like Monick's reflections, from a more sober and insightful perspective. Being a classic if unwitting account of how unevenly valorized binary oppositions have their origin in human experience, that is, in the realities of human nature, Freud's essay in fact warrants extended attention. (See Sheets-Johnstone 1994b and 2000 for both more detailed expositions of the origin of unevenly valorized binary oppositions and more detailed examinations of Freud's essay.)

In "The Acquisition of Power over Fire," Freud points out that a man cannot urinate if he is on fire, that is, if he is in the heat of desire, and conversely, he cannot be on fire if he is urinating. Freud likens this natural opposition to the myth of Prometheus, in which Prometheus hides the fire he has stolen in a hollow rod—a fennel stalk. If we interpret the myth as a dream, Freud says, then the rod signifies the penis, and what "man harbours in his penis-tube . . . is the means of extinguishing fire" (Freud 1957, 289). The question is why the stealing of fire would be considered a crime. Freud answers by saying that "primitive man could not but regard fire as something analogous to the passion of love. . . .

The warmth radiated by fire evokes the same kind of glow as accompanies the state of sexual excitation, and the form and motion of the flame suggest the phallus in action" (291). He furthermore calls attention to the symbolic similarity between fire and passion in terms of "daily consumption and renewal," that is, of how "the appetite of love" is gratified daily . . . [and] daily renewed." In this context, he recalls the phoenix, which, "as often as it is consumed by fire, emerges again rejuvenated," stating that "probably the earliest significance of the phoenix was that of the revivified penis after its state of flaccidity" (291–92). He concludes that "[t]he male sexual organ has two functions, whose association is to many a man a source of annoyance" (293). There can be no doubt but that the distinction Freud is at pains to describe is a *natural opposition:* there is nothing cultural about the fact that a man cannot urinate and copulate at the same time. But there is something unequivocally cultural about acquiring power over fire, for to have *power* over fire—to have absolute control over "the flame of love"—is to have the power of *the phallus,* which is equivalent to perpetual erection, a thoroughly unnatural state of affairs. Indeed, power over "the flame of love" means leaving the natural everyday body behind. In effect, the natural opposition that Freud initially describes and that has its roots in the natural reality of male bodies is superseded by an unevenly valorized binary opposition having its roots in a culture-spawned symbol that turns what is by nature impermanent into a totem of eternal power.

Male transcendence over nature is virtually a pan-cultural artifact.[13] Anthropologist Clifford Geertz seems to affirm the reality of this claim enthusiastically when, after averring, "Our ideas, our values, our acts, even our emotions are, like our nervous system itself, cultural products—products manufactured, indeed, out of tendencies, capacities, and dispositions with which we were born, but manufactured nonetheless" (Geertz 1973, 50), he goes on to state, "It is no different with men: they, too, every last one of them, are cultural artifacts" (51). What happens to females in this nature-transcending cultural production hardly needs specification: females menstruate, they give birth to young, and they nurse them. They are natural entities through and through, one might say, permeated and indelibly scripted by Nature. Moreover, they have dark genitalic insides, which links them with the unknown, hence with danger. Since they are hard put to enshrine themselves as cultural artifacts apart from being objectified—or from objectifying themselves—as sex objects, they have no power comparable to the phallus, and even as sex objects, they have lesser status precisely because they are real. As sex objects, they are the embodiment of raw nature; they are not symbolic, i.e., of refined culture (see Sheets-Johnstone 1994b for a critical discussion of the Lacanian distinction between the real and the symbolic). Along with Nature herself, they too are transcended by the eternal power of the phallus.

*From the Perspective of Practices in Present-Day Western Science*

Since the time of Francis Bacon—the "father of modern science"—scientific efforts have consistently aimed at transcending Nature, not by cultural productions as such, i.e., by mythologies, religions, and symbols, but by the cultivation of means—implements and instruments—that control Nature and control it absolutely. Scientific efforts to understand human life constitute efforts to understand how it can be preserved, programmed, extended, freed of disease, and so on. The efforts are in pursuit of more life, i.e., a staving off of death, disease, old age, and other natural physical eventualities that diminish, impoverish, or nullify human life. The efforts cannot be labeled 'pure research' as in physics; they are pointedly tethered to a domination of nature with respect to the vicissitudes of human bodies. Moreover whether in the material form of genes, brains, livers, or what have you, and whether in the experimental form of humans, macaques, cats, or mice, the goal is to unveil the mysteries of natural bodies and to master them, and, in effect, to enrich, heighten, or prolong human life through transplantations, "gene therapy," and the like. The practice of cloning and the creation of virtual realities are further testimony to this pursuit. The quest for the fountain of youth is thus not dead; it is alive and well in the twenty-first century in a different form. Indeed, twenty-first-century technology has allowed it to be reformulated in far more striking and concrete ways. With an ever-expanding technological ingenuity, Western science promotes itself as offering true and certain passage to the wellspring of life itself and to bona fide understandings of what it is to be human. It thus positions itself as keeper of "the keys of the kingdom" (Matthew 16:19). In the process, understandings of human nature disappear into laboratory effluvia—recordings of neuronal firings, mappings of the human genome—human nature being transmogrified into purely material entities.

It is not medical technologies alone that testify to the quest for the fountain of youth. Combined with the hard science of chemistry, engineering feats herald a new era in which humans will be chemically engineered organisms—a new breed of CEOs (Chief Executive Officers, as corporate and company presidents and directors are now succinctly labelled). Such a future is implicit in the remarks of chemical and biomedical engineer Robert Langer. In the December 1999 issue of *Chemical and Engineering News,* Langer writes that, thanks to chemistry and biotechnology, "by the end of the next century disease as we know it today will no longer pose a major threat to human life" (Langer 1999, 92). This sanguine prediction has multiple and interrelated shadow sides. The end of disease as we know it today will entail the demise of nature as we know it today, not only our own nature but Nature in the large sense of an ecologically interconnected biosphere, and this because it will entail the demise of natural selection as eons of ages have known it. Chemically engineered organisms are by definition out of step with the natural order of the universe; they are essentially death-defying creatures whose values, because they extend no further than themselves, are out of tune with the natural cyclings of evolutionary life. In effect, with such CEOs at the helm, a far more radical violence is carried out than that specified by Hume when he characterizes acts motivated by selfishness. To amplify an earlier quotation from Hume: "[A]cquiring goods and possessions for ourselves and our nearest friends is insatiable, perpetual, universal, and directly destructive of society. There scarce is any one, who is not actuated by it" (Hume [1739] 1888, 491–92). The violence is far more radical because the prolongation of human life, the eradication of human disease, the fixing of genetic defects, the correction of wayward tissues, cells, and cell components, the creation of replacement tissue and organs—all chemical and engineering modifications Langer itemizes—can only come at the expense of natural selection, of other animals, and of the environment, thus, at the expense of the ecological sanity, diversity, and beauty of the biosphere and of the planet called "earth." In short, *an unnatural species,* by its very creation, creates an unnatural Nature in which, to paraphrase Geertz—or perhaps better, to carry Geertz's claim to its logical conclusion—"Everything is a cultural product. It is no different with nature: every last corner and inch of her is a cultural artifact."

## From the Perspective of the Cultural Practice of War

The natural divide between life and death may be muted by religious immortality ideologies, or be chemically, genetically, or surgically manipulated by Western scientists, but a more subtle mode of dampening and control is also possible, subtle in the fact that it is a matter of collective rather than individual belief, and of collective rather than individual preservation. Indeed, though immortality ideologies are clearly expressed in and sizably fueled by certain religious beliefs, and though chemical and engineering feats promised by Western science may unnaturally extend human life and free it of disease, human illusions concerning life and death can derive from a different source altogether; science and religion are not alone in fostering or supporting them. To cite contemporary examples, China's cultural revolution, Germany's Thousand-Year Reich, and Russia's first-ever socialist state are testimony to the seductive ideological power of nationalist programs that aim at once toward an enduring exaltation and veneration of a nation, its leaders and citizenry, its political standards and values. Nationalist immortality ideologies blur the line between the living and the dead by creating everlasting glories in which nationally privileged humans can participate. Indeed, they demonstrate to members of the nation how life can emerge triumphantly victorious, suppressing the finality of death, for where the nation ideologically endures, though death may still threaten, it is not fatal. Its fatality is only for those who threaten the nationalist ideology from an alien and philistine outside, and who, making true and authentic life unlivable for the citizens within, perish with irredeemable finality.

As the above examples show, humans are powerfully conditioned by nationalist immortality ideologies. The ideologies bear a strong resemblance to the nature of war as Hobbes described it. "For WAR," Hobbes wrote,

> consisteth not in battle only, or the act of fighting; but in a tract of time where in the will to contend by battle is sufficiently known; and therefore the notion of *time*, is to be considered in the nature of war; as it is in the nature of weather. For as the nature of foul weather, lieth not in a shower or two of rain; but in an inclination thereto of many days together: so the nature of war, consisteth not in actual fighting; but in the known disposition thereto, during all the time there is no assurance to the contrary. (Hobbes [1651] 1930, 252–53)

Hobbes's keen description pinpoints the mindset that drives war: the "will to contend by battle" is an unwavering attitudinal disposition. Ian

Buruma's characterization of dictators as "compulsive warrior[s]" who are never satisfied with a single victory echoes and strongly supports Hobbes's description. Buruma, a socio-political historian and journalist, writes, "Like any gambler, the compulsive warrior has to keep on upping the ante . . . gambling for ever bigger stakes" (Buruma 2005, 36). Whether described as will or compulsion, human reality indicates that war is a perseverating competitive state of mind. Indeed, in just the context of "the will to contend by battle," Hobbes recognizes the need of "a common power" to keep men "quiet" (Hobbes [1651] 1930, 252): "without a common power to keep them all in awe" (252), "every man is enemy to every man; . . . men live without other security, than what their own strength, and their own invention shall furnish them" (253). Accordingly, in the absence of that common power, there is "continual fear, and danger of violent death; and the life of man [is] solitary, poor, nasty, brutish, and short" (253). But a common power may itself harbor a perseverating competitive state of mind. In other words, while Hobbes recognizes the need for a common power to keep "the known disposition" (253) toward war in check, it is clear that the common power itself may have a "will to contend by battle," thereby enforcing its particular immortality ideology. The examples of China, Germany, and Russia are cases in point. But a further dimension is apparent, a dimension that in fact underlies and explains the known disposition itself, whatever the level at which it is expressed. War is a competitive display of power that has antecedents in evolutionary history, specifically in the phenomenon of male-male competition, a phenomenon Darwin describes in great detail in his study of sexual selection across the animal kingdom (Darwin [1871] 1981, 2 vols.). Recognition of its evolutionary antecedents not only supports Hobbes's description of war as a naturally perseverating competitive state of mind and his specification of competition, fear, and glory as the "principal causes of quarrel" (Hobbes [1651] 1930, 252), but also supports the claim that wars fueled by nationalist immortality ideologies are rooted in that natural disposition and readily driven by it. Nationalist immortality ideologies, in short, are the cultural elaboration of what is evolutionarily given; a national call to arms catapults male-male competition to a national level.

Two aspects of the relationship of nature to culture are of additional significance to the cultural practice of war. An examination of the one will illuminate in finer terms how individual features of male-male competition are maximized when males join forces and abilities (to use

Hume's apt terminology) to serve the immortal glories of their nation; an examination of the other will illuminate the ultimate irony of a species-specific designation that vaunts human intelligence. Let us look at each in turn.

Size and power are distinctive features of male-male competition, whether the competition takes place in happenstance encounters or in leks—special male battlegrounds of some species of birds, insects, and mammals. The male having the greater (or greatest) size and power is champion—the one with privileged access to females. But males can of course also compete to gain authority or dominance, territorial rights or resources, and so on. In other words, beyond access to females, males can compete to obtain power, possessions, and other advantages that secure them a superior standing within their group. This individual form of male-male competition can readily become a group form of competition if males band together toward a common end. The human phenomenon of war is a unique, unparalleled, and exceptional instance of this transformation. Indeed, the various forms of social cohesion that remedy what Hume identifies as individual "inconveniences"—i.e., the limited power, ability, and security of a single individual—can have a sizably expanded function: forms of social cohesion can be pooled not only to maximize individual subsistence but to maximize national prosperity, territory, power, and so on. In a word, they can serve to maximize and perpetuate the glory of a nation. As Hume rightly observes, "By the conjunction of forces, our power is augmented" (Hume [1739] 1888, 485), but augmented in this instance not to allay individual "ruin and misery" (485), but to bring ruin and misery on another nation or nations for the greater power and eminence of one's own. In effect, force and ability are nationally co-opted to the taking of lives as well as land, wealth, and the like. Most important, they are nationally co-opted for securing and perpetuating the beliefs and values of one's own nation over those of another. It is no surprise then that the human battlegrounds that define war are in actuality competitive display grounds where the victor not only takes all, but destroys what is axiologically and ideologically anathema to his nation. In this way, the victorious ones preserve the illusion that death will not touch them and that only the true and authentic meanings of life emblematic of their nation alone will live on.

Hume's view of the benefits of society and Hobbes's acute observations of human nature vis-à-vis the cultural elaboration of the evolutionary practice of male-male competition notwithstanding, an ironically different aspect of the nature/culture relationship comes to light when the relationship is put in the evolutionary perspective of *Homo sapiens sapiens*, with all that that self-referential taxonomic label indicates about the species' epistemological prowess. Put in that perspective, war may be justly described as the unenlightened and in turn inevitable result of a recalcitrant human ignorance and self-deception. Nineteenth-century philosopher Herbert Spencer succinctly captured these dual human shortcomings—shortcomings in self-knowledge—in his descriptive account of "the confusion of ethical thought," an account that, given recorded human history, has a timeless character as well as a decisively veridical twentieth/twenty-first century ring:

> When, throughout a whole community, daily acts are at variance with feelings, these feelings, continually repressed, diminish, and antagonist feelings, continually encouraged, grow. . . . Whatever injures foes is then thought not only justifiable but praiseworthy, and a part of duty. Success in killing brings admiration above every other achievement; burning of habitations and laying waste of territory become things to be boasted of; while in trophies, going even to the event of a pyramid of heads of the slain, the conqueror and his followers show that pride which implies the consciousness of great deeds. (Spencer [1892] 1978, 345)

Spencer's subsequent remark, that "in most minds the virtues of the warrior take the first place," encapsulates the irony. Rather than pursuing knowledge of human nature that would shed light on oppressive practices and correlative antagonistic feelings, specifically, how those feelings take root and are encouraged to grow, the doubly rational species turns its back on self-knowledge, cultivating warriors instead who will do battle for the community or nation, who will kill others, who will despoil their property, who will bring trophies of their conquests back to their confreres and fellow citizens, and who themselves will be hallowed for their great deeds that preserve the values, traditions, beliefs, and glory of their community or nation.

Human history from earliest times in fact gives consistent and ample testimony to the need of one human community or nation to protect itself from the aggressive incursions and violent acts of other human communities or nations. The notion of a "pacified [human] past," as archaeologist Lawrence Keeley convincingly shows, is a romanticized fiction (Keeley 1996). It is hardly surprising, then, that warriors are prized above all "in most minds"; that is, humans know themselves to be at risk with respect to other humans, who can and do oppress them, enslave them, sell them, mutilate them, rob them, and so on. In turn, it is hardly surprising that nationalist immortality ideologies spawn not simply combatants but warriors, men who, in the classical sense, aggressively defend, uphold, and secure the honor of their country. While the virtues of the warrior might be thought to be essentially the virtues of the mythic hero, whose strength, courage, and ability allow him to rise to any challenge, to face the unknown and to vanquish it, thereby liberating his people from oppression, insuring their customs and institutions, and preserving their well-being, the resemblance is superficial. The mythic hero does not train himself nor is he trained by others to kill. The warrior, as his name indicates, distinguishes himself by fighting, by battling and killing others. He is admired and hoisted to fame by those on whose behalf he kills, and brings eternal glory to himself in the process. Unlike the mythic hero, the warrior does not so much grapple with the unknown as simply live his profession to the full: fight and kill. Thus, while the warrior's virtues, like those of the mythic hero, might be similarly subsumed in a goodness capable of subduing the forces of evil—they are life-enhancing virtues that keep the threat of communal or national death at bay—the warrior is fundamentally unlike the mythic hero in important respects. Moreover unlike the mythic hero, the warrior acts not alone but is one brave man among a contingent of brave men. His competitive powers are thereby maximized, and his abilities to fight and kill are proportionally augmented. In sum, his ethos is far less to protect than to fight, annihilate, and destroy. Honing his competitive skills to a perfection worthy of his chosen profession, he both trains himself to fight and is trained to fight. Being a warrior is indeed a profession.

What is ironic—and puzzling—of course, is that *Homo sapiens sapiens* does not use its doubly vaunted intelligence toward peaceful international ends. It is as if the biologically rooted impulsion toward male-male competition were indelibly inscribed at a national level, making human males in general powerless to ameliorate their disposition to war, and fraternally confederated killings and oppressive acts implacable male built-ins. The lapse in intelligence, and in effect, the moral blindness, is all the more ironic given that the cycling relationships between oppression and resentment and resentment and aggression are all but transparent: cycles of feeling perpetuate cycles of killing that are endless, oppression breeding resentment and resentment breeding violent retaliation. The affective cycles present so simple and natural an affective lesson to learn, especially since they have been reiterated over centuries of human history. The irony is furthermore compounded by the fact that, in not utilizing its prized intelligence toward peaceful ends, the species actually makes Nature dominant over Culture. Indeed, if cultures are helpless against male-male competition at group and national levels, then war is indisputably in the genes of males, their hormones, their wiring, their brains. Set within this reductive cul-de-sac, the self-congratulatory self-labelling by which humans set themselves categorically apart from other species counts for nought, or rather, it counts only in the service of the cultivation and training of warriors, whose indomitable and valorous will-to-kill and indifference to mutilation and torture secure and perpetuate "the will to battle," and culminate in both their own glorification and the eternal glory of their nation.

The compounded irony, however, is oddly enough reversed if viewed from a different vantage point. If nations, in their cultivation and training of warriors, are actually not in thrall to Nature but are reworking Nature to their own ends, then Culture overrides Nature and ultimately reigns supreme. In other words, by conjuring the warrior out of the biological disposition to male-male competition and idealizing and enshrining his feats, nations are culturally elaborating what is evolutionarily given. In so doing, they are consecrating and sanctifying the warrior as keeper of "the keys of the kingdom" in a different but no less elevated sense than that of science. The nation's warriors are keepers of the keys not through a cultivation of knowledge that promises humans *more*—more life in the form of some duly engineered fountain of youth—but through a cultivation of human ignorance and self-deception that together fuel barbarous acts that promise eternal national glory. One might accordingly conclude that nationalist immortality ideologies are fabricated not by *Homo sapiens sapiens* but by a different species altogether: *Homo nescius et barbarus*.[14]

VII. CONCLUSION

The foregoing four perspectives illustrate the motivating power of the human life/death polarity to promote and support immortality ideologies of one sort or another and in the process dramatize the different ways in which Culture rescues or otherwise delivers humans from Nature. They show at an even deeper level how humans are motivated to adopt self-protective attitudes, beliefs, and values against the lesser—and feared—member of the polarity, or in other words, to embrace cultural tenets and meanings that give enduring significance to their lives and, in effect, outstrip death. These foundational motivations have moral significance and are not themselves discovered in mythologies, religion, patriarchal symbolism, the practices of present-day Western science, or the cultural practice of war. On the contrary, legendary stories, theological ideologies, totemic dreams, engineering feats, and cultural practices pit themselves in one way and another against the natural realities of human life, perpetuating illusions of infinite wisdom, eternal power, epical grandeur, everlasting life, and so on. Clearly, those foundational motivations of humans having moral significance are discovered by an examination of human nature itself, and entail elucidations of the natural social proclivities of humans, their ontogenetic and phylogenetic lineages together with their cultural elaborations, distortions, exaggerations, and suppressions (see Sheets-Johnstone 1994b for a further analysis and discussion of how cultures transform nature).

In sum, taking the fundamental human nature of human morality seriously means cultivating philosophical, ontogenetic, and phylogenetic understandings of human nature. Aided by a methodology proper to the task, the project of this book is to set forth just such understandings. Human morality is not an add-on to human behavior or human thought, but, as indicated above, the expression, distortion, elaboration, neglect, or suppression of social proclivities foundational to human nature together with the distinctive attitudes, beliefs, and values that ensue therefrom. Short of elucidating these proclivities and the binary modes of thought to which they give rise, one consistently falls short of fundamental understandings of human morality. In turn, one can only continue wringing one's hands at the disastrous doings of humans—doings that are disastrous not only to themselves but to a stunning diversity of other living beings, and to the earth that is the very condition of the possibility of these lives at all. Especially now, in these early years of an unrelentingly violent and bellicose new century, questions about human nature need to be resurrected and deep and rigorous inquiries made into the nature of that nature.

## NOTES

1. Philosopher Eugen Fink, the last of phenomenologist Edmund Husserl's dedicated assistants, wrote of the necessity of a "constructive phenomenology" with respect to birth and death, experiences that are non-accessible. See philosopher Ronald Bruzina's excellent translation of Fink's *Sixth Cartesian Meditation* (Fink 1995). See also Sheets-Johnstone 1999b, chap. 5.

2. For example, in his discussion of sympathy, Darwin notes that in communities in which members are sympathetic to one another, people aid and defend each other, and thus "flourish best and rear the greatest number of offspring" (Darwin [1871] 1981, 1:82).

3. Spitz presents a "brief review of our knowledge regarding the preliminary stage of visual differentiation between animate and inanimate during the first year of life." He writes, "Already a few weeks after birth we can isolate two visual stimuli which reliably provoke the infant's attention and his response to the living. First, the percept of the human face and eyes, to which the infant reacts already at four to six weeks of age by following them with his eyes. The other stimulus is the perception of movement of any kind" (Spitz 1983, 149).

He later points out that at two or three months, a child's reaction will be the same whether the human face is real or "an inanimate artifact, as long as they both fulfill the conditions of the privileged Gestalt plus movement" (149). A six-month-old infant, however, will no longer react in the same way: "Endowing the inanimate with the privileged Gestalt and with movement is of no avail. Indeed, it would seem that, *the more the inanimate artifact approaches the living prototype, the more anxiety-provoking it becomes*" (149; italics added). Spitz's observation strongly suggests that something that looks alive but is not alive is strange, alien, unknown, thus precipitating fear, and indeed he goes on to delineate a response that he terms *"eight-months anxiety"* (150), a phenomenon commonly designated as "fear of strangers." A detailed discussion of these infant responses figures centrally in the Epilogue of the present text.

It should be added that there is good reason to think the distinction between the inanimate and the animate and the privileged status of movement is not unique to human infants but a pan-animate distinction. Nonhuman animals make their living and defend themselves on the basis of movement, recognizing a possible meal or possible predator, for example, as when a spider senses movements at a place on its web or an antelope perceives movement just beyond the water hole where it is drinking.

4. It could, of course, be claimed that mental dispositions, especially pan-cultural mental dispositions, are as natural as binary oppositions, but this conception is antithetical to the thrust of Needham's inquiry. As will become evident, his intent is to show how fundamental pan-cultural binary oppositions are social constructions through and through.

5. See anthropologist F. H. Cushing's illuminating article "Manual Concepts" (Cushing 1892).

6. This is not to suggest that all thinking modeled on the body is along the lines of binary oppositions. On the contrary, analogical thinking is a fundamental form of thinking, a form that is the basis of primary modes of symbolization. See Sheets-Johnstone 1990.

7. It may happen that a particular valuing in one society is antithetical to that of another society. Thus, for example, left might be positively valued over right. Lloyd comments that right and left "tend to be used as the symbols of opposite spiritual categories *whichever of the two is believed to be the superior*" (Lloyd 1966, 39, italics in original). Though most humans are right-handed and thus naturally favor the right over their left hand, in cultures in which humans work for their own subsistence, both hands may be

equally valued (see Cushing 1892). Though having nothing to do with left and right, equal valuing is paradigmatic of the Eastern opposites, yin and yang, for example, and of Jung's "unity of opposites," which epitomizes the conjunction of spirit and nature—or spirit and instinct—and engenders a similarly equal valuing.

8. Malinowski continues: "Death is the gateway to the other world in more than the literal sense. According to most theories of early religion, a great deal, if not all, of religious inspiration has been derived from it—and in this orthodox views are on the whole correct. Man has to live his life in the shadow of death, and he who clings to life and enjoys its fullness must dread the menace of its end. And he who is faced by death turns to the promise of life. Death and its denial—Immortality—have always formed, as they form today, the most poignant theme of man's foreboding" (Malinowski 1948, 29).

Malinowski notes too that emotions in face of death are extremely complex and even contradictory: "[T]he dominant elements, love of the dead and loathing of the corpse, passionate attachment to the personality still lingering about the body and a shattering fear of the gruesome thing that has been left over, these two elements seem to mingle and play into each other" (30).

9. To be reincarnated is not necessarily to be rewarded in a positive sense. If one has not learned one's lessons well in how to live while living, one may, according to some forms of Hindu thought, be reincarnated in a lower form. See, for example, Kinsley 1993.

10. Religious scholar Theodore M. Ludwig's well-informed explication of temporally sensitive observances in terms of "sacred time" is particularly instructive. See Ludwig 1994, 16–17.

11. Poet and novelist Robert Graves offers several differing accounts of the relationship of Zeus to Nemesis in his commentary on the myth of Leda. The first of these begins: "Some say that when Zeus fell in love with Nemesis, she fled from him into the water and became a fish; he pursued her as a beaver [?], ploughing up the waves. She leaped ashore, and transformed herself into this wild beast or that, but could not shake Zeus off, because he borrowed the form of even fiercer and swifter beasts. At last she took to the air as a wild goose; he became a swan." Of Nemesis herself, he writes that she "was the Moon-goddess as Nymph . . . and, in the earliest form of the love-chase myth, she pursued the sacred king through his seasonal changes of hare, fish, bee, and mouse—or hare, fish, bird and grain of wheat—and finally devoured him. With the victory of the patriarchal system, the chase was reversed: the goddess now fled from Zeus." See Graves 1960, 1:206–7.

12. Bataille is commonly regarded a philosopher by philosophers who appear oblivious of his diverse writings. He is more widely regarded a sociologist, but was actually a librarian by profession. In addition to being the author of obscene novels written under a pseudonym (see McCully 2002, in particular, p. 26), he authored unusually sexualized interpretations of paleolithic cave art (see Bataille 1989).

13. "Virtually," because there is at least one society in which the phallus does not make an appearance, and this because the penis itself is perpetually under wraps from the time a male child is four or five years old (see Heider 1979; see also Chapter 4 of the present text).

14. I am deeply indebted to Lowell Bowditch, Professor of Classics at the University of Oregon, for enlightening me as to the most appropriate Latin term to designate a lack of self-knowledge. My original designation, *Homo ignorans et barbarus*, while grammatically correct, was semantically inexact, suggesting more a lack of acquaintance with a person or thing than an absolute ignorance or lack of knowledge of something. I learned too that *insipiens* is technically the opposite of *sapiens*, but is less exact with respect to my intended meaning, i.e., a lack of knowledge, *insipiens* (or with a few authors, *insapiens*) meaning "unwise," "senseless," or "foolish."

# PART I

# 1

## Size, Power, and Death:
## Constituents in the Making of Human Morality

> There is no mistaking a dominant male macaque. These are superbly muscled monkeys. Their hair is sleek and carefully groomed, their walk calm, assured and majestic. They move in apparent disregard of the lesser monkeys who scatter at their approach. For to obstruct the path of a dominant male or even to venture, when unwelcome, too near to him is an act of defiance, and macaques learn young that such a challenge will draw a heavy punishment.
> —SAREL EIMERL AND IRVEN DEVORE, *The Primates*

> The cause of all these evils was the love of power, originating in avarice and ambition. . . . Striving in every way to overcome each other, they committed the most monstrous crimes; yet even these were surpassed by the magnitude of their revenges which they pursued to the very utmost, neither party observing any definite limits either of justice or public expediency, but both alike making the caprice of the moment their law.
> —THUCYDIDES, *The Peloponnesian War*

> The fear of death, simple and natural though it appears, is actually complex. If we are to comprehend a little of the world about us, it is imperative that we gain as much understanding as is possible of the complexity of this fear.
> —GREGORY ZILBOORG, "FEAR OF DEATH"

## I. INTRODUCTION

Any explanation of the origin and nature of human morality must take into account a powerful and inescapable pan-cultural human awareness. Death is the great pan-cultural human leveler and human awareness of death is a near life-long awareness. However metaphysically or religiously conceived, however long postponed by medical science, however softened by belief or by faith, the basic human fact and fear of death cannot be denied. Neither, in opposition, can the basic human craving for more life.

---

This chapter is an expanded version of an article that first appeared in the *Journal of Consciousness Studies* (Sheets-Johnstone 2002b).

The awareness that death awaits us all, that our lives are on the line and will be on the line until we die, is an awareness unique to humans. Humans are the only animal species who know they lead a punctuated existence. Their awareness of the no-moreness of death is a formidable and heavy life sentence. It is only natural, then, that the sentence should figure prominently in human morality and in theoretical formulations of human morality.

The purpose of this chapter is to show how size, power, and death are interrelated constituents of human morality and how, from the perspective of their interrelationship, the roots of morality are submerged in an awareness and fear of death. A full account of the basic constituents of human morality requires a study of affinitive constituents of human morality, notably, caring, empathy, trust, and play, and these from both an ontogenetic and phylogenetic perspective. The second part of this book will examine these fundamental, morally weighted aspects of human nature in depth. In effect, this beginning chapter, like those following in the first part of the book, present structural constituents of human morality from one side only.

The chapter begins with a discussion of size as a biological marker of power. It then shows how vulnerability is a biological fact of life and how power is a bulwark against vulnerability. It goes on to identify ways in which the biological value of size, i.e., power, is culturally transformed and how, as transformed, it is tied to the biological fact of death. The chapter draws critically and constructively on the work of researchers in evolutionary ethics and in cultural studies of evil and death. Major implications of the analysis, discussed in the last section, show that pancultural dimensions of human nature cannot be omitted from investigations of human morality short of rendering the investigation incomplete at best and inaccurate at worst, or, in other words, that the uniquely human awareness and fear of death are impervious to any form of reductionism—whether genetic, neuronal, modular, algorithmic, or computational.

## II. SIZE AND POWER

Size plays a decisive role in animal power relations. Darwin called attention to its significance in both natural and sexual selection (Darwin [1859] 1968, [1871] 1981). Other biologists and zoologists have similarly signalled its importance. Consider the following description by primatologist Frans de Waal of chimpanzee society:

> [The] habit of making the body look deceptively large and heavy is characteristic of the alpha male. . . . The fact of being in a position of power makes a male physically impressive, hence the assumption that he occupies the position which fits his appearance. The impression of a connection between physical size and social rank is further strengthened by a special form of behaviour which is the most reliable indicator of the social order, both in the natural habitat and in [captivity]: the *submissive greeting.* . . . [T]he subordinate assumes a position whereby he looks up at the individual he is greeting. In most cases he makes a series of deep bows which are repeated so quickly one after the other that this action is known as bobbing. Sometimes the "greeters" bring objects with them (a leaf, a stick), stretch out a hand to their superior or kiss his feet, neck or chest. The dominant chimpanzee reacts to this "greeting" by stretching himself up to a greater height and making his hair stand on end. The result is a marked contrast between the two apes, even if they are in reality the same size. (de Waal 1982, 87)

Size is clearly a biological marker of power. Its value in the evolutionary world is readily apparent: those who are large by nature and those who can increase their size—by inflating themselves or a part of themselves, e.g., the common European toad, male sea elephants (Attenborough 1979, 140; Darwin [1871] 1981, 2:278)—gain an upper hand in defending themselves, in attracting a mate, or in competing with others. Humans are by no means unaware of the potential advantage of their given size, of giving the illusion of being larger than they actually are, or of actually making themselves larger through cosmetic surgery, as in present-day breast and penis enlargements. The value of size in the human world has moreover been evident over centuries in practices such as lip enlargement, buttock enlargement (steatopygia), tendril-like nail elongations, and head elongations (Rudofsky 1971), all of which practices are thought to enhance one's power in some way.

Size and power, implicit in de Waal's descriptive account of an alpha male, are equally implicit in anthropologist Christopher Boehm's conception of an alpha male (see below). They are bona fide constituents of morality in nonhuman animal societies,[1] and this even though there is no threat of *death*, no fear of *death*, no urge to *kill* another individual in either de Waal's or Boehm's accounts, or in any other researcher's account of alpha males, and even though the threat, fear, or urge do not figure in accounts of aggressive social relations in nonhuman animal societies generally. Richard Wrangham and Dale Peterson's account of "demonic" chimpanzee males, for example, provides ample evidence of maiming and mutilating, but the motivation, as Wrangham and Peterson suggest, seems to lie as much in "excitement" as in "gratuitous cruelty" (Wrangham and Peterson 1996, 70; see also 6, 14, and 17). While untempered brutality and ultimately fatal injuries undeniably enter the scene, *death* does not enter the scene. It is important to point out that this is not because nonhuman animals lack *the word* "death"; it is because the concept of death is lacking (Boehm 1992, 165),[2] but it is not lacking because there is no awareness of, and no feelings about, the disappearance or permanent inanimation of a friend, for example, or of a baby (Goodall 1971). The concept is lacking because it is contingent on an objectification of one's own body and because nonhuman animals do not have physical bodies *as such*—an object of such and such parts, for example, or such and such placement with respect to other parts, and so on (Sheets-Johnstone 1986a, 1990). Nonhuman animals make no analytical distinction between what in traditional phenomenological terms (e.g., Sartre 1956, Merleau-Ponty 1962) is called the physical and lived body (cf. Humphrey 2000 on "sensation" and "perception"). They experience themselves and their fellow creatures dynamically and physiognomically—as animate forms, not as objects made up of arms, heads, legs, feet, eyes, tongues, and so on. Kanzi, a male bonobo who mastered language on his own, does not apply himself to learning words for parts of his own body, "even though these are words that have been on his keyboard for some time" (Savage-Rumbaugh 1993). He experiences himself not as having a physical body *as such*, but as a dynamically engaged body immersed in some activity and affectively and cognitively caught up in it. What one nonhuman animal experiences in experiencing another is similarly not a physical body *as such* but a portentous physiognomy of some kind: threatening, caring, playful, fearful, curious, and so on. In short, in the nonhuman animal world, what is experienced or what appears is not a material body abstractively separated or analytically separable from the animate and animated body that the individual is.[3] In consequence, nonhuman animals have no fear of their bodies, of what their bodies might do, of what they might become. Hence there is no future fate that awaits them in view of their being material bodies. The origin and import of the fear of one's body are, in contrast, significant aspects of human morality.

Size and power have the potential to answer to the basic vulnerability of all animate life. The vulnerability of humans, however, is complicated by the fact that we humans know ourselves to be vulnerable. We are subject to disease, illness, accidents, earthquakes, tornadoes, volcanoes. We are vulnerable always and without appeal by the mere fact of our being alive. Our size may be the source of a natural or cultivated strength whereby we defeat an illness, escape a tornado, or survive an accident. But merely being alive makes us susceptible, keeping us always on the edge of a possible calamity or affliction. We are in fact all ultimately overtaken by death in some way (for a medical analysis, see Nuland 1994). Size and power thus eventually count for nought. But the plot is far thicker than mere aliveness, especially as concerns morality, for death can come not only at the hands of Nature; it can also come at the hands of others. It is here that the social significance of size and power comes decisively to the fore.

Our primary vulnerability is corporeal; our bodies are ever open to injury and to death from the violence of others who can maim, torture, and kill. Mental harm by others is a more sophisticated form of violence. Recognition of others as having the power to harm us and to do us in is a potent awareness. The recognition intensifies our basic felt vulnerability and compounds the possible ways in which others might channel power. Others have verbal powers, for example—to abuse, insult, or cut down; in many cultures, they have metaphysical powers, most notably through the evil eye (Dundes 1992); they have ideational powers—to plot insidious, destructive schemes, for example—and politico-military powers—to rape, ravage, and plunder. Size may be directly related to power as in the latter instances, or it may figure indirectly or play only a supportive role if any, as with verbal and metaphysical powers. The social power of humans clearly comes in multiple forms, any one of which may be easily converted into violence, which itself comes in multiple forms and is accomplished by multiple means. Power is thus diversified in human terms; it is open to elaboration along different lines, but lines that consistently terminate in pain, in bodily felt vulnerabilities. In consequence, the social situation of humans is tenuous: humans are at risk with one another. They know they are at the mercy of the goodness of others, that their lives are or might at any moment be at stake, as when one person clandestinely compromises the lives of all others within the group, state, or nation by acts of treason, or that should their relations with others deteriorate or not be consistently and closely monitored, they may pay for it, as when an employee or a student compromises the lives of others by shooting them. Thus, humans are at risk not only by the mere fact of being alive, but *of being alive among other humans.* In the most elemental sense, humans know they have the power to make life not just painful for others but the power to inflict the tortures of hell on them. They know, in short, that they have the power to bring hell to life and to extinguish life altogether. The fear of death is thus clearly a built-in of human life. The violence of others is always potential and death is always a possibility.[4]

How do we come to know that the bodies of others are vulnerable, that we can torture them by cutting them, tearing them, hacking them, dismembering them, blinding them, starving them? Clearly, we know that we ourselves are quintessentially vulnerable in just such ways. We know that we have physical bodies *as such*.

### III. CULTURAL TRANSLATIONS OF BIOLOGICAL FACTS

The biological value of size as a measure of power is rooted in the body, generating certain intercorporeal meanings and specific interanimate behaviors with respect to both the height and bulk of interacting individuals and to their interanimate spatial positionings, precisely as indicated in de Waal's descriptive account (see also Sheets-Johnstone 1994b). These same intercorporeal meanings are enacted by humans—by Britons, for example, in deference to royalty, by the people of Tikopia in their greetings and in their apologies to one another, and by Catholics in their ordination rites (Firth 1978). But in human societies, the biological value of size as a measure of power goes further than these intercorporeal meanings. While the value of size is rooted in the body and retains its natural value in that domain, it is at the same time elaborated along cultural lines. The size-is-power equation is converted into territory, for example, as measured by size of home or number of homes, for instance, or number of building properties, or number of real estate investments; into mates as measured by number of wives, for instance, or incidental sex partners, or mistresses; into food resources as measured by number of livestock, for instance, or size of daily rations, or amount of subsistence budget; into monetary accounts as measured by number of securities, for instance, or certificates, or bonds; and so on. In other words, the biological value of size as a marker of power translates culturally into the size of one's personal holdings. Their sheer size buys not simply territorial, sexual, provisional, or monetary securities but emotional securities that offset the awareness and fear of death. In effect, one's personal holdings afford one an abundance of life, an abundance sufficient to mask anxiety about death, even great enough to forestall it. The abundance not only literally protects one from disaster—from starvation, homelessness, loneliness, meaninglessness, or possible death from hopeless abjectness or exposure to the elements of Nature—but provides a barrier between oneself and death.

Although the no-moreness of death prompts the desire for ever more life—more food, drink, sex, property, money, stock, fame—the no-moreness of death eventually triumphs because the ultimate abundance desired—*more time*—is not to be had. All cultural elaborations of life in the form of abundance—all cultural cultivations of power—ultimately fail. However much wool we pull over our eyes, we are stuck with death. Depending on who we are and on what our life experiences have been, when the fact of our own mortality surfaces—not intellectually, contemplated as a vague future event, for example, but affectively as a vibrant but impermanent aliveness felt here and now—we feel impelled to protect ourselves from the thought or to offset knowledge of our own potential sufferings and ultimate death, particularly since the thought or knowledge may create monstrous anxieties, make us intolerably angry or unbearably sad, decrease our sense of power over our lives, and in fact make us not just *feel* acutely uncomfortable and uneasy but motivate us to *act* in ways commensurate with these feelings. The thought or knowledge may in fact motivate us to deeds most foul. Fear of our own death may turn silently into a rage against Nature, a rage that opens the possibility for retaliation: why not commandeer the power of Nature to oneself—the power to dole out misery, harm, pain, disease, and death to others? Arrogating to oneself the power of Nature—the power of "the gods"—one wreaks havoc on others, gets even as it were, and outlives one's own otherwise mortal destiny by timeless acts that live on in history.[5] Indeed, what humans do or can do to others is in part precisely what Nature does or can do to humans: infect them, crush them, kill them. In sum, the thought or fear of death may turn silently into a rage against Nature and the rage against Nature into a rage against others. Rage against the impermanent nature of life is thereby transformed into a rage for the power of death. One takes the no-moreness of death into one's own hands.

## IV. CULTURAL TRANSFORMATIONS AND EVOLUTIONARY ETHICS

In an edited volume on evolutionary ethics (Katz 2000), evolutionary anthropologist Christopher Boehm presents a persuasive account of how despotic societies ruled by alpha human males were superseded by egalitarian societies formed and maintained by coalitions of people. These latter societies, which reached their full flourishing in the Late Paleolithic (Boehm 2000a, 94), did not support dominant/subordinate relationships; they dealt with "deviants"—those who were bullies or tyrants—by suppressing them in some way. Boehm's account is evolutionarily grounded in a method that he terms "triangulation": he hypothesizes a common ancestor of humans and the two *Pan* species—chimpanzees (*Pan troglodyte*) and bonobos (*Pan paniscus*)—on the basis of extant behaviors of each *Pan* species and on studies of extant human nomadic and hunter-gatherer societies, i.e., present-day societies that are egalitarian. On the basis of his method of triangulation, Boehm proposes that the common ancestor lived in an alpha male society that was tempered by reconciliatory and pacifying intervention behaviors, behaviors that reduced or placated conflicts. He proposes that human societies were initially alpha male societies and that egalitarian societies implemented a form of social control to counter natural alpha male behavior directly. He states that at the time of the Paleolithic,

> People had a high degree of what I have called 'actuarial intelligence', which helped them to set up cooperative systems of sharing and to calculate the damage that uncontrolled conflict might do to the group. While active conflicts were 'managed' as much as possible, as with Pan [chimpanzees], the group also was able to *anticipate* conflict on a long-range basis and to manipulate the behaviours that were likely to produce it. These were basics of moral life. (95)

Boehm earlier poses the question of how the societal transformation was actually accomplished, how "an innately despotic species manage[d] to become phenotypically egalitarian" (85). He speculates that people in the first egalitarian societies might have either directly addressed themselves to the solution of socio-political problems that attend alpha male behaviors or that other societal changes eliminated the alpha male role as a by-product. In lieu of these alternatives, however, he actually opts for what he terms "a more general hypothesis that helps to account for either of these possibilities," namely, and as suggested above, conflict management and social control. What is startling and notable is that immediately after proposing his "more general hypothesis," he states, "The striking anomaly for this hypothesis is murder. Hunter-gatherer homicide is quite frequent, and it usually takes place because of problems with male competition over women" (Boehm 2000a, 85–86). Moreover adultery is common in these societies and seemingly "insusceptible of definitive control" (86). Thus, although a dominance/submission hierarchy is not pronounced in extant hunter-gatherer egalitarian societies "because individual rank is not a major factor in reproductive success, and because leaders are not very dominant" (84), murder is not uncommon. Vulnerability is, *pari passu,* not uncommon then either: humans are at the mercy of other humans, depending upon what they and other humans choose to do and not do, choices commonly being socially opaque until enacted. Boehm's further observations underscore the point. He notes that while murder is "wholeheartedly condemned, internecine killing is not well controlled by the group" (86), and that, with respect to adultery, "this major cause of homicide is difficult to detect, and therefore difficult to suppress" (86). In explanation of the homicides, he alludes to the genetic basis of adultery, saying that it is "firmly grounded in sexual selection, and the motives would appear to be powerful" (86).

The earlier elucidation of the relationship between size, power, and death offers a quite different perspective on the "anomaly." When one male encounters another who competitively threatens to deprive him of abundance in the form of a woman, he acts accordingly: he deprives the other conclusively of abundance, i.e., of life; when one male's personal holding is sexually compromised by another, he acts accordingly: he deprives the other conclusively of his holding, i.e., of life. To kill is to increase one's power by insuring and perpetuating unquestioned access to abundance and by nullifying in absolute terms any threat to one's own life. Killing, insuring, perpetuating, and nullifying are not a matter of selfish genes; they are a matter of life and death. Death meted out to others is a yea-saying of one's own life, complete with all the abundance it can possibly sustain, and at the same time, a nay-saying of one's own death in the sense that meting it out to others keeps the fear of one's own death at bay and is a deterrent to what might be one's own always untimely death. Having the power of death is, in effect, having the power of life. Power is thus the essential biological game for humans.[6] As Boehm himself says, "[H]umans are innately disposed to vie for power and position" (Boehm 2000a, 83). In this game of power, one plays first and foremost—naturally—in the currency of the body.

An earlier point is relevant in this context. Fighting, not killing, is what basically structures nonhuman primate male-male competition and internecine competition generally, and fighting successfully means simply having the greater size and power. In other words, wounds are inflicted, skin is torn off, bodily parts are maimed or bitten off, *but not because the victor is out to kill*. To bring death willfully and knowingly to another is a human motivation and act—a human invention.[7] Even Wrangham and Peterson's descriptions, showing that wanton cruelty—not just fighting—is part of the behavioral repertoire of male chimpanzees, provide no counterevidence (Wrangham and Peterson 1996). This is in part because none of their descriptions records an actual kill. After witnessing a severe mutilation, for example, observers note that the victim disappears, either immediately or eventually, and is not seen again.[8] Judging from the descriptions, one would say that the chimpanzees neither assure themselves that their victim is *lifeless*—nor do they appear concerned with whether it is or not. On the contrary, the descriptions implicitly suggest that what is central to the chimpanzees' attacks are the violent actions themselves: pummeling, biting, battering, dragging, tearing, stomping, striking. In line with this centrality is the fact that, as noted earlier, excitement appears to be as much a factor as gratuitous cruelty. For example, of one victim, Goliath, Wrangham and Peterson write, "His aggressors showed their excitement in a continuous barrage of hooting and drumming and charging and branchwaving and screaming. They kept up the attack for eighteen minutes, then turned for home, still energized, running and screaming and banging on tree-root buttresses" (17). The excitement strikes a common chord with humans on the battlefield: Churchill remarked that "[N]othing in life is so exhilarating as to be shot at without result" (Becker 1975, 106); anthropologist Harry Holbert Turney-High—one of the "architects of [the] concept of *primitive war*" (Keeley 1996, 9)—believed, "Not only could war be useful, especially in a civilized context, but it was also an exciting diversion" (10). War is exhilarating because it makes men feel vibrantly alive, and to feel vibrantly alive is to defy death.

In sum, through his method of triangulation, Boehm presents a provocative, thoroughgoing analysis of the evolution of social control, but the singularly human awareness of death must be factored into the analysis, and in a foundational way. In light of evidence of hominid burials in the Late Paleolithic, the singularly human awareness is all the more essential to recognize. In his brief discussion of the social life of Late Paleolithic humans, Boehm mentions that "[t]hese people sometimes seem to have cared for the injured, and they sometimes buried their dead—an act also performed by Neandertals" (Boehm 2000a, 80–81).[9] Thus, by the Late Paleolithic when, as per his account, humans shifted from alpha male to egalitarian societies, burials took place. *The concept of death was necessarily present.* The concept is not just one more in the conceptual arsenal of humans. It is a concept that is inextricably tied to life in awesome, dreadful, frightening ways; it is a concept that in competitive circumstances might easily reverberate daily and disquietingly in the course of food procurement, mating, and predator avoidance. One might in fact wonder whether an awareness and fear of death was already present in earlier Paleolithic times or whether the shift from despotic to egalitarian tribal communities was fueled, even generated, by an awareness and fear of death. Whatever the answer, the impact of the concept of death must be taken into account. Human mortality is a core element of human morality. "Deviants," as Boehm labels those who oppress others, are bullies and tyrants who must be contained, dissuaded, or thwarted if society is to function peacefully. But killers are also deviants, and those who kill are strikingly difficult to control, precisely as Boehm indicates in his discussion of homicide in extant hunter-gatherer societies. Why would this be, one might wonder, if not that the awareness and fear of death are perpetually beyond absolute moral containment by moral rules, that is, that the urge to kill and the power to kill continually arise in human societies because the prospect of death is a continual if muted presence in human life, and being a continual presence, is continually invoked in proportion to anything that threatens one's own abundance and one's own craving for more life?

## V. IMMORTALITY IDEOLOGIES

We can examine this possibility most effectively from the perspective of immortality ideologies, notably, as they have been analyzed by cultural anthropologist Ernest Becker—in a preliminary way in his Pulitzer Prize–winning book *The Denial of Death* and more fully in his last book, *Escape from Evil*—but also as they have been presented by psychologist Jordan Peterson.

Becker's thesis, which is spelled out basically in his persistent psychoanalytic probings of culture and in his cultural analyses of ritual, money, and other societal artifacts, is epitomized by his summary statement that "what people want in any epoch is a way of transcending their physical fate, they want to guarantee some kind of indefinite duration, and culture provides them with the necessary immortality symbols or ideologies; societies can be seen as structures of immortality power" (Becker 1975, 63). Becker exemplifies the thesis when he shows how ritual, for example, provided earlier humans with a way to achieve immortality—e.g., through ceremonies and offerings that venerated rulers or gods, through the sacrifice of animals or other humans, and so on. He comments that through his offerings and sacrifices "the ritualist has done nothing less than enable life to continue; he has contributed to sustaining and renewing the universe" (14). He has perpetuated—or bought—more life.[10]

Power figures centrally in Becker's account, power seen through the eyes of culture, i.e., minus recognition of its foundational biological value and equation with size. Power fundamentally sustains life: food is power, skill is power, money is power, and so on: "It is easy to see the significance of power for the human animal; it is really the basic category of his existence, as the organism's whole world is structured in terms of power" (45). More particularly, Becker's claim is that cultural power is sacred because it buys immortality: "All power," he writes, "is in essence power to deny mortality. Either that or it is not real power at all, not ultimate power, not the power that mankind is really obsessed with. Power means power to increase oneself, to change one's natural situation from one of smallness, helplessness, finitude, to one of bigness, control, durability, importance" (81). With respect to the history of culture, Becker's contention is that certain individuals came to rule over others because they showed themselves to have extra powers: they distinguished themselves in hunting, or were extraordinarily skillful or strong, or they displayed a "special fearlessness in warfare," and so on (46). These persons were privileged and treated accordingly; they were revered because "[they] were thought to have an extra charge of power or mana" (46). Though they are not called such by Becker, they are clearly alpha-males. From a cultural perspective, immortality power attaches to alpha-males. People follow them. The fear of death is suppressed in the presence of the mighty; power is released, life is full, vibrant, and meaningful; one does anything the alpha-male commands. As Becker (1973, 29–30) states, "If we had to offer the briefest explanation of all the evil that men have wreaked upon themselves and upon their world since the beginnings of time right up until tomorrow, it would be not in terms of man's animal heredity, his instincts and his evolution: it would be simply in *the toll that his pretense of sanity takes*, as he tries to deny his true condition," namely, that he is an abysmal worm, an insignificant nothing, and that his fear of death is *dreadful*, too dreadful to be faced. Where man turns against others in harmful and murderous ways, he turns in defiance of his own death: "If we don't have the omnipotence of gods, we at least can destroy like gods" (85).

Becker's psycho-cultural analyses of the fear of death are indisputably insightful, at times profoundly so. They are, however, situated within naive, i.e., unexamined, natural attitudes (see Husserl, e.g., 1977, 1983, 1989) grounded in unevenly valorized binary oppositions, notably, nature/culture, female/male, body/mind. For example, Becker tells us that "Nature's values are bodily values, human values are mental values" (Becker 1973, 31); "symbols" spell "freedom"—"body spells "fate" (44); "woman, as a source of new life, [is] a part of nature" and "nature" as "mere physical sense experience" runs counter to "human nature," which is *"symbolic"* (170, 185, respectively). Peterson's account of the moral force of the human awareness and fear of death is similarly tied to unevenly valorized binary oppositions. Though his equally asymmetrical account is anchored in mythical-religious-Jungian thought—in the Great Father and the Great and Terrible Mother, and the Hero—he arrives at the same conclusion: fear of the unknown, notably death, prompts "Man" to dark deeds. Fear of death is the motivating source of evil (Peterson 1999, e.g., 310, 347, 454, 460, 466). It motivates "Man" to "torture his brother and dance on his grave" (347).

What is significant about both Becker's and Peterson's cultural analyses is their agreement on the ontological motive that drives "Man" to murder, massacre, butcher, starve, blind, and so on, namely, the fact of man's own inescapable death. As is apparent from his explanation "of all the evil that men have wreaked upon themselves and upon their world," Becker affirms that there is nothing inherent in man's inhumanity to other humans. Peterson says nothing of an inherent motivation apart from his attempt to tie left and right brain hemispheres to the known (already explored territory, hence safe) and the unknown (unexplored territory, hence dangerous), respectively (Peterson 1999, 67ff.). Yet clearly, the claim 'no inherent motivation' can be elaborated. The allegory of selfish genes aside (of which more below), there is nothing innate that goads, motivates, or drives humans to mutilate and kill each other. The motivating source of these pan-cultural human behaviors lies in the pan-human knowledge of the impermanence of the human ontological condition and in the affective reactions of humans to that impermanence: *the fear of death and the transformation of that fear into a rage against Nature—in all her forms.* This elaboration of the claim will be documented in what follows.

In their strikingly persuasive cultural analyses of human knowledge and fear of death, Becker and Peterson both single out the Hero—"the 'real' man," as Becker calls him at one point (Becker 1973, 86)—the one human capable of looking at death squarely and leading lesser men away from wanton, evil acts of destruction and toward positive moral values—what Peterson calls our "infinite capacity for good" (Peterson 1999, 456).[11] Toward the end of his last book, Becker wonders what the human world would be like if the leaders chosen by people—the heroes—were those who "know the reality of death as a primary problem" (Becker 1975, 167). Indeed, he wonders, what if these leaders "were conscious of *their own* fear of life and death"? (167). His point is a psychoanalytic one, i.e., "well-analyzed men" (167) might be different leaders altogether. His narrow, that is, strictly psychoanalytic, view of what is needed for man's enlightenment is both puzzling and curious. Not that psychoanalytic work would not be productive, but it is not the only possibility. Particularly from a cultural viewpoint, a strictly psychoanalytic solution bypasses non-Western possibilities such as Buddhism, for example. Buddhism appears to be the only complex system of thought that, in its penetrating examination of the human condition and mind, takes the challenge of an in-depth examination of death seriously, facing the fear of death directly and unswervingly.[12] Peterson does not appeal to psychoanalysis but prominences Christianity and the figure of Christ in his quest for an enlightened humanity, underscoring the possibility

of self-understandings in light of our awareness of death, self-understandings that would lead us "inexorably upwards, toward a consciousness sufficiently heightened to bear the thought of death" (Peterson 1999, 468).

However thoughtful their respective Heroics in face of what is inescapable, the heroics are in each instance hemmed in by liabilities in the form of Cartesianism, patriarchal views, and a man-*über-alles* mentality. In other words, unevenly valorized binary oppositions compromise their analyses, claims, and appeals, skewing their vision and limiting their conclusions. Becker and Peterson are in essential ways men writing about men, not humans writing about humans.[13] For example, both Becker and Peterson overlook the fact that throughout recorded human history, it is specifically, universally, and virtually *only* males who kill. Though they discuss leaders and rulers at length, prominencing and extolling the virtues of the Hero, the man who "has transcended himself" (Becker 1973, 86), the man who, archetypally, "makes order out of chaos, brings peace to the world, and restructures society when it has become rigid and anachronistic" (Peterson 1999, 93), they say nothing of violence and murder being virtually exclusive to males, much less to hierarchical societies that position and support alpha males. Most important, while they explicitly, consistently, and exclusively speak of "man," even about "the society of men" and of "the patriarchal kingdom of human culture" (Peterson 1999, e.g., 224, 99), *they do not call into question the patriarchal values within this very culture* that feed "Man's" motivation to turn against other humans.[14] Moreover in all the cultures they analyze, nature—or better, Nature—is portrayed as evil, not only in causing earthquakes, tornadoes, and so on, but most significantly, for bringing time, illness, and death into human lives.

Becker's and Peterson's portrayal of Nature as evil is conceptually of a piece with biologist George Williams's portrayal of "Mother Nature" as a "wicked old witch." Williams complains how Nature denies man's aspirations and values,[15] how "organisms constantly engage in activities that violate the dicta of human ethical systems and moral sensitivities" (Williams 1993, 228); he underscores "the moral perversity of natural selection" (230). Mother Nature is "immensely powerful," but also "abysmally stupid." Only because of an "abnormal modern environment" in which there are "biologically abnormal manifestations" of "kin selection and reciprocity" is "compassion towards strangers and even animals" possible (229). The conceptual coincidence is striking and warrants extended attention for the light it sheds on unevenly valorized binary oppositions.

Like Becker and Peterson, Williams personifies nature, but with the weight of selfish-gene science behind him, a science that operates in a theoretical, Galilean vacuum and is more profitably read as a truth-telling allegory of the human pursuit of more life—abundance—than as a scientific truth either about the whole of human nature or about what foundationally motivates the pursuit of abundance.[16] What is astonishing is that neither Williams nor Becker nor Peterson stops to question the personification *Mother* Nature: why they so christen *her*, for example—is it because *she* supplies them the basic stuff of life?—food, materials to construct shelters, materials for tool-making, and so on—or why they qualify nature with a certain sense of *her* (motherly) power together with a certain sense of their desire to overcome that power. Certainly the personification has a long history: "For you have but to follow and as it were hound nature in her wanderings, and you will be able, when you like, to lead and drive her afterwards to the same place again. . . . [Man ought not] to make scruple of entering and penetrating into these holes and corners [i.e., into "the secrets of nature"], when the inquisition of truth is his sole object" (Bacon 1883, 296). Its long history, however, does not authorize its being treated as received wisdom. What is reiterated reflexively without thought is epistemically at risk; mindless reiteration may be deceptive, nothing more than self-serving judgment, for example. In the present instance, it may even be self-incriminating since, if nature is "abysmally stupid," then surely men are abysmally stupid since they are part of nature, no matter how much they might wish to dissociate themselves from "her." Moreover Williams especially seems not to realize that creation and destruction define reality; that is, creation and destruction describe the earthworld as it is, and life, being part of the earthworld as it is, creation and destruction are of the nature of life.

The denigrations of nature by all three men are from this perspective anti-realist, not in the academic philosophical sense of disavowing the possibility of knowledge of the world as it really is or of disavowing there being a world at all apart from a subject, but in the everyday sense of refusing acknowledgment of reality, in this instance, the double reality of nature (cf. Keith: "I look on the duality of a human nature [as per Spencer's code of amity and code of enmity] as an essential part of the machinery of human evolution" [cited by Alexander 1987, p. 195; see also Ardrey 1966]). However destructive of life, nature is undeniably bountiful, not only in the creation of a diversity of life but in the sustenance of that diversity through flowing waters, methods of pollination, decaying old growth that supports new life and environing ecological systems, accommodations of poikilotherms and homeotherms alike, and so on. The destructive facts of nature may clearly appear to "human sensitivities" to be sad ones, or most especially with respect to the ultimate destructive fact of death, to be a hateful, rage-producing fact, but they are nevertheless true facts, and the true one that is death is the crowning one that humans in their privileged wisdom are burdened to face and face alone.

Of particular interest in this context of truth is Becker's citation of psychoanalyst Otto Rank, whose work is the foundation of Becker's own. Rank writes that "[e]very conflict over truth is in the last analysis just the same old struggle over . . . immortality." Becker continues Rank's thought in a long, perspicuous statement that merits quotation in full:

> If anyone doubts this [that conflict over truth is a struggle over immortality], let him try to explain in any other way the life-and-death viciousness of all ideological disputes. Each person nourishes his immortality in the ideology of self-perpetuation to which he gives his allegiance; this gives his life the only abiding significance it can have. No wonder men go into a rage over fine points of belief: if your adversary wins the argument about truth, *you die*. Your immortality system has been shown to be fallible, your life becomes fallible. History, then, can be understood as the succession of ideologies that console for death. Or, more momentously, *all* cultural forms are *in essence sacred* because they seek the perpetuation and redemption of the individual life. This is the breathtaking import of Rank's attempt to see history as stages or successions of immortality ideologies. Culture *means* that which is super*natural;* all culture has the basic mandate to transcend the physical, to permanently transcend it. All human ideologies, then, are affairs that deal directly with *the sacredness of the individual or the group life,* whether it seems that way or not, whether they admit it or not, whether the person knows it himself or not. (Becker 1975, 64; all italics in original)[17]

The truths of culture ideologically supersede the truths of nature because immortality ideologies defy death. But culture supersedes nature to begin with because, as indicated earlier, culture and nature—along with their conceptually related cousins, mind and body, and male and female—are unevenly valorized binary oppositions. Being unevenly valorized, the lesser member of the opposition may in each instance be heroically, i.e., manfully, overpowered. Denigrations are thus easily braided together into a powerful rage against death: a rage against nature for bringing death, a rage against the body for being helpless, a rage against females—especially as personifying Mother Nature—for being creative sources and carriers of life, for being the ones on whom males are initially dependent, and for being, by associative personification, the source of death. The rage is readily played out in some form of combat as the quotation from Becker suggests, but as the quotation also suggests, whether ideological or physical, the combat has mortal effects: its aim is to perpetuate one's own life at any price. The immortality ideology of selfish-gene theory flawlessly exemplifies this aim no less than does an SS trooper carrying out the orders of his superior. Combat aside, two aspects of the rage itself warrant comment.

First, a rage against death follows from the fear of death, and it is the rage, not the fear, that opens one's vision to the possibility of retaliation, i.e., Why not commandeer the power of Nature to oneself—the power to dole out misery, harm, pain, disease, and death to others? As noted earlier, by arrogating to oneself the power of Nature—the power of "the gods"—one wreaks havoc on others, gets even as it were, and outlives one's own otherwise mortal destiny by timeless acts that live on in history. The "society of men" that cries out "I am threatened with death—let us kill plentifully" (Becker 1973, 149) thus blindly turns the fear of death into an unquenchable rage against other bodies at the same time that it transmogrifies the power of Nature into man-made death machines, instruments of pain, weapons of destruction, cascading armies that plunder, rape, and kill. In brief, the fear of death is subverted into a rage against Nature and the rage in turn appropriates the very powers it rails against and is helpless to foil.

Second, the fear of death is tied to the body, The fear of death may in fact be manifest as fear of one's body—of what it might do or what it might become. What links morality to death, what in fact grounds morality and *makes it fully real*, is foundationally one's own body. It is one's own body that is vulnerable and ultimately impotent, that is affectively experienced as exposed, assailable, open to pain, disease, and suffering, and that is affectively experienced as ultimately out of one's control. It is thus hardly surprising that individuals harm others first and foremost in bodily ways; being vulnerable and ultimately impotent, bodies can be made the powerless targets of a fear of death turned into a rage against Nature.

## VI. IMPLICATIONS

Two major implications follow from the above analysis of size, power, and death as constituents in the making of human morality. The implications are less consequences than implicit dimensions of the analysis. They might rightly be spelled out as awakenings, for radical changes would be mandated in sociobiological theory and in the practice of the human sciences generally if the analysis is sound. Since the implications are intimately related to the idea of a universal morality, it is fitting to identify them by way of this idea.

A universal morality must necessarily rest on universal foundations; that is, it must logically derive from what is pan-cultural. As this chapter has shown, the biological value of size, the biological and cultural equations of size and power, and the human awareness and fear of death are pan-cultural phenomena that are conceptually linked and that structure hierarchical systems of human morality. If a universal morality were to be cultivated and achieved, then an appreciation of pan-cultural similarities would have to balance an appreciation of cultural differences and similarities in particular would have to be explicitly recognized and attended to accordingly. Further, the conceptually divisive underpinnings of 'Us against Them' mentalities would have to be elucidated, and in ways that would bring the conceptual infrastructure of hierarchically structured human morality, with its complex linkages to human mortality, to light. In effect, *subjective dimensions of life* could not be dismissed because they constitute the driving force of human morality: human awareness and fear of death are pan-culturally subjective phenomena that are foundational to human morality.

Disdain for the subjective may well be a scientifically sanctioned way of denying death and of keeping the fear of death at bay. In other words, the subjective too may be regarded the lesser member of an unevenly valorized binary opposition, a member that is not only axiologically but epistemologically overpowered: only "the objective," the Galilean ideal, guarantees true knowledge. But neither the awareness of death nor the fear of death can be objectified or measured. The awareness of death and the fear of death are not to be found in a segment of human DNA or in a certain cluster or sequence of neuronal firings or in a certain module of the brain or in any other objective piece of matter; neither the awareness nor the fear can be reduced to genes or to brains, or to any other material structure. The awareness and the fear are tied to a concept: the concept of death (Sheets-Johnstone 1990). This concept is a specifically and uniquely human concept which no form of material reductionism can capture.

The first implication of the analysis therefore specifies an awakening to and an incorporation of the subjective. People within the human sciences who are engaged in studies of human morality or whose work dovetails with studies of human morality—not only sociobiologists but medical personnel, cognitive scientists, and evolutionary psychologists, for example—are charged with awakening to the way in which the subjective is bound up with what they consider "the objective."[18] Further, they are obliged to reckon with the subjective because it is a foundational dimension of human life whose ramifications cannot be avoided without compromise to the integrity of their investigations of human morality.[19]

The subjective presents a methodological problem, but only for those raised and bred on a diet of behaviorism and later twentieth- and twenty-first century sciences. In earlier times, introspection was the method of choice. With the ever-growing rise of Western science, however, knee-jerk dismissals of introspection became and continue to be common. For example, with respect to the possibility of determining by introspection whether one's actions derive from egoism or altruism, Sober and Wilson write, "Introspection is misleading or incomplete in what it tells us about other facets of the mind; there is no reason to think that the mind is an open book with respect to the issue of ultimate motives" (Sober and Wilson 2000b, 198). Batson is strongly supportive of the judgment: "Sober and Wilson rightly observe that we cannot rely on introspection to identify an ultimate goal; we must infer the ultimate goal by looking at the pattern of behaviour across systematically varying circumstances (Batson 2000, 208). In the pursuit of theoretical ultimates, introspection can play no part. What is essential to recognize, however, is something quite other than theoretical ultimates. Introspection is at the core of the human awareness of death; it is at the core of the human fear of death; and most significant, it is at the core of the human ability to face death head-on. A universal morality would from this vantage point require introspective courage of all humans.

As with the subjective, introspection too might be perceived as a threat, personally as well as professionally. Getting too close to self-examinations, self-reflections, self-inquiries may, after all, be uncomfortable, anxiety-producing, and the like—most certainly with respect to death, that is, to investigating one's feelings, attitudes, and thoughts about one's own mortality. One might well feel that one's own death is best left unexamined. Individual introspective courage might accordingly be fostered and nurtured by cultures. In fact, a universal morality would demand cultural involvement and support. What human awareness and fear of death demand are cultures sophisticated enough to deal with the terror of individual mortality without turning that terror into a rage against others and against Nature. Awareness and fear of death at the individual level indeed pose an enormous cultural as well as individual challenge.

In sum, evolutionary explanations of human morality need to reckon with the concept of death because the roots of human morality are submerged in the human awareness and fear of death. To deny death is to deny vulnerability, and to deny vulnerability is to pretend to powers beyond one. Such is the power of ideologies that have fueled human cultures for ages and prompted their bellicose displays of power. To face the impermanent reality of the human condition opens one to the possibility of a universal morality. Weaning oneself from immortality ideologies and aspiring to a universal morality requires both introspective courage and a positive recognition of the subjective. To live with the truth of the human condition entails both learning to separate the truth from immortality ideologies and learning to forego ultimate answers. Weaning is not easy, but it opens us to the possibility of a universal morality grounded in the foundational truth of human existence.

## NOTES

1. It is not uncommon to use the label "protomorality" (or "prosociality") to describe nonhuman animal moral behaviors. The terminology is self-servingly anthropocentric, linguistically colonizing, and evolutionarily skewed insofar as it is based on the notion of progress-toward-the-human. Evolutionary linkages may be studied without adopting a prejudicial perspective that belittles the moral (or social) relations obtaining

in other species and in turn jeopardizing the possibility of knowing other species in their own terms.

2. Christopher Boehm offers a practical perspective on why chimpanzees do not have a concept of death: "Chimpanzees appear to lack a cognitive tradition that includes any very focused implicit conceptualization of death and, therefore, of killing as the immediate cause of death. It may be that the lack of any practical need to develop a definitive *coup de grace* in hunting helps to leave chimpanzees cognitively unprepared to be efficient killers conspecifically; i.e., prey animals, once disabled, are killed incidentally in the process of being consumed as meat, while adult conspecific strangers who are savagely attacked and then abandoned to die of their wounds (or possibly recover) are not eaten" (Boehm 1992, 165).

3. Consider, for example, the phenomenon of recognition in a penguin rookery. There is no reason to think penguins recognize their own mates and offspring among thousands of others in any way other than the way humans, searching for friend in a crowd, come finally to recognize an overall facial form or style of walking—a certain "pattern of wholeness" (Scheler 1954, 264). Recognition of the pattern is not a matter of analysis but of physiognomic form (for further discussion, see Sheets-Johnstone 1986b and 1990).

4. Spencer's and Keeley's different perspectives on human aggression (each of them cited in the Prologue) lend weight to the notion that humans know themselves to be at risk with respect to other humans. The "confusion of ethical thought" that Spencer describes, namely, the way in which positive feelings of those within oppressed communities are repressed and in turn replaced by antagonistic feelings that are played out in violent acts against the oppressors, culminates in what might well be termed "the pan-cultural cult of the warrior," whose virtues, as Spencer notes, take "first place" (Spencer 1978, 345). In his elucidation of "the myth of a pacified [human] past," Keeley, writing approximately a century after Spencer, remarks, "Our capacity for organized violence, the universal ugliness of war, and the intricate difficulties of keeping a peace are part of the 'pain' of being human." In mustering evidence against a pacified human past, he shows that the pain reaches far back into human history and across all kinds of societally-organized human cultures. Failure to recognize the truth of our past, he states, "encourages us to neglect solving these universal problems in the only place we can—in the present, among ourselves" (Keeley 1996, 171).

It is perhaps not too much to claim that from the time humans arrived at the concept of death, they were from then on infatuated with it, learning what accidents or methods might bring it about, examining in detail how individuals meet with death, met with death, or might meet with death, executing outright killings themselves, torturing others to death, and so on.

5. After recalling Hegel's claim that morality is irrelevant to world history-making heroes, historian Alan Bullock describes Hitler and Stalin precisely as two men who considered themselves "exempt from the ordinary canons of human conduct" (Bullock 1992, 348). Both saw themselves as saviors of their nations—Hitler "to rescue the German people from the humiliation of defeat and the decadence of Weimar [and] to restore them to their rightful historic position as a master race"; Stalin "[to turn] a peasant society into a modern industrialized country and at the same time . . . [into] the first socialist state in the world" (348). Bullock comments, "Neither task could be carried out without countless material and human sacrifices, but on the stage of world history on which they were actors the cost had never counted. History would justify and forgive them, as it had forgiven their predecessors—provided they were successful" (348). Thus Hitler's "Thousand-Year Reich" and Stalin's first-ever communist regime would outlive each man respectively.

6. It can also be and most often is the essential socio-political game, as witness the

following headline in the 2 May 2005 electronic edition of the *Washington Post:* "Both sides of the debate . . . will insist they're fighting over facts. But in reality the fight is over what it always is in Washington—power."

7. In his book *The Company of Strangers,* economist Paul Seabright attempts to link the murderousness of human males to the murderousness of other primate males. In particular, he attempts to put the fact that human males kill one another in evolutionary perspective, claiming through an "evolutionary argument" (Seabright 2004, 51) that nonhuman primate males likewise kill one another. He states, for example, "When unconstrained by fear of reprisals, many other primates systematically exploit opportunities to kill individuals who are not related to themselves" (52). Infanticide, a phenomenon he briefly cites in support of his claim, has certainly been documented in the literature on nonhuman primates, but is not wholly to the point and in fact wide of the mark, i.e., *murder* specifically carried out by adult human males is not of infants but of other adult human males. In the context of his "evolutionary argument that human beings, especially males, are likely to be strongly disposed to kill other, unrelated individuals in the appropriate circumstances" and that chimpanzee males are similarly disposed, he states, "Among chimpanzees, related males regularly cooperate to launch violent, unprovoked attacks against isolated and defenseless members of other troops, even when such attacks yield no food or other resources" (51, 52). In his effort to make an evolutionary connection, he embellishes field studies by primatologists of nonhuman primate raids (seemingly Wrangham and Peterson 1996) with false claims regarding kinship, with adverbs like "systematically" and "regularly," and so on, the whole seemingly conjured in ways that will firmly harness the murderousness of human males to the "murderousness" of nonhuman male primates. The harnessing, however, will not hold: Seabright's anthropocentric attributions are unsupported—nonhuman primate "violence" (Seabright 2004, 52; 262 n. 7) is not equivalent to murder—and in fact are insupportable in default of a concept of death. Moreover Seabright skirts around the biological matrix of male-male competition, alluding to it only indirectly by way of rivalry "for the sexual favors of females" (49). Rather than acknowledging what Darwin described at great length as "the law of battle" (Darwin [1871] 1981), he instead emphasizes and prominences "the tendency on the part of females—far from universal, but sufficient to make a difference—to be drawn sexually to those who have displayed prowess in contests of force" (Seabright 2004, 50). For an extended examination of the biological matrix of male-male competition, see this text, Chapters 3 and 4.

8. In the one instance described as a "freshly killed body," observers were led to the body by "a party of Kahama males" (Wrangham and Peterson 1996, 14).

9. Researchers of our hominid past might find it of considerable interest to explore the possibility that anatomically modern humans and Neandertals, being equally aware of their mortality, were aware of their vulnerability and of their potential to kill. Such an exploration would seem pertinent to those who think anatomically modern humans and Neandertals warred with each other and that the former exterminated the latter.

10. An unusually fine similarity obtains between the ritualist and the lumbering robot of sociobiologist Richard Dawkins (Dawkins 1989). By passing on his genes, the lumbering robot, like the ritualist, also does "nothing less than enable life to continue." See also this chapter, n. 16; Chapter 2, n. 11.

11. The fundamental problem is that human history attests over and over to a different brand of hero, notably those "heroes" who lead multitudes of "lesser" men to murderous acts: Hitler, Stalin, Mao, and Milosevic in recent times, Tamerlane (fourteenth century) and Basil II (eleventh century), for example, in earlier times.

12. Buddhist practitioners are directed either to observe decaying dead bodies or to visualize vividly a body in various states of decay. The practitioner/meditator applies what he/she sees to him/herself: "Verily, this body of mine, too, is of the same nature as that body, it will become like that, and will not escape it" (Thera 1965, 67).

13. The same may be said of sociobiologists such as David Barash: "If men are ever to be at peace, ever certain that their lives have been lived as they were meant to be, they must have, in addition to paternity, culturally elaborated forms of expression that are lasting and sure. Each culture—in its own way—has developed forms that will make men satisfied in their constructive activities without distorting their sure sense of their masculinity" (Barash 1979, 116). It is significant that females have their lives cut out for them and are of small cultural, that is to say, male, concern, as Barash's next sentence affirms: "Fewer cultures have yet found ways to give women a divine discontent that will demand other satisfactions than those of childbearing" (116).

14. Daly and Wilson claim (1983, 285) that uncertainty about paternity motivates homicide and that "[i]f a marriage contract provided a man with a magical guarantee of paternity, the world would be a more peaceable place!" A ready, pan-culturally supportable response to the exclamatory inanity of the claim would affirm that the sooner humans learn to accept the fact that they are mortal, the more peaceful this planet will be.

15. See also Alexander 1987, 62: "[A]s we age, and as senescence proceeds, large numbers of potential sources of mortality tend to lurk ever more malevolently just 'below the surface,' so that, unfortunately, the odds are very high against any dramatic lengthening of the maximum human lifetime through technology." Thus, try as we might to realize *more*, we are limited by "malevolent" sources of death: Nature "lurk[s] ever more malevolently just 'below the surface'."

16. The bounds of this book preclude a full substantiation of this claim. Suffice to note:

First, sexual selection mandates nothing in the way of behavior, thus nothing in the way of the biological imperative "Pass on your genes!" To say, for example, "It is correct beyond question that genes shape brains that induce individuals to do whatever best gets copies of those genes into future generations" (Nesse 2000, 229) is thus misguided.

Second, the pseudobiological directive takes no notice of the fact that humans of any age are vulnerable simply in virtue of their being alive among other humans. This ontologically fragile and continuous dimension of human life is nowhere inscribed genetically; it is nonetheless a basic fact of human life. Sober and Wilson come close to recognizing it when they briefly recognize "the dark side" of group selection. "Group selection," they write, "does not eliminate conflict so much as elevate it to a new level in the biological hierarchy, where it can operate with even more destructive force than before" (Sober and Wilson 2000a, 264). They thus skirt along the edge of a recognition of the fundamental human vulnerability: *being alive among other humans*. This "dark side" of group selection is essential to elucidate, and in depth. The "universal morality" that Sober and Wilson allude to hangs in the balance and, as others have noted, is contingent on an understanding of human nature (Boehm 2000c, 149, 179–80; Boehm 2000b, 212; Carling 2000, 122; Mysterud 2000, 226). The understanding is incomplete short of a recognition of the foundational pan-cultural human awareness and fear of death and of the vulnerability that is the ontologically continuous if muted complement of that awareness and fear.

Third, the pseudobiological directive "Pass on your genes!" is similar to the biblical directive "Go forth and multiply" (Genesis 28). This ideational conjunction of science and religion is perhaps a function of human male mentality in that it is preeminently male humans who formulated the directives and to whom the directives are addressed. One might easily be led to think that, in drafting and codifying the directives, males were/are simply writing about and justifying themselves. But this judgment, by itself, ignores the task of understanding the profound influence that knowledge of human mortality has on both human morality and formulations of human morality.

Fourth, the notion of genes as ultimates throws a genetically reductive net over living subjects. If one can boldly state that "ethics . . . is an illusion fobbed off on us by our genes to get us to cooperate" (Ruse and Wilson 1985, 51), or wonder whether "after the new Darwinism [i.e., evolutionary psychology] takes root, the word *moral* can be anything but a joke" (Wright 1994, 326), then clearly, the reductive net has been effectively cast. The net transforms sexual selection into something other than a scientific construct based on observations of life and converts the living reproductive success of animate forms into an *immortality ideology of genes*.

And fifth, an immortality ideology is not just transparent but explicitly affirmed by Richard Dawkins, the originator of "selfish genes": "What I am doing is emphasizing the potential near-immortality of a gene, in the form of copies, as its defining property" (Dawkins 1989, 35). Genes, Dawkins proclaims, "are denizens of geological time: genes are forever" (35). We humans thus have a piece of immortality; we are made up of "immortal replicator[s]" (266). See also Dawkins's conception of "God's covenant with Abraham" (Dawkins 1998).

Biologist Brian Goodwin has argued persuasively for a broader biological perspective, one that takes "complex wholes" into account, "complex wholes such as organisms, communities, and ecosystems" (Goodwin 2001, viii). He observes that "[d]espite the power of genocentric biology to explain an impressive amount of biological data, there are basic areas where it fails. One of these, the most important, concerns its claim that understanding genes and their activities is enough to explain the properties of organisms. . . . The position I am taking in biology could be called organocentric rather than genocentric" (3).

Of particular further interest is the fact that, in the course of presenting his broader perspective, Goodwin takes forthright cognizance of the immortality ideology inherent in genocentric biology. For example, with respect to nineteenth-century zoologist's August Weismann's experimental conclusions, he notes that "organisms [were separated] into two distinctly different parts, one mortal and transient (the body) and the other potentially immortal, the transmitter of hereditary instructions (the chromosomes in the germ cells)" (27–28); with respect to present-day molecular biology, he notes that "we can identify DNA as the potentially immortal hereditary stuff of life, while protein is the mortal material that makes up the transient body of the organism" (28–29).

17. Cf. Hume, who introduces his *Treatise on Human Nature* with the following thought: "Nothing is more usual and more natural for those, who pretend to discover any thing new to the world in philosophy and the sciences, than to insinuate the praises of their own systems, by decrying all those, which have been advanced before them" (Hume [1789] 1888, xvii).

Attention might also be called to the startling verb Merleau-Ponty uses in seeking to define the kind of history of philosophy he wishes to write vis-à-vis the philosophy of others. He states that it would not be "a flattening of history into 'my' philosophy—and . . . would not be idolatry." Instead, he writes, it would be a "history of philosophy as a *perception* of other philosophers, intentional encroachment upon them, a thought of one's own that does not kill them, either by overcoming them, or by copying them" (Merleau-Ponty 1968, 198). The physically invasive sense of "intentional encroachment upon others" ("*empiètement intentionnel sur eux*"; Merleau-Ponty 1964, 251) together with a felt but properly restrained underlying urge to do away with, to kill, what is contrary ("*pensée propre qui ne les tue pas*"; 251), appear to be strong human dispositions in the realm of ideas.

At a purely ideational or theoretical level, ideological disputes can indeed be a metaphorical matter of life and death, as Becker (via Rank) affirms. At the level of actual living bodies, however, ideologies can be a literal matter of life and death, as is evident in socio-political dictatorships that efface all signs of the past in forging an entirely new society. Such socio-political dictatorships reach as far back as 221 B.C. when the emperor of Qin unified China, to the twentieth century when Hitler, Stalin, and Mao unified their respective countries. Ian Buruma writes perceptively of such dictators, characterizing their effacements as creating "a tabula rasa which cannot be challenged by meddlesome priests or fussy scholars. The immediate past is by definition inferior, even evil" (Buruma 2005, 35).

18. In this context, recognition should be given to the well-known studies of Giacomo Rizzolatti, Vittorio Gallese, Leonardo Fogassi, and other researchers at the University of Parma—the "Parma group," as an anonymous reviewer of this book referred to them. They are indisputably adding to our knowledge of the primate brain through their experimental studies of macaque monkeys and human subjects. Researchers following the footsteps of this group are being similarly productive: they too are giving us insights into the neural substrates that are activated functionally and in integrated ways when we do such everyday things as grasp a cup or infer what someone is intending to do. The insights allow us to correlate the neurology of the brain with actual experience—with the "subjective." It is important to emphasize that the relationship is correlational. Were one to reduce "subjective" experience to neurological happenings in a brain, one would diminish or otherwise discount first-person experience, and, in effect, diminish or otherwise discount the need to elucidate the realities of first-person experience. In short, neurological happenings in primate brains are not constitutive of experience but are, as indicated, functionally integrated aspects of animate experience. The point warrants elaboration from both a conceptual and an evolutionary perspective.

Consistent use of the term "embodied" by researchers in cognitive neuroscience appears to be a direct effort to avoid reductionist modes of thinking, but it is itself a radically problematic term. As I have elsewhere shown, the term "embodiment" and its derivatives are a lexical band-aid covering a 350-plus-year-old wound (Sheets-Johnstone 1999a, 1999b). The favored derivative term "embodied" is indeed today everywhere bandied about, not only in the present-day designation of cognitive neuroscience as "'embodied' cognitive neuroscience," but in virtually all subjects discussed under its heading, and in neurophenomenology as well. Thus we have, for example, texts and discussions of "embodied experience" (e.g., Gibbs 2006), "embodied simulation" (e.g., Gallese, Keysers, and Rizzolatti 2004; Gallese 2005; Gallese, Eagle, Migone 2007; Gallese 2007a), "the embodied mind" (Thompson 2007), "an embodied perspective" (Gibbs 2006), and even "embodied movement(s)" (anonymous reviewer). In reality, the term perpetuates a schizoid metaphysics. As I have pointed out elsewhere (Sheets-Johnstone 1999a, 1999b), in reality, we do not look around and see *embodied* beings or experience ourselves as *embodied*—unless, of course, we experience others and ourselves precisely as *packaged* in some way.

Researchers in the new "embodied" cognitive neuroscience and in neurophenomenology as well (e.g., Thompson 2007) emphasize the interaction of brain, body, and world, not only presumably to avoid a reductionist mode of thought but to situate the brain in the realities of life itself. Yet no matter how insistently and strongly they emphasize the interaction, the separation of brain and body preserves the notion of a "headquarters" distinct from an instrument that, through its sense organs, receives information from the outside world and moves about in that world. Through its artificial separation from the body, *the brain* in a quite literal sense loses its natural footing in the world. Though *action understanding*, for example, as the "Parma group" commonly shows, is based on the firing of "mirror neurons" (see, for example, Rizzolatti and Craighero 2004 and Freedberg and Gallese 2007) and is hypothesized to be of primary importance in neurological investigations of a range of human experiences, from social cognition to aesthetic experience, the natural kinesthetically experienced dynamics of action are unacknowledged, much less analyzed. Indeed, while a sensory-motor system is at times mentioned, the dynamic realities of animation are absent (e.g., Gallese 2005). Further validation of this fact is found in the consultation of the index of texts in embodied cognitive neuroscience and neurophenomenology: there is virtually no entry for proprioception, kinesthesia, or movement, or if an entry exists, a single page or sometimes two is indicated (see, for example, Thompson 2007 and Gibbs 2006).

As the present chapter goes on to show, there is a methodological problem as well for people in the human sciences in incorporating the subjective. It is edifying in this context to recall Darwin's observation of how best to proceed to understandings of mind. Darwin wrote, "Experience shows the problem of the mind cannot be solved by attacking the citadel itself.—the mind is function of body.—we must bring some *stable* foundation to argue from" (Darwin 1987, 564). His observation is doubly significant: it calls our attention to the fact that mind and morphology evolve together and that a proper methodology is the key to our enlightenment concerning "the problem of the mind." Several points may be made with respect to his doubly significant observation.

To begin with, what Darwin meant by saying "Experience shows" may be interpreted in two ways. He may have been referring to philosophers and scientists who attempt to show the nature of mind by attacking the citadel itself. But he may also very well have meant that *his own experience*—his own first-person experiences of animate life—showed him that the mind was not something distinct from the body but precisely, as he states, a function of body. In effect, animate bodies are mindful bodies. What Darwin observed in his travels and in his home studies as well, especially his extended study of worms in his last years (Darwin [1881] 1976), was movement—the habits and practices of living creatures. He observed that what they did and how they did it made sense in terms of survival. It is thus hardly surprising or odd that he should write what he did. The idea that mind and morphology evolve together surely makes evolutionary sense. The idea that mind is rooted in nature is moreover methodologically significant. Darwin's ending line intimates as much; that is, "we must bring some *stable* foundation to argue from" is quintessentially a question of methodology. But what methodology, one might properly ask? Just what constitutes a *stable* foundation?

Surely we can take a further cue from evolutionary biology, specifically, a cue from Darwin's formulation of the origin of species, of the descent of man and selection in relation to sex, and the expression of the emotions in man and animals (Darwin [1859] 1968, [1871] 1981, [1872] 1965, respectively). We can in other words take a cue from his basic writings about the animate world. They all have a stable foundation. They are based on observations of animate creatures making their way in the world, on the animate forms and dynamics of life itself. But that is not all. Darwin meticulously transcribed what he observed into a language that both captured and preserved the uniqueness of those animate forms and dynamics. The stable foundation from which he argued was thus not initially explanatory or theoretical in nature, but *descriptive*. His consequent thesis concerning evolution and his explanations of the interconnectedness of animate life rest on *descriptive foundations* (Sheets-Johnstone 2002a; see also Sheets-Johnstone 2007).

If we ask what the specific import might be of descriptive foundations for understandings of mind, it is apparent that they elucidate the actual living phenomenon itself, whatever it might be, and thus provide not only a *stable* foundation from which to argue in pursuit of explanations or theories, but a *stable* foundation from which to pursue scientific investigations in the first place. What prompts and drives investigations in embodied cognitive neuroscience and neurophenomenology is, after all, life itself. That being so, descriptive analyses of human experience as it is immediately and directly lived are foundational to the scientific enterprise; they detail and bring to light the living and lived-through realities of experience, its complex and subtle relationships and dynamics. Descriptive foundations are moreover the empirical point of origin for verification by others who can corroborate or question the authenticity and aptness of a descriptive analysis, or amplify it in greater detail in an effort to specify the complexities and subtleties of the subject of investigation more fully or with greater precision.

In sum, the Darwinian foundation on which evolutionary biology rests is clearly already grounded in bodily life; the living subjects it describes thus need no "embodying." Indeed, at the very core of the distinction between investigations in both the new "embodied" cognitive neuroscience and neurophenomenology and the descriptive literature on the experiential dynamics of life itself is the outright omission in the former of what earlier famed neurophysiologists realized, namely, the living significance of movement: Roger Sperry concluded that the brain is an organ of and for movement; Alexander Luria wrote of complex sequential activities such as writing one's name and calculating sums as "kinetic/kinaesthetic melodies" (Sperry 1952; Luria 1973; see also Sheets-Johnstone 2003b). Sperry and Luria recognized that animation is at the heart of our aliveness as it is at the heart of the aliveness of all forms of animate life. Clearly, in the new "embodied" cognitive neuroscience, the brain is no longer akin to a brain in a vat, as it was in the former computational and connectionist modes of cognitive neuroscience, but it remains artificially separated from a properly recognized and properly described proprioceptively and kinesthetically alive body. The singular item needing to be "embodied" and in fact warranting "embodiment" is thus actually the brain itself. The brain is indeed in reality an *embodied* brain, a brain that, like the beating heart and the dynamics of breath, is part of a living whole.

For an additional discussion of mirror neurons specifically, see Chapter 5, note 37.

19. Cf. Goodwin's "science of qualities," in Goodwin 2001, chap. 7.

# 2

## Death and Immortality Ideologies in Western Philosophy

> I have seen men of reputation, when they have been condemned, behaving in the strangest manner: they seemed to fancy that they were going to suffer something dreadful if they died, and that they could be immortal if you only allowed them to live.
> 
> —SOCRATES, *Apology*

> Quotation of the Day [*New York Times*]—"Thirty-six hours, then we'll be in the history books forever."
> 
> —MAJOR MORRIS T. GOINS, Army's Third Infantry Division, speaking to some soldiers before the push to Baghdad, April 13, 2003

### I. INTRODUCTION

Focused attention on central figures in Western philosophy will effectively highlight the abiding place of death and immortality ideologies in human life, bringing facets of the essential relationship of death to immortality ideologies to the fore along with human preoccupations with their own mortality.[1] In particular, this chapter will show in detail how the finality of death may be suppressed by an immortality ideology that transfigures the reality of death. It will do this by drawing on the writings of three notable figures in Western philosophy—Descartes, Heidegger, and Derrida. The aim is both to exemplify immortality ideologies in concrete instances and to examine Rank's psychoanalytic writings on immortality ideologies more closely. The chapter in no way presents an exhaustive examination of immortality ideologies in Western philosophy, and the notable figures on which it focuses are in fact highly selective. They are chosen in view of the methodologically diverse and emblematic ways in which they proceed: through rational argument, through a descriptive metaphysics, and through deconstructive techniques, respectively. As will be evident, Heidegger's immortality ideology differs radically from that of Descartes and of Derrida. Being

This chapter is a slightly modified version of an article that first appeared in *Continental Philosophy Review* (Sheets-Johnstone 2003c).

anchored in the thinking of the "they," the ideology is critically assailed rather than hopefully or discreetly pursued.

Because immortality ideologies were originally recognized and in fact so named by Rank, a close examination of his writings on the subject is not only apposite but is itself philosophically rewarding, providing ample grounds for philosophical thought. Rank was a Freudian dissident who, in introducing the concept of immortality ideologies, traced out historical and psychological roots of "soul-belief" (*Seelenglaube*). A section of the chapter is devoted not only to an examination of his thesis but to its psycho-socio-political elaboration by cultural anthropologist Ernest Becker. In *The Denial of Death* and *Escape from Evil*, Becker analyzes and documents in fine detail the *raison d'être* and psychology of Rank's concept of immortality ideologies, delving deeply into Freudian psychoanalysis in the process, but anchoring his work consistently in Rankian thought. A later section of the chapter demonstrates the relevancy of Rank's correlative thesis of 'the Double' (*Der Doppelgänger*). It shows in particular how Rank's concept of 'the Double' provides deepened understandings of immortality ideologies in general and a deepened analysis of Derrida's immortality ideology in particular. Finally, a concluding section points up the extraordinary cogency of Rank's distinction between the rational and the irrational to the question of the human need for immortality ideologies.

In preface to what follows, a word should be said about the term "ideology." An immortality ideology is precisely a story: a belief structure either without empirical foundations or going beyond empirical foundations as in a belief in procreative immortality, i.e., living in generations to come through one's children, their children, and so on. A belief in personal immortality or in the immortality of "the soul" is from an empirical perspective unwarranted. While humans have given reports of near-death experiences, for example, none has given a report of *after-death experiences. Some philosophers might nonetheless be disposed to think that if a position is rationally defensible, it is not an ideology. Rational defensibility, however, does not confer ideological immunity where it is a question of *immortality*. Though humans may desire immortality, they have no knowledge of it, hence no grounds for reasoning about it. They can in fact offer only indirect reasons to sustain their belief in it. Rank's explanation of the motivation for immortality ideologies is of particular interest in this context. He suggests in his psychoanalytic study of the soul and of spiritual belief from earliest human times onward that the denial of death, i.e., belief in immortality, keeps fear of death at bay. The same thought is echoed in his epigrammatic quotation of astronomer-physicist Sir Arthur Stanley Eddington: "[R]eality is a child which cannot survive without its nurse, illusion" (Rank 1950, 13–14, 168, respectively).[2]

II. DESCARTES

*On the Purpose of the* Meditations *as Specified in the Synopsis*

Sustained focus on the mind/body problem has long deflected attention away from the ultimate purpose of Descartes's *Meditations:* to prove, by argumentation, that "the mind ["or the soul of man"] is immortal by its very nature" (Descartes 1984, 10). To arrive at this proof, Descartes affirms it necessary "to form a concept of the soul which is as clear as possible and is also quite distinct from every concept of body." He believes such a concept to be "the first and most important prerequisite for knowledge of the immortality of the soul" (9). In effect, while his proof rests on a distinction between mind and body, that distinction is not the *raison d'être* of his *Meditations,* at the very least not as originally envisioned.[3] Moreover contrary to what one might think, his purpose is not either to show that the external world really exists or that people really do have bodies. Not only does Descartes state that "no sane person has ever seriously doubted these things" (11), but he states explicitly that the purpose of his *Meditations* is to show that arguments leading to "knowledge of our own minds and of God" are more "solid" and "transparent" than arguments demonstrating the existence of the external world and of bodies, and that, as objects of knowledge, mind and God "are the most certain and evident of all possible objects of knowledge for the human intellect" (11).

It is odd—even ironic given his perdurable influence on Western culture—that Descartes's fundamental claim in his Synopsis to the *Meditations* has not received primary or even secondary attention. Bernard Williams gives testimony to this fact when, in his *Encyclopedia of Philosophy* article on Descartes, he remarks that "[t]he influence of Descartes has been enormous" (Williams 1967, 354), but nowhere mentions anything of the guiding and ultimate purpose of his *Meditations.* Interestingly enough, however, he does so in passing in his later book on Descartes, the first time in a footnote where he points out that the original edition of the *Meditations* carried the subtitle "in which are demonstrated the existence of God *and the immortality of the soul*" (Williams's italics); the second toward the end of the book where he points out, with respect to Descartes's denial that animals have souls, that "[f]or him, soul meant separable soul, and separable soul meant the possibility of immortality" (Williams 1978, 105, 287, respectively). As with most discussions of the *Meditations*, Williams's focus is on epistemological concerns: certainty, the foundations of knowledge, philosophical methodology, and so on.[4] On the other hand, Anthony Flew's article on immortality in the *Encyclopedia of Philosophy* (Flew 1967), though not highlighting Descartes's *Meditations* as meditations providing a rational basis for a belief in immortality, discusses other works in which Descartes argues for and makes claims about immortality.

Descartes's *Meditations* do not merely lay out rational grounds for a belief in immortality, grounds that may be examined and subsequently accepted, refuted, or elaborated; they constitute an immortality ideology, a credo or doctrine concerning human death. The ideology is constructed on the basis of an immaterial mind, a mind exempt from destruction and death because it is *supernatural*, beyond the reach of nature and natural forces. A brief review of mind as immaterial substance, in Descartes's understanding of the term *substance*, will show how its supernatural status is the foundation of its immortality, thus how Descartes's immortality ideology is constructed.

*Mind as Immaterial Substance*

By demonstrating how, unlike the body, the mind does not decay, change shape, and so on, Descartes eventually arrives at what he claims is a clear and distinct conception of the mind, one that shows it to be an altogether different substance from the body. In his *Principles of Philosophy*, he defines substance as "a thing which exists in such a way as to depend on no other thing for its existence" (Descartes 1985b, para. 51, p. 210). He goes on to expand this definition in two interrelated ways: with respect to created things and to God. Mind and body, he says, are both substances that are created and that do not depend on other things but "need only the concurrence of God in order to exist" (para. 52, p.

210). He subsequently characterizes mind as "created thinking substance" (para 54, p. 211). Part of the characterization derives from experiences spelled out in the *Meditations;* that is, on the basis of his experiences of doubting, Descartes finds mind to be a substance that *thinks,* doubt being a form of thought. That mind is a created substance, however, and that its existence is dependent on God, are expanded facets of the original definition that, in contrast, derive not from experience but from arguments Descartes offers on their behalf. It is perhaps for this reason that, in his Synopsis to the *Meditations,* Descartes says only that arguments in his Second Meditation—which show that the "decay of the body does not imply the destruction of the mind"—are sufficient "to give mortals the hope of an after-life" (Descartes 1984, 10). In other words, rational principles being less solid than he would like, Descartes appears to acknowledge that he does not—and indeed, cannot—actually *prove* immortality but can only show there is reason to hope. His immortality ideology might therefore be summed up in the words, "Whosoever believeth in my arguments shall have hope everlasting."

Considered from the perspective of his arguments in the *Meditations* and their expressed aim, Descartes's resolution of mind into a "created thinking substance" is less an experientially-tethered understanding of mind than a specification of it as something outside Nature. His methodology undergirds the specification. It is less pointed toward an investigation of mind *in situ,* so to speak, than toward a contemplation of it removed from its everyday commerce with the world. In particular, by casting an all-pervasive doubt on everything experienced, his investigational procedure is akin to typical laboratory practice in which one puts certain strictures on experimental subjects, Descartes's stricture of doubt functioning as a blanket skepticism with respect to beliefs, opinions, and so on. Moreover by methodologically specifying mind in terms of what mind *does,* Descartes emphatically undergirds its specification as something outside Nature: Nature is material substance through and through; what mind *does* has no comparable material substance. Doubts, understandings, affirmations, denials, willings, refusings, imaginings, and so on (19), are all doings or functions that have no physical reality. In effect, the created thinking substance that is mind, being totally unlike the created extended substance that is body, is of just the character necessary to constitute the supernatural foundation of his immortality ideology.

## Mind and the Question of Time

Descartes's functional understanding of mind takes no notice of its temporal nature and, in effect, no notice of a certain linkage with Nature in virtue of its temporal nature. His functional identification of mind occludes recognition of the experienced flux and impermanence of thoughts, motivations, images, plans, memories, and so on; in a word, the actual temporal flow of mind fails to come into view. Accordingly, it might on the contrary, and on the basis of experience, be argued—and persuasively—that mind mirrors Nature quite strikingly in its ongoing, ever-changing flow of thoughts, ideas, images, feelings, moods, and so on. "Nature is a principle of motion and change," as Aristotle pointed out (Aristotle 1984b, 200b12–14), and mind is no exception to this principle. Indeed, temporally speaking, mind is of the very nature of Nature. Furthermore, and again, on the basis of experience, it might be argued that coincidental with a recognition of the experienced temporal nature of mind comes a recognition of the experienced quasi-autonomy of mind. Hence it might be argued further that experience shows mind to have a spontaneous character, one that may in fact be at odds with an individual's predilections and desires, as when unwanted thoughts or fears, or disturbing images intrude. In Descartes's wide sense of thinking, what experience leads one to recognize is that there are indeed thoughts without a thinker:[5] ideas, images, sentiments, memories, feelings arise on their own and unfold on their own—in a manner not altogether unlike sleep and hunger. From this experiential vantage point, one might say that minds have minds of their own. Their inherent spontaneity gives further weight to a linkage with Nature since Nature too is inherently spontaneous: sun spots form, comets streak by, winds come up, the earth quakes suddenly. What arises in Nature appears too to arise *causa sui*.

The above considerations clash with a Cartesian supernatural view of mind, but they also lead to a fundamental insight. The Cartesian mind is not different from the body merely in the fact that it is a thinking as opposed to an extended substance and thereby immaterial as opposed to material. In other words, it is not simply that mind is a *non-spatial* substance. It is also in a Cartesian sense a *non-temporal* substance in that it is impervious to time. Descartes does not specify the non-temporal nature of mind directly but implicitly indicates it in specifying temporal aspects of the body: the body moves, decays, and changes shape—all in virtue of its materiality. An immaterial mind does none of these things. Non-spatiality is thus the gateway to non-temporality: the mind's immateriality makes it impervious to all things temporal. It abides without change and in this sense is outside time—in effect, immortal. It is thus not thinking substance itself, but *the non-temporal nature* of thinking substance that ultimately anchors Descartes's immortality ideology and gives it its force.

In fairness to, and in support of Descartes, one might respond that temporal possibilities and temporal aspects of bodies are of course not applicable to mind since mind does not gad about in the world, and though it changes with age—in normally standard ways in infancy and childhood, in quite variable ways in late adulthood—those changes are of a quite different order from those of an extended substance. Yet one might question such a response by noting that acknowledgment of the temporal possibilities that *are* applicable to mind—flux, impermanence, coming to awareness, fading away—rests not on an examination of what minds *do* and how they function, but on an examination of how they are experienced. Temporal aspects are discovered not by ascertaining what capacities mind evinces—affirming, denying, and so on—but by attending to the actual course of its activities. Such attending discloses a temporality characterized by impermanence: thoughts arise and vanish, images appear and disappear, feelings wax and wane. In a sense, mortality is a built-in of mind. The "substantizing" of mind fails to do justice to its streaming, fluctuating, unceasingly changing flow. Indeed, from a Buddhist perspective, nothing mindful lasts except the possibility of mindfulness itself. Hume approximates this experience of the temporal reality of mind when he describes mind as a theater of impressions, an ongoing coming-to-be and disappearing of perceptions, thoughts, and so on. In Descartes's *Meditations,* the inherently motional nature of mind never surfaces. In turn, its temporal metaphysics never surfaces. Only the body has a temporal metaphysics, as Descartes specifies in *The Passions:* when we die, it is not that the soul takes leave of the body, thereby depriving it of heat and movement, but that bodily heat and organs decay on their own, and with their decay, the soul takes leave of the body (Descartes 1985a, para. 5, 329). Thus, death is death of the body, not the soul. The soul—or the mind—is immortal.

If one asks why Descartes would seek a proof for immortality and provide arguments for hope, the reason is not difficult to find. The spectre of death looms large for many if not most humans, larger perhaps at times than the phenomenon of life itself. Immortality ideologies are created to subdue death, to circumvent it, or to outlive it. The understanding of an immortality ideology thus depends on fine-grained analyses of both human knowledge of death and human fear of death. We should perhaps again note that the concept of death is peculiar to humans (see Chapter 1). While many non-human animals are well aware of the sudden disappearance of individuals from their midst and of stark changes in individuals, notably, changes in their responsivity and animation (see, for example, Goodall 1971, 214–24), they do not have a concept of death. Hence, they are not aware that they too lead a punctuated existence, that their life too is on the line, that *in time,* they too will die. A fear of death is thus absent. Without a concept of death, there can be no foreknowledge of one's own death, hence no fear that *in time,* one's life will come to an end—or alternatively, no fear that one might be killed suddenly in some way by something or someone in the otherwise nonviolent course of everyday life.

### III. HEIDEGGER AND IMMORTALITY IDEOLOGIES

In describing inauthentic Being with respect to death, Heidegger describes ways in which humans avoid acknowledgement of their own death, and ways in which their anxiety about death is transformed into what he terms an "ambiguous" fear of death (Heidegger 1962, 297, 298). Though their aim is altogether remote from such an end, Heidegger's descriptions underscore the reality of immortality ideologies. Indeed, Heidegger's critique of the "they" with respect to death may be read both as an implicit condemnation of immortality ideologies and an implicit undermining of them through an exposition of their driving motivations, namely, a denial of one's mortality and a concealment of one's anxiety about death. His descriptions merit attentive study from this perspective.

Writing of the "average everyday Being-towards-death" (296), Heidegger begins by pointing out how death is "'known' as a mishap which is constantly occurring," and which, because of its constant occurrence, is simply an everyday event consumed in "idle talk" and thereby "inconspicuous": it is someone else or "one" who dies, not oneself (297). The possibility of one's own death is perpetually concealed. So also is what Heidegger calls the "nonrelational" character of the possibility of one's death: the possibility is devoid of any connection whatsoever to others; it has no outward ties. Furthermore, the possibility of one's death cannot be "outstripped": it cannot be exceeded or out-run in any way (297). All three aspects of death as Dasein's possibility are concealed in the "everydayness of Dasein" (296). Heidegger not only makes explicit, but underscores the reason for the concealment when he observes, "*The 'they' does not permit us the courage for anxiety in the face of death.* . . . The 'they' concerns itself with transforming this anxiety into fear. . . . In addition, the anxiety which has been made ambiguous as fear, is passed off as a weakness with which no self-assured Dasein may have any acquaintance" (298). In effect, in its cowardly everydayness, Dasein envelopes itself within protective ways of thinking, speaking, and acting that keep its mortality and anxiety of death at bay. As indicated above, Heidegger does not describe the concealment in such terms, but the concealment clearly shields Dasein with an immortality ideology, protecting Dasein from its own possibility of death.

We see more deeply into what motivates the immortality ideology, its everyday imperviousness as reflected in everyday Dasein's stolid attitude toward death, in Heidegger's affirmation that "Death is the possibility of the absolute impossibility of Dasein" (294). The possibility of the *absolute* impossibility of Dasein not only leaves no doubt about the finality of death; *it leaves no room for an immortality ideology that might appease or temper the finality*. The impossibility of Dasein, the closure of Being, is indeed absolute. It is without appeal. Authentic being for Heidegger means precisely facing the possibility of absolute impossibility without veiling it with an immortality ideology, in effect facing the possibility as an indubitable and inescapable certainty. Indeed, authentic being means having no comforting but illusory place to hide from the absolute impossibility of being. Authentic being is distinguished from inauthentic being in just such terms. Authentically being-towards death, one can no longer say, for example, "One dies too, sometime, but not right away" (299); one can no longer allow "the 'they'" to cover up "what is peculiar in death's certainty—*that it is possible at any moment*" (302); one can no longer act in "everyday matters" in ways that conceal the indefiniteness of death, anymore than one can continue to act in "everyday matters" in ways that conceal its certainty (302). On the contrary, death is "a possibility of *Dasein's* Being," and Dasein's Being is a Being-towards death" (305).

Clearly, what Heidegger is implicitly calling humans to confront is their inmost existential condition: the possibility of their own death, the possibility of their own ultimate non-being. He is calling them away from the immortality ideologies that define everyday human life and that veil both the possibility of death and its indefiniteness. His judgment is unequivocal with respect to immortality ideologies. He reiterates many times over that death is *"the end of Dasein"* (303), and that the possibility of death is *"one's ownmost, . . . [that it] is non-relational, . . . [and that it] is not to be outstripped"* (303; also 294, 296, 299). As indicated above, his descriptive metaphysics leaves no doubt about the finality of death and no room for an immortality ideology. Living authentically takes courage precisely because it means "penetrat[ing] into . . . *the possibility of the impossibility of any existence at all"* (307). But furthermore, his descriptive metaphysics leaves no correlative doubt and no correlative room with respect to authentic being either. That is, authentic being faces death not as some actual event, but as the indubitable and inescapable possibility of existential nothingness, a possibility that looms ahead, but looms ahead always presently in the form of anticipation. Heidegger characterizes this ontological form of anticipation in ways that unmistakably accentuate once again the immortality ideology that sustains everyday Dasein but that at the same time unmistakably accentuate the anxiety that conclusively marks the impossibility of an immortality ideology at all. He writes, "[A]nticipation *reveals to Dasein its lostness in the they-self, and brings it face to face with the possibility of being itself . . . in an impassioned* **freedom towards death**—a freedom which has been released from the Illusions of the 'they', and which is factical, certain of itself, and anxious" (311; Heidegger's italics and bold). In sum, in anticipation, one comes face to face with the certainty and indefiniteness of one's death and lives it without recourse to an immortality ideology that might promise one hope or save one from one's authentic ontological possibility: the "Being-towards-death [that] is essentially anxiety" (310).[6]

Present-day Continental concerns with *Other, Others,* and *Otherness*—concerns related at times to seemingly near fanatical concerns with *difference*—can be curiously deflective with respect to death, successfully eliding the possibility of what Heidegger specifies as being face-to-face with oneself (see, for example, Heidegger 1962, 233). At the same time, they can be curiously suggestive of an undercurrent theme of death in focusing on something nameless, something that is an unspecified unknown, something that is thus an easy stand-in for death.[7] In this respect, they can appear even to exemplify everyday Dasein in its veiling of death and anxiety of death. The *Other, Others, Otherness,* and *difference* can certainly be a source of worry, threat, and danger, but one can address and analyze "the problem of" the *Other, Others, Otherness* and *difference* with far less anxiety than one can address and analyze "the problem of" death (see, for example, Bell 1998). In fact, current social as well as philosophical dispositions are to evade confrontations with anxiety, precisely as Heidegger indicates: "existential angst" on behalf of one's own possibilities is muffled. Everyday killings and destruction, for example, happen 'out there', in places one is not and to people one is not. As Heidegger recognizes, it is "the everyday publicness of the 'they', which brings tranquillized self-assurance . . . into the average everydayness of Dasein" (Heidegger 1962, 233).[8] But everyday Dasein's tranquility—by whatever means it is bought—is bought at an ontological price, for "Dasein is anxious in the very depths of its Being" (234). Moreover only through a recognition of its anxiety does authentic Being come to light: "Anxiety brings Dasein face to face with its *Being-free for* . . . the authenticity of its Being, and for this authenticity as a possibility which it always is" (232). Indeed, anxiety shows itself in ways that shame, for example, or remorse, that is, other "personal emotions," do not. Anxiety individualizes one without relief. In shame, there is a drama in which the Other figures centrally; in remorse, there is similarly a drama in which the Other and/or a particular situation figures centrally. In anxiety, there is oneself and oneself alone. From this perspective, one might read the whole of *Being and Time* as a fine-grained existential analysis of how the core and essential meaning of Being is death: *how to be is to die*.[9] Whatever their particular form, immortality ideologies as instantiated by the "they" suppress this meaning. They effectively hide what Sartre later describes as the "Nothingness [that] lies coiled in the heart of being—like a worm" (Sartre 1956, 21).

IV. PSYCHOLOGICAL UNDERPINNINGS OF IMMORTALITY IDEOLOGIES

It is especially relevant to examine Rank's writings on immortality ideologies and their elaboration by Becker in the context of Heidegger's pointed concern with death and its consistent veiling by everyday Dasein who has not the courage to face it. The writings and elaboration elucidate multiple psychological dimensions of the "they" of whom Heidegger writes. Accordingly, by spelling out Rank's concept of immortality ideologies and Becker's elaboration, we will gain substantive psycho-social perspectives on Heidegger's portrayals of the "they," and correspondingly, keener psycho-social understandings of his depiction of the natural attitude toward death. But we will also ultimately gain a sense of how illusion is or can be psychologically justified, that is, how, in the end, Heidegger's call to authentic Being can go unheeded and a need for immortality ideologies can be upheld.

Through his investigations of ancient and modern human history, myths, and anthropological field reports, and through his examination of contemporary cultural practices—notably, psychology and psychoanalysis—Rank found that assuagement of the fear of death through soul-belief pervades all human cultures, from the earliest known human societies or groups onward (Rank 1998). He found too that it is variable: soul-belief can and does change over time within particular groups or cultures, and it can and does take on different guises from one individual to the next, as Rank shows with respect to prominent figures in psychoanalysis (see below). A soul-belief is thus a belief that may take one of several possible ideological forms: it may anchor a belief in individual immortality, a belief in collective immortality, or a belief in generative immortality. That is, the belief may specify eternal life for no more than a single individual, as in the doctrine of Christian salvation; or it may encompass the immortality of a collective soul, as evidenced in the epics and myths of a community or group, and in religions in which ancestors are actively honored; or it may specify immortality through one's descendants, i.e., through procreative acts that beget children. Whatever its form, the ideology has a complex structure embodying values, proscriptions, punishments, sufferings, and so on, all conceptually joined to the same end, namely, the affirmation of an imperishable soul. Thus, however different primitive soul-belief might be from ancient Greek soul-belief, for example, or soul-beliefs codified in myths from soul-beliefs in present-day religions, they are all driven by the same human constants: fear of death and the desire for eternal life.

Rank's intent, however, was to demonstrate something more than a psycho-historical phenomenon. It was to show how psychology, by becoming a science that rejects the subjective, compromised its originating source. Psychology, and by extension, psychoanalysis, transformed the fundamental human fear of death and the concomitant human desire for eternal life, abandoning all talk of soul and turning itself into a superficial materialist enterprise: "Psychoanalysis arrived to save the human soul in a materialistic era sick with self-consciousness and threatened by loss of belief in immortality and in its public expression, religion.... But realistic psychology is the death knell of the soul, whose source, nature, and value lie precisely in the abstract, the unfathomable, and the esoteric" (23). Rank points up the disturbed relationship with a telling contrast. He writes, "With psychoanalysis people try to hold on to what they need and want; in this *'psychology without a soul'* they seek a doctrine of redemption that science cannot be, although in therapy we still find clear echoes of the will to rescue the soul and spiritual well-being. This works only to the extent that psychoanalysis can support the illusion of the old soul-belief and give us *soul without psychology*" (23).

Rank's disillusionment with Freud, Jung, and Adler centers precisely on their forsaking *psyche,* Freud abandoning it for biology, Jung for religion, and Adler for sociology. An ironic twist is evident in this context. The term *psychology* derives from Psyche, which word itself derives from Greek *psychein:* to breathe, blow, hence live; *Psyche* is "the animating principle in man and other living beings, the source of all vital activities" (OED). Thus, psychology's—or *Psyche's*—attachment to soul is fundamental. In the course of relating the complex psycho-history of soul-belief and its eventual interspersion with sexuality and procreation, Rank explains how, from being totemized in animals, soul-belief came to be connected with woman:

> [W]oman became the soul-animal [i.e., the former totem animal as, for example, the phoenix or soul-bird] who harbored the souls of the dead until as a mother she brought them to life again. As wife and mother, woman was now as sacred as the totem—the immortal soul that could not be hurt or killed—had been. First its medium, then identical with it, woman represented the soul. This is the meaning of Psyche, the later conscious representation of the feminine soul, patron saint of our science, which is named for her. (19)

In his critique of psychology, Rank shows how this older conception of soul gave way to heroic formulations, but then eventually lost all connection with animate life, whether nonhuman or human. Soul-belief gave way in modern times to "scientific intellectualism" and became embodied in the "new god" of *truth* (59). At this point in his narrative, Rank makes a particularly provocative observation. He writes, "All truth-seeking is in the end the old struggle for the soul's existence and its immortality" (60). Not only in psychology and psychoanalysis, then, but in all fields of inquiry, soul-belief lives on in the guise of truth-seeking.

Becker takes up this broader theme, elaborating Rank's observation in a striking way. As the beginning lines of the extended quotation from Becker in Chapter 1 specify, if anyone doubts Rank's conception of truth-seeking as an immortality ideology,

> let him try to explain in any other way the life-and-death viciousness of all ideological disputes. Each person nourishes his immortality in the ideology of self-perpetuation to which he gives his allegiance; this gives his life the only abiding significance it can have. No wonder men go into a rage over the fine points of belief: if your adversary wins the argument about truth, *you die*. Your immortality system has been shown to be fallible, your life becomes fallible. History, then, can be understood as the succession of ideologies that console for death. (Becker 1975, 64)

Becker's incisive contributions to an understanding of the psychological underpinnings of immortality ideologies lie by way of anchoring the Rankian thesis in just such everyday dramas of human life. But they also lie by way of extending the thesis to the larger specifics of socio-political life. He observes, for example, that "[t]he thing that feeds the great destructiveness of history is that men give their entire allegiance to their own group; and each group is a codified hero system. Which is another way of saying that societies are standardized systems of death denial; they give structure to the formulas for heroic transcendence" (153–54). By heroic transcendence, Becker means the forms by which a society indoctrinates its citizens to conform to its values. It is not just that with the French Revolution, for example, a particular type of modern hero was codified, namely, "the revolutionary hero who will bring an end to injustice and evil once and for all, by bringing into being a new utopian society perfect in its purity" (154–55), but that "[m]ore cars produced by Detroit, higher stockmarket prices, more profits, more goods moving—all this equals more heroism" (154). Becker's insights here take on a sweeping and even prescient character now, in these early years of the twenty-first century, as when, in considering leaders and the need for a veritable science of society, he speaks of the need to expose both the talents and the shortcomings of leaders, noting that "[t]his [exposure] is, after all, the dearest and grandest feature of a democracy, that it tries to keep these critical functions alive" (166). The need is pressing, he says, because "[t]he problem has always been that the leader is the one who usually is the grandest patriot, which means the one who embraces the ongoing system of death denial with the heartiest hug, the hottest tears, and the least critical distance" (166). In light of the socio-political stakes, Becker pleads not only for a veritable science of society but an enlightened society and concomitantly enlightened leaders. He suggests that "we already know what we would want our leaders to be like: persons . . . who took each single life and its suffering full in the face as it is. Which is another way of saying that they would know the reality of death as a primary problem" (167). On this basis, and carrying forth his broadened Rankian thematic, he suggests that what we really want are "well-analyzed" men as our leaders, namely, men "conscious of *their own* fear of life and death" (167).[10]

As is evident, Becker's elaborations of Rank's thesis are spelled out by way of persistent psychoanalytic probings of everyday behaviors—neurotic and otherwise—and of their socio-political motivations and consequences. But they are also spelled out in cultural analyses of ritual, money, and other societal artifacts. The elaborations from this perspective are epitomized by his summary statement that "what people want in any epoch is a way of transcending their physical fate, they want to guarantee some kind of indefinite duration, and culture provides them with the necessary immortality symbols or ideologies; societies can be seen as structures of immortality power" (63). Becker exemplifies this Rankian theme in many ways, showing, for example, as we saw in Chapter 1, how ritual provided earlier humans with a way to achieve immortality—e.g., through ceremonies and offerings that venerated rulers or gods, through the sacrifice of animals or other humans, and so on.[11]

In sum, Rank and Becker open our eyes to the Heideggerian "they" in ways that clarify, augment, and deepen the psychological dimensions that Heidegger disdained and left untouched. In doing so, they bring into sharp focus the severity of the human affliction and of the fact that, as both men maintain, illusion is necessary. Rank's earlier-cited epigram from the writings of Sir Arthur Eddington indicates as much. Humans cannot live with the truth of death. "To be able to live one needs illusions," Rank writes, "not only outer illusions such as art, religion, philosophy, science and love afford, but inner illusions which first condition the outer" (Rank 1968, 250). Becker clarifies the inner illusions, defining them as "a secure sense of one's active powers, and of being able to count on the powers of others" (Becker 1973, 188–89). Both Rank and Becker thus affirm the necessity to compensate for the overwhelming reality of death. No matter, then, Heidegger's calling us to an authentic *Dasein*. Authentic *Dasein* is an impossibility; *Dasein* must sustain itself by illusion.

V. DERRIDA'S IMMORTALITY READING OF HUSSERL AND DERRIDA'S OWN IMMORTALITY IDEOLOGY

Derrida's immortality reading of Husserl and his own immortality ideology are doubly instructive: they engage the spectre of death in ways markedly different from those of Heidegger and they exemplify the making of an immortality ideology that, in hovering between the lines rather than being straightforwardly set forth, is guilefully more sophisticated than Descartes's.

Derrida's immortality reading of Husserl is succinctly highlighted in the following analysis he offers of "phenomenology's 'principle of principles'": "The relation with the presence of the present as the ultimate form of being and of ideality is the move by which I transgress empirical existence, factuality, contingency, worldliness, etc.—first of all, *my own* empirical existence, factuality, contingency, worldliness, etc." (Derrida 1973, 53–54). In other words, according to Derrida, the relation with presence that Husserl describes puts one beyond the bounds of any empirical reality, hence beyond death. In effect, Derrida projects an immortality ideology onto Husserl, one which he repudiates at the same time that he produces an immortality ideology of his own. As for his projected Husserlian immortality ideology, Derrida specifies it more finely when he proceeds to show how transgression of the empirical into the transcendental[12] only putatively preserves being, for "[t]he relationship with *my death* (my disappearance in general) lurks in this determination of being as presence, ideality, the absolute possibility of repetition" (54). The transcendental move is ineffective as an immortality move because, as Derrida declares, it fails to recognize its relation-

ship to death in "the sign." On the other hand, the transcendental move *is* effective according to Derrida because Husserlian presence will not be affected by what he (Derrida) terms "my death": "presence [is] the universal form of transcendental life," and, says Derrida, speaking in the voice of Husserl, "I have a strange and unique certitude that this universal form of presence . . . will not be affected by [my absence, i.e., my death]" (54). Derrida thus affirms that Husserl is certain—however "strangely" and "uniquely"—that in transcendental subjectivity, he has found a (the?) road to immortality.

At this juncture in his critical commentary, Derrida interposes and explains his interpretation of language in terms of "the sign." He states first that the experience of the possibility of death or disappearance is nowhere to be found in an *I* "experienced only as an *I am present*" (54). In other words, in virtue of transcendental certainty, this *I* is unaffected by the possibility of disappearance or death. What Derrida specifies as "the relationship with *my death*" is mediated by "the sign," namely, by the *I* in *I am*, a sign which, he says, is "originally a relation with its own possible disappearance" (54). In particular, the sign *I* mediates in that it carries with it the possibility of *not I*—or perhaps better, *no I*. Derrida straightaway interprets this possibility as a mortality claim: "*I am* originally means *I am mortal*" (54). He thus passes over into a specification of how, *originally*, signs indicate death, a theme later spelled out in more detail in terms of the trace (via effacement) and of *différance*. At the same time, he jumps nimbly from " 'transcendental life' " (6)—from Husserl's practice of phenomenology—to language, ultimately linking *the experience of presence*—whatever that experience might be[13]—to the experience of signification, understood as *différance* that is both distinctive—nonidentical with itself (82)—and endlessly iterable or repeatable. By ruling out any "pre-expressive stratum of sense" (69) or "pre-expressive sense" (87)—there is no "signification" before language, "no such thing as perception" (103)—Derrida deftly places "the sign" at the center of life, thereby refuting his projected Husserlian immortality ideology.

Through the sign, however, Derrida spells out an immortality ideology of his own. He writes, "The move which leads from the *I am* to the determination of my being as *res cogitans* (thus, as an immortality)—the move by which Husserl transgresses the empirical—is a move by which the origin of presence and ideality is concealed in the very presence and ideality it makes possible" (54–55). In a word, and *contra* Husserl's "transcendental life," it is the sign that is the origin of presence and ideality, that makes presence and ideality possible to begin with. Derrida thus effaces the distinction between experience and language, including the distinction between experience and language in the very experience of language.[14] Experience *is* language in one form or another—internal monologue, speech, hearing, writing, reading; it is a play of signs.[15]

When Derrida specifically considers the experience of self-presence in an internal monologue, he denies that the experience has "nothing to reveal to itself by the agency of signs." He finds, on the contrary, that hearing oneself speak is a unique experience, "an auto-affection of a unique kind" (Derrida 1973,78), "the sole case to escape the distinction between what is worldly and what is transcendental" (79). Indeed, "the unity of sound and voice . . . makes that distinction [between the worldly and the transcendental] possible." Not only is there "no consciousness . . . possible without the voice" (79) but "the voice *is* consciousness" (80). Derrida thus gets a decisive, one could almost say, defiant, linguistic foot in the phenomenological door, transgressing and displacing Husserl's transcendental sanctum. Moreover he brings writing with him, for "the possibility of writing dwell[s] within speech, which [is] itself at work in the inwardness of thought" (82). In other words, talking to oneself presupposes the purely temporal nature of the "expressive" process, i.e., speech *and* writing. What Derrida wants to show by "auto-affection," an "exercise of the voice" that affects oneself, is not only that self-presence is contingent on auto-affection—the latter is the "condition for self-presence"—but that auto-affection makes "pure" transcendental reduction impossible (82). He thus cuts the transcendental legs from under phenomenology. Rather than a transcendental immortality, there is an auto-affectively generated immortality, which, because it "seems not to separate itself from itself" (77), is self-present to itself. In fact, Derrida states explicitly that auto-affection—the experience of hearing oneself speak—"*does not risk death in the body of a signifier that is given over to the world and the visibility of space*" (77–78; italics added). Signs thereby lay claim to immortality. Words—*bodies of signification*—that are voiced internally or externally or that are scribed on paper are idealities that are immortal: "The ideal object is the most objective of objects; independent of the here-and-now acts and events of the empirical subjectivity which intends it, it can be repeated infinitely while remaining the same" (75). But writing has the edge and in fact, Derrida's immortality ideology is made explicit with respect to writing: "[T]he total absence of the subject and object of a statement—the death of the writer and/or the disappearance of the objects he was able to describe—does not prevent a text from 'meaning' something. On the contrary, this possibility gives birth to meaning as such, gives it out to be heard and read" (93)— over and over again, obviously. When Derrida specifies writing as "the common name for signs which function despite the total absence of the subject because of (beyond) his death" (93), he leaves no doubt about his immortality ideology. The signifier *"that is given over to the world and the visibility of space"*—in a word, *writing*—lives on. It is beyond the death of its author. In fact, the death of its author is essential to the life of the text. The text otherwise has no life of its own and thus cannot lay claim to immortality.

VI. THE DOUBLE: A FURTHER SIGN OF DERRIDA'S IMMORTALITY IDEOLOGY

The immortality claim of Derrida's *signs* is powerfully heightened when viewed in the psychological prism of the Double. The thematic of the Double is thus well worth pursuing. It runs through Western literature, most famously perhaps in Dostoyevsky's *The Double* and Stevenson's *The Strange Case of Dr. Jekyll and Mr. Hyde*.[16] Moreover the topic of the double in literature is itself a literature; that is, critical writings on the double constitute a literature in itself. In both respects, certain analogies exist between literary and philosophical literatures. In a quite specific sense, Descartes's double is *res cogitans;* Nietzsche's double is *Zarathustra;* Heidegger's double is *Dasein*, and *Dasein* is itself double in that it has the possibility of being either authentic or inauthentic *Dasein*. Whether in the form of *res cogitans*, *Zarathustra*, or *Dasein*, the double endures beyond the philosopher and is itself the subject of critical writings. Along the same line, and following Derrida's deconstructive reading, *transcendental subjectivity* is Husserl's double, one Derrida explicitly conceives as deathless. The subject of transcendental subjectivity likewise endures in a critical literature beyond its originating philosopher. Further still, *voice* is Derrida's double, or rather, the double he initially sets forth in the course of his critical reading of Husserl's "Theory of Signs." Deconstructively glossed as auto-affection, voice is the initial ground on which Derrida's double appears, *his double proper, however, being his texts*, which are untouched by death and which will endure in a critical literature beyond their author.[17] One might say that any philosopher concerned with mortality and/or death is liable to create a double—or implicitly to reject any possibility of a double, as in recent analytical treatments of the topics (see, for example, French and Wettstein 2000).

The intriguing analogy between literary and philosophical writings notwithstanding, the concern here is not with the double *in* literature—whether literary or philosophical—but with the double that *is* literature, i.e., *the double that is the text in relation to its author*.[18] It is here that, as indicated, we find a further sign of Derrida's own immortality ideology, a sign that, again as indicated, rests on the already cultivated ground of Derrida's deconstructive rendering of the auto-affective phenomenon of speech. In fact, Derrida's specification of auto-affection as true self-presence not only presages the double but is itself brought into view by way of "a double exclusion or double reduction" (Derrida 1973, 70): in hearing itself speak, "the phenomenological voice" (75) sets up a relationship of otherness to itself and separates expression from sense. In auto-affection the subject is thus double to itself in the very unity of its being. As we have seen, "the unity of sound and voice, which allows the voice to be produced in the world as pure auto-affection, is the sole case to escape the distinction between what is worldly and what is transcendental; by the same token, it makes that distinction possible" (79). *The same* here is, in effect, nonidentical with itself; that is, auto-affection produces self-presence on the background of the double. In Derrida's words, "the exercise of the voice" "*produces* sameness as self-relation within self-difference" (82; italics added). This doubling of self is at metaphysical odds with Heidegger's existential determination of death as non-relational. Moreover, other aspects of an auto-affective nonidenticality of self are similarly inconsistent with Heidegger's existential determinations. Because these aspects are set in high thematic relief by Rank in his book, *The Double,* we will turn attention first to Rank's analysis.

Rank begins by taking literary doubles seriously from a psychological perspective. He moves from a discussion of examples, including ones associated with well-known fictional characters—Dorian Gray, William Wilson, Peter Schlemihl, Titularrat Golyadkin, for instance—to a consideration of the authors themselves—Oscar Wilde, Edgar Allan Poe, Adalbert Chamisso, Fyodor Dostoyevsky—finding that, with respect to the authors, a disposition "toward psychological disturbances is conditioned to a large degree by the splitting of the personality, with special emphasis upon the ego-complex, to which corresponds an abnormally strong interest in one's own person, his psychic states, and his destinies" (Rank 1971, 48). In a word, Rank presents evidence showing that the author himself is psychologically troubled in some way. But Rank also states that the specific ways in which the created double appears do not jibe with the author's living personality: "to a certain degree they seem to be alien to it, inappropriate, and contrary to his way of otherwise viewing the world." Put more explicitly, literary doubles are "odd representations of the double as a shadow, mirror-image, or portrait, the meaningful evaluation of which we do not quite understand even though we can follow it emotionally. In the writer, as in his reader, a superindividual factor seems to be unconsciously vibrating here, lending to these motifs a mysterious psychic resonance" (48).

Following his examination of a number of literary authors of doubles and of the peculiar relationship of the doubles to their authors, Rank turns to an examination of the double from an anthropological viewpoint, i.e., from the perspective of cultural beliefs and practices. Though he focuses at first on "superstitious" understanding of the shadow (e.g., not letting one's shadow fall upon a corpse, not stepping on the shadow of a pregnant woman), he soon concentrates on the shadow as covalent to the soul, a covalence supported by all folklorists (57). Citing Sir James Frazer as well as a wide range of other anthropological sources, Rank concludes that the series of "folkloric investigations has shown without any doubt that primitive man considered his mysterious double, his shadow, to be an actual spiritual being" (58). This spiritual being, however, is actually corporealized; that is, it assumes a corporeal form. Rank in fact underscores the fact that for "primitive peoples living with nature—as well as [for] . . . ancient civilized peoples [e.g., Greeks, Egyptians] . . . *the soul figured as an analogon to the form of the body* (59; italics in original). He takes up this "primitive monism" in his next and final chapter, "Narcissism and the Double," which begins with the observation, "By no means can psychoanalysis consider it as a mere accident that the death significance of the double appears closely related to its narcissistic meaning" (69). Again, after consulting and discussing a variety of works, literary as well as psychoanalytic, i.e., Freudian, Rank finds that "[a]mong the very first and most primitive concepts of the soul is that of the shadow, which appears as a faithful image of the body but of a lighter substance" (82). Thus, *narcissism*—what Rank identifies more specifically as "pure-ego interests" (78)—*is tethered to the body*. Commonly specified in terms of "self-preservation," pure-ego interests emanate actually from self-love; self-love motivates self-preservation, generating at the same time the fear of dissolving into nothingness. The body is the locus of these feelings: "Primitive narcissism feels itself primarily threatened by the ineluctable destruction of the self. Very clear evidence of the truth of this observation is shown by the choice, as the most primitive concept of the soul, of an image as closely similar as possible to the physical self, hence a true double. The idea of death, therefore, is denied by a duplication of the self incorporated in the shadow or in the reflected image" (83). Furthermore, Rank finds that not only primitive but culturally developed peoples held to the same "primitive monism": "the most primitive concept of the soul of the Greeks, Egyptians, and other culturally prominent peoples coincides with a double which is essentially identical with the body" (83). He concludes not only that there was originally a "'primitive monism of body and soul'" (83), but that only with "the increasing reality-experience of man" and the reluctance "to admit that death is everlasting annihilation" did the material origin of soul give way to an immaterial conception (84). Non-identity thus came to define the relationship of soul and body in Western culture. If the soul is to last, it must transcend the body in some way—*precisely as by Cartesian argumentation*, for example, *or by Derridean declaration*: "*there is nothing outside of the text*" (Derrida 1976, 158; italics in original).[19]

Four themes are significant in the above exposition of Rank's broad and probing investigations. There is first the idea that doubles are created by people who have "an abnormally strong interest in [their] own persons, [their] psychic states, and [their] destinies." At the same time, however, the created doubles are "odd representations" insofar as they go beyond the author: a "superindividual factor seems to be unconsciously vibrating here, lending to these motifs [e.g., shadow, mirror-image, or portrait] a mysterious psychic resonance." Third, "the idea of death . . . is denied by a duplication of the self incorporated in the shadow, or in the reflected image." Finally, echoing the three previous themes as a unit, is the theme of narcissism: the double is a narcissistic creation, the meaning of which is tied to self-preservation and the denial of death.

Further aspects of Derrida's double—aspects that in deconstructive terms are in excess of a basic nonidenticality of self—correlate with the above themes and deepen understandings of his immortality ideology in significant ways. Taking the themes in order, we find first that death is a consistent theme across the writings of Derrida, apparent not only in his attribution of an immortality ideology to Husserl and in the formulation of an immortality ideology of his own, but in specifically addressed texts: *The Gift of Death, Aporias,* and *Adieu to Emmanuel Levinas* are focal examples. That his own "person, psychic states, and destiny" are on the line in these writings is hardly debatable. Yet consistent with the second theme, Derrida's double does not lend itself to easy formulation. It is indeed an "odd representation," one that, through *différance*, shows itself in every way to be precisely a "superindividual factor" that "[lends] a mysterious psychic resonance." His double is here, there, and nowhere in his texts; it cannot be pinned down.[20] All the same, and consistent with the third theme, a "duplication of the self" is undeniably there in the "reflected image" that is the text. A relational Otherness or Other has been created that embodies at the same time that it exceeds and will continue to exceed its own Other by the sheer timelessness of its endurance. Finally, Derrida's deconstructive writings are unique in the way that hearing one's own voice is "unique" (Derrida 1973, 78): just as there is no mistaking the voice that is pure auto-affection, there is no mistaking a Derridean text. In effect, his signature is not effaceable, which is to say, his double is "pure auto-affection" but in an added, exorbitant sense. "Pure auto-affection" signifies not just "'hearing oneself speak'" (78): it signifies self-love, a narcissistic self-love expressed here not in a "primitive monism" but in a corporeal form nonetheless. If there is indeed "nothing outside of the text," then there is indeed nothing outside of the text, i.e., only an absolute void. Texts are instantiations of soul, embodiments that protect one from what Rank describes as the "everlasting annihilation" of death (Rank 1971, 84), engendering traces of what was once present and of what is to come in the form of endless possible exhumations and understandings.

Given Derrida's elemental conceptual and philosophical affinities to Heidegger,[21] his textual double has an ironic ring. Death, Heidegger repeatedly insisted, "is *that possibility which is one's ownmost, which is non-relational, and which is not to be outstripped* (Heidegger 1962, 294; italics in original). He insisted further that "*Authentic* Being-towards death can *not evade* its own-most non-relational possibility, or *cover up* this possibility by thus fleeing from it, or *give a new explanation* for it to accord with the common sense of the 'they'" (304–5; italics in original). Heidegger thus eschews an immortality ideology, insisting that the possibility of one's own utmost impossibility must be faced directly. What the tenets of deconstruction limn—through *différance,* the play of traces, iterability, and so on, all of which are "not deconstructible" (Derrida and Caputo 1997, 101)—is, in contrast, the possibility of an eternal double, a double bodied forth in texts. This textual double endures beyond one's ownmost, and in so enduring, both escapes the non-relational character of death and outstrips death. Indeed, Derrida's non-deconstructible textual double draws an enduring presence in its wake, a presence created by an auto-affection that is "of a unique kind," being produced by the writing that "dwell[s] within speech" and the self-love that fears death (Derrida 1973, 78, 82, respectively). That created presence is no longer linked to a nonidentical self-presence, but is a free form, so to speak, immortalized for others by the very nature of signs, which live on through endless acts of repetition: "[T]exts are a little legacy, a perpetual gift that keeps on giving and (quasi-) living, long after the death of their authors" (Caputo 1997, 175).

VII. THE LAST WORD AND THE ULTIMATE MORTAL QUESTION

The last word belongs to Rank, whose conception of rationality and irrationality has a historical and socio-psychological dimension that is distinctive in itself and that resonates in distinctive ways with the philosophical perspectives of Descartes, Heidegger, and Derrida as discussed above. In fact, as we will see, an unasked question lingers in Rank's conception, a question that brings to the fore and accentuates the tension between Descartes and Derrida on one side and Heidegger on the other.

For Rank, culture is "a continuous translation of supernatural conceptions into rational terms . . . an expression of the irrational self seeking material immortalization in lasting achievements" (Rank 1958, 84). In discussing the doubles Dostoyevsky created in the persons of Golyadkin, Stavrogin, and Ivan Karamazov, for example, and how each embody terrifying or irrational aspects of self, Rank notes how in tragical literary permutations of folk-beliefs about doubles, about the soul, and about immortality, "the artist not only disposes of his irrational self in his work but at the same time enables the public to detach itself from both the writer and his creation." He points out, "Such artistic transformation of a primitive motif differs . . . from the historical detachment of scientific classification in that it appears as a living expression of powerful personalities still under the spell of those irrational forces. In giving them form, that is, rational expression, the artist enables the public to feel sufficiently removed from the irrational elements to dare vicariously to participate in them" (83). As is evident even from this brief example, by 'irrational' Rank does not mean a lack of mental clarity, madness, or the like. He means, on the contrary, a keen and profound awareness that the world and the events of one's own personal life are not fully explicable, controllable, or justifiable, and that, efforts toward mastery are, as a commentator of Rank bluntly states, "overwhelmingly governed by the rational at the expense of the irrational," the "attitude of omnipotence lead[ing] to a failure on the individual level to accept the nature of life and to deal creatively with its inevitabilities—especially with the fact of death" (Menaker 1982, 88).

From this Rankian perspective, we find—most self-consciously in Derrida, less so in Descartes—a renewal of the "hero-artist" who, through his activity, "give[s] rise to a new belief in the immortality of creation" (Rank 1958, 101), and who thereby contributes to culture as "an expression of the irrational self seeking material immortalization in lasting achievements" (84). But we have also found the voice of a different "hero-artist" who, contrary to both Rank and Becker, and contrary to Descartes and Derrida, summons us away from illusions, assails us for our cowardice, and charges us to face the anxiety of death: "the possibility of the absolute impossibility of Being." The question is thus: Do humans need illusions in order to live? Do they need to become hero-artists, immortalizing themselves "in lasting achievements"? Or alternatively, do they need hero-artists—leaders of one kind or another—who, through their "rational expression" of "irrational forces," sustain and protect them?

The answer must surely be "no," simply in view of the possibility itself, that is, the possibility of living without illusions. In fact, the negative answer can be sketched out along Heideggerian lines that Heidegger himself might have followed but left virtually unexplored, lines suggested in passing in the above citations from Rank highlighting artistic creation, but lines that are also literally prefigured in Heidegger's text itself. For example, creativity calls "Dasein's Self from its lostness in the 'they'" (Heidegger 1962, 319) no less than "[the] *voice of conscience*" (313) calls "Dasein from its lostness in the 'they'." Indeed, creativity is an ontological dimension of Being no less than conscience.[22] As with the call of conscience, the call of creativity "is precisely something which *we ourselves* have neither planned nor prepared for nor voluntarily performed, nor have we ever done so." In both instances, "'It' calls . . . 'it' does the calling" (320, 321). Moreover in both instances the call "calls Dasein forth to its possibilities" (319), awakening its ownmost potentiality-for-Being; the call of creativity attests too to "Dasein's ownmost potentiality-for-Being—an attestation which *is* in Dasein itself" (341). Further still, creativity like conscience is "futural" through and through: it opens not only on an unknown but on a blank future, a "nullity" (329) that is not a *not-yet* but a *not-at-all* "in which Dasein, in its ownmost potentiality-for-Being, comes toward itself" (373). Ontologically, it is even conceivable that creativity is the wellspring of authentic Being, arising ontologically as a direct answer to the existential *angst* that keeps Dasein tethered to the 'they', muffled by its inauthentic everydayness, in effect, summoning Dasein not from what one might term the "ontologically moral," but from the ontologically anxious depths themselves.[23] Creativity is thus a clue to living without illusions. It constitutes *"Being towards a possibility"* (Heidegger 1962, 305), a *"Being toward"* that springs from within and bounds beyond itself, moving toward something rather than nothing, something that is potentially of value in and of itself and lays no other claim. Indeed, only the author of the work can make the further claim; that is, only the author can double himself in the work, whether discreetly or indiscreetly, transforming the ontology of creativity into an immortality ideology.[24]

NOTES

1. As should be clear, immortality ideologies are not the preserve of Western philosophers. Scientists' quest for immortality is dramatically brought to the fore, for example, in clinician and surgeon Sherwin Nuland's review ("Killing Cures") of the well-intentioned but failed lifework of two twentieth-century psychiatric surgeons. See Nuland 2005.

2. Sir Arthur is not of course alone in his assessment. T. S. Eliot echoes the same thought in lines from "Burnt Norton": "human kind / Cannot bear very much reality" (Eliot 1943, 4).

3. The first edition of the *Meditations* (*Meditationes de Prima Philosophiae*), published in 1641, carried the subtitle "in which are demonstrated the existence of God and the immortality of the soul." The subtitle was changed in the 1642 edition to read: "in which are demonstrated the existence of God and the distinction between the human soul and the body." See Descartes 1984, 1, "Translator's Preface."

4. A striking exception to the general omission of non-epistemic concerns is a recently translated and edifying article by Walter Schulz. Schulz states that "Descartes is essential in illuminating the structure of the metaphysical conception of immortality

insofar as he unifies both the objective and the subjective approaches." He points out specifically that the *Meditations* "[seek] to prove the existence of God and the differentiation between the human soul and its body" and that "Descartes clearly recognizes that immortality is based solely on this differentiation." See Schulz 2000, 475.

5. See Mark Epstein's 1995 book *Thoughts Without a Thinker*. Epstein is a psychoanalyst and Buddhist.

6. It is of interest to point out that, his early theological training seemingly to the contrary, Heidegger does not soften or attempt to soften the ontological reality of death and attendant ontological anxieties by appeal to religion, i.e., to the possibility that religious convictions, practices, and the like might soothe one if not save one. But see also note 23.

7. Sartre, for example, in his perspicuous and trenchant analyses of The Look, writes of how the Other usurps my freedom and fatally threatens my existence: "The Other is the hidden death of my possibilities in so far as I live that death as hidden in the midst of the world"; "[B]eing-seen constitutes me as a defenseless being for a freedom which is not my freedom. . . . [I]n so far as I am the instrument of possibilities which are not my possibilities . . . I am *in danger*. This danger is not an accident but the permanent structure of my being-for-others" (Sartre 1956, 264, 267–68).

8. Heidegger's pithy insight is *uncannily* descriptive of the attitude of the current U.S. (Bush) administration and seemingly of many if not most Americans toward civilian Afghanistan people killed in the months following the terrorist attacks in New York City on September 11, 2001. It is similarly *uncannily* descriptive of the attitude toward Iraqi civilians killed in the Iraq war.

9. Compare the way in which philosopher John Caputo particularizes dying in relation to Dasein: " 'the certain but indefinite possibility,' the futural possibility of an impossibility, that haunts and, by haunting, awakens Dasein's freedom and *Sein können*, that gives Dasein the gift of an authentic *Zu-kunft*" (Caputo 1997, 83).

10. Becker goes on to speak of "the cultural system as a way of heroic transcendence," i.e., illusion is necessary in order to live, a theme deriving from Rank. (See further in this text.)

11. Again (see Chapter 1, n. 10), we might note the unusually fine similarity between the ritualist and Richard Dawkins's "lumbering robot" (Dawkins 1989) who, by passing on his genes, also does "nothing less than enable life to continue." Unlike the lumbering robot, however, the ritualist is a *corps engagé*, that is, a living being quintessentially caught up—both affectively and cognitively—in meaning and in a life of meaning.

12. Since Derrida is criticizing Husserl, we can presume he is using the word "transcendental" in the Husserlian sense of a meaning-bestowing subject, though insofar as he does not specify the meaning of the term (except in its opposition to "empirical"), we cannot be sure that he is. It is pertinent to note with respect to both Derrida's critique and Husserl's central concern with meaning that Derrida dissociates meaning from the transcendental, thus leaving the latter term free for his consequent transcendentalization of *the sign*, i.e., the placement of the sign in the realm of *différance*. The transformation is accomplished by his Saussurean distinction of sound and voice, the latter being tied not to the production of meaning but to the production of signs—*signification* proper, according to Derrida.

13. Derrida gives no examples other than that of talking to oneself because only talking to oneself qualifies as "auto-affection." One might wonder, however, why dancing by oneself, or meditating as in Vipassana (Buddhist) meditation, or walking with full attention to the movement of walking (as one walks in meditational practice), might not also qualify, for these experiences also meet the rules Derrida specifies for "auto-affection": not passing through "what is outside the sphere of 'ownness' " and having a claim to "universality" (Derrida 1973, 78). Derrida unwittingly intimates as much when

he writes that the "proximity" of signifier to signified "is broken when, instead of hearing myself speak, I see myself write or gesture" (80). Clearly, Derrida overlooks tactile-kinesthetic experience in favor of the visual, and this even though articulatory gestures constitute speech in a literal and empirical sense as well as enter into its constitution in a phenomenological sense. Hence, when Derrida later asks, "But, . . . are there not forms of pure auto-affection in the inwardness of one's own body which do not require the intervention of any surface displayed in the world and yet are not of the order of the voice?" and answers that "these forms remain purely empirical, for they could not belong to a medium of universal signification" (79), he throws off to empiricism anything outside language and ignores dancing, meditation, and the meditational practice of walking as "mediums of universal signification." Yet like the voice, they too are "absolutely at our disposition" to signify (79); and like the voice, they too may be said to escape, "the distinction between what is worldly and what is transcendental" and "by the same token, . . . [make] that distinction possible" (79).

14. With respect to the latter distinction, he effaces the experience of breathing and the experience of articulatory gestures in the act of speaking, which, however horizonal, are of the essence of sound-making.

15. Philosopher David Loy captures a sense of this absorption of experience by language when he points out that the metaphysical path Derrida wants to navigate between the philosophically new and the philosophically old specifies a liberation that is "only *textual*," clarifying the point by saying, "The difference is between being stuck somewhere within language and being free within language" (Loy 1992, 240).

16. One might also cite the appearance of the double in present-day science, as in the practice of cloning and the technological creation of virtual realities. People appear to have the notion or impression that *they*, as the individuals they are, can in some manner live on. The science of cryogenics earlier held out the promise of just such a possibility: freeze oneself now; thaw and wake later. Clearly, science and technology are not excluded from the "culture of the copy." Although his discussion across a range of cultural practices does not include discussion of Rank's own wide-ranging discussion of the double, see Hillel Schwartz's book *The Culture of the Copy* (1996) and note too his witty index entry on Derrida.

17. We should note that in the contemporary modern world *textual doppelgängers* are not the only possibility. *Technological doppelgängers* may also be cultivated. See Epilogue, note 31.

18. Derrida's writings on Artaud's theater dramatize the relation in terms of theatrical voice rather than in terms of author, but like his writings on voice as auto-affection, his histrionic comments bear witness to language—the text—as double. In particular, in "La Parole Soufflée," Derrida underscores the absence of the authorial script, or, in positive terms, the presence of the breath, which surpasses the authorial script: "To let one's speech be spirited away [*soufflé*] is, like writing itself, the ur-phenomenon of the *reserve*: the abandoning of the self to the furtive, to discretion and separation, is, at the same time, accumulation, capitalization, the security of the delegated or deferred decision. To leave one's speech to the furtive is to tranquilize oneself into deferral. . . . To reject the work, to let one's speech, body, and birth be spirited away [*soufflé*] by the furtive god is thus to defend oneself against the theater of fear which multiplies the differences between myself and myself" (Derrida 1978, 189–90).

19. The statement, of course, is a double entendre: outside the text is a void of being.

20. The situation recalls philosopher Dermot Moran's judgment that "it is always difficult to get from Derrida a clear, unambiguous statement of his claim" and that while "[Derrida] would agree that our grasp of the meaning of a sentence is *incomplete*, provisional . . . he denies that this provisional meaning is to be measured against the impossible ideal of the complete meaning of the sentence. Rather the meaning of the

sentence will always involve some 'slippage' . . . so that we will never actually master the meaning of any sentence" (Moran 2000, 471). Such a situation, of course, preserves the text in perpetuity since the last word on it can never be uttered. Derrida's double is, if not an eternal double, a thoroughly open-ended one.

21. See, for example, Evans 1991, xix–xxi, and Allison and Garver 1973. David B. Allison and Newton Garver, translators of Derrida's text, write, for example, "[I]t is wiser not to try a direct translation from Derrida's Heideggerian language" (ix), and "Working within a Heideggerian framework, Derrida . . ." (xiii). See also Derrida's text itself.

22. The affinities between creativity and conscience are indeed striking; that is, the ontology of conscience that Heidegger describes accords with ontological dimensions of creativity. Further instances of the accord could be given beyond those that follow in this chapter. For example, the call of creativity, like the call of conscience, "will not let itself be coaxed" (Heidegger 1962, 319); "the call may undergo a different interpretation in the individual Dasein in accordance with its own possibilities of understanding" (318); "In the tendency to disclosure which belongs to the call, lies the momentum of a push—of an abrupt arousal" (316).

23. One might consider Heidegger's theological background with respect to his choice of conscience as the "saviour," so to speak, that calls Dasein from its self-forgetfulness in the "they." In particular, and in a straightforward ontic sense, one might wonder whether Heidegger found that he could not in good conscience believe in doctrines of immortality, salvation, and the like, as preached and promulgated by theologians and philosophers. As philosopher John van Buren indicates in his account of Heidegger's path in theology, Heidegger began with strong ties to Luther, developed a growing and avowed sense of devotion to being not a philosopher but a "'Christian theo*logian*,'" and by "sometime around 1930 . . . began to identify with the experience of 'the death of God' in Nietzsche and Hölderin, as well as with their aspirations toward the Parousia of a new and more Greek God" (van Buren 1994, 173, 174, respectively). In short, one might wonder whether conscience awakened Heidegger from his own lostness in the death-denying "they" of traditional Christianity.

24. Noted modern dancer and choreographer Merce Cunningham's observation is provocative in this context: "you have to love dancing to stick to it. it gives you nothing back, no manuscripts to store away, no paintings to show on walls and maybe hang in museums, no poems to be printed and sold, nothing but that single fleeting moment when you feel alive. it is not for unsteady souls" (Cunningham 1968, unpaginated).

# 3
## *Real* Male-Male Competition

> Man is the rival of other men; he delights in competition, and this leads to ambition which passes too easily into selfishness.
> —CHARLES DARWIN, *The Descent of Man, and Selection in Relation to Sex*

> Relations between men centre around the struggle for power; whether individually or in a group, they are permanent rivals in the appropriation of women, wealth and glory.
> —EMMANUEL REYNAUD, *Holy Virility*

> Aggression in animals is primarily a way of competition, not of destruction. . . . aggressive episodes rarely inflict damage in Old World monkeys under natural conditions.
> —UELI NAGEL AND HANS KUMMER, "Variation in Cercopithecoid Aggressive Behavior"

## I. INTRODUCTION

What helps to sustain immortality ideologies and to quell the fear of death? The answer certainly involves no labored reflection. The cultural honing of heroes and the cultural adulation of warriors have been human constants for centuries and even millennia. What necessitates labored reflection are understandings of the origin of such constants and their cultural elaborations. In this chapter, we will examine in detail the evolutionary genesis of heroes and warriors in the biological phenomenon of male-male competition and exemplify the kind of cultural practices and values that both support and fuel the competition. The chapter that follows will offer extended psychological and socio-political analyses of the bio-cultural phenomenon as it has been exemplified most commonly and uniquely by humans, namely, in their inveterate killings of each other in the persistent practice of war. Especially in light of the biological perspective, and as suggested by the opening epigraph above, the fact that nonhuman animal competition among males is nota-

---

This chapter is an expanded version of a keynote address presented at the Pacific Division meeting of the Society for Women in Philosophy, University of Oregon, Eugene, November 2003.

bly different from competition among human males warrants emphasis from the beginning. In the latter instances, competition is not uncommonly lethal and even aims at being lethal. We might recall Boehm's observations cited in Chapter 1, i.e., that homicide "usually takes place because of problems with male competition over women." We might equally cite the biologically unique human practice of war.

Since evolutionary biology describes sexual bodily differences in terms of both natural selection and sexual selection, it will be instructive first to differentiate between the two, and then consider more closely Darwin's specification of sexual selection, that is, consider the morphological-behavioral evidence he brings forth in its support. On the basis of these empirically grounded fundamentals of evolutionary biology, we can then turn to a central aspect of sexual selection that has not received the attention it warrants—and warrants especially now in a violence-ridden human-made and human-dominated world—and show how this central aspect has been exapted, to use a term Stephen Jay Gould and Elizabeth Vrba coined to specify traits that have been co-opted for a purpose other than the one they originally served (Gould and Vrba 1982). Curiously enough, this central aspect has been omitted from investigations by feminist theorists, who have been more concerned with exposing intersexual inequities than with exposing intrasexual ones, and who have, by extension, been more concerned with examining ways in which intersexual rather than intrasexual inequities are culturally played out. I hope through the course of this chapter to awaken interest in male-male competition—*real* male-male competition—specifically as it is humanly played out and has been played out for centuries and even millennia in its most radical form: war. My aim is to show that war is a cultural elaboration of human male-male competition, a competition whose stakes are sanctified by one's most entrenched beliefs, dearest values, and utmost longings concerning life and death, whose ferocity and atrocities can be and often are proportionately exacerbated by religious doctrines that promise one salvation, eternal life, or some form of immortality, and whose enactment at the same time makes one's life immediately and indelibly meaningful. We will initially examine the distinction between natural and sexual selection in the context of certain feminist writings because I want to emphasize from the very beginning the critical role of Nature in our humanity.

II. ON NATURAL AND SEXUAL SELECTION

A decade and more ago, it was fashionable to discredit Nature, to deny that there was such a thing. "The natural body is . . . a discursive phenomenon," wrote philosopher Ladelle McWhorter (McWhorter 1989, 612); "There is not . . . such a state as 'being' female," wrote feminist and social theorist and critic Donna Haraway (Haraway 1985, 72). "The ostensibly biological reality that we designate as sex is an historical construct," wrote philosopher Judith Butler (Butler 1989, 261). All of these views have a certain creationist ring, creationist not in a biblical sense—though the views might well be compared with biblical positivism—but creationist in the sense of being thoroughly ignorant or thoroughly dismissive of evolutionary facts of life and of evolutionary history. We are each the product of a sexual union between a male and a female, a union that is not peculiar to twentieth- or twenty-first-century humans, but a union that has been enacted over millions of years—and not just between human animals. Indeed, we are all here today, thanks to the sexual intercourse not only of our respective fathers and mothers, but of their respective fathers and mothers, and of the respective fathers and mothers of their fathers and mothers, and so on, and so on, back thousands and even millions of years to *Homo erectus, Homo habilis,* and still earlier hominid species. The sexual differences between males and females make new life possible: they are the source of millions of ongoing species including the species known colloquially and honorifically as human beings. Most importantly, they are what make a range of variations possible in any animal population and in turn make plasticity possible; that is, they are the basis of the ability of certain individuals within a population to find additional resources, to initiate new patterns of movement, to meet novel and unexpected challenges, and so on. Parthenogenesis—self-reproduction—admits of variation only through the occurrence of a mutation, not through a mixing of genetic material, the mutation generating a new line, but a new line incapable of generating anything other than itself. In contrast, variation is the basic stuff of natural selection, and in effect, constitutes the cornerstone of organic evolution, the evolution of animate forms.

Sexual bodily differences are thus significant in the double sense of being the source of new life and the source of variations in the production of new life. In effect, having a vagina or a penis (and having or not having breasts) makes a difference essential both to the creation of new humans and to variations among humans. These corporeal matters of fact are elementary. Whatever the theory, it cannot argue with these corporeal matters of fact, or rather, it can argue with them only at the risk of self-inflicted ignorance. Accordingly, what should substantively support a theory with respect to sexual dimorphism are the morphological matters of fact that specify sexual dimorphism in the first place. In this respect, a further elementary morphological fact is and has been apparent to observers of mammalian life: in general, males tend to be both stronger and larger than females. What is crucial to emphasize in face of this fact is, again, variation, the first tenet of evolutionary theory as originally specified by Darwin. Variations exist along multiple dimensions: within any group of animals of the same species, some are more alert than others, some more curious, some more docile, some more aggressive and ready to fight, some more wily in escaping predators successfully, some keener in locating new food sources, and so on. Such variations condition natural selection in that some individuals are able to sustain themselves more capably than others, sufficiently so to survive and reproduce. But variations also condition sexual selection, and in fact a given variation may overlap both forms of selection. Males who are stronger than others can use their greater strength not only to outrun predators but to subdue other males in the pursuit of females; males who have greater endurance than others or are more persistent than others can use those capacities not only to keep up a chase but to hold their ground in battle with other males over females. From the viewpoint of sexual selection, the differential in certain attributes is first and foremost a male-male differential expressed in the phenomenon of male-male competition. In effect, differential attributes such as being stronger and larger may not be simply markers that separate males from females, but markers that differentiate one male from another. Indeed, the prime arena of sexual competition is not that of males and females but of males.[1] Males compete not *with* females but with other males *for* females. Within evolutionary biology, this fact too is elementary.

In light of these facts, I suggest that we look Nature directly in the eye, that we read what Darwin, ethologists, evolutionary biologists, and natural historians describe on the basis of their first-hand experiences of Nature, and that we then reflect and ask ourselves what Nature has to teach us about ourselves as sexually dimorphic creatures. As I hope now to show, consideration of the nature of Nature in the lifeworld, in particular, male-male competition, opens the way to possible insights into the historically validated conflict-ridden nature of human nature.

### III. DARWIN'S SEMINAL INSIGHTS INTO MALE-MALE COMPETITION AND THEIR TOTAL NEGLECT IN CURRENT RESEARCH

In *The Descent of Man and Selection in Relation to Sex*, Charles Darwin detailed his observations on male-male competition, at one point noting quite specifically that

> When the two sexes follow exactly the same habits of life, and the male has more highly developed sense or locomotive organs than the female, it may be that these in their perfected state are indispensable to the male for finding the female; but in the vast majority of cases, they serve only to give one male an advantage over another. . . . In such cases sexual selection must have come into action, for the males have acquired their present structure, not from being better fitted to survive in the struggle for existence, but from having gained an advantage over other males, and from having transmitted this advantage to their male offspring alone. It was the importance of this distinction which led me to designate this form of selection as sexual selection. (Darwin 1871, 1:256–57)

In contrast to Darwin's detailed elucidation of sexual selection and the real-life phenomenon he designates as "the law of battle" and exemplifies in male animals all the way from beetles to birds to mammals, including "man," *real*—one is even pressed to say, *honest-to-goodness*—human male-male competition is no more highlighted by biologists in present-day discussions of sexual selection than it is highlighted by feminists in their present-day discussions of sex. At the center of current biological attention is *sperm* competition (e.g., Birkhead 2000, Parker 1998, Simmons 2001). Fascinating theoretical comments abound in texts on sperm competition. For example, in a discussion of why females might or might not remate—"the costs of repeated harassment from males [might] outweigh the costs of additional matings"—Simmons writes, "In general, the resolution of sexual conflict over mating is likely to reflect the relative costs and benefits of remating for females, since male interests will always be best served by copulation" (Simmons 2001, 12). Simmons later states that

> Sperm selection is the extension of female choice at the gametic level and has also been termed female sperm choice. The mechanisms by which females could actively select particular sperm to fertilize their eggs are unclear, and indeed the occurrence of sperm selection itself is equivocal. Nevertheless, females have ultimate control over the utilization of sperm within their bodies so that observed patterns of sperm precedence could at least potentially reflect adaptive fertilization strategies of females. Sperm selection is fundamentally different from sperm competition in that sperm selection requires the evolution of traits by which females can circumvent the outcome of sperm competition when there is sexual conflict over which sperm are to be utilized. If there were not sexual conflict over sperm utilization, sperm selection strategies in females would not arise. (26)

As further example, consider an essay titled "The Evolution of Ejaculates," in which biologist G. A. Parker writes, "In this chapter, I consider the problem of how a male should allocate sperm among different ejaculates and summarize a model framework for the analysis of this problem" (Parker 1998, 4). In a section of his essay titled "The Logic of Sperm Competition Games," he states,

> Recently, a new theoretical basis for the analysis of the evolution of ejaculate characteristics in terms of sperm size and number has been developed.... I have termed these models 'sperm competition games' to stress that they are evolutionary games between rival males, whose ejaculates compete for the fertilization of the ova. Pay-offs to competing males depend on the ejaculation strategies played by other males in the population; their analysis requires an evolutionarily stable strategy approach and hence forms a part of evolutionary game theory. (5)

Clearly, sperm competition sidelines if not totally obliterates *real* male-male competition as a bona fide and centrally significant *human* subject for human study. The reductionist move and agenda are in keeping with the fact that sexual selection was itself earlier displaced by genocentric thinking in contrast to Darwin's organismic thinking (see Goodwin 1994, 3). As well-known evolutionary biologist Ernst Mayr points out, "When the mathematical population geneticists declared the individual gene to be the unit of selection and defined fitness as the contribution of such genes to the gene pool of the next generation, there was little room left for sexual selection" (Mayr, 1988, 505). With the rise in sociobiological thinking, interest in sexual selection grew, but only in the guise of reproductive cost-benefit analyses having to do with cuckoldry, paternity certainty, parental investment, and homicide (see especially Trivers 1972, Daly and Wilson 1983). Male-male competition, in other words, degenerated into a purely theoretical phenomenon, males themselves being nothing more than robots obeying their communal internal dictum, "Pass on your genes!"—an aptly worded command, we might note, not only in terms of immortality ideologies as pointed out earlier in a note in Chapter 2, but in terms of the act of intromission. Indeed, theory has taken over to the extent that absurd conclusions may be reached, conclusions strikingly epitomized in sociobiological psychologists Martin Daly and Margo Wilson's declaration (footnoted earlier in Chapter 1), "If a marriage contract provided a man with a magical guarantee of paternity, the world would be a more peaceable place!" (Daly and Wilson 1983, 285).

Given this state of affairs, it is not surprising that empirical studies of *real* male-male competition have fallen from sight, as some ethologists and ecologists have already pointed out. Malte Andersson, for example, states that

> the greatest obstacle to understanding [sexual selection] now seems to be shortage of adequate empirical tests, not lack of theoretical ideas. Maynard Smith . . . remarked that no topic in evolutionary biology has presented greater difficulties to theorists than sexual selection. One might add that critical empirical testing of some aspects of the theory seems even more difficult than formulating it. Many kinds of tests are needed, based on combinations of observations, experiments, and comparative analyses. (Andersson 1994, 436)

Along similar lines, biologist J. Van den Assem points out that "[s]ince any population is composed of living individuals, their behaviour must play an important role in producing the effects in which ecologists are most interested, and the study of relevant behaviour patterns may help in a better understanding" (Van den Assem 1967, 2). Van den Assem's point is that ecology requires a study of behavior, a study of real-life happenings in the lifeworld (3). His point is strongly underscored by ecologists Morton and Stutchbury, who write, "To be a first rate empirical theorist takes a lifetime of devotion and a great amount of experience with fieldwork and learning how to observe and be observant" (Morton and Stutchbury 1998, xi). They furthermore remark that "[r]ecently, behavioral ecologists have begun to realize their science lacks a foundation of the mechanics of behavior—how it works, its pragmatic effects" (xi).

A further reason why attention to *real* male-male competition as a specifically human phenomenon appears to have been suppressed is interest in female choice, the correlative factor in sexual selection theory. As Darwin points out, the two factors can be difficult to distinguish: "Our difficulty in regard to sexual selection lies in understanding how it is that the males which conquer other males, *or* those which prove the most attractive to the females, leave a greater number of offspring to inherit their superiority than the beaten and less attractive males" (Darwin 1871, 1:260–61; italics added). Though the nature and question of female choice has received comparatively more attention in recent times, it too is investigated less as a *real-life* phenomenon than as a reductive and theoretically modeled vaginal tract/ovular phenomenon.[2]

The lack of commensurate attention to *real* male-male competition is striking considering how specifically Darwin identified morphological and behavioral differences entering into male-male competition and ultimately influencing female choice, differences he spelled out not only in terms of "weapons of offence and the means of defence possessed by the males for fighting with and driving away their rivals" but in terms of male "courage and pugnacity" (257–58). Darwin in fact devoted twelve chapters—upwards of 460 pages—to intra-male morphological and behavioral differences, beginning with the secondary sexual characters of molluscs, annelids, and crustaceans, moving from there to spiders, beetles, and other insects, from there to butterflies and moths, from there to fish, amphibians, and reptiles, from there to birds (four chapters), mammals (two chapters), and man (two chapters).

Has *real* male-male competition as it was finely delineated by Darwin been driven out by sperm competition, by population genetics and sociobiological theory, and by a greater concern with female choice? Or do people believe that Darwin observed essentially everything there is to observe about *real* male-male competition in general, and that more recently and in particular, zoologists, especially avian zoologists, have observed everything there is to observe about *real* male-male competition in their studies of leks, localized arena display grounds where males compete for attention by females, grounds that Darwin more briefly described?

Let us reflect a moment, examining the topic at closer range precisely by turning attention to those special grounds of male-male competition that in many species, i.e., not just species of birds, are traditionally returned to year after year at mating season, males enacting what might well be termed a ritual practice (see avian biologist Alan Lill's fine-grained empirical study of the Trinidadian Golden-headed Manakin, 1976; Höglund and Alatalo 1995; Johnsgard 1994).[3] Those males who win the competition are those who secure the best territory within the lek, as with Topi antelope, or who show through competitive displays any one of a number of other talents that attract females, as, for instance, orchid bees in their performance of certain bodily movements, including sound-making body movements, or bowerbirds in their construction of highly ornamented bowers, or hammerhead bats in their performance of sequences of honking calls together with wing-flapping, and so on (Attenborough 1990). As the examples suggest, while the term "lek" most commonly and prominently refers to the special ground on which avian males compete with each other, leks are actually formed by species of insects, flies, butterflies, wasps, lizards, fish, frogs, toads, newts, bats, walrus, deer, wildebeest, and antelope. Leks are, in other words, not exclusively avian creations. The character of male-male competition with respect to each species, however, is notably different. Several of Darwin's observations warrant mention in this respect.

Darwin points out that "Male birds sometimes, though rarely, possess special weapons for fighting with each other" and that they are more given to ornamental, vocal, or movement displays.[4] All the same, "Almost all male birds," he says, "are extremely pugnacious, using their beaks, wings, and legs for fighting together. We see this every spring with our robins and sparrows. The smallest of all birds, namely the humming-bird, is one of the most quarrelsome" (Darwin 1871, 2:40). He also notes specifically that "The males of many birds are larger than the females, and this no doubt is an advantage to them in their battles with their rivals, and has been gained through sexual selection" (43). But he also later observes that although "The season of love is that of battle[,] . . . males of some birds, as of the game-fowl and ruff, and even the young males of the wild turkey and grouse, are ready to fight whenever they meet" (48).

Darwin's descriptive study of mammalian male-male competition is equally informative and suggestive. In his beginning chapter on the topic, in a section titled "the law of battle," he opens with the observation that "With mammals the male appears to win the female much more through the law of battle than through the display of his charms" (239). He observes further that "The law of battle prevails with aquatic as with terrestrial mammals," that "[a]ll male animals which are furnished with special weapons for fighting, are well known to engage in fierce battles" (240), and that only in reindeer are special weapons—horns—also a female feature (243). He points out further that overall size differences and strength differences obtain between males and females, that males have larger canines, that "male quadrupeds are . . . more courageous and pugnacious than the females" (260), and that, with few exceptions, males are "the best armed" of the two sexes (399).

Extended reflection on the foregoing close-up observations of sexual selection leads to significant questions concerning *real* male-male competition in humans, questions that are epistemologically broadening rather than reductive in perspective, that are empirical rather than theoretical, and that, rather than being overshadowed by other concerns, stay tethered to the phenomenon at issue. Indeed, the questions come readily into view when we turn attention to actual human male-male competitive behaviors. Several examples will give an idea of the import of these behaviors. In particular, the examples will first demonstrate concretely how particular human male behaviors are exaptations of the basic biological phenomenon of male-male competition, the exaptations being cultural elaborations of what is evolutionarily given (for more on cultural elaborations of what is evolutionarily given, see Sheets-Johnstone 1994b). They will subsequently provide empirical grounds for showing elementary and even strategic correspondences between human and nonhuman male-male competition, specifically correspondences between human and nonhuman primates.

IV. EXEMPLIFICATIONS

In his classic study *Homo ludens,* in a chapter titled "Play and War," cultural historian Johan Huizinga discusses the practice of dueling in the Middle Ages and beyond. He writes that "[t]he last 'trial by battle' in a civil suit"—in 1571—was "on a battle-ground sixty feet square specially marked off for the purpose. The combat was permitted to last from sunrise 'until the stars grow visible'," or until one of the combatants uttered a certain word, "thereby avowing himself beaten" (Huizinga 1955, 93–94). Huizinga describes too how in early Greece, the battle between two Euboean cities in the seventh century B.C. "was fought wholly in the form of a contest," in which rules were set beforehand as to "the time and place for the encounter" (96). Writing of the modern duel in which a male does not fight to the death but only until blood is drawn, he again underscores the precise patterning of the contest: "The spot where the duel is fought bears all the marks of a playground; the weapons have to be exactly alike as in certain games; there is a signal for the start and the finish, and the number of shots is prescribed" (95). Moreover he underscores precise patterning again in speaking of medieval history generally. He writes, for example, "In the year 1400 a certain Count of Virneburg offered battle to the town of Aachen on a fixed day and place. . . . Such appointments regarding the time and place of a battle are of the utmost importance in treating war as an honourable contest which is at the same time a judicial decision" (98). In short, battles were rule-governed in a spatio-temporal sense: battlegrounds were clearly marked and the battles themselves were temporally limited.[5]

Whether in the form of duels, community clashes, or national conflicts, the battleground was akin to a lek. It was not a natural but consentiently chosen ground where combatants fought according to certain rules for a specified duration and a winner emerged. Such human patterning of male-male competition was not in the service of winning females, though winning females might have been a spin-off of a particular battle or contest,[6] but in the service of publicly acknowledging honor or justice, for example. The point is not that such a form of human male-male competition may be *modeled* on lek behavior, but that the formalized, strictly ordered, rule-governed male-male competition *exemplifies* lek behavior. Lek behavior is a biological matrix, that is, an archetype of male-male competition in which battles and battleground are prearranged, and in which, age differentials aside, i.e., as when a juvenile or immature male fights with a mature one, the contestants are matched; they are true antagonists, as Huizinga repeatedly emphasizes, equal contestants in the contest or *agon*. The archetype is co-opted—exapted—precisely to the extent that it no longer serves its original purpose, that is, when weaponry and/or abilities that evolved originally and specifically for the purpose of sexual pursuit and conquest are utilized to a different end, as when, for example, they are utilized to satisfy honor or justice. The further point is *not* that lek competitions were formerly in the behavioral repertoire of humans to be exapted directly—we will never know whether hominid males once engaged in lek competitions or not.[7] The point is rather that the archetypal or matrical form of male-male competition was co-opted. Serving a purpose other than its original one of winning females, lek competitions among human males was for winning in a psycho-social, socio-political, or socio-economic sense over other males.

Though Huizinga writes that war is a "development of the agon" and that the ludic function [is] inherent in the agon" (1955, 90), he also later states. "It is difficult to assess the agonistic element in warfare proper." Indeed, the archetypic contest between and among males has not simply been co-opted by humans. It has been culturally elaborated in highly variable and diverse ways, ways that precisely exceed "warfare proper." When Huizinga specifies forms of combat such as "the surprise, the ambush, the raid, the punitive expedition and wholesale extermination" as *non*-agonistic, and points out how "political objectives of war"— "conquest, subjection or domination of another people"—similarly define *non*-agonistic combat (90),[8] he implicitly documents variable and diverse ways of exceeding "warfare proper." Wherever such *non*-agonistic combat defines war, the battle does not in truth constitute a true contest (90). On the contrary, Huizinga declares,

> We can only speak of war as a cultural function so long as it is waged within a sphere whose members regard each other as equals or antagonists with equal rights. . . . This condition changes as soon as war is waged outside the sphere of equals, against groups not recognized as human beings and thus deprived of human rights—barbarians, devils, heathens, heretics and "lesser breeds without the law." In such circumstances war loses its play-quality altogether and can only remain within the bounds of civilization in so far as the parties to it accept certain limitations for the sake of their own honour. (89–90)

In sum, where antagonists are not equal, or where there is no forewarning of an attack or battle, or where the intent is to punish or to kill, and so on, war is not a civilized undertaking. Huizinga's comment, "In the very earliest phases of culture fighting lacked what we would call fair play—that is, it was largely non-agonistic" (95), is of interest in this regard insofar as it accords with Keeley's debunking of "the myth of a pacified [human] past." Keeley's extensive and finely detailed studies show that deaths from modern warfare are, in populational terms, minuscule in comparison with those in primitive societies. One of a number of his statistical graphs, for example, shows that "[a] typical tribal society lost about .5 percent of its population in combat each year." Keeley points out that were this casualty rate applied to earth's twentieth-century populations," it would predict "more than 2 *billion* war deaths since 1900" (Keeley 1996, 93; see also 89).[9] In short, his archaeological studies of human societies of all description—prehistoric, primitive, tribal, nonstate, hunter-gatherer, and modern—offer striking testimony to the phenomenon of *real* human male-male competition in its most radical form, wars that in Huizingan terms are indubitably non-agonistic. Although Huizinga would insist that such wars have no cultural *function*, they are rooted in an archetype no less biologically generated and culturally honed than agonistic wars. Both forms of war are, in other words, culturally elaborated on the basis of what is evolutionarily given: *real* male-male competition.

V. EVOLUTIONARY CONSIDERATIONS

Let us look more closely now at the phenomenon of *real* male-male competition as it is consistently described in the literature on primates, primates being the biological order to which humans belong. Such competition in nonhuman primates is routinely conceived and categorized in terms of dominance, specifically primate male dominance hierarchies. A display of might or power is a bid for dominance that might happen anywhere at any time, as when, by suddenly making a spectacle of himself, for example, a male primate frightens other males, in turn subjugating or otherwise oppressing them. Consider the following extended description by Jane Goodall, in which a male chimpanzee, attempting to rise to the top of the "adult male dominance hierarchy," not only makes a spectacle of himself but does so with the added benefit of artificial weaponry (Goodall 1971, 112–13):

A group of five adult males, including top-ranking Goliath, David Graybeard, and the huge Rodolf, were grooming each other. The session had been going on for some twenty minutes. Mike was sitting about thirty yards apart from them, frequently staring toward the group, occasionally idly grooming himself. All at once Mike calmly walked over to our tent and took hold of an empty kerosene can by the handle. Then he picked up a second can and, walking upright, returned to the place where he had been sitting. Armed with his two cans Mike continued to stare toward the other males. After a few minutes he began to rock from side to side. . . . Gradually he rocked more vigorously, his hair slowly began to stand erect, and then, softly at first, he started a series of pant-hoots. As he called, Mike got to his feet and suddenly he was off, charging toward the group of males, hitting the two cans ahead of him. The cans, together with Mike's crescendo of hooting, made the most appalling racket: no wonder the erstwhile peaceful males rushed out of the way. Mike and his cans vanished down a track, and after a few moments there was silence. . . . After a short interval that low-pitched hooting began again, followed almost immediately by the appearance of the two rackety cans with Mike close behind them. Straight for the other males he charged, and once more they fled. . . .

Rodolf was the first of the males to approach Mike, uttering soft pant-grunts of submission, crouching low and pressing his lips to Mike's thigh. Next he began to groom Mike, and two other males approached, pant-grunting, and also began to groom him.

Though on an infinitesimally smaller scale than the scale of possible human attempts at dominance, Mike's bid for dominance is readily comparable to human male bids for dominance, and not only individual male bids but national bids, bids in the form of displays that break into otherwise peaceful relations, that utilize immediate attention-getting objects, that provoke fear, and by provoking fear, aim to subdue or subjugate others. Piercing through ordinary activities of everyday life, such human displays of power can and do generate unendurable tensions that readily leave vengeful, rancorous figures in their wake as well as cringing, submissive ones. Where the intent is to dominate others, the display, after all, can be one in which anything goes. It can take the form of a surprise attack, for example, a massacre, or a technological assault calculated to produce shock and awe. Where Huizinga's cultural proprieties of war go unrecognized and political objectives are the driving force, the display of power is in the service of dominance. The human urge to dominance may be specifically driven by the idea that "might makes right," a characterization that, interestingly enough, Huizinga finds apposite and links to archaic systems of thought. In such systems of thought, he says, "One wages war in order to obtain a decision of holy validity," the decision being "'a judgement of God'": "might makes right" is "'the will of the gods'" or "'manifest superiority'." Indeed, Huizinga provocatively states that in archaic thought, "war itself might conceivably be regarded as a form of divination" (Huizinga 1955, 91). In these divine instances especially, dominance clearly exceeds mere power, the compass of the aim of dominance being greater than that of mere power. It is, in other words, not mere glory and superiority that are desired, but the enshrinement of one's own beliefs and values, and in turn, the subjugation of others to one's own will, a social relation that demands subservience, precisely as in acts of grooming, pant-grunting, and the kissing of a thigh, though in these instances without any doxic or axiological trappings.

From a human perspective, the range of responsive options to a non-agonistic bid for dominance appears, theoretically at least, to be greater than grooming, pant-grunting, and the kissing of a thigh. That is, theoretically at least, what happens next depends on the motivations and reflective intelligence of those on the receiving end of a bid for dominance. In this respect, however, the motivations of Mike, and actually, of those whom Mike upends as well, are critical to consider. Might we not liken Donald Rumsfeld, the former U.S. secretary of defense, to Mike, for example? As described by Goodall, Mike's display of power was clearly productive of shock and awe—the fear aspect of awe, not its wonder. Rattling his technological cans, Rumsfeld's strategy was akin to Mike's shock and awe strategy for establishing himself at the top of the adult male dominance hierarchy, akin in terms of subduing others, establishing the beginnings of a dominance hierarchy in the Middle East, and indeed, rising to the top of a global hierarchy. As a result, could and should Americans not glory in their nation, not feel proud and duly avenged for the events of September 11, 2001? Moreover could and would they not feel the "holy validity" of their war? Huizinga's

1938 historical observations are prescient in this regard. He writes, "The great wars of aggression from antiquity down to our own time all find a far more essential explanation in the idea of glory, which everybody understands, than in any rational and intellectualist theory of economic forces and political dynamisms. The modern outbursts of glorifying war, so lamentably familiar to us, carry us back to the Babylonian and Assyrian conception of war as a divine injunction to exterminate foreign peoples to the greater glory of God" (90–91).

Darwin does not broach the subject of war in his discussion of male-male competition and "the law of battle." As indicated by the above empirical facts and discussion, however, war is a form of human male-male competition, such competition being exapted and put in the service of agonistic or non-agonistic combat. As we have seen, a major reason the co-optive transition is not recognized is that male-male competition has been put in either of two reproductive boxes, one labeled "sperm competition," the other labeled "Pass on your genes!" Where theory rather than real-life happenings determine truth, investigations and appreciations of evidence in the form of empirical matters of fact fall by the wayside. *Real* male-male competition clearly warrants investigation. Feminists would indeed do well to turn attention to the ways in which human history attests to biological realities that have a central part in explaining the phenomenon of war—right up to the present. Males wage war. The only female army was a mythological one; however memorialized on Greek vases, Amazons are long gone. Male-male competition is at this very moment being played out by a few, but on a global field where virtually no one is safe.[10] The competition is ostensibly in pursuit of power, an end in itself, but it reeks with dominance and divine injunction. In this competition, hosts of males are conscripted ideologically as well as militarily in the service of a leader whose values and beliefs they come to embody: as with Mao, Stalin, and Hitler, so with present-day organizations and nations. The psychological spin-off for the indoctrinated masses as for the actually recruited is sizable. The meaning and value of one's life is sustained by an immortality ideology, be it in the form of nationalism or religion—or both—or in the form of any other nobly enshrined value and belief system. Of course, not all are seduced by the rhetoric, but for those who are, an incontrovertible and absolute meaning is given to their lives.

VI. A METHODOLOGICAL IMPERATIVE AND A CLOSING APOLOGUE

In sum, war is a cultivated human taste, the cultural magnification of the biological archetype of *real* male-male competition, co-opted from its original sexual context and put in the service of dominance *über alles* and all that dominance *über alles* brings with it. In the late twentieth and early twenty-first centuries especially, war has become less and less a matter of true antagonists than of unequal contestants and armaments, inequalities that mirror the dominant and subjugated class system that moneyed interests can establish and that a degenerate capitalism can and does so admirably support. Coincident with these summary observations is a critical methodological imperative and a brief story that poignantly and profoundly points up the urgency of the imperative. With respect to the imperative, I elsewhere urged—and at some length—that we practice philosophy close-up, that is, that we immerse ourselves experientially in our questioning, feeling the ground underneath our feet directly as we explore it such that it touches us directly and nothing professional separates us from it. To win our freedom, I said, we must practice philosophy close-up (Sheets-Johnstone 1999b). A brief apologue, however anecdotal it might be, is a testimonial to this methodological urgency: A Native American grandfather was talking to his grandson about how he felt about the tragedy on September 11. He said, "I feel as if I have two wolves fighting in my heart. One wolf is vengeful, angry, violent. The other wolf is loving, forgiving, compassionate." The grandson asked him, "Which wolf will win the fight in your heart?" The grandfather answered, "The one I feed."

VII. AN AFTERWORD

The above detailed analysis of the bio-cultural phenomenon 'real male-male competition' is clearly of signal importance. In the broadest sense, the analysis underscores the importance of understanding natural and cultural histories; in a more focused sense, it demonstrates the importance of understanding those dual histories to understandings of sociopolitical human violence, a violence not only readily apparent across untold centuries of human history, but apparent in today's global human world; in a fine-edged critical sense, it provides an otherwise rare opportunity to acknowledge briefly but pointedly that Nature gives us other options, options that we can, if we choose, cultivate in lieu of *real* male-male competition.

Other significant aspects of male-male competition warrant attention as well, aspects that hinge not on a lack of academic research on the biocultural realities of the phenomenon, but on unwitting personal prejudices and inadvertent leaps of language. These aspects can be brought to the fore most incisively by examining Ernest Becker's last published article before his death, "Towards the Merger of Animal and Human Studies" (Becker 1974), an article in which Becker attempts to incorporate biological studies into his socio-psychoanalytic framework. Precisely because his writings on the denial of death, the perpetration of evil, and the love of violence offer such penetrating insights into the human condition and human behavior, his complete omission of any mention of male-male competition makes the significance of the phenomenon all the more striking.

Becker's stated aim in the article is to bridge the gap between biology and culture, "to show that the two camps could easily be reconciled if they so desired, that there is obviously secure truth in both," sufficient to "make mutual capital out of their profound insights into the human condition" (235). He uses ethologist Konrad Lorenz's book *On Aggression* and evolutionary anthropologists Lionel Tiger and Robin Fox's joint book *The Imperial Animal* as biological stepping-stones, but then charges both Lorenz and Tiger and Fox with, as he puts it, "speaking the truth 'falsely'" (240); in different ways, Becker says, they lock humans tightly into a "biological imperialism" (243, 249), Lorenz by his "instinct theory" of war, what he—Lorenz—terms "militant enthusiasm," Tiger and Fox by their "biogram" of man the hunter, a wired-in disposition to killing and physical dominance. What Becker in essence wants to do is to supplant such biological understandings of "the human condition" with psychoanalytic and socio-psychological truths. In particular, he wants to show how "insignificance and death" (251), the two evils of creatureliness, are at the center of man's existence. In supplanting biology in this way, he of course sizably if surreptitiously changes the nature of the bridge he wants to build. But let us follow him through on this shift and outline its highpoints.

Equating Nature with creatureliness, Becker speaks of man's need for "heroic transcendence" over his animal nature, namely, over the fact that all animals, humans included, are born and die. Thus, when he writes of "man's basic animality" (244), he is writing basically about nothing more than the mortality of creatureliness. He thereby virtually dismisses any biological dispositions, not only when he criticizes Lorenz's "instinct theory" of aggression and Tiger and Fox's hunter theory of male aggression, but when he speaks of Darwinian thought as no more than "[a] reminder about the human condition" (248), for example, and claims that zoological texts are *"thin"* (249). By such remarks, he leads the reader to think that he is to a surprising degree unacquainted with Darwin's writings, notably, *The Descent of Man and Selection in Relation to Sex*. The impression is considerably strengthened when he urges that, to speak the truth of biology truthfully, we need to move to "a more general level of theoretical explanation" (241), one that fastens on motivation, and in particular on "the explanation of motives that has come out of the best distillation of psychoanalytic theory, specifically in the work of Otto Rank, Norman O. Brown, and Robert J. Lifton, . . . [who show] "that the things that drive men are their urges to self-perpetuation and heroic victory over evil" (242). He affirms that "when we consider man as the culturally modifiable creature that he is, . . . we still get the scientific and moral lesson that Lorenz wants, but we get it not on the basis of exact homology between animals and men" (242). The bridge to be built is, in effect, not one between biology and culture but between science (particularly psychology and psychoanalytic theory) and culture. And indeed, in his final section, Becker distinguishes animals and man on the basis of man's being unconsciously driven by the irrational, that is, by the fear of death. He states, "We know that the irrational in man's inner life is his unconscious horror of insignificance and death" (251), later affirming that "[T]he real problem of the human condition is terror of death and the need for heroic transcendence" (251). So all his talk about understanding "man's basic animality" amounts to understanding man's motivation to transcend mortality by heroic acts. War, in effect, is an immortality game or "hero-game" (242) as Becker aptly describes it, but a game with no connection whatsoever to biology. Indeed, the last section of his paper is titled, "The drawbacks of the zoological approach to man" (248).

Now a central but unnoticed fact, surprisingly unnoticed even by Becker himself, is evident in the course of the article. When Lorenz, Tiger and Fox, *and Becker* speak, respectively, of militant enthusiasm, male-hunting biograms, and heroic transcendence, they are not *really* talking about humans, that is, about the genus *Homo;* they are talking about *males*, human males to be sure, but incontestably *male* humans. Militant enthusiasm, male-hunting biograms, and heroic transcendence are notably *male* occupations or preoccupations. The surreptitious slide from talk of humans and the human condition to talk of "man" is what might be termed an unwitting linguistic legerdemain; what is identified as human to begin with is in actuality a wholly male phenomenon never boldly and straightforwardly affirmed as such, not even when Becker quotes Tiger and Fox's suggestion that "the phenomena of human cruelty, blood-craving, sacrifice, and pseudo-specific killing and abuse are directly related to the sense of personal manly validation individual men feel in terms of their male groups" (245), and their later depiction of Nazis, Black Muslims, and Ku Klux Klan members as "men feeling relatively deprived to establish themselves as full and effective men," that is, as "the expression of a need to be a man among men" (245). Indeed, the underlying biological phenomenon of male-male competition that grounds male-hunting biograms as it grounds militant enthusiasm and heroic transcendence is masked in talk of aggression, of dominance, or of victory over evil. With respect to Becker, we could straightaway critically say that he wrongfully omits females; but we could more germanely say to begin with that he rightfully focuses exclusively on males, but fails to hit the biological nail on the head.

Of particular interest in this context are passages in the probing and at times moving interview that Sam Keen, a psychology editor and religion scholar, conducted with Becker. In interviewing Becker in the last days of his life, Keen effectively draws out theoretical aspects of Becker's work, and at times just as effectively comments on it. At a point midway through their conversations, Keen observes,

> It seems to me that in some way your thought is excessively masculine, that is—it is natural enough—you are a man—but when you talk about the human project of consciousness, . . . I wonder if the condition that you portray is not more the masculine condition than it is the human condition and if it isn't largely a condition which is at least exaggerated by the kind of culture in which the rational, the driving, the competitive, the masculine, the rational elements, have been the formative ones. How do you think if you had been a woman that your approach would have been different? (Keen, n.d., 20)

Keen's insight into Becker's unwitting linguistic sleight of hand—his *male* rather than *human* focus—is in fact readily evident not only in Becker's writings, but in his interview with Keen. In his first response to Keen, for example, who proposes the interview as "a test of your theory," Becker answers: "It's a test of everything I've written about death. How does one die? And I've got a chance of showing how one dies. The attitude one takes. Whether one does it in a dignified, manly, way . . ." (1).

Several pages later, looking at his work in its historical context, he speaks of the intellectual's work in today's world being "to elaborate his picture what it means to be a man and what is the condition of man" (6) and again, several pages later, he states that theologians like Paul Tillich and he were "trying to . . . answer the same questions," namely, " what makes people act the way they do and what does it mean to be a man?" (9). Moreover with respect to Keen's specific question as to whether his approach would have been different, "if [he] had been a woman," he responds immediately, "That is some question. I don't know." In musing to some degree on the question, he alludes to "the tremendous roles the German women played in Nazism, encouraging this kind of heroics," and then, adding to Keen's follow-up observation, "Women create out of their biological given, in a way that we [men] do not," he states, "Which leads probably to less competitiveness among women" (20). Shortly after this interchange, he offers the following more personal reflection: "I think I am talking more about men than about women when I talk about the drive to be a hero and the need to stand out as a creative person. Men are very competitive in that. The whole drama of history is a drama of men seeking to affirm their specialness, isn't it?" (21).

Clearly, the interview sensitively limns Becker's open and honest responses to questions about his work, and in the process substantively highlights the fact that he unwittingly converts "the human condition" into "the male condition." Several of Becker's responses, however, merit deeper attention in this context. First, there is no denying that females can and do encourage male heroes, precisely as Becker suggests in his comment on German women in the Third Reich. From a biological perspective, females are attracted to male heroes. The attraction is an expression of female choice, the female biological equivalent of male-male competition (see Darwin 1871, vol. 1, chap. 8; Eberhard 1985; Sheets-Johnstone 1994b, chap. 3, sec. 6). Thus, and as will be evident in a fuller discussion in the Epilogue, females can certainly support the honing of warriors, they can share in the glories of war, and so on, but they themselves are not riveted on training themselves to fight and kill nor are they in any way primarily those who are trained to fight and kill: they are not warriors nor are they motivated to be warriors. Second, to assay the competitiveness of females in relation to the competitiveness of males, i.e, to ponder the probability that there is "less competitiveness among women," is not of biological moment, at least not in this context. What is of biological moment is twofold: the fact that accruing resources, seeking power and glory, achieving heroic transcendence over "man's basic animality," and the like, are all preeminently male occupations or preoccupations, and the fact that correlative to these occupations or preoccupations is the biological matrix of male-male competition. Male-male competition is foundational to the challenges posed by the occupations and preoccupations. The significance of this biological truth will surface in later chapters and fuller discussions will be offered, but a related aspect warrants extended discussion here.

When it was stated earlier that Becker's wrongful omission of females was less immediately germane than his exclusive focus on males, it was not to minimize—and certainly not ignore in any way—the psychologically and psychoanalytically recognized truth that males distance themselves from females for a reason: for a man to be a man, he must dissociate himself from all that is female. Fear of the feminine is thus understandably of a piece with the cultivation of heroes, for heroes—*real* warriors—can only be contaminated by what is female. An exclusive masculine focus is from this perspective not just an avoidance or omission of the feminine, but indeed, a fear of the feminine. A true male—a man who is truly a man—recoils categorically from anything even remotely female, for even what is female only by decree or cultural convention—natural human feelings of fear or hurt, for example—can only defile and dishonor what is truly male. A male worth his manly salt thus denies his wounds and fears; either this, or his society denies them for him, branding him a coward (see the discussion of Marlowe's study of war in the Epilogue). Psychoanalysts and psychologists offer provocative and insightful perspectives on the manly point at issue, namely, fear of the feminine, and in turn, show why the omission of females is not simply a critical point to be raised reactively against Becker, but a germane topic in its own right.

In three essays in particular,[11] psychiatrist D. W. Winnicott traces fear of the feminine to "fear of Woman," "Woman" in the sense that "each man and woman *came out of a woman*" (Winnicott 1986, 191). He states that "the trouble is not so much that everyone was inside and then born, but that at the very beginning everyone was *dependent* on a woman" (191; italics in original). Though no one remembers being dependent, there remains "a vague fear of dependence ... always including the fear of domination" (125). There is a difference, however, between the sexes with respect to the vague fear of dependence in that "Women have it in them to deal with their relation to WOMAN by identification with her" (192). Nevertheless, Winnicott declares, "The awkward fact remains, for men and women, that each was once dependent on woman, and somehow a hatred of this has to be transformed into a kind of gratitude if full maturity of the personality is to be reached" (193).

In the present context, the most interesting aspect of Winnicott's perspective has to do less with a transformation of hatred into gratitude than with the socio-political consequences of "the fear of domination." Winnicott notes that "Unfortunately, the fear of domination does not lead groups of people to avoid being dominated; on the contrary, it draws them towards a specific or chosen domination. Indeed, were the psychology of the dictator studied, one would expect to find that, amongst other things, he in his own personal struggle is trying to control the woman whose domination he unconsciously fears, trying to control her by encompassing her, acting for her, and in turn demanding total subjection and 'love'" (125). He follows up on this socio-political theme in another essay, noting that the "fear of WOMAN is a powerful agent in society structure, and it is responsible for the fact that in very few societies does a woman hold the political reins.... [A] man who in a political sense is at the top can be appreciated by the group much more objectively than a woman can be if she is in a similar position" (252–53). He points out again, but in this instance more emphatically, that the motivations of a dictator *"can be a compulsion to deal with this fear of woman by encompassing her and acting for her,"* and specifies the connection more closely when he notes that

> the tendency of groups of people to accept or even seek *actual* domination is derived from a fear of domination by *fantasy woman*. This fear leads them to seek, and even welcome, domination by a known human being, especially one who has taken on himself the burden of personifying and therefore limiting

> the magical qualities of the all-powerful woman of fantasy, to whom is owed the great debt. The dictator can be overthrown, and must eventually die; but the woman figure of primitive unconscious fantasy has no limits to her existence or power. (253)

It is worth noting too that Winnicott poses the question of why males seek danger, and ties the answer to the fact that men not only envy the danger that women go through in childbirth, but "moreover, they feel guilty because they cause pregnancies and then sit pretty and watch women going through it all, not only the childbirth, but the whole confinement and the terribly restricting responsibilities of infant care. So they take risks too. . . . They are trying to break even. But when a man dies he is dead, whereas women always were and always will be" (193).

In sum, Winnicott's psychoanalytic explanation of the "fear of WOMAN," of the consequences of that fear, and of the feelings associated with it, is anchored in biological and developmental human realities. A wholly different perspective, yet one offering basically the same explanation, is taken by educational psychologist Chris Blazina. As prelude to his discussion of "fear of the feminine," he briefly sketches how a fundamental character of the hero abides across human history:

> We see the Indo-European hero as one who must break free of the safety of the community to do battle with demons, dragons, monsters, and the like in order to reach the goal of being a successful warrior who has achieved the fame that does not decay. There is an emphasis upon valor. Breaking free of the safety of maternal care allows for the seeking of a male mentor who will infuse the neophyte with masculine virtues. This theme is recycled as the backdrop for the successful masculine neophyte who must now [in the nineteenth and twentieth centuries] do battle with dangers of a different kind—engulfment by caregivers. In this case, hero status is the achievement of successful masculine identity through emotional independence and psychological separation. Whether we approach these hero's journeys from an objective perspective or engage the passionate pleas of advocates for a kinder, gentler way to raise boys, we are witness to how this part of the masculine paradigm has remained in the

forefront of discussions of masculine identity. (Blazina 2003, 68–69)

Though expressed in the mythical language of the hero and the search for true masculinity, the theme of psychological disengagement is not only again in evidence, but is again tied to a basic biological fact: in the beginning, males are dependent on females. If they are to realize themselves as males, they must dissociate themselves emotionally and psychologically from caregiving females; they must precisely battle any such bonds. The basic biological fact is thus taken to be an emotional and psychological straitjacket from which any male who would be a man must free himself.

The emotional and psychological straitjacket is perspicuously analyzed by psychologist Silvan Tomkins in his dense and probing sociopsychological excavations of the genesis and scripting of affectivity in human development and behavior (but see also, for example, Seidler 1997).[12] Affective stratification is necessary to the cultivation of warriors—*real* men; that is, feelings proper to *real* men must be separated out from feelings that are proper to females. Accordingly, feelings of shame, timidity, distress, humility, and so on, are transformed into feelings of anger, violence, excitement, risk-taking, contempt, disgust, and so on. Tomkins terms this unevenly valorized categorization of feelings "affect stratification," which he analyzes as both a familially and societally generated phenomenon. In his analysis, he shows how affects are divided into two quite separate categories, those of the warrior and those of women and other lesser individuals, and how "powerful magnification of the warrior affects guarantees that the feminine affects will become as alien as they are seductive" (Tomkins 1995, 163). In effect, males and females are fundamentally distinguished and distinguishable by the feelings they have and do not have, the feelings being those that are either countenanced or not countenanced, and in turn fostered or not fostered. In a certain sense, males are parentally and culturally goaded into being males. But in another quite real sense, the goading builds on what is evolutionarily given. When Tomkins suggests that "[s]ocial stratification rests upon the affect stratification inherent in adversarial contests" (163), he offers a keen analysis of how affect stratification arises, but without any reference to male-male competition. His analysis is instructive and of considerable interest in this sense and warrants extended quotation.

118    Part I

> There is no other single influence which so governs our affective postures than ideology, because discrimination of all kinds, exploitation of all kinds, and derogation of all kinds cannot be justified without reason. The reason, I submit, came many thousands of years ago when in response to perceived scarcity of food, stratification began. Sanday (1981) [*Female Power and Male Dominance*] has reviewed the evidence using 150 primitive societies, and found in general that where there was no real scarcity there was differentiation between the genders and between the ages, but not stratification. Stratification began when, given serious scarcity, human beings began to pillage and rape other tribes, to take prisoners, and to defeat them in mortal combat. That was the beginning of human slavery. Anybody who commands the life of another human being has all the power there is to have. It began in adversarial contests. (356)

Tomkins presents a compelling descriptive account of the affect stratification that is the result of adversarial contests:

> When one man could kill another man, or have him at his mercy, the ultimate bifurcation of primary affects into feminine and masculine affects occurred. The masculine affects were anger, excitement, and dissmell ["a distancing response"; see Tomkins 1991, 24], which the victor showed the defeated other, who was granted his life as the victor's slave. . . . The slave's affects were defined as the feminine ones. He was to tremble in fear, and he did not have to be told that, because he had a knife at his throat. Furthermore, he had to be humble and ashamed, just as the victor was proud and arrogant and contemptuous. Thirdly, he had to cry for his life. (Tomkins 1995, 356–57)

Tomkins writes that "the definition of woman" comes from the defeated male: "humble, timid, loving, not angry, not dissmelling," and that the affect stratification was thus not limited to women but to anyone who failed to be a man (357.)

Finally, it is of moment that while Tomkins gives socio-political examples from contemporary life to validate the repudiation of males who have "no fire in the belly" (357; see also Keen 1991b), he basically links stratification to scarcity:

> When men contest for scarce resources, they become adversarial, and when they become adversarial, life becomes, as Hobbes described it, nasty, brutish, and short. That is inherent in adversarial living. We will never be free of it entirely. We may civilize it, we may tame it, but we will forever be vulnerable to it, so long as there is scarcity. And scarcity does not simply refer to money. It can refer to how many citations there are in the literature to one's latest work. It can make people very nasty. There are all kinds of limitations in the world that evoke the masculine-feminine affect stratification. (Tomkins 1995, 357)

Tomkins clearly sees adversarial contests not as biologically driven but as existentially driven. Male-male competition is, in other words, not recognized as the biological matrix that it is. One can readily and with solid reason, however, take the realities of evolutionary biology into account and at the same time strongly uphold Tomkins's thesis regarding affect stratification. To wit, male-male competition is essentially about privileged access to resources; male reaction to scarcity, whatever its form, elicits and builds on the biological matrix of male-male competition.

The foregoing psychoanalytic and psychological observations are clearly perspicuous and keenly instructive in their elucidation of the fear of the feminine. With their neglect of the reality of *real* male-male competition, however, they show that neither Becker nor Lorenz, nor Tiger and Fox are alone either in their exclusive focus on males *or* in their misdirected focus on aggression, dominance, or violence; they too overlook male-male competition as the fundamental biological phenomenon. Focal exclusivity and misdirection are in fact pervasive in the literature generally.[13] For example, throughout zoologists J. D. Carthy and F. J. Ebling's edited book on *The Natural History of Aggression*, not only is no mention made of male-male competition by any of the essayists, but their common inadvertent leap from talk of humans to talk of "man," not as a commonly used synonym for "human," but in pointed reference to "man's destructiveness," man's "innate aggression," man's aggressive propensity to war (Carthy and Ebling 1964, 4), and so on, unequivocally testifies to the same linguistic sleight of hand: what starts out as "human" is in reality exclusively male. *Real* male-male competition may furthermore be ignored not so much by a linguistic sleight of hand than by an outright obliviousness of the basic maleness of aggression to begin with, and this even in instances where ethological sources in particular and biological sources in general are consulted. For example, psychiatrist Anthony Stevens writes that "Readiness to do battle is one of the less appealing characteristics of our *species*" (Stevens 1983, 232; italics added); and further, that "[a]ggression . . . is an ineradicable feature of human nature, and its manifestations in battle with outsiders for territory and resources and in struggle with insiders for power and prestige are everywhere characteristic of the life of mankind" (234).[14] In short, that it is not a question of humans generally but of males in particular is everywhere evident but nowhere acknowledged. Moreover in neglecting any mention of the biological phenomenon of male-male competition in discussions of aggression, whether the natural history of aggression or the psychological aspects of aggression, writings on the subject testify to an absorption in what is derivative rather than what is original, i.e., from a biological perspective, *male-male competition feeds aggression, and not the reverse*. In particular, from a biological perspective, aggressive actions against others are in the service of procuring females, maintaining one's place in a dominance hierarchy, attaining the more favorable resources, and so on. The actions are driven by the biological matrix of male-male competition. How any particular competition plays out depends on just those biological variables Darwin discussed in his explanation of natural and sexual selection: some males are more pugnacious than others, just as some are more eager than others, some more amicable than others, some more tense, more energized, more docile, more vocal, more alert, and so on, than others. It is furthermore notable that Darwin called attention to the fact that there is greater variability in secondary sexual characters in males—characters such as pugnacity and eagerness—than in females (Darwin 1871, 1:274–75). Aggression—a ready kin of what Darwin describes as "pugnacity"—is a biological variable that exists along a socio-psychological affective gradient, a gradient that may, to be sure, be culturally influenced toward one extreme or the other in humans, but a biological variable all the same. In contrast, male-male competition is a biological matrix that exists directly along a *cultural* gradient in human males, a gradient readily exemplified in the degree to which, and the ways in which, a culture can and does promote competition, honing heroes and prominencing warriors in the pursuit of power, glory, and so on. Recognition of the biological matrix of male-male competition is elided in discussions of "the natural history of aggression," just as it is elided in Becker's socio-psychoanalytical theory of death and evil, in Lorenz's instinct theory of aggression, and in Tiger and Fox's biogram theory of dominance. It is as if the biological matrix would contaminate any one or all of these theories. But of course it does not. Male-male competition grounds the pan-cultural human practice of war. The practice is in fact the ultimate human testing ground of male-male competition. To this end, aggression is cultivated; the pan-cultural practice of war is contingent on its cultivation, that is, on a forcefully positive value and meaning being placed on "pugnacity"—on actual acts of violence: killing, mutilating, massacring, torturing. The honing of aggressive males, the cultivation of *real* warriors, has the power not only to bring glory to the nation, tribe, or group that engages in warfare, but to annihilate the enemies, aliens, and ideological adversaries that threaten the nation's, tribe's, or group's lasting identity, wealth, power, and the like, and to sustain the immortality ideologies of the warriors who die so valiantly in the fight. Male-male competition is the biological ground on which cultures hone aggression in males, sharpening their taste and capacity for violence.

Yet Becker is surely correct when he observes that "the real step to large-scale evil in the evolution of man was when he switched from a merely physical self-perpetuation to a symbolic self-perpetuation based on the absolutes of his cultural world view. Man was the first animal who could aggrandize himself infinitely in his fantasy, and this is what began to take such a toll of pulsating life" (Becker 1974, 247). What Becker tries to show is what we might well label "a complementarity of motives in zoological man and psychoanalytical man." What he in fact does not realize, however, is the complementarity itself, and he does not realize it because he nowhere acknowledges the biological matrix of male-male competition. The complementarity of motives resides in the fact that male-male competition is at the heart of the toll that Becker so poignantly recognizes as exacting suffering on "pulsating life," for self-aggrandizement (national aggrandizement, tribal aggrandizement, group aggrandizement) always comes at the cost of other lives, other peoples, other beings, and even of the planet itself. Fantasies of power, of glory, of heroic transcendence are fantasies in which males precisely compete with one another. To use Becker's language, "symbolic perpetuation" has its roots in "self-perpetuation." In effect, one does not "switch" from one form of "perpetuation" to the other. Symbols do not descend from the blue but remain tethered to their point of origin. They have their roots in analogical thinking and thereby remain rooted in life's realities. (For a fuller discussion of symbols and analogical thinking, see Sheets-Johnstone 1990 and 1999b, chap. 1).

A final note should be added. As we have seen, present-day biological investigations of *real* male-male competition are egregiously lacking, having been replaced in the main by *sperm* competition. The situation is unfortunate, for what we want to understand is how *real* male-male competition, a bona fide *human male biological* disposition—just as it is a male biological disposition in other animal species—plays out culturally, that is, precisely how cultures rework what is evolutionarily given. In just this context, it is possible to answer to the charge that Becker raises against Lorenz, namely, how, if militant enthusiasm is an instinct, there can be cultures in which war is unheard of. Moreover it is possible to answer to the charge that Becker raises against Tiger and Fox, namely, that their male biogram is reductionistic, overdetermining man, or as he puts it, their biogram overdetermines "the *nature* of the evil that we must hunt down" (Becker 1974, 247) and thus fails to address man's symbolic modes of self-perpetuation. The answer in each instance is that cultures can suppress, elaborate, exaggerate, or distort human biological dispositions. I have exemplified these four elemental cultural variations on a biological theme at length in *The Roots of Power: Animate Form and Gendered Bodies* (Sheets-Johnstone 1994b). The point here, however, is not to answer on behalf of Lorenz and of Tiger and Fox to Becker's charges, but to illuminate obstacles in Becker's own path, or in other words, to show how Becker can marry biology in the form of evolutionary matters of fact to culture in the form of his psychoanalytic and sociopsychological theories by recognizing what is foundationally covert and amiss in his own theoretics and analyses—just as it is covert and amiss in the theoretics and analyses of other scientific researchers in similar pursuits—and to show this in ways that strengthen and enhance his thesis and analyses.

In sum, humans are free to choose what they affectively cultivate, precisely as the Native American grandfather wisely explains to his grandson. When males realize this existential fact of human life and open to their full humanness, they realize they are not locked in. Nature gives them other options. Turning away from these other options, they compromise their intelligence. The species *Homo sapiens sapiens* in turn suffers; it has yet to cultivate and realize its vaunted wisdom.

## NOTES

1. Writing of the "Mechanisms of Sexual Selection," and in particular of "Darwin's 'Law of Battle'," biologist Peter O'Donald observes that "[f]ighting is perhaps the simplest and most direct form of competition" (O'Donald 1980, 28). He later observes that "[m]ales may compete for females in more subtle ways than merely by fighting for them. They may compete in the size of the territories they hold and by the intensity of their display and courtship" (29).

In his book *Sexual Selection*, biologist Malte Andersson writes that "[s]exual selection will often favor traits that improve the endurance of a male, enabling him to remain longer at a breeding site and mate with females that otherwise would mate with other males" (Andersson 1994, 11). Echoing Darwin, he states, "Fights over mates select for strength, often achieved by large size, and for weapons such as antlers, horns, and spurs," and notes, "In addition to large sensory or locomotory organs and weapons, males in many animals have conspicuous ornaments or behavioral signals" (11). He also notes that "Competition for mates is the defining aspect of all forms of sexual selection" (12).

Andersson's observations concerning variations and display are equally worth citing. For example:

> More or less discontinuous variation in male structures and behavior occurs in many species; the cause often appears to be sexual selection in [the] form of male contest competition over mates. Some examples in fishes and arthropods are aggressive behavior, large body size, weapons, or other secondary sex traits, versus small size and sex traits, and inconspicuous mating behavior. (395)

> Energetic and physiological constraints can limit male display behavior and mating success. There is increasing evidence that display rate is important for mating success, but sexual display is often among the most energy-demanding activities of an animal, raising the metabolism 15–20 times. Sexual selection should therefore strongly favor good phenotypic condition and the ability of displaying at a high rate over extended periods, in many species based on resources stored over a long time. (440)

2. But see biologist William Eberhard's real-life rendition of sexual selection in Eberhard 1985.

3. Alan Lill comments on the number of years lek-displaying birds return to the same site. He states that when his study in Trinidad ended in 1971 that "[a]s in other lek-displaying birds, arenas were persistent at particular sites. In the lower Arima Valley two leks were known to have persisted at the same sites at least 2.5 years, one at least 4.5, three at least 5.0 and one at least 12.0" (Lill 1976, 14). (The Arima Valley in Trinidad is located in the northern mountain range of the country, and Lill's research station was in the center of the range.) Also to be noted in this context is the rather low-key and seemingly little-recognized observation of avian biologists Jacob Höglund and Rauno Alatalo that "a typical feature of many vertebrate lekking species is the mobility of females" (Höglund and Alatalo 1995, 187).

4. Indeed, actual avian fights are rare. See, for example, Lill (1976, 16) on the Golden-headed Manakin: "Ritualized encounters [of males] at territory boundary zones rarely erupted into fights." For a general discussion with a range of examples, see Attenborough 1990.

5. Huizinga, however, also mentions Herodotus's disapproval of the practice of setting a place for battle in advance (Huizinga 1950, 96–97).

6. Territory counts, for example, in rivalry among three-spined sticklebacks: "Rival males appear to influence each other in settling success [how and whether a male "claims an area as his territory"], in choice of a nest site, in building proper, and in activity-pattern characteristics of the post-building phases. Aggression shown by males present in a rival situation is correlated with the respective sizes of their holdings, and something like a rank order is established" (Van den Assem 1967, 4). Van den Assem also points out, "[T]erritories are exclusively connected with breeding activities. It should be clear that a territory in itself is non-existent, it always is inseparably connected with appropriate behaviour of its owner" (3).

7. In fact, it seems unlikely that they did since, though nonhuman primate males fight for dominance, they do not compete in a special place or follow any rules.

8. Cf. Van den Assem on "sneaking" by male sticklebacks (1967, 100–111).

9. Political scientist David Wilkinson's finely detailed conclusions concerning *Deadly Quarrels* is based on his computerized reappraisal of Lewis Fry Richardson's earlier statistical studies of the causes of war (most notably as detailed in Richardson 1960). His itemized conclusions under several different headings give considerable pause for thought, particularly in today's twenty-first-century world. Wilkinson carried out his "timely reappraisal" of Richardson's work in order "to see whether it has been assimilated into political science as fully as it deserves, or whether there is still more to be learned by reading or analyzing, imitating or extending it" (Wilkinson 1980, 116). Examples of several of his conclusions will indicate just how timely his reappraisal is. Under the heading "Complex Wars," one of Wilkinson's conclusions affirms that "[r]eduction or elimination of long-range weapons systems (navies, air forces, missile forces), dissolution of peacetime alliances, and political unification of independent neighbor states would all probably tend to reduce the incidence of complex wars, which are particularly damaging" (119). Under the heading "Participation," he states, "It is . . . particularly important to pacify great powers and harmonize their interrelations—or to abolish such powers" (119). His first conclusion under the heading "Ethnocultural Factors," reads as follows: "The propensity of any two groups to fight increases as the differences between them (in language, religion, race, and cultural style) increase. A homogeneous world would probably be a more peaceful one" (119). In his first conclusion under the heading "Miscellaneous Factors," he states, "It appears that 'militant ideology' is a cause of war. 'Ideological disarmament' is therefore more closely tied to peacemaking and detente than some choose to admit. Evidence for the belief that collective worldwide prosperity is possible within the current world order would tend to promote ideological disarmament" (120).

10. Where formerly males carried off females won in the course of winning over other males, they now rape females on the spot.

11. The three essays, all of them in Winnicott 1986, are "The Mother's Contribution to Society," "This Feminism," and "Some Thoughts on the Meaning of the Word 'Democracy'."

12. Speaking for "men," sociologist Victor Seidler writes, for example, "Rather than disconnecting with our emotions so that we can control them, we have to learn to acknowledge and express them in appropriate situations. . . . Gradually we might begin to recognize emotions where before we did not know them. We might be all too familiar, for example, with our anger as men, so it could be surprising to uncover the fear and vulnerability. Life can be something that we are constantly learning from rather than controlling (Seidler 1997, 130). A page later, he notes, "Withholding ourselves emotionally can be a form of control." Earlier, he observes, "Within modernity men learn to be 'independent' and 'self-sufficient' through *denying* emotional needs and desires. It is

'others,' namely women and children, who show their weakness by having needs. . . . This is a myth that many men find . . . hard to break with, for we fear the weakness and inadequacy that it will show. We fear losing face in front of others and our place on the hierarchy of power positions" (46).

13. But see also ethologist Irenäus Eibl-Eibesfeldt, who, in preface to itemizing "mechanisms of aggression control" such as smiling that can tone down aggressive encounters, states, "Competition *leading to* aggressive interactions are frequently observed among children, in the Kalahari Bushmen, Yanomami, and Papuan, as well as in Europeans" (Eibl-Eibesfeldt 1980, 67; italics added). An implicit recognition of the priority of competition (whether for dominance, resources, or whatever) appears evident.

14. Of further note in the context of aggression is Stevens's statement, "There are and always have been women of outstanding ability, but even the brightest of them seem to lack those para-intellectual qualities which determine success in creative work, namely, perseverance, *aggression* and ambition—all of which are known to be enhanced by the presence of testosterone in the bloodstream and are probably due to differences in cerebral development as well" (1983, 189; italics added).

# 4
## On the Pan-Cultural Origins of Evil

Let me have war, say I; it exceeds peace as far as day does night; it's spritely, waking, audible, and full of vent. Peace is a very apoplexy, lethargy; mulled, deaf, sleepy, insensible; a getter of more bastard children than wars a destroyer of men. . . .

Ay, and it makes men hate one another. . . . Reason: because they then less need one another.

—WILLIAM SHAKESPEARE, *Coriolanus*, act 4, scene 5

> Start with an empty canvas
> Sketch in broad outline the forms of
> men, women, and children.
> Dip into the unconscious well of your own
> disowned darkness
> with a wide brush and
> stain the strangers with the sinister hue
> of the shadow.
> Trace onto the face of the enemy the greed,
> hatred, carelessness you dare not claim as
> your own.
> . . . . . . . . . . . . . .
> When your icon of the enemy is complete
> you will be able to kill without guilt,
> slaughter without shame.
>
> —SAM KEEN, "To Create an Enemy"

There never was a good war, or a bad peace.

—BENJAMIN FRANKLIN, letter to Quincy

## I. INTRODUCTION

The pan-cultural origins of evil clearly have their roots in the evolutionary heritage of humans, though just as clearly those roots stretch from the biological to the cultural. What is evil if not warfare, massacres, ethnic cleansings, and so on, and what is war to begin with if not male-male competition? In particular, what is war *fundamentally* if not an expression of the biological matrix of male-male competition raised from the size and power of an individual male to the size and power of a group of males? On the other hand, what is war if not *armed* conflict? Weaponry, not fisticuffs, is the stuff of war, and for weaponry to exist, a culture supporting the technology of weaponry must exist. Moreover not only the technology but the history of war and cultural dispositions to war are transmitted from one generation to the next. War is thus clearly a socially–elaborated biologically derived phenomenon.

The aim of this chapter is to unravel the pan-cultural origins of evil through a focal, phenomenologically informed attention to war. It is fitting to note in preface that war is commonly conceived as a purely cultural phenomenon, never as an activity that sets "man" apart from other animals—"the beasts." Accordingly, killing their own kind is never mentioned as a behavior that makes humans unique in the animal world. One might question, however, whether the omission is due wholly to the fact that killing one's own kind is considered a purely cultural phenomenon or whether it is due also to the fact that killing one's own kind is a singularly *unlaudable* practice, far from the honorific practice of language, for instance, and all those other fine practices offered in praise of human civilization. In other words, since war is a beastly practice, it can hardly differentiate "man" from "the beasts," and differentiating man from the beasts is not only easily done by way of culture, but is vital to the self-esteem of *Homo sapiens sapiens*. Arguing in essence along the lines of a purely cultural explanation of war, sociologist Stanislav Andreski, for instance, reasons as follows: "Fisticuffs usually end with thrashings or the flight of the beaten; . . . But . . . if weapons are used, . . . then he who stabs or shoots first wins, and under such circumstances it is safest to kill one's enemies. Anyway, in all fighting where weapons are used some of the participants are likely to get killed. So we are justified in saying that the prevalence of killing within our species was made possible by the acquisition of culture" (Andreski 1964, 130). Although ethologist Irenäus Eibl-Eibesfeldt is at pains to point out biological dispositions underlying the human practice of war—fear of strangers, territorial claims, bonding patterns—he argues along similar lines when he states, "The important point to bear in mind is that destructive war is a result of cultural evolution" (Eibl-Eibesfeldt 1979, 123). Only with the introduction of weapons, he declares, is there a "basic difference [in group defense of a territory] between human conditions and those we encountered among the chimpanzees," for with weapons, men are enabled to kill one another (123).

Thus, while *aggression* is "biological,"[1] while group defense of a territory is "biological," and while "our innate rejection of strangers, which leads to the demarcation of the group" is "biological" (122–23), the real-life phenomenon of war appears virtually untainted by biology: there is nothing biological about war.

How male-male competition can be disregarded in this context is startling and inexplicable. With quite minor as well as altogether rare exceptions in the long course of human history, it is males who plan wars, who initiate wars, who fight wars, and who win and lose wars. Indeed, the omission of male-male competition is odd in the extreme, but then few humans seem prepared either to examine close-up the biological basis of war, *or* to acknowledge something "beastly" as that which in fact readily distinguishes human animals from their nonhuman counterparts.

Several points warrant clarification in preface to what follows. Murder, rape, and thievery are also pan-cultural human acts, and such acts are or may well be described as evil. Moreover females as well as males murder and steal, albeit in so far lesser numbers that their commission of these acts is negligible. The acts, however, are clearly not on the scale of war, of massacres, of ethnic cleansings. Though they may take place in the context of war—and rape is a notably prime act in this respect—they are epiphenomenal to war itself. Most importantly, and as will be evident, murder, rape, and thievery are not evolutionarily grounded human acts and are not motivated as war, massacres, and ethnic cleansings are motivated. Further still, as will also be evident, they do not give meaning to one's life as war gives meaning to one's life. In short, murder, thievery, and rape are individual acts structured neither in a biological matrix nor in the wider framework of enmity and amity, preeminently social structures that make war distinctive. These distinctions decisively separate the pan-cultural evil that is war from the individual pan-cultural evil practices of murder, thievery, and rape. Indeed, human history not only attests to the distinctions incontrovertibly but attests to the foundational banality of the pan-culturality of evil that is war.

## II. THE BANALITY OF EVIL

Hannah Arendt[2] dissociated evil from religion and from attendant questions about the goodness of God and placed it solidly in the everyday human realm, a realm characterized by a thoughtless diligence to duty. In her well-known report on "the banality of evil" ensuing from her experience of the trial of Adolph Eichmann, she concluded "on the strictly factual level" that Eichmann's "diligence in itself was in no way criminal"; he *"merely . . . never realized what he was doing"* (Arendt 1977, 287). As she describes his evil actions in an earlier chapter (252), his "fearsome, word-and-thought-defying *banality of evil"* was not a matter of wickedness but of a mindless diligence to authority. Though Arendt does not pointedly call attention to the relative ease with which humans can and do accede to decimating other humans, her observations on Eichmann's mindless diligence, and more broadly, on the Nazi regime and on German people living under that regime, readily testifies to it. In particular, in her chapter on "Duties of a Law-Abiding Citizen," she details how Eichmann managed to do his "duty." She notes in the beginning his avowal that he lived according to the Kantian notion of duty and quotes his answer to the judge who questioned him about his Kantian ethics: "I meant by my remark about Kant," Eichmann states, "that the principle of my will must always be such that it can become the principle of general laws" (136). She points out that Eichmann later confesses that he failed to live up to the Kantian ethics when he became aware of the Final Solution and that he "consoled himself with the thought that he no longer 'was master of his own deeds', that he was unable 'to change anything'" (136). But as she also acutely observes, Eichmann did not actually reject Kant's principle; he distorted it. The distortion is explicit in Hans Frank's paraphrasing of " 'the categorical imperative in the Third Reich'," which Arendt quotes and which, she says, "Eichmann might have known": "Act in such a way that the Führer, if he knew your action, would approve it" (136). In short, while the arbiter of the general law changed, Kant's imperative remained the same, thereby facilitating a relatively easy shift within moral conscience and a consequent relative ease in either doing evil directly or participating in evil deeds.

The relative ease is again implicit but in broader terms in the end paragraph of the same chapter, which Arendt begins with the general observation, "[J]ust as the law in civilized countries assumes that the voice of conscience tells everybody 'Thou shalt not kill', even though man's natural desires and inclinations may at times be murderous, so the law of Hitler's land demanded that the voice of conscience tell everybody: 'Thou shalt kill', although the organizers of the massacres knew full well that murder is against the normal desires and inclinations of most people." She follows this general observation with a more specific one: "Evil in the Third Reich had lost the quality by which most people recognize it—the quality of temptation" (150). She then points out—in ultimately poignant terms—the double-sided character of temptation: "Many Germans and many Nazis," she writes, "probably an overwhelming majority of them, must have been tempted *not* to murder, *not* to rob, *not* to let their neighbors go off to their doom . . . and not to become accomplices in all these crimes by benefiting from them. But, God knows, they had learned how to resist temptation" (150).

The anguish in Arendt's closing sentence is near palpable, but certainly she is alone in her anguish; that is, she gives no indication of anguish on the part of those who were tempted *not* to murder but who "learned how to resist temptation." Neither does she give any indication of how the probable "overwhelming majority" in fact learned to resist. Yet how they not only learned but learned with seeming ease to participate in evil is a pressing question. At the end of her next chapter, "Deportations from the Reich," however, Arendt presents evidence that precisely indicates how the requisite learning was so easily accomplished. Indeed, she writes, "How easy it was to set the conscience of the Jews' neighbors at rest is best illustrated by the official explanation of the deportations given in a circular issued by the Party Chancellery in the fall of 1942: 'It is the nature of things that these, in some respects, very difficult problems can be solved in the interests of the permanent security of our people only with *ruthless toughness*'—*rücksichtsloser Härte*'" (161; Arendt's italics). The appeal to violence and the appeal to callousness are appeals made explicitly on behalf of one's own security and on behalf of "one's own" people. In effect, they make possible a relatively easy learning and social conversion. But they do so not simply by turning people readily away from judging their own acts, as Arendt would insist they do, or away from reflectively pondering their morality through a Kantian-anchored imagination that allows them to envision the plight and viewpoint of others, as Arendt would also insist they do. In the most basic sense, the appeals turn people readily away from empathy: the appeals motivate people to numb any positive social sensibilities toward others who, they are told, jeopardize their own security and group. In effect, the relative ease with which humans can and do accede to decimating other humans is not unmotivated, but traceable to an affective narrowing, a closing off of civil social feelings and a cultivation of brutality, precisely as mandated by those in authoritative power, in this instance, the Party Chancellery. The moral lapse that allows one to accede with relative ease to decimate others is thus not basically a matter of absolving oneself of the responsibility of judging, as Arendt indicates, when, for example, she ironically comments on Eichmann's reaction to the Wannsee Conference, where German leaders and bureaucrats "were vying and fighting with each other for the honor of taking the lead in these 'bloody matters.'" To Eichmann's statement, "At that moment, I sensed a kind of Pontius Pilate feeling, for I felt free of all guilt," Arendt caustically comments, "*Who was he to judge?*"

Her emphasis on a lack of judgment and on a mindless diligence at work notwithstanding, Arendt herself implicitly suggests that something more is involved in the banality of evil, not only by her reference to a temptation to do or not to do evil and her acknowledgment that Eichmann had to "console himself" that he could not do otherwise than what he was doing, but in her postscript chapter where she mentions in passing that "[e]xcept for an extraordinary diligence in looking out for his personal advancement, [Eichmann] had no motives at all" (287). The question of *motives* is of foundational import to understandings of human morality. Motives are the generating force propelling one to act in particular ways and are at bottom a question of affect. In each of the above instances—the *temptation* to do or not to do evil, the need to *console* oneself with respect to doing what one is doing, an exclusive *concern* with one's personal advancement—a person is specifically motivated to do or not to do something, and whatever the particular motivation, it is through and through affectively charged. Indeed, affectivity is the bedrock of motivation: feelings drive action; they impel one, *and are experientially felt to impel one*, toward a certain doing or not doing (see Sheets-Johnstone 1999a and 1999b; see also Bull 1951). However complex the run of feelings might be in any situation, the action one takes is ultimately an action taken in conjunction with those feelings, and the action's aftermath is similarly saturated in feelings, whether of accomplishment, regret, or whatever. In effect, the choices one makes with respect to one's actions are essentially choices not on behalf of abstract, intellectualized values, but on behalf of those affectively charged values that color and entwine themselves about abstract, intellectualized values in the first place, and that motivate one in a bodily felt sense toward a doing of some kind—toward action. In short, affectively charged values are the point of departure for thoughts about what to do and for ensuing deliberations and choices. From this perspective, and as suggested above, the relative ease with which humans can and do accede to decimating other humans is traceable first and foremost to an affective narrowing of social concern and caring. Ruthless toughness toward certain others demands no less: delimiting lines are strictly drawn around those privileged ones who matter.

III. AFFECTIVE ELABORATIONS OF THE BANALITY OF EVIL

In his book, *Perception, Empathy, and Judgment,* philosopher Arne Vetlesen devotes an early chapter to a detailed examination of Arendt's moral presentation of Eichmann and in fact, in his book as a whole, focuses almost exclusively on Nazi Germany and the Holocaust as an empirical point of reference. In the chapter on Arendt, he develops critical theses that, in certain respects, are akin to those specified above that draw on and amplify implicit aspects of Arendt's trial report. Vetlesen's overall aim, however—as the title of his book indicates—is to present a critical case for taking emotion and perception into moral account (Vetlesen 1994, 85). Though he does not address the issue of relative ease or raise the question of motivation, he skirts close to both the issue and the question in his attention to indifference toward others and hatred of others, feelings that, he argues at length, are adducible to a lack of empathy, which itself, he later argues far more briefly, is ultimately traceable to a lack of perception and empathy on the part of caregivers in infancy, adult individuals who set the emotional preconditions for instilling moral performance in children. Vetlesen thus opposes his own characterization of Eichmann as an "emotional failure" on the level of empathy (106) to Arendt's characterization of Eichmann as a "cognitive failure" on the level of judgment (85). He substantiates his characterization by showing in beginning ways the crucial importance of empathy to moral performance. For example, he shows how, in perception as in judgment, there is both a cognitive and emotional component, both of which are *"indispensable"* (104), and how, it is in turn requisite to "differentiate between a cognitive and an emotional aspect of moral judgment" (115). In the course of his critical commentary on Arendt's notion of moral judgment, he emphasizes the wholly intellectual nature of her account. He points out, for example, that "Arendt puts forward the claim that Eichmann failed to judge, because he was incapable of representing others in his own mind" (98), and that "It is in the *refusal to judge* that Arendt locates the greatest evils in the political realm; the evil of totalitarianism epitomized in Eichmann was manifest in his lack of imagination" (98). Quoting Arendt, he limns the latter capacity in universalizing terms as the capacity "of having present before your eyes and taking into consideration the others whom you must represent" (98), hence, an ability to envision "how I would think and feel if I were in [another's] place" (97)." In short, and coincident with the earlier critical look at Arendt's assessment, Vetlesen's examination is riveted on the fact that, for Arendt, "Eichmann was not wicked but thoughtless" (94): his moral lapse rests on a purely mental or intellectual inability, i.e., an inability to imagine or represent others.

As is apparent, what Vetlesen wants to argue is that if moral judgments are disinterested and impartial representations or products of the imagination, as Arendt insists, that is, if they are devoid of an emotional component, then empathy plays no part (117–18), and if empathy plays no part, then "humanity's basic emotion faculty" (105, 119, 125) is ignored. In consequence, the capacity to bring together an "I" and an "Other" in "a meeting of particulars" (114) is nullified. Vetlesen describes what he means by the latter locution in terms of Eichmann: "I claim that moral judgment as exemplified by Eichmann has to do with the meeting of particulars; judgment in the sense here intended comes about when the person who judges frankly *confronts his or her own particularity with the particularity of that which is to be judged*" (114). The point is of considerable import in view of the force with which authoritative power can hold sway. As Vetlesen earlier recognizes, demanding that an individual not allow himself or herself "*to become incapable of judging . . .* means demanding that the individual always question the legitimacy—as opposed to the factual legality—of the institutional framework he or she is about to enter, *before* becoming its helpless victim" (108). Moreover as he also previously argues, the roots of indifference that foster evil

> must be sought not in the psychology of the individual but in the bureaucratic institutions that structure modern life, make killing abstract, and undermine the actor's sense of responsibility by fragmenting his or her acts as well as comprehension of the acts' final consequences. Failing to achieve an overview of the administrative body to which he or she belongs, always one

among many and as such perfectly exchangeable, the individual is less inclined to assume responsibility; failing to see the people affected by his or her actions as humans rather than as dull objects, or *Sachen* (things). (108)

Vetlesen's consequent argument—that "the question of individual responsibility must take the form of *not allowing oneself to become incapable of judging*" (108)—is central to his thesis. In particular, the capacity to see others as human beings is contingent on the emotional capacity to appreciate the direness and difficulties of their situation, and accordingly, "to develop empathy toward them" (106). Vetlesen in fact at one point remarks, "[T]here is no way in which any one of us can comprehend the murder of millions.... What we can hope for and strive toward is comprehension of the murder of one human individual" (114). His focus on the individual nature of moral judgments implicitly underscores the fact that *morality is an individual matter,* that rules and regulations from on high, while dictating certain societal moral norms and taboos, require individual sanction, which means not blind compliance but affective ratification of values. Moral judgments, in other words, emanate from individuals in particular circumstances. This real-life, individualized and situationally resonant view of morality coincides with certain classic empirical socio-psychological studies that will be discussed in Section IX, the Afterword of this chapter. In their investigations of obedience to authority, these studies raise fundamental moral questions concerning precisely the human capacity for "perception, empathy, and judgment."

In a later chapter, "Emotions and Immorality," Vetlesen attempts to flesh out his principal thesis along ontogenetical lines, explaining that his claim that "a lack of empathy is due to a lack of empathy" means that "one must have been the object of empathy in order to evolve into its subject" (266) His attempts to anchor his thesis in ontogeny, however, remain abstract. He offers no concrete ontogenetical details to back up his explanation, but examines instead the theoretical writings of Max Horkheimer and Theodor Adorno, Erich Fromm, and others. In short, his claim that hatred and related emotions have their origin in a lack of empathy (221–22) reduces to the claim that the "ontogenetical origin of human destructiveness and hatred" (221) lies not in negative human proclivities but in the absence of the primary positive emotional bond that defines empathy. In effect, whether a matter of indifference, hatred, or sadism, a lack of empathy prevails, a lack traceable to an ontogeny that thwarts and impairs emotional growth and thereby thwarts and impairs "moral performance" (222). Vetlesen's account of "a lack of empathy" is in fact admittedly not empirical but theoretical (259). The empirical, he states, applies only to a particular case, whereas what he wants to pinpoint is the theoretical that addresses or uncovers "[the] principle in question" (259). Thus, he speaks in broad terms of "the failure of the self-object [i.e., the mother or care-taker] to meet the relational needs in question," a failure that "helps cause . . . an *arrest in development*" (265). The result is a theorized account of the "emotional preconditions" of moral perception and judgment (266) that, while in many respects persuasive and edifying, remains unanchored in precisely the way it needs to be anchored in order that the ontogeny of empathy and the ontogeny of a lack of empathy are fittingly and precisely delineated.[3]

A parallel lack of anchorage detracts from Vetlesen's final chapter in which he expressly defends his thesis as offering a non-gendered account of morality, i.e., it is applicable to all humans irrespective of sex. His claim in part is that in the well-known writings of men such as Lawrence Kohlberg and Jürgen Habermas, there is "an exaggerated preoccupation with the demand for impartiality in moral reasoning" (357). The claim in essence echoes the claim of Carol Gilligan, whose equally well-known work Vetlesen discusses. In his closing pages he in fact quotes "two points of lasting importance in Gilligan's work," the first to the effect that there is a "propensity of moral philosophers of various persuasions to paint a 'male' picture of what moral reasoning consists of" (355); the second to the effect that mainstream theory—as exemplified by men such as Kohlberg, Rawls, and Habermas—"defines the moral domain and what is to count as a moral issue" (355). Vetlesen in fact commends feminist theorists such as Gilligan and Seyla Benhabib for throwing light on why "the emotional abilities in 'man' at the center of my study are largely overshadowed by cognitive and intellectual ones," that is, by the disposition of males to narrow "the moral universe" (357). Given the straightforward recognition of the narrowing and its source in male propensities, definitions, and assessments, it is all the more striking that readily identifiable, historically enduring male proclivities and practices enter neither into a critique of the "'male' picture" of moral reasoning nor into a critique of what defines the domain of the moral, and that, in fact, the proclivities and practices fail to be a moral issue at all, indeed, given human history, that male-male competition and war—perduring, actual, real-life activities of males, in historically appropriate dynamic systems terms, *real-time* male activities—fail to be a central and persisting pan-cultural moral issue of human life. That the moral challenge these activities present falls squarely on the shoulders of men is hardly debatable. That in her perspicuous renderings of political life Arendt did not call attention to the pointedly male challenge and that Vetlesen did not do so either in his emendations of Arendt's account may not be surprising, but the enormous proportions of the moral oversight are hardly debatable either.

## IV. TOWARD PAN-CULTURAL UNDERSTANDINGS OF THE BANALITY OF EVIL

The banality of evil is unquestionably a rich concept. Arendt's insights are profound and provocative in themselves and seminal to Vetlesen's painstaking examination of the perceptual and affective aspects of the banality of evil. Yet deeper grounds remain to be uncovered, not only as shown with respect to questions of relative ease and of motivation, but to intimately related questions of ontogeny and phylogeny that speak directly to the need to examine *the nature of human nature*. The banality of evil is indeed pan-cultural, not simply in the immediate sense of being a present-day world-wide human phenomenon, but in the perseverating sense of being a chronic historically laden human phenomenon. Battlefields stretch all the way from archaeological records and chronicles of war to a multitude of contemporary conflicts. Leaving their mark in one way and another, they testify to the banality of evil as a historical pan-cultural fact, hence to foundational if unacknowledged aspects of human nature. In finer terms, human history testifies to both the relative ease and ready motivations with which humans kill and maim each other, and, in turn, attests to a natural history that undergirds the banality of evil, a history that, cultural variations notwithstanding, has phylogenetic roots. To trace these roots to their sources requires an elucidation of the nature of human nature in evolutionary terms that do justice to both the essential realities and intricate complexities of the human capacity for evil. Deeper understandings of the banality of evil and of human morality hang in the balance.

The merest glance at human history readily points us in the direction of these understandings, concretizing the historically embedded nature of the pan-cultural human capacity for evil. World events past and present are witness to the fact that "the banality of evil" is not peculiar to the Nazis and their programs of extermination. Tamerlane, whose "undisciplined hordes" displayed "ferocious cruelty" in Central Asia in the fourteenth century, ordered the execution of hundreds of thousands of Hindus, devastated their property, plundered, and made slaves or prisoners of thousands (Wright 1985, 593); the Byzantine emperor Basil II in his defeat of the Bulgarians at the dawn of the second millennium took fourteen thousand prisoners whom he first blinded, then sent back home in groups of one hundred, each led by a one-eyed man (Sherrard 1966, 62). Recent events similarly demonstrate what is traditionally termed "man's inhumanity to man," and quite apart from the events of September 11, 2001, and its aftermath. A wide array of articles appearing in the *New York Review of Books* in 1999 and 2000, for example, succinctly attests to the pan-cultural human capacity for evil in such titles as *Divine Killer*, featuring Mao Zedong (Buruma 2000); *Always Time to Kill*, focusing on the First and Second World Wars, and the Vietnam War (Epstein 1999); *Milosevic's Final Solution*, recording Serbian atrocities (Zimmermann 1999); *The Worst Place on Earth*, reporting on brutal maiming and savagery in Sierra Leone (Traub 2000); and *Death in Kashmir*, detailing internecine battles in India (Mishra 2000), to name only a few.[4] As if this contemporary evidence were not compelling enough, one need only recall Keeley's archaeological studies over the past few decades that were cited in the last chapter, showing that deaths from modern warfare are statistically minuscule in comparison with those in primitive societies.

Surely we should ask: What is at the bottom of this enduring pan-cultural phenomenon? What motivates man's easy assent to kill, mutilate, and torture others? Is there a *pan-cultural motivation*? That is, coincident with the pan-culturality of evil, is there something pan-culturally human—some aspect or character of human life—that motivates humans to evil deeds? An inquiry into the origin of the pan-cultural human capacity for evil—in essence, an attempt to flesh out in phenomenological terms an answer to the question, what *motivates* evil? will show how a universal dimension of human life is, if not the abiding mainspring of evil, a consistently present element in its historical enactment.[5] The inquiry will thus attempt both to deepen and to extend

Arendt's disconcerting but keenly accurate concept of the banality of evil.

As is fitting to an inquiry into origins, we begin with a consideration of behavioral evolutionary relationships, probing our animal heritage for clues to the pan-culturality of evil.[6] In so doing, we will expose sizable evolutionary roots, but we will also show that something more complex is involved in the banality of evil and in the motivation to do evil, something wholly specific to humans, something that ultimately spawns immortality ideologies, the foundations of which are encased in unevenly valorized binary oppositions emblematic of the fear of death.

V. BEGINNING EVOLUTIONARY CONSIDERATIONS

The following descriptive account of a raid succinctly captures essential features underlying evolutionary commonalities and might well be taken as a paradigmatic portrayal of evil:

> It began as a border patrol. At one point they sat still on a ridge, staring down into [the valley] for more than three-quarters of an hour, until they spotted [X], apparently hiding only twenty-five meters away. The raiders rushed madly down the slope to their target. While [X] screamed . . . he was held and beaten and kicked and lifted and dropped . . . and jumped on. At first he tried to protect his head, but soon he gave up and lay stretched out and still. His aggressors . . . kept up the attack for eighteen minutes, then turned for home, still energized, running and screaming. . . . Bleeding freely from his head, gashed on his back, [X] tried to sit up but fell back shivering.

The raid could be fact or fiction: it could recall a television documentary or a film, an anthropological study or a scene from a novel. In actuality, it is a description of a group of male chimpanzees from Kasekela assaulting a male from nearby Kahama Valley (Wrangham and Peterson 1996, 17). In their study of "demonic males," anthropologists Richard Wrangham and Dale Peterson link this kind of "chimpanzee violence" to "human war" (71). They state that "these raids are exciting events for [the chimpanzees]." They point out that in these raids, "the mayhem visited on . . . victims looks a world apart from the occasional violence that erupts during a squabble between members of the same community" and that "the attackers act as they do while hunting monkeys, except that the target 'prey' is a member of their own species" (70). They say furthermore, in explicitly comparing chimpanzees and humans, that "The appetite for engagement, the excited assembly of a war party, the stealthy raid, the discovery of an enemy and the quick estimation of odds, the gang-kill, and the escape are the common elements that make intercommunity violence possible for both"(71).[7] In short, what male chimpanzees of one community do to chimpanzees of a different community appears to have certain motivational links to what male humans of one community (tribe, state, nation) do to humans of a different community (tribe, state, nation). In both instances there is an inclination (appetite, craving, desire) for excitement and a concomitant physical disposition toward wanton brutality. Moreover though not "spritely," actual engagement is "waking, audible, and full of vent," precisely as Aufidius's servant states in Shakespeare's *Coriolanus*.

Wrangham and Peterson, however, overlook a crucial difference and are inexact in their comparative description. Not only is *war* not a practice in chimpanzee societies and hence *"war party"* not a "common element" of chimpanzee and human "intercommunity violence," but gang-*kill* is not to be found within the behavioral repertoire of the common chimpanzee.[8] As noted in Chapter 1, Wrangham and Peterson record no direct observations of *a kill*:[9] after witnessing a severe mutilation, they and other observers have simply noted that the victim disappeared, either immediately or eventually, and was not seen again. Furthermore, as also noted in Chapter 1, to judge from observational reports one would with good reason conclude that attacking chimpanzees neither assure themselves that their victim is *lifeless* nor do they appear concerned with whether it is or not. While wounds are inflicted, skin is torn off, and bodily parts are maimed or bitten off, *it is not because the attackers are out to kill*. What the descriptions implicitly suggest is that what is motivationally central to chimpanzee attacks are the violent actions themselves. In line with this motivational centrality is the fact that, as Wrangham and Peterson indicate, excitement is as much a factor as wanton violence.

Wrangham and Peterson nowhere mention motivation in their account, yet the question of motivation is implicit in their inquiry and the two constituent motivational elements are adumbrated in their observations: "Based on the evidence of the chimpanzees' alert, enthusiastic behavior, these raids are exciting"; the chimpanzees' assaults "are marked by a gratuitous cruelty—tearing off pieces of skin, for example, twisting limbs until they break, or drinking a victim's blood—reminiscent of acts that among humans are regarded as unspeakable crimes during peacetime and atrocities during war" (70). Motivation does indeed appear to lie not simply in radically unrestrained physical dispositions—tearing, twisting, breaking, and the like—but in radically unrestrained dispositions heightened by an inclination or craving for excitement. In sum, raids are rousing and exhilarating; they make an individual's blood flow. All that physical pummeling, striking, jumping, and tearing is stimulating.

Sheer physicality and excitement are essential realities of the chimpanzee raid. They are similarly essential realities in the human capacity for evil. They in fact constitute the ground for the cultivation of warriors. Warriors are fearless, and as is evident in the dynamic conjunction of sheer physicality and excitement in the chimpanzee raid, there is no fear. While the chimpanzee raid is a non-agonistic battle, as Huizinga would characterize it in that its combatants are unequal, it is nonetheless a combative encounter, a veritable intercorporeal assault in which the sheer actions themselves and the sheer excitement of engaging in them are dynamically enthralling. A concentrated intensity reigns in which one is wholly present to doing what one is doing and to feeling what one is feeling in doing it. The pan-cultural cultivation of warriors has roots in just this evolutionary fact of life. Sheer physicality and excitement are precisely the foundation for the cultivation of warriors, men who lock themselves in battle and whose lives are dedicated to fighting and killing. The ritual warfare of Dani peoples, one group among untold numbers of other possible examples all the way from epic histories to present-day wars, provide exacting documentation of these evolutionary roots. The Dani's ritual war practices were stopped in the 1960s by the Dutch and Indonesian governments, who used armed police and then military units to put an end to them, but secular wars were not eliminated (Heider 1979, 111–12). It is mainly, however, the Dani's ritual war practices that are of moment in what follows, in particular, their battles and raids, each of which, we might note, conforms to and exemplifies in general terms Huizinga's original distinction between rule-governed contests—true *agons*—and "uncivilized" contests in which fair play is absent.

In his book *Grand Valley Dani*, anthropologist Karl Heider begins his description of battles as follows: "Battles are formal events involving hundreds of men which take place for a few hours at midday on one of the battlefields in no-man's-land" (93).[10] After describing the care with which men prepare themselves for battle—smearing themselves with cosmetic pig grease, arranging feathers in their hair, adjusting various ornaments—and noting that "[e]veryone is attired differently, but all are elegant" (94), he goes on to state that men are armed either with spears or bows and arrows. Their long spears are for jabbing, their shorter ones for throwing. Heider then describes the physical nature of the battlefields and the way in which a battle proceeds, noting, for example, that "The front continually fluctuates, moving backwards and forwards as one side or the other mounts a charge" (96). He then states,

> Battles are exhilarating. There is danger, of course. Many men walk away with painful arrow wounds and some must be carried home to spend weeks recovering. But for most, a battle is full of excitement. There is a tremendous amount of shouting, whooping, and joking. Most men know the individuals on the other side, and the words which fly back and forth can be quite personal. . . . But as lighthearted as the atmosphere sometimes gets, battles are definitely not just a game, not merely a welcome change from the routine life of sweet potato farming and pig herding. They are fun, entertaining, and adventurous, but battles, and war in general, are a more important core of Dani life. (96–97)

Differences certainly obtain between a Dani battle and a chimpanzee raid, not least in terms of Huizinga's distinction. One can nevertheless with good reason claim that "descent with modification" aptly captures the relationship between the battle and the raid. Though it is a question of many against one in the latter instance and of equally matched antagonists in the former instance, for example, and in turn a question simply of withstanding an onslaught in the one instance as opposed to dodging as well as shooting arrows and avoiding spears as well as jabbing with them and throwing them in the other instance, a basic similarity is unmistakable: sheer physicality and excitement constitute the essential realities of both raid and battle. They are the driving force of both. As noted earlier, the sheer actions themselves and the sheer excitement generated in engaging in them are dynamically enthralling. Whether pummeling another or shooting arrows, whether beating another or jabbing with a spear, whether hooting and screaming or shouting and whooping, the actions consume and enrapture those engaged.

More is clearly involved, however, in a Dani battle than in a chimpanzee raid, and concomitantly, more is clearly involved in the way of motivation. These further facets do not in any way lessen or detract from the basic motivation exemplifying descent with modification, but warrant extended attention in their own right, specifically with respect to killing, death, and fear, elements that are precisely absent in a chimpanzee raid. What requires clarification in particular is the way in which killing, death, and fear enter into the banality of evil as a pan-cultural phenomenon, and the way in which all three elements are motivationally entwined. A closer examination of Dani warfare will allow us beginning points of entry into this clarification.

## VI. CLARIFICATIONS ALONG MOTIVATIONAL LINES

In their book *Gardens of War: Life and Death in the New Guinea Stone Age*, Heider and fellow anthropologist Robert Gardner present graphic as well as textual evidence of what Margaret Mead describes in her introduction to their book as a "long, relentless cycle of killing and being killed" (Mead 1968, viii). From the very beginning, Dani children learn a way of life without any formal instruction. "They are schooled by direct contact with virtually all the major events of life by the time they are five years old" (Gardner and Heider 1968, 64). In particular, by simply observing and listening, and by playing war-like games, they learn from experience about "magic, death, war, gardening, house building and pig keeping" (64). Commenting specifically about young boys, Gardner and Heider state, "They learn to be warriors not only by listening to men talk about wars, but by having their own *weem yelés*, or war games. Just as *weem yelés* gives young boys practice in dodging arrows, so does *sigogo wasin* give them a chance to perfect their aim with spears" (64). After describing games that train young boys "to appreciate the more brutal aspects of war" (64), they remark, "As they play at sudden death, the children are learning important facts of life" (65).

In their final chapter, "Violence," Gardner and Heider describe the important differences between a ritual battle and a raid, the latter being "a desperate attempt to take an enemy life," an attempt that "has none of the theatricality of a formal battle" (142). Raids, however, like ritual battles follow "a set procedure" in which stealth plays a central role, the one "great difference between battles and raids [being] the matter of surprise: it is never known when the enemy will try to sneak through one's defenses and kill, whereas the whole countryside is aware of an impending battle" (141). Thus, each alliance has watchtowers with guards who are there from dawn till dark; there is a "no-man's-land" between neighboring groups; various other defense manoeuvres are practiced, including most prominently magical ones. What one might find astonishing about the necessity of such defensive practices and about surprise attacks to begin with is the fact that the Dani constitute a single people who in fact speak the same language. Indeed, it is of particular interest that, as Gardner and Herder point out, "Since they share a common culture, the same considerations motivate them" (136), considerations that are later limned in terms of a "delicate balance . . . between chance and competence, between the competing needs of life and death" (139).

Clearly war is at the center of the balance between life and death, the grounds on which the "competing needs" of each are played out. We readily appreciate this fact in the many statements Gardner and Heider make that underscore the centrality of war. For example, "It must be remembered that all Dani men are professional fighters. They have been trained since learning how to walk in all the techniques of war" (136). An extended quotation, however, aptly details the concentrated attention that is fixated not only on war but on killing and death:

> One of the most dramatic expressions of the interplay between forces that affect the well-being of the living is in intertribal hostilities. When a member of one warring faction has been killed by his enemy, there is set in motion an elaborate sequence of events whose purpose is to kill a person on the offending side. However the motive is not simply revenge. Nor do these people enjoy killing for its own sake. Instead, there is a complex process of reasoned behavior that occurs between deaths, and leads to the inevitable climax of another killing. When a person has been killed, the village of the deceased immediately starts funeral preparations. On the day following death the corpse is cremated in a large public ceremony, and for another four days the traditional rites accorded death are performed. During this

period, beginning with the moment when the corpse is laid on the fire and his ghost is released, all people connected with the deceased must assume a special role in relation to the new-made ghost. It is axiomatic in Dani reasoning that such a ghost will not rest until the living avenge it. Its unrest is the principal concern of its living relatives and associates, for the ghost turns to them for satisfaction. (88–89)

One killing is thus always followed by another: "Killing an enemy inevitably brings death to oneself or one's friends" (92). Moreover "Since the enemy also die and become ghosts, and since the Dani are a warrior society, it is not strange that the ghosts of both sides continue the hostilities they began in life" (93). In short, one can well appreciate that war, killing, and death are the central and ongoing focus of attention of the Dani. Indeed, as Gardner and Heider write, "In large measure, their health, welfare and happiness depend on the pursuit of aggression against their traditional enemies" (136). And as Heider states in his own later book, a book that, incidentally, is the result of an initial stay of approximately twenty-six months and of visits of various durations thereafter (Heider 1979, 16), "War was an immediate part of Dani life. Every Dani alliance was constantly at war with at least one of its neighboring alliances. Every individual Dani was touched by war" (88).

With the exception of their chapter on ghosts, however, in which Gardner and Heider attempt to detail Dani beliefs and practices about the dead, the linkage of death with war and killing remains largely unexamined. Even with respect to ghosts, the linkage is chiefly a matter of explaining that, the behavior of ghosts being unpredictable, magical ceremonies are required in order that the ghosts, as the Dani people state, "'stay where they belong', that they 'do not come around bothering us'" (88). A somewhat fuller understanding of the linkage is implicit in Gardner and Heider's identification of ghosts as "the shades of deceased relatives and friends, the insubstantial survivors of the intermediate crisis of death" (Gardner and Heider 1968, 87), and in their labeling the ghosts "'living dead'." If death is an "intermediate crisis," however, then a certain continuity obtains between living and dead, but a continuity fraught with fear since whatever one does to placate the "living dead" or to avenge them might be insufficient; they might not "stay where they belong." The elemental nature of this fear is suggested by Gardner and Heider when they write that the Dani "are religious for many reasons, but the principal one, as perhaps for most other people, is that they are sometimes afraid" and that "since they believe that humans linger after death, their religion is largely concerned with guiding and controlling the ghosts" (93). As they later state, "to ignore the demands of unavenged ghosts" is the greatest danger to their lives, more dangerous than engaging in battles and raids (136).

Since safety demands that ghosts be avenged, the problem of safety is approached by way of both common sense and magic (92). Safety thus dictates "the necessity of a noman's land, of watchtowers, of men spending much of their time on guard duty and making weapons, of keeping the grass short wherever the enemy might try to set up an ambush, of maintaining artificial ponds where ducks will rise if someone approaches, and of an elaborate set of magical practices that safeguard the system of defenses and warriors who man it" (141). It becomes evident, then, how fear is a primary element, motivationally linked to the manning of watchtowers, performance of funeral rites, and so on. That "it is a long time before anyone's death is forgotten, either privately or ritually, even when an enemy is killed and a victory has been celebrated" (96) attests to a foundational ongoing fear, to a belief that ghosts perpetuate hostilities, and to a consequent necessity of both common sense and magical practices. In sum, any death is portentous; one's own life and livelihood and the lives and livelihood of one's relatives are always on the line in face of it. Yet in spite of fear, "The Dani fight because they want to and because it is necessary. They do not enter into battle in order to put an end to fighting. . . . The Dani are warriors because they have wanted to be since boyhood, not because they are persuaded by political arguments or their own sentimental or patriotic feelings" (135).

## VII. KILLING, DEATH, FEAR: ELEMENTARY FACTS OF HUMAN LIFE

Rooted in human evolutionary history, the pan-culturality of evil is precisely culturally elaborated, induced, and perpetrated along a diversity of lines. Its common source lies in the fact that humans are alive among other humans—for Dani, and perhaps other peoples as well, that they are alive not only among other *living* humans but among *dead* humans, e.g., ghosts. One can always come to harm or death through the actions of others. Along with the fear of death itself, the fear of other humans and of what they might do might thus be taken as the core meaning of Heider's remark that, though "battles, and war in general" are "fun, entertaining, and adventurous," they are "a more important core of Dani life" (Heider 1979, 97). Battles, and war in general, are an enactment of the existential human condition of being both alive in itself and alive among other humans and of the attempt to subdue and even transform the fear embedded in that condition. Among one's own kinsman, one's own group, or one's own nation, one is relatively safe, but insecurity reigns elsewhere and precautions must be taken with respect to others. Thus, as we have seen, the Dani erect watchtowers, arrange a no-man's-land between their own group and their neighbors, and so on. Concerted action is taken against others for fear of what they would do if measures were not taken to impede them. But taking measures does not guarantee safety. The all too familiar human penchant for killing is always present. It is exemplified by "the great massacre of 1966," the secular Dani war that Heider briefly but pointedly alludes to. "Hundreds of men of the northern Gutelu," he writes, carried out a surprise attack against "the nearest compounds of the Wilhiman-Walalua." He does not describe how the massacre took place, but states simply, "In an hour they had killed about 125 people and burned many of the compounds" (104). Though surely not on the scale of Saddam Hussein in Iraq, of Slobodan Milosevic in Serbia, of Hitler in Europe, nor of multiple other genocides carried out in the "civilized" world of the twentieth and twenty-first centuries, let alone earlier centuries, the 1966 Dani massacre was not essentially unlike other massacres: certain others are exterminated because they pose a threat to one's well-being or to the meaning of one's life, or both. A basic fear subtends massacres: one kills those who might otherwise take one's life, one's goods, one's property, and so on, or who, by impairing one's well-being in some way, might otherwise divest one's life of its meaning, and not only by the bare might of their arms and weaponry, but by the ideological might of their belief system and values, which threaten to overpower one's own, nullify them, and indeed obliterate them. Religious wars over human centuries as well as more recent national wars attest with special force to the fear that not just one's life but the beliefs and values that inform it are on the line.

From this all too human perspective, warfare is a seemingly ineradicable human institution erected on the seemingly ineradicable foundations of human fear, foundations that themselves have their roots in the ineradicable unpredictability of humans and their ineradicable end in death. The fear of death and the decimation of others through warfare—only seemingly paradoxical facets of human existence—can thus be seen to lie at the heart of the banality of evil.

Montaigne aptly termed warfare a "human disease" (Braudy 2003, 291). Most certainly the disease is fed by motivations other than fear—by cravings for power, revenge, territory, resources, and so on—but battlefields are the basic ground on which men prove their mettle and prove it by being dauntless warriors, scuttling fear first of all in the sheer physicality and excitement of battle. Only then are acts of bravery and courage possible; only then is the warrior born. Indeed, while courage and bravery are the mark of the warrior, fear is necessarily their source, fear that must precisely be overcome if courage is to arise. The valuing and glorying of courage would otherwise have no reason. It is notable that while the warrior might be compared to the mythic hero in terms of his courage and bravery, the resemblance quickly ends, for, as pointed out in the Prologue, the mythic hero neither trains himself nor is he trained to kill.[11]

Fear in being alive among other humans is never-ending—or ends only with one's own death. Magic, religion, mind-altering drugs, and so on, may be powerful antidotes, ways of keeping fear at bay, but fear of harm or death at the hands of others is as existentially endless as the warfare it generates. Heider's "A Chronology of War: An Account of Battles and Raids on the Southern Frontier, April–September 1961" (Heider 1979, 90–92) well illustrates the endless misery that follows on endless fear: it shows that if violence never ceases, it is because fear never ceases, and if fear never ceases, it is because "the enemy" might call a battle or carry out a raid at any time. Battles were called on 10 April and 15 April, for example, in which men were wounded but none killed; on 11 May, however, in a raid, a man is killed in his watchtower. Other battles and raids ensue, and on 4 June, following a raid, a watchtower is burned. On 7 June, in another raid, a shelter is burned, potato vines are uprooted, tobacco plants are trampled, a dam is broken, and so on, and on 10 June a young boy is killed in an ambush. More battles and raids follow, and on 6 August, an attempt to raid gardens fails, but the attempt is followed by a battle between boys on either side of a stream. As Heider describes it, there are "[b]oys as young as six, standing on either side of the stream, shooting arrows at each other, coached by older men" (92). Heider concludes the chronology in early September, when another young boy is killed in a raid.

Heider's pithy distinction between ritual warfare, as in the above instances, and secular warfare, as in the 1966 massacre, is initially compelling. He writes that secular warfare "is rare, it is short, it is very bloody; women and children, as well as men, are killed; property is destroyed and plundered; and it is done for motives of secular revenge" (105). The term "enemy," however, which Heider alone and Gardner and Heider use in their descriptive accounts of both secular and ritual war, belies the distinction: *enemy* signifies an ever-present alien ever ready to harm, to kill, or to inflict damage, hence one who must be killed. Gardner and Heider speak of "dead enemy warriors," for example (Gardner and Heider 1968, 137), and of the fact that "warriors in the forward and middle positions watch their enemy with mounting alertness" (138); Heider states, "The Dani know how to kill an enemy" (Heider 1979, 102), that "there are always ghosts to be placated and enemy to be killed" (106), and that following victory, a ceremony takes place on a special field "in plain view of the enemy" and that the noise they generate in celebrating "probably reaches across to where the enemy are holding the funeral [for their dead]" (103).[12] Surely, there can only be an *enemy* if there are others who threaten one's life, one's resources, one's values, and so on, or even others who, as Heider states in speaking of the 1966 massacre, are the source of "endless annoyances" (105).

Moreover the closing paragraph of Gardner and Heider's book confutes Heider's seemingly easy assessment of the effects of pacification by the Dutch and Indonesian governments—"[it] seemed to make little immediate differences to [the Dani] way of life" (Heider 1979, p. 112). Their closing paragraph epitomizes the cultural preeminence of war: "War is one of the paramount institutions of Dani life. With agriculture and pig raising, it constitutes one of the few major focuses of all people's interest and energy. Without it, the culture would be entirely different; indeed, perhaps it could not find sufficient meaning to survive except parasitically as the novelty of missionaries or policemen" (Gardner and Heider 1968, 144).[13] While Gardner and Heider attempt to capture Dani life precisely before pacification, their final comment regarding parasitic survival is notably ironic: in light of obvious domination and subjugation, conflict between groups of men continue; only the cast of characters changes.[14]

Descriptive accounts of the lives of other people are clearly of consuming interest in both the insights they generate and the questions they raise, questions that exceed simple points of information, reverberating instead in deep, self-questioning ways. Of considerable interest in this regard is Gardner's film on the Dani and his commentary in the film, both of which are discussed by Heider in an appendix to his book. The title of the film—*Dead Birds*—is explained by Gardner in the opening lines of the film and is quoted by Heider: "There is a fable told by mountain people living in the ancient highlands of New Guinea about a race between a snake and a bird. It tells of a contest which decided if men would be like birds and die, or be like snakes which shed their skins and have eternal life. The bird won and from time to time, all, men, like birds, must die" (Heider 1979, 145). After quoting the lines, Heider goes on to consider "Gardner's own philosophy vis-à-vis the Dani," stating that "It is well summed up by Gardner's own words":

> A Dani is a plumed warrior in his most desirous state. What I have done is to acknowledge this indubitable fact and be glad for its wry, perhaps ironic, implications. I saw the Dani people, feathered and fluttering men and women, as enjoying the fate of all men and women. They dressed their lives with plumage, but faced as certain death as the rest of us drabber souls. The film attempts to say something about how we all, as humans, meet our animal fate. (145)

Gardner's so-called philosophy is more than a mere personal impression or anthropological take on a foreign culture. A subtle immortality ideology informs Dani culture, precisely as Gardner implicitly indicates. The ideology weaves its way in what the descriptive accounts in both books state about the Dani's belief in ghosts and what they do not state about the Dani's belief in ghosts, namely, that in time, the living too will be ghosts; they too will need to be placated; they too will demand and direct the avenging arrows and spears of the living. Though they die, they too will be "living dead," and though the living will want them "to stay where they belong," they too will be treated with respect. Death is merely a halfway station, "an intermediate crisis" between living and ghostly presence.

As we have seen in earlier chapters, immortality ideologies answer to the fear of death, and the Dani immortality ideology is no exception. It too bridges the chasm between life and death. Though the immortality ideology is latent in the descriptive accounts, never surfacing directly, its subtlety should blinder us neither to the ideology itself nor to the fact that the ideology is akin to other immortality ideologies. At the simplest level, a Dani's ghost is akin to Descartes's soul, which similarly achieves immortality by being immaterial, perduring beyond actual life in the form of an imperishable substance rather than an imperishable presence. In more complex ways, Dani ghosts are akin to Derrida's texts, which achieve immortality not merely by not dying, but by directly influencing the ways of the living. Indeed, the texts, like Dani ghosts, lose nothing of their power over the living, but on the contrary, shape the thoughts, pursuits, and beliefs of the living. That immortality ideologies are pan-cultural can hardly be doubted. Their pan-culturality is testimony to the abiding challenge of death, the abiding human fear of mortality, and the abiding fact that humans are at risk in being alive among other humans.

VIII. WARRIORS AND THE HEROIC HONING OF MALES

That a warrior society is man-made is obvious, and that Gardner and Heider's book, in pictures as well as text, centers almost exclusively on males is also obvious. Heider himself writes, "We—male as well as female anthropologists—have traditionally concentrated on the men, who were the more obvious focus of power and excitement" (1979, 10–11). Especially in conjunction with these facets of the obvious, it is notable that Gardner and Heider mention only in passing that, as part of traditional Dani funeral rites, fingers of young girls are cut off. An explanatory caption of a picture showing just such young girls states,

> These young girls with bandaged hands have just lost one or two fingers early on the second day of the funeral ceremony. After the hand has been numbed by a blow on the elbow, the fingers are chopped off with a blow from a stone adze. Like pigs and shell goods, the fingers are gifts considered necessary to placate the ghosts. Although nearly every Dani girl loses several fingers, as a woman she does a wide range of work, from gardening to making nets, with great manual skill. (Gardner and Heider 1968, 100–101)

At an earlier point, Gardner and Heider mention—again in passing—that "the child," that is to say, the young girl, "may cry or not, depending on its age and temperament. Each knows that what has happened had to happen, and that it will happen again. When they were infants their own mothers had held them and played with them using hands that were mostly thumbs" (96).[15] While the practice of finger mutilation ceased with a government-imposed end of ritual warfare, it is nonetheless remarkable to consider that when an act of a warrior basically generating sheer physicality and excitement results in a tribesman's or tribesboy's death, it can require brutal acts practiced on innocent others quite outside the circle of warriors.

Traditional Dani warfare and its attendant ritual practices, though ended, remain a microcosm of human history: war in all its brutal dimensions is perpetual. Psychologist Lawrence LeShan's distinction between mythical and sensory perceptions of war is instructive in this context. LeShan notes that before on-the-scene reports of war, which began in the 1830s and 1840s with the advent of foreign correspondents and the telegraph, "wars were generally regarded as distant affairs fought by glorious Homeric warriors for a noble (ours) or evil (theirs) cause" (LeShan 1992, 60). With on-the-scene reportage, news of actual battle "made the fighting men and the conflict itself appear heroic" (60). In effect, warriors along with war itself came to be perceived in what LeShan terms "the 'mythic' mode, as opposed to the 'sensory' mode of perception we ordinarily use" (31): warriors became heroes in the heroic cause of war. But LeShan also attempts to identify what attracts individuals to war in the first place, specifying four aspects, the first two of which coincide with the thesis that war allows fear to be contained in the sense of allowing its energies to be transformed into something positively exhilarating, the second two of which coincide with the thesis that immortality ideologies underlie and suffuse the human practice of war. With respect to the first two, LeShan writes, "War offers us a wonderful target for the tensions and angers we feel toward others who are close to us . . . such as colleagues and superiors at work, [and when] we are offered a way of channeling these tensions to people far away, and we are socially encouraged to use it, our close relationships then improve rapidly and strongly" (94). Furthermore, war "also helps to ease the stresses within ourselves [such that what] is most disliked and rejected about the perceived self—what gives us the most pain or anxiety or depression—can now be projected far away from us, again with full social approval" (94–95). In essence, what LeShan is saying is that war gives its warriors a ready emotional outlet for difficult feelings by providing them with a flesh and blood enemy on which to vent them. With respect to the first of the second two aspects, LeShan states, "The intensity of feeling in war—the danger, the excitement, the implied (and accepted) promise that everything will be vastly better after victory, the engagement in a great crusade for a noble cause—all make our life more exciting and meaningful" (95). Moreover "as crusaders," he writes, "we are very much a part of a group; the more enthusiastic we are, the more dedicated and involved, the more we are accepted into that group" (95). In short, war infuses not only fighters but non-fighting members of the tribe or country with excitement and glory at the same time that it provides them a sense of belonging, a belonging definitively etched in a history that will be commemorated by future generations for years to come. War thus intensifies the meaning of life for both the individual and the group.

These aspects of war are far removed from the actual sensory realities of war—the corpses, the stray body parts, the bloodied bodies, the raping of women, the killing of children, the dead comrades, and so on. It is of particular interest to note how journalist Chris Hedges, writing of his experiences on many war fronts and following along the lines of LeShan's distinction, highlights just how the actual realities of war differ from the "mythic" notion of war. "Once in conflict," he states, "we are moved from the abstract to the real, from the mythic to the sensory," and with this move from the abstract, the "rhetoric of patriotism is obliterated, exposed as the empty handmaiden of myth. Fear brings us all back down to earth" (Hedges 2002, 40). As LeShan emphasizes in his book, "In order for war to retain its mythic aspects, and thus increase the intensity of meaning in our lives and bond us more completely as group members, enough of the real facts of how war is waged must be concealed" (LeShan 1992, 61). In effect, war is heroic and warriors become heroes to the populace only when fear is sidelined and when reportage shows the country's warriors miraculously and with derring-do vanquishing "the enemy" and proving themselves victors in battle.

From a real-life, non-mythic perspective, the heroic honing of males might in contrast be described as a near pan-cultural obsession in response to an existential fear that is defused in the aura of the sheer physicality and excitement of actual fighting, but that is nevertheless sustained by the actual fighting, since whatever the war, and whenever it ends, humans will continue to live among other humans, and wars will continue to loom on the horizon. It is thus not simply that the history of victories and grievances are passed on from generation to generation, but that the affective charge of those victories and grievances never wanes. Even if centuries have elapsed, the affective charge persists, as the celebration of Orangemen's Day confirms, for example, in its commemoration of a battle and victory fought over three hundred years ago. Correlatively, antagonistic feelings of those who are subdued and subjugated do not disappear. Whenever those feelings ripen, then, as 19th century philosopher Herbert Spencer perceptively noted, "Whatever injures foes is . . . thought not only justifiable but praiseworthy, and a part of duty" (Spencer [1892] 1978, 345 [but see also Spencer's "General Preface," 23]). Kosovo is an exemplary instance. In the 1389 battle of Kosovo, Serbs were conquered by Turks. Three hundred and forty years later, part of what was Serbia was reclaimed by Serbia, but not until the Balkan War of 1912–13 was the part of Serbia that included Kosovo liberated from Turkish domination. The massacre in Kosovo in the 1990s by Serbians cleansed Kosovo of all non-Serbs. Clearly, those who are conquered and oppressed by others become resentful of them. Spencer's insight seems so simple an affective lesson for humans—*Homo sapiens sapiens*—to learn.

When war transforms the energies of fear into something positively exhilarating, it not only enlivens the lives of warriors but gives them a special power, namely, the power of life and death over other humans. Such power is exhilarating. It recalls Becker's perspicuous observation that where "man" turns against others in harmful and murderous ways, he turns in defiance of his own death: "If we don't have the omnipotence of gods, we at least can destroy like gods" (Becker 1973, 85). The heroic honing of males is thus doubly enticing: fighting is exhilarating in itself, and in actually killing others, one exhilarates in one's power of life and death over them. These doubled feelings of exhilaration effectively smother fear of one's own death and fear of other humans. Recall from Chapter 1 Churchill's remark that "Nothing in life is so exhilarating as to be shot at without result" and Turney-High's comment that war is "an exciting diversion." One finds substantive echoes of these exhilarative feelings in a diversity of writings, from popular historical texts to historical treatises to journalist reports. Describing the life of the Celts, for example, Norton-Taylor writes, "[T]hey were avid hunters and they fought each other at the drop of an insult—fiercely, and often for the sheer joy of physical combat" (Norton-Taylor 1974, 10). Calling attention to the enduring historical fascination of war, well-known historian

Arnold Toynbee takes a broader view: "Wars are exhilarating when they are fought elsewhere and by other people. Perhaps they are most exhilarating of all when over and done with; historians of all civilizations had traditionally regarded them as the most interesting topic in their field" (Toynbee 1957, 2:356). From his journalist's perspective, Hedges comments, "The rush of battle is a potent and often lethal addiction, for war is a drug . . . [that] is peddled by mythmakers—historians, war correspondents, filmmakers, novelists, and the state—all of whom endow it with qualities it often does possess: excitement, exoticism, power, chances to rise above our small stations in life (Hedges 2002, 3). In sum, and as noted in Chapter 1, fighting and killing are exhilarating because they make men feel vibrantly alive and to feel vibrantly alive is to defy death, defy it even as one is surrounded by it. Moreover the invigorating power of sheer physicality and the concomitant rush of excitement experienced in actual battle can be transliterated into a variety of related cultural forms, as military parades, air shows, monuments to fearless warriors, and the like, demonstrate. Whatever the form, the basic meaning remains constant: war is dynamically enthralling. In effect, a society's need for heroic men is never ending.

Historian Leo Braudy captures the nature of beliefs and judgments in the heroic honing of males in his discussion of nationalism and war in his book, *From Chivalry to Terrorism: War and the Changing Nature of Masculinity*. Though never mentioning the banality of evil and its acute and chronic pan-culturality, his observations document both unequivocally:

> National stereotypes in particular gather strength from wars and foment new wars in return—especially when the propaganda of war needs to justify a conflict with the Antichrist, the Infidel, or just the Other. The issue is not only "Who is the enemy?" but also "Who are we?" And the answer is often "We are men, and they are not." Just as popes and antipopes learned to preach and war against each other from the Crusades, the incessant exhortations to destroy the infidel stand like a grim shadow behind the nationalist antagonisms, both internal and external, of the next several centuries. From the expulsion of the Jews from Spain in 1492, to the burning of Mayan books by the Spanish conquistadors in the early sixteenth century, to the English selling of rebel Scots and Irish as slaves in the late six-

> teenth and mid-seventeenth centuries, to the policies of Louis
> XIV that provoked so many Huguenots to leave France after
> 1685—the urge toward national "purity" is often predicated on
> seeing the enemy as less than human, opposing his culture and
> eradicating his life. (Braudy 2003, 135)

Seeing the enemy as less than human, a second-class citizen, a subhuman, and so on, is indeed a common justification of war. When Spencer remarks that "the virtues of the warrior take the first place," he notes not only that the warrior's deeds are praiseworthy, but that his actions against an enemy are sanctioned by civilians, who offer "no protests against the massacres euphemistically called 'punishments'" (Spencer 1978, 345). Thus, whoever the enemy might be—"the Antichrist, the Infidel, the Other"—he deserves what he gets, indeed, what he must get, because he does not measure up.

The dehumanization of others is clearly a vital aspect in the heroic honing of males, but the need to separate negative beliefs and judgments about others from motives to harm or kill them is imperative if the pan-cultural heroic honing of males and the banality of evil are to be fully understood. While actions perpetuating the banality of evil may certainly be buttressed by beliefs and judgments about others, those beliefs and judgments are not their driving force. They fuel the actions from an intellectual remove, as it were, and are not their prime movers. On the other hand, a lack of empathy is not a motivation, any more than is a lack of judgment. Neither lack explains an outright motivation to harm or kill others. Moreover neither does the feeling of indifference explain motivation. Something more basic motivates acts that harm and kill others, something that in fact needs honing, and this because the human capacity for evil is just that: a capacity. It is not the banality of evil itself but only its potential. In short, the human capacity for evil is latent in human nature, latent in the sense that torturing others, maiming them, killing them are possible human acts, acts that, as human history shows, fall definitively within the human repertoire and define all of us. The capacity is thus not a ready-made, but an ability to do that may be realized or not, hence a potential that can be tapped into, drawn on, encouraged, nourished, promoted, and so on. So cultivated, the capacity produces males who are exemplars of the banality of evil, males who, as Peterson writes (see Chapter 1), willingly "torture [their] brothers and dance on [their] grave[s]." The challenge of deepening understandings of the motivation to harm and kill—in essence, acceding to deeper understandings of the heroic honing of males—thus remains a pressing task. It is apparent at this point only that, since the capacity must be tapped and nurtured in order to flourish, humans are neither born evil nor do they have a natural penchant for evil; what they do have is a capacity to harm and kill other humans, a capacity that can be culturally fostered and valued to the point that tribes, governments, military powers, and so on, train and sanction males to go forth and inflict the tortures of hell on anyone deemed "the enemy."

IX. A FINER ANALYSIS OF MOTIVATION

Warriors are the cultural elaboration of the basic biological phenomenon of male-male competition. The connection between evolutionary biology and human cultural practice is all but transparent to anyone who looks closely at "the law of battle" (see Chapter 3) and the long-documented human practice of war. Thus, to whatever the degree the heroic honing of males is a veritable cultural obsession, there is no doubt but that cultivation of the capacity for evil and the practice of making war have the same biological roots. Both are firmly anchored in the biological matrix: male-male competition.

Active cultivation of the capacity builds on those exhilarating death-defying realities described earlier in the discussion of raids and battles that epitomize the positive affective side of human male-male competition. The realities might be motivationally encapsulated in the slogan, "Whatever is dynamically enthralling is worth doing." Warriors are basically motivated in just this way: they are bred to fight, exhilarating in the sheer physicality and excitement of battle and in their power of life and death over others. In the most fundamental sense, war-making itself is just so motivated, enlivening those who plan it, initiate it, and direct it, and enlivening equally those who watch it from the sidelines. The inherent potency of war-making to enliven in fact aptly explains why war can be a satisfying and wholly engaging spectator sport, emotionally akin to the gladiatorial contests in the Colosseum of ancient Rome. Though on an infinitesimally smaller scale than war, those contests—in which people were compelled to fight to the death—were captivating, engaging events. But while sheer physicality is invigorating and stimulating and the excitement generated by sheer physicality compounds the pleasure, and while the power of life and death over others is gratifyingly sweet in light of one's own mortality, heightening one's own feelings of aliveness, sheer physicality, excitement, and power do not exhaust the array of human motivations. On the contrary, a warrior's motivations can be intricately complex. Resentment, vengeance, status, fame, glory, rage, and obedience to authority—all are possible motives over and above the enthralling dynamic realities of actual battle. Indeed, the array of possible motives makes the banality of evil intricately complex at the same time that it makes it a historically common and seemingly indelible human reality.[16]

Insights into its complexity and indelibility are implicit in Arendt's singular statement about Eichmann's motivation, i.e., his having no motivation for doing what he was doing outside of a desire for personal advancement. The statement indicates that cultivation of the capacity for evil deeds is tied in one way or another to self-interest, that is, to what in some way brings more life to the doer: more power, status, privilege, females, fame, resources, and so on. It is striking that in their zealous preoccupation with getting from an "is" to an "ought," philosophers have failed to look precisely at what *is*, specifically, what is in the form of male-male competition and of an abiding human male competitive practice: war, a practice that, alongside art, is the most salient feature of human civilizations.[17] The remains of the latter are treasured and prominently housed in museums or performed on stages and in concert halls; the remains of the former are treasured and prominently housed in cemeteries or have monuments and memorials erected in their honor. What *is* and what thereby warrants focal attention is the competitively based practice of killing, not for food and not for "sport"—as in bullfights and hunting—but for death-defying, life-tethered reasons that, one might say, are in a bio-cultural sense umbilically bound to oneself: killing one's own kind to aggrandize one's life and life possibilities.[18] Indeed, an array of possible motivations for harming and killing other humans centers on *more*, not just in the sense of maximizing one's holdings, making oneself richer in one way or another, and so on, but in the sense of extending one's life and safeguarding that extension. In a word, the mere fact of being alive carries with it the desire for *more*. It is thus not surprising that the meaning of one's life readily becomes attached to *more* in the form of a meaning that endures beyond one's lifetime, precisely in the way the meaning of the life of a noble warrior who fights in a noble cause lives on after he is dead. The desire for more is thus not limited to the desire for more life, but extends to the desire to give eternal meaning to one's life.

We find this theme not only in Rank's perspicuous and subtle insights into the nature of immortality ideologies and in Becker's elaborations of Rank's original writings, but in a diversity of writings as well. We find it, for example, in Hedges's *War Is a Force That Gives Us Meaning*. Participating in, or belonging to something larger than oneself, Hedges says, something ennobling, gives one's life a larger-than-life significance. Accordingly, though "[w]ar exposes the capacity for evil that lurks not far below the surface within all of us, . . . [i]t can give us what we long for in life. It can give us purpose, meaning, a reason for living. . . . [W]ar is an enticing elixir. It gives us resolve, a cause. It allows us to be noble" (Hedges 2002, 3).[19] What Hedges, following LeShan's distinction between the mythic and the sensory, pinpoints in a range of literary descriptions as "the myth of war"—its ennobling character, its heroics, and so on—skirts the edges of a crucial psychological dimension of immortality ideologies, ideologies in the name of which wars are fought. In particular, war "gives us meaning" because it provides not simply the opportunity to give immediate meaning to one's life, but to commemorate that meaning in the course of living it.

This living commemorative dimension is dramatically illustrated in observations Arendt makes about the importance of time to totalitarian leaders generally and to Nazi officials specifically. She calls attention to "the emphatic assertions by totalitarian rulers that they consider the country where they happened to seize power only the temporary headquarters of the international movement on the road to world conquest, that they reckon victories and defeats in terms of centuries or millennia" (Arendt 1958, 411). In support of this observation, she notes, "The Nazis were especially fond of reckoning in terms of millennia. Himmler's pronouncements that SS-men were solely interested in 'ideological questions whose importance counted in terms of decades and centuries' and that they 'served a cause which in two thousand years occurred only once' are repeated, with slight variations, throughout the entire indoctrination material issued by the SS-Hauptamt-Schulungsamt" (411 n. 66). In short, Arendt's observations implicitly underscore the importance of time and the desire of humans to leave their mark in history, to be remembered for their valiant and glorious deeds, and in being remembered, to attain historical immortality.

Interestingly enough, Toynbee emphasizes the same desire but from a broader historical perspective in a chapter of his *Study of History* titled "The Mirage of Immortality." Writing of "universal states," such as the Roman Empire, the Ottoman Empire, and the Egyptiac culture, he explains,

> If we look at these universal states, not as alien observers but through the eyes of their own citizens, we shall find that these not only desire that these earthly commonwealths of theirs should live for ever but actually believe that the immortality of these human institutions is assured, and this sometimes in the teeth of contemporary events which, to an observer posted at a different standpoint in time or space, declare beyond question that this particular universal state is at that very moment in its last agonies. (Toynbee 1957, 14)

Toynbee quotes a number of ancient writers to document his claim; for example, Tibullus (of the first century B.C.) who "sings of 'the walls of the eternal city'," and Virgil (of the same century) who "makes his Iuppiter, speaking of the future Roman scions of Aeneas' race, say: 'I give them empire without end'" (14). He quotes Livy, Horace, and others all to the same point, and later remarks on the "halo of an illusory immortality, worn by moribund universal states" (15).

Empires, cultures, nations, ethnic groups can—and most often do—carry above them just such a halo. As Toynbee observes, however, its illusory nature goes unrecognized. On the contrary, by identifying with and participating in the battles of their political states, individual citizens believe they can reap immortal rewards along with their leaders. It is no wonder, then, that the heroic honing of males can through and through become a veritable cultural obsession. By putting their lives, their beliefs, their values on the line, warriors make immortality—the crowning touch of *more*—available to all within their culture. What greater motive could be had than to gain immortality?

Two widely observed and highly significant evolutionary phenomena—one having to do with territory, the other with dominant males—emerge in this socio-political context. In both instances, humans as a species show themselves to be of a piece with other animal species. A consideration of each phenomenon in turn will demonstrate again that descent with modification is to be taken seriously: it is an evolutionary fact of human life.

X. BROADER SOCIO-POLITICAL UNDERSTANDINGS OF THE HEROIC
HONING OF MALES: A RETURN TO EVOLUTIONARY CONSIDERATIONS

Territory is an integral part of the national history of a people. It is thus not surprising that, in a pan-cultural sense, war shapes and patterns human life. But territory has a much longer and more complex history, being an integral part not only of the national history of a people but of the natural history of humans. Its national history is in fact the cultural elaboration of its natural history, that is, an elaboration of what is evolutionarily given, as evidenced in the territorial behaviors of nonhuman animals, including the behaviors of other primates, and, given the human archaeological record and recorded human history, the behavior of early hominids. We can glimpse the beginnings of these evolutionary relationships in Robert Ardrey's *The Territorial Imperative*. Ardrey, playwright and author of an earlier 1960s text on the science of man (Ardrey 1961), opens *The Territorial Imperative* with a definition: "A territory is an area of space, whether of water or earth or air, which an animal or group of animals defends as an exclusive preserve" (Ardrey 1966, 3). He goes on immediately to state, "The word is also used to describe the inward compulsion in animate beings to possess and defend such a space. A territorial species of animals, therefore, is one in which all males, and sometimes females too, bear an inherent drive to gain and defend an exclusive property" (3). He thus identifies certain socio-political behaviors—gaining and defending territory—as species-specific behaviors and roots these behaviors primarily in the male of the species. Given this evolutionary basis for "the territorial imperative," Ardrey fittingly identifies human nations as biological entities, showing how they are an extension of the territorial claims of nonhuman animals, a domain of research he documents extensively. In addition to dwelling pointedly on the concept of *a biological nation,* he dwells at length on Spencer's concept of amity and enmity that identifies the dual moral codes informing human action, emending the concept along the lines of evolutionary thought. Indeed, Ardrey remarks on the fact that, despite Spencer's knowledge of and obvious ties to evolutionary thought, his dual codes remain devoid of evolutionary reference: "Oddly enough, it is Spencer, the evolutionist, who seems by some quirk to have clung to a belief in man's original good nature. He saw the code of enmity as something laid onto man, something that history must one day wash away" (286).[20]

In contrast to Spencer, Ardrey anchors enmity firmly in the very nature of human nature.[21] On the basis of the territorial imperative, he formalizes the relationship of amity and enmity, commenting, for example, that "What we call patriotism . . . is a calculable force which, released by a predictable situation, will animate man in a manner no different from other territorial species" (232). But he points out too that anthropologist Sir Arthur Keith was actually the first to take up Spencer's dual codes in a true biological sense, giving them a firm footing in territorial behavior, and quotes Keith's basic claim: "Human nature has a dual constitution; to hate as well as to love are parts of it; and conscience may enforce hate as a duty just as it enforces the duty of love. Conscience has a two-fold role in the soldier: it is his duty to save and protect his own people and equally his duty to destroy their enemies. . . . Thus conscience serves both codes of group behavior; it gives sanction to practices of the code of enmity as well as of the code of amity" (287–88).

What Keith was at pains to show was the central significance of territory in his "group theory of human evolution" (Keith 1968, 12), in particular, how tribes occupying specific territories were the original human "evolutionary unit" (Keith 1946, 142), how nations are "the lineal successors of tribes" (146), and how amity binds the tribe or nation together in *"group affection"* and enmity separates the tribe or nation from other tribes or nations in *"group aversion"* (Keith 1968, 14). Of particular note is his emphasis upon *fear* as the basis of the "enmity complex": "Fear is the tribal sentinel," Keith states. "Even at peace, fear is not asleep," but is present in suspicions, dislikes, contempt, and so on (Keith 1946, 143–44). When roused by a perceived threat, fear sets off a "state of warlike exaltation [in which] there is pressed into action a passion to destroy, to kill, to exterminate the enemy, to terrify him by acts of cruelty and of inhumanity" (144). In short, Keith's insights into human nature and its capacity for evil run deep, including not only understandings of the power of fear but the power of ambition to precipitate war. At the base of man's "competitive complex," he states, is "man's desire for place and power—ambition" (Keith 1968, 58), a desire he elsewhere speaks of as "the most compelling of human passions" and, as noted, specifies as one of the two causes of war (Keith 1946, 145, 141, respectively).

Both Keith's and Ardrey's conceptions of the dual codes are firmly grounded in the field research of psychologist C. R. Carpenter, whose studies of the behavior of social animals is seminal to their theses. Carpenter's extensive studies of primates in such diverse places as Panama, India, and Thailand included species ranging from howler monkeys to red spider monkeys, macaques, gibbons, and orangutans. His studies are in fact valued worldwide; his research in the 1930s "established many of the motivations, goals, methodologies, and basic concepts of the subsequent work in this field [of nonhuman primate social behavior]" (Southwick 1963, 2). It is instructive to cite a number of his observations pertaining to primate territorial behavior that appear in the essay "Societies of Monkeys and Apes," for they capture the import and practice of territoriality in close-up terms and provide a finer comprehension of evolutionary linkages in territorial behaviors.

To begin with, Carpenter speaks of "territorialism," defining the term as involving "inter-group antagonisms, adjustment to or learning of a given area, homing and group defense." He points out that "The organized groups of every type of monkey or ape which has been adequately observed in its native habitat, have been found to possess territories and to defend these ranges from all other groups of the same species. . . . Territorialism of groups would seem to be a primitive basic characteristic of non-human primate groupings and the analogies with human behavior are close and strikingly evident" (Carpenter 1963, 37). Addressing the question of group stability in this context, he states, "Through continuous association and reinforcement by various incentives, the territory becomes familiar to most all individuals of a group and is reacted to positively; surrounding new territory is unfamiliar or unknown and is reacted to negatively. Thus territorialism may importantly influence social integration because a number of animals are adapted to a common environment" (38). Carpenter does not draw on Spencer's concept of amity, but it is obvious that, enhanced by "territorialism," group stability is linked to amity: what is familiar is what is expected, hence congenial rather than fearsome or disturbing. In contrast, what is strange and unfamiliar provokes fear: one does not know what to expect from alien surrounds—or alien others. Such surrounds may in fact harbor alien others who will threaten and jeopardize one's security, one's resources, and so on. Alien others from a human primate perspective are readily perceived as just such threats; moreover they can call one's values and beliefs into question as well as endanger one's life. In short, analogies to humans clearly hover at the edge of Carpenter's many observations on nonhuman primate territorialism. A particularly striking instance concerns the relationship between a lack of federation, the presence of inter-group dominance, and the lack of inter-species dominance:

> The characteristics of primate societies which cause them to react antagonistically to other groups of the same species and to defend a limited territorial range, prevent the *federation* or *combining* of organized groups, . . . [but] intergroup dominance exists among primates . . . [and] is dependent upon the relative dominance of the respective autocratic males in the interacting group. . . . Whereas an organized primate group does not tolerate another of the same species, a group of another species may mutually share a territorial range. I have seen howlers feeding in the same trees with capuchin monkeys, gibbons feeding with siamangs or with macaques, and macaques feeding in the same trees with langurs. I have never observed organized groups of the same species *peacefully* associated. (38–39)

When Carpenter observes that "intra-species competition and group antagonisms are much stronger than [competition and antagonisms] between groups of different species or genera," he implicitly specifies not "the characteristics" but the prime character "of primate societies which cause[s] them to react antagonistically to other groups of the same species and to defend a limited territorial range," namely, enmity. The character is finely illustrated in the example Carpenter gives of a howler monkey inter-group encounter:

> Coincident with the approach to, or entry of, the territory of one howler group by another, the barking roars of this species are normally exchanged between the two groups. A truly vocal battle between the males of the groups, supported by whines of females and young, ensues and continues usually without actual fighting, until one group retreats. Most often the retreat is made by the encroaching group, i.e., the home team usually wins. The territory is defended and inter-group dominance is asserted through the medium of strong and persistent sound production. (50)

It is of moment to note that, in this essay originally printed in 1942, Carpenter goes on to remark that "The functions of a League of Nations is at least as old as the non-human primate family, and even on this level of evolution, vocal expressions of aggression may substitute for actual battle!" (50).

Though the oppositional notions of amity and enmity never enter into Carpenter's descriptions and discussions as such, they are supported by his observations of nonhuman animal territorial behaviors and by their ready analogies to human territorial behaviors. Described and discussed in terms of a positive intra-group and negative inter-group species accord, they are equipotential characters. While Ardrey utilizes Carpenter's studies, he does not weigh the accords equally. On the contrary, in Ardrey's formulation, which he states is "for purposes of illumination, not definition"—"an expression of probability, not determination" (Ardrey 1966, 272)—enmity rules over and above amity. Enmity is in fact the binding force of amity: $A = E + h$, where h stands for all those hazards to life that arise from without, whether in the form of other species or of environmental happenings such as floods and droughts. Enmity is defined by "those forces of antagonism and hostility originating in members of one's own species" (272), or as he later puts it: enmity is "hostility for others of one's kind" (273). In effect, "enmity is the root of all goodness" (273). It draws individuals of one group together in virtue of their shared hostility toward all others of the same species. Though Ardrey recognizes "innate" amity (271), he declares it too negligible to be of significance (271–72). He mentions a natural amity in connection with mother-infant relationships, for example, but considers it a short-term phenomenon connected simply with dependence (273–74), and as for long-term family or marriage bonds, he quickly puts the bonds in the context of death and divorce, contexts in which "in a dirty twinkling such sentiments [as amity] vanish. Property is king" (274). Thus, as for "innate" amity, he says, "we may promptly forget it" (272).

However hasty and peremptory his dismissal of natural amity—a positive affective bond readily evident in empathy and in child's play as we will see in Chapters 6 and 8—and in turn sorely biased his view of human nature, Ardrey's basic insight into the evolutionary nature of territorialism and the centrality of territory in human affairs is significant: the relative ease with which humans can and do kill and maim each other has sizable roots in "the territorial imperative." A summary and strikingly contemporary way of specifying these roots appears in the course of his prescient observations on the "state of Israel and the Jewish people." He discusses "certain theoretical consequences" of "a territorial interpretation of the Jew." Hypothesizing first, "if territory has transmuted the Jew, physically and psychically, into another being called the Israeli . . . ,"Ardrey then points out the breach between those who portray "the Israeli [as] a chauvinist, . . . a man who has lost his world view and no longer acts according to his conscience, as one who has somehow betrayed the most profound ideals of a people," and the Israeli him/herself who dismisses the "moralizer whose sermons if put into practice would mean death to Israel." Ardrey affirms that "[w]hat neither understands is that natural law has intervened; that they [Jew and Israeli] are no longer the same people sharing the same conscience and the same amity-enmity complex" (310). In short, the division between Jew and Israeli is a matter of territory, and territory—or territorialism—is precisely at the heart of an abiding and altogether central Middle East problem. Like the pan-cultural phenomenon of war, it structures human life in a social dynamics played out equally along the lines of amity and enmity: the tightening of inward bonds at the same time as a loosening of outward antagonisms against others. With respect to the problem, Ardrey writes that "it will be solved or it will destroy the nation" (311). Though not speaking of territory but of land, political historian Amos Elon echoes the same theme in "War Without End," which assesses the failed "peace process" between Israelis and Palestinians (Elon 2004, 29), a process in which the possibility of a two-state solution appears an increasingly less likely possibility. At the root of the conflict is land as well as religion (27–28).

War and territory are inextricably linked because hatred of and antagonism toward alien outsiders of the same species—toward strangers—is a biological disposition. War itself, however, is hardly a biological disposition, and the maiming and killing of others outside one's group is hardly a biological mandate. War is the cultural elaboration of what is evolutionarily given: male-male competition. When that competition takes the form of a radical and willful territorialism in which claims of one group or nation are deemed by its leader imperative to pursue and its citizens duly follow along the imperative of their leader, the claims are imperiously and ruthlessly so pursued. National history and natural history are thereby inextricably linked.

Of utmost relevance to a further validation of the link between evolution and culture, and to further evidential support for human analogies to and extrapolations from Carpenter's studies of territorialism, is a consideration of early hominids themselves. Biological anthropologist Jonathan Kingdon's thesis concerning the evolution of hominids is of utmost significance in this respect. In *Lowly Origin,* Kingdon sets forth two original and evidentially persuasive theses concerning early hominids, both of which are substantively related to an understanding of how the natural history of territorial behaviors is fundamental to understandings of national histories, and in turn, to understandings of the human practice of war.

Kingdon's first thesis concerns the advent of consistent bipedality. Building on anthropologist Clifford Jolly's original seed-eater hypothesis (1970), Kingdon deftly shows how the origin of hominid bipedality lies in squatting postures that built spinal support for the upper torso and head independently of legs. To allay any misconceptions, it should perhaps be noted specifically that early hominids did not adopt squatting postures in order that later generations of hominids might one day arrive at bipedality—any more than one fine day, early hominids decided they had squatted enough and simply stood up and began walking about on two legs, however hazardously, and subsequently perfected the technique. The squatting posture of early hominids, Kingdon shows, was an ecologically advantageous posture that allowed foraging on the forest floor. What it required were progressive structural changes from a relatively platelike spinal column to a curved one and related functional changes from a "top-heavy" body (Kingdon 2003, 127) to a body whose shoulders and arms were operatively distinct from hips and legs. In "squat-feeding," as Kingdon terms it (21), stability is achieved through pelvis and legs. This stable base of support makes possible a variety of upper-body movements including forward bending and full straightening of the back, twisting of the shoulders and head, and flexibility at the waist, movement possibilities that would otherwise be hindered and even opposed by upper-body weight-bearing functions. As Kingdon remarks, "I think that what took place was less a case of bipedalism initiating new behaviors than the removal of frustrating constraints on many existing talents. . . . Before becoming bipedal, the potential for more effective manual manipulations of foods or fellows must have been curtailed by the persistent intrusion of weight-bearing duties" (126). In short, structural transformation and functional enhancement evolved together in conjunction with squat-feeding: the spine was structurally transformed and the mobility of the upper torso and head was functionally enhanced prior to the advent of bipedality, the major base of support ultimately shifting from pelvis and legs to feet.

One might well wonder what these structural and functional changes associated with squat-feeding and antecedent to bipedality have to do with territorialism and war. The answer is weaponry. There are no wars without weapons with which to fight them. Thus it is not that, like soft tissue and speech, fistfights do not fossilize, but that whether engaged in or not, fist fights are not the stuff of war. The archeological record documents weaponry in the form of spears, bludgeoning instruments, arrow points, and so on, and thus attests to the practice of war. But a further critical point is easily passed over. Weaponry demands not simply the technological skill to make weapons; it demands certain movement possibilities in the absence of which weapons would never be made. These movement possibilities provide the basis for both conceptualizing the very idea of weaponry to begin with and the envisioning of certain weapons in particular. In other words, one does not make a tool, much less a weapon, one cannot wield: one designs tools and weapons congenial to the body one is and to the use they will be put (Sheets-Johnstone 1999b). Physical anthropologist Milford Wolpoff makes this point indirectly with respect not to weaponry but to toolmaking, in particular, to "the Levallois technique" of the middle Paleolithic period, when he states, "It is apparent that forms were preconceived and that greater and greater effort was made to flake the implement into the desired shape. . . . When tools are made by direct (or indirect) percussion, there is an immediate feedback as the stone is being worked, since each step makes it look more like the desired form. The Levallois technique does not have this feedback potential because the core does not look like the Levallois flake that will be struck from it" (Wolpoff 1980, 242–43). A tool "preconceived" according to a "desired shape" is in actuality a tool "preconceived" according to certain patterns of movement possible to the individual who uses the tool. The point of moment in this regard is that movement possibilities expanded radically with bipedality. The latter did not merely facilitate jumping, leaping, hopping, kicking, and so on, but enhanced throwing, hurling, slinging, and the performance of a host of other ballistic movements in which, precisely, the force and spatial possibilities of the whole body, and the enhanced functional strength and mobility of the upper body, could be put in service of the task, venture, or goal at hand.

Kingdon's squat-feeding thesis thus has sizable significance with respect to war, for with squat-feeding, movement possibilities of the upper body and the body as a whole were vastly expanded. Commensurate with these possibilities, a range of technological possibilities opened, not just in terms of tool production and the use of tools by individuals, but in terms of weaponry and the use of weaponry by groups initiating the practice of war. It is commonly said that upright posture freed the hands for tool-carrying and for seeing at a greater distance. However true these hypothesized functions, what the early functional separation of upper and lower torso in the course of squat-feeding together with the later development of consistent bipedality made possible was the use of weapons, instruments that are used not merely to secure food—in other words, instruments that are not properly speaking *tools*—but instruments that are used to kill for the sake of killing and are indeed *weapons*. Several of Kingdon's remarks in the context of his discussion of tool use originating from "two different behaviors—solitary foraging and social aggression" (Kingdon 2003, 252) are notable in this respect. Kingdon specifies the use of spikes—"[a] minor tool type to begin with"—in foraging "to impale, perforate, loosen, or degrade," and then notes that, in their "larger morphs," spikes "would become the spear, javelin, sword, and dagger." He remarks further with respect to hammers that "[h]ammering can also have a rarer aggressive connotation in which the arm's action simulates fist pummeling" (253). Certainly with the advent of bipedality and an enhanced upper-torso strength and mobility, groups of early hominids did not immediately begin devising weaponry to have at each other. The practice of war evolved as a practice. Interestingly enough, Wolpoff implicitly suggests just this when he points out that the archaeological record documents "different distinguishable tools" such as hand axes and cleavers at the time of *Homo erectus* (Wolpoff 1980, 204), and "projectile weapons" that effectively harm or kill at a distance at the time of early *Homo sapiens* (225). Use of the word *weapons* in the latter instance and *tools* in the former is already suggestive of the idea that instruments that kill are different from instruments that, for example, split, slice, or butcher. The distinction furthermore implicitly suggests that instruments used for hunting in the form of distance killing were likely to have been and probably were co-opted for war, not only because they were effective at a distance, but because they could be effectively used by a group of individuals against a common target. So used, they were indeed no longer tools but veritable weapons. In effect, hominid hunting techniques were culturally exapted[22] for a new purpose, i.e., war-making.

This evolutionary thesis is not altogether new, but certainly its evidential base and reasoning are. In his first book, *African Genesis,* Ardrey proposed what is popularly known as the "killer-ape hypothesis." Though questionably linking the hypothesis to ethologist Desmond Morris[23] as well as to Ardrey, Wolpoff nicely summarizes the hypothesis as follows:

> Humans originated when a group of pongids became savanna-dwelling carnivores (i.e., "killer apes"). To varying degrees, they [Ardrey and Morris] hold this unique hominid heritage to be responsible for what they see as the "aggressive instincts" in modern humans. Their writings have led to the idea that many undesirable elements of human behavior, ranging from mob behavior to crime and ultimately warfare, are the result of this heritage and are somehow coded in our genes. (91)

Wolpoff's probing comments on the hypothesis testify to its continuing importance:

> The killer-ape model . . . has come to be more than a hypothesis about hominid origins. Its implications extend to claims about the basis of behaviors in living humans. The model of how cultural behaviors may have inherited aspects . . . suggests it is unlikely that any *specific* behaviors (aggressiveness, war making, etc.) could be inherited. However, the question remains of how important carnivorous behavior was in hominid origins, and what if any effects this might still have on human behaviors. (91–92)[24]

The "hunting-to-mobbing-to-war" connective tissue of the killer-ape hypothesis is persuasive. Yet its basis in "aggressive instinct" does not enlighten us about the motivation to war or about the pan-cultural banality of evil. The hypothesis is in fact surprisingly deficient in light of its being a biological explanation. In its concentration on "aggressive instincts," specifically with respect to human aggression (a consuming and popular topic in evolutionary biology, anthropology, and ethology in the 1940s, 1950s, and 1960s [e.g., Lorenz 1966, Malinowski 1948]), it omits not just a pivotal and crucial factor of evolutionary theory, but a pivotal and crucial aspect of male animate life on which the pivotal and crucial factor of evolutionary theory rests, namely, male-male competition.[25] Male-male competition is the biological matrix of war. In default of that matrix, there would be no ground on which the pan-cultural phenomenon of war itself and particular cultural elaborations of warfare would develop. Talk of aggressive instincts masks what is out there for all to see. It puts the cart before the horse: *aggression devolves from competition*, and not the reverse. The motivation to war from a biological perspective lies in male-male competition, in the sheer physicality and excitement that that competition engenders and in the power and resources that attach to the winner. What Kingdon's first thesis offers is a sturdy bodily basis for male-male competition over and above—that is, in excess of—the classic biological competition for females. It offers a sturdy bodily basis for the build-up of technological prowess coincident with technological innovations. As Kingdon himself states. "Humans, like chimps, are aware that 'expertise' confers power, and the display of a good command of skills would have been a prime tenet of prehistoric education from the earliest times" (Kingdon 2003, 279). He in fact goes on to remark, "It is, therefore, possible that the social knapping of hand axes might have become an occasional 'recreational' activity, conducted in a spirit of mild rivalry" (279).

The second equally compelling thesis Kingdon presents concerns another hominid behavioral practice having to do with food, this one not with postural feeding practices but with a food-procurement practice that is in essence territorial. Kingdon terms the procurement practice "niche-stealing" and "niche-thievery." He shows how niche-stealing was a foraging technique based on two skills already possessed by early hominids and numerous other species, especially predators: "the close observation of other species," and a "predatory intolerance of competitors" (219). These skills were connected to scavenging in a particular sense, namely, obtaining another animal's food through "particularly acute sensitivities to other animals as guides to hidden or potential food sources" (218). Scavenging in this sense, Kingdon points out, "could have provided a major mechanism not only for expansion out of the forest, but for a diversification of diet that led away from species-specific diets and, even more significantly, a rapid elaboration of flexible technologies for obtaining food" (218). Dietary flexibility is a likely development for a species without adaptive bodily specializations such as claws and canines that commonly determine diet in bounded ways. Such flexibility allows a greater range of edibles, provided one is aware of them and can recognize their location, and provided one can edge out other actual or potential feeders. Kingdon explains the new food procurement practice, distinguishing it from classic notions of scavenging, precisely in these terms: "Combining the predator's alertness to other species' behavior with a periodic intolerance of actual and potential competitors . . . might better be termed 'niche-stealing' than scavenging" (219).

Kingdon describes in detail how niche-thievery defines the evolutionary life of hominids from their lowly beginnings in squat-feeding to their "entirely new way of earning a living," i.e., through "tool-assisted 'niche-stealing'" (247), a practice humans ultimately honed to the point of taking over lands belonging not just to others of their own species but to other animals altogether. Summing up his earlier view of "periodic intolerance," Kingdon recalls his own family's experiences of "fleeing chimps" in Africa, that is, of "an image of black bundles in hasty retreat" from humans (111). He points out that "Humans and chimpanzees are too closely related not to have been long-term competitors," and in terms painfully pertinent to present times, remarks topically in relation to his subsequent chapters, that "our own intolerance of other species has been integral to the development of bipedalism and to the elaboration of a unique relationship with nature" (112).

Niche-stealing and territorialism obviously go hand in hand. Basing his reconstruction on fossil evidence, Kingdon proposes that southern Africa was the point of radiation of hominid evolution. As the *Australopithecus africanus* lineage (the "South African man-apes" [147]),

> extended its range into the uplands, a prime challenge . . . would have been to get access to resources that were contested or preempted by a variety of other species, mostly mammals. . . . [T]hese hominins[26] might have become "niche-thieves" because they pursued technological and behavioral solutions to get access to foods that were previously only accessible to *other* species (ones that had evolved the techniques or physiologies to bypass or outwit their prey's defenses). In a sense, all adaptive advances involve moving in on the niches of precursors, but I am proposing a much faster type of takeover in which tools, techniques, and strategic intelligence all played pivotal roles. (199–200)

In sum, "the thieving of niches" has ecological and technological significance: it means a way of making a living that is wrapped up in territory and tools, the latter becoming at some point weapons used against one's own kind. Kingdon's two theses provide formidable support for a view not of human aggression, but of warfare and the banality of evil.

Practical as well as deep psychological lessons are to be learned from the hard and perduring realities of animate life such as those Kingdon presents, lessons that should not be beyond the ken of humans. Indeed, "man, the rational animal" otherwise fails to live up to his self-exalted billing. Freud suggests as much, though far too glibly and irresponsibly when, in explanation of the human barbarities of World War I, he writes, "In reality our fellow-citizens have not sunk so low as we feared, because they had never risen so high as we believed" (Freud 1915 [1958], 218). The star-billing humans accord themselves clearly requires serious examination, as Freud implies, but it can hardly be seriously examined if one is theoretically tethered elsewhere, e.g., to infant sexuality, and myopically explains away the barbarities he witnesses. Those committing these barbarities are not aptly identified as "our fellow-citizens" but as males. In short, and again, an acknowledgment of male-male competition is mandatory.

## XI. CLASSIC STUDIES: AN AFTERWORD ON HISTORY AND SCIENCE

One can barely pick up a text on human history, past or present, without falling upon accounts and descriptions of war, its influences, its causes and consequences. Indeed, the most famous historical texts—the classics—are precisely treatises on war, from Herodotus's *The Persian Wars*, Thucydides's *The Peloponnesian War*, Julius Caesar's *The Gallic War*, Polybius's *The Rise of the Roman Empire*, to Bruce Catton's trilogy on the Civil War and Winston Churchill's *The Second World War*. Toynbee's observation that "historians of all civilizations had traditionally regarded them [wars] as the most interesting topic in their field" lends weight not simply to the focal attention of historians on war, but to the perduring phenomenon of war itself in human history: it is a readily available "interesting topic" because it is a regularly occurring human reality in which one group of humans is intent on decimating or vanquishing altogether another group of humans.

War, by its very nature, necessitates obedience to authority; it requires concerted action—hence a cooperative obedience toward a common end—and thus a bonding among fighting males in subservience to a leader all recognize as authoritative. In their classic review of the literature on sex differences in their book *The Psychology of Sex Differences*,[27] psychologists Eleanor Maccoby and Carol Jacklin call attention to the fact that competition involves just such "cooperation." After noting on the basis of their thoroughgoing and painstaking review that "[t]he evidence for greater male aggressiveness is unequivocal," they state that "a different picture emerges from the research on competitiveness and dominance." In particular, "Male competition in real-life settings frequently takes the form of groups competing against groups . . . an activity that involves within-group cooperation as well as between-group competition, so that cooperative behavior is frequently not the antithesis of competitiveness." Moreover they go on to state, "Most research on competition has been conducted in contrived situations that fail to take account of this fact and that do not correspond well with the naturalistic conditions under which competitiveness is most intense" (Maccoby and Jacklin 1974, 274). What Maccoby and Jacklin have in mind with respect to "most intense" competition is sports, not war, but their observation is surely applicable to war. Indeed, the intense competition of war does not simply involve cooperation but requires it.

We can profitably consider two classic experimental studies in social psychology that show that "contrived situations"—i.e., experimental science—need not be so artificially dissimilar from real life happenings that they fail to accord with "naturalistic conditions," the second study in particular with "naturalistic conditions" that, though not in fact recognized as such, are grounded in competition, competition that if not "most intense" is readily enough intense. The issue and the studies themselves have sizeable epistemological implications with respect to understandings of human nature and the contentious place of history and science in those understandings.

In the first classic social psychology study, a subject is told by the experimenter to give an electric shock of increasing intensity to "a learner" whenever the learner fails to give the proper answer in a paired-word test. The learner never actually receives a shock but is in fact an actor playing a role in the experiment. Social psychologist Stanley Milgram, who designed and carried out multiple experiments on this basic theme and discusses them at length in his book *Obedience to Authority*, states, "The point of the experiment is to see how far a person will proceed in a concrete and measurable situation in which he is ordered to inflict increasing pain on a protesting victim. At what point will the subject refuse to obey the experimenter?" (Milgram 1973, 3–4). As Milgram himself notes, such an experiment recalls Arendt's analysis of Eichmann, and the controversy that attended Arendt's contention "that the prosecution's effort to depict Eichmann as a sadistic monster was fundamentally wrong, that he came closer to being an uninspired bureaucrat who simply sat at his desk and did his job" (5). On the basis of his multiple experiments with all their subtle and rich variations on obedience to authority, Milgram states, "After witnessing hundreds of ordinary people submit to the authority in our own experiments, I must conclude that Arendt's conception of the *banality of evil* comes closer to the truth than one might dare imagine. The ordinary person who shocked the victim did so out of a sense of obligation—a conception of his duties as a subject—and not from any peculiarly aggressive tendencies" (6).

Yet it is not only a lack of judgment in Arendt's sense that Milgram observes in his experimental studies, but "empathic cues," cues that support Vetlesen's sense of "moral performance" as a conjunction of "perception, empathy, and judgment." In particular, varying the degree and kind of physical closeness of subject and learner, i.e., subject and learner may be visually, auditorily, or tactilely distanced or in contact with each other, results in different responses by the subject. Milgram observes, for example, "Obedience was significantly reduced as the victim was rendered more immediate to the subject" (34–36). On the other hand, in a distanced auditory or tactile situation, he comments, "[the subject] is aware, but only in a conceptual sense, that his actions cause pain to another person; the fact is apprehended but not felt" (36). He suggests that visual awareness of suffering "trigger[s] empathic responses in the subject and give[s] him a more complete grasp of the victim's experience." But he also suggests that "empathic responses are themselves unpleasant, possessing drive properties which cause the subject to terminate the arousal situation," and concludes that "[d]iminishing obedience, then, would be explained by the enrichment of empathic cues in the successive experimental conditions" (38).

Milgram's experiments, all of which save one were conducted with males,[28] were replicated in South Africa, Australia, Jordan, Austria, Italy, West Germany, and Spain (Blass 2000, 59), and the results obtained were similar to those Milgram himself obtained. It is of interest to note, however, that in a comparison of the many experiments utilizing male subjects to the single experiment conducted with female subjects, the same rate of obedience prevails in both females and males (65 percent; see Blass 2000, 47–50), but obedient females differ from obedient males in terms of greater nervousness and observed tension (Milgram 1973, 63 and 207 n. 6; see also Blass 2000, 50). One female subject, for example, pleads with the experimenter, "Can't we stop? I'm shaking. I'm shaking. Do I have to go up there [give the learner the higher voltages]?" (Milgram 1973, 80).[29] In the course of detailing the progression and results of his experiments, Milgram in fact emphasizes that tension is at times high, that some subjects are distressed, that some protest to the experimenter, but that even as they "tremble and sweat" (43), they nonetheless continue to administer the shocks. In light of the rate of compliance, Milgram comments, "It is the extreme willingness of adults to go to almost any lengths on the command of an authority that constitutes the chief finding of the study and the fact most urgently demanding explanation" (5). In the Preface to his book, he supplies the explanation by way of responsibility: if one does not feel responsible for one's actions—if one is just carrying out orders—then one is not acting in a morally aberrant way but is merely the instrument of another person's demands. Since this "adjustment of thought," he writes, allows one "to engage in cruel behavior," then the same justifications are at work whether one is "in a psychological laboratory or the control room of an ICBM site. The question of generality, therefore, is not resolved by enumerating all the manifest differences between the psychological laboratory and other situations but by carefully constructing a situation that captures the essence of obedience—that is, a situation in which a person gives himself over to authority and no longer views himself as the efficient cause of his own actions" (xii). At a later point, he comments, "The most far-reaching consequence of the agentic shift is that a man feels responsible *to* the authority directing him but feels no responsibility *for* the content of the actions that the authority prescribes. Morality does not disappear, but acquires a radically different focus: the subordinate person feels shame or pride depending on how adequately he has performed the actions called for by authority" (145–46). At the conclusion of his book, he comments,

> The results, as seen and felt in the laboratory, are to this author disturbing. They raise the possibility that human nature, or—more specifically—the kind of character produced in American democratic society, cannot be counted on to insulate its citizens

from brutality and inhumane treatment at the direction of malevolent authority. A substantial proportion of people do what they are told to do, irrespective of the content of the act and without limitations of conscience, so long as they perceive that the command comes from a legitimate authority. (189)

In sum, Milgram's experimental studies are not run-of-the-mill laboratory studies. They are designed in such a way as to create a highly realistic situation in which what is demanded runs experientially counter to an individual's normal, everyday moral sense. In such a situation, *immoral* performance is centrally adducible neither to a lack of empathy nor to a lack of judgment, but to another factor altogether: obedience to authority. This factor, historically in evidence at the Nuremberg Trials in the form of an individual's proffered reason for having done what he had done, is kaleidoscopically highlighted in Milgram's laboratory studies in ways that throw light on the actual experience of obeying an authority to harm another, its real-life, lived-through dynamics. As the foregoing account of his studies clearly shows, obedience to authority most commonly subverts both empathy and judgment: it succeeds in requiring an individual to act in ways beyond his or her normal moral bounds. What commonly feeds such obedience is the notion that authorities know what they are doing—they are people in a better position than "I" to judge what must be done or what is best. Eichmann's Kantian ethics exemplifies just this notion in its dictum that one's acts are to be judged with respect to what the Führer would approve. Even so, exactly what triggers the genuflective behavior is difficult to pinpoint. With respect to understandings of human nature and the place of science and history in those understandings, it is interesting that Milgram points to ontogeny, hence to a form of history, for an answer: obedience to authority derives from childhood, from both familial authority and institutional, i.e., school, authority (135–38). In effect, he implicitly suggests that history and experimental science—in essence, accounts of real life and of life in the laboratory—can each contribute to an illumination of the nature of human nature. What should be pointed out, however, are the subtleties, thoroughness, inventiveness, and overall intelligence of Milgram's experimental studies[30] in contrast to those "contrived" scientific studies of which Maccoby and Jacklin write, studies that tell us little about "the naturalistic conditions" of actual life. As Milgram himself indicates, however, his observations do not provide a complete picture. Answers to questions about obedience to authority must also derive from human ontogenetical history.

Given the twentieth and twenty-first centuries' prominencing of science, an age in which, typically, other disciplines do not measure up, brief mention should be made of common troublesome views of history and its relatively low axiological place in the popular as well as academic world. In his introduction to *The Greek Historians,* Francis Godolphin, briefly takes up the question of the relationship of history and science, alluding to "the long-standing debate on the nature of history as an art or a science," and to the fact that the results of historical research or investigations "cannot be formulated in strictly scientific terms," but involve "the problem of form and interpretation" (Godolphin 1942, 1:xiii). Set in such a perspective, one may readily accede to the idea that history is anecdotal and must somehow be validated by science to rise to authenticated status, or to the idea that history offers only an "interpreted" account of what happened, not the real thing. In effect, the idea proliferates that history is not something that is or can be accredited in its own right. Yet what better demonstration of the integral worth of history than its testimonials to male-male competition and war? Further still, what better demonstration than its testimonials to human obedience to authority, not only with respect to childhood but with respect to war? Who can argue with the in-the-flesh cooperative obedience that subserves war and without which wars could not be fought? Obedience to authority indeed appears to be a pan-cultural element that grounds the cooperative spirits and deeds vital to male-male competition in war. Military psychiatrist David Marlowe's brief but finegrained and astute historical analyses of wars from the viewpoint of combat and deployment, with special emphasis on the Gulf War on the basis of his own first-hand experiences, strongly attest to the importance of group cohesion. Troops unified by ongoing comradely bonds and by a known and unchanging authority are more skillful and better able to cope with insecurity, tension, and fears than troops lacking cohesion (Marlowe 2001, see especially 73–90; see also a further discussion of his analyses in the Epilogue of the present text). Such military psychiatric studies apart, science cannot replace historical accounts of real-life events that are lived through and that are in fact the bedrock of the information they proffer. History testifies to the human realities of war as it testifies to the human realities of childhood: by way of real-life events that need no validation by science. But most crucially too, history can itself be scientific, not in an experimental sense but in an evolutionary sense. Indeed, such history is essential to human self-understandings because human phylogeny, like human ontogeny, shapes human nature.

Social psychologist Philip Zimbardo's classic Stanford Prison Experiment might appear to substantiate this claim by bringing to life the complexities of "situational power" (Zimbardo, Maslach, and Haney 2000, esp. 204–11). In truth, the experiment does just this, but in a way removed from the way in which its investigators analyze and discuss the experiment, and in fact, removed from the way in which the experiment is interpreted and discussed.[31] As indicated above, the key conceptual element in the experiment is identified by Zimbardo as "situational power"—and by extension, powerlessness. The brief review of the experiment that follows, however, and that is based on Zimbardo's own synopsis of the research, will expose a quite other key element that is in fact not a theoretical construct or framework but a human reality that literally animated the experiment from beginning to end.

A prison was constructed in the basement of a building on the Stanford University campus and was filled with nine prisoners and nine guards, the latter "supplemented by backups on standby call" (199–200). Prisoners and guards were college students selected from an original seventy who applied to be participants in the experiment, which was to last up to two weeks. No behavioral instructions were given to prisoners or guards: "The guards were merely told to maintain law and order, to use their billy clubs as only symbolic weapons and not actual ones, and to realize that if the prisoners escaped the study would be terminated" (200). The first day was "marked by awkwardness between both groups of participants" (200). Several prisoners led a rebellion, however on the second day. Calling in standby guards, the guards "crushed the prisoner rebellion and developed a greater sense of guard camaraderie, along with a personal dislike of some of the prisoners who had insulted them to their face" (200–201). Moreover the guards "generated a psychological tactic of dividing and conquering *their enemies* [italics added] by creating a 'privilege cell' [for cooperative prisoners]." Over the next several days, "the guards steadily increased their coercive and aggressive tactics, humiliation, and dehumanization of the prisoners," and in fact, people in charge of the experiment "had to remind the guards frequently to refrain from such abuses" (201). One prisoner had to be released after 36 thirty-six hours because of suffering seemingly "pathological" effects (201), but prior to his release, he warned the other prisoners that "they would not be allowed to quit the experiment even if they requested it," an assertion that "jolted" the other prisoners, generating absolute conformity in some, but generating also an imitation of "craziness" by some in order to force the experimenters to release them early (201–2). After six days, the experiment was terminated "because too many normal young men were behaving pathologically as powerless prisoners or as sadistic, all-powerful guards" (202). Zimbardo notes that "the immediate impetus for terminating the study came from an unexpected source, a young woman . . . [who] saw the raw, full-blown madness of this place that we all had gradually accommodated to day by day . . . [and who] challenged us to examine the madness . . . that we had created" (203). The woman, Christina Maslach, was not a casual visitor but a social psychologist.

It bears notice that Zimbardo attributes the behaviors of guards and prisoners to prior acculturation, i.e., to "the participants' own experiences with power and powerlessness, of seeing parental interactions, of dealing with authority, and of seeing movies and reading accounts of prison life" (206). In other words, guards and prisoners fell into ready-made social "roles," roles society already furnished them (206). Thus, in a sense comparable to Milgram, but without the latter's more focal emphasis on ontogeny, he sees participant behaviors as originating in some form of prior social conditioning. He states, "Good people can be induced, seduced, initiated into behaving in evil (irrational, stupid, self-destructive, antisocial) ways by immersion in 'total situations' that can transform human nature in ways that challenge our sense of the stability and consistency of individual personality, character, and morality" (206). Though he goes on to recall Nazi concentration guards, "destructive cults," and other "evils" (206), he appears to conceive the real-life value of the experiment to lie mainly in its relationship to actual prison life (207–11). Most importantly, he defends his experiment along with those of Milgram with respect to their "'mundane realism'" (207); that is, countering critics who "deride such research as limited by context-specific considerations," he upholds the experiments as the "psychologically *functional* equivalent of a real-world process or phenomenon" (207). He conceives them to be "naturalistic equivalent[s]" (207). In effect, he would maintain that Maccoby and Jacklin's charge could not be lodged against the Stanford Prison Experiment.

In actuality, the charge could be far more strongly countered were the experiment freed of its conceptual "situational" tethering and its social dynamics more finely consulted. Indeed, three inter-related aspects of the experiment stand out precisely because they are passed over in both Zimbardo's and Maslach's analysis and discussion of the experiment and passed over as well in a further commentary by social psychologist Craig Haney, a co-investigator in the experiment. It is strikingly odd, even incredible, that no one makes mention of the fact that the experiment is an *all-male* experiment; that *a woman*, who is not merely "an outsider," but indeed a female, is the person who sees "the madness"; and that "the madness" is viewed as something *"we had created."*[32] In different ways, each of these aspects veils over the phenomenon of male-male competition. However much experimental research studies on competition commonly fail to correspond to the "naturalistic conditions of the most intense competition," as Maccoby and Jacklin affirm, Zimbardo's classic study in social psychology surely does correspond. The fact that it does, however, is lost because males go unrecognized *as males*. In turn, male behaviors in the experiment are neither perceived in competitive terms nor given any natural historical placement linking them to biological dispositions within human nature, an omission that is particularly remarkable in light of Zimbardo's passing references to a number of wars—e.g., to indoctrination methods of the Korean War and to anti–Vietnam War demonstrations (ibid., 204), to World War II and to "atrocities committed in Bosnia, Kosovo, Rwanda, and Butundi" (206): wars are the cultural embodiment of male-male competition *par excellence*. In short, that prisoners and guards are *males*, and males involved in male-male competition, are facts unmentioned in any documentation of the experiment. When these facts are brought to light, it is immediately evident that Zimbardo and colleagues did not *create* the competitive disposition of prisoners and guards to win out over each other, to dominate each other. That disposition is part of the biological heritage of males and is palpably evident in the behavior of the guards and prisoners. It is thus also evident that battles and struggles for power emanate basically not from "situations" or from "roles" that situations engender, but from male-male competition: their roots are biological, not social.

When we hone in on the social dynamics of the experiment, male-male competition is all but transparent. What more summary demonstration of it than the prisoners' rebellion on the second day of the experiment? Moreover not only do descriptions of the day to day behaviors of prisoners and guards attest to male-male competition—behaviors in which "guards steadily increased their coercive and aggressive tactics, humiliation, and dehumanization of the prisoners" as "observed and documented on videotape" (201)—but an entry in a guard's diary, quoted by Zimbardo, dramatically testifies to it: "During the inspection," the guard writes, "the prisoner . . . grabbed my throat, and although I was really scared, I lashed out with my stick and hit him in the chin" (194). Prisoners and guards clearly vied with one another in sheer physical ways in an attempt to gain power over one another. The competitive social dynamics persisted until prisoners were duly subdued and guards became dominant, a dominance played out in a different dynamics but a dynamics secured and held in place by the undergirding competitive social dynamics. Maslach's description of an "amazing transformation" in a guard's behavior attests to the succeeding social dynamics of dominance. She states that she spoke to the guard early in her visit on the fifth evening of the experiment and found him "very pleasant, polite, and friendly, surely a person anyone would consider a really nice guy" (215). Later in the evening, however, she finds that of all guards on the late-night guard shift, " 'John Wayne' [the nickname given to the guard by the experimenters] . . . was the meanest and toughest of them all. . . . I was absolutely stunned to see that [he] was the 'really nice guy' with whom I had chatted earlier. . . . He was yelling and cursing at the prisoners . . . going out of his way to be rude and belligerent."[33] The "amazing transformation" that Maslach reports is at bottom not the result of "situational power" or even of a difference between male behavior toward females and male behavior toward other males. It is fundamentally the result of male-male competition, a competition previously played out in sheer physicality and daring, and played out now in the subjugating and verbally abusive power of a dominant male. Maslach furthermore provides a striking glimpse of male fascination with, and excitement over the social dynamics of male-male dominance when she recounts what happened later that same night at the time of the prisoners' "bathroom run." She writes, Zimbardo "excitedly told me to look up from some report I had been reading: 'Quick, quick—look at what's happening now! . . . Do you see that? Come on, look—it's amazing stuff!' " (216). Maslach states, "I couldn't bear to look again, so I snapped back with, 'I already saw it!' " (216). What she saw were what she describes as "totally dehumanized" males (216).

In sum, the "mundane realism" of the experiment lies not in "situational power" but in male-male competition and its aftermath in dominance and subjugation.[34] Male-male competition not only initiates the prisoners' rebellion on the second day but is attested to in episodes such as that recorded in the guard's diary, in the fact that a cooperative male bonding was established among the guards as it was among the prisoners when they mounted their rebellion, and in Zimbardo's statement, "It became my job to hold in check the growing violence and arbitrary displays of power of the guards" (194). It is attested to equally but in different and seminally important ways by the fact that guards were "team player[s] . . . conforming to or at least not challenging what seemed to be the emergent norm of dehumanizing the prisoners in various ways" (205) and in Zimbardo's excited observation of males engaged in displays of power and subjugation, displays that testify to a competition no longer being played out but won, and enacted now in displays of dominance.[35] The dehumanizing realities of male-male competition constitute the subtext underlying the whole of the unfolding prison drama—the living events themselves. Male-male competition in the experiment might indeed be described as a nano-exemplification of male-male competition in war: one billionth the evil proportions of the latter, but in essence cut of the same cloth.

The value of identifying male-male competition as the subtext is not to affirm, much less to suggest, that human male-male competition is a predetermined biological program, a genetic built-in of males from which there is no escape, in effect, that human males are irremediably out to dehumanize one another and irremediably wired for war. It is rather to affirm that the pan-culturality of evil warrants both historical and scientific investigation and that male-male competition is undeniably pivotal, the *sine qua non* of the investigative enterprise. It is the essential core not in terms of causes but in terms of origins. As we have seen, innovatively designed experimental studies can give us miniatures of the truths of human nature when elucidated along the lines of natural history, even resonating with an experiential clarity that approximates to phenomenologically informed analyses. What thereby begins to dawn are insights into the nature of fundamental human proclivities without the theoretical and conceptual draperies that define everyday natural attitudes. Such insights into origins can in turn be utilized as points of departure—in more formal phenomenological terms, as transcendental clues—toward understandings of human nature, in the present instance, understandings of the dark underside of human nature, namely, the pan-culturality of evil. Indeed, the relationship between male-male competition and war is for some reason kept under wraps; perhaps it is an embarrassment. Perhaps male-male competition can be culturally recognized only when it occurs in a sports environment where it is sanctioned and even celebrated.[36] History and science, however, clearly have the possibility of exposing it, and in turn, the possibility of contributing to our understandings of the pan-culturality of evil. Male-male competition is written between the lines in histories of war and is palpably evident if unacknowledged in Zimbardo's study. Moreover the truth of its history is apparent not only between the lines but *in* lines themselves. Francisco Goya's riveting artistic depictions of war in the *Desastres* constitute a classic historical text about the brutalities and horrors produced by male-male competition. His artistic renderings of the Peninsular War (1808–14) between the Spanish and the French are akin to Heider and Gardner's study of Dani warfare: both attest to, and are a microcosm of, the pan-culturality of evil. The *banality* of evil is indeed its very pan-culturality. A lack of judgment, a lack of empathy, obedience to authority—all may contribute incisively and even definitively to the banality of evil, but the banality of evil is most fundamentally not an individual but a pan-cultural phenomenon. The biological disposition that makes the doing of evil pan-cultural is what grounds the possibility of an individual's doing evil. Morality is thus an individual matter, as Vetlesen affirms, but its roots lie in human evolutionary history. The pan-culturality of evil is thus a fitting subject for both history and science. It is in fact a pressing subject for both history and science in this twentieth/twenty-first-century globally intermeshed human world. When what is there dispositionally is both vigorously and subtly cultivated, subtly in the name of patriotism, for example, or of an otherwise deficient masculinity, it can gravely impact not just humans but all living beings and the entire planet, menacing habitats and the entire ecology of the earth. Art and cultural historian Robert Hughes succinctly captures this fact in describing Goya's grisly, mutilated bodies and destitute landscapes: "The ruin of the human body is paralleled . . . by what Goya sees inflicted on nature itself. Nature suffers a similar death. . . . The backgrounds to the *Desastres* are pared down to their simplest constituents. . . . This is a landscape without resources. Its physical exhaustion is an emblem of the human moral exhaustion of war" (Hughes 2003, 295).

The pan-culturality of evil is indeed in need of serious study and lessons from that study are in serious need of being learned. Everything earthly hangs in the balance.

NOTES

1. Aggression, as we have seen, subserves competition and dominance, not the reverse. Aggression in other words emanates from competition: it is apparent in the practice of competition and in the striving for dominance, and not the reverse. Dominance itself is not a constitutional disposition any more than aggression is "instinctive"; it results from competition and is thus a key element in and of male-male competition. Aggression may furthermore be readily linked to sheer physicality and excitement, that is to say, to the elemental bodily-felt surges of energy and thrill that go with competition. Finally, although the term "aggression" is used by many researchers and its fundamental basis in male-male competition and dominance overlooked, its proper evolutionary placement in the perspective of male-male competition and dominance is essential to recognize, a fact this text tries firmly to establish.

2. It is notable—and lamentable—that in the 1967 edition of *The Encyclopedia of Philosophy*, there is no entry for Hannah Arendt, although there are entries for Martin Heidegger and Karl Jaspers.

3. A complete analysis of what is pan-cultural in human morality requires a study of empathy, beginning with its ontogeny. The foundations of this phenomenological-empirical study are laid out in Chapter 5.

4. See also across the same two years Ignatieff 1999, Perutz 2000, M. Robinson 2000, Simic 2000, and Urquhart 2000. Books such as Jonathan Glover's *Humanity: A Moral History of the Twentieth Century* (Glover 2000) attest similarly to pan-cultural atrocities: in Rwanda, Cambodia, Hiroshima, and so on.

5. A particular practice within present-day Western science ironically exemplifies the motivation for evil even as its practitioners think of themselves as ridding the world of evil. The inhuman, i.e., *brute*, use of nonhuman animals by humans in research that has no other purpose than to eradicate human disease and thus to prevent humans from suffering and dying was most recently shown to be only 1 to 3.5 percent instructive or effective (Bekoff 2000). Nonetheless, usage not only continues but has recently escalated to include genetic creation (and will likely escalate eventually to genetic breeding). The creation of a genetically engineered rhesus monkey, for example, was applauded as "a first"—by scientists and by the media (see, for example, Milius 2001). The rhesus monkey and all future such rhesus monkeys will serve as "models for research on human diseases" (38). In other words, they will be infected with cancer or afflicted with Parkinson's, Alzheimer's, or any number of other human diseases. Clearly, the banality of evil is not restricted to Nazi practices, nor to human inhumanities to humans alone.

6. These clues are similar to those everyday clues that serve as points of departure—"transcendental clues"—in the practice of phenomenology. The starting point in each case is, as Husserl points out, "the object given 'straightforwardly'" (Husserl 1973, 50).

7. Wrangham and Peterson's comparison is actually between chimpanzees and the Yanomamö. I have generalized their comparison because their specific comparison aims at the generalization. But I have generalized it also because the findings from the anthropological studies of Napoleon Chagnon of the Yanomamö, studies that constitute the foundation of Wrangham and Peterson's comparison, were under investigation as having been in part orchestrated by Chagnon himself. See, for example, Bower 2001.

8. There are in fact two species of *Pan*, the common chimpanzee (*Pan troglodytes*) and the pygmy chimpanzee (*Pan paniscus*), the latter being the smaller species.

"Bonobo" is the preferred name of this species because the animals should be classified "as a fully distinct species, rather than as, so to speak, the poor man's miniature chimp" (de Waal and Lanting 1997, 7).

9. As noted in Chapter 1, in the one instance that Wrangham and Peterson mention a "freshly killed body," they state that they were led to the body by "a party of Kahama males" (Wrangham and Peterson 1996, 14).

10. It is notable that the battles accord with Huizinga's classic account of agonistic encounters as specified and discussed in the previous chapter.

11. The warrior might be thought akin to the earlier mythic hero who risks his life on behalf of his people, but the warrior is a brave man among many, that is, among a contingent of brave men who risk their lives on behalf of their group, tribe, or nation.

12. Many other allusions to the enemy dot Heider's text. Heider speaks of "[t]he only time that a warrior does not look at what his enemy is doing" (Heider 1979, 139), of "the enemy [having] a magical defense post" (143), and of "an intention to overcome or dominate an enemy" (107), for example.

13. "Policemen" were in fact Dutch and Indonesian men who were instrumental in trying to end Dani fighting (Heider 1979, 111–12).

14. See further in this chapter the discussion of Spencer's remarks on subjugation and his code of amity and enmity.

15. Why children should be made to suffer on behalf of the beliefs and dispositions of their parents—and of adult members of their culture generally—is a question that can be asked not only with respect to the Dani, but with respect to long-nourished religious conflicts, ethnic wars, and so on.

The banality of evil is clearly not a contained adult preserve, but affects young children and affects them directly. Indeed, it can affect them physically as well as ideologically and affectively, as the Dani instance indicates. Because of their commonly lesser size and strength, and also because of their commonly lesser status, female children are particularly vulnerable in this respect. As Gardner and Heider comment at one point with respect to funerals, "a male death is more important" (1968, 93).

A further critical aspect is equally obvious. The banality of evil encompasses females, but on an infinitesimally smaller scale and on markedly different motivational grounds than males. It is not sheer physicality and excitement that motivate females toward wanton brutality or violent acts. Mothers who drown their children, for example, or who otherwise kill them or mistreat them are not motivated along such lines. Psychological and psychiatric studies describe such mothers as "disturbed," limning their motivation along distinctively psychological rather than physical lines.

It is also notable that while females do not band together to beat, torture, and mutilate others, they can nonetheless join predominantly male groups for this purpose, playing essential roles in the banality of evil, as the treatment of Iraqi prisoners and of Guantánamo Bay "detainees" by females in the service of the United States Army demonstrates. Yet while females may take on such roles and while they might also be heroic as Joan of Arc and Cleopatra were heroic, they are not trained to be warriors. Indeed, a *real* woman is not tested on the battlefield.

16. Since motives may be personally generated—as with serial killers, snipers, and psychopaths, for example—rather than socially generated, it is obvious that the motivation to hone one's capacity to harm or kill others may stem from personal resentment, rage, or vengeance rather than from social resentment, rage, or vengeance, and, in turn, be restricted to a far smaller number of others. A personal motivation toward the cultivation of evil may thus be distinguished from a social motivation.

Alternatively, however, the personal and the social may conjoin, the social indoctrination of hate and rancor toward a certain group of others, for example, being socially cultivated and internalized as part of one's personal acculturation into society. Thus, while single-person assaults upon others—as, for example, the erratic killings of Charles Whitman in Texas in the 1960s—are different from group assaults, both draw upon something basic in the nature of human nature: feeling power and satisfaction in one's capacity to physically harm or destroy others, and finding in that power and satisfaction the possibility of satisfying other feelings—of hatred and rage, for example, by giving vent to them. Moreover those feelings of hatred and rage may, as shown in Chapter 1, be fueled by an underlying fear. Indeed, fear may be socially manipulated into rage, vengeance, and rancor, and those feelings actively conscripted in the service of national agendas. The motivation to hone one's capacity for evil may indeed be intricately complex.

17. At the end of the epilogue to his book where he voices concern about "the possibility that human nature, or—more specifically—the kind of character produced in American democratic society, cannot be counted on to insulate its citizens from brutality and inhumane treatment at the direction of malevolent authority," Milgram incorporates a memorable quotation from Harold J. Laski's 1919 article in *Harper's Monthly Magazine*: "Civilization means, above all, an unwillingness to inflict unnecessary pain. Within the ambit of that definition, those of us who heedlessly accept the commands of authority cannot yet claim to be civilized men" (Milgram 1973, 189).

18. The overworked problem of converting an *is* into an *ought* constitutes precisely a concern with moral reasoning, a concern that overlooks the essentially affective ground on which morality and moral questions arise in the first place. Harming others is a practice that is first and foremost a bodily phenomenon, a physically injurious assault or impoverishment of some kind that is affectively motivated.

19. Hedges's further comments along these lines merit attention. He states, "Combatants live only for their herd, those hapless soldiers who are bound into their unit to ward off death. There is no world outside the unit. It alone endows worth and meaning. Soldiers will rather die than betray this bond. And there is—as many combat veterans will tell you—a kind of love in this" (Hedges 2002, 40).

20. On the other hand, it is, oddly enough, Ardrey who, even with his recognition that virtually all territorial behavior is vested in the male of the species, does not specifically place the behavior within the realm of male-male competition, competition that indeed takes forms other than territorial, as Ardrey himself specifies when he writes, for example, of the arena behavior of a bowerbird: "Like the male member of any arena species, he competes with other males, by inward compulsion, to achieve status" (Ardrey 1966, 76). Ardrey even speaks at an earlier point of territory and status as "the market places of male competition" (71).

What Ardrey wants to argue in the chapter is that arena behavior is on behalf of the survival of the group, and that seen in this context, male arena displays are directed not toward the winning of females, but toward the achievement of status with respect to other males. The winning of females is, in other words, a by-product of male competitive behavior, not its aim. In support of this claim, Ardrey summarizes zoologist Helmut Buechner's conclusions, drawn from Buechner's study of Uganda kob. The first concluding point is that "[m]ales compete for real estate, never for females. The kob's territorial and sexual appetites are so profoundly intermeshed that fights generate sexual stimulation. The champion whom we watched in a twenty-minute defense of his property had an erection through most of the combat" (51). Moreover in the context of discussing ornithologist C. B. Moffatt's thesis that male displays are to repel other males rather than to attract females, Ardrey writes, "What is eternally bothering the male is not female estimate, but how he is doing in the eyes of his fellows. Many a contemporary school of psychology would regard this as a homosexual tendency. Nature sighs" (55).

21. Spencer's codes of amity and enmity are not commonly cited in the literature of the past fifty years, but as Ardrey recognizes, they are the proper conceptual bedrock

for understanding territorial behavior. Analyses and accounts of human behavior, such as those of LeShan (1992) and Braudy (2003), which recognize the phenomenon of group solidarity against a common enemy, strongly testify to the dual fundamental affective dynamics of human group behaviors identified in Spencer's codes.

22. The verb *exapt* (and noun *exaptation*) comes from "Exaptation—A Missing Term in the Science of Form," by biologists Stephen Jay Gould and Elizabeth Vrba (1982).

23. Wolpoff aligns Morris with Ardrey, but Morris is quite specific about *not* envisioning the naked ape as a killer. In concordance with the observations of Nagel and Kummer (see epigraph, Chapter 3), Morris states, "Defeat is what an animal wants, not murder; domination is the goal of aggression, not destruction, and basically we do not seem to differ from other species in this respect" (see Morris 1967, 143–44).

24. In the same decade that Ardrey and Morris were writing of the evolutionary basis of human aggression, well-known evolutionary biologist John T. Robinson was writing along similar lines, but on the basis of fine-grained analyses of fossil specimens and with no reference to human aggression. He found that in the evolutionary transition from vegetarian ape with sizable canines to carnivorous ape with no specialized dentition came "a premium on tools" and ultimately, "the emergence of *Homo*" (Robinson 1962, 293, 294, respectively). In short, Robinson's fossil-based hypothesis of a shift from a vegetarian diet to a meat-eating or omnivorous diet specifies the need for tools; that is, in the absence of canines and other bodily resources, hunting requires implements for catching and killing prey animals. Extrapolating from Robinson's hypothesis, one can readily see that proficiencies developed in the course of tool-making and tool-using could be co-opted for war-making.

25. As noted in the previous chapter, the only wars fought by females were the fictional wars of the Amazons.

26. Kingdon uses the Latin root or stem form *homin* rather than hominid.

27. This classic text is in large measure developmentally oriented in a solidly detailed ontogenetic sense.

28. It is of interest to note that in no experiment, even the one in which subjects were females, was the "learner" a female. See Milgram's comments (Milgram 1973, 62–63), among which: "It would be especially interesting to place women in the position of authority. Here it is unclear how male subjects and other women would respond to her"; "The women were studied only in the role of teachers [i.e., subjects]. . . . As victims, they would most likely generate more disobedience, for cultural norms militate against hurting women even more strongly than hurting men" (63).

29. Blass comments, "[T]he fact that the same observable behaviors—identical rates of obedience (65%) in men and women in a baseline condition—were accompanied by different levels of nervousness should alert us to the importance of trying to identify the underlying processes involved in acts of obedience and defiance, whether they involve the Milgram paradigm or not" (Blass 2000, 50).

30. See Takooshian regarding Milgram as a researcher: he has "no peer as an inventive researcher"; he is "a social scientific artist whose research illustrates and clarifies human reality using methods we have never encountered before" (Takooshian 2000, 12).

31. In his *Science News* article, ironically titled "To Err Is Human," and in which he discusses both Milgram's and Zimbardo's experiments, science writer Bruce Bower grossly misrepresents the facts. He states that Milgram studied "obedience to a *malevolent* authority figure," that "an experimenter *relentlessly* ordered participants to deliver what they thought were even stronger electrical shocks," and that "[a]s many as 65 percent of participants administered *what they must have thought* were highly painful, and perhaps even lethal, voltages" (Bower 2004, 107; italics added). Bower not only egregiously classifies all experimenters as "malevolent" and conjures what participants "must have thought," but apparently did not read the whole of Milgram's study and

acquaint himself at any depth with the different experimenters, their different reactions to their task, and their different choices of action, all of which aspects of the study would have made for deeper and more complex as well as truer understandings.

32. Maslach presents herself strictly as "an outsider" to the experimental situation (see Maslach's specific account in Zimbardo, Maslach, and Haney 2000, 214–20).

33. Maslach in fact writes of "John Wayne": "With his military-style uniform, billy club in hand, and dark, silver-reflecting sunglasses to hide his eyes [what one might aptly term in a *double entendre* "shades of the Panopticon"], this guy was an all-business, no-nonsense, really mean prison guard" (Zimbardo, Maslach, and Haney 2000, 216).

34. By way of conclusion, it is important too to note in conjunction with what was said earlier of aggression that Zimbardo is in error when he writes of Milgram's experiment that its contribution "was to quantify aggression and thus the extent of obedience" (Zimbardo, Maslach, and Haney 2000, 194). If it quantifies anything, the experiment quantifies obedience and thus the extent of aggression. Subjects were in other words *not* told to be aggressive but to be obedient. Their compliance can in no way be classified as an unprovoked assault, an outlet of frustration, *or* a competitive move; hence, aggression played no part in their behavior.

Zimbardo appears to confuse his own Stanford Prison Experiment with Milgram's obedience experiments. His experiments *are* about aggression, not directly, but as the vehicle by which power is secured and maintained. Subjects in his experiment were directly aggressive—"sadistic" (Zimbardo, Maslach, and Haney 2000, 201, 202, 213). In truth, however, and as has been repeatedly emphasized, aggression subserves competition and dominance, and not the reverse.

35. The remarkably succinct but sterling description of a dominant male macaque that was included as the lead epigraph of Chapter 1 aptly captures the perks of dominance. Just as there is no mistaking a dominant male macaque, so there is no mistaking a dominant male human.

36. Though not terming it such, physiologist-geographer Jared Diamond gives a fascinating account of male-male competition on Easter Island in the form of enormous statues up to thirteen feet high and 500 feet wide that were erected by competing clans. In the course of his review of two recent books on the subject of the statues, he notes that "the excellent quality of Rano Raraku volcanic stone for carving eventually resulted in chiefs competing by erecting statues representing their high-ranking ancestors on rectangular stone platforms," and that about six and a half centuries after the practice was first initiated (circa A.D. 1000 or 1100), "rival clans switched from erecting increasingly large statues to throwing down each others' statues by toppling them onto a slab placed so that the statue's neck would fall on the slab and break" (Diamond 2004, 8, 10, respectively).

# PART II

# 5
# Empathy

> The first thing constituted in the form of community, and the *foundation for all other intersubjectively common things,* is the *commonness of Nature,* along with that [*commonness*] of the *Other's organism and his psychophysical Ego,* as paired with *my own psychophysical Ego.* . . . These two primordial spheres, mine which is for me as ego the original sphere, and his which is for me an appresented sphere—are they not *separated* by an abyss I cannot actually cross, since crossing it would mean, after all, that I acquired an original (rather than an appresenting) experience of someone else? If we stick to our de facto experience, our experience of someone else as it comes to pass at any time, we find that actually the *sensuously seen body* is experienced forthwith as *the body of someone else* and not as merely an indication of someone else. Is not this fact an enigma?
> —EDMUND HUSSERL, *Cartesian Meditations*

I. INTRODUCTION

The phenomenological analysis of empathy that follows constitutes the beginning of an attempt to map fundamental aspects of what Hume would term the "sympathetic" side of humans. Together with the three subsequent chapters—on child's play, trust, and caring—this chapter describes a dimension of human nature that is not an add-on in some sense or other but defines a native human capacity. It is important to underscore the natural ground of these capacities, for they are not uncommonly deemed vague, fuzzy, frivolous, or altogether dispensable and in turn not infrequently underestimated, undervalued, or ignored. So judged and neglected, an awareness of their centrality to a fully resonant human life is straightaway obliterated, and indeed, what presents itself as human is summarily crippled and warped. The significance of these aspects is, on the contrary, essential to the development and realization of a fully resonant human, one capable of opening to both the density of his or her own bodily being and the density of the bodily being of others.

The phenomenological analysis of empathy originates in clues found in Husserl's Fifth Cartesian Meditation. The clues, discussed in an earlier publication (Sheets-Johnstone 1999c; but see Sheets-Johnstone 2006a for emendations), highlight ways in which empathy is generated on the basis of kinetic/tactile-kinesthetic bodies. Their further significance here lies in grounding the claim that empathy is basically a form of sense-making that is rooted in movement. After a brief review of the clues, I turn attention to philosopher Søren Overgaard's perceptive amplifications of Husserl's archival writings on pairing that prominence movement, and offer important clarifications of the nature of kinesthesis. Examinations of infant psychiatrist Daniel Stern's descriptions of affect attunement and his distinction between attunement and empathy follow the clarifications. I proceed to a thoroughgoing elucidation of empathy as a form of sense-making. As preface to that elucidation, a critical point is in order. Husserl speaks of empathy as the ground of a public communal world. Empathy gives us access to the mental acts and processes of others. We know, through empathy, what the feelings and values of others are, what their convictions are, and so on. Through our capacity for empathy, we ultimately share what Husserl describes as an intersubjective world, that is, *a communally intelligible world*. Though the critical point goes unnoticed, it is clear that in empathy, we basically make sense of each other in ways outside language. In this sense-making, movement is our matchpoint (Sheets-Johnstone 1999b).

## II. EARLY CLUES AND HUSSERL'S ARCHIVAL TEXTS

Though in his Fifth Meditation Husserl explains the basis of empathy as resting on pairing and on analogical apperception, he does not offer an extended descriptive analysis of the experience of empathy. He does, however, leave three clues that might lead to such an analysis. In particular, certain unspecified aspects of empathy appear in his reduction of the sense of self to what he terms a "sphere of ownness" (Husserl 1973, 92–99). The first clue turns on the fact that the five characteristics he cites as belonging to the sphere of ownness—fields of sensation, I govern, I cans, self-reflexivity, and psychophysical unity—are all rooted in experiences of our kinetic/tactile-kinesthetic bodies. The second clue has to do with similarity. Husserl speaks of similarity as undergirding my pairing of myself with others, ostensibly tying similarity simply to formal appearance, but intimating a similarity in kinetic dynamics by references to a person's *style* and *conduct*. Such references indicate that a similarity in dynamics as well as form binds me to others in a common humanity and even in a common creaturehood, and this because others present themselves as *animate,* and in their animation, move in ways dynamically similar to the ways in which I move. Again, we are pointed in the direction of kinetic/tactile-kinesthetic bodies. The third clue has to do with harmoniousness. Husserl speaks of "harmonious behavior," "harmonious systems," and "harmonious verification," all in the context of explaining the analogical in analogical apperception. He gives no extended example of harmoniousness, though he remarks, for example, that "the outward conduct of someone who is angry or cheerful . . . I easily understand from my own conduct under similar circumstances" (120), and that when someone behaves in a discordant manner, we regard that someone as a "pseudo-organism" (114). If we take harmoniousness as a clue, however, we are readily led to a kinetic dynamics. In other words, at the most basic level of analysis, harmoniousness points us not toward *behaviors* as such but toward movement; it refers to a *kinetic,* not a behavioral attribute. In effect, we are led once again to kinetic/tactile-kinesthetic bodies.

On the basis of his readings of Husserl's archival texts on intersubjectivity, Overgaard shows how Husserl prominences movement in attempting to elucidate the nature of pairing. By calling attention to this prominencing of movement, Overgaard sizably enriches our understanding of Husserl's analysis in the Fifth Meditation. His exegetical aim is not to explicate intersubjectivity, but to answer to the question of how pairing is possible to begin with. His amplifications of Husserl's texts, however, are of considerable import for the former enterprise, for they show—not explicitly but in a readily discernible manner—that Husserl approaches the problem of pairing from a direction essentially different from that in the Meditations. Rather than the problem of pairing being a problem of *the other body*, it is a problem of *my body*. In other words, what Husserl attempts to pinpoint in his archival investigations of intersubjectivity is not how the other body is a lived body but how my body is "a physical, spatial body," that is, an object in the world. As Overgaard shows, "Husserl . . . reaches the insight that kinesthetic, 'subjective' movement must at the same time be 'objective' (physical, spatial) movement," that "the 'internal' and the 'external' of my movement are inseparably realized (*verwirklicht*) as one." Overgaard tells us that Husserl "sometimes underscores [this conclusion] by saying that "the kinesthetic movement brings with it *its* external side, and that the kinesthesis itself *is* the spatial movement" (Overgaard 2003, 63).

Overgaard's illumination of how pairing could even get started, in essence answering the question of what motivates it, vindicates Husserl's notion of pairing at the same time that it deepens our understanding of it by focusing attention on self-movement and what it reveals. Phenomenological understandings of self-movement nonetheless remain incomplete. They remain incomplete because the phenomenon of self-movement is under-examined, specifically in terms of what Husserl and Overgaard term "kinesthetic movement." From a phenomenological perspective "kinesthetic movement" can only mean the actual experience of one's own movement, an experience, we might note, that is readily accessible to any human even if readily passed over by many. An examination of the experience reveals not only the fact that any movement creates its own qualitative dynamics, including specifically *spatial* dynamics, i.e., directional and areal qualities, but that the mover has the possibility of experiencing space in an objective sense in any act of moving merely by paying attention to the three-dimensionality of his or her movement. There is thus no reason for "musts," as in the above statement, "'subjective' movement *must* at the same time be 'objective' (physical, spatial) movement"; or, for example, in the statement, "there is a way in which my movement can and indeed *must* have the status of an external movement for me" (64; italics added). "Musts" are properly replaced by descriptive accounts of kinesthetic/kinetic experience, that is, by a bona fide phenomenology of self-movement. A phenomenological examination of kinesthetic/kinetic experience readily shows that both spatial qualities and three-dimensionality are manifest in self-movement. In effect, any movement I make creates a certain qualitative dynamic in virtue of its spatial qualities and is at the same time a three-dimensional happening.[1]

Perceiving my movement as a three-dimensional happening, i.e, perceiving myself moving in a three-dimensional expanse, is *not* contingent on vision. Movement has both an "inner" and an "outer" that is directly experienced (or experience-able) in movement itself. Indeed, it is inherently spatial in the double sense that when I move, I kinesthetically feel a certain qualitative spatial dynamics—curved, jagged, twisted, straight, constricted, confined, expansive, open, and so on—and perceive the three-dimensional reality of my movement. (We might note in passing phenomenologists' dedicated attention to the double sense of touch—"the touching and the touched"—and their remarkably blindered and consequentially far-reaching neglect of the double sense of movement.)

When I hammer a nail, for example, I experience space objectively in the three-dimensional expanse in and through which my downward-arcing arm moves, and at the same time experience a certain qualitative spatial dynamic; when I scratch my head, I experience space objectively in the form of the three-dimensional expanse through which my arm moves in traveling to my head, and at the same time experience a certain linearly reiterative spatial dynamic in the movement of my fingers back and forth on my head. Correlative spatial experiences obtain with any other so-called "kinesthetic movement." There would in fact be no space—no objective "out there"—short of movement; there would be no concept of space or of being "in space" to begin with. The concept derives from movement. It is anchored in kinesthetic/kinetic experience, specifically in the dual experience of a qualitative spatial dynamic and the three-dimensionality of movement.

The problem of trying to get my movement "in space" is thus a pseudo-problem when the experience of self-movement is phenomenologically examined and understood. We are alerted to this understanding even by neurophysiologists. In *Scientific Bases of Human Movement*, Barbara Gowitzke and Morris Milner state, "The voluntary contribution to movement is almost entirely limited to initiation, regulation of speed, force, range, and direction, and termination of the movement" (Gowitzke and Milner 1988, 193). Though their way of putting the matter is negative because of their central focus on what is neurophysiologically transpiring in self-movement, that is, on what is involuntary rather than voluntary, their straightforward acknowledgment of range and direction (among other facets of movement) leaves no doubt but that movement is inherently spatial and, being voluntary, is open to experiential investigation. In the present instance, the challenge is to flesh out the nature of that spatiality as it enters into the constitution of intersubjectivity; in particular, it is to show precisely, through a phenomenological analysis of movement, how it is that "the kinesthesis itself *is* the spatial movement." Further clarifications—or perhaps better, admonishments—warrant mention in the context of this challenge.

Overgaard remarks that "[s]ome of [Husserl's] most fascinating reflections center on the ... notion of something appearing 'there', in near- and far-perspectives," and that "[t]here would be no space, and nothing at all would appear 'out there', according to Husserl, if I myself—with my kinesthetic movements—did not move *in* space" (Overgaard 2003, 62). Ironically, the concern with "here" and "there," and with "near" and "far" leads one to conceive of pairing in static rather than dynamic spatial terms. In fact, the common understanding of empathy in terms of "here" and "there," i.e., my *imagining* myself there where the other is, is grounded in static images. Movement is implied but precisely not prominenced in the foundationally dynamic way it should be prominenced, "should" not out of theoretical or explanatory necessity, but in recognition of the fact that movement *is* in fact central, quintessentially so. The same is true of "near" and "far": space is implied by way of movement, and movement is itself merely implied. Moreover the very words—"here," "there," "near," "far"— take for granted the very *space* they want to instantiate and document by way of experience. This may well be because space itself is already construed as a static container, a holder of things that are "here" or "there", "near" or "far." Husserl's conclusion—that "the kinesthesis itself *is* the spatial movement"—is from this perspective less a point of arrival than a point of departure for a phenomenological analysis of self-movement that would do justice to the dynamics of pairing and in turn ground the dynamic underpinnings of intersubjectivity and empathy.

Furthermore, in following through on that phenomenological analysis of self-movement, the sphere of ownness that Husserl describes would be properly augmented to include feelings. Feelings are a vital dimension of the sphere of ownness.[2] As Freud rightly observed, we have both sensations and feelings "from within" (Freud 1955, 19). But it is important that we distinguish between the two. In particular, we do not have *sensations* of movement—as we have sensations of touch or smell, or as we might say we have sensations of light and of sound; we have *feelings* of movement, just as we have motivational feelings—urges and impulsions—and affective feelings. The assumption that we have sensations of movement distorts the dynamic reality of self-movement. The terminological problem is complex. The common distinction between sensation and perception commonly rests on a distinction between inner and outer: whatever the modality of objects sensed "out there" in the world, we have *perceptions* of them; whatever the modality of objects sensed in our bodies we have *sensations* of them. The sensation/perception distinction, however, does not hold when it comes to self-movement. Self-movement is not sensational like pains, itches, a scratchy throat, and so on. Sensations are not dynamic events but punctual ones having no inherent connection or flow. Movement is in contrast an *unfolding dynamic event*, and as such, demands close analysis and elucidation in its own right. We in fact have *perceptions* of movement as well as *feelings* of movement, precisely in terms of our double spatial sense of movement: we perceive our movement as a kinetic three-dimensional happening; we feel the qualitative dynamics of our movement kinesthetically.[3] It is notable in this respect that in the Fifth Meditation, Husserl remarks that empathy is through and through "indicated somatically," even to "the *'higher psychic sphere'* " (Husserl 1973, 120). As shown earlier by way of clues in the Fifth Meditation, he could equally say that everything is indicated somatically in the sphere of ownness. In both instances, it is not merely a question of a body, but of a body-in-movement. Husserl's further statement underscores this very point: "Higher psychic occurrences," he observes, "diverse as they are and familiar as they have become, have furthermore their style of synthetic interconnexions and take their course in forms of their own, which I can understand associatively on the basis of my empirical familiarity with the style of my own life" (120). Whether put in terms of *style* or *conduct*—or in terms of "I govern" or psychophysical unity or self-reflexivity, as in the sphere of ownness—the core phenomenon is not simply a body but a *moving* body. Accordingly, we should be considering not intersubjectivity and *embodiment*, the latter a thoroughly static concept like sensations, but intersubjectivity and *animation*, a dynamic concept proper to the phenomenon being investigated and described.[4]

Given the foregoing phenomenological findings and clarifications, we can show how infant psychiatrist Daniel Stern's descriptive account of affect attunement resonates with Husserl's notion of harmoniousness, but take into serious account too Stern's distinction between attunement and empathy. On this basis, we can proceed to show how a kinetic dynamics mediates across sense modalities, and how in doing so, accords not only with Stern's descriptive illustrations of mother-infant attunement, but with Aristotle's seminal notion of movement as a *sensu communis*. Following this path will furthermore lay the ground for examining the relationship between the kinetic and the affective. In particular, it will allow us to show how a dynamic congruency obtains between the kinetic and the affective, and how cognitive understandings enter into the congruent dynamics of both attunement and empathy via recognition of the dynamics themselves.

## III. AFFECT ATTUNEMENT AND THE QUALITATIVE NATURE OF MOVEMENT

Stern's descriptions of infant-mother affect attunement implicitly testify to a dynamics that is kinetically articulated. His later identification of intensity, timing, and shape as primary dimensions of attunement further testify to that kinetically articulated dynamics, as for example, when he describes how a mother's "prosodic contour" matches her child's "facial-kinetic contour," and how an infant's up-and-down rattle-shaking prompts his mother to an up-and-down head movement that keeps "a tight beat with her son's arm motions" (Stern 1985, 141). As Stern points out, attunement is not an imitative phenomenon; the modality of the infant is not that of the mother. Rather, he says, "some form of [cross-modal] matching is going on" (141). In trying to spell out the nature of that cross-modal matching in a later section on the unity of the senses, he observes that "shape, intensity, and time can all be perceived amodally" (154). In this context, he recalls Aristotle's notion of a common sense that is not tied to any particular modality, but he does not connect attunement specifically to motion as a common sensible; he merely mentions motion as one of the common sensibles specified by Aristotle. In short, Stern comes close to realizing that movement is at the heart of affect attunement, that it is our original and abiding intersubjective matchpoint, but he is more interested in affirming the unity of the senses, and attunement as an instance of that unity—along with synaesthesia—than he is in finding the key to the unity, a key that, ironically, is as palpably present in his fine-grained descriptions of affect attunement as in his identification of intensity, timing, and shape as its defining dimensions.

From a Husserlian perspective, it is notable that Stern concludes the section on the unity of the senses by stating, "The point of this discussion about the unity of the senses is that the capacities for identifying cross-modal equivalences that make for a perceptually unified world are the same capacities that permit the mother and infant to engage in affect attunement to achieve affective intersubjectivity" (156). In phenomenological terms, our capacity for cross-modal equivalences is a constitutional capacity, the foundation of both a coherent objective world and an intersubjectively paired one. It is not surprising, then, that Stern's descriptions and discussions of affect attunement complement Husserl's concept of harmoniousness: they give the concept concrete exemplification in experience even as they fall short of identifying the unifying key of the basic capacity. Intensity, timing, and shape are basically and originarily not dimensions of attunement, but dimensions of movement; they are integrally related dynamic aspects of movement and become dimensions of attunement only by way of movement. In short, what is essential to both attunement and harmoniousness is pairing by way of a kinetic dynamic. Attunement and harmoniousness are rooted alike in the capacity to feel and to perceive movement as a dynamic happening, and in turn, in Stern's words, to *"achieve"* an affective intersubjective world through attunement (156), in Husserl's words, to *constitute* an intersubjective world through harmonious pairing.

We should perhaps emphasize that the experience of a kinetic dynamics is neither an idiosyncratic form of movement experience nor an experiential feat to be mastered, but a kinetic matter of fact: movement *creates* a kinetic dynamic because movement—any movement—creates its own space, time, and force. That it does so—that it creates a particular spatio-temporal-energic patterning—is what allows cross-modal matching and thereby affect attunement to take place. Stern's descriptions of mothers *creating* a kinetic dynamic analogous to the one their infants create exemplify the kinetically founded relationship. Affect attunement may indeed be phenomenologically described as a form of harmonious pairing. As described in "Re-Thinking Husserl's Fifth Meditation," where harmony is evident, *"intercorporeal harmonies are livingly present"* (Sheets-Johnstone 1999c, 102).[5] Affect attunements are just such livingly present intercorporeal harmonies. Intercorporeal harmonies, on the other hand, may be, but are not limited to, just such affect attunements. Given its genesis in ontogeny, however, affect attunement is a primordial form of intercorporeal harmony and hence constitutes a primordial form of harmonious pairing.[6]

Recognition of the intercorporeal dynamics undergirding affect attunement opens the possibility of fleshing out the connection between the kinetic and the affective. His richly kinetic descriptions notwithstanding, Stern does not make explicit the dynamic concordance between movement and affect not only because he conceives attunement in terms of cross-modal equivalences and the unity of the senses, but because he conceives what he clinically observes in terms of behavior rather than movement: behavior is the external or overt phenomenon; feeling is the internal or inner phenomenon. Thus, for example, he explains attunement in contrast to imitation as "referencing the inner state rather than the overt behavior" (Stern 1985, 142 n. 1), and later speaks of how "mirroring" and "echoing" "represent attempts to grapple with the issue of one person reflecting another's inner state" (144). Clearly, the issue cannot be resolved by appeal to behavior, but can only be resolved by way of movement, the dynamic phenomenon itself, and by recognition of the dual nature of the experience of movement as a kinesthetic/kinetic phenomenon. In effect, resolution of the issue mandates phenomenological understandings of self-movement. On the basis of these understandings, it is possible to elucidate how movement bodies forth affectivity, precisely as a mother's "prosodic contours" affectively body forth the affectively charged "facial-kinetic contours" of her infant. In default of this elucidation, affect remains something totally "within," i.e., devoid of connection to anything "without." Again, we can appreciate the necessity of focusing attention not on a *behaving* body or on an *embodying* body, but on a veritable *animate* and *animated* body, and in turn, undertaking a phenomenological analysis of movement. The following sketch should suffice to show the relevance of such an analysis to understandings of affect attunement, and ultimately, of how empathy develops as an outgrowth of affect attunement on the basis of its shared origin in kinetically dynamic pairings.[7]

The formal dynamics of movement are articulated in and through the qualities of movement as they are created in the act of moving. Even a sneeze has a certain formal dynamic in which certain suddennesses and suspensions of movement are felt aspects of the experience. The aspects are qualitative features of movement. A phenomenological analysis of movement discloses four primary qualities: tensional, linear, areal, and projectional (Sheets-Johnstone 1966 [1979/1980], 1999b). We might note that in a quite general sense, intensity is coincident with tensional quality, timing with projectional quality, shape with linear and areal qualities. In other words, Stern's defining dimensions of attunement coincide in broad terms with phenomenological findings. Primary qualities of movement, however, are open to a far more detailed and coherent analysis, and this because movement is a complexly integrated dynamic phenomenon. Linear quality, for example, encompasses both the linear design and linear pattern of a moving body, its forward diagonality in walking against a strong wind, for instance, its zig-zag trajectory in avoiding obstacles along the way. Moreover the complexity of linear quality is greater than these simple examples of design and pattern indicate. A moving body carves multiple lines simultaneously. Walking against the wind, a body tilts forward as a whole against it, but at the same time, arms are swinging, legs are striding, and in so doing, make linear designs and linear patterns of their own. The synthesis of primary qualities in any actual movement is similarly complex, significantly so, and is describable in far more detail than might ordinarily be supposed, as we will presently see in describing an emotion as it is actually experienced.

Before proceeding to this descriptive account, a beginning clarification is apposite concerning the relationship between attunement and empathy. Stern observes that both attunement and empathy "[start] with an emotional resonance," but that attunement "takes the experience of emotional resonance and automatically recasts that experience into another form of expression" (1985, 145). He affirms in fact that attunement "occur[s] largely out of awareness and almost automatically," while empathy "involves the mediation of cognitive processes" (145). In this general categorical way, he distinguishes between attunement and empathy. Although the distinction might appear intuitively tenable, it requires finer examination and specification; in other words, while we might agree with Stern that affect attunement shares features with empathy but is not equivalent to empathy, we need finer understandings of their similarities and differences. Indeed, by turning closer attention to similarities and differences, we have the possibility of acceding to understandings of how affect attunement as a primordial form of harmonious pairing opens out into empathy through more and more complex forms of harmonious pairing. In turn, we have the possibility of a keener grasp of continuities in *the development of intersubjectivity* and indeed a keener grasp of the structure and increasing complexity of intersubjective experience. To arrive at this possibility, it is necessary first to show how a dynamic congruity obtains between emotion and movement, or, in Sternian terms, to broaden and in turn deepen understandings of the "emotional resonance" that, according to Stern, grounds both attunement and empathy.

IV. EMOTIONS AND MOVEMENT

Previous research setting forth a beginning empirical-phenomenological analysis of the relationship between emotion and movement (Sheets-Johnstone 1999a) began with a summary and discussion of three psychiatric-psychological studies of emotion, showing how each study, though differently focused and employing a different methodology, specifies an intimate relationship between emotion and movement. The summary and discussion were followed by two descriptions of fear, one by a well-known ethologist (Konrad Lorenz), the other by a well-known novelist (William Faulkner), *fear* being chosen because it is both a common emotion and an exceptionally well-researched one. It was notable that both descriptions relied pivotally on kinetic terms—e.g., "hurried," "anxious" movements, "hesitant" movements, stop-and-start movements, "surging," "springing," "scrambling" movements—to capture the experience of fear. Finally, a phenomenological description of fear was presented that took as its context the experience of being pursued by an unknown assailant at night in a deserted area of a city. The experience was described as follows:[8]

> An intense and unceasing whole-body tension drives the body forward. It is quite unlike the tension one feels in a jogging run, for instance, or in a run to greet someone. There is a hardness to the whole body that congeals it into a singularly tight mass; the driving speed of the movement condenses airborne and impact moments into a singular continuum of motion. The head-on movement is at times erratic; there are sudden changes of direction. With these changes, the legs move suddenly apart, momentarily widening the base of support and bending at the knee so that the whole body is lowered. The movement is each time abrupt. It breaks into an otherwise unrelenting and propulsive speed of movement. The body may suddenly swerve, dodge, twist, duck, or crouch, and the head may swivel about before the forward plunging run with its acutely concentrated and unbroken energies continues.

The phenomenological account reveals in greater detail what the psychiatric-psychological studies and descriptive accounts of fear reveal: that a dynamic congruency obtains between the kinetic and the affective and that *emotions move us*. In classical terms, they move us to move toward or away or against. Spatio-temporal-energic qualities of movement weave together an ongoing kinetic form that is dynamically congruent with the form of ongoing feelings. Whether a matter of fear, sadness, joy, disgust, shame, or whatever, emotions first and foremost motivate us to move. When they move us, we move in ways we are moved to move. There is not an identity but a formal dynamic congruency between the kinetic and the affective. Unified by a congruent dynamics, the two modes of experience are simultaneous; they are temporally conjoined.

That emotions move us to move and in ways dynamically congruent to their own energies is borne out by the evolutionary studies of emotion by biologist Manfred Wimmer. At the most primitive level of life, Wimmer observes, "disturbances and motoric pattern are combined in a unit" (Wimmer 1995, 43). "Primary emotion" is thus equivalent to disturbances of homeostasis and prompts "motoric action" (43). Wimmer observes further that "the unit "becomes segregated at higher levels of organisation" (43). He describes in particular how initial "kinesis reactions" in unicellular organisms undergo an evolutionary shift toward differentiation in "taxis reactions," reactions that are both stimuli-determined and internally determined, and cites as an example the differentiated behavior of a turbellarian worm: a hungry one "will move towards the feeding site, while the 'satiated' organism does not react" (43). Wimmer emphasizes, however, that the differentiated response is always tethered to the organism's internal state, hence—in Wimmer's adopted Piagetian vocabulary—to "centration" (44). His evolutionary thesis of the origin of emotion thus affirms that whatever the degree of development of an organism's differentiated response, i.e., whatever the degree of development of its *cognitive processes*, its response remains tethered to its internal state. In effect, emotions move us to move and in ways consonant with their own internal energies or dynamics.[9]

Psychiatrist Luc Ciompi's construct of affect-logic resonates in similarly complementary ways. Ciompi's psycho-socio-biological approach to the understanding and treatment of schizophrenia underscores the integrative way in which emotions shape what we do: they are "motivating and mobilizing" forces, having "major energizing . . . effects on cognition." They are furthermore pivotal in organizing cognitions—for example, with respect to attention and memory (Ciompi 1997, 161).[10] Of further interest is Ciompi's utilization of concepts in nonlinear dynamics to explain breaks in psychic functioning, that is, breaks in the constellations of affect-logic that structure and inform normal everyday lives— "fear-logic," "anger-logic," "sadness-logic," "happiness-logic," and so on (162)—and that structure and inform pathological lives no less. Explaining psychotic breaks by way of nonlinear dynamics, Ciompi writes that "Clinically, as well as theoretically, it seems very likely that unspecific emotional tensions (such as those created in a vulnerable individual, e.g., by 'high expressed emotions', or by other psychosocial or biological stressors) function in mental systems as relevant control parameters which, when modified to a critical point, are capable of provoking a nonlinear shift to psychosis" (166). Clearly, Ciompi conceives "mental systems" dynamically. Though the dynamic congruency of the affective and the kinetic goes unrecognized, it is implicit in his descriptive account of how "overall feeling-thinking-behaving patterns" can shift suddenly in nonlinear ways as a result of "strong emotions" (Wimmer and Ciompi 1996, 43) that propel an individual toward a distinctively different but still normal mode of feeling-thinking-behaving or, in pathologically disposed individuals, toward psychosis. Indeed, basic to his thesis of psychic functioning is the idea that "'integrated feeling-thinking-behaving programs' . . . develop through action" (37). In affect-logic-*kinetic* terms—terms that justly describe in a complete way "feeling-thinking-behaving programs"—one would say that "strong emotions" and various forms of stress can trigger sudden shifts in everyday "affect-logic-kinetic programs," veering a person toward a radically different way of being kinetically in the world, even to the point of schizophrenia. In short, while Ciompi's "programs" are conceived in behavioral (or action) terms, self-movement is clearly at their core, engendered in the very idea of emotions being "motivating and mobilizing" forces, i.e., forces that move us to move. As Ciompi himself pointedly affirms, "[A]ctions without emotions do not exist" (41).

Neurologist Antonio Damasio's conception of how emotions evolved expands the framework of complementary perspectives along further lines. Damasio ties emotion at its inception to what amount to "kinesis reactions," thereby complementing Wimmer's evolutionary thesis. He ties emotion at a later evolutionary stage to cognition and action in ways that complement Ciompi's thesis of affect-logic. His tenuous distinction between emotion and feeling aside, we readily discern the two complementary strands in the following remark: "The first device, emotion, enabled organisms to respond effectively but not creatively to a number of circumstances conducive or threatening to life—'good for life' or 'bad for life' circumstances, 'good for life' or 'bad for life' outcomes. The second device, feeling, introduced a mental alert for the good or bad circumstances and prolonged the impact of emotions by affecting attention and memory lastingly . . . [leading] to the emergence of foresight and the possibility of creating novel, nonstereotypical responses" (Damasio 2003, 80). Damasio's concept of the origin and evolution of emotion clearly underscores the basic "motivating and mobilizing" energies of emotion, affirming that emotions do indeed move us to move. Moreover when he writes that "In the beginning was emotion, but at the beginning of emotion was action" (80), he again echoes Wimmer's evolutionary thesis and Ciompi's psychiatric one, but in reverse so to speak, calling attention to the essentially *responsive* rather than essentially *motivating* significance of emotion, in other words, calling attention to the fact that *the original telos* of emotions was—and still is—to move us to move. In so doing, he implicitly acknowledges the dynamic bond between the affective and the kinetic. Indeed, he acknowledges in reverse fashion Ciompi's affirmation: "[A]ctions without emotions do not exist.

When we translate the affective-kinetic bond reflected in the initial thesis and its complementary perspectives into Stern's language of attunement and empathy, we readily find an "emotional-*kinetic* resonance." Emotional resonance—"the resonance of feeling state" (Stern 1985, 145)—is kinetically manifest. It is kinetically manifest in the intersubjective accordances of attunement and empathy just as it is kinetically manifest in "kinesis reactions" and "taxis reactions," in hurried and anxious movements, in scrambling movements, in swerving and twisting movements, and so on. In a word, emotions move us to move in shared experiences with others no less than they do in unshared individual experiences. In empathy, however, emotional resonance is not—to use Stern's term—"recast" (142 n. 1); that is, it is not reconfigured kinetically into a different sense modality as in attunement. In fact, in empathy bodily movements tend to be similar. In empathizing with someone in grief, for example, one similarly sinks heavily downward, perhaps also moving one's hand to one's brow and closing one's eyes; in empathizing with someone in joy, one similarly moves expansively, perhaps also raising one's arms overhead and punctuating that expansiveness with a clap of the hands. The resemblant kinetics are dynamically congruent with affect in the same way that the modally differentiated bodily kinetics of attunement are dynamically congruent: in both instances we find a ready validation of the dynamic congruency between affect and movement; in both instances, we move in ways we are moved to move. In empathizing with another person, however, we move in ways that tend to resemble the kinetic ways of that person not only because kinetic dynamics are congruent with affective dynamics, but because both kinetic and affective dynamics spring from a common human evolutionary heritage even as they are elaborated along the lines of particular cultural traditions. In other words, elemental forms of harmonious intercorporeal pairing reach back to infancy and beyond, to a common primate heritage. Because they do, a phenomenological account of intersubjectivity must ultimately reach back through phenomenologically informed readings of empirical literature, tracing out those relational ways of moving and feeling that our common evolutionary lineage defines and that cultural traditions inflect and temper.[11] Only through these readings can the phenomenology of intersubjectivity avoid a simple "mirroring" or "motor mimicry" explanation of similarity—of a resemblant kinetics—in empathy; that is, only through these readings can the phenomenology of intersubjectivity describe how affective intercorporeal harmonies of empathy have their origin in a human repertoire of movement and affect such that what is intercorporeally articulated is articulated dynamically along similar kinetic lines.[12]

## V. SPONTANEITY

That the harmonious pairing movements of empathy are *spontaneous*, just as they are spontaneous in the ontogenetically earlier intersubjective phenomenon of attunement, is of primary significance. Stern's description of attunement as "occurring largely out of awareness and almost automatically" is—or can be—misleading in this respect. Neither the expressed kinetic dynamics of attunement nor those of empathy are mechanical reactions performed unconsciously or executed on the basis of habit. The kinetic dynamics are in each instance spontaneous responses that are volitional in the sense of being *motivated:* the individual is precisely *moved* to move.[13] Whatever the flow of movement, it is not planned, thought about, or selected in advance, but is the result of affective-kinetic-cognizing awarenesses. As such, it makes sense. One might indeed speak of a bodily logos (Sheets-Johnstone 1990) or, as above, of an affect-logic-kinetic, both terms centering attention in different ways on the disposition and aptitude of animate forms to move spontaneously in ways that make sense. The implications of kinetic spontaneity in attunement and empathy are thus sizable and the necessity of deepening understandings of spontaneity along the lines of a bodily logos—along the lines of sense-making—is as requisite as broadening understandings through investigations into evolutionary affective-kinetic repertoires and cultural groomings. Indeed, the deepening and broadening lines converge in an evolutionary semantics (Sheets-Johnstone 1990, 1999b, 1999d) or biosemiotics (Hoffmeyer 1996), interdisciplinary areas of study that, as we shall see, highlight both the responsivity of animate forms and the way in which animate forms are primed for meaning to begin with, that is, how they are disposed to make sense spontaneously in the double sense of sense-making: making intelligible and creating meaning.

Just such spontaneous sense-making is not only palpably present in Stern's descriptions of affect attunement, but might well be elaborated by infant and mother alike in ways that give rise to more complex intercorporeal pairings. Consider, for example, that affect attunement is not necessarily limited to, or by, a mother's response. While a mother's spontaneous kinetic response in essence constitutes the attunement in each of Stern's experimental studies and descriptions of attunement, the experience of the infant is of moment in its own right, and this beyond the fact that, as the first criterion for treating an interaction as an attunement, the infant "[make] some affective expression," and as the third criterion, the infant see, hear, or feel the mother's response (Stern 1985, 147). In particular, an infant might do more than "[make] some affective expression" and perceive the mother's response: it might respond in turn. Attunement might, in effect, continue beyond the experimental protocol, generating a more complex pairing. An infant might, for example, spontaneously respond to its mother not only by repeating its movements but by increasing their intensity, by slowing them down or speeding them up, by making them bigger or smaller, by making movements similar to its mother's, by transposing the same kinetic dynamics to a totally new modality, and so on. Indeed, though Stern's experimental protocol understandably requires a clean stopping point—"Entry criteria were set up to identify points at which to jump into the stream of interaction. . . . When an event meeting these criteria was viewed, the videotape was stopped and the questions were asked" (147)—there is no reason to think any "stream of interaction" would actually end coincident with the protocol. The "roles" of infant and mother might thus be reversed in a continuing interaction, the infant being the one to constitute an attunement by spontaneously creating a complementary kinetic dynamic, one that reiterates the original or offers a harmonious embellishment upon it. Not only this but in creating a complementary dynamic, the infant would offer its mother a further opportunity to respond, whether in a spontaneously comparable or more complex dynamic. Attunement might thus conceivably take the form of turn-taking, an elemental dyadic form of interaction that one prominent infant researcher describes as the distinguishing feature of intersubjectivity: "Intersubjectivity is expressed in different ways and makes use of different behaviors, but its hallmark is turn taking" (Bloom 1993, 74).

Turn-taking is in fact a well-researched and commonly studied phenomenon in linguistic (and linguistically conceived) infant-mother interactions. Its reality as a non-linguistic, i.e., *kinetic*, phenomenon goes largely unnoticed, and this in good measure because movement is commonly submerged in thoughts and talk of behavior.[14] In consequence, that movement is our original and abiding mother tongue—as affect attunement and empathy show—that it is indeed our original and abiding matchpoint with the world (Sheets-Johnstone 1999b; see also Spitz 1983, Bower 1971) goes unrecognized. Equally unrecognized is its spontaneity: movement flows forth in attunements between infants and mothers and in empathic affective moments from joy to grief with neither proddings nor promptings. The possibility of spontaneous ongoing attunements—kinetic turn-takings or dialogues-in-movement—is in fact of considerable importance in showing a developmental continuity from affect attunement to empathy. Through just such spontaneous ongoing harmonious pairings, an infant itself can open the door to further possibilities of attunement, and in the process, to the possibility of developing its capacity for more and more complex pairings. An indication of these developmental possibilities is implicit in psychologist Andrew Whiten's study of early infant-mother interactions in which responses that a mother and infant make to each other alternately are considered a "turn" (Whiten 1977, 415). Whiten makes no mention of spontaneity, but the "turns" he identifies are clearly spontaneous: no one enters into the interactions urging mother or infant to move in any way, whether to touch, smile, laugh, or vocalize in response to the other; neither mother nor infant are following a manual, a guide to forging intersubjective relations, as it were; and so on. The fact that the maximum number of turns in a response sequence increases from the time an infant is one month old to the time it is four months old—from 0.8 to 2.3 to 4.0 to 6.8 (414–18)—testifies to the development of more complex pairings; that is, infant and mother are responding to each other mutually and successively. Given the increase in turns and their relatively rapid chronological development, one can readily understand how turn-taking might spontaneously develop within an affect attunement and similarly result in more complex spontaneous intercorporeal pairings. One can readily understand too how these more complex spontaneous intercorporeal pairings might provide the spawning ground of empathy.

The challenge in concretizing and substantiating these dual understandings is to start from scratch: from the bodily logos or affect-logic-kinetic of infancy rather than from assumption-laden adultist perspectives that appeal to theory or invoke entities to explain human behavior in advance of describing "the things themselves." Indeed, a constructive phenomenology is called for to elucidate on the basis of pairing how empathy is a spontaneous outgrowth of affect attunement. Such a phenomenology would bring to light ontogenetic continuities, continuities that need investigation no less than phylogenetic ones. In fact, the relationship of the one history to the other is in need of elucidation, not that ontogeny *repeats* phylogeny, but that ontogeny carries forward affective-kinetic patterns that are evolutionarily given, patterns such as smiling, turning toward, turning away, reaching for, and so on.[15]

A further aspect of spontaneity is of critical significance in this context. In affect attunement as in empathy, it is the responding individual who solidifies meaning. As primatologist Thelma Rowell observed, "Once an intention movement has acquired meaning, or predictive value, and this is a matter of the evolution of the receiver rather than the animal making the movements, it may presumably come under selection pressure as a signal" (Rowell 1972, 94; see also Sheets-Johnstone 1999b). In Stern's studies, it is thus the mother who establishes the kinetic-semantic relationship. The infant is not a passive or oblivious partner, however, but is precisely attuned to the kinetic-affective pairing created by its mother's dynamics, as Stern implicitly indicates in his third criterion for judging an interaction to constitute an attunement.[16] Moreover the infant is attuned not only to its mother's response, but to its own capacity to create meaning, the dynamic affective-kinetic meaning to which its mother has in fact responded. In other words, an infant is not only semantically receptive but semantically creative, and spontaneously so in each instance. In each instance, sense-making and movement go hand in hand. They are in fact essentially intertwined in both the natural world, as exploratory and appetitive patterns of movement across the animal kingdom show, and in the natural interanimate world, as an evolutionary semantics shows (Sheets-Johnstone 1990, 1999b, 1999d). It is not surprising, then, that a kinetic-semantic relationship is empirically evident in affect attunement and in its development into more complex forms of pairing, such as, for example, linguistic turn-taking and empathy. These more complex forms also arise on the basis of our spontaneous capacity to move ourselves, not just randomly but in coordinated meaningful ways, ways that, as we develop and mature, become both more compounded and more subtle. Our spontaneous capacity for sound-making, and for discovering more and more intricate ways of making sound as we move from babbling, to vocalizing, to articulating, to speaking is a notable instance in point. In sum, our spontaneous capacity to move ourselves and to be both kinesthetically aware of the dynamics of our own movement and kinetically aware of the dynamics of the movement of others is the foundation of our interanimate sense-makings. That capacity generates the possibility of affect attunement, and in turn, the possibility of empathy. Animation thus indeed holds the key to understandings of intersubjectivity.

## VI. THE KINETIC FOUNDATIONS OF "KNOWING OTHER MINDS"

Kinetic dynamics are congruent to affective dynamics: the dynamics rise and fall, wax and wane, expand and constrict, surge and fade together. But the dual dynamics are additionally congruent to beliefs, judgments, and values. Indeed, the dynamics at any particular time are indicative of particular beliefs, judgments, and values, as, for example, my sudden spurt into a run is indicative of my belief and judgment that I might thereby catch the bus that I am desperately anxious to catch in order to arrive at an important meeting on time. Thus, it is not only *that* one moves, but *how* one moves that is doxically and axiologically meaningful, and for others as for oneself. It is not simply a matter of moving or of being at rest, but a matter of the livingly present qualitative dynamics of movement. Kinetic dynamics can be indicative of convictions, for example; one creates a different spatio-temporal-energic dynamic according to whether one is assured, doubtful, determined, or hesitant, for instance. The dynamics can be equally indicative of preferences—one's likes, dislikes, or indifferences, as when one approaches something rapidly, turns brusquely away from it, or shrugs one's shoulders with reference to it. They can furthermore be indicative of appraisals, whether of a situation or an idea, as when one opens bodily toward it indicating that one judges it positively and can or will accommodate it with ease and enthusiasm, or recoils from it bodily, indicating that one judges it negatively and can or will accommodate it only with difficulty and trepidation. As such examples attest, in the most basic sense we know what we call "the minds" of others by way of their moving bodies: we know their beliefs, judgments, and values by their manifest qualitative dynamics. Everything is indeed "indicated somatically," as Husserl observed, even to the *"higher psychic sphere."*

The *problem* of other minds is thus *originally*, i.e., at its source in our common ontogeny, "the problem" of other moving bodies. From this ontogenetic perspective, and as suggested in the previous section, the problem of other minds as conceived by adult humans is in truth an *adultist* problem: that of marginalizing moving bodies and thinking that whatever is cognitive is tucked away "inside," literally all in the head—a matter of *the* brain. Indeed, given that movement is our mother tongue, that it is our original and abiding matchpoint for making sense of the world, the problem of other moving bodies is not a problem to begin with. On the contrary, movement is the focal point of attention of infants from the beginning (e.g., Bower 1971, Bruner 1990, Baldwin and Baird 1999, Poulin-Dubois 1999, Spitz 1983, and Bloom 1993; see Sheets-Johnstone 1999b, chap. 5, for review and discussion). Not only this, but infants make sense of movement, as point-light studies by Bertenthal and colleagues show (Bertenthal and Pinto 1993; Bertenthal et al. 1984), and as imitation studies by Meltzoff (e.g., Meltzoff 1990, 1993, and 1995), agent-action studies by Bruner (Bruner 1990), object studies by Bower (Bower 1971, 1979), and studies by other infant researchers also show. It is hardly surprising, then, that from our common infancy onward, moving bodies are the foundational dynamic channel by which we forge understandings of others, coming to know their beliefs, judgments, and values through their movement. Such knowing—as the above examples of conviction, preference, and appraisal show—is a *semantically richer form of knowing* than knowing *the purpose* of another's movement, i.e., conceiving the other's movement simply in terms of "goal-directed behavior," a not uncommon way of conceptualizing intentionality and the relationship of intentionality to action (e.g., Baldwin and Baird 1999). It is similarly different from philosopher John Searle's quasi-first-person distinction between "intentions in action" and "intent to act," with its finer distinctions between presentation and representation, and mind-to-world and world-to-mind direction of fit, and its focus on conditions of satisfaction (Searle 1983). Essentially separating bodies from mind, Searle's distinction between "intentions in action" and "intent to act" sets apart what biologist Jaak Panksepp glosses as "higher forms of cognitive consciousness" and "ancient forms of affective consciousness" (Panksepp 2000, 39), and in the process bypasses the integral relationship between the cognitive and the kinetic, i.e., between everyday movement and central dimensions of intentionality that both perfuse everyday movement and are kinetically manifest.

Given our common kinetic point of departure for knowing "the minds" of others, our challenge as adults is first of all to give our common point of departure its due, recognizing the semantic power of movement, and on this basis elucidating how we come originally to know the beliefs, judgments, and values of others. It should be noted—and emphasized—that this elemental kinetic understanding is forged prior to language, that language is indeed properly described as *post-kinetic* (Sheets-Johnstone 1999b), and that this elemental kinetic understanding does not disappear with language (see also Stern 1990). The privileging of language is in fact, from this ontogenetic perspective, an unjustifiable practice if not a conceit. As infants learn to speak and enter into the language-tethered, language-centered world of adults, the linguistic simply tends to swallow up the kinetic. Thus, not only talk and thoughts of *behavior* prevent a kinetic dynamics and in turn the foundational relationship obtaining between movement and sense-making from coming to light, but talk and thoughts of *language* do. Movement can in fact be muffled in a number of ways, not only by researchers in their investigations, but by the force of cultural tradition. Language in everyday adult Western life becomes a convenient shorthand for finding out what another believes, what he or she judges to be the case, what he or she values, and so on. It becomes a shortcut to sense-making, relieving the sense-maker of what Husserl describes in various ways as "seeing deeply into the depths of another" (Husserl 1989, e.g., 286, 310, 341). Yet however covered over with words, movement remains the bedrock of language as it remains the bedrock of behavior: whether a matter of articulatory gestures or writing, or of eating, mating, provoking, consoling, hitting, grasping, accommodating, cooperating, competing, or any other behavior, movement is its foundation, not in the simple sense of being an instrumental means, but in the sense of being *the dynamic sine qua non* of the phenomenon. While "seeing deeply into the depths of another" is obviously metaphorical, it describes something experienced: feelings, motivations, beliefs, thoughts, attitudes, judgments, and values of another come to light precisely as they are manifest in what Husserl terms "the exterior" of movement, an exterior whose foundational significance is strikingly underscored by Husserl himself in his statement that everything psychic is "indicated somatically" even to "the *higher psychic sphere*."

The "exterior" is thus clearly not only a three-dimensional happening but a qualitative kinetic dynamics—a dynamics that is livingly present even in postural attitudes and bodily orientations. Elemental kinetic understandings are grounded in these dynamics. The understandings are not a matter of "body language," hence not a matter for itemization in a kinetic lexicon. Elemental kinetic understandings direct us not toward lexical compilations but toward a kinetic semantics, that is, toward an analysis of movement that does justice both to its complexity and to the complexity of its qualitatively present affective-cognitive dimensions, dimensions that constitute and substantively testify to its semantic richness. Such attention to movement has the power to launch us into a bona fide phenomenology of intercorporeality and thereby into foundational understanding of what we call "intersubjectivity." Indeed, by examining the biologically recognized pan-animate phenomenon of responsivity (Curtis 1975), inquiring specifically how it is that the responding individual certifies meaning (Sheets-Johnstone 1999d), we can place elemental kinetic understandings within the larger framework of an evolutionary semantics, and in so doing describe basic dimensions of a bona fide phenomenology of intercorporeality, arriving in turn at fundamental aspects of intersubjectivity, notably those underlying the advent of a particular form of interanimate meaning: empathy.

VII. RESPONSIVITY

Interanimate sense-making depends on the individual who certifies meaning, the one who *understands* what the other is perceiving, feeling, thinking, saying, and so on. As Stern indicates through his criteria of affect attunement, and as Meltzoff and Moore show in their studies of neonates' ability to imitate adult mouth gestures (Meltzoff and Moore 1977, 1983), human infants certify as well as create meaning. In a word, they are *responsive*. In being responsive, they ratify the meanings of adults, showing they make sense of—they understand—adult movements and gestures. Responsivity thus suffices to explain such phenomena as affect attunement and imitation; that is, one need not go beyond a native disposition to turn toward movement in the double sense of being attentive to movement and being kinetically responsive to movement—in dynamic systems language, to turn toward movement as an *attractor* in the same double sense.

This dual disposition is a biological disposition of all animate forms that move themselves.[17] It is, as indicated, a *sense-making disposition* in the double sense of that term. Indeed, the dual disposition is such an obviously basic disposition of animate forms as they go about making a living for themselves in the world that it goes virtually unnoticed, perhaps being considered too simple-minded a fact to warrant attention. Yet to neglect attention is to fail to perceive, and perceive in the strongest empirical sense, that movement is our matchpoint with the world, and indeed the matchpoint of all animate forms that move themselves. Moreover it is the matchpoint in a concomitantly critical sense for social species: intersubjective meanings are transduced in and through movement. A male gelada baboon raises its brows, thus displaying a white spot above its eyes; it yawns, thus displaying formidable canines; and so on. The baboon to whom it directs its escalating threat movements retreats, sufficiently threatened to desist in doing whatever it was doing, knowing at the same time that by continuing to perturb the male it will be attacked in some way. Conversely, in seeing the threatened individual retreat, the threatening male desists in his threat displays. In effect, one does not need theory—simulation theory or theories of mind—to explain intersubjectivity among gelada baboons. By the same token, one does not need theory—simulation theory or theories of mind—to explain the foundations of intersubjectivity among humans, whether an infant's ratifying perception of its mother's attunement, or its ratifying imitation of an adult's mouth gesture. In each instance, the infant's response hinges on recognizing a qualitatively animated other, i.e., the movement dynamics of another individual. As shown earlier, harmonious pairing in attunement is experienced by an infant through its kinesthetic-kinetic consciousness of a particular spatio-temporal-energic dynamics, a dynamics that has been sensorily transduced, from the kinesthetic to the visual or from the kinesthetic to the auditory. The *sensu communis*—the common sensible—that is movement engenders the same dynamics across sensory fields. A similar harmonious pairing is experienced by the infant in its imitation of adult gestures: a particular spatio-temporal-energic dynamic unfolds in the visual world and that dynamic is replicated kinesthetically by the infant in its own movements.

That responsivity, like metabolism and organization, is a prime biological marker of the animate as distinguished from the inanimate (Curtis 1975) testifies unequivocally to the fact that movement is meaningful. It attests not simply that in the above instances a kinetic-semantic relationship obtains, but that kinetic-semantic relationships obtain across the animal kingdom. Taking responsivity seriously thus means taking an evolutionary semantics seriously. An evolutionary semantics has the breadth necessary to an elucidation of just such relationships, showing how cognitive as well as affective dimensions enter into responsivity, and in particular, how responsivity is not a matter of "unconscious" or "reflex" reactions but a matter of intelligent responses, i.e., of epistemically rich movement. In this respect it perhaps warrants notice—if not emphasis—that humans are not above evolution. Responsivity is an evolutionary fact of life, and evolutionary facts of life apply equally to humans. We can readily appreciate the reality of human responsivity in the phenomenon of infant affect attunement and of infant imitation. We can appreciate its reality equally in the development of progressively more complex forms of responsivity as infants mature, and who, in their maturation, come to richer and more complex affective-cognitional awarenesses and correlatively, richer and more complex affective-cognitional responses. As an infant learns its body and learns to move itself it comes to have progressively more possibilities of movement, for example, possibilities that give rise to certain beliefs, judgments, and values: it can reach out for and touch, but not quite grasp, its favorite toy; it can walk to a table without falling down; by kicking its leg, it can make a mobile move that is attached by a string to its foot; and so on. The beliefs, judgments, and values that are embedded in the development of "I cans" (Husserl 1989, 1970a,, 1973, 1980) and in growing awarenesses of if-then relationships (Husserl 1989, 1970a; see also Stern 1985 on "consequential relationships" and Bloom 1993 on "relational concepts") are not linguistified formulae. An infant does not think in propositions; it thinks in movement (Sheets-Johnstone 1999b). In reaching for something it cannot quite grasp or in walking without falling or in kicking its leg to move a mobile, it is responsive to its own movement every literal or figurative step of the way, learning its body, the ways of the world, and the ways of things in the world in the process, and tempering its movement accordingly.

As infants mature, they come to see others similarly thinking in movement: someone opening a certain door is going to go outside; someone seeing a ball being thrown into the air is running to catch it; someone sweeping a floor rids it of crumbs; and so on. Movement generates meanings along more and more complex lines. As infants see others *move*, they come to know increasingly more about them through analogical kinetic apperceptions grounded in their own dispositional habit of thinking in movement: they come to see not only that others are *feeling* their own movement, that they too have an inner life of its dynamics, a tactile-kinesthetic/affective life, but that that life is suffused with particular beliefs, judgments, and values as they move about in the world. Opening, running, and sweeping are for infants not *behaviors*, but semantically inflected movement patterns by which they begin to "see deeply into the depths of another." In short, intersubjective understandings derive foundationally not from theory but from a bodily logos, a bodily logos that is from the beginning not only drawn to movement, but responsive to its semantic richness.

The kinetic-semantic relationship that fundamentally constitutes responsivity generates a critical question: how is it that an individual—an infant of a social species, for example, or in more general terms, a displayed-to animal—comes to validate the movements or gestures of another as meaningful? The question is indeed in a phenomenological sense a constitutional question fundamental to the origin of semiosis. It is furthermore a fundamental question with respect to species-specific and species-overlapping movement repertoires, hence a basic question within the larger framework of an evolutionary semantics. It is equally a fundamental question in the context of biologist Jesper Hoffmeyer's notion of "semiotic freedom" (Hoffmeyer 1996) insofar as semiotic freedom poses the question of how "increases" in meaning originate (61). That questions about origin cut across disciplines is significant. How things come to have the meaning and value they do is both a foundational question in phenomenology (Husserl 1970a, 1973) and a question quintessentially pertinent to understandings of the origin of semiosis in the sense Rowell's statement and Hoffmeyer's "semiotic freedom" indicate.[18] Clearly, as formatively realized over the course of evolution, sense-making has involved the constitution of new interanimate meanings on the basis of new corporeal acts, dispositions, discoveries, and so

Empathy    219

on. Because in all such instances it is a question of meaning and not reference (or information, for that matter), understandings of the origins of interanimate sense-making necessarily require understandings of the living organisms that define natural history, in particular, understandings of the diverse ways in which they both move about in, and experience the world. An unusually graphic instance of a newly minted interanimate meaning, though one that has not entered the repertoire of the species, is described by primatologists Michael Tomasello and Josep Call in their book *Primate Cognition*:

> [T]he initiation of play often takes place in chimpanzees by one juvenile raising its arm above its head and then descending on another, play-hitting in the process. This then becomes ritualized ontogenetically into an "arm-raise" gesture in which the initiator simply raises its arm and, rather than actually following through with the hitting, stays back and waits for the other to initiate the play, monitoring its response all the while.... If the desired response is not forthcoming, sometimes the gesture will be repeated, but quite often another gesture will be used. In other situations a juvenile was observed to actually alternate its gaze between the recipient of the gestural signal and one of its own body parts; for example, one individual learned to initiate play by presenting a limp leg to another individual as it passed by (an invitation to grab it and so initiate a game of chase), looking back and forth between the recipient and its leg in the process. (Tomasello and Call 1997, 244)

How, we may ask, does any so-designated "recipient" know that the gesturing individual wants to initiate a game of chase? A quite sophisticated meaning is intended, after all, by the combined gesture and look. Two captioned pictorial examples provide additional perspectives on the question and underscore in further ways the complexities and challenges of elucidating responsivity, the gestures in these instances being gestures in the species' repertoires. The first example is striking in the sense that we might have thought the gesture a uniquely human one. The caption reads—"Gorilla using hand clapping as auditory attention-getting gesture" (248). That hand clapping has human affinities is of considerable significance for an evolutionary semantics, and particularly from the viewpoint of origins. To clap one's hands to get attention is to have a sense of oneself as a sound-maker, hence to have not only a sense of oneself as an individual but a sense of oneself as an agent within a social group or communal setting, someone who can make things happen, and happen precisely by way of movement, exactly as a human does when he or she claps his or her hands to get people's attention at a gathering. Clearly, interanimate meanings are tied to movement possibilities and movement possibilities for any particular individual are tied to its being the body it is. In broader terms, movement possibilities are the ground on which a repertoire of "I cans" is generated, "I cans" that define not only individual but species-specific and species-overlapping repertoires.

The second example includes two pictures and is tantalizingly under-explained. The pictures show two hamadryas baboons, and the caption simply reads: "The young adult male gives his one-year-old female a gestural invitation to climb on his back; he then carries her across a difficult passage in the sleeping-cliff" (Kummer 1968, 302). However deficient its description, the gestural invitation testifies to at least three distinct awarenesses on the part of both male and female baboon: an awareness that the expanse or jaggedness of the cliff is too difficult for the young female to manage; an awareness that the male can cross the passage himself; an awareness that the male can transport the female on his back across the passage. Because the male's backward-turning of his head is not described, one wonders: does he jerk his head slightly toward his back, pointing as it were with his head—in the same way that a human might when he or she specifies "over there" with a head gesture? Does he look directly at the female at the same time that he gestures with his head? If so, there is a basic similarity between the baboon's gesture and look and the chimpanzee's gesture and look, the difference being that the baboon looks and gestures simultaneously and the chimpanzee alternates his gaze between his limp leg and the passing individual with whom he wants to play.

An important aspect of gesturing—of *kinetically instantiating intercorporeal meanings*—warrants mention in this context. Primatologist Emil Menzel (1973; see also Lieberman 1983) observed that chimpanzees do not point manually but use their whole bodies in a deictic manner as when, by bodily orientation, they point in the direction they will go and want others to go.[19] Looking back and forth between one's limp leg and a passing individual does exactly this: the back and forth look is a way of pointing with one's body. In effect, what a human finger does and does effectively is what other parts of the body or the body as a whole can do and do effectively. Moreover there is an iconic aspect to what we may call corporeal pointing with one's body, just as there is an iconic aspect to dexical manual pointing. Tomasello and Call virtually dismiss the possibility of nonhuman iconic relationships. With respect to a report that a bonobo male's gestures to a female are iconically based sexual invitations, they state that "the 'iconic' relationship of the gestures to the desired action may be from the human point of view only, as for the bonobo they may just signal the desired action in the same way as other ritualized signals, that is, based on the mutual shaping of behavior in previous interactive sequences" (Tomasello and Call 1997, 247). Their explanation clearly sidesteps the question of how the gestures originated, that is, how the recipient comes to authenticate the meaning of the gestures, literally solidifying the gesturing individual's intended meaning. Moreover to suggest ritualization rather than iconicity and in turn clothe the answer in talk of "mutual shaping" and "previous interactive sequences" merely poses the question anew. Such talk, while ostensibly taking one step forward, in truth takes two steps back.

In all three examples, there is no doubt but that the gesturing individual intends a meaning, but why should hand clapping make others turn in the direction of the clapper?; why should a backward turn of the head and backward glance toward another individual constitute for that individual an invitation to climb on the other's back?; why should the offering of a limp leg and a direct gaze at a passing individual constitute for that individual an invitation to play chase? To describe interanimate meaning consistently in terms of what is commonly termed "the displaying" rather than "the displayed-to" individual, and in fact to put interanimate meaning in the perspective of movement possibilities and "I cans," appears to preclude any answers by inverting the question, focusing on the "sender" instead of the "recipient." Indeed, rather than shedding light on how one individual knows what another intends and in turn how it comes to respond in a harmonious way, the examples seem to specify how one individual might go about motivating or encouraging another individual to do something. To see the examples in this inverted way, however, misses the point. What the examples show is not just that movement is used by an individual as an attractor in an attention-getting sense; they show that *movement is known to be a social attractor, a semantically rich social attractor, and that being so, it will generate a response*.[20] From the viewpoint of certifying meaning, then, the question is not *why*, but *how:* how is it that the individual to whom the gestures and looks or gestures and sounds are addressed grasps the meaning?

The answer to the question—in essence, the answer to the question of responsivity—is rooted in *animate* understandings, specifically, in deepened animate understandings of what primatologist Stuart Altmann terms comsigns (Altmann 1967). Acknowledgment of the corporeal-kinetic underpinnings of comsigns—acknowledgment of species-specific kinetic capacities, dispositions, and possibilities—is at the core of understanding interanimate responsivity. By showing how the corporeal-kinetic underpinnings of comsigns are species–specific, we will be able to show how interanimate responsivity—responding harmoniously in some way to the movement of another—is a built-in of animate forms.[21]

We should note to begin with that short of species-specific kinetic/tactile-kinesthetic invariants,[22] there would be—and could be—no species-specific intercorporeal communication. This claim is validated not only by the hand-clapping gorilla, the gesturing and visually oriented male hamadryas baboon, and the gesturing and visually oriented chimpanzee. All forms of intended kinetically enacted intercorporeal meanings are contingent on a common body of experience, hence on species-specific kinetic dynamics and tactile-kinesthetic invariants. A honeybee's dance, a human's speech, a wolf's submissive "signalling behavior," and so on, would be meaningless in the absence of kinetic/tactile-kinesthetic invariants. They would be meaningless because short of these invariants, there would be no common point of departure, no common body of reference, on the basis of which the individual to whom the intended semantically laden kinetics was addressed could make sense.[23] This is precisely the phenomenological import of Altmann's concept of comsigns. What the term "comsign" pinpoints is the fact that most primate signals are part of the repertoire of *all* members of the species or particular group in question, at the very least for some period in each animal's life.[24] What is true of primates is equally true of wolves, ravens, bees, humans, and other social animals. Kinetic/tactile-kinesthetic invariants anchor *interchangeability:*[25] they anchor the possibility of a perceiving animal being the acting animal and the acting animal being the perceiving animal; they anchor the possibility of comsigns. Moreover a fundamental *formal* similarity obtains between movement and meaning in comsigns; that is, there is a kinetic-semantic relationship that is basically iconic rather than arbitrary (see below for further discussion). A common species-specific (and possibly species-overlapping) body of movement, potential as well as actual, and, correlatively, a common species-specific (and possibly species-overlapping) body of meanings, ground one individual's understanding of the movement pattern or gesture of another. In the most fundamental sense, one body understands another body to the degree it not only *resembles* that body, but moves and gestures or has the possibility of moving and gesturing in ways similar to the ways in which that body moves and gestures, and in moving and gesturing or in having the possibility of moving and gesturing in ways similar to the ways in which that body moves and gestures, has perceptual experiences similar to that body, perceptual experiences that consistently combine certain tactile-kinesthetic/affective feelings with certain contextually situated kinetic-visual (or kinetic-auditory as in human speech or kinetic-tactile as in the honeybee dance) awarenesses.[26] Meaning is thus in the most fundamental sense corporeally structured; it is articulated along the lines of moving bodies.[27]

When we take seriously the question of how new interanimate meanings are minted, in particular, how it is that one individual knows what another individual means when the latter does something the former has not seen done before or heard before, we come to realize the importance of a common body of movement, a species-specific (and possibly species-overlapping) kinetic repertoire. But we realize something further too, namely, that it is necessarily the perceiving rather than acting individual who solidifies meaning. An individual can, after all, move or gesticulate endlessly, even making all kinds of sounds in the process, but unless and until the individual on the perceiving end responds, and responds in a way coincident with the intended meaning of the movement or gestures, the intended meaning goes unrecognized. The earlier-cited passage from Rowell makes this very point: unless and until the receiver certifies meaning, the gestures or sounds will not enter the communicative repertoire of the species or group in question. In Altmann's terms, the gestures or sounds will not become a comsign. The question of how a displayed-to animal comes to validate the movements or gestures of another as meaningful is thus of critical importance. Darwin did not consider the question in his rich and pioneering work, *The Expression of the Emotions in Man and Animals*, but he presented three principles[28] in explanation of how "movement or changes in any part of the body,—as the *wagging* of a dog's tail, the *drawing back* of a horse's ears, the *shrug-*

*ging* of a man's shoulders . . . may all equally well serve for expression" (Darwin 1872 [1965], 28; italics added). In his clear recognition of the *kinetics* of emotional expression, Darwin implicitly affirms the species-specific kinetic foundation of comsigns. Indeed, his explanatory thesis coincides in key ways with the thesis presented here: that the affective and the kinetic are dynamically congruent, that communal bodies of movement—kinetic/tactile-kinesthetic bodies—are the foundation of comsigns, and that comsigns are the foundation of interanimate communication.

We might note that in his discussion of ritualization, i.e., in his discussion of how "certain movement patterns lose, in the course of phylogeny, their original specific function and become purely 'symbolic' ceremonies" (Lorenz 1966, 54–55), ethologist Konrad Lorenz speaks of the "reactor," the one to whom a gesture or movement pattern is addressed, as having "an innate understanding" of the gesture or pattern (63). He later specifies that "[t]he direct cause of changes in behavior [that is, the direct cause of ritualization] is to be sought in the selection pressure exerted by the limitations of the 'receiving set' which must respond correctly and selectively to the signal emanating from the 'sender,' if the system of communication is to function properly" (73). Again, the individual on the receiving end is highlighted, but without specification as to how the "'receiving set'" comes to "respond correctly." Yet on what could the understanding of a "'receiving set'" rest if not on species-specific kinetic/tactile-kinesthetic bodies and invariants? In other words, on what could a receiver's correct and selective response rest if not on species-specific movement with its common kinetic/kinesthetic dynamics, and hence its foundational possibility of "sender" and "receiver" interchangeability? In short, Lorenz's observations coincide with Rowell's and support the same explanation of how interanimate meanings are forged, namely, through species-specific kinetic/tactile-kinesthetic invariants that underpin the invention of comsigns and the interchangeability of "sender" and "receiver."

Species-specific tactile-kinesthetic invariants go a long way toward answering the question of how interanimate meanings are constituted precisely because they signify a body of common experiences. Tactile-kinesthetic invariants furthermore predispose organisms toward *iconically* rather than arbitrarily structured meanings because the most easily formulated, consistently utilizable, and readily understood signals are those that are structured in bodily movements and experiences shared by all members of the species.[29] If we ask how the offering of a limp leg, for example, is an iconically rather than arbitrarily structured meaning signifying an invitation to a game of chase to a passing individual, we see first off that it is a gesture centered precisely on that part of the body that is kinetically central to a game of chase. Since running is integral to chasing and since one's legs do the running, it makes sense to invite someone to a game of chase by extending one's leg: a conceptual relationship obtains between gesture and meaning. The gesture is iconic in the further sense that the leg offered is a *limp* leg. A limp leg is a caricature of a leg, so to speak; it is a farcical condition for a leg to be in. It implicitly suggests fun in just this sense: the desired chase is playful and would be enjoyable. Iconicity is thus in this instance a conceptual marker with respect both to the leg itself and to its limpness, the marker leading one to conceive of chasing in a way that is not serious but fun.

VIII. DEEPENED UNDERSTANDINGS OF EMPATHY

Deepened understandings of responsivity, of its basis in both comsigns and interchangeability, and of the basis of comsigns and interchangeability in species-specific kinetic/tactile-kinesthetic invariants, provide the grounds for elucidating the interanimate phenomenon of empathy. Empathy is a form of responsivity: in the most fundamental sense, and like attunement and imitation, it ratifies meaning. But empathy goes further, enriching meaning in virtue of affective-cognitive understandings of the other as the other him/ herself experiences and understands his/her situation. These understandings are not mental constructions: empathy is neither an imaginative playing back and forth of a "here" and a "there," nor a rationalized transformation of the visual into the tactile-kinesthetic and of the tactile-kinesthetic into the visual. Empathy emerges directly from the empirical realities of animation; it is a spontaneous response to direct experiences of what is foundationally a corporeal-kinetic dynamic, a dynamic that, as experienced, and from its foundations in affect attunement, comes to disclose progressively richer and more complex dimensions of another animate being amid the challenges, vicissitudes, and joys of a common lifeworld. In just this sense, empathy is a seeing deeply into another. A twinge, a drooping somberness, a sudden raising of eyebrows, a lightness, a raptness—in each instance, a particular dynamic unfolds and is experientially evident. The dynamic articulates a kinetic pattern of being that resonates in kinesthetically recognizable ways, and precisely as kinesthetically recognizable, generates affective-cognitive understandings: that the other is feeling the sting of another's insult, or is engrossed in thought about what to do, or is ecstatic about a new job, or is wanting to avoid another person, or is eager to leave, and so on. In the most fundamental sense, what another is thinking and feeling is indicated somatically, yet not *"somatically"* as mere physical event or as semiotic signpost, but *dynamically*: affective-cognitive dimensions are livingly present in a kinetic dynamics that reverberates kinesthetically–affectively–cognitively in our own being. Responding empathically, we experience the density of another person, the meanings that are livingly present for him or her.

These deepened understandings of another are not ready-mades but mature progressively as we ourselves mature. In other words, empathic moments are the products of our own experience and in this sense are self-fueled. While we may cultivate empathy for others and in fact be taught from early childhood on to be empathic toward others, empathy comes on its own: it is a spontaneous response to others, a response that may wax and grow, shrivel and die, be selectively nurtured with respect to some and willfully nurtured negatively with respect to certain others, be pathologically absent, or be individualized in a variety of other ways. When it does flourish and grow, it comes spontaneously to incorporate richer and more intricate understandings of others: the other is not just feeling eager, but is eager to leave a painful situation; the other is not just engrossed, but engrossed in thought about a complex family problem; and so on. We grasp at ever deeper levels what another is living through because we have ourselves grown in life experiences and become more intricate persons ourselves in the process. In this respect, what we share verbally with others is significant. A friend relates to us that he has lost his job, or that he is getting a raise, or that he is getting married, or that his child has been diagnosed with leukemia, or that he just won the lottery, or that he has had to cancel vacation plans. Whatever his life experience, we respond empathically in hearing of it. Here too, however, meaning is dynamically indicated. When empathically understood, verbal meanings are grasped in a dynamically felt sense: the speech of another is heard not as a series of factual statements or informational reports, but as livingly present dimensions of an animate being that resonate in the voice as in the flesh.

While some empathic experiences obviously require language or are enriched by language, it would be a mistake to think their origins lie in merely or wholly verbal understandings. An original kinetic semantics subtends verbal meanings as it does the capacity for language itself, i.e., our capacity to speak. Articulatory gestures are in fact themselves dynamic phenomena: humans generate speech through movement and learn to speak to begin with by mastering the articulatory gestures of a particular language. It is not surprising, then, that articulatory gestures are open to prosodic inflection. Indeed, the prosodic contours of speech are, from the beginning, integral to language-learning, and are as much a part of the dynamics of empathy as specific word meanings.[30] As indicated above, what is related to us in language and what we respond to empathically are not factual statements or informational reports, but dimensions of animate life as it is lived through. Moreover reading descriptive accounts of the plight or joy of other humans, as in novels or in newspapers, we empathize precisely to the degree we awaken to that original kinetic semantics and in turn have a dynamically felt sense of the experiences of others, what they are living through as animate beings.[31] In sum, however much we learn how to do things with words[32] in the course of language-learning or in the course of learned discourse, we learn how to do them through movement, through a sense of their kinetic dynamics. Empathic understandings are thus readily generated by way of the human voice and texts.[33]

In view of its origin in a kinetic dynamics, the emergence and development of empathy clearly turns on a particular kind of noticing and sensitivity, both of which are epitomized in an infant's exquisite disposition toward movement. An infant's attentiveness and responsivity to movement inform its capacity to perceive and respond to what Stern terms "vitality affects"—"elusive qualities" that, as he describes them, "are better captured by dynamic, kinetic terms, such as 'surging,' 'fading away,' 'fleeting,' 'explosive,' 'crescendo,' 'decrescendo,' bursting,' drawn out,' and so on" (Stern 1985, 54). Vitality affects indeed describe kinetic dynamics. It is thus not surprising that vitality affects as experienced—"[t]he manner of performance of a parent's act" (56), such as combing the infant's hair or putting on its diaper, for example—are a gateway to the harmonious pairing of attunement, and in turn to the analogical apperception that constitutes empathy. Whatever their particular form and context, when we notice and are sensitive to kinetic dynamics, we reawaken our mother tongue and become open to the possibility of empathy. We are in touch with our original matchpoint with others and with the kinetic semantics that grounds analogical apperception. From this vantage point, we can appreciate in a further respect the significance of Overgaard's elucidation of pairing in Husserl's texts on intersubjectivity, and how Husserl's prominencing of movement, when fully elaborated, obviates the need to invoke acts of imagination, imitation, or translation. When we see someone twinge, we do not need to imagine ourselves over there where the other is, or try twinging ourselves in like fashion in order to discover what the person is feeling, in effect prompting ourselves to empathize. We already know in a dynamically felt sense what twinging feels like. The *sensu communis* that is movement is the key to our empathic understandings, the natural bridge that joins us empathically to another. In broader terms, the kinetic-semantic infrastructure of sense-making discloses a dynamic that, when we notice and are sensitive to it, brings us spontaneously to empathize. The foundations of that sense-making—the foundations of empathic responsivity—reach back to our first relationships to others. When the kinetic noticings and sensitivities inherent in and essential to that sense-making are submerged in the platitudes and chit-chat of everyday speech or hidden from view in the theoretical and abstract concerns of learned discourse, we lose touch with our mother tongue. Methodologically going back to beginnings, we have the possibility of reawakening—or as Husserl would say, of reactivating—the dynamic kinesthetic/kinetic, intercorporeal-interanimate ground on which empathy originates and develops, the ground on which everything is "indicated somatically," even to "the *higher psychic sphere.*"

## IX. A POSTSCRIPT ON ORIGINS, HISTORY, AND METHODOLOGY

If the above phenomenological analysis of empathy holds, that is, if a kinetic semantics does indeed ground the harmonious pairing that developmentally comes to constitute empathy, then the origin and development of intersubjectivity is open to a genetic phenomenological analysis similar in kind to any other historically developing pan-cultural phenomenon of the human world. In fact, as a phenomenological topic, the origin of intersubjectivity bears extraordinary resemblances to the origin of geometry as Husserl conceived it in his essay of the same name (Husserl 1970b). Its dissimilarities from the essay are equally significant, centering as they do on language, specifically, on what Husserl terms the "linguistic embodiment" of geometry (358) and the basic difference of that "embodiment" from a kinetic semantics. An examination of both resemblances and differences will highlight the extraordinary if overlooked relevance of ontogenetic and phylogenetic studies to phenomenology, precisely in view of their being *built-in historical* facets of human life. In other words, it is not just *human productions* like geometry—*human-made* histories—that are open to genetic analysis; it is humanness itself. Humanness itself has a history, an ontogenetic-phylogenetic history that in essential ways is not relative, but on the contrary, grounds dimensions of humanness in pan-human capacities, dispositions, and possibilities. Because the difference between linguistic embodiment and a kinetic-semantics is in itself significant and because it is furthermore of central import in demonstrating analogical confluences between the origin of intersubjectivity and passages in Husserl's text on the origin of geometry, it will be instructive to consider it first.

Husserl speaks of "linguistic embodiment" in the context of asking how the ideal objects of geometry, i.e., geometrical meanings first arising in a single person, become "ideal objectivities," i.e., common knowledge. He states, "In advance we see that it occurs by means of language, through which it receives, so to speak, its linguistic living body" (358). In short, geometric truths are passed on from generation to generation through language, just as history itself is passed on through language. It is not uncommon to conceive intersubjectivity as a kind of "linguistic embodiment," or better, as a *problem* of linguistic embodiment. Under the paradigm of language, intersubjectivity is commonly conceived as a problem of *translation,* namely, translation from the visual to the tactile-kinesthetic. Philosopher Max Scheler called attention to this problem in the early 1900s, for example,[34] as did sociological phenomenologist Alfred Schutz in a later essay (Schutz 1966). More recently, philosopher Shaun Gallagher specifies the problem when he writes, "For the infant to be able to imitate a displayed facial gesture, it must be able to translate a visual display into its own motor behavior" (Gallagher 2000, 15; but see Gallagher 2001 for an "action-based" understanding of intersubjectivity). In general, the tendency is to think that language is the fundamental interpersonal medium of human communication, and accordingly, to think along the lines of language when questions of interanimate communication arise. As we have seen, however, the common sensible that is movement makes language, i.e., translation, unnecessary. In attunement, imitation, and empathy, intersubjective meanings are precisely *not* translated. To think they are is to be misled by language. When perceived dynamically as the interanimate phenomena they are, i.e., kinetically and kinesthetically, and in turn conceived in terms of a movement dynamics, one finds no foreign language relationship to obtain and no need for a foreign language relationship to obtain between the visual and the tactile-kinesthetic.[35] In each instance, intersubjective relations are transduced in and through movement. Being inherently dynamic, movement unfolds a particular spatio-temporal-energic patterning that is in each instance perceived by "sender" and "receiver" alike, sender and receiver having different sensory but dynamically congruent or dynamically matching experiences.

The foundational kinetic-semantic relationship that originally and developmentally binds humans together in a common humanity structures intersubjectivity and is the condition of its possibility. Intersubjective relations are thus neither built on language to begin with nor are they carried forward by language, i.e., by "linguistic embodiment," in a historical sense. They are basically nonlinguistic phenomena whose experienced meanings are corporeally sedimented and carried forward kinetically, i.e., in movement. The challenge they present is precisely *the challenge of languaging experience* (Sheets-Johnstone 2002a, 2003b). Husserl's comment about language that warns of passive understanding is strikingly apposite in this context. Speaking of how our "originally intuitive life . . . falls victim to the *seduction of language*," Husserl astutely observes, "Greater and greater segments of this life lapse into a kind of talking and reading that is dominated purely by association" (Husserl 1970b, 362; italics in original). The singular and notably neglected point he underscores in this passage is that *language is not experience*. Instead of inquiring into origins and following the chain of meanings that have developed, we passively accept what we hear, speak, and read, failing to question, investigate, explicate, or elucidate the epistemological ground of our knowledge, thus failing to arrive at actively experienced meaning. Assumptions about translation, about the absolute incommensurability between and among sensory modalities, and a consequent drive to find explanations for observed human "behavior" lead precisely to the epistemological void Husserl identifies. In a word, language-tethered assumptions overlook movement. It is thus not surprising that present-day researchers in a variety of fields search for or identify intersubjective "translators" of one kind or another[36]—a "body schema" (e.g., Meltzoff and Moore 1995; Gallagher and Meltzoff 1996; DePraz

2001), "mechanisms" (e.g., a "psychological primitive," a "supramodal representational system" [Meltzoff 1990]), "modules" (e.g., an "intentionality detector," an "eye-detection detector" [Baron-Cohen 1995]), "mirror neurons" (e.g., "'motor labeling," "action coding," [Rizzolatti and Gallese 1997; Iacoboni et al. 2005; see also, Hurley 2007, Jacob and Jeannerod 2007, Goldman 2007, Csibra 2007, Gallese 2007])[37], for example—and this even though the real thing, the dynamic phenomenon itself, is, as it were, staring us in the face. The result is that, as with geometry and other "segments of this life," the history of intersubjectivity remains buried; self-evidence is not brought to light but is hidden under the weight of language.

As one reads Husserl's essay, one senses more and more analogies between the "origin of geometry" and the "origin of intersubjectivity." That both are *historical* phenomena is a basic fact that fundamentally ties the two phenomena together: neither is given full-blown but develops over time. Indeed, in perhaps the most general and simplest of senses, a cultural-individual historical analogy is evident, geometry originating and developing over centuries "[in] a lively, productively advancing formation of meaning" in the world of mathematics (Husserl 1970b, 365), intersubjectivity originating and developing in the course of ontogeny and into and through adulthood "[in] a lively, productively advancing formation of meaning." Their analogically related histories temper the notion of a hard and fast opposition between culture and nature: one can "get back" with respect to each; both are open to genetic phenomenological elucidation. Moreover if there is a cultural history, or in fact, cultural histor*ies,* there is also and to begin with a natural history, a history that phenomenologists are ultimately obliged to take into account as the fulfillment of a notable direction in Husserl's writings: Husserl takes nature into account, prominently in *Ideas II;* he consistently—and uniquely among philosophers generally as well as uniquely among phenomenologists—mentions and comments upon nonhuman animals in the course of discussing animate being (e.g., *Ideas II, Ideas III*); he grapples with the challenge of *human history* in preeminently cultural terms, terms that reverberate along natural lines because what arises culturally does not arise *deus ex machina* but has its origin in nature, i.e., in natural proclivities, dispositions, capacities, possibilities, and so on. Notable too is the fact that there would be no phenomenology without transcendental clues. They are the lifeblood of phenomenology in the sense of constituting the point of departure for phenomenological studies. *Nature* is just such a clue, opening on a vast area of investigations into human possibilities, capacities, and so on. Indeed, phenomenology does not need to be naturalized; it is already natural in view of its subject, who is a product of natural history and whose historical lineage delineates quintessential dimensions of humanness. Its natural history encompasses ontogeny as well as phylogeny, constituting the subject in living ways along maturational as well as evolutionary lines. The subject of phenomenology, after all, is not born into the world as an adult, but has a developmental history that begins pan-culturally in infancy and as such has natural dimensions open to phenomenologically informed analyses.

Sizable correspondences in fact come to light as one reads Husserl's essay and realizes that a phenomenon does not have to be a *cultural* phenomenon in order to be open to genetic analysis. On the contrary, natural phenomena, and in particular, the phenomenon of intersubjectivity as it arises in the course of each human life, are open to historical analysis, i.e., to genetic phenomenological investigation. Nature is indeed not a deterrent but a challenge to phenomenology. Clearly, human life is a natural phenomenon that is not given all at once any more than an object in the world or a human invention such as geometry is given all at once. In each instance, an origin is no longer present, but can be reconstructed, or in phenomenological terms, "reactivated." Husserl demonstrates this possibility in "The Origin of Geometry," and his insights are clearly—one might even say, uncannily—descriptive of the origin of intersubjectivity. The sequence of quotations that follows brings seminal analogies to light, each citation testifying to the fact that what Husserl affirms of the historical genesis and development of geometry can be equally affirmed of the historical genesis and development of intersubjectivity.

"[Geometry] must have arisen out of a *first* acquisition.... We understand its persisting manner of being: it is not only a mobile forward process from one set of acquisitions to another but a continuous synthesis in which all acquisitions maintain their validity, all make up a totality such that, at every present stage, the total acquisition is, so to speak, the total premise for the acquisitions of the new level" (355).

"[T]he *total* meaning of geometry ... could not have been present as a project and then as mobile fulfillment at the beginning. A more primitive formation of meaning necessarily went before it as a preliminary stage, undoubtedly in such a way that it appeared for the first time in the self-evidence of successful realization" (356).

"[M]eaning is grounded upon meaning, the earlier meaning gives something of its validity to the later one, indeed becomes part of it to a certain extent. Thus, no building block within the mental structure is self-sufficient" (363).

"[W]ithout the actually developed capacity for reactivating the original activities contained within its fundamental concepts, i.e., without the 'what' and the 'how' of its prescientific materials, geometry would be a tradition empty of meaning" (366).

"[A]ll new acquisitions are in turn sedimented and become working materials" (369).

"[T]o understand geometry or any given cultural fact is to be conscious of its historicity . . . it is something constructed through human activity" (370).

"[Geometry] bears, with essential necessity, the horizon of its history within itself" (370–71).

"[H]istory is from the start nothing other than the vital movement of the coexistence and the interweaving of original formations and sedimentations of meaning" (371).

In sum, the history of intersubjectivity has originary and developmental affinities with the history of geometry. Not only is what originates and develops in the course of many lifetimes temporally analogous to what originates and develops in the course of a single lifetime, but the chain of propagated and progressively augmented and enriched meanings of geometry is structurally analogous to the chain of propagated and progressively augmented and enriched meanings of intersubjective experience. The chain in each instance becomes more complex as it evolves. Empathy in particular is not a singular and monolithic thing but a shifting and variable accomplishment. Husserl himself suggests as much when he speaks of the possibility of new understandings of another (Husserl 1973, 120) and of the possible experience of "discordant" others (114). Furthermore, precisely with reference to the histories of geometry and intersubjectivity as forward movements over time from a point of origin, an oppositional conception of culture and nature is not viable: not only do geometry and intersubjectivity both bear "the horizon of their history within themselves," but their respective horizons overlap precisely in that language—what is said or written—is, as indicated earlier, grounded in a foundational kinetic semantics.[38] It is in fact notable that geometric truths are originally articulated in movement, i.e., in the drawing of lines and the discovery of linear relationships. Moreover deepening understandings of language—deepening understandings of the ways in which it modulates, enriches, or diminishes its foundational kinetic semantics—would deepen understandings of intersubjectivity, bringing to life horizons within the history of intersubjectivity, particularly with respect to empathy. Indeed, rather than treating intersubjectivity generally, and empathy in particular, as ahistorical phenomena, as static and unchanging "accomplishments," we would do well to attend to their origin and history, and with even more urgency than we would attend to the origin and history of geometry insofar as intersubjectivity and empathy are quintessential dimensions of our humanness. Both are natural in a phylo-ontogenetic sense and naturally open to nurturing and to later personal cultivation or neglect. Whatever their particular cultural and individual inflections, those inflections do not descend from the blue, *deus ex machina*, but are grounded in what is evolutionarily and ontogenetically given (cf. Sheets-Johnstone 1994b). In other words, what humans nurture and cultivate is what they are naturally capable of nurturing and cultivating. The ethical implications of our common phylo-ontogenetical disposition and capacity for empathy and for intersubjective sense-making generally are not only substantial but have a decisive Socratic cast: an ever-expanding capacity and disposition to see deeply into another is a seeing commensurate with an ever-expanding capacity and disposition to see deeply into oneself.

## NOTES

1. Of course, any movement I make creates not just a spatial dynamic but a spatio-temporal-energic dynamic. Because space and physicality are of specific moment here, I omit the fuller descriptive term.

2. Husserl's omission of feeling from his account of the "sphere of ownness" and his specification of "fields of sensation" within that sphere, blind us to the dynamics of self-movement and to the foundationally kinetic nature of empathy.

3. It is both curious and ironic that phenomenologists are notably focused on—one might even say mesmerized by—the dyad touched/touching, and appear wholly oblivious of the double aspect of movement and its foundational import.

4. Husserl himself intimates as much when he speaks of "the animate bodily organism of the other Ego" (Husserl 1973, 122).

5. I called attention also in "Re-Thinking Husserl's Fifth Meditation" to the fact that "[t]he deeper understanding of harmony has implications for deeper understandings of empathy, not only with respect to humans and to human intersubjectivity, but with

Empathy    235

respect to nonhuman animals and to human-nonhuman intersubjectivity" (Sheets-Johnstone 1999c, 102).

6. Attunements are not imitations. Hence, an infant's imitative capacities constitute a different kind of pairing. See further in this text for citations of the work of Andrew Meltzoff on infant imitation.

7. For a full phenomenological analysis of movement, see *The Phenomenology of Dance* (Sheets-Johnstone 1966 [1979/1980]) and *The Primacy of Movement* (Sheets-Johnstone 1999b).

8. Very early on, in *Ideas I*, Husserl underscored the possibility of using imaginary as well as perceptual experience as a point of departure for eidetic studies. See Husserl 1983, 11–12.

9. Wimmer discusses the origin of emotion in Piagetian terms, namely, centration and decentration, "internal homeostasis" exemplifying the former term and offering a "'yardstick' for 'knowledge' of the world" (Wimmer 1995, 42), more complex behaviors exemplifying the latter term but being still "in a close relation to a centrating base" (44).

10. An article co-authored by Wimmer and Ciompi (1996) shows how affect and cognition "form a [sic] inseparable interactive unit," both ontogenetically and phylogenetically.

11. For analyses and discussions of how cultures inflect and temper—by elaborating, distorting, neglecting, or suppressing what is evolutionarily given—see Sheets-Johnstone 1994b.

12. In 2002, I was invited to give a paper at a conference titled "The Perils and Promises of Interdisciplinary Research" at the Center for Subjectivity Research at the University of Copenhagen. The topic I chose was "Preserving Integrity Against Colonization," a topic of specific concern here with respect to avoiding a simple "motor mimicry" explanation of empathy. The paper, subsequently published in *Phenomenology and the Cognitive Sciences* (Sheets-Johnstone 2004), addresses the problem of reconciling first- and third-person methodologies and knowledge, particularly with respect to phenomenology and cognitive neuroscience. The article has both a critical and constructive section. The critical section assesses the idea that one must build bridges across an epistemological divide, that one can make experiential ascriptions to brains (e.g., the brain "infers" [Crick and Koch 1992, 153], the brain "ascertains" [Zeki 1992, 69]), and so on. Of moment here, however, is the constructive section, which spells out evidence supporting the claim that "genuine reconciliation is mediated by phenomenally-based conceptual complementarities." In particular, conceptual complementarities of mirror neurons with Husserl's notion of *Einfühlung* are identified in terms of the tight connection Rizzolatti and Gallese postulate between movement and meaning (Rizzolatti and Gallese 1997), as in "Action appears to represent the founding principle of our knowledge of the world" (227), and in terms of the correlation of neuronal firings with specific movements, indicating a quintessential coherence of physical and lived bodies (see Sheets-Johnstone 1986a for an evolutionary account of the quintessential coherence). An overall phenomenal conceptual complementarity is shown to be rooted in a kinetic dynamics that articulates an intercorporeal semantics, a semantics Rizzolatti and Gallese identify from a third-person standpoint as a 'motor vocabulary' (Rizzolatti and Gallese 1997, e.g., 220).

For a fuller discussion of these particular conceptual complementarities and for the identification and discussion of complementarities with respect to studies of dynamic systems, notably those within the domain of coordination dynamics (see Kelso 1995), and to an innovative use of functional MRI in conjunction with Husserl's analysis of time-consciousness, the reader is referred to the article. Along with the discussion of mirror neurons, these further examples support the thesis that life is a unifying concept across disciplines and a concept consistently exemplified in movement. The thesis indeed informs the entire article.

A highly significant aspect of the thesis warrants emphasis in light of recent developments in the new "embodied" cognitive neuroscience and neurophenomenology, an aspect that did not surface at the time of the paper or the article, but that has since been written of in another article (see Sheets-Johnstone 2003b). What needs not simple attention but underscoring—not mere recognition but phenomenological elucidation at length and in depth—are the living kinetic dynamics of movement. Those dynamics cannot properly be brushed aside in passing talk of the sensory-motor system or transmogrified in talk of "corporeal sensations," "motor acts," and so on, all of which lack any reference to kinesthesia (see, for example, Gallese and Lakoff 2005, Gallese 2005 and 2007b, and Thompson 2007; see Sheets-Johnstone 2003b and 2005 for a critique of the erroneous use of the term "sensations" to describe the experience of "action" and Sheets-Johnstone 2003b for a critique of the term "motor" in describing first-person experience), any more than the *"dynamic congruity"* of movement and affect (Sheets-Johnstone 1999a) can be adequately understood when casually invoked without elaboration much less proper scholarly citation (Gibbs 2006) or when discussed in purely third-person terms, remaining unanalyzed phenomenologically (Freedberg and Gallese 2007). In this respect the projects of neurophenomenology (e.g., Thompson 2007) and of naturalizing phenomenology (e.g., Petitot et al., 1999) appear doomed to failure, for the at-length and in-depth experiential analyses that would sustain the *phenomenology* are nowhere in sight. In short, integrity is *not* preserved but gives way to colonization.

13. In a wider context of intersubjective relations, an individual may be moved *not* to move in a spontaneous pairing, i.e., empathically, *indifference*, for example, being precisely an affective motivation. Philosopher Arne Vetlesen implicitly exemplifies a possible kinetic mode of this feeling when he writes of a person walking along who sees another person being beaten and who does *not* respond, whose response is precisely not to care, who "feels nothing in particular," and who "proceed[s] with his walk" (Vetlesen 1994, p. 159). For an example at the opposite extreme of indifference, see philosopher Martha Nussbaum, who writes that the tendency of emotions is "to take over the personality and move one to action with overwhelming force" (Nussbaum 2003, pp. 272–73). In both instances, a strong conceptual accord is evident with Ciompi's "affect-logic," or more specifically with his (amended) "affect-logic-kinetic," the conjoint nature of the affective and the kinetic being duly if implicitly recognized.

14. Movement may be equally submerged in talk of action, as in Searle 1983 and Baldwin and Baird 1999.

15. For analyses and discussions of how what is evolutionarily given is culturally played out, specifically with respect to power, see Sheets-Johnstone 1994b. For analyses and discussions of how smiling is an evolutionarily derived human phenomenon, see van Hooff 1969 and 1972.

16. The first criterion is "that the baby [makes] some affective expression—facial, vocal, gestural, or postural"; the second is "that the mother [responds] in some observable way" (Stern 1985, 147).

17. Sessile organisms do not move themselves in self-governing, self-directed ways. While they are responsive, their response is passive. They are moved to move by the waters surrounding them, for example, as with an adult tunicate.

18. Husserl's essay "The Origin of Geometry" (1970) shows in a particularly exacting way how a genetic phenomenology is concerned with the origin and constitution of meaning, thus how a phenomenological methodology is particularly suited to a search for origins. (To avoid possible misunderstanding, it should perhaps be noted explicitly that Husserl's term "genetic" has nothing to do with genes; it specifies origins, as does the common English word *genesis* and the word "gene," of course.)

19. "[O]ne good reason that chimpanzees very seldom point manually is that they do not have to; rising to a quadrupedal position, glancing at a follower, and orienting 'out there' conveys all the directional information one could ask for" (Menzel 1973, 218).

20. The hand-clapping example shows further that making sounds by way of movement can enhance the semantic power of movement, even to the point of specifying what is or was moving, precisely as *hands* clapping.

21. The term "harmonious" should not be taken as meaning an "always pacific" mode of relating to another. After all, anger and fear, jealousy and resentment, to name perhaps the most outstanding non-pacific emotions, are also ways of relating to another. "Harmonious" thus refers to the fullest possible spectrum of affective-cognitive understandings of another, and include, for example, understandings of another's motivations and intent to insult (prompting anger), or to menace (prompting fear), or to possess (prompting jealousy) or to flaunt (prompting resentment). In other words, anger, fear, jealousy, resentment, and other such emotions are the motivating force for a *response* to an analogically based understanding: they move an individual to move. The threat example in the text demonstrates this relationship: the individual to whom the threat is made desists in doing what he/she was doing.

22. For a detailed treatment of tactile-kinesthetic invariants, see Sheets-Johnstone 1990, chap. 15.

23. Kinetic/tactile-kinesthetic invariants similarly anchor Bertenthal and Pinto's basic notion of complementary processes undergirding the perception and production of human movement (Bertenthal and Pinto 1993) and Liberman and Mattingly's earlier idea that complementary processes anchor speech perception and speech production (Liberman and Mattingly 1985).

24. Altmann points out that some comsigns (which he conceives as *behaviors* rather than as dynamic patterns of movement) are peculiar to the males or the females of a species. He mentions among other examples the roar of an adult male gorilla and "intromission," stating that "intromission (but not mounting) by females will be impossible in all [primate] species" (Altmann 1967, 336).

25. See linguist Charles Hockett's identification of interchangeability as a "design feature" of human language in his article "The Origin of Speech" (Hockett 1960).

26. For a comparative analysis of primordial/present-day human language and the Tanzsprache (the honeybee dance), see Sheets-Johnstone 1990.

27. That primordial language was structured analogically along the lines of the body should give pause for thought. Received wisdom urges us to think that language is made up of vocal sounds that are arbitrarily formed and arbitrarily linked to objects in the world, and that naming things and naming them by way of arbitrary sounds is the crowning mark of human achievement (see, for example, Hockett 1960 and his specification "duality of patterning," a preeminent "design feature" of human language). However brief, the foregoing evolutionary perspective—from Precambrian semiosis to morphological and kinetic corporeal representation—challenges the wisdom of that view. More than that, it challenges the empirical evidence—or in truth, lack of evidence—for that view. Indeed, taking a cue from biologists Stephen Jay Gould and Richard Lewontin's critique of adaptationist stories with its cautionary emphasis against taking present-day utility of a trait or behavior as reason for its origin (Gould and Lewontin 1979), we may similarly issue a cautionary note against taking the arbitrary counters of present-day human languages as the defining feature present at the origin of human language. Linguist Mary LeCron Foster's comprehensive studies of languages worldwide point us in precisely this direction, presenting us with a formidable array of evidence supporting the conclusion that the symbolic structure of primordial language was through and through analogical; particular meanings followed along the lines of the bodily dynamics constituted by particular articulations of the supralaryngeal tract. See Foster 1978, 1990, 1992, and 1996.

28. The first principle is termed "the principle of serviceable associated Habits"; the second, "the principle of Antithesis"; the third, "the principle of actions due to the

constitution of the Nervous System" (Darwin 1872, 28–29). All three principles are spelled out in terms of movement.

29. It is important to emphasize that the disposition toward iconicity is not necessarily a conscious disposition, nor are any of the associated kinetics necessarily consciously planned and executed. Interanimate communication is structured not in reflective acts—e.g., "I think I'll make up a movement pattern and see what happens"—but in prereflective corporeal experience; it is the spontaneous product of certain species-specific bodily experiences. What Freud said of the dreamer is thus more than likely true of dispositions in interanimate communication: "The dreamer's knowledge of symbolism is unconscious" (Freud 1963, 148).

But while the symbolizing animal is, like the dreamer, unaware of its symbolizing behavior as such, *unlike the dreamer*, it is not unaware of its movement. It is conscious of its own actions; it experiences its own body; it experiences its own appetites, desires, and proclivities toward movement and communication. Its thinking is tied to these experiences, which are essentially kinetic experiences. A disposition toward iconicity is thus a disposition toward *analogical thinking*. In turn, to say that analogical thinking is at the root of interanimate communication is to identify a process of thinking in which what is thought is thought along the lines of the body. Analogical thinking is foundationally a process of thinking not in words but in movement. Analogical thinking as a *reflective* act is an elaboration of this basic kinetic dispositional capacity (see Sheets-Johnstone 1990).

30. See, for example, Eimas 1975 and Mehler et al. (n.d.) on the significance of prosodic elements in infant speech perception.

31. Visual artists and art critics stress for good reason the movement in painting and sculpture. Even in newspapers and magazines, pictures of animate creatures present a condensed, stilled version of a particular kinetic semantics, precisely as Ekman's facial expression studies show (see, for example, Ekman 1989 and 1992).

32. See Austin 1962 and Searle 1969.

33. People can feel empathy even for those distant from them. Reading about an earthquake that has devastated thousands, for example, people can respond empathically, and this even if they have never themselves lived through an earthquake. They can imagine what it is like to have the ground move and shake beneath their feet, have their homes crumble, and so on. Similarly, people can see pictures of starving children in third world countries and empathize with them even though they themselves have never been without food.

34. The first edition of Scheler's book—subsequently titled *Wesen und Formen der Sympathie* and translated into English as *The Nature of Sympathy* in 1954—was published in 1913. Scheler writes, for example, that "we are indeed conscious of our expressive movements, but apart from mirrors and suchlike, such consciousness takes the form, merely, of intentions to *move*, and of the consequences which follow from sensations of movement or state; while in the case of others, the primary data are represented by the visual images of such movements, which have *no* sort of immediate resemblance or similarity to the data encountered in our own case" (Scheler 1954, 240). What Scheler overlooks, in addition to the fact that movement is a common sensible, are the *dynamics* of movement: movement is not *sensational*.

35. Berkeley (1709 [1929]) wrote of the incommensurate difference between the visual and tactile in a highly object-tethered sense; that is, he did not consider movement and its kinetic dynamics as a common sensible, nor did he consider self-movement.

36. The facile invocation of a body schema to explain intersubjectivity and empathy in present-day philosophic circles is akin to the well-entrenched practice of cognitive scientists and neuroscientists to invoke entities—"feature analyzers" and "cognitive maps," for example, as well as various mechanisms and detectors noted in the present text—to explain what is puzzling or otherwise inexplicable. The invocation in each

instance specifies a "structure" in the brain that is dedicated to carrying out whatever performance is in need of explanation. The practice is unfortunate, since in each instance knowledge is not actually furthered. For additional discussion of the issue, see Sheets-Johnstone 2003b.

37. See also Hurley 2007, Jacob and Jeannerod 2007, Goldman 2007, Csibra 2007, and Gallese 2007b. These five articles can be found in the May 19, 2007, issue of the on-line journal *Interdisciplines,* under the heading "What Do Mirror Neurons Mean?" The very question indicates that there are language-tethered ambiguities as to what the term 'mirror neurons' signifies, and in connection with those ambiguities, assumptions about the explanatory scope and role of mirror neurons. Indeed, Gallese's response apart, in quite different ways, Jacob and Jeannerod, Goldman, and Csibra strongly challenge the meaning of mirror neurons with respect to social cognition and the mechanism through which social cognition ostensibly operates, i.e., what Gallese and Rizzolatti term 'embodied simulation'. Rizzolatti and Gallese's research nonetheless merits serious attention. Though they do not interpret their findings in terms of a kinetic dynamics, their research on mirror neurons underscores the centrality of movement to intersubjective understandings. They write, for example, that "action understanding . . . discussed here in neural terms, appears very close to the notion of *Einfühlung* as discussed by Husserl" (Rizzolatti and Gallese 1997, 227; see also Gallese et al. 1996 and Rizzolatti et al. 1996).

38. As the previous analysis and discussion has shown, empathy is a natural phenomenon in a double sense: it has an evolutionary lineage as well as a developmental history, and both enter into its accomplishments.

# 6

## Child's Play:
## A Multidisciplinary Perspective

Two chess masters may *play* a friendly café game; in a tournament they *compete*.... [T]he degree of 'playfulness' in an action decreases in proportion as the exploratory drive is adulterated by *other drives;* or to put it differently: as the self-arousing and self-rewarding nature of the activity, ... yields to striving for specific rewards.
—ARTHUR KOESTLER, *The Act of Creation*

Adult contests are becoming the means of younger and younger children as they feel our fears and inherit our struggles. There is a vicious cycle of adults shortening childhood and pressing adulthood onto younger and younger children, followed by younger and younger children acting out adult contests, followed by cries of frightened adults for adult punishments for younger and younger children....

Contest is a centrifugal force, scattering and atomizing people as groups and individuals whose self-awareness depends on identifying others as outsiders.... Our self-esteem is built upon the quicksand of lowering the esteem of others. Our only sense of personal meaning is derived from a contest in which every victory is a funeral.... In its most primal form a contest requires the taking of that which is most valuable, including another's life.... This 'dying' may take many forms from failure in school tests, sporting events, political elections, and corporate takeovers in which one feels 'as though' he died.
—O. FRED DONALDSON, "Belonging: That Bargain Struck in Child's Play"

A play ethic is anything but trivial, although it may be somewhat childlike. It cannot guide us toward the acquisition of power over others or over events, and it is unlikely to create wealth or status, as the work ethic has done. Instead, play grows from our sense of freedom. It produces strength and skill for the players, stimulates the imagination, and encourages agility and self-confidence.... If we were to have a Bill of Rights for Play, it might include the following:

- All players are equal or can be made so.
- Boundaries are well observed by crossing them.
- Novelty is more fun than repetition.
- Rules are negotiable from moment to moment.
- Risk in pursuit of play is worth it.
- The best play is beautiful and elegant.
- The purpose of playing is to play, nothing more.

—JOSEPH W. MEEKER, "Comedy and a Play Ethic"

This chapter—minus the epigraphs—originally appeared in *Human Studies* (Sheets-Johnstone 2003a).

## I. INTRODUCTION

Child's play supports and fosters those empathic understandings that undergird a harmonious communal life. Two passages from the writings of psychiatrist Stuart Brown do not merely exemplify the foundational import of child's play but succinctly dramatize it with respect to its enduring and immediate significance. The first passage is taken from an in-depth psychobiological study of Charles Whitman, the Texas tower mass murderer of the late 1960s, a study commissioned by then-governor of Texas John Connally. In Brown's words, "We had originally expected to discover a brain tumor and drugs as primary causal agents, but our intensive investigation weighted abuse and playlessness as *the* major factors placing him and his future victims at risk" (Brown 1998, 248).[1] The second passage is taken from an unpublished manuscript "Play Maxims" and concerns a Little League player who could make or break the game. The coach did not tell him to "Go out there and by God make the point or else!" but told him that whatever happened, they'd all go out for pizza after the game.

Where competition drowns out play, in particular, the bodily play originating in infancy and typical of young children, it undermines its own foundations, foundations that are phylogenetic as well as ontogenetic. In so doing, it transforms its otherwise low-profile place in early life and gives rise to an altogether other social activity, an activity whose ethos is driven by a premature aggression and whose asocial end is one-dimensionally self-serving. Competition in such instances is not a matter of play become serious, but a matter of no play at all. The motivations and meaning of movement have changed, obliterating the possibilities of play. The name of the game is win, and win at all costs.[2]

I hope to make good on this complex claim, first by considering ethological research on both rough and tumble play and locomotor-rotational play in young human and nonhuman animals; second by examining laughter ontogenetically as a kinetic marker of play and noting its phylogenetic correlates; and third by specifying the foundational moral significances that come to light when child's play is examined in multidisciplinary perspective. My abiding aim in the course of these substantiations—in essence, this exploration of the nature and import of early play without objects—is to provide a deeper appreciation of the original and perduring significance of child's play and the consequent need to preserve its integrity against the premature ingress of adult competition, which, in proportion to its presence, is a perversion of play. Indeed, to discourage, curtail, or otherwise suppress the natural disposition of young humans to play is not only a morally questionable act, but, as the first cited passage from Brown indicates, an act that can have sizable moral consequences for both the deprived individual and for society.

II. ROUGH AND TUMBLE PLAY

Rough and tumble play was first put on the ethological map by N. G. Blurton Jones in his study of three to five year-old nursery-school children in London. Taking the descriptive term "rough and tumble play" from Harry and Margaret Harlow, who used it in their study of social deprivation in monkeys, Blurton Jones found this kind of play to be distinguished by "seven movement patterns which tend to occur at the same time as each other and not to occur with other movements," such as those involved when a child paints, for example, or works with clay (Blurton Jones 1969, 450). The distinctive movements are running, chasing and fleeing, wrestling, jumping up and down with both feet together, beating at each other with an open hand without actually hitting, beating at each other with an object but not hitting, and laughing. Blurton Jones also mentions that falling "seems to be a regular part of this behaviour," and that "if there is anything soft to land on children spend much time throwing themselves and each other on to it" (450).

It is of interest to note that the seven movements—what I would call *the kinetic markers* of rough and tumble play—have received comparatively little attention, though ironically, just such observed movements would seem to have influenced both earlier adultist definitions of play as purposeless, irrational activity, and later functionalist explanations of play as motor training and as practice for adult behavior. Earlier researchers might have observed rough and tumble play and asked: What does jumping up and down accomplish? What does laughing accomplish? What is the rational point of beating without hitting? Later researchers, in contrast, attempt to pin down the adaptive value of such movement. With respect to both earlier definitions and later explanations, however, one might well ask another question: why should early childhood social play center on rough and tumble play, in particular, on pretend attack and defense movements? William James (James 1890

[1950], 429n) posed a similar question when he stated, in answer to a psychologist who claimed that there is no play instinct but only an *"aversion to remain unoccupied,"* "No doubt this is true; but why the particular forms of sham occupation?"[3]

Present-day ethologists regularly note the relationship between attack and defense movements and both human and nonhuman play, but they commonly give an adaptive explanation as above. Robert Fagen, an animal ethologist whose 1981 detailed study of animal play is a landmark volume, wrote more ambiguously on the subject. Stating early on that "[t]he most familiar form of animal play, playfighting and play-chasing[,] consists of cooperative nonagonistic chasing, wrestling, and hitting" (Fagen 1981, 5), he highlights the non-aggressive nature of play, but underscores its equally competitive aspect as well. He begins his chapter "Biology of Social Play" by stating, "Social play at its cooperative best is a biological showpiece. Evenly matched and closely related partners cooperate in apparent mutual physical training and skill development. Their play is non-injurious. It does not harm their social relationship and may even strengthen long-term prospects for their cooperation. An older individual may play altruistically with its younger sibling. Special communicative signals and stabilizing techniques ensure that play is fair to both participants" (387). But Fagen points out too that "[p]lay between individuals is less idyllic when partners are not evenly matched, are not close genetic relatives, and can exploit play interactions for ulterior purposes. Social manipulation, cheating, bullying, and intimidation may then become the norm" (387). While noting further how sociobiologists unsuccessfully insist on a view of play as "damaging competitive behavior" (competitive, that is, in the self-interest of reproductive success), he himself nevertheless emphasizes that play has a tactical objective, and that "[t]he tactical objective of social play is . . . to achieve control of the opponent without being controlled" (411). On this basis, he goes on to vindicate a view of playfighting as having a winner and a loser. Yet, somewhat astoundingly, in the same context he states, "The apparent purpose of play is some form or forms of experience occurring while attempting to achieve a positional objective against a partner's defensive moves or while defending against a partner's attempts to achieve it" (411), and proceeds to quote evolutionary anthropologist Donald Symons, who, in his extended observations of rhesus monkeys (Symons 1978), found that "the striving or competition" (rather than mere achievement or defense of the goal) "appears to be its own reward" (Fagen 1981, 411). In sum, mixed characterizations abound, and they abound not simply because play is a complex kinetic phenomenon and Fagen's coverage of it is extensive and meticulously detailed, but because experiential-semantic levels of discourse remain unexamined, and remaining unexamined, remain conceptually at odds with levels that are.

Other researchers have looked along developmental lines at the relationship between attack and defense movements and rough and tumble play or playfighting, noting, for example—as Karl Groos (1901) did long ago—that "rough and tumble becomes rougher with age, . . . although it is still fundamentally distinct from hostile fighting" (Humphreys and Smith 1984, 255). Other researchers have looked along sexual lines, noting, for example, that boys engage in more rough and tumble play than girls, not only in our own culture but in cultures different from our own. In the context of such developmental and sexual data, researchers of child behavior have noted a relationship between unpopularity and aggression: "Rejected (unpopular) boys, who lack the skills to engage in the cooperative games that build social support and status in adolescence, are much more likely than peers to express dominance and aggression in their play. More than others, rejected boys use rough and tumble to bully and victimize vulnerable lower-ranking children" (Biben 1998, 175).

All such empirical studies present abundant evidence for the distinction between play and competition or aggression, and abundant evidence for developmental and sexual differences in play as well, but none satisfactorily answers the question of why the social play of youngsters centers on rough and tumble play or playfighting. Deeper reflection on the kinetic markers of play is of substantial help in this regard. Blurton Jones originally noted, for example, that playfighting and aggression are facially distinct: rough and tumble play is associated with laughing; aggression with frowning and fixating (Blurton Jones 1969, 451; see also Humphreys and Smith 1984, 251–52). If we eschew the common antithesis between cooperation and competition—the first of these terms being an unelucidated cliché concept with respect to social play—and discount a concern with winners and losers as well, and if we hew instead to kinetic markers, keeping in mind even if not commenting directly upon the increasing roughness of rough and tumble play with age and the difference between girls and boys in amount of rough and tumble play, we perforce anchor attention on bodies and movement. In particular, we anchor attention on bodies and movement *from the beginning* and thereby have the possibility of deeper insights into rough and tumble play and early bodily play in general. As I hope to have shown elsewhere (Sheets-Johnstone 1999b), in the beginning we all learn our bodies and learn to move ourselves—without an owner's manual and without instruction. What I have not shown elsewhere but hope to show here is that in learning our bodies and learning to move ourselves, we first learn the vulnerabilities of being a body—our own vulnerabilities and the vulnerabilities of others in our movement interactions with them.

Rough and tumble play is a way of coming to grips with our vulnerability, indeed, of playing with it, at times literally wrestling with it in the form of another individual. In learning our bodies and learning to move ourselves in the course of rough and tumble play, we learn that we can be hurt: others can shove us too hard, kick or slap us inadvertently, and so on. Rough and tumble play is all the same a sane and safe way of putting our vulnerability on the line, of experiencing firsthand the ultimately fragile bodies we are. It is a self-teaching exercise in corporeal care and survival, not only corporeal care of ourselves and our own survival, but corporeal care of others and their survival.

When we learn our bodies and the bodies of others, we learn a common kinetic language, becoming as kinetically attuned to the movements of others as we are kinesthetically attuned to our own. As noted in the previous chapter, primatologist Stuart Altmann coined the word *comsigns* to designate social behavioral patterns—play signals, for example, or threat gestures—that are common to an animal species or group. Expanding his concept along experiential-semantic lines, we readily see that comsigns are part of a common kinetic language structured in common movement patterns emanating from a common body and having common experiential dynamics and common meanings. From this experiential-semantic perspective, rough and tumble play, like bodily play in general, can hardly be categorized as Johan Huizinga of otherwise well-deserved *Homo ludens* fame and other researchers of play have categorized it, namely, as purposeless and irrational activity. What is kinetically pervasive among individuals and has commonly experienced dynamics and commonly recognized meanings can be judged neither purposeless nor irrational. From this same perspective, neither can rough and tumble play nor bodily play in general be adequately explained as motor training or practice for adult behavior. Indeed, adaptive scenarios are no more help than non-adaptive scenarios in understanding play, and this because play, as noted, is a complex kinetic phenomenon demanding close attention in its own right as the developmental, evolutionary, and *experientially meaningful* phenomenon that it is. It in fact calls for a triumvirate of perspectives: ontogenetic, phylogenetic, and philosophical. Short of the latter perspective, foundational understandings of the nature of play are short-circuited. So too are deeper significances that, on the one hand, are concealed in the question: why these movements—running, chasing, beating without actually hitting, laughing—and not others?; and on the other hand, are couched in awarenesses of what it is to be the body one is and what it is like to be the body one is not. Experience and meaning are not subsidiary, empirically dispensable aspects of a behavioral package marked "play," but non-expungeable dimensions of the phenomenon itself, and this because they in fact constitute its *raison d'être*. As Fagen and Symons obliquely indicate, the motivation to play and the import of play lie in the experience and meaning of play itself.

In effect, when vigorous—and vigorously promoted—competition prematurely intrudes on play, it diverts the attention of children from their still growing bodies. It robs them of the space they need to explore their strengths, their weaknesses, their endurance, their agility, their capacity to think in movement in the immediacy of the moment, their kinetic ingenuity, and so on. It catapults them beyond their years and their abilities, deflecting them from testing their possibilities and recognizing their limitations in relatively risk-free ways. It shunts their attention from the care and survival of others in concert with their own to a quest for dominance over others. It focuses attention on something altogether different: winning.

We should note that the learning of vulnerabilities is not mediated by language; indeed, it is not linguistified nor is it even necessarily 'linguistifiable'. It is not and cannot be codified into a series of rules. Neither is it nor can it be tested, measured, and quantified; it is not translatable into objective formulas. While an infant or child may be verbally admonished not to shove or hit because he or she can hurt another in doing so, the verbal admonishment only vaguely captures the desired *nonlinguistic* awarenesses and *corporeal concepts*. The awarenesses and concepts go beyond mere verbal prohibitions and cause-effect statements. In this respect, nonhuman animals are one step ahead of their human counterparts. Nonhuman animals know the so-called rules of social play kinetically, and know them kinetically from the start:

claws are automatically retracted, bites are not actual bites, and so on (e.g., Fagen 1981, 395–96). There is no adult individual admonishing a younger one to back off in some way or other and to think about how one can hurt another individual.

We should note too that though one might insist that learning one's vulnerabilities is adaptive (i.e., it is in the service of fitness for reproductive success), such a conception de-personifies, or better and more inclusively, de-animates living bodies, bodies that initiate movement, that terminate movement, that can speed up or slow down in the process of moving, that can intensify their efforts, expand the range of their movement, change direction, and so on. Living bodies are motivated bodies that move voluntarily in the course of learning vulnerabilities; they are neither automatons nor lumbering robots at the command of their genes. Moreover that vulnerability is *learned*, and learned first and foremost in the course of moving, means that it is *experienced*, which in turn means that corporeal-kinetic meanings resonate in living ways and become engrained in the kinetic lifestyle of the living animal, and that a kinetically discriminating intelligence, a bodily logos, is cultivated and constituted in the process. In short, to insist that learning one's vulnerabilities is simply adaptive is to insist that learning one's body and learning to move oneself are adaptive, which is to insist that virtually everything in the end is adaptive, the bottom line being in its ultimate formulation a *reductio ad absurdum:* being alive has survival value and is adaptive for reproductive success!

Put in a wider philosophic-scientific perspective as above, it is readily apparent not only that rough and tumble play is play with the vulnerabilities of being a body—play with the fears, inhibitions, hesitations, worries, and so on, that arise in the course of learning our bodies and learning to move ourselves—but that rough and tumble play is at the same time fun—most commonly, great and overriding fun! This integral and preeminent dimension of play was actually recognized early on by researchers of play[4] and cannot reasonably be written off in the current manner of sociobiologists who are content to claim that animals find "sweet" the activities in which they engage (Barash 1982, 147). To begin with, pleasure is not a kind of background music provided by wholly theoretical genes to keep us interested, focused, and on target—whether a matter of mating, hunting, or eating. Most important, applied to play, the purported *sotto voce* accompaniment is a gross distortion. Experience, in particular, kinetic/tactile-kinesthetic experience in rough and tumble play, and in bodily play generally, cannot be reduced to an accompanying sweetness no matter how much ultimate causation is pedestalled over proximate causation. Pleasure or fun in running, chasing, laughing, jumping, beating, and so on, is quite literally pleasure or fun in the flesh. It is not an accessory to a main event, but the main event itself. Close examination of locomotor-rotational play will corroborate this fact precisely because, whether socially situated or not, it is a matter of individual experience.

III. LOCOMOTOR-ROTATIONAL PLAY

Consider the following description by A. S. Einarsen (1948, 122), a wildlife specialist:

> Coming cautiously one day over a rimrock at Spanish Lake, I saw a group of seven antelope kids with their mothers on the hard shore-edge of the receding lake. The mothers were contentedly resting in the warm June sun, apparently at ease and unaware of my approach. The kids were having a great time in a quite highly organized game. Rushing away across the flat rim of the lake shore, as though started by a lifting of a barrier on a race track, they ran neck and neck, swung in a wide arc and then thundered back, their tiny hooves beating in unison as they soared rather than ran, their bodies parallel to the earth. Upon nearing the starting point they drew up to a stiff-legged stop at their mothers' sides, gazed with dreamy eyes around the immediate vicinity, then wheeled away on another flight, with apparently enough power and enthusiasm to drive them to the summit of the Rocky Mountains 1,000 miles away.

Ethologist John Byers comments that Einarsen's description of pronghorn play emphasizes "what all ungulate young do when they play. They run" (Byers 1984, 43). More broadly, Fagen notes, "The best-known locomotor-rotational movements are leaping, rolling, headshaking, body-twisting, neck flexion, rearing, and kicking" (Fagen 1981, 48). Fagen remarks further that "[c]ommon usage gives these lay movements special status by employing unique terms: gambol, caper, romp, scamper, frolic, rollick, frisk, jink, cavort, ragrowster, *gambader* (French), and *balgen* and *tollen* (German)" (48).

Now it would be as absurd to dismiss these "unique terms" as mere anthropomorphic, subjective, or literary glosses as to dismiss tactile-kinesthetic experience as mere behavioral gloss. Moving—running, leaping, rolling, cavorting—is clearly fun, whether you are a harbor seal, a pygmy hippopotamus, a giant panda, a caviomorph rodent, or a human child—animals who have all been observed by ethologists to gambol, caper, romp, frolic, and so on (48). Given this ethological perspective, we can begin to appreciate how and why movement can itself be a motivating force, or correlatively from a dynamic systems perspective, how and why movement can itself be an attractor. Movement is enjoyable, pleasurable; for the moving individual, it produces a high, an elevated sense of aliveness, a delight in the kinetic dynamics that is under way. We can furthermore readily understand the regular emphasis on both the vigorous and remarkable nature of play movement. When Fagen, for example, writes, "Play is rich in brisk and lively body movements" (287), and Byers (Byers 1984, 47) writes that ungulate play is "often spectacular and dramatic," and evolutionary psychologist K.R.L. Hall writes that the social play of patas monkeys is "exceedingly vigorous and spectacular in the wild, much of it being high-speed chasing—some of it mock-fighting" (Hall 1967, 277), each is giving voice to the fact that movement itself is compelling, compelling in both a motivating sense and in an attention-getting sense; it is itself both a sufficient reason to move and a sufficient reason for attention. In the latter sense, it is indeed a magnet, capturing the attention of human and nonhuman animals alike. Though not stopping to remark on its significance, ethologists S. M. Pellis and V. C. Pellis note the magnetic pull of movement in their observation of magpies in the midst of swarming beetles. Rather than following the behavior of adult magpies who walk slowly and catch beetles that fall to the ground, younger magpies run after a beetle, but as soon as it drops in the grass and another beetle flies by, they chase the new beetle each time. "The juveniles," Pellis and Pellis remark "were clearly distracted by, and attracted to, movement" (Pellis and Pellis 1998, 131). Their assessment agrees with the experimental findings of psychologist T. G. R. Bower, who found that infants "ignore features [of objects] to such an extent that I would suggest that they respond *not to moving objects but to movements*" (Bower 1971, 37; italics added). In short, movement is primary in early animate life, the attractor *par excellence*.

The doubly compelling nature of movement is further reason why kinetic pleasure cannot be marginalized as mere *sotto voce* phenomenon in the lives of animals, human and nonhuman. Adult humans who cannot grasp the pleasure in bodily play may well be out of touch with themselves as moving bodies and therefore out of touch with the kinetic joyride that movement affords (Sheets-Johnstone 1986a, 242). Several of Darwin's observations on pleasure and movement are instructive in this regard. To begin with, although Darwin speaks of "purposeless movements" in the context of pleasure, it is not with dismissive, deprecatory, or trivializing intent. He points out (1872, 76) that

> [u]nder a transport of Joy or of vivid Pleasure, there is a strong tendency to various purposeless movements, and to the utterance of various sounds. We see this in our young children, in their loud laughter, clapping of hands, and jumping for joy; in the bounding and barking of a dog when going out to walk with his master, and in the frisking of a horse when turned out into an open field. Joy quickens the circulation, and this stimulates the brain, which again reacts on the whole body.

He goes on to observe that "with animals of all kinds, the acquirement of almost all their pleasures, with the exception of those of warmth and rest, are associated, and have long been associated with active movements, as in the hunting or search for food, and in their courtship," and then points out, "Moreover, the mere exertion of the muscles after long rest or confinement is in itself a pleasure, as we ourselves feel, and as we see in the play of young animals" (77). He concludes that "on this latter principle alone [i.e., the pleasure of bodily play] we might perhaps expect, that vivid pleasure would be apt to show itself conversely in muscular movements" (77).

Now obviously, when Darwin says that joy and pleasure are expressed in purposeless movement, he does not mean that joy and pleasure are purposeless. But neither does he mean that purposeless movement is insignificant or meaningless. On the contrary, he pointedly suggests that movement is self-stimulating when he notes that "joy quickens the circulation," and explicitly observes that movement can itself be a source of pleasure, not only in the fact that "active movement" is associated with pleasurable activities, but in the fact that "the mere exertion of muscles"—movement—is a felt pleasure.[5] In short, movement is in and of itself engaging, fun, and delightful, and it is engaging, fun, and delightful because it resonates in feelings of aliveness radiating dynamically through a kinetic/tactile-kinesthetic body.

It is important to emphasize that one does not have to language the experience of movement to appreciate such feelings. It is quite unnecessary to think to oneself or say aloud, "Oh! Does this ever make me feel vibrant, lively, and spirited! How great it is to be alive!" One appreciates the feelings directly in the kinetic/tactile-kinesthetic experience itself; one savors the experience of kinetic fun—kinetic fun in being a body, kinetic fun in the flesh—without words. Nonhuman animals are thus experientially not at a loss for words but can in fact, in their bodily play, teach humans something basic and important about themselves, something that, as a nonlinguistic and in essence non-linguistifiable experience, they may have trivialized or suppressed.

Byers's evolutionary view that locomotor-rotational play is the progenitor of play is relevant to consider here, though in ways that go beyond his adaptive valuation of it in terms of a "common ancestral function," namely, motor training (Byers 1984, 60). His descent with modification thesis—that more sophisticated forms of play—social play and play with objects—were spin-offs from locomotor-rotational play—is significant in terms not only of what we might call the complexification of fun and pleasure, but what we might call the complexification of vulnerabilities in the evolution of play. As indicated earlier, as corporeal-kinetic knowledge of one's own vulnerabilities and capacities is built up and integrated, it grounds knowledge of the vulnerabilities and capacities of others in one's social play with them. The most basic form of social knowledge is thus empathic in character and its foundations lie in intercorporeal understandings generated in and by corporeal-kinetic knowledge of one's own body. More finely stated, empathic understandings of others come by way of corporeal-kinetic transfers of sense. The transfers are not reasoned out connections, but neither are they on that account what some, following scientist-turned-philosopher Michael Polanyi (1969), might call a form of "tacit knowledge." On the contrary, by turning full attention to bodies and movement, we can trace out ways in which corporeal-kinetic understandings of the vulnerability of our own body is built up, and in being built up, is the basis of our understandings and appreciations of the movement possibilities and limitations—the vulnerabilities—of others in our movement interactions with them. In phenomenological terms, we can come to understand how a repertoire of "I cans" and "I cannots"[6] comes literally into play in the constitution of our own bodies in experiences of play and, in turn, in the constitution of the bodies of others in our experiences of play with them.[7] By the same token, we can trace out ways in which play opens up corporeal-kinetic possibilities and thereby opens up space for innovation, a field in which creative energies can surge.[8] Complexification of fun derives from the basic ability to think in creative kinetic ways in the moment, expanding a range of "I cans" and thereby achieving greater degrees of freedom. In play with others, these creative energies and degrees of freedom are compounded so that play can be and often is on the verge of breaking out into something new at the same time that it is intercorporeally structured in the kinetically and kinesthetically known. Playing with others at the cutting edge of innovation complexifies the fundamental pleasure, fun, and delight of movement.

IV. PLAY AND LAUGHTER

What is commonly termed "display behavior" corroborates and points up the import of experientially resonant, semantically laden intercorporeal awarenesses and restraints structuring the intercorporeal-kinetic bonds of rough and tumble play and playfighting, what we might broadly designate *play sport*, including under its aegis locomotor-rotational play as well. Social semantic understandings are of course critical to the relationships of social animals generally, but they are particularly critical to the initiation and continuance of play since what actually ensues in the interaction is contingent on the recognition of a play signal (or play-promoting signal [Pellis and Pellis 1996]). In canids (dogs, wolves, coyotes, and so on), for example, the play signal is a "play bow," a lowering of the forelegs, and thus the forward end of the body, the hindlegs remaining upright (Bekoff 1995). What I want to consider here, however, is a signal more closely aligned with an element of human play: laughter. The relaxed open-mouthed face of most primate species—the play face—is homologous to human laughter (van Hooff 1969, 1972). (The silent bared-teeth face, it might be noted, is homologous to human smiling.) The relaxed open-mouthed primate face initiates play and occurs during play, and sounds regularly emitted during its expression are glossed as "ah, ah." Detailed phylogenetic analyses linking the nonhuman primate play face and sounds to the face and sounds of human laughter were carried out by ethologist J. A. R. A. M. van Hooff, the relationship being further commented upon by Blurton Jones in his studies of children's rough and tumble play (Blurton Jones 1969, 1972). Psychologist Anthony Ambrose's study of the original bivalent affective nature of human laughter, though unconcerned with phylogeny, is relevant to the phylogenetic analysis.

The aim of Ambrose's study is to show how infant laughter is motivated by "ambivalent tendencies," and how these ambivalent tendencies are manifest in particular patterns of behavior. On the basis of his own observations and the research studies of others, Ambrose notes first that infants commonly laugh in three types of situation: in being suddenly surprised, in being tickled, and in exploratory play or in the noticing of something new (Ambrose 1963, 170).[9] He comments that when looked at from the viewpoint of ambivalent tendencies, it is apparent that each situation "has a dual effect on the infant": at the same time it elicits fear or anger, it is "enjoyable or relieving" (171).[10] Where fear or anger predominate, a "stimulus-terminating tendency" predominates and crying results; where enjoyment or relief predominate, a "stimulus-maintaining tendency" predominates and laughter results. Giving an example of each situation in turn, he shows how in laughter, enjoyment is "tinged" with fear (171).[11] Turning attention to differences in patterns of behavior between enjoyment and fear, he descriptively pinpoints differences in movement and posture. In the fear response of crying, "There is tenseness of muscles, the fists are often clenched, and arms and legs move and kick spasmodically"; eyes are closed, the forehead is furrowed, and "the mouth assumes a rather rectangular form." In enjoyment—not in laughter specifically yet, but in enjoyment generally—eyes are open, there are "more or less rhythmic arm and leg movements which are free from restraint" and "movements of incipient approach rather than withdrawal" (172). Most notably, there is a fundamental difference in respiration between fear and enjoyment, a difference that, as Ambrose shows, is precisely homogenized in the phenomenon of laughter: as in enjoyment, there is "heightened inspiration . . . interrupted by . . . expirations"; as in crying, there is a continuous series of expirations, "shorter at each occurrence," and interrupted by vocalizations which emerge "in the form 'ha-ha-ha'" and are "lower pitched than in crying" (173). In fact, Ambrose observes, "laughter generally begins with a vigorous expiration, rarely with an inspiration," though deep inspirations occur during laughter and usually on its termination (173).

Particularly in view of his bivalent characterization of laughter, it is odd that in his observations of respiration, Ambrose does not consider the initial gasp of fear. As Sir Charles Bell[12] noted in his third edition of *The Anatomy and Philosophy of Expression*, published in 1844, "the first sound of fear is in drawing, not in expelling the breath; for at that instant to depress or contract the chest would be to relax the muscles of the arms and enfeeble their exertion." In fact, to make the point more strongly, Sir Charles asks the reader to imagine two men wrestling in the dark, asking whether "the violence of their efforts" would not be apparent from the sounds they make: "The short exclamation choked in the act of exertion, the feeble and stifled sounds of their breathing, would let us know that they turned, and twisted, and were in mortal strife" (Bell 1844, 190–91). In short, while the gasp of fear is an outright response to felt vulnerability, laughter is an outright affirmation of its successful subduction in play. From the perspective of respiration, laughter is a defusion of fear: the gasp of fear is released in bursts of exhalation. In effect, from the perspective of play, laughter defuses vulnerability at the same time giving voice to the edge of fear that vulnerability provokes.

These deeper understandings of the relationship between respiration and fear aside, Ambrose's empirical data and thesis make sense phylogenetically as well as ontogenetically. For example, Darwin long ago observed that tickling elicits the same response in chimpanzees as in humans: "If a young chimpanzee be tickled—and the armpits are particularly sensitive to tickling, as in the case of our children, . . . [a] chuckling or laughing sound is uttered; though the laughter is sometimes noiseless. The corners of the mouth are . . . drawn backwards; and this sometimes causes the lower eyelids to be slightly wrinkled. But this wrinkling, which is so characteristic of our own laughter, is more plainly seen in some monkeys" (Darwin 1872, 131). Van Hooff's more recent descriptions of the nonhuman primate play face show that our phylogenetic ties run even deeper.

> In the majority of primates [the relaxed open-mouth play face display] has much in common with the aggressive *staring open-mouth* display. [It should be noted that "A monkey is rarely purely aggressive, without being a little fearful as well." Thus

the term "agonistic," which designates conjoined "aggressive and fearful behaviour" (Rowell 1972, 93).] It is likewise characterised by a rather widely opened mouth, and lips that remain covering all or the greater part of the teeth. It differs from the *staring open-mouth* display by the free and easy nature of the eye and body movements and by the fact that the mouth-corners are not pulled forward. (van Hooff 1972, 217)

The mouth and body gestures van Hooff describes clearly coincide with the ambivalent tendencies Ambrose describes. The subducted edge of fear in primate tickling and play generally is readily explainable in terms of an inability to predict with certainty what will happen next.[13] The inability extends in more and more complicated ways as infants mature and engage in more vigorous bodily play with others. Indeed, all social animals are at risk with respect to conspecifics, who can bite them, kick them, even cripple or disfigure them. As pointed out in Chapter 1, humans hurt each other bodily first and foremost. The same is obviously true of all animals. Our primary vulnerability is corporeal: our bodies are ever open to injury and to death from the violence of others.[14] Indeed, and again, as pointed out in Chapter 1, we humans are at risk not only by the mere fact of being alive, but *in being alive among other humans*. That ethical studies do not begin with a recognition of this fundamental fact of life but are instead regularly caught up from the start in theoretical inquiries about moral agency, moral status, rights, moral obligations, and so on, is peculiar, particularly since the fundamental fact of life is evident from the beginning, both ontogenetically and phylogenetically.

Ambrose's data and thesis are relevant in a further phylogenetic sense. Laughter did not suddenly emerge from the mouths of hominids, but evolved on the basis of already extant movements and gestures within the corporeal-kinetic repertoires of ancestrally related primates, those movements and gestures having affective components akin to enjoyment and fear. In a related way, laughter issues from the mouths of babes on the basis of developmental affectivities as they unfold and open the door to playfulness and play.

V. MORALITY AND CHILD'S PLAY

In conclusion, I would like to highlight three critical aspects in the relationship between morality and child's play.

First, competition and the perversion of child's play should be a topic of pressing interest, even urgency. The incursion of competition into child's play accelerates a child's motivations and satisfactions beyond its years. When power, dominance, fame, and fortune overturn a child's motivation to play, they become the motivating sources of sport and define its felt satisfaction or pleasure. Winning becomes the sole goal because—power, fame, and fortune aside—it alone certifies achievement, mastery, and categorical superiority. The rest is silence and oblivion.

Second, child's play is not lacking in either complexity or meaning. Neither is it "something easily done," as the dictionary states and metaphoric usage maintains. Moreover while child's play is neither purposeless nor irrational, and while it is not adequately explained as motor training or as practice for adult behavior, it is not either properly viewed as an innocent, carefree activity. Such notions of child's play are adultist in conception, and ontogenetically, phylogenetically, and phenomenologically uninformed. Drew Hyland's engrossing and stimulating book *The Question of Play* is of moment precisely in this context, specifically at the point when Hyland wants to show how child's play, "with its connotations of spontaneity, freedom, whimsicality, purposelessness, unpredictability, and irrationality," is "an important alternative" to his own view of play (Hyland 1984, 79). He proceeds to discuss the important alternative by showing how the paradigm of child's play as carefree, purposeless, and so on, undergirds decisive aspects of the philosophy of Nietzsche, Heidegger, Gadamer, Fink, Derrida, and Foucault, and how it is a limited conception of play, failing to do justice to the richness and significance of play. In his critique, however, he never mentions ontogeny or phylogeny, and thus fails to put in perspective the origin, nature, and development of child's play itself. The romanticized notion of child's play that he criticizes is not in fact child's play at all and is misguided in whatever philosophical guise it appears. What requires elucidation, and from a multidisciplinary perspective, is precisely the play that *is* child's play. A societal ethics hangs in the balance, for what is there *and what is not there* in the otherwise natural experiences and meanings of child's play is quintessentially related to what is there *and what is not there* in the play of adults. Child's play is the original sport. It is there naturally before any developmental shifts toward competition, dominance, or aggression. It constitutes a kinetic engagement with one's own body and the bodies of others, an engagement which is great fun and at the same time fearsome in varying degrees in bringing vulnerabilities to the fore. Precisely because play begins in ontogeny and not in adult life—play in fact peaks before adulthood—there is further reason for averring that child's play is a pressing topic to be examined, not only by teachers in early childhood education and by public school physical educators, but by researchers engaged in the study of sport.

In its concern with rules, a further passage from Hyland's critique is relevant. Hyland notes that all the philosophers he discusses cite the same fragment from Heraclitus, which he translates as: "Time (or lifetime) is a child playing at draughts. Kingship belongs to a child" (82).[15] He points out that draughts is actually "a game with rules and ordered moves" (82), that time (or lifetime) is thus "a rule-governed game" (92), and hence that it is something other than child's play as understood by the philosophers he discusses. A different interpretation of the fragment, however, aptly captures the philosophical allure of Heraclitus's epitomization of time as child's play. The interpretation sheds light on Hyland's parenthetical alternative or disjunctive "lifetime" in relation to time proper and thereby highlights a third critical aspect in the relationship between morality and child's play.

A child is ignorant of death; it plays at draughts as time plays with mortal humans. Time and child are alike oblivious and imperturbable,[16] caught up in the flow of their activity, each of them undistracted by mortally aware humans. Time and the draughts-playing child are in fact one with Heraclitus's famous river. The river too is caught up in its own activity, undistracted and essentially unperturbed by the footsteps of mortal humans. Hyland seems to recognize this thematic obliquely when he says that "we can share with these thinkers [philosophers] a recognition of the significance of finitude" (109). He seems to recognize it obliquely too in his later discussion of risk-taking, where he points out that one can risk not merely physical injury, as in some contact sports, but that in sports such as rock climbing and automobile racing, one takes "the genuine risk . . . of death" (127). In sports such as skydiving and race car driving, one does indeed play with death, putting one's vulnerability on the line, betting that one can get the better of it or outwit it. A short-lived immortality ideology is enacted each time one comes through alive. Playing with death in these ways is playing against the oblivious, imperturbable child rapt in its game of draughts, but the oblivious, imperturbable child, having the kingship in its hands, will always win. Time will always be the victor because life is a rule-governed game, a *single* rule-governed game. No one knows when the rule will be enforced, but death is inevitable—even if no one thinks the rule applies to him or her personally. The draughts-playing child is thus most certainly playing a rule-governed game, but one in which, "ordered moves" or not, it cannot predict with certainty what will happen next, how and when the game will end, when kingship will be claimed. The single rule is as unpredictable as it is inviolable. As if crystallizing this uncertainty, the rule-*un*governed, hence free, structure of early childhood play brings the experience of our fundamental ontological reality to the fore. Its rule-*un*protected openness accentuates and intensifies vulnerability, making it fearsome, the stark uncertainty of what will happen next at times exceeding the possibility of laughter.[17] If not for our quintessential vulnerability, trust would hardly figure as a crucial factor in play, not only for Hyland, who specifies among his examples, trust in the driving ability of other drivers, trust that one's squash opponent is not intentionally going to hurt one, but for infant-child psychoanalyst Erik Erikson (1950), who, in his influential systemization of the critical developmental stages of human life, lists feelings of trust or mistrust in the world as the first and most basic psychosocial crisis of infancy.[18] Where would the roots of the need or desire for trust lie if not in feelings of vulnerability? Further still, what is risk-taking if it is not a measure of our foundational vulnerability?

Rough and tumble play and locomotor-rotational play are clearly not games "with rules and ordered moves" nor is kingship their ultimate end. They are not in fact games at all except in the sense of posing a kinetic challenge. As indicated above, they are more aptly categorized *play sport* and the putative rules that apply to them are more properly termed *principles*.[19] The principles of play sport are learned kinetically. They are not game-specific but undergird all games later played across the domain of sport. They are learned kinetically because they are in fact kinetic. Indeed, this is why they are foundational to all later rule-governed games. In a wider sense, this is why they are foundational to human morality. They embody, in a literal kinetic sense, a repertoire of "I cans" and "I cannots" with respect to others. They are beginning moral precepts in that they constitute the base line of a social morality, namely, the recognition of other humans as equal to oneself in vulnerability. The kinetically learned principles of play sport are, in effect, foundational principles not just for sport but for life.

## NOTES

1. Brown's subsequent participation in studies of young murderers throughout the state of Texas and in a multidisciplinary, federally funded auto accident study eventuated in a similar finding with respect to play: *"normal play behavior was virtually absent throughout the lives of highly violent, anti-social men"* (Brown 1998, 249).

2. War is the ultimate instantiation of this game. As shown in Chapters 3 and 4, there is little indication in the literature—in the sciences or the humanities—that a concrete biological-cultural relationship exists between male-male competition and war, but male-male competition is surely a driving force in the instigation and pursuit of war. Broadly stated, the uniquely human game of war is the ultimate cultural manifestation of the biological phenomenon of male-male competition. A bio-developmental analysis of the relationship would show that as rough and tumble play is the ground on which human male-male competition develops and comes to the fore, so war is the most extreme terrain on which it is honed and pursued. That Konrad Lorenz does not mention this relationship in his study of aggression (Lorenz 1966) is surprising.

Johan Huizinga's characterization of war is of interest in this context. In his chapter titled "Play and War" in *Homo ludens*, Huizinga discusses medieval tournaments, chivalric behavior, codes of honor, and such, distinguishing these realities of "archaic warfare" that had a "play-element" from the realities of modern "total war" (Huizinga 1955, 91, 103; 90): "The modern outbursts of glorifying war, so lamentably familiar to us, carry us back to the Babylonian and Assyrian conception of war as a divine injunction to exterminate foreign peoples to the greater glory of God" (90–91). In archaic warfare the time and place of war was decided in advance, for example, and actual killing was often avoided by diplomatic action. Though in his discussion of such warfare, Huizinga speaks of honor, chivalry, and the like, and not of vulnerability, there can hardly be doubt that along with "the desire for prestige and all the pomps of superiority" (90) was a recognition of vulnerability—one's own vulnerability and that of others. After all, unless one survived, there would be no prestige or pomp to be had.

The strategies of opposing military leaders who, by conferring or warning each other in advance of their moves, avoided actual conflict appear strikingly similar to the strategies of baboons and other primates who, through threat, bluff, and the like, avert an actual fight. Primatological psychologist K. R. L. Hall writes that "[r]elationships between baboon groups are characterized by mutual tolerance or mutual avoidance according to the nature of the habitat" (Hall 1968, 154), the characterization resting on the fact that "[n]o aggressive interactions between groups have ever been recorded by Hall and DeVore in over 2000 hours of observation" (155). Zoologist Peter Marler concurs: "Physical combat [between groups of primates] seems to be uncommon, except in some populations of rhesus and irus macaques" (Marler 1968, 424–25). Similarly, primatologist Kenji Yoshiba (Yoshiba 1968, 235), in his observations of Hanuman langurs, writes that "[i]ntertroop aggressive encounters seldom develop into severe fights between members of the two troops, but sometimes the leader and the females of one troop will slap and bite those of the other troop, although no animal is usually hurt in such encounters."

A further aspect of the similarity between human primate archaic warfare and nonhuman primate intertroop interactions is of interest. At the time the above-cited field researchers were conducting their studies, evolutionary anthropologist Sherwood Washburn and psychologist David Hamburg were urging caution with respect to just such judgments of aggression between same-species groups of nonhuman primates. They wrote, "It is our belief that intertroop aggression in primates has been greatly underestimated" (Washburn and Hamburg 1968, 470). Primate field studies certainly support diplomatic solutions as exemplified above, but instances of aggression are not lacking.

For example, and as described in Chapters 1 and 4, primatologists Richard Wrangham and Dale Peterson, in their book *Demonic Males*, recount how, with no provocation, chimpanzees of one group brutally assault isolated chimpanzees of another group. Such instances, however, appear to be less instances of intertroop aggression—they involve a single individual from "the other side"—than instances of heightened excitement and frenzied attack, in essence, aggression *tout court*, as Wrangham and Peterson themselves indicate (Wrangham and Peterson 1996, 70; see also 6, 14, 17). Moreover recent field studies of intertroop exchanges uphold the judgments of earlier researchers. For example, evolutionary anthropologist Shirley Strum, who conducted field observations of olive baboons over a period of fifteen years, states, "Interactions between troops varied a great deal, from peaceful mingling, with the two groups appearing as one to an untrained observer, to active aggression between certain members of each troop. Aggression occasionally escalated: one troop would mob the other more or less the way they mobbed a particularly aggressive male from their own group" (Strum 1987, 92), namely, by pushing the offender "beyond the edge of the group" by a "mobbing vocalization" (88).

In a later discussion of aggression from an evolutionary viewpoint, Strum asks, "Shouldn't the same evolutionary processes that developed aggressive capabilities also have developed alternatives to aggression, as potential losers sought a way to not always be a loser?" her point being that "[i]f aggression existed, then alternatives should also [have] exist[ed]," even though "all species might [not] be capable of finding such alternatives" (Strum 1987, 146). Strum's point should be well taken, since self-assertive aggression that brooks no obstacles to its attacks may be self-defeating in its inflexibility—it may, for example, be overthrown by group action, precisely as mobbing behavior suggests.

Finally, it should be noted that several field researchers remark upon the fact that, with respect to *intra*-group aggression, actual fighting between male baboons is rare. Strum notes the fact briefly (Strum 1987, fig. 15); Hall does more extensively:

> Fighting amongst the adult males is extremely rare, the demonstrations between them consisting mainly of, to the onlooker, impressive, noisy chases without physical contact being made. These "threat displays" are probably less stereotyped than those described for other nonprimate mammals, but are likely to have the same social significance. Discipline within the group is usually very adequately maintained by threat, or by beating and biting of the subordinate on the nape of the neck which very rarely result in any visible injury to the victim. The overall picture of group organization in these animals is of a sensitive balancing of forces. . . . In other words, physical prowess may not be actually tested, the confident usurping animal achieving his end simply by some of the forms of threat display and moving toward the other animal."
> (Hall 1968, 154)

Surely if there are human lessons to be learned about war and peace, some of the lessons are to be learned at the knees of our primate relatives. Huizinga's rendition of what one might think of as "the niceties" of archaic warfare, the anthropology of war tells another story. See archaeologist Lawrence Keeley's detailed analysis and provocative discussion of the myth of a peaceful hominid past in *War Before Civilization* (Keeley 1996), a topic and work cited in Chapter 3.

3. In his *Principles of Psychology* (vol. 2), James actually paid surprisingly little attention to play. He concludes his short section on play with the statement, "The immense extent of the play-activities in human life is too obvious to be more than mentioned" (James 1890 [1950], 429).

4. See, for example, Pycraft 1912, Tinkelpaugh 1942, and Bolwig 1963. See also well-known animal psychologist Frank Beach (Beach 1978, 531), who, writing of the *joie-de-vivre* hypothesis of play, states that "its uncritical adoption tends to discourage and render apparently unnecessary any further attempt to examine in detail the real nature of the reactions thus 'explained'." Earlier, he states, "The first and most obvious objection is that this so-called interpretation does not interpret nor explain. . . . [There is] no advance in the understanding of basic causal relationships responsible for the outward activity" (530). It is obviously difficult to credit an experiential explanation of play if experience is discounted. It is correlatively difficult to specify the nature of the experience of play if meaning is discounted. It would seem that, for Beach as for many if not most contemporary scientists, the spectre of subjectivity is too closely aligned with play for experience and meaning to be acknowledged and investigated. Such investigations would elucidate not causal relationships "responsible for the outward activity," but reasons for engaging in "the outward activity" in the first place.

5. Again, we see that it is quite inadequate to say that animals find "sweet" the activities in which they engage.

6. The concept "I can" comes from Husserl and figures centrally in his epistemological understandings of "the kinestheses." See, for example, Husserl 1983 and 1970a, 106–8, 161, 217, 331–32. See also Sheets-Johnstone 1990, 1994b, and 1999b. The concept "I cannot" is of equal significance and warrants elucidation in its own right. For a beginning sketch, see Sheets-Johnstone 1994b, 131–34.

7. Hume took transfers of sense for granted in terms of sympathy in his *Treatise of Human Nature*, stating, for example, "The minds of all men are similar in their feelings and operations. . . . As in strings equally wound up, the motion of one communicates itself to the rest; so all the affections readily pass from one person to another, and beget correspondent movements in every human creature" (Hume [1739] 1888, 575–76).

As shown in Chapter 5, Hume's account of sympathy as a natural human affection can be both deepened and enriched by phenomenological, ontogenetic, and phylogenetic analyses and understandings of empathy. Through this deepened and enriched perspective, we can readily see that it is not simply that comsigns can be performed by all members of the same species or group, but that *the tactile-kinesthetic feel* of these comsigns is virtually the same for all, and tactile-kinesthetic feeling being virtually the same for all, affective meanings are virtually the same for all. In brief, we see that empathic understandings underpin the actual functionality of comsigns and that lacking empathic underpinnings, comsigns are shells of behavior bereft of meaning.

8. This characterization of play as opening a field of possibilities is akin to Hyland's primary characterization of play as a "responsive openness" (Hyland 1984).

9. Ambrose notes that infants begin laughing at approximately four months and that laughter "has precursors that are manifested from the first week of life" (Ambrose 1963, 170), "precursors" alluding most probably to the fact that smiling occurs prior to laughing. The prior occurrence of smiling has been noted over many years by many people, including Darwin (see, for example, Sully 1907, Stearns 1972, and Darwin 1872).

10. Cf. D. W. Winnicott's psychoanalytic of play (Winnicott 1971). Although his theoretics of play is more closely tied to the realities of psychotherapy than to everyday life, Winnicott's descriptive account of play closely echoes Ambrose's bivalent account. He writes, for example, that "[p]laying is inherently exciting and precarious" (52). Its precariousness derives from the fact that "it is always on the theoretical line between the subjective and that which is objectively perceived" (50), the objectively perceived being "actual, or shared reality" (52). The precariousness of play that Winnicott describes can correlatively be seen as deriving from a tension between the unknown and the known, insecurity and security—or between fear and laughter.

11. Ambrose refers consistently to fear *or* anger, stating early on that "since it is

not clear which [emotion the infant is experiencing], the stimulus-terminating tendency activated will be referred to as 'fear-anger'" (Ambrose 1963, 171). To simplify the summary of his account and at the same time to accentuate certain observations concerning fear that are presented later in this text, the infant's "stimulus-terminating" tendency will be specified as fear.

12. Darwin highly esteemed Bell's observations on expression, referring not only to his reputation—"so illustrious for his discoveries in physiology"—but to his stature as a scientist engaged in the study of expression: "He may with justice be said, not only to have laid the foundations of the subject as a branch of science, but to have built up a noble structure" (Darwin 1872, 1, 2).

13. It should perhaps be explicitly noted that the startle reflex is not limited to humans (see, for example, Chance 1980; see also Darwin 1872 on astonishment and fear). Being suddenly surprised may thus elicit the equivalent of laughter and fear in nonhuman primates.

14. To accentuate the primacy of the body with respect to experiences of vulnerability, it should be added that mental harm is a more sophisticated, i.e., developmentally later or adult, form of violence, a form which, we may also note, however "mental," resonates corporeally in unmistakable and formidable ways.

15. Wilbur and Allen's translation: "Time is a child playing a game of draughts; the kingship is in the hands of a child" (Wilbur and Allen 1979, 66).

16. With respect to the child's obliviousness and imperturbability, see Winnicott: "To get to the idea of playing it is helpful to think of the *preoccupation* that characterizes the playing of a young child. The content does not matter. What matters is the near-withdrawal state, akin to the *concentration* of older children and adults. The playing child inhabits an area that cannot be easily left, nor can it easily admit intrusions" (Winnicott 1971, 51).

17. In their chapter on rough and tumble play, Humphreys and Smith point out that some teachers whom they consulted prior to their study "saw such activity [rough and tumble play] as harmless fun, and were happy to let it carry on provided nobody was in danger of getting hurt, while at the other extreme, some saw all such behaviour as aggressively motivated and forbade it" (Humphreys and Smith 1984, 253). They point out further in relation to their study that "those [teachers] objecting most strongly to rough-and-tumble tended to be those in charge of older children (9- to 12-year-olds)" (253–54). Projected fears of adults may preclude play, as may adult uncertainty about the uncertainty of play itself, which, depending on the children involved, may increase with age.

18. See also Winnicott 1971, 102: After quoting a passage from Jungian analyst Fred Plaut—"The capacity to form images and to use these constructively by recombination into new patterns is . . . dependent on the individual's ability to trust"—Winnicott comments, "The word *trust* in this context shows an understanding of what I mean by the building up of confidence based on experience, at the time of maximal dependence, before the enjoyment and employment of separation and independence." One can not only readily understand, but understand all the more why trust is of quintessential significance in infancy given our "time of maximal dependence."

19. There is, of course, no guarantee that the principles will not be subverted, that is, that knowledge of the vulnerability of others will not serve violent ends. Intentional harm of others is rooted precisely in knowledge of their vulnerability.

# 7
## On the Nature of Trust

Trust or trustworthiness is not something one can install or inject. . . . To force trust is like forcing spontaneity; if it worked it would not be genuine.
—BART NOOTEBOOM, *Trust*

The generally familiar surrounding world of persons has for everyone an open horizon of unfamiliarity.
—EDMUND HUSSERL, *Ideas II*

I. INTRODUCTION

Trust is grounded in a nonlinguistic sense of others that is rooted in sensitive and deep awarenesses of the feelings, dispositions, and intentions of others toward us. It is basically an intercorporeal attitude that, from its very beginnings in infancy and early childhood, centers on our vulnerability in relation to others. The questions of how this attitude develops and of how it is conditioned by the freedom of others constitute basic questions concerning human relationships.

This chapter conjoins and explores the two questions under two general headings: the learning of trust and the existential meaning of uncertainty. Its aim is to elucidate the fundamental nature of trust, its origin and development. The themes are developed with specific attention to sociologist Niklas Luhmann's noted monograph on trust. The purpose is to expand Luhmann's trenchant functionalist analysis of trust, opening up and examining more fully two dimensions that, as his own analysis shows, rightfully belong to it, namely, affective experience and human freedom. In keeping with the chapter's aim, the point of departure for considering these dimensions is ontogeny. I begin with a basic claim concerning ontogeny, a claim that is itself empirically grounded

An earlier version of this chapter was presented as an invited paper at an international "Symposium on Trust" at the École des Hautes Études en Sciences Sociales in Paris in September 2003 and was subsequently published in *Les moments de la confiance* (see Sheets-Johnstone 2006b).

and that ultimately provides both an empirical basis for, and a theoretical development of, Luhmann's theoretics of trust.

It should be noted in preface that Luhmann's writings are more widely known in Europe than in the United States. What makes his monograph on trust particularly appealing as a basic text on trust is its broad theoretical base and analytical scope, which together provide both a sturdy foundation for critical thinking on the subject of trust and a profitable if neglected starting point for a broad range of individuals—parents, teachers, medical professionals, philosophers, psychologists, psychiatrists, political scientists, sociologists, and more. Trust is indeed a generally neglected topic in medical and academic research. As political scientist Russell Hardin points out from an academic perspective, "Philosophers, economists, psychologists, and political theorists, especially those in the tradition of John Locke, have addressed trust and have given interesting insights; but there is surprisingly little in all of these disciplines." His subsequent observation that "[d]iscussions of trust are almost entirely missing from moral philosophy" (Hardin 2002, xix) implicitly underscores the egregious lack of interest in a topic—indeed, in a human experience—basic to understandings of human morality.

## II. LEARNING TO TRUST: UNCOVERING AFFECTIVE AND EXISTENTIAL REALITIES

From an ontogenetic viewpoint, the learning of trust begins in nonlinguistic experience, i.e., in tactile-kinetic social interactions, notably those in the context of nurturing and play. In such infant/adult interactions, affective experiences are generated. In particular, feelings of ease (e.g., comfortableness, pleasure, contentment) and uneasiness (e.g., apprehension, startle, fear) are generated. These primary experiences, documented in a variety of literature on human infant and child development (for example, Stern 1977 and 1985, Trevarthen 1977, and Bugental et al. 1991)—and on nonhuman infant behavior as well (for example, Goodall 1971, Strum 1987, and Dolhinow 1972)—are the foundation of developing attitudes of trust; they are the ontogenetic basis of learning to trust.

When Luhmann states that "trust . . . has to be *learned*, just like any other kind of generalization" (Luhmann 1979, 27), he appears tacitly to recognize just such experiential ontogenetic foundations, all the more so since he immediately alludes to infancy. He does so, however, in a rather puzzling way. He claims that the learning process of trust has "underlying assumptions that are laid down in infancy" (27), but gives no clue as to what the underlying assumptions might be, how they are laid down in infancy, or how he knows or why he thinks there are underlying assumptions in the first place. In consequence, one readily wonders what he means by "underlying assumptions" and how our common state of infancy is their spawning ground.

If we attempt to satisfy the wonder by following Luhmann's line of thought, it appears ever more likely that "the underlying assumptions" of the learning process of trust are foundationally tied to ontogenetic affective experiences of ease and uneasiness, and that, because these ontogenetic affective experiences are nonlinguistic, the original affective ground, from a functionalist's point of view, remains murky, at best hard to discern, perhaps never to be known with assurance. Quite simply put, the original affective ground has no symbolic structure. It may be for this reason that, after alluding to the learning process of trust in infancy, tying it to the family as a social system, and noting that "the learning process does not end there" (28), Luhmann declares, "Our understanding of this learning process is still far from complete" (28). He goes on all the same to affirm a quite specific "starting point" for the learning. He states that rather than thinking the initial learning of trust to be a matter of generalizing from specific experiences "in which trust was not betrayed, . . . one has to proceed from the starting point that the learning process is mediated by *the experiences of the learner with himself* and is controlled by *the self-developing (also learned) identity of the learner*" (28; italics added).[1] He thus affirms that the process of learning to trust originates and develops in conjunction with self-experiences and in the growing sense of a "self" to begin with. His "starting point" strongly supports the notion that "experiences of the learner with himself" are primarily affective experiences since feelings of ease or comfort, and of uneasiness or discomfort, are primary experiences of infant life. Though non-symbolic, they have precisely the power to generate and ultimately mediate a sense of trust and distrust, respectively.[2]

Surprisingly enough, Luhmann contradicts his affirmation that the learning process is mediated and controlled by self-experiences in a double-edged statement couched in an obligatory logic. In a subsequent paragraph, he states, "If the child establishes his own self by differentiating 'I' and 'You', the first thing he has to do is *forget his first, practically unmotivated, act of trust* and find a form of trust which takes account of this differentiation" (28; italics added). His obligatory logic categorically nullifies his initial "starting point" for the learning of trust, i.e., "the experiences of the learner with himself"; and his claim that the learner establishes a self "by differentiating 'I' and 'You'" negates his previous suggestion that the self-developing identity of the learner is linked to self-experiences. His double negation together with his emphatic directive that the learner forget "his first, practically unmotivated, act of trust" denies a continuity that, on the basis of affective "underlying assumptions," and an affectively charged "starting point," might well be characterized as moving from a predominantly tactile-kinesthetic, self-centered psychological trust to a broader and richer other-oriented sociological trust. Why Luhmann would deny such a continuity is puzzling, especially in light of his concern with the *process* of learning to trust, and with what he himself designates as the necessity of moving from one "form of trust" to another. Continuity is precisely what needs spelling out.[3] Luhmann's claims about "underlying assumptions" and a "starting point" for learning to trust otherwise slip away unelucidated and trivialized. So also does his reference to a "first, practically unmotivated, act of trust," namely, an infant's initial native disposition to turn openly and receptively toward the world. Attention to continuity mandates an analysis of the developmental passage from that initial native disposition to a substantive form of 'I' and 'You', a developmental passage that again substantiates the idea that the *process* of learning trust unfolds on the basis of affective ontogenetic experience; that is, if, in the beginning, the act—or we might say better, the nature—of trust is "practically unmotivated," it is because it has as yet no definitive social context, but only a spontaneously generated affective character of ease or uneasiness with respect to others.

The import of explicitly acknowledging an infant's native disposition to trust is certainly not to identify some module of trust in the human brain,[4] but to trace out the learning process of trust from its beginnings: how it is that an infant-child moves beyond his/her native disposition to trust as reflected in his/her openness toward the world and his/her spontaneous affective experiences of ease or uneasiness with others, and toward precisely what Luhmann identifies as a differentiation between 'I' and 'You'. The task necessarily requires that we take seriously Luhmann's richly textured and provocatively detailed theoretical analysis of trust. At the same time, it requires that we take ontogeny seriously and honor ontogenetic matters of fact over adult—or adultist[5]—theoretical claims.

The dual requirement is well illustrated in a consideration of Luhmann's continuing remarks on the topic that support and solidify the foregoing ontogenetic clarifications, even as they raise a fundamental problem that cuts widely across disciplines. Luhmann declares, "The learning process will not force the separation of I and You into complete and absolute distinction. On the contrary," he says, "the You stays as 'another I'" (28). His categorically assured but conceptually difficult and empirically unsubstantiated pronouncement surely demands more than a reference to G. H. Mead's notion that "the learning of an individual self through experiences with others" is "reciprocal" and his own guarantee that "[i]t is a question here of complementary aspects of a unitary process" (31). The "unitary process"—if such it be—calls out for a painstaking and thoroughgoing empirical-phenomenological resolution of a long- and still-standing multidisciplinary problem, what is commonly termed the problem of intersubjectivity or the problem of other minds.[6] It calls out even for a painstaking and thoroughgoing evolutionary analysis of the problem in terms of species identity and attachment.[7] I will not attempt even a brief sketch here of the challenges of either analysis, but will for exegetical reasons simply take the pronouncement at face value.

Luhmann mitigates the opaqueness of the pronouncement to a degree by specifying how, on the basis of the incomplete and non-absolute distinction—the You "stay[ing] as 'another I',"—the generalization of experiences of trust comes to be.[8] He states, "The learner reasons from himself to others and is thus in the position to generalize from his experiences with others." He thus appears to affirm that the capacity to trust proceeds from self-experiences to others, and from experiences of others to a generalized attitude of trust. It is notable that he specifies reasoning to be operative at this point in the learning process, with no reference to "underlying assumptions," starting points, or "practically unmotivated acts," but that he nevertheless continues to ground the process basically in the self-experiences of the learner himself, that is, in the psychologically rather than sociologically cognitive. Significantly too, he seems to see the process as moving *from* the psychological—reasoning *from oneself* to others—*to* the fully fledged sociological—generalization on the basis of experiences of others. His immediate gloss on the statement, however, complicates if not confuses matters considerably. He states: "Because [the learner] feels he is prepared to honour the trust of some unknown person, he is also able to show trust to others" (1979, 28). He thus claims that the learner's experience of a stranger's trust in him—the learner—provides grounds for him—the learner—to trust others generally, i.e., to arrive at a generalized, bona fide social sense of trust. The reasoning is thus far more complex than appears at first glance, and is certainly far more complex than any reasoning one might attribute to a young child.

The reasoning is in fact clearly sophisticated. It involves not known but wholly unknown others from start to finish. It thereby involves generalizing from the unknown to the unknown: "If I can honor the trust in me of an utter stranger, then I, in turn, can trust all other utter strangers." Moreover a sizable other unknown compounds the rationalized unknownness. As Luhmann elsewhere emphasizes, trust is always a matter of the present; the future is always uncertain.[9] Hence trust, as Luhmann conceives it, is actually doubly fraught with uncertainty: it is, one might say, two hundred percent risky. On the one hand, trust in the full social sense begins with trusting the trust of a stranger in oneself and ends by one's generalizing that trust to other strangers on that basis. On the other hand, trust is itself always an expectation about the future; it guarantees nothing. While the temporal compounding of risk is certainly of moment, what concerns us here is the reasoning that anchors Luhmann's thesis of social trust. It pivots not on a familiar other but on an unfamiliar other and is from this perspective odd as well as sophisticated. Indeed, not just the reasoning but the life situation Luhmann describes is odd, uncommonly so, to the point it hardly seems a credible basis for the learning of trust. A preparedness to honor the trust of a stranger in oneself—minding a stranger's child or car, here in a parking lot, while the stranger returns to his office a block or two away to get some papers, for example, or minding a stranger's wallet, here at a beach, while he goes scuba-diving—hardly seems a credible anchorage for learning to trust others. Moreover as the ground experience for trusting others, it seems to come rather late in life.[10] Most important, given the scenario, reasoning from oneself to others amounts to reasoning on the basis not of *trusting someone*, but of *being trusted by someone*. The scenario thus reverses the preceding logic of reasoning from oneself to others in that it is the experience of a stranger's trust in oneself, not the experience of one's own trust in another, that is generalized. In fact, the firsthand experience of trust that is wanted seems to be missing: the very person who needs the experience of trusting others in order to generalize it to others does not have it. In short, what Luhmann proposes is that one learns trust by being trusted.

Is this claim tenable? If one does not oneself have the experience of trusting others and thereby know what it is to trust someone and what it entails, can one even know that it is trust that a stranger is placing in one when he asks if he might leave his child or his car or his wallet? Can one be prepared to honor something one has not experienced firsthand, or is being on the receiving end of someone else's trust equivalent to bestowing trust in another, as Luhmann infers? In broader terms, is the trust of an unknown person in oneself sufficient grounds for one's trusting other persons in general, or is Luhmann's "starting point" of trust elided in such a scenario? To put the question in even broader perspective and at the same time heed Luhmann's affirmation that trust is "an attitude which is neither objective nor subjective" (1979, 27), would recognition of a continuity from the psychological to the sociological sustain the coherency of the learning process of trust that Luhmann seeks to define?

Luhmann speaks at several points of the foundation of trust. He states, for example, "Familiarity is the precondition for trust as well as distrust" (19),[11] and subsequently adds, "Of course, trust is only possible in a familiar world; it needs history as a reliable background. One cannot confer trust without this essential basis and without all previous experience" (20). Later, he states, "Trust is founded on the motivation attributed to behaviour" (41); still later, he states that "the "general structure of emotional relationships shows . . . a generalized medium of problem-solving, an equivalent for certainty, of the type which we are seeking as a foundation for readiness to trust" (81); further still, he states that "emotions form a foundation for entering into relationships of trust with other people to whom the emotion itself does not extend" (81).

Surely in light of these comments, the trust of a stranger in oneself cannot be the foundation of trust. In turn, Luhmann's trenchant and compelling thesis that the reduction of complexity is the motivating factor—"what constitutes the background to all trust [is] the problem of complexity" (63)—cannot be the whole story. From a foundational perspective, what remains hidden in his account of the learning process of trust is precisely a further powerful dimension of the underlying motivation to trust. The dimension is encapsulated in the notion of uncertainty, a notion that surfaces frequently in Luhmann's account, but a notion that is inadequately understood simply as an aspect of trust with respect to others or with respect to the future. In a word, uncertainty is a foundational aspect of *the motivation* to trust. It may in fact be characterized precisely as Luhmann characterizes familiarity: like familiarity, uncertainty structures "existence, not action" (19). In other words, uncertainty—the unknown—like its general opposite, familiarity—the known—is an existential not performative dimension of human life and is thus understandably a precursive spring to trust. Before proceeding to an elucidation of its foundational motivational import, I turn to the penultimate chapter of Luhmann's monograph, "Readiness to Trust," a chapter that substantiates and underscores the foregoing ontogenetic expansions and critical questions of his thesis.

## III. A CRITICAL EXAMINATION OF LUHMANN'S THESIS OF A "READINESS TO TRUST"

Luhmann begins the chapter on readiness by specifying what he has been considering to this point: "predominantly . . . aspects of the formation and use of trust external to the system." He states that his account "would remain incomplete . . . if the conditions for the formation of trust *internal* to the system were not also brought into consideration" (Luhmann 1979, 78). After initially showing that readiness to trust "does not consist in an increase of security with a corresponding decrease in insecurity," but rather, "conversely in an increase of bearable insecurity at the expense of security" (79–80), he goes on to speak of "internal mechanisms for the reduction of complexity," and singles out two of these as exemplary: "emotional cathexis and assurance in self-presentation." It is the first of the two that is of moment here, "assurance of self-presentation" being obviously an arrived-at juvenile to adult possibility. Emotional cathexis, in contrast, ties in conceptually with what was said earlier of both an infant's native disposition to trust and its affective experiences of ease or uneasiness with others.

At the beginning of his discussion of emotional cathexis, Luhmann states, "One of the most elementary mechanisms of complexity reduction is *the stabilization of feelings* towards particular objects or people" (80; italics added). It is not surprising, then, that his ensuing discussion of feelings resonates substantively with my earlier claims regarding affective ontogenetic experience and a needed expansion of his thesis.

Indeed, as Luhmann himself states categorically, "The emotional cathexis of the child with his family is . . . the foundation for the learning of all trust" (81). Moreover he follows this categorical statement with a highly significant comment: "In this way readiness to trust can survive as an habitual and proven attitude long after the emotions to which it owes its existence have faded" (81). He thus implicitly affirms continuity from the psychological to the sociological, from an initial native disposition to turn toward the world—to trust—and from early affective feelings of ease with others to an attitude of trusting and ultimately of a generalized social attitude of trust. Though the initial feelings fade in the course of maturation, they remain substantively formative, sufficiently so to send the infant on its sociologically trusting way.

Luhmann, however, proceeds to modify and even undercut his affirmation of the foundational role of emotions. As he puts it, "[A] mobile, highly differentiated social system . . . cannot content itself with this foundation of trust alone. . . . It increasingly demands trust for systems for which one can have no feeling" (81–82).[12] With this judgment, he proceeds to discuss *"assurance in social self-presentation,"* which he describes as the alternative "problem-solving" mechanism that can "partly replace feeling as a basis for trust and partly restrict it to increasingly private functions" (82). He later gives more weight to self-presentation than to feeling as a means for reducing complexity, but he also states, "Whether readiness to trust is achieved more through emotion or more through flexibility of self-presentation" depends on "the *structure* of the systems which confers trust." He thus moots the value of feeling and self-presentation with respect to a readiness to trust, implicitly suggesting that different people come to confer trust on the basis of different experiences, needs, motivations, circumstances, and so on. Most important, however, he ends by denying that a readiness to trust is foundational at all in the sense of constituting an 'internal' condition for the possibility of trust. Trust, he declares, "does not depend so much on the readiness to trust"; readiness is merely a variable of the trust system (84). Thus, individuals, i.e., "trusting systems," are "relieved of responsibility for their trust" (84). In a surprisingly casual and offhand manner, he states, "Trust is created—one way or the other" (84). With such words, he seems to take back all claims regarding foundations. Trust is, as it were, merely in the air, varying according to "social conditions"—social conditions that, for example, allow in particular ways for "the expression of emotion or successful self-presentation" (84), just as they allow in particular ways for what he terms "communications media" such as money and truth.

That Luhmann abruptly makes feeling a mere variable in the trust system comes as a particular surprise. The move might be mandatory for theory, but it is consistent neither with the realities of ontogeny nor with Luhmann's own analysis of trust over his previous ten chapters. By canceling out his previous analyses and claims, he not merely equivocates, but equivocates at a critical juncture. Seemingly, he wants to say that only if feelings are looked at from a psychological point of view are they foundational. If they are looked at from within the whole of the trust system, they are not foundational, for the trust system is more than a psychological reality. But then what is theoretically lacking just as it is empirically lacking—again—is an analysis of the passage from 'I' to 'You', the constitution of intersubjectivity, the relationship of the psychological to the sociological, and with it, the generalization of social trust. Such an analysis would necessarily focus more keenly on uncertainty and on the insecurity or risk element of trust, themes that Luhmann emphasizes throughout. The keener focus would not be to the exclusion of the function of trust as a means of reducing complexity, but would take its place alongside that function, and this precisely because uncertainty is a precursor of trust, and like trust itself, it is spawned in the psychological realities of ontogeny. In short, uncertainty defines the functional value of trust no less than the reduction of complexity.

As a brief developmental example, consider what is consistently described as stranger anxiety: "[J]ust prior to infants' entry into the people/object stage (nine to twelve months), [infants] start manifesting a novel sense of exclusivity with their primary caretakers, reacting with marked anxiety when encountering or left alone with a stranger ('eighth-month' or 'stranger anxiety')" (Rochat 2001, 162; see also, for example, Bower 1979 and Bowlby 1973). Stranger anxiety is tied to what psychologist Philippe Rochat—a prominent infant researcher—terms "social selectivity," that is, "the growing attachment and selective attention of infants toward certain individuals in their environment" (Rochat 2001, 166)—what Luhmann refers to in psychoanalytic terms as the emotional cathexis of an infant with his family, "the foundation for the learning of all trust."[13] If just such social selectivity is claimed to be foundational to trust not only in the sense of coming first chronologically, but in the sense of being an originary developmental character that undergirds future social interactions—readiness to trust, as Luhmann tells us, becomes "an habitual and proven attitude"—affective attachment clearly has sizable functional value. In view of this value, it is difficult to see how *feelings* can be so easily relativized and in essence marginalized. Moreover if trust is an attitude that is neither objective nor subjective (Luhmann 1979, 27), but conjoins both external and internal structures, then clearly, its dual faces must be understood equally, and the relationship of the dual faces to each other must be clarified. Luhmann's previously cited affirmation concerning the starting point of the learning process of trust further strengthens the importance of this psychological-to-sociological reading of his work and the importance of working through an analysis that brings the reading to light. Working through such an analysis leads us to inquire into affective experiences that subtend the development of trust, and correlatively, that subtend distrust via feelings of uncertainty, insecurity, or risk.

IV. AFFECTIVE EXPERIENCE, HUMAN FREEDOM, AND UNCERTAINTY: DEEPENED UNDERSTANDINGS OF TRUST

Let us begin with a range of examples from Luhmann's monograph. Luhmann speaks of the freedom of the other in terms of "his disturbing potential for diverse action" (Luhmann 1979, 39); more broadly, he speaks of "other people's uncontrollable power to act" (41). He states, "As soon as another person figures in consciousness not simply as an object in the world but as *alter ego*, as freedom to see things differently and to behave differently, the traditional taken-for-granted character of the world is upset and its complexity manifest" (19). He speaks of "the possibility of excessive harm arising from the selectivity of others' actions" (24); of "[c]ertain dangers" (25); of "leftover uncertainties" (25); of "uncertainty in behaviour" (91); of "the leap into uncertainty" (33); of the fact that trust is "an internally guaranteed security" against "missing information" (93); that trust is "a risky undertaking" (27);[14] and so on. With respect to his earlier discussion of the "problematic relationship" of trust to time (10), he later declares that "rather than being just an inference from the past [based on familiarity], trust goes beyond the information it receives and risks defining the future" (20). At the very beginning of his text, he says that "if chaos and *paralysing fear* are the only alternatives to trust, it follows that man *by nature* has to bestow trust" (4; italics added).

The range of examples leaves no doubt that experiences of uncertainty are fundamental to trust and to understandings of trust. It thereby shows that feelings cannot be suddenly "reveal[ed] as a variable" (84) and that rationality alone cannot explain trust. Feelings of uncertainty, danger, risk, insecurity, and so on, reverberate affectively in living ways through living bodies: in fear, in anxiety, in dread. Though it is certainly not his intent, Luhmann puts the source of these corporeal matters of fact in a nutshell when he speaks in passing of another's "disturbing potential to diverse action" and of "other people's uncontrollable power to act." However brief the statements, they call attention to the fact that we never know with certainty what others will do to us. Indeed, what others choose to do to us—their "selectivity of action," as Luhmann so genteely puts it—knows no bounds, as even the most superficial readings of human history attest. Others can not merely lie to us, deceive us, hit us, and kick us, they can beat us, blind us, maim us, torture us, kill us. They can, as described in Chapters 1 and 4, wreak the tortures of hell on us. When Luhmann mentions "the possibility of excessive harm arising from the selectivity of others' actions" (24), he gives voice to the socio-affective subtext on trust that runs through his monograph. The subtext of *Trust and Power* is written in the language of uncertainty, insecurity, risk, danger, and harm. It testifies to a sizable and foundational dimension of human psycho-social reality, a dimension that is charged with feelings, various facets of which are internal or external—present in either the system or the environment, to use Luhmann's terminology. Feelings of uncertainty—of possible danger in foreign surrounds, for example, of possible punishment or retaliation for what we do or words we utter, of the possibly harmful effects of following a superior's orders, of the depth of commitment in a friendship—all testify to the fact that we are perpetually open to possible suffering at the hands of others. Moreover in a highly sophisticated technological world in which arrogant nationalists and religious fanatics are indifferent to social relations except in the form of "Us against Them," a world in which 'might makes right' and the decimation of innocent civilians is regarded "collateral damage," humans are inescapably open to harm by means ever more inventive and extreme.

Trust assuages feelings of vulnerability, anxieties about what others might do to us. Thus, if trust is an alternative to "paralysing fear," and if we humans are "by nature" obliged to bestow trust, as Luhmann doubly affirms, then there is clearly something we humans are as social beings that needs explaining beyond the notion of complexity. More pointedly put, if we are obliged *by nature* to bestow trust not simply to avoid chaos—i.e., not simply to avoid being irremediably submerged in complexity—*but to avoid paralysing fear,* then there is no doubt but that the functional value of trust amounts to something more than the reduction of complexity, and that to understand trust, human feelings and not just human rationality must be taken fully into account.[15] Indeed, basic affective aspects of human psycho-social reality must be uncovered and acknowledged. The "possibility of excessive harm" in fact puts affective corporeal matters of fact lightly. The sheer capacity of humans to harm others—to cheat and lie to their own monetary advantage; to devise instruments of torture to persecute, weaken, or destroy; to starve, lynch, butcher, and outright kill—is not simply a capacity that has been culturally honed in myriad ways and seemingly knows no bounds, but a capacity that *naturally* puts humans at risk with respect to one another because it is a capacity *naturally* present in all humans and one that can be willfully cultivated.[16] In short, it is not simply *other people* who have "an uncontrollable power to act," but that all humans have *by nature* a certain freedom to act and are thereby *by nature* at risk with respect to each other. We are each of us one of those other people with "an uncontrollable power to act." Indeed, there is no absolute assurance that respect and kindness will prevail in us or toward us, and that, in effect, an enduring trust will be won. As Luhmann perceptively points out, "Trust rests on illusion" (32). It is not surprising, then, that "[t]he possibility of excessive harm arising from the selectivity of others' actions" gives rise, and naturally, to a functional aspect of trust on par with the reduction of complexity. Whether the context is social, psychological, economical, or political, a common thread runs through acts of trust. Feelings of uncertainty, insecurity, or risk define the common socio-affective thematic, namely, the possibility of harm at the hands—and minds—of others.

As suggested, trust is a palliative to fearful feelings: it diminishes fear, but neither automatically nor necessarily banishes it conclusively. Bodily feelings of fear and trust, however, are oppositional. The dynamics of fear are in a corporeal-kinetic sense antithetical to trust. Fear *moves through* the body in ways different from trust, and *moves* the body in ways different from trust. In effect, the emotional resonance of the feelings is such that the two cannot be present simultaneously. A striking resemblance in fact obtains with the relationship Epicurus observed between life and death: when fear is present, trust is not; and when trust is present, fear is not. Moreover at any moment fear may banish trust just as, at any moment, trust may banish fear. The political relationship between the George W. Bush administration and the electorate in the United States in a post–11 September world is a sterling example. Trust in one's federal government keeps fear of terrorism at bay, but fear of terrorism can be—and was—willfully injected into public life precisely in order to secure the public's trust in the federal government. Periodic injections of fear—there may be a terrorist attack on the Golden Gate Bridge or the Brooklyn Bridge; smallpox inoculations are necessary; duct tape should be purchased to secure windows; and so on—kept trust in the federal government alive, bolstered it, and strengthened its social hold. In a word, trust was politically cemented by the social manipulation and control of fear.

The oppositional dynamics of trust and fear testify affectively to the fact that trust, as Luhmann affirms, "rests on illusion" and is "a risky investment." Yet however illusory and risky the nature of trust, it is in our interest to trust and to cultivate trust,[17] both in ourselves and in others, for in a way totally unlike other creatures, humans are at risk not only by way of natural accidents or aging; as emphasized in Chapters 1, 4, and 6, they are at risk in being alive among their own kind, they are at risk *in being alive among other humans*. The existential value of trust is to mitigate this human condition, that is, to preserve human sanity by mitigating the potential threat of others and the concomitant anxiety that that threat poses. To put the value in terms of sanity is not to say that the relationship of uncertainty to trust is a reasoned out relationship, i.e., "other people have an 'uncontrollable power to act'; I cannot be certain what they will do, therefore I will trust them to offset my anxieties about what they might do." As shown earlier, trust originates in ontogeny, in feelings of ease, and in subsequent feelings of attachment. It thus develops naturally in specific sociological ways on the basis of its natural affective origins. Precisely as Luhmann affirms, trust is in the very nature of human nature. Its existential value is in turn a naturally arising value. Luhmann implicitly recognizes this value when, as we have seen, in introducing his discussion of emotional cathexis, he states, "One of the most elementary mechanisms of complexity reduction is the *stabilization of feelings* towards particular objects or people" (80; italics added).

In sum, trust has sizable socio-affective compensations for all its risks.

Its power to stabilize feelings of ease in a world of others is a substantive part of its nature. In effect, while trusting others reduces complexity in "a mobile, highly differentiated social system," it also clearly reduces something else at same time: it reduces anxiety about harm from others, just as it undoubtedly reduced anxiety about harm from others and continued to reduce anxiety about harm from others long before human society became "a mobile, highly differentiated social system." Luhmann's allusion to a "pre-social sense" of other people's freedom of action is thus not a sense present-day humans have outgrown or something that a reduction of complexity dissolves or obliterates. Anxiety about harm is at the heart of trusting others. Feelings of ease and uneasiness are primary affective dimensions of human social relations from the very beginning.[18] Just such feelings motivate attitudes of trust and distrust.

A pressing question surfaces in just this context: why should strangers evoke uneasiness, insecurity, apprehension? After all, it is not as if they are some other species; they are humans, just like oneself. That they evoke such feelings commonly goes unquestioned. Yet the feelings should be cause for wonder: what reasons do we have for feeling uneasy with strangers? The question can be answered in part on phylogenetic grounds: xenophobia is not restricted to humans but is an evolutionary character (Holloway 1974). But the question can also be answered at closer range by consulting human history, which is replete with instances in which one group of humans, whose social organization as a whole—whose values, ways of behaving, styles of living, and so on—is different from that of another group of humans, attacks the alien group for the purpose of taking its land and resources, or of eradicating it altogether. In other words, different social practices, beliefs, behaviors, and so on, are perceived as a threat: they are strange and in turn a danger to one's known social order. At an individual level, a stranger is by definition the embodiment of just such a threat. Precisely because what he does is strange, he is unpredictable and hence the embodiment of possible harm.[19] It is not surprising, then, that strangeness motivates feelings of distrust.[20] Luhmann's description of the person who distrusts in fact brings to the fore in reverse terms the threat posed by a stranger. He describes the person who distrusts as virtually paralyzed. He states that because distrust involves preeminently positive expectations of injury, "strategies of distrust become correspondingly more difficult and more burdensome. They often absorb the strength of the person who distrusts to an extent which leaves him little energy to explore and adapt to his environment in an objective and unprejudiced manner, and hence allow him fewer opportunities for learning" (Luhmann 1979, 72). In essence, what Luhmann tells us from a reverse perspective is that strangers evoke distrust and distrust motivates one to curtail one's freedom in an effort to avoid injury. He does not mention fear directly, but why else would someone impose restrictions on his movements, on his learning, on his curiosity about the world, except out of fear of what might befall him at the hands of others? Such fear is the affective embodiment of an attitude of distrust. In fear as in distrust, the possibility of impending disaster hangs in the air. Voluntary curtailment of one's freedom is thus indeed self-protective; it is in the service of self-preservation.

Because its cognitive structure is always open to affective inflection, that is, to being affectively reconfigured or dislodged by some form of fear, the cognitive structure of trust is unstable. In turn, and *contra* Luhmann, trust is not a generalization that is learned like any other generalization.[21] Luhmann speaks of trust as "fragile" and "precarious," but not in an affective sense. For him, trust is "fragile" and "precarious" because, like all generalizations, it inevitably simplifies the world (28). In a more basic sense, however, trust is "fragile" and "precarious" because, quite *unlike* all generalizations, the generalization it instantiates rests on human affect and freedom of action. In other words, trust is not affectively neutral like other generalizations; it is affectively vulnerable. Moreover its affectively vulnerable cognitive structure is invariable, whether a matter of economics, politics, or whatever. Generalized social attitudes of trust can be upset in any domain because harm at the hands of others is always a possibility. Indeed, the fragility of trust can nowhere be tempered.

In sum, a corollary needs to be added to Luhmann's affirmation that "[t]he complexity of the future world is reduced by the act of trust" (20); namely, "The uncertainty of the basically free actions of others is reduced by acts of trust." Similarly, the fundamental nature of risk needs full disclosure. Luhmann's affirmation that "[t]rust reduces social complexity, that is, simplifies life by the taking of a risk" (71) enlightens us only by half. Trust reduces fear no less than social complexity. The socio-affective underside of risk—fear of potential harm by others—is indeed not a variable of social complexity but a structural built-in of human nature, precisely as Luhmann implicitly affirms when he speaks of another's "disturbing potential to diverse action," of "the possibility of excessive harm," and so on. Recognition of the uncertainty of the actions of others and their power to harm is thus not simply a matter of an unknown future, but a matter of the freedom and unknown motivations of others. Short of this freedom and motivational opacity, there would be no reason to trust—or not to trust. An understanding of trust thus requires deepened understandings of intersubjectivity, beginning with the intricately woven psycho-sociological dynamics of the passage from "I" to You." We might note that the empirical staples of infant/child development studies—joint attention, imitation, and turn-taking—document early intersubjective relations, but they do not answer the question of how an intersubjective world is constituted, and how, in a psycho-sociological sense, that intersubjective world both shapes development and is itself shaped in the course of development. Until we arrive at more fully realized understandings of intersubjectivity and the affective foundations of trust, we can hardly arrive at a full understanding of the cognitive structure of trust.

NOTES

1. It should be noted that when Luhmann writes that the initial learning of trust cannot be based on a generalization issuing from an instance in which trust was not betrayed (1979, 28), he is conceptually ahead of himself. His statement is indeed conceptually problematic, since within the experience he rejects as the ultimate basis of learning to trust, trust is already in place as an attitude and therefore cannot be "being learned." That is, if trust is not betrayed, then trust has already been learned. Theoretically, and specifically in terms of betrayal, however, Luhmann might claim that trust is not learned directly, but learned only when one discovers that it has been betrayed, betrayal awakening one to the fact that, to this point, one has been trusting. The claim would substantiate and in fact exemplify his basic claim concerning intersubjectivity: differentiating between "I" and "You" requires first and foremost that the child "forget his first, practically unmotivated, act of trust." Betrayal, he might argue, would prompt just this move on the part of the child.

2. Moreover when Luhmann affirms that the process of learning to trust originates and develops in conjunction with a developing sense of self-identity, he affirms a clearly psychological origin and maturation of trust, psychological in the sense of Husserl's notion of "I govern"—e.g., an infant feeling and following through on its own progressively complex motivations—and his notion of "I can"—e.g., an infant feeling itself capable of progressively more complex movements and acts (see Husserl 1973 and 1989)—and psychological in the sense of developing a sense of self relative to feelings of security or insecurity—e.g., an infant feeling itself progressively more secure in the dark, in tactile-kinetic interactions with others, and so on.

3. If "man *by nature* has to bestow trust," then one might take a cue from Linnaeus: *Natura non facit saltus*—"Nature does not proceed by leaps." Moreover while Luhmann implicitly preaches discontinuity in his dictum to forget one's "first practically unmoti-

vated, act of trust" and to find a form that takes account of the differentiation between "I" and "You," he need not jettison continuity either to promote a social sense of trust or to preserve it. Not only does his theory of the learning process of trust confirm continuity in its allusions to "underlying assumptions," a starting point, and a "first, practically unmotivated, act of trust," but as indicated, an analysis of the initial spontaneous affective disposition of an infant toward others and to the ways in which that initial disposition becomes socially individualized through those who initially nurture it, who minister to it and play with it, i.e., through those whom Luhmann already specifies as "the family system," would prominence the very process of socialization that Luhmann is intent on highlighting with respect to complexity.

4. A necessary counterbalance, as it were, to the not merely hypothesized but taken-as-fact brain module for cheating and deception. The brazenly conjured spatial entity in the brain is featured in the writings of evolutionary psychologists Leda Cosmides and John Tooby. See Barkow, Cosmides, and Tooby 1992.

5. For detailed explications of the term "adultist," see Sheets-Johnstone 1994b, 245; and 1999b, 232, 243, 260.

6. Luhmann's comment that "one would have to work out some kind of phenomenological psychology of everyday behaviour" to determine which events "accelerate or brake the process of the formation of trust or distrust" (1979, 75) not only supports my claim but testifies to the fact that further work needs to be done on the intersubjective process of learning to trust. Luhmann's earlier remarks about the anonymous constitution of meaning and world (18) are markedly insufficient in this respect.

7. The question of species identity and attachment is not a compelling topic today, but it warrants study. A number of essays in M. Aaron Roy's *Species Identity and Attachment: A Phylogenetic Evaluation* offers a provocative sense of the import of the topic. We might note that Luhmann's claim that "the You stays as another I" appears definitively linked to the question of species identity and attachment, i.e., on what grounds other than species identity and attachment would "the You stay as another I"?

8. That the "You" *stays* as "another I" strongly suggests an allegiance to received wisdom, i.e., belief in an "undifferentiated" infant, the infant being, from the beginning, merged with its mother. This still prevalent notion has been shown to be false by a number of psychiatrists and psychologists. See, for example, Stern 1985, 1990; Butterworth 1983; Meltzoff 1990; and Meltzoff and Moore 1977, 1983.

9. He writes, for example, that "the theme of trust involves a problematic relationship with time" (Luhmann 1979, 10), that "trust can only be secured and maintained in the present" (12). He states specifically that "[t]o show trust is to anticipate the future ... to behave as though the future were certain" (10), and that "trust is required for the reduction of a future characterized by more or less indeterminate complexity" (12).

10. Indeed, in this respect, the scenario might even be said to have a dubious ring about it, the learner not learning to trust in such a situation, but being impressed that a stranger can trust *him*, he who has to this time such a mixed life record of trustworthiness.

11. As will presently be evident, just as "[f]amiliarity and trust are ... complementary ways of absorbing complexity and are linked to one another" (Luhmann 1979, 20), so familiarity and trust are complementary ways of absorbing uncertainty and are linked to one another.

12. With this remark, Luhmann's strong claim about fading emotions seems itself to have faded, i.e., his claim that "a readiness to trust can survive *as an habitual and proven attitude long after the emotions to which it owes its existence have faded*" (81; italics added).

13. Rochat's terminology—"social selectivity"—in fact accords nicely with Luhmann's central concept of selectivity, that is, his concept of the individual or social system as "selecting" certain courses of action from among possibilities of action in the

environment. An infant precisely "selects" among possible objects of attachment in the environment.

14. Communication is also "a risky undertaking" (Luhmann 1979, 40).

15. But of course the relationship of feelings to rationality must also be understood.

16. The story related of the Native American grandfather in Chapter 3 speaks eloquently to this very point. (See also Sheets-Johnstone 1994b, as noted in Chapter 3, for analyses and discussions of the ways in which cultures inflect and temper in various ways what is biologically given.)

17. If one were a sociobiologist rather than a systems theorist, one would attempt to show that trusting and cultivating trust are behaviors enhancing reproductive success rather than reducing complexity; that is, one would attempt to explain trust adaptively in terms of ultimate causation rather than functionally in terms of proximate causation. The explanations, however, would run basically along similar lines, i.e., they would determine "the benefit" that comes from trust. In contrast to posing and answering the questions, what is it good for? or how does it work?, one could pose and answer the question, where does it come from? If phenomenologically inclined, one might thereby trace out the origin and development of trust, elucidating it as an existential condition of human aliveness.

18. As humans mature, the relations expand; and particularly in "mobile, highly differentiated social systems," they come to include progressively more and more unfamiliar as well as familiar others, any one of whom might be trusted or distrusted, feared straight-off, or come to be feared. In other words, that another individual or other individuals are familiar does not automatically ensure their being invariably trusted.

19. It is of interest to note that the origin and development of contemporary Western science is conceptually rooted in the idea of Nature as a stranger. The quest of modern science is thus to make the unknown known and to tame the unpredictable, the desire being to create a totally controllable world that is not subject to the "unfamiliar."

20. As Luhmann himself tells us, distrust—like trust—is "controlled by subjective processes" (1979, 74). Luhmann does not specify what he means by "subjective processes," but if we inquire into what they might be, it is clear that they revolve about fear, anxiety, worry, or apprehension of what is strange, foreign, or unknown. To use Luhmann's words, they revolve about fear of "other people's uncontrollable power to act."

21. Of course, like all generalizations, trust can come undone because one finds exceptions to the generalized rule—the grocery clerk shortchanges me; with no warning, the driver of the car in front of me abruptly stops—or because one makes a judgmental error in generalizing—the person I thought to be my friend turns out to be duplicitous; the verbal promise of a raise by my employer is not honored.

# 8

## The Rationality of Caring:
## Forging a Genuine Evolutionary Ethics

> No man is an *Island*, entire of it self; every man is a piece of the *Continent*, a part of the *main;* if a clod be washed away by the *sea, Europe* is the less, as well as if a *promontory* were, as well as if a *manor* of thy *friends* or of *thine own* were; any man's *death* diminishes *me,* because I am involved in *Mankind;* And therefore never send to know for whom the *bell* tolls; It tolls for *thee.*
> —JOHN DONNE, "Meditation 17," in *Devotions upon Emergent Occasions*

> Every realm of nature is marvellous. . . . [W]e should venture on the study of every kind of animal without distaste; for each and all will reveal to us something natural and something beautiful.
> —ARISTOTLE, *Parts of Animals*

> For man, as for flower and beast and bird, the supreme triumph is to be most vividly, most perfectly alive. Whatever the unborn and the dead may know, they cannot know the beauty, the marvel of being alive in the flesh. The dead may look after the afterwards. But the magnificent here and now of life in the flesh is ours, and ours alone, and ours only for a time. We ought to dance with rapture that we should be alive and in the flesh, and part of the living, incarnate cosmos. I am part of the sun as my eye is part of me. That I am part of the earth, my feet know perfectly, and my blood is part of the sea.
> —D. H. LAWRENCE, *Apocalypse*

> So what is this relationship between one human being and another that will be called fraternity? It isn't the relationship of equality. It's the relationship in which the motivations for an act come from the affective realm while the action itself is in the practical domain. That is, the relationship between a man and his neighbor in a society in which they are brothers is primarily affective and practical. . . . All human beings will be in a state of fraternity with each other when they can say of themselves, through all our history, that they are all bound to each other in feeling and in action. Ethics is indispensable, for it signifies . . . a future based on principles of common action, . . . which is to say, what I have is yours, what you have is mine; if I am in need, you give to me, and if you are in need I give to you—that's the future of ethics.
> —JEAN-PAUL SARTRE, *Hope Now: The 1980 Interviews*

> The objection will perhaps be raised that Ethics is not concerned with what men actually do, but that it is the science which treats of what their conduct *ought* to be. Now this is exactly the position which I deny. . . . the conception of *ought* . . . is valid only in theological morals, outside of which it loses all sense and meaning. . . . there remains no way of

discovering the basis of Ethics except the empirical. We must search and see whether we can find any actions to which we are obliged to ascribe *genuine moral worth*.
—ARTHUR SCHOPENHAUER, *The Basis of Morality*

## 1. INTRODUCTION

In the same way that the chapter on the pan-cultural origins of evil offers deepened understandings of male-male competition, so this chapter on the rationality of caring offers deepened understandings of empathy. This essential purpose notwithstanding, the chapter can be read from other perspectives and even as having aims in other directions. First, particularly in light of its indebtedness to Edmund Husserl's densely rich but narrowly appreciated analysis of empathy, it can be read as a detailed vindication and elaboration of Husserl's Fifth Cartesian Meditation. In this context, it can be also read as a critique of sociologist Alfred Schutz's major criticism of Husserl regarding the incommensurability of one's felt body and another's visual body, and as a critique as well of philosopher John Sallis's criticism of Husserl regarding the impossibility of "total reflection." Second, in its own right, it can be read as a vital step in the establishment of a bona fide and comprehensive, i.e., genuinely interdisciplinary, philosophical zoology[1] spelled out in a phenomenological deepening of Charles Darwin's natural history of the moral sense. Finally, and again in its own right, it can be read, and hopefully will be, as an attempt to show the inherent link between ethics and biology, thereby laying the ground for a genuine evolutionary ethics.

A genuine evolutionary ethics must indeed be a *living* ethics, one rooted in the biological realities of everyday life. In finer terms, it must be rooted in the very nature of human nature, in as sturdy and ever-present human characters as animation, sense-making, learning, and intercorporeal understandings. Because such characters are shared by many nonhuman animals, their origin is traceable to a common evolutionary heritage. The rationality of caring emerges precisely from this common evolutionary heritage. In other words, built-ins of biological life are at the foundation of the rationality of caring, and in turn provide the basis for a natural ethics, an ethics in which values are embodied in fundamental facts about the world and in fundamental intercorporeal facts of animate life.

We can see these built-ins first of all in the compound transfers of sense that anchor the rationality of caring and that progressively conjoin in a systematic reasonableness of intercorporeal meanings. The transfers are all contingent on original tactile-kinesthetic/affective experiences, that is, on experiences of one's own body as it itself is felt in touching and moving as it touches and moves both itself and objects in the world, and on experiences of one's own body as it is distinctively felt in distress, contentment, fear, anger, joy, grief, disgust, desire, and so on. In the transfers of sense integral to the rationality of caring, what is actually there, sensuously present in experience—the directly perceived body of another—coexists with what is not sensuously present but is just as immediately given in the experience—the *ap*perceived tactile-kinesthetic/affective body of the other.[2] Apperception in these instances contrasts with apperception in other everyday instances—for example, seeing *a book* where in fact only a two-dimensional surface is evident—in that it is analogically rooted: one's own body is the standard upon which the plight, concerns, thoughts, and feelings of another are grasped. In short, one's own body is a semantic template for those intercorporeal understandings that ground the rationality of caring and in fact generate caring as an attitudinal affect.[3] Hence the contingency of all transfers of sense upon original tactile-kinesthetic/affective experience.

Insofar as the compound and progressively entwined transfers of sense engender understandings of another's movements, gestures, words, cries, postures, and expressions, i.e., another's behavior in the widest possible sense, they indicate a capacity for empathy, a capacity to enter in a dynamically and affectively intuitive sense into the life of another.[4] To uncover the rationality of caring and show how it grounds a genuine evolutionary ethics is thus necessarily to recognize the kinetic-affective dynamics that are the basis of empathy as elucidated in Chapter 5. But as intimated above, the task of elucidating the rationality of caring demands further analyses and is clearly not a singular but a twofold task. On the one hand, it demands further analyses of those experiential structures of bodily life that give rise to intercorporeal, i.e., social, meanings; it demands, in other words, a further examination of how analogical apperception makes transfers of sense possible. On the other hand, it demands further explications of those evolutionary commonalities in the bodily life of human and nonhuman animals that give rise to social behaviors and understandings; it demands, in other words, a further elucidation of evolutionary continuities. Seen in this perspective, the task is defined methodologically by both a phenomenological and a hermeneutical strand (see Sheets-Johnstone 1990), in broad terms, by both descriptive and interpretive analyses. Woven together, the strands provide the basis for a genuine evolutionary ethics. Such an ethics makes explicit the epistemological structures of caring at the same time that it anchors those structures in corporeal facts of evolutionary life. The significance of this epistemologically grounded, bodily based evolutionary ethics lies both in its demonstration of the foundation of an evolutionary ethics of caring and in its own standard as an ethical credo: a genuine evolutionary ethics shows how "facts of life" are tied to values—*literally, to valuings*—of the living world and the lifeworld.

## II. TRANSFERS OF SENSE: THE GROUND OF CARING

Compound and progressive transfers of sense undergird caring, each of them distinguished by their corporeal point of origin—one's own body or the bodies of others—and by the sensory relationships and complexities of their intercorporeal structure. The transfers of sense are not reasoned-out associations, nor are they language-dependent. They are spontaneous sense-makings of corporeal facts at hand. As indicated above, all derive in an originary sense from first-person tactile-kinesthetic/affective experiences. These experiences originate in infancy and even before, in the womb—a period not normally remembered but not by that measure unexperienced—and ground transfers of sense from one's felt body to one's visual body. A three-month-old infant in rapt visual attention to its hand, indeed at times seemingly mesmerized by its hand—its shape, its topography, its opening and closing into a fist, for example (see Piaget 1968, e.g., ob. 60, p. 90; ob. 67, p. 96; Bower 1979)[5]—is discovering its felt hand as a visual entity. Its discovery consists precisely in finding this complex visual object to be its own, a visual analogue of its familiar tactile-kinesthetic body. As its felt hand moves, for instance, as it turns over, the shape of its visual hand changes; similarly, as its felt hand closes into a fist, its visual hand shrinks in size. Through such experiences, an infant comes to claim its visual hand as a worldly counterpart of its felt body, and in the process discovers certain powers and causal regularities: such and such hand movements, such and such capabilities and such and such visual forms. Its tactile-kinesthetic body is primary in these experiences; transfers of sense are effected through moving or having moved. In effect, the direction of transfer is consistently from the kinetic to the visual, the kinetic dynamics of the felt hand being transferred to the hand as a visual form.[6] The *pairing* of tactile-kinesthetic and visual bodies that results from these experiences is the most primitive form of pairing insofar as it is played out on the ground of one's own body.

Because it is played out on the ground of one's own body, the transfer of sense at this initial stage is neither apperceptive nor analogical in an intercorporeal sense. Others have no part in these experiences: there is no firsthand evidence "outstanding," so to speak, nor are others already there in any way, adumbrated in the experiences, "foreshadowed" horizonally either in themselves or in cultural objects of one sort or another. The evidence is purely and wholly *self-evidence*, and it is all there, actually or potentially, in the original tactile-kinesthetic and visual experiences of one's own body.[7] A sphere of ownness, to use an apt phrase from Husserl (Husserl 1973, 92–99), is alive and well in these tactile-kinesthetic/visual experiences. Moreover this original transfer of sense is critical, since before one can apperceive the tactile-kinesthetic bodies of others, one must first be a tactile-kinesthetic body oneself and a visual body for oneself. It is only then, through a compound and reciprocal transfer of sense emanating from one's own tactile-kinesthetic body to the visual bodies of others and from the visual bodies of others to one's own visual body, that one can *see* oneself as being *like* others and in turn *see* others as being *like* oneself, in effect, that one can begin to make the kind of intercorporeal sense integral not only to empathy but to caring.[8]

Psychologists Andrew Meltzoff and M. Keith Moore's classic experiments on infant imitation cited in Chapter 5 are of singular moment in the present context as well. In imitating an adult's mouth gestures, a newborn infant is learning its body and learning to move itself. It engages in a "kinetic-kinesthetic *dynamic* matching" (Sheets-Johnstone 1999b, 261), a transfer of sense from the visual body of another to its own tactile-kinesthetic body, discovering the dynamic possibilities and actualities of its own moving body in the process. Though not described or analyzed in such terms, the experiments testify to this fact just as they testify to responsivity and ratification of meaning, as shown in Chapter 5. Such testimonials notwithstanding, an infant's actual transfer of sense from the visual body of another to its own tactile-kinesthetic body is unexplicated. While its impetus toward matching clearly lies in its own kinetic liveliness—its "primal animation" (Sheets-Johnstone 1999b) or what dynamic systems theorist and innovator J. A. Scott Kelso aptly terms its "intrinsic dynamics" Kelso 1995—and in its dynamically attuned body, as detailed in the earlier chapter, its actual transfer of sense remains topologically unexplained: how, in broad terms, does the infant know that the deformations it sees are replicable by deformations it can enact? The answer lies in both movement and topology, namely, in the fact that one changes shape as one moves, and in moving, changes shape in invariant ways. The topological connection is experienced. In other words, self-movement is topologically distinct. It is experienced as distinct because topological specificity is inherent in the dynamics of self-movement, i.e., in kinesthesia. Thus, when a fetus, even at eleven weeks, opens and closes its mouth, and later, at four-and-a-half to five months, slips its thumb into its mouth and sucks it (Furuhjelm et al. 1976), it is becoming topologically familiar with its body, specifically its mouth, the first and pivotally central topological attractor of human infancy (Spitz 1983; note too Furuhjelm et al. 1976, 52: "We develop from the head downward"). Moving mouths are primary centers of attention for infants, as documented in the tongue protrusions, lip roundings, and lip protrusions of Meltzoff and Moore's experiments. In these experiments, the kinetic dynamics of movement play out with topological specificity both on and within the body: they are felt by the viewer and seen by the infant, and in turn felt by the infant and seen by the viewer. Just as an infant's responsivity and its ratification of meaning have their origin in the *sensu communis* that is movement (as explained in Chapter 5), so do its foundational topologically informed transfers of sense. Indeed, its responsivity and ratification of meaning are grounded in topologically informed transfers of sense rooted in the *sensu communis* of movement, movement that is both self-movement and the movement of others.

From this vantage point, what are commonly termed *cross-modal matchings* in scientific studies of infants are in reality topologically informed transfers of sense. Cross-modal matchings are indeed *sense-making acts*. They are alive with meaning, acts in which an infant makes simultaneous sense of others and of itself. Moreover as detailed in the earlier chapter, an infant's capacity to transfer sense is rooted not simply in movement but in its capacity to *think in movement*, and in thinking in movement, precisely to learn its body and learn to move itself. Further still, as intimated by *transfers of sense* and references to *sense-making*, thinking in movement is more than the ground of an infant's corporeal-kinetic learnings: it is the bedrock of an infant's developing rationality, the abiding foundation of its attainment of a progressively systematic reasonableness of meaning in its engagements with others and with the world. An infant's capacity to think in movement is indeed something more than simply a pragmatic for getting about efficiently and effectively in the world; it is ultimately the *sine qua non* of its making sequences of intelligible articulatory gestures itself in communication with others and of its understanding the articulatory gestures of others, of its playing with others without hurting either itself or them, of its nondestructive action with respect to the world, and so on. In a phylogenetic sense, it is the *sine qua non* of communal work, as in carrying out successful hunting strategies in concert with others, in putting together even the simplest of architectural constructions with others, and so on. In short, Meltzoff and Moore's experiments attest to the fact that transfers of sense, and all they require and entail in the way of sense-making and thinking in movement, are fundamental to rationality. Indeed, before being able to give reasons for one's actions and beliefs, one must be able to act reasonably in the world and to have reasonable beliefs about it, and to act and to believe in this way, *one has first to make sense* of the world and of oneself and others as living, animate creatures within it.

The discovery of one's own body as itself a visual form is the cornerstone of progressive intercorporeal sense-makings. For instance, the whole of one's felt body cannot be seen; one's own visual form is in fact always incomplete. Initial visual discoveries are in consequence progressively filled out in ways beyond actual or potential firsthand experience, that is, through analogical apperceptive transfers of sense from the bodies of others to oneself. In this way, one's own visual form takes shape through what one knows and comes to know of the visual form of others.[9] These visual to visual transfers of sense are not limited to very young and growing children. Transfers from the visual bodies of others become not only an apperceptive dimension of one's body per se but a dimension within one's social relations with others, defining not only one's public self, i.e., the person one presents to others as described in Jung's psychoanalytic, but one's friends who commonly resemble oneself, i.e., they look the same age, dress similarly, and so on. One's friends may of course also be visibly different—of a different race, sex, or culture, for instance, as well as shorter, taller, thinner, and so on. The point is that the visual form of others reverberates along strongly personal lines, but does so on the basis of the original discovery of one's felt body as a visual form. In virtue of that discovery leaching out, as it were, one comes over time to "see" oneself as a body both like and unlike other bodies, as a body that will grow, and then grow no more, that will age and visibly change in ways coincident with aging, and so on. Indeed, as individuals increase in years and become adults, they monitor their changing visual form apperceptively and analogically along a continuum of life with respect to the visual forms of others and monitor the changing visual forms of others as well.

As suggested above, a fundamental transfer of sense substantively grounds these complex sense-makings and ongoing visual elaborations of oneself. Through this transfer, one originally links oneself visually to others. One does so not only as a visual form *simpliciter* but as a physiognomically and dynamically changing body, *un corps engagé et expressif*. This further transfer of sense is contingent on the first, i.e., on those original tactile-kinesthetic experiences that ground visual sense-makings of one's own body in the first place. Unlike the first transfer, however, the second transfer is both *apperceptive* and *analogical* in an intercorporeal sense. Moreover as indicated, it becomes doubly analogical: sense-makings from corporeal facts at hand flow both ways, from myself to others and from others to myself. A reciprocal transfer is thus evident. For instance, I myself cry, pull back, go forward hesitantly, smile, frown, laugh, stretch out my arms, and so on—not that I *name* these things that I do; rather that from the very beginning, I *feel* the dynamics of these affective/tactile-kinesthetic experiences. Equally, I see others cry, pull back, go forward hesitantly, smile, frown, laugh, stretch out their arms, and so on. All of these visual apparencies appear portentously to me; each has a certain qualitative physiognomic and dynamic character, a certain lightness, heaviness, tenseness, softness, openness, warmth, and so on. The body of the other is clearly in each case a qualitatively different visual form. My understandings of its qualitative aspect derive from tactile-kinesthetic/affective experiences of my own body—its tenseness, warmth, or heaviness in experiences such as crying, frowning, and laughing. The seen bodies of others are in effect alive with tactile-kinesthetic/affective meanings because I apperceive their ever-changing physiognomies and dynamics in light of tactile-kinesthetic/affective meanings originating in my own felt sense of myself as an animate form. As is evident, language itself offers us straightforward clues to this fact: I see tenseness, lightness, warmth, ardor, brusqueness, heaviness, or vigor in other bodies—I see *qualities having nothing inherently visual about them at all*, qualities originating in experiences quite distinct from *vision* as a discrete sensory modality. By the same original tokens of tactile-kinesthetic/affective experience, I see fear, surprise, anger, indifference, joy: I see eyebrows raise, mouths open, fists shake, bodies stiffen, not as objective visual happenings but as dynamically affective physiognomic ones. A particular qualitative affective character is evident on the basis of the same original analogical apperceptive transfer of sense from my own felt body to the body of the other. In the recognition of like qualitatively dynamic physiognomies—similar expressive, gestural, kinetic, postural qualities—I *see* others apperceptively as having a tactile-kinesthetic/affective life. On the basis of this original pairing, I come in turn to *see* my own feelings apperceptively mirrored in a visual form; I come to have a sense of what I look like when I smile, for example, or when I am pensive or angry. Reciprocality thus enters into this second fundamental transfer of sense because apperception becomes here *doubly* analogical: my own body is the standard upon which I apperceive the other; the body of the other is the standard upon which I come to apperceive myself as a visual form.

A further and equally significant dimension of this original analogical pairing is apparent. Certain possibilities of action are mine. I stretch my legs, for example, or reach for something, turn something over, or shake it. I feel myself moving, touching things, and being touched in the process. Equally, I see others doing things, and in the doing of them, touching and being touched. The others' bodies are topologically dynamic insofar as they are in virtually constant movement: bending, reaching, turning, lifting, opening, walking, talking, gesturing, sitting down, standing up, and so on. They change shape as they move and move as they change shape. From such dynamic perceptions of myself and others, a further pairing takes place. Just as I do certain things and in the doing of them both intend certain things and feel various complex dynamic patternings of movement in the process—of stretching, retracting, twisting, and so on—and still other various complex apparencies such as hardness, sharpness, coolness, heaviness, so I apperceptively perceive others to have the same intentional possibilities as I, the same possibilities of movement and touch, and the same or similar experiences ensuing from these possibilities. In this recognition of an intentional life, of powers of action and of sentience, there is again an *analogical apperceptive* transfer of sense from my felt body to the moving visual bodies of others. On the basis of this fundamental pairing of others with myself, I come also to pair the moving visual bodies of others with my felt body. There is thus again a reciprocality in corporeal sense-making: the body I feel is, like the moving bodies I see, a moving visual form, an animate form *for others*, the locus of intentionalities, of topologically distinctive postures, movement patterns, orientations, spatial relationships, and so on; correlatively, the moving bodies I see are, like my felt body, dynamic centers of movement and meaning, of sentience and animation.

The preceding *sensory-kinetic* descriptive analyses (Sheets-Johnstone 1990) show how the transfers of sense that ground empathy are rooted in tactile-kinesthetic/affective experience. The felt body is the source of our original pairing of our felt and visual bodies, and of our compound and reciprocal analogical pairings of our felt and visual bodies with the visual and felt bodies of others. Through these pairings, we come to *see* others as feeling, purposefully acting, self-governing bodies; we come to realize that like ourselves, they too are free to move, to do; that they too choose certain courses of action; that they too feel joy, sadness, fear. Equally, we come to *see* ourselves as moving visual forms of ever-changing physiognomies. These beginning empathic associations that develop among like creatures, these *intercorporeal sense-makings* that arise spontaneously and that would be phenomenologically described in terms of passive syntheses, describe an intersubjectivity that is in actuality a thoroughgoing *intercorporeality*, a way of living together in harmonious understandings. Husserl's emphasis upon *harmonious* behaviors as the principle of verification in empathic understandings of others is again substantively significant. Beginning empathic associations generated in the second transfer of sense consistently bring the seen world into systematic correspondence with a felt world; they tether sense-makings—of myself and others—to fundamental constancies of tactile-kinesthetic/affective life. In doing so, they anchor social life in a rational system of meanings. Precisely because they do, they make a life-enhancing sociality possible. Bodies that share a common ground, a kindred animate form and correlative tactile-kinesthetic invariants, have the possibility of understanding one another quite apart from verbal language. In fact hominids originally depended on that common ground of intercorporeal understandings in their very invention of a verbal language in the course of evolution (Sheets-Johnstone 1990). Human infants similarly depend on that common ground of intercorporeal understandings in learning their native tongue, as do humans learning a second or third language. Such intercorporeal understandings are in fact not limited to humans but can be illustrated in ways that link them decisively to evolutionary life. So illustrated, they bring to light the beginnings of a natural history of sense-making, and as will be evident, a natural history of the foundations of caring. *Comsigns* in particular exemplify the evolutionary conjunction. As a paradigm of intercorporeal sense-makings and their evolutionary significance—in essence, a paradigm of the way in which forms of life are rich in possibilities of self- and other-understandings—comsigns demonstrate conclusively the inherent *value,* indeed, the necessity, of intercorporeal understandings to the evolution of human life.

III. COMSIGNS: THE EVOLUTIONARY BASIS OF INTERCORPOREAL LIFE

As discussed in Chapter 5, the term *comsign* is a neologism for identifying behavioral possibilities common to all members of a particular species or society if only for a brief period of time within their lives. Altmann introduces the term in the context of analyzing linguist Charles Hockett's "design features" of human language, in particular the feature "interchangeability," a feature that in fact describes not an aspect of language but, as described in Chapter 5, the capacity of a single individual to be on either the sending or receiving end of a communication. Insofar as they are within the behavioral repertoire of all members of a species, comsigns are clearly fundamental to social communication. Indeed, social communication could hardly be stabilized in life-enhancing ways were modes of social communication idiosyncratic. So long as everyone can perform the same gestures, movements, and acts, there is a common communicational frame of reference. Comsigns are *rational* in this respect; *a systematic repertoire of bodily meanings is possible.* Altmann implicitly underscores this fact not only in his definitional exemplification of comsigns, but in his specification of a second "property" of interchangeability: *interpersonal* signs as well as comsigns undergird interchangeability. What one individual does—presents, speaks, or yawns, for example—will be understood in a particular way by all other individuals of the same species or group, hence interpersonally.[10] In other words, whether all other individuals can perform the movement, speech, or gesture themselves or not, and allowances for individual differences aside (e.g., sex, age), they will understand and respond to the movement, speech, or gesture of another in predictable, stable ways. Altmann distinguishes between the two kinds of "signs" in terms of "a mute who understands all that he hears" and "[a] deaf person who talks," the former being conversant exclusively in comsigns, the latter exclusively in interpersonal signs (Altmann 1967, 336). Interpersonal signs are equally *rational: systematic understandings of bodily enacted communications are possible,* and not only possible but readily evident in the fact that primatologists, for example, can study nonhuman primate behavior and *themselves* profess to understand what is consistently meant even though they themselves do not normally perform or cannot perform the gestures, movements, or acts. That a further elaboration of analogical apperception underlies their understandings is to be noted but will not be pursued here except to remark that short of analogical apperception, inter-species understandings—not only of nonhuman primates by human ones, but also of human primates by nonhuman animals, including not only nonhuman primates, but nonhuman animals such as horses and dogs—would otherwise be impossible. Analogical apperception is the basis of the intercorporeal logos that structures comsigns. In light of the analysis set forth in Chapter 5 of the conditions of possibility of the interchangeability of "senders" and "receivers," we will take the term *comsign* to specify both the power to produce communal gestures, movements, and acts oneself and the power to understand the same gestures, movements, and acts in others rather than make a distinction between two "properties" of interchangeability as Altmann does. In effect, *comsign* designates species-specific *communal powers of communication.* Those communal powers constitute a communal repertoire of "I cans."

Social animals know that they are seen by other members of their group, that is, that they are *visual* bodies and that by moving in certain common public ways, they have the possibility of controlling the behavior of others to their advantage. This is true not only of baboons and chimpanzees, for example, in what is called "tactical deception" (Whiten and Byrne 1988), but of felines such as lionesses. Zoologist George Schaller observed several instances in which a lioness, after a kill, would "sit down and look around casually, as though nothing had happened, until other lions could no longer observe her; then she began to eat" (Schaller 1972, 268; also cited in Peters and Mech 1975, 292). Comsigns used for tactical deception on one's own behalf, however, are only half the story. Schaller's observations of the hunting techniques of lionesses are equally enlightening with respect to the other half. He writes, for example, that during stalking manoeuvres, a lioness "is fully aware of the advantage that cover confers" (Schaller 1972, 247),[11] and that in group hunting manoeuvres, lionesses coordinate their actions "by observing each other's posture and movement" (251). In the latter manoeuvres especially, comsigns must be at maximum efficacy; intercorporeal understandings undergird group survival in the sense that as a *socially undertaken enterprise*, successful hunting is contingent on movement patterns being readily and effectively read by others. The only way they can be so read, of course, is if "observing" means "analogically apperceiving another's intentions." Lionesses understand each other's postures and movements on the tactile-kinesthetic ground of their own bodies and can thus coordinate their efforts toward a successful end. In broader terms, because tactile-kinesthetic invariants undergirding the movement patterns of social hunting animals are species-specific, the patterns are meaning-specific/meaning-consistent for all in the group. We might note that tactile-kinesthetic invariants similarly undergird human speech perception, a phenomenon that also depends for its success on meaning-specific/meaning-consistent patterns (see Sheets-Johnstone 1990 and 1999b). Comsigns are indeed at the core of intercorporeal intelligibility.

A sense of oneself as a visual form and of the visual impact of one's movements can be translated into certain rudimentary causal notions, or in other words, into certain relational awarenesses: if I do such and such, then others will not likely notice me eating; if I do such and such, then the other will likely stop chasing me (see Whiten and Byrne 1988). Comsigns from this perspective are not merely visual signals but epistemically rich *rational* signals that allow individuals of a group to make sense of each other, in effect, to live as *social* animals. Not only do all individuals know how to perform them (or how they are performed); all know what they mean and what their effect is likely to be, and this on the basis of their own tactile-kinesthetic powers of articulation, powers that translate into ways of intercorporeal knowing. Comsigns—the kinetic basis of intercorporeal sense-makings—attest to the evolutionary foundations and significance of an intercorporeal logos that anchors social communication. The rationality of the universe is a rationality of structures of the animate as well as the inanimate. Not only is the world semantically coherent with *its* regularities; creatures themselves are semantically coherent with *their* regularities. Indeed, if social meanings are corporeally enacted, intercorporeal sense-making only makes sense.

The claim that nonhuman animals do not have physical bodies *as such* was spelled out and documented at length in an earlier book, specifically in a chapter devoted to the origin of the concept of death (Sheets-Johnstone 1990); it was more summarily presented in Chapter 2 of this book. The claim is of considerable import in linking the having of physical bodies *as such* to the concept of death and to the concept of one's body as being susceptible to ageing, to disease, to woundings and tearings at the hands of others, and so on. The claim certainly neither asserts nor entails that nonhuman animals feel no apprehension about being hurt by another, for example, or that they feel no pain. It asserts only that they have no concept of the body as *flesh*, that is, of being a physical body separate from their living body, and as being vulnerable to all those things to which flesh is heir, most notably, death and wanton killing or mutilation by others. Though nonhuman animals may certainly be threatened by each other in the course of everyday exchanges as we saw in Chapters 1 and 4, for example, they have no sense of the possibility of *being killed* by each other. As described earlier, nonhuman animals perceive each other as dynamically moving forms, forms whose affectively charged and changing physiognomies remain consistently familiar in the course of everyday comportments and gestures. In fact, a decided shift occurs in the presence of atypical actions or strange behaviors. For example, when a chimpanzee becomes partially paralyzed by polio and its gait becomes queer, the chimpanzee is shunned by others as an alien (Goodall 1971, 221–22). In such circumstances, the familiar comsigns of everyday social life are either radically altered or missing altogether. The queer behaviors and atypical physiognomies do not result in *explanations*. They do not precipitate investigations at the level of fleshly realities, physical facts. They are taken and understood for what they are: a queer gait, a changed visual form, and the like. Jane Goodall gives many examples of how chimpanzee mothers solicitously cradle or groom their injured infant, sometimes even their dead infant, but do not examine the infant to find the cause of its distress, or indeed, make judgments about its lack of liveliness (Goodall 1968). A caveat is in order, however. Though explanations are not sought with respect to injured physical bodies or to once animate forms, sense-making is far from absent with respect to the physical presence of living bodies. As described in Chapter 6, for example, allowances are made by larger individuals for smaller individuals in the context of play. Moreover a sense of vulnerability is palpably present in comsigns of threat and retreat, kinetic and gestural forms in which warnings of an impending attack are given and heeded. An essential, altogether basic sense-making thus exists with respect to physical bodies, an elemental rationality with respect to one's own body and that of others, but in a wholly living, here-now context. Similarly, a sense of vulnerability, one's own and that of others, is decidedly present, but in a wholly living, here-now context. In other words, the essential and altogether basic sense-making and sense of vulnerability are not tied to matters of life and death, to the physical body *as such*. The concept of death and the fear of death, both of which are tied to the physical body *as such*, are absent. In consequence, sense-making and the sense of vulnerability are not of the scope potential in human primates. As emphasized in Chapter 1, what links morality to death, what in fact grounds morality and *makes it fully real*, is foundationally one's own body, one's own *physical* body, which is vulnerable and ultimately impotent, that is, which is affectively experienced as exposed, assailable, open to pain, disease, suffering, and death, and which is affectively experienced as ultimately out of one's control.

The existential depth of such affectively experienced physical bodily realities is unfathomable by sense-makings on the order of "why is life fraught with pain?" "why are there diseases?" and so on: whatever the physical bodily reality, the existential impact of the experience simply is what it is. But a rationally unadorned and unadornable existential awareness of oneself and other living beings as exposed and open to pain, suffering, and death, as quintessentially vulnerable by the mere fact of being alive, of being first and foremost a physical body, has the possibility of giving rise to sense-makings going beyond, yet still rooted in, those already described. Indeed, the further sense-makings that link all humans in a common humanity and common creaturehood, and a common humanity and common creaturehood to a common natural world, build on the foundational sense-makings of analogical apperception and the intercorporeal semantics of comsigns, sense-makings that essentially connect one individual to another. As we have seen, these rationally ordered structures of intelligence allow individuals to understand one another and to communicate with one another. Sense-makings that build on this foundation have the possibility of opening upon ever deepening understandings of the vast world of Nature and awakening the attitudinal affect of caring.

## IV. THE RATIONALITY OF CARING: LAYING THE GROUNDWORK

Caring is not a ready-made of sentient life but requires the profoundly deepened form of sense-making potential in, and unique to, the species that christens itself *Homo sapiens sapiens*. The potential was undoubtedly present in incipient ways in earlier hominid species in the course of their burial practices and their ministerings to wounded and ill others, and possibly too in their territorial expansions, explorations of new resources, appreciations of new and different forms of life, awarenesses of cosmic phenomena such as eclipses and star-laden skies and of cosmological regularities in the form of changing seasons, and so on. This more profound form of sense-making is rooted in the apprehension and comprehension of the interconnectedness of life, of all forms of life and of life in all its forms to the universe, thereby an interconnectedness of sweeping historical as well as livingly present dimensions. In its manifold evolutionary unfoldings, and in the dependence of those unfoldings on the earth itself—on air, water, gravity, and myriad other physico-chemical phenomena—and on the biodiversity of animals and sentient beings in general—all the way down to worms as Darwin so attentively and perspicuously shows us and of which more presently—the interconnectedness foundational to caring is palpably evident. Nature indeed *non facit saltus*, and if nature *non facit saltus*, then that principle exists not in the abstract but in and across the livingly present and historical particularities of Nature, and as such, should surely be discernible by the vaunted intelligence of humans.

As a classic theoretical doctrine, rationalism is narrowly understood as a vision of—and a credence in—rational man reading the rationality of the universe. The understanding is narrow because rational man himself must be held up to the light and rationally examined. The actual scope of rationality is thus far broader. So realized, rationality encompasses an awareness of the ties that bind humans as much in a common humanity and a common creaturehood as to a common evolutionary heritage and to a common world. The possibility emerging from this awareness is that of living the rationality of one's own being, that is, experiencing in the ongoing living present one's interconnectedness to the whole of Nature. Such a rationality does not proceed in the direction of Heidegger's ontology of care with its focal concern on a radically heightened sense of *individual* human being, i.e., *Dasein* (of which more later), but in the direction of what one might term a metaphysical plenum of being, a sense of the pan-animate oneness of, and oneness with, the natural world. This rationality is essentially *creative* rather than *conscience-driven* (see Chapter 2); it is perpetually open to discovering new connections and thus lives on the edge of new insights. The epigraph from Donne at the beginning of this chapter epitomizes with eloquent clarity, even *ecological* eloquent clarity, just such a rationality. So also does the epigraph from D. H. Lawrence. Sense-making in the deepest sense is indeed an expansion, not a contraction of the rational.

The very rationality epitomized in the epigraphs from Donne and Lawrence is substantiated in detail by Darwin, for example, in his descriptions of ecological differences such as those ensuing between an untouched barren heath and an enclosed one planted with Scotch fir where "we see how potent has been the effect of the introduction of a single tree" (Darwin 1859, 123). It is substantiated further in the fact that cattle "absolutely determine the existence of the Scotch fir" (124); and in a still further instance, in the fact that "in several parts of the world insects determine the existence of cattle" (124). A diversity and multiplicity of examples are in fact readily available in Darwin's writings. Indeed, through his patient and thorough observations Darwin shows not only "how complex and unexpected are the checks and relations between organic beings, which have to struggle together in the same country" (123), but "how plants and animals, most remote in the scale of nature, are bound together by a web of complex relations" (124–25). He later remarks pointedly on the fact that "when a plant or animal is placed in a new country amongst new competitors, though the climate may be exactly the same as in its former home, yet the conditions of its life will generally be changed in an essential manner" (128).[12]

The depth of insight of Darwin, Donne, and Lawrence into the interconnectedness of all living forms and of life to the earth itself testifies to the rationality potential in humans, to the *sapience* that actually defines them as a species and that underlies caring. Caring is an extension of that rationality, an affective and attitudinal extension of the capacity to see lucidly into the nature of life on earth. The rationality of caring thus has nothing to do with cost-benefit analyses and similar kinds of assessments and calculations of gainful or otherwise advantageous personal spin-offs that one may expect as a result of "caring." Indeed, *that* kind of caring is not in the least equivalent to the caring that is an extension of rationality. But neither is caring a rationalized fabrication, an invented, constraining, or justifying product of moral thought. It is a potential attitudinal and affective dimension of one's own being, one's own *human* being that is capable of apprehending and comprehending the rationality of the universe and oneself as part of the universe. It bears emphasis with respect to this genuinely sapient rationality that before being able to give reasons for one's actions and beliefs—the common criterion of rationality—one must be able to act reasonably in the world and to have reasonable beliefs about it, and to act and to believe in this way, one has first *to make sense* of the world and of oneself and other animate forms as living creatures within it. To live the rationality of one's own being in this sense is to apprehend and comprehend the interconnectedness of Nature in all her forms; it is to live the powers of insight potential in experiences of the natural world, including and even beginning with oneself. Thus, insight into the nature of Nature and into the nature of human nature is necessarily at the heart of caring: sensemaking is its foundation; it literally informs caring from the start.

An elucidation of caring that brings to light the living rationality in which it is structured is thus necessarily an elucidation of how rationality is *the very condition of the possibility of caring*. Hobbes's characterization of the natural state of humans as "solitary" is instructive to consider in this context, as is Schopenhauer's notion of egoism. In their respective descriptions of an aspect of human nature antithetical to its realization, both philosophers, in markedly different but incisive ways, indirectly clarify caring and the condition of its possibility. Moreover Schopenhauer's further exposition of *compassion* as a fundamental human motive provides concrete grounds for considering directly the metaphysics of caring. Let us consider each philosopher in turn.

Hobbes's pithy description of human life in a state of nature is commonly reduced to the last three of its original five characteristics, his thesis being in essence that no inherent beneficent sociality informs human life. He writes that in a state of nature, "the life of man . . . [is] solitary, poor, nasty, brutish, and short" (Hobbes 1930, 253). A moment's reflection shows that the first characteristic is of particular moment from the viewpoint of caring. Not only is a solitary existence both pivotal to, and portentous of, a life that is poor, nasty, brutish, and short, but it is both pivotal to, and portentous of, a life essentially driven by fear. "The life of man" could, after all, be poor, nasty, brutish, and short in ways neither fundamentally grounded in, nor heightened by, the fear-laden challenges of solitary existence. Hobbes in fact minces no words in emphasizing the elemental fear natural to solitary existence and in citing everyday instances of it. He writes, for example, that in a state of nature, i.e., "without a common power to keep them all in awe" (252), each man relies purely on himself, "without other security, than what [his] own strength, and [his] own invention shall furnish [him] withal" (253), and that in such a condition, what is "worst of all" is that he lives in "continual fear, and danger of violent death" (253); he states, "[E]very man is enemy to every man" (253), that "all men against all men" (266) or "all against all" (267) is the rule; and so on. Moreover it is not surprising that fear of death looms large since "[a]ll men in the state of nature have a desire and will to hurt" (262). At a later point, Hobbes explains that "the most frequent reason why men desire to hurt each other, ariseth hence, that many men at the same time have an appetite to the same thing; which yet very often they can neither enjoy in common, nor yet divide it; whence it follows that the strongest must have it, and who is strongest must be decided by the sword" (263).

Self-interest in the preservation of one's own life and resources is in consequence foremost. Hobbes points to an assortment of everyday facts that readily exemplify how each man defends and protects himself and his belongings. When a man goes to sleep, for example, "he locks his doors," and even when he is in his own house, "he locks his chests" (253); he arms himself when taking a journey; and so on. Moreover a man does these things even when he lives with others in obeisance to a common power or authority, i.e., even when "he knows there be laws, and public officers, armed, to revenge all injuries shall be done him" (253). In short, a man's elemental fear of his fellow citizens is transparent in everyday behaviors; at its core, "mutual fear" (261), not an inherently amicable sociality, informs the solitary life of man.

In his lengthy explanation of how man is *not* "born fit for society" (258), Hobbes in fact avers that "solitude is an enemy," and this because from the very beginning man is at the mercy of others: "infants have need of others to help them to live, and those of riper years to help them to live well" (258). It is less the need, however, than the unfitness that solitude engenders that is of fundamental significance: "[A]ll men, because they are born in infancy, are born unapt for society" (258). Moreover, though men are "made fit for society not by nature, but by education," it happens that "[m]any . . . perhaps most men, either through defect of mind or want of education, remain unfit during the whole course of their lives" (258). The bleak picture of solitude that Hobbes presents is compounded by his later warning that "an error proceeding from our too slight contemplation of human nature" (259) may lead us to think that when men do come together in a civil society, they do so in genuine sociality, whereas the opposite is true. It is not for the benefit of true camaraderie that a man seeks society but for the motive of profit or gain of some sort. If men meet for trading or communicative exchanges of some kind, for example, "it is plain every man regards not his fellow, but his business; if to discharge some office, a certain market-friendship is begotten, which hath more of jealousy in it than true love" (259); and so on. In sum, each man is impelled by nature to pursue "what is good for him" and to shun "what is evil, but chiefly the chiefest of natural evils, which is death" (263); each man is thus naturally impelled to protect himself and his belongings. Only "the fundamental *laws of nature*" (258), i.e., societal laws, serve to protect him and his interests, for in binding him and others like him to a common authority, the laws mitigate the absence of justice and injustice, of *"mine"* and *"thine"* (256), absences that, Hobbes observes, define the "ill condition" that is solitude (257). These fundamental laws define the liberties and rights in civil society generally and require conformance to rules and principles that give each man the right "to use his own power, as he will himself, for the preservation of his own nature" (268).

Hobbes's description of humans in a "state of nature" coincides in certain respects with prime aspects of human nature analyzed and discussed in Part I, most notably with the fact that humans are at risk among other humans: the fundamental vulnerability of humans lies in their being alive among others of their species. Placed in a broader perspective on human nature, however, Hobbes's thesis, like Part I, clearly enlightens us only by half. As the foregoing chapters in Part II suggest, human nature has another side. "The life of man" that begins in infancy is part and parcel of human nature, but the true nature of that beginning life is unjustly limned by Hobbes in his summary picture of infants as "unapt for society"—or rather, with proper and due respect, in the summary picture Hobbes limned more than three hundred and fifty years ago. In a word, capacities discovered over the past fifty years and more through firsthand observations, extensive psychological and developmental studies, and experimental research show that infants are neither socially incompetent nor socially inadequate. Their capacities for imitation, affect attunement, and play, for example, substantiate a markedly different assessment of the beginnings of human nature. Moreover a substantively defining social character of infancy—to be more fully elucidated in the Epilogue—warrants attention in this context. The character is succinctly captured in an especially relevant way in one of Darwin's trenchant observations: "Seeing a Baby (like Hensleigh's) smile & frown, who can doubt these are instinctive—child does not sneer" (Darwin 1987, Notebook M, no. 96, p. 542). It is indeed noteworthy that the first "essentially social manifestation" of an infant (Spitz 1983, 100) is a smile and not a sneer—and not any other kind of disdaining or aggressive social gesture either. Since others have been there consistently for the infant from the time it was born, it could conceivably sneer—or curl its lips, or spit—at any one of them. But it is with a directed smile that, at about three months of age, it first socially recognizes another, doing so in a totally friendly and open way. Darwin's simple observation is of additional import in underscoring the wholly spontaneous nature of the smile: the smile is "instinctive." Not only does nothing duplicitous enter, but there is no attempt at putting a smile together, as it were, as infants sometimes attempt to put together—to perfect—their imitation of an adult's mouth gesture (Meltzoff and Moore 1983). The smile is a natural sign that is immediately and fully present. Further still, the fact that blind infants smile (Fraiberg 1987; Bower 1979) rules out the possibility that an infant's smile is no more than a reflex response to seeing an adult smile. In fact, the idea that a baby's smile is a response[13] may be misleading; that is, an infant's smile is developmentally a *causa sui* act whose self-spontaneity and meaning is easily elided when categorized as a "response." Precisely as Darwin indicates in describing it an "instinctive" gesture and in contrasting it with a sneer, the smile is essentially an *initiatory* act rather than a responding one. Through its smile, an infant greets a world of others, greeting it even indiscriminately, as we will see in the following chapter through a consideration of psychiatrist René Spitz's many ingenious experiments. In sum, in contrast to Hobbes's negative assessment of infant sociability, Darwin's observation vividly captures the natural character of an infant's burgeoning sociality, its initially open and unconditionally positive sense of another human. An essential condition of the possibility of caring rests on just such an affectively charged, attitudinally positive sense of the other.

Now when Hobbes states that, with respect to "the ill condition, which man by mere nature is actually placed in," there is "a possibility to come out of it," he specifies the possibility in terms of "passion" and "reason": "The passions that incline men to peace, are fear of death;

desire of such things as are necessary to commodious living; and a hope by their industry to obtain them." As for reason, it "suggesteth convenient articles of peace, upon which men may be drawn to agreement. These articles . . . are called the Laws of Nature" (Hobbes 1930, 257). It is clear, however, both from the above discussion of what Hobbes considers the state of nature and its fundamental solitude and from his subsequent elaboration of the "Laws of Nature" that steer men toward peaceful coexistence, that "the dictate of right reason" (268) that subtends the laws and that leads to social conformity is driven by fear of death, not caring. The point is that, so long as caring plays no part, war will be unending, for what individuals give up, sovereign leaders can readily take up in the form of superordinate power, power that can fuel intermittent if not insatiable cravings for *more:* an expanded dominion, greater wealth, greater glory, and so on. Through war, sovereign leaders lay claim to history; as we have seen in Chapter 4, they believe their deeds will make them and their nations of lasting historical significance if not immortal. Hobbes himself writes that "in all times, kings, and persons of sovereign authority, because of their independency, are in continual jealousies, and in the state and posture of gladiators; having their weapons pointing, and their eyes fixed on one another; that is, their forts, garrisons, and guns upon the frontiers of their kingdoms; and continual spies upon their neighbours; which is a posture of war" (256).

Thus, Hobbes's "Laws of Nature" are not sufficient to establish peace, and education as Hobbes pictures it through the "Laws of Nature" is clearly not only not enough but ineffective. The kind of education needed to cultivate peace, as we shall see more fully in the Epilogue, is precisely of the sense-making kind undergirding the insights of Donne, Lawrence, and Darwin. Their rational readings of the universe draw on their own native capacity for sense-making and both their readings and the native capacity on which they are based are at the foundation of the rationality of caring, a rationality that is itself the foundation of a humanly peaceful world. An education built on their insights would encompass fundamental understandings of the nature of Nature, including of course the nature of human nature. Moral precepts would arise naturally in the course of such an education; they would readily ensue from fundamental understandings of the interrelatedness of the whole of Nature. Thus, human morality would originate not in rules and principles or in "information"—whether about oneself or the world—but in personal understandings and verifications of the insights of others that span Nature as a whole and engender attitudes, feelings, and motivations commensurate with those understandings.

Like Hobbes's notion of the state of nature, Schopenhauer's notion of egoism is significant in specifying an aspect of human nature that highlights by antithesis the phenomenon of caring. Egoism is in fact what Schopenhauer specifies "the chief and fundamental" antimoral incentive (Schopenhauer 1915, 150). Egoism, he writes, is "the urgent impulse to exist, and exist under the best circumstances" (150). Fear of death per se does not enter into his discussion, but "the urgent impulse" is clearly a different face of what, in Hobbes, man constantly seeks to avoid: "the chiefest of natural evils." Schopenhauer's analysis of the egoist centers on the latter's limitless concerns with himself: "'All things for me, and nothing for others' is his maxim" (151). At a later point, Schopenhauer notes that "at its worst" the maxim is "[H]elp no body, but rather injure all people, if it brings you any advantage" (157). Acting wholly from antimoral incentives, among which Schopenhauer lists "gluttony, lust, selfishness, avarice, covetousness, and injustice" (157), the egoist can hardly perform any deed of "genuine moral worth" (148, 162). Because his motives perpetually derive either to some degree or to the full from self-interest, the moral value of his acts is either "lowered by the disclosure of an accessory selfish incentive" or the value "is entirely destroyed" (163). Thus, Schopenhauer states, "The absence of all egoistic motives is . . . the *Criterion* of an action of moral value" (163). As will be evident, he finds this criterion in compassion.

It is notable that in the course of his analysis, Schopenhauer calls attention to the fact that if a man obeys "some absolute command issued by an unknown, but evidently supreme power," he is at bottom acting egoistically, out of fear of punishment for being disobedient (167–68). Hence, religiously motivated acts are either to some degree or entirely devoid of moral value, for wherever and whenever "the actual weal and woe of the agent himself is the real motive . . . what he does is *egoistic*, and therefore *without moral worth*" (168). In contrast, it is when the weal and woe of someone else is the consuming motivation that an action has "the stamp of moral worth": an act "is carried out, or omitted, purely for the benefit and advantage of another" (168–69).

The stringency of Schopenhauer's moral determinations is pointedly evident in his identification of three fundamental motives that drive any and all human acts: "(a) Egoism; which desires the weal of the self, and is limitless. (b) Malice; which desires the woe of others, and may develop to the utmost cruelty. (c) Compassion; which desires the weal of others, and may rise to nobleness and magnanimity" (172). Schopenhauer has comparatively little to say about malice; he concentrates efforts toward showing how compassion is "the ultimate basis of morality" and underlies all acts of true justice and lovingkindness (171). Thus, while all three motives are within the compass of human nature, compassion alone is "the only true moral incentive" (165ff). In the process of substantiating this claim, Schopenhauer confronts the critical question of how the weal and woe of another comes to be "my *motive*" (169), that is, how it is that "I suffer with [another]" (169). He answers that "for this to be possible, . . . the *difference* between myself and him, which is the precise *raison d'être* of my Egoism, must be *removed*, at least to a certain extent" (169–70). He later refers to the removed difference as "this extraordinary phaenomenon" and adds that its explanation is "not so easy" (174). He states that its "key can be furnished by Metaphysics alone" (175), and goes on to provide that metaphysics in his concluding chapter, though at the end he characterizes what he has written as "hints towards the elaboration of a metaphysical basis for Ethics" (281).

The immediate point of moment is that, however tentative and metaphysically incomplete Schopenhauer's answer, it coincides with Donne's, Lawrence's, and Darwin's sense-makings of the universe: a 'difference removed' testifies to the reality of interconnectedness. Moreover in spelling out actions emanating from "the only true moral incentive," Schopenhauer names two principles: *"Neminem laede; immo omnes, quantum potes, juva,* (Do harm to no one; but rather help all people, as far as lies in your power)" (175). While some might argue that each principle as enacted might be either admittedly self-interested or perceived or interpreted as self-interested, it may as readily and more strongly be argued that when motivated by a lack of difference "between myself and him," each principle takes on an altogether different character. To see this, however, is to delve more deeply into the "extraordinary phaenomenon" of removed difference, a phenomenon Schopenhauer at other points terms *"mysterious"* (204) and an "almost incomprehensible paradox" (206), and duly recognizes to begin with and in closing as "the great mystery of Ethics" (170, 278). In short, it is to delve more deeply into precisely the metaphysical basis of ethics.

In his closing chapter, Schopenhauer attempts to ground the "primal ethical phaenomenon" (255) in the Kantian thought that plurality is but appearance: that "there is but one and the same entity really existing, which is present and identical in all alike" (270). He points out that this thought is considerably older than its Kantian expression, citing the Hindu Vedas, Pythagoras's Eleatic School, Sufi mysticism, and a good many other religious and philosophic traditions and formulations. In other words, whatever its particular instance, the thought centers on a dissolution of difference between the ego and the non-ego, a dissolution that, as he has earlier shown, is the source of compassion and therefore the metaphysical foundation of ethics (273). When he writes, "My true inmost being subsists in every living thing" (275), he is in essence giving a metaphysical reading of the rationality of the universe as suggested above, indeed, elaborating on Donne's opening meditation line—"No man is an *Island*, entire of it self; every man is a piece of the *Continent*"—and the penultimate line, "any man's *death* diminishes me because I am involved in *Mankind*." In contrast to Donne, however, and stretching his metaphysics beyond its natural limits, i.e., beyond its natural living expression in compassion, Schopenhauer casts an immortality ideology over the 'primal ethical phaenomenon', stating, "He . . . [who] has broken the fetters of the *principium individuationis* . . . embraces all his countrymen, and in them lives on and on." For such a man, he declares, "death is no more than "a wink of the eyelids, so momentary that it does not interrupt the sight" (278–79).

The immortality ideology is in fact an unnecessary addendum to "the great mystery of Ethics." If the metaphysics that grounds ethics, as Schopenhauer describes it, is the common being of ego and non-ego, an identification in which "the individual directly recognizes in *another* his own self, his true and very being" (274), then that metaphysics clearly encompasses the reality of death, i.e., the death of another as one's own eventual reality, and does so without the need of an immortality ideology, which indeed, as Schopenhauer specifies it, re-fetters man to the *principium individuationis*. On the contrary, what threads its way through the whole of Nature, joining all to all, is in and of itself metaphysically significant; that is, its import lies in its living reality, not in an immortality ideology. It is in fact the experience of its living import that is in want of further elucidation, for it is its living import that awakens a moral sensibility to what is. Schopenhauer's description of a 'removed difference', Donne's meditation, Lawrence's panegyric to life, Darwin's descriptions of the interconnectedness all forms of life resonate with a sense of the ties that bind us in a common humanity, a common creaturehood, a common existence with all. What we need to understand is precisely how this sense gives rise to caring.

## V. THE LIVING IMPORT OF THE "METAPHYSICALLY SIGNIFICANT": THE EXPERIENCE OF INTERCONNECTEDNESS

The existential roots of caring may be elucidated from two convergent directions: the experience of interconnectedness—or "removed difference"—and the principle of not harming. A metaphysics of the nature of human nature, or more properly, a bio-metaphysics of the nature of human nature, is required to illuminate each source, a *bio*-metaphysics in the sense of being Nature-tethered and grounded in sense-makings of Nature. In this sense, the bio-metaphysics is experientially tethered and aims at descriptive rather than explanatory accounts; that is, it asks not "how does it work?" but "where does it come from?" precisely as a central concern with the roots of morality mandates. Further, the answers it seeks do not assume caring an all-at-once, full-blown phenomenon, but a developmental phenomenon, an affective attitude toward the world and others that grows commensurate with one's sense-makings. From this perspective, it is clear that studies outside as well as inside what is nominally considered the domain of ethics can condition the real-life emergence of caring and that such studies can in fact be deeply illuminating of the sense-makings that condition its emergence. On the other hand, subjects commonly treated as basic ethical touchstones or as bearing strongly on ethics may also shed light on caring by setting the phenomenon in relief. Extended critical examinations of two such touchstones—altruism as evolutionarily rendered by a variety of researchers and care as ontologically rendered by Heidegger—will exemplify both sources of knowledge, i.e., how studies both inside and outside the domain of ethics can be decisively edifying, enhancing our understandings of caring in seminal ways.

In the introduction of their target article on unselfish behavior, philosopher Elliott Sober and evolutionary biologist David Wilson state, "Evolutionary altruism is not the same as helping" (Sober and Wilson 2000b, 185). They proceed to a discussion and validation of the biological concept of group selection in relation to both evolutionary altruism and psychological altruism, the former being a matter of fitness, the latter a matter of motives and desires. Their article and the ensuing interdisciplinary commentaries exemplify typical present-day concepts of concern with respect to the topic of evolutionary altruism: group selection, kin selection, and selfish genes. It is significant in light of these concepts that the term altruism, taken in its original, which the OED suggests comes from Auguste Comte who "perh[aps] coined it, on the model of *égoisme*," means simply "[an] unselfish concern for or devotion to the welfare of others." In other words, it is tied to individual everyday human reality, not scientific discourse and analysis. In contrast, a second meaning, given in Webster's 1996 Unabridged Dictionary under the category *"Animal Behavior,"* follows along the latter lines; it reads: "behavior by an animal that may be to its disadvantage but that benefits others." In effect, while the non-theoretical first meaning has nothing to do with fitness, selection, or genes—whether genes conceived anthropomorphically as selfishly concerned with their own reproduction (Dawkins 1989, Nesse 2000) or non-anthropomorphically as elemental molecules of living beings—the second meaning most definitely does, and in fact constitutes the sparring ground of conflicting biological, psychological, and philosophical perspectives on altruism. When Sober and Wilson write, "Evolutionary altruism is not the same as helping," they are making just such a distinction between the first and second meanings of the term 'altruism'.

It is equally significant in light of typical present-day concepts of concern that contemporary discussions of altruism emanate from Darwin's original observations of caste systems and reproduction in social insects, and that, in his studies of these insects, Darwin was not concerned with altruism and in fact never uses the word. His concern was wholly in showing the difficulties that the caste systems pose for the theory of natural selection, and in turn, how the theory is not undermined by them. In the concluding chapter of *The Origin of Species*, he puts the difficulties in the context of human expectations of perfection, i.e., Nature should be "perfect." After pointing out that natural selection "adapts the inhabitant's of each country only in relation to the degree of perfection of their associates; so that we need feel no surprise at the inhabitants of any one country . . . being beaten and supplanted by the naturalised productions from another land," he states, "Nor ought we to marvel if all the contrivances in nature be not, as far as we can judge, absolutely perfect; and if some of them be abhorrent to our ideas of fitness." He proceeds then to caution against human expectations of perfection vis-à-vis the apparent destructiveness and wastefulness of nature, remarking, "We need not marvel at the sting of the bee causing the bee's own death; at drones being produced in such vast numbers for one single act, and being then slaughtered by their sterile sisters; at the astonishing waste of pollen by our fir trees; ... and at other such cases" (Darwin 1859, 445). He affirms quite the contrary: "The wonder indeed is, on the theory of natural selection, that more cases of the want of absolute perfection have not been observed" (445).[14]

It is notable, of course, that "marveling" at the want of absolute perfection in nature is foundationally—if covertly—tied to matters that matter most to most human beings: life and death. In other words, though not specified by Darwin as such, a human concern with Nature's lack of "perfection" follows from the quintessential human concern with human mortality, precisely as exemplified in Williams's "Wicked Old Witch" depiction of Mother Nature discussed in Chapter 1. Given their subtext in human mortality, human expectations of, or desires for, perfection in Nature constitute a bona fide area of inquiry in evolutionary studies of human morality. Such expectations and desires are invested with feelings—of dread, yearning, hope, or anxiety, for example—precisely as are human motivations; and as we have seen across the last six chapters through analyses and elaborations of Rank's and Becker's work on immortality ideologies, of male-male competition and the pan-culturality of evil, and of empathy, play, and trust, how humans behave toward one another depends on how they are motivated. Expectations and desires concerning the perfection of Nature may thus implicitly or explicitly motivate human behavior, and in particular, selfish rather than altruistic behavior. The latter, in its original sense, is obviously motivated in ways patently free of any expectations or desires of perfection in Nature. From this perspective, however, altruism and selfishness enter equally into the real-life equation of affect and action; that is, both are forms of human action that spring from and are driven by human affects. It follows that if humans look Nature in the eye and see death, destruction, and waste, and thereby intimations of their own mortality, they may readily feel that since Nature sets such an imperfect example, why should human nature in general and human acts in particular be different? More specifically put: Why should *I* be anything other than selfishly inclined? Why should *I* be moved to act altruistically? The impending motivation to selfishness is akin to the spite-laden anguish Becker epitomizes when he writes: "If we don't have the omnipotence of gods, we at least can destroy like gods" (Becker 1973, 85; see Chapter 1).

Debates about the perfection or imperfection of Nature have no place in present-day debates about altruism—indeed, there is no mention of the topic in the literature cited. Such debates would plainly center not on different forms of selection, on genes, or indeed on "mechanisms" of any kind, but rather on the living reality of altruism, selfishness, and human mortality. Of critical moment here is not whether such debates might take place but the fact that all contending views are anchored in the original, non-theoretical meaning of altruism without which they would not exist: short of the straightforward concept of unselfish behavior embedded in the original meaning, the broader "animal behavior" meaning would have no foundation. The theoretical concept of "selfish genes" is a sterling example of this dependency. Given the interdisciplinary appeal of "selfish genes" (see, for example, Tooby and Cosmides 1992, Pinker 1997, and Nesse 2000), the dependency is worth spelling out.[15]

To label genes "selfish" is to personify them; what is properly characteristic of individuals is ascribed to molecular parts of individuals. The practice of personification not only obscures the "real-life, real-time"—to use dynamic systems terminology—meaning of altruism, but is emphatically ironic in the context of a reductionist program. When evolutionary psychiatrist Randolph Nesse, for example, in his commentary on Sober and Wilson's target article, derides those who veer from the path of "selfish genes" in their attempt to "reclaim altruism," he speaks of "the mist that descends when the language of morality is used as a metaphor for the process of natural selection" (Nesse 2000, 227), a language he later specifies as making altruism "impossible" (229). At the same time, however, he fails to see that his own language with respect to selfish genes is a lexical excess, a *façon de parler* (Sheets-Johnstone 1999b, 1996 n. 37; 1992 n. 33) that is egregiously sweeping in its claims and that itself makes altruism "impossible." He states, "Calling genes 'selfish' was inspired. It accurately describes how they create organisms designed wholly to increase the copies of their genes in future generations" (Nesse 2000, 228). Shortly afterward he proclaims, "It is correct beyond question that genes shape brains that induce individuals to do whatever best gets copies of those genes into future generations" (229). He maintains that it is when the latter "principle" is erroneously combined with "our intuitive notion that altruism consists of costly acts that benefit others" that "altruism is impossible" (229).

While Nesse seeks to differentiate selfish genes from selfish individuals (for example, 227, 229), claiming that just because genes are selfish, people are not necessarily so, and while he wants to keep moral issues properly "at the levels of the individual and society" (230), and while both aims are noble from the perspective of recognizing different levels of investigation and discourse, the aims are vitiated by egoistical-intentional ascriptions anchored in a "language of morality" that covers over not only the fundamental source of altruism but of selfishness as well. Indeed, according to Nesse, morality issues only from brains led by selfish genes to produce morality through genetic competition (229, 230, 231). Simple reflection shows that it is these reductionist circumstances, not a "principle-cum-intuition," that make altruism impossible, for in these circumstances organisms along with their behaviors are put into genetic straitjackets and morality loses its real-life significance. However "mindlessly" selfish genes "advance their own interests" (228), their conceptual swaddling in selfishness makes a living morality disappear into molecular theoretical mists.[16] The basic question from a reductionist perspective is thereby itself put in question; that is, is the reductionist's basic question, "Can genes somehow induce individuals to be moral?" as Nesse insists, or is it, "Can genes *seduce brains* into thinking they can induce individuals to be moral?" Either way, selfish genes continue on what is essentially their immortality ideology pilgrimage (see also earlier, Chapter 1), a pilgrimage that is a universe away from everyday human morality where feelings are felt, thoughts are thought, and certain actions are taken or not taken.

In sum, the very notion of "selfish genes" exemplifies a *façon de parler* parasitic on real-life experience: if unselfish behavior had not been observed—for example, seeing one animal risk her life to save another (Relethford 1990, 139)—and an initial concept of altruism formed coincident with this observation, there would be no such phenomenon as altruism to analyze in the first place, and in turn no expansion of concepts into notions of selfish genes or, at an equally abstract level, of proximate and ultimate causation. That the originally observed phenomenon, the source of the concept of altruism, remains largely unexamined in evolutionary literature on morality is an oversight in patent need of correction. Indeed, when we are "at the pains of a little thought" (Berkeley [1709] 1929, 85), we readily see that altruism depends on intercorporeal sense-makings. It depends on analogical apperception and on comsigns. Whatever the altruistic behavior, it is basically anchored in species-specific intercorporeal meanings, meanings that have the potential in some instances to be understood and even generated across species—for example, the care of one species by another, as in Darwin's account of a baboon guarding and carrying about the young of other species (Darwin 1871, 41). Altruism is an empirical fact of animate life, the understanding of which rests on genealogical understandings of its source in intercorporeal sense-makings. Altruism is in fact not simply an instance but a paradigm of analogical apperception: one individual sees that a smaller individual needs help or special treatment, as in play (see Chapter 6); one individual sees that an individual is being chased aggressively by another individual and intercedes; and so on. One can readily see in view of just such genealogical underpinnings that altruism is a paradigm of the sense-makings underpinning the metaphysical experience of caring. Concern and devotion to the welfare of others such as to enhance their life in some way involves *actions* and *behaviors* that are intelligent.

Caring is not altruism but is grounded in such intelligence. It is not an act or behavior but an attitudinal affect anchored in an intercorporeal logos that encompasses all beings: animate and inanimate, sentient and insentient, one's own body and the entirety of bodies one is not. In caring, to paraphrase Donne, I am "involved" not just in *Mankind*, but in *Nature*. In effect, the sense of interconnectedness that grounds caring articulates a wide and deep metaphysics that encompasses Nature as a whole, and not merely in a spatial sense but in a temporal sense. Indeed, Nature is not a photographic harmony of the moment but an ever-changing constellation of harmonies that are dynamically melodic rather than statically chordal:[17] the air we breathe is always there; the earth on which we walk is always there; always there, but always different. Caring emanates from experiences of just such ever-changing harmonies and resonates alike with their creation and destruction, their endlessly coming into being and passing away. Hence, while humans might expect or want "perfection" from Nature in the form of life everlasting, Nature's perfection lies elsewhere. It lies in the shifting but perduring harmonies of all with all, harmonies aptly symbolized in the Hindu God/Goddess Shiva, who both creates and destroys. Darwin was not only acutely aware of these harmonies, that is, of how creation and destruction together wend their way through Nature, but eloquently described them in his final book, *The Formation of Vegetable Mould through the Action of Worms with Observations on their Habits*. In this intricately detailed and absorbing study, the intertwined creative and destructive faces of Nature are seen not just minutely but across centuries, and not just locatively but globally. Psychiatrist Adam Phillips memorializes Darwin's final book in a book of his own: *Darwin's Worms*, a book that is both trenchantly observant and sensitive, and that, interestingly enough, is subtitled *On Life Stories and Death Stories*. It is worthwhile pausing over Darwin's worms. Their labors epitomize facets of the interconnectedness of Nature and enhance understandings of the attitudinal affect of caring. Indeed, their labors show how elemental empirical truths of Nature have metaphysical significance, generating insights into the natural universe as a whole.

It is remarkable, even striking, that Phillips remarks specifically on the fact that the labors of worms are "inadvertently generous; not designed for altruism" (Phillips 2000, 57). Indeed, worms are first and foremost living creatures, and their labors are first and foremost the labors of all living creatures: to find food and feed themselves. Such labors are clearly neither altruistic nor selfish, and it would be an error to interpret them as either. Moral ascriptions to worms and moral judgments concerning their labors are in consequence out of place. On the contrary, and as Phillips implicitly suggests, it is the *inadvertent* generosity of the labor of worms that is morally significant, for it is in that generosity that we see limned the interconnectedness of Nature. What the labors of worms do inadvertently for others—their intimate relationship to the growth and well-being of seedlings and plants, for example—endows their labor with moral import. Indeed, understanding what their labors do for others is a lesson in the rationality of caring, part of the substrate of the intercorporeal logos that is witness to the interconnectedness of all to all. What is noteworthy in this instance is the lowly estimation and regard for worms that contrasts so conspicuously with the heights of awareness to which Darwin's treatise leads us, heights that allow us to see the essential conjunctive perfection of Nature, the shifting but perduring harmonies of all with all that in turn have the potential to set us on the path to caring.

Phillips writes that at the end of his life, Darwin turned to the morality of Nature, a Nature that "has no theological sanction, and is unavailable for wishful idealization" (55). He comments, "Perhaps it is not strange that as Darwin gets so close to his own death he starts writing about worms." He then remarks,

> [W]hat is striking about this last book is that . . . [i]t celebrates the inexhaustible work that makes the earth fertile. . . . Indeed, it proposes what might be called a secular after-life: the life of the world that continues after one's own death. The battle, the struggle, the war of life are omitted in this book; it is the sheer resilience and inventiveness of nature—"how strong worms are" and "the earth which they so largely consume"—that Darwin wants largely to emphasize at the end of his life. (55–56)

And indeed, as Darwin renders the lives of worms in fine detail, telling us how they "swallow an enormous quantity of earth, out of which they extract any digestible matter which it may contain" (Darwin 1881 [1976], 33) and how they plow the soil with their burrow excavations and form castings with the earth they eject along with intestinal secretions (65–70), he marvels at their intelligence and industry, at one point noting that their burrows "are not mere excavations, but may rather be compared with tunnels lined with cement" (64). At an earlier point, he observes that neither chance nor instinct alone can account for their discriminating actions, and that "[i]f worms have the power of acquiring some notion, however rude, of the shape of an object and of their burrows, . . . they deserve to be called intelligent . . . for they then act in nearly the same manner as would a man under similar circumstances" (58); at a later point, he remarks, "Archaeologists ought to be grateful to worms, as they protect and preserve for an indefinitely long period every object, not liable to decay, which is dropped on the surface of the land, by burying it beneath their castings" (146).

Phillips succinctly summarizes the significance of Darwin's worms when he comments, "They preserve the past, and create the conditions for future growth" (Phillips 2000, 56). Worms are indeed living testimony to the ongoing creative and destructive faces of Nature. Their literally foundational contribution to the continuity of life and preservation of earth is commemorated by Darwin himself at the conclusion of his book where he writes, "The plough is one of the most ancient and most valuable of man's inventions; but long before he existed the land was in fact regularly ploughed, and still continues to be thus ploughed by earthworms. It may be doubted whether there are many other animals which have played so important a part in the history of the world" (Darwin 1881, 148). In sum, the "inadvertent generosity" of worms that creates and destroys is part of the ongoing interconnectedness of all natural phenomena. Being aware of that generosity, indeed, being able to perceive its empirically based realities at all, is a human possibility, an exalted one in the natural world, a gift of Nature that is an "inadvertent generosity" in its own right and that warrants "marveling." It follows that caring is itself an inadvertent generosity of Nature. As we have seen, it is an existential attitude born of sense-makings and experiences of interconnectedness, an attitudinal affect toward others and the world. The attitudinal affect is not temporally riveted to a particular life, incident, or reading, and is thus not a momentary or passing *now* experience, but an ongoing attitude toward the plenum itself—the plenum of Nature spanning the cosmic and animate alike. Eighteenth-century scientist James Hutton's famous conclusion regarding earthly origins, "no vestige of a beginning,—no prospect of an end" (Hutton [1795] 1960, 1:200)—majestically captures this virtually timeless plenum of Nature.[18]

Set within this virtually timeless character, caring differs radically from care as Heidegger elaborates it in his ontology. Care is decidedly temporal, but it is neither worry about the future nor a practical as opposed to a theoretical stance toward something in the immediate world (Heidegger 1962, 237–38). Nor is it the result of some prior condition; as Heidegger cautions, "[C]are cannot be traced back to some ontical 'primal element'" (241). On the contrary, care is ontologically primary. It structures Dasein's Being (235–41) as a temporally inflected ontological trilogy: "Being-ahead-of-oneself . . . Being-already-in . . . [and] Being-alongside" (237, 241). Declined specifically in terms of Dasein, these modes are, respectively, existence (projection), facticity (thrownness), and falling (235, 329), the final term not having any "negative evaluation" but specifying "an absorption in Being-with-one-another, in so far as the latter is guided by idle talk, curiosity, and ambiguity"; in other words, falling is "a quite distinctive kind of Being-in-the-world—the kind that is completely fascinated by the "world" and by the Dasein-with of Others in the "they" (220). (We might note parenthetically that *falling*, though not identified as such, was discussed in Chapter 2 in terms of the "they," of immortality ideologies, and of the contrast of both with authentic Being—e.g., "When the call of conscience is understood, lostness in the 'they' is revealed" [354] and

Dasein realizes its own ownmost potentiality for Being, its "authentic potentiality-for-Being-a-whole" [365]). The point of moment here is not Dasein's lostness in the "they" and in immortality ideologies, but the totally individualized nature of care and its resolutely directed temporality. As will be evident, these aspects of Dasein's "care-structure" (see throughout 241–364) are significant for what they both say and do not say about the mystery of "removed difference."

The call of conscience is the call of care. In attesting to the possibility of authentic Being, the call of care "individualizes" Dasein and does so inexorably: "Relentlessly it individualizes Dasein down to its potentiality-for-Being-guilty, and exacts of it that it should be this potentiality authentically" (354). Being-guilty means "being-the-basis of a nullity" (331), of a *not* that is the existential sense of guilt. Though in foundational ways distinct from Heidegger's "nullity," this *not* is ontologically akin to what Sartre later describes as the "[n]othingness [that] lies coiled in the heart of being—like a worm" (Sartre 1956, 21). The radical individualization of authentic Being in Heidegger marks not just the singular distinctness of *Dasein* but the futural emphasis of that distinctness. In authentically "Being-ahead-of-itself" toward death, Dasein comes toward itself, toward its full individual potentiality of Being, comprehending the "not" or nullity of its ek-sistence, its "Being-toward-the-end" (Heidegger 1962, 365). To be responsive to the call of care and thereby the nullity of Being, Heidegger states, is to face death with "anticipatory resoluteness," a resoluteness that is part of the structure of care that holds to the constant certainty of death (356). Moreover "[a]uthentic thinking about death" is a manifestation, an expression of care (357). The call toward authentic Being is, in effect, both a call toward a radical, inmost individuality, an individuality of Being totally apart from the "they"—or any others—and a call toward the primordial temporality that constitutes Dasein's care-structure and that leads Dasein to comprehend (in the sense of "taking on" as well as of understanding) the nullity that "permeate[s]" its Being and its own ultimate death (331).[19] Indeed, Heidegger states, "Dasein's Being is care" (329) and "Care is Being-towards-death" (378).

Heidegger's own call that summons humans away from immortality ideologies and what Becker terms "a denial of death" is insistently and emphatically heightened in his dense and lengthy analyses of care. In the course of his unwavering focus on Dasein as *individual* human marked for irreversible, ultimate, and certain *individual death*—on

Dasein's "ownmost, non-relational possibility, which is not to be outstripped" (309)—Heidegger points out, for example, that "[d]eath does not just 'belong' to one's own Dasein in an undifferentiated way; death *lays claim* to it as an *individual* Dasein. The non-relational character of death . . . individualizes Dasein down to itself. This individualizing is a way in which the 'there' is disclosed for existence. It makes manifest that all Being-alongside the things with which we concern ourselves, and all Being-with Others, will fail us when our ownmost potentiality-for-Being is the issue" (308).

Such passages underscore the fact that the "there" is not—or can no longer be—a refuge when Dasein confronts its very Being. In effect, in making Dasein's ownmost potentiality-for-Being the issue,[20] that is, in making understanding Being definitive of Dasein, Heidegger is not simply identifying a particular form of self-understanding, but transforming a wholly *ontological* form of self-understanding into a wholly individual human imperative, even *the* fundamental human imperative.[21] Granted, Heidegger is not writing an ontological ethics or an ontology of morality. He nonetheless affirms that his ontology grounds morality in that the latter presupposes a dimension of care, that is to say, being-guilty (332).[22] Even more important, his ontological categories of the *authentic* and the *inauthentic* and his *ontological phenomenology of care*, especially with its derivatives of *concern* and *solicitude* and its *call to conscience*, have a determinative and incontestable moral tone. When he writes that a concern with things and a solicitude for Others are factical dimensions of Dasein, i.e., everyday aspects of care in everyday life, and that concern and solicitude are authentic only when Dasein answers to the call of its ownmost potentiality-for-Being, that moral tone is readily apparent. It is all the more apparent when he writes that when Dasein heeds the call of conscience and turns toward itself, authentic care with respect to things and to Others not only becomes possible, but *changes the nature of Dasein's everyday concern with things and solicitude for Others*. Indeed, Heidegger states that in everyday life where the call goes unheeded, Dasein is not only chained to "the entertaining 'incidentals' with which busy curiosity entertains itself" (358), for example, but "maintains itself . . . for the most part in the deficient modes of solicitude" (158). Only when one is "*authentically* bound" with the Other does one liberate rather than dominate the Other, free the Other through one's solicitude rather than make the Other beholden (159). More specifically and most significantly, in authentic care, one "helps the Other to become transparent to himself *in* his care and to become *free for* it" (159).

The helping relation Heidegger specifies has an inescapable moral character: to help the Other, especially without making the Other beholden to one, i.e., to act "selflessly," is to act morally—one might even say, to act altruistically. Thus, whatever his explicit protestations to the contrary, as when, in his "Letter on Humanism," he states, "The thinking that inquires into the truth of Being and so defines man's essential abode from Being and toward Being is neither ethics nor ontology" (Heidegger 1977a, 235–36), and later maintains that thinking simply brings Being into language (239), morality suffuses his existential analysis.[23] Either this or his "fundamental ontology" (238) and fundamental ontological imperative fail to carry any ontological force: individualizing Dasein "down to itself" is pointless; self-understanding is pointless; Dasein itself is pointless. All are pointless because Dasein's existence is totally insular. It is ringed with an individuality so egocentrically bound that it fails to resonate in the very world that constitutes Dasein's Being-in-the-world, a world in which being *"authentically* bound together" is a possibility, in which authentically helping another is a possibility. Though Heidegger specifically detaches what we might call "Dasein-analysis" from any practical or theoretical effect or result (236), it is nonetheless evident that if nothing is gained from Daseinanalysis except the bringing of Being into language, that is, the rendering of Being in words so that "language is the language of Being, as clouds are the clouds of the sky" (242), then authentic existence drifts off into *the said*, into a world apart from a living world of Others, and indeed, into a private language of Being.

The morality that suffuses Daseinanalysis, on the contrary, says something of profound importance to humans in its insistence on "thinking existence," in its emphasis on "Being-toward-death," in its recognition of the everyday "theyness" of everyday life. At the same time, however, Daseinanalysis leaves much of profound importance unsaid with respect to its ingrained morality. Heidegger nowhere spells out the nature of being *"authentically* bound together," for example: he gives no substantive descriptive account of "authentic care" in the form of solicitude as he gives substantive descriptive accounts of "inauthentic care"; he gives no intimation of just how authentic Dasein "helps the Other to become transparent to himself *in* his care," that is, how Dasein liberates the Other; and so on. In short, the real-life nature of *authentic* tetherings of solicitude needs detailed descriptive specification. If help is given to another in such a way as to release the Other to the most profound depths of Being, a moral relationship is defined. Indeed, an *interconnectedness* of Being obtains. When Daseins "devote themselves to the same affair in common" and "become *authentically* bound" in such a way that each "frees the Other in his freedom for himself" (Heidegger 1962, 159), then in the deepest of ontological senses, difference is "removed." What is left unsaid is both how this common binding and mutual liberation come to pass. Surely analogical apperception and pairing ground the possibility of both the binding and the liberation; that is, surely sense-makings are foundational to the care-structure of Dasein, not as stand-ins for, or catch-all alternatives to, Heidegger's ontological fore-structures of understanding—fore-having, fore-sight, and fore-conception (188–95)—but as real-life epistemological phenomena in which transfers of sense, intercorporeal meanings, affect attunement, and empathy semantically build on one another and become experientially significant aspects of human morality.

Heidegger in fact leaves sense-making behind, just as he leaves the ontology of change from "inauthentic" to "authentic" Being-with Others behind. These observations are less a critique of Heidegger than a statement of fact critical to understandings of the morality that is both said and unsaid within his ontology of care. Sense-making, while admittedly not part of that ontology, is necessarily a part of it in a real-life sense. Real-life sense-makings in fact *ground* ontology generally, and this because, before something has stature as existing, it must stand out as something meaningful, something distinct, something of interest, something noticed, indeed, something of which one is aware in the first place as *being alive*, or as being *an aspect of being alive*, or as *being present* in the world, or as *being a happening or an aspect of a happening* in the world. For example, our "thrownness," as Heidegger designates it, is an aspect of our being—of Dasein—but our awareness of that aspect of our being is conditional on our sense-makings of ourselves, of others, and of the world about us. All the more so since our 'thrownness' is not of our accord; we do not choose to be born—any more than we choose to die; we are indeed thrust into the world. In short, our understanding of our facticity comes not from fore-knowledge of any kind but from our sense-makings. Moreover, and most significant, sense-makings are the *sine qua non* of the concept of death. Although Heidegger disdains concepts in favor of language as the source of the truth of Being (Heidegger

1977a, 235), he cannot accord to language a conceptual awareness that has no basis in experience without invoking some kind of "natural light," an inborn knowledge, in this instance of death.[24] His sophisticated and adultist rendition of death in fact takes for granted the epistemological origin of *thanatos*. The concept of death does not—and did not originally—descend from the blue. The concept was forged on the basis of the experience of other once-living beings. The knowledge of a "punctuated existence," of an "I too," comes not from Being, but from real-life worldly experiences (Sheets-Johnstone 1990). The concepts of solicitude and concern, of Being-with and Being-alongside, of authentic and inauthentic Being, of conscience, of helping, of freeing, and so on, are indeed, like the concept of death, sophisticated, adult concepts that no child in any culture is born with. All are concepts that develop over time in the course of sense-makings. True, there is a human aptitude or disposition toward such concepts. True, other forms of life have either no such particular concepts or less highly elaborated ones. But it is the pan-animate capacity for sense-making that is the foundational aptitude and disposition, and it is on the basis of this pan-animate epistemological capacity that an ontology is even possible.

In sum, experiences of interconnectedness are rooted in epistemological foundations that undergird both one's own being and a world of others from the beginning. As we have seen, virtually nothing of these beginning and developmentally enduring sense-makings threads its way into Dasein's insulated ontological universe. Indeed, Dasein is untethered to the epistemological foundations that ground its existential interpretation as care. It is perhaps not surprising, then, that Dasein's insulated ontological universe, its Being-in-the-world, has a predominantly cultural aura about it, precisely as with its useful things that are "ready-to-hand," its existent things that are "present-at-hand" (Heidegger 1962, e.g., 67, 98), and its world of "encountered" Others who are there too, *"environmentally"* (155). Moreover, in this insulated ontological universe, the "bodily nature" of Dasein is minimally recognized; it is described solely in terms of direction and deseverance (which may be loosely glossed as "closing a distance"), Heidegger adding in parenthesis at the end of his account of these two "bodily" aspects, "This 'bodily nature' hides a whole problematic of its own, though we shall not treat it here" (143). Clearly, Heidegger's world is unrelated to the global world of Nature, the cosmos, or to the natural world to which "man" belongs.[25] It is tethered to the immediate world of "things"—tools, furniture, rooms, and so on—and to the immediate world of Others who are *"like"* Dasein, who *"are there too"* (154), who have the "same kind of Being as Dasein" (162), and who constitute an existential dimension of Dasein's Being: Being-with.[26] Thus, in Heidegger's world, there are Others—other Daseins and even earth, trees, and so on—but difference is not "removed," not even in virtue of the "sameness of Being" that ontologically defines all Daseins (154). What is "removed," but in a wholly other sense, is individual Dasein itself. If not a Special Creation, Dasein is a Special Being, one who holds sway by dint of language and is set apart from *physis*, a Being whose special "mission" is to think, and in thinking to become authentic. If Dasein arrives at being *"authentically* bound" with an Other (Dasein), it is through language, not through any natural proclivities or intercorporeal sensibilities and insights. In effect, being *"authentically* bound together" heralds not an experience of interconnectedness but a paean to Dasein who can bear witness to the Other in language. The same holds true for Nature more generally. If the earth is the earth only in virtue of a work of art—for example, a building such as a Greek temple *"lets the earth be earth"* (Heidegger 1977b, 171)—and if plants and animals "have no world" but "only belong to the covert throng of a surrounding [world] into which they are linked" (170), then, by the same token, there is no experience of an interconnectedness with animals, earth, trees, mountains, and so on, but a paean to Dasein who can bear witness to them in language. In short, clouds and earth may make an appearance, but only as summoned by language. Nature is nowhere in sight. There are no Darwinian worms.

## VI. THE LIVING IMPORT OF THE METAPHYSICALLY SIGNIFICANT: INTERCONNECTEDNESS, THE PRINCIPLE OF NOT HARMING, AND "DIFFERENCE REMOVED"

Evolutionary altruism and Heideggerian care are at diametrically opposite theoretical extremes, neither of which approximates to the living import of the interconnectedness of Nature so evident in the cited writings of Darwin, Donne, and Lawrence, or to the sense-making grounding that import. Neither can in consequence provide the basis for a genuine evolutionary ethics, which clearly requires a genuine historical and not either merely reproductive or personal foundation. But it is notably significant as well that even altruism pure and simple—what might be termed "genetically unmodified altruism"—cannot ground a genuine evolutionary ethics, and this because before one can concern oneself with the welfare of another, that is, before one can *help* another, one must first have a sense of the other, and a sense of the other as needing help or as possibly prospering from help. In particular, one must not only have made sense of the other as an animate being, but one must understand suffering from first-person experience and in turn understand that others can suffer in the same way as oneself or in like ways. Crying is a clue to just such understandings among humans. Crying is a wholly natural human expression of suffering from the beginning of human life. Over time, infants and young children make sense of the crying of others on the basis of their own first-person experiences of suffering: the sounds and tears alert them to the suffering of others. Such sense-making goes beyond entrainment, i.e., beyond the "empathic distress" cries observed and studied in newborns (see, for example, Sagi and Hoffman 1976). Indeed, in the most fundamental sense, crying is a symptom of one's own vulnerability of being a body and the harm one can suffer, and correlatively, a sign of the bodily vulnerability of others and the harm they can equally suffer. One's motivation to help others and one's actual acts of altruism build on just such foundational symptomatic and signal bodily experiences. In other words, whatever the act of genetically unmodified altruism, it is grounded in a living sense of vulnerability and suffering: an awareness that, like oneself, others are open to bodily harm.

Further perspectives on a genuine evolutionary ethics warrant attention in this context. To begin with, it is precisely with respect to evolution that the question of why humans kill each other is both a pressing question and one that cannot be ignored—any more than the killings can be marginally treated simply as "the dark side" of human nature (Sober and Wilson 2000a, 264). The wholesale slaughter and mutilation of humans by humans is a blight on the species *Homo sapiens sapiens*. If evolutionary altruism or Heideggerian care could genuinely ground an evolutionary ethics, it would be able to explain how and why it is that, century after century, across all civilizations, nations, and tribes, under the aegis of religion, nationalism, territorialism, racism, ethnicism, and so on, humans continually and in vast numbers kill and maim one another. It is worth noting that Hobbes addressed the pressing question and in doing so came close to articulating truths of human nature seminal to a genuine evolutionary ethics. When he observed that competition, glory, and fearfulness (i.e., "diffidence"; see Malnes 1993, 26–27) are the fundamental causes of social conflict, that apart from societal laws, i.e., in the state of nature, there is no justice or injustice, "no *mine* and *thine* distinct; but only that to be every man's, that he can get; and for so long, as he can keep it" (Hobbes 1930, 256), he implicitly recognized that each man is not just out for himself but out to harm others (252–53). Indeed, as noted earlier, he stated, "All men in the state of nature have a desire and will to hurt" (262). It is equally worth noting, particularly in light of Hobbes's observations on the nature of human nature, that Schopenhauer gives priority to "not harming"—"do not harm; but rather help"—specifying it the first moral principle and thereby suggesting that not harming is prior to helping. Of course, he could well have written the reverse—"help rather than harm"—but here too the directive to hold oneself back from doing others ill appears a necessary antecedent, a non-action on which the helping of others depends. Through ignorance, that is, through a deficiency in sense-making, one could in fact inadvertently harm in attempting to help "as far as lies in your power." Moreover, when put in the context of an inherent bodily vulnerability, the first principle is of a conceptual piece with the "extraordinary phaenomenon" of "difference removed." When an "individual directly recognizes in *another* his own self, his true and very being" (Schopenhauer 1915, 274), he "directly recognizes" the other's vulnerabilities of being a body, his openness to harm at the hands of others.

As we have seen, fear of harm by others follows from the basic truths of vulnerability and the power if not the disposition of humans to kill and maim. The broader truth of the amity/enmity complex follows in turn. Fear of strangers is a fear of those who are different and whose behaviors are therefore unpredictable. Moreover as we have seen, their differences can put cherished beliefs and values at risk such that not only one's life but the very meaning of one's life is at stake. The double risks readily pit "Us" against "Them," and the larger truths of fear just as readily hover over "Us": the fear of death along with what serves to assuage that fear, namely, an immortality ideology in the form of religion, nationalism, power, glory, or whatever beliefs, identifications, and/or acquisitions take the sting of nothingness away. Clearly, openness to harm at the hands of others has formidable aspects and consequences.

Not harming thus warrants recognition beyond Schopenhauer's identification of it as the first ethical principle. It warrants recognition as the first moral principle within a genuine evolutionary ethics.[27] The principle is not a law or rule ordained from on high to be dutifully obeyed, but a spontaneous self-generated stance or attitude toward other humans and the whole of the natural world. This stance or attitude carries with it not a tinge of "ought," any more than it carries with it the weight of a decision, even a rational decision. Its motivation springs from sense-makings and caring, from the realization of an interconnectedness of being, indeed, of manifold interconnectednesses of being stretching across evolutionary time and embracing untold millions of beings. A genuinely *evolutionary* ethics requires precisely such a realization: a recognition of both the awesome diversity of Nature and the awesome enormity of Nature, not only the extant 10 million species but the four billion years that life has existed on earth and the evolutionary changes and products that have emerged since it first arose. Accordingly, a genuine *evolutionary* ethics requires a recognition of the interconnectedness of all animate life, of all animate life to its surrounding world, of its surrounding world to the global world, and the global world to the evolution of the cosmic planet itself. In short, a genuine evolutionary ethics requires a recognition of Nature in both her virtually timeless character and her virtually limitless diversity. Set in this natural perspective, "difference removed" is indeed an awesome difference, and makes an awesome difference. In the experience of this "extraordinary phaenomenon," animate beings and the natural world are comprehended as existentially bound together, and bound together over eons of time. The wondrous, intimate, and fragile character of the natural world and all manner of its living relationships become apparent, not in a simple recognitional sense, but in a reflectively reverberating sense that generates the attitudinal affect of caring. The non-act of not harming follows in turn. Motivated by sense-makings and caring, the primary non-act of not harming is the touchstone of moral acts, of a morality generated in and by a genuine evolutionary ethics.

A fundamental clarification is nonetheless essential with respect to an understanding of "difference removed." The latter is not synonymous with incorporation, consolidation, melding, absorption, and the like; it is altogether distinct from the idea of a mergence of oneself with another. In the most elemental sense, to recognize one's own self in another is to apperceive the other along the lines of one's own body, that is, as an animate form. Indeed, it is precisely through analogical apperception that one recognizes the vulnerability of another human. To speak of "difference removed," however, goes a step further, a step that might be misread as indicating that "two become one." The "mystery" of "difference removed" is not a matter of the latter and in fact not a mystery at all. Understood in terms of interconnectedness, the experience of "difference removed" hinges on the experience of existential ties to something existentially distinct in its own right, something that stands apart, separate from one even as a radically different living form or non-living form altogether, or remote from one even across eons of time. In other words, whatever the "difference"—morphological, kinetic, spatial, temporal, and so on—insight into the ties that bind one in a common humanity, a common creaturehood, and to a common world of Nature, give rise to the experience of interconnectedness. In effect, existential ties close the distance between oneself and something other. But they do not close the distance entirely. If they did, the other—whatever its nature—would disappear as the being it is; or one would oneself disappear as the being one is. A distance remains that is equally an existential distance, that is, a distance in which oneself and something other in the natural world—a cloud bank, a fellow human, a herd of elephants, a volcano, a worm—retain their individuality even as they are existentially bound together. As indicated, the experience of *interconnectedness* could otherwise not be. The ties that bind together in fact heighten the wondrous, intimate, and fragile individuality of each individual or phenomenon even as they heighten the wondrous, intimate, and fragile character of the interconnected relationship itself.

The clarification of "difference removed" as a closing but not effacement of distance is in certain respects akin to the attitude of "psychical" or "aesthetic" distance in art, an attitude elaborated in a classic study in aesthetics by philosopher Edward Bullough. "Psychical distance" is instructive not by way of aestheticizing a moral phenomenon, but by way of throwing further explanatory light on existential distance. Bullough describes how psychical or aesthetic distance "lies between our own self and such objects as are the sources or vehicles of [our] affections," the latter term "in its broadest sense [meaning] anything which affects our being, bodily or spiritually" (Bullough 1959, 647). Being a matter of both the individual and the object, psychical distance describes both the spectator's attitude toward the finished art object and the attitude of the artist in her/his creation of the art object. When the spectator personalizes the artwork, thus *under*-distancing it, he/she fails to "appreciate and enter into [it]" (651); when the artist personalizes the work in the process of creating it, similarly *under*-distancing it, he/she fails to "formulate it artistically" (651). Such personal involvements obtrude upon or obviate altogether the possibility of an aesthetic experience or of an aesthetic object being created in the first place. Yet a personal relationship is crucial to both aesthetic experience and the creation of an art object. Bullough formulates the paradox in terms of "the antinomy of distance" (650), which he later specifies as "the *utmost decrease of Distance without its disappearance*" (651; italics in original).[28] Though he does not speak in terms of intrinsic value, it is evident that with "the utmost decrease of Distance without its disappearance," the work as created by the artist attains intrinsic value; it stands wholly on its own. Correlatively, its intrinsic value is the bedrock of its aesthetic appreciation; it is the intrinsic value of the work that gives rise to aesthetic experience.

A similar kind of "antinomy of distance" holds with respect to the experience of interconnectedness: the personal is present, but in a distinctively muted way. It is not overrun by practical, material, economic, theoretical, or experimental concerns, for example. Such concerns would close out the possibility of interconnectedness. They would not allow the intrinsic value of the other—whatever kind of natural object the other might be—to come forward and remain foregrounded. On the other hand, the personal undergirds and even structures the experience of interconnectedness. It undergirds the experience precisely in its capacity for sense-making and its capacity to open outward and toward the natural world rather than remain anchored in individual interests with respect to that world. In so doing it establishes a metaphysical bond, a bond clearly outside practical, material, economic, theoretical, experimental, or other such interests. The bond rests on rational readings of the rationality of the universe, on experiences of the ties that bind the whole of Nature in all its stunning diversity and sweep across time. It thus rests on deep personal understandings of Nature and on empirical matters of fact. But with "the utmost decrease of distance without its disappearance," these understandings and empirical matters of fact give rise to a preeminently existential meaning in which the living import of the bond—of interconnectedness—is brought to light. Its metaphysical character is palpable in the epigraph from Lawrence's writings cited at the beginning of this chapter. Indeed, Lawrence articulates the bond from a cosmic perspective, that is, from the perspective of humans in a full-bodied, wholly animated, and dynamic relationship with Nature. Moreover Lawrence articulates the bond as a call in a near Heideggerian sense, a call to awaken to being alive and to a celebration of what is. When Lawrence writes, "We ought to dance with rapture that we should be alive and in the flesh, and part of the living, incarnate cosmos," he is summoning us to an awakening of both our own being and of our connection to the whole of the natural world: our connection to what is. In fact, in Lawrence's prose, we see clearly that there is not a mergence of two into one, but on the contrary, an existential distance that allows us to awaken both to the wonders of being alive and to our interconnectedness to the whole of Nature.

### VII. A CLOSER LOOK AT THE FIRST MORAL PRINCIPLE AND THE CHALLENGE OF HUMAN EXISTENCE

A strikingly apposite formulation and example of the principle of not harming comes from American history, specifically from the pen of John Adams and the orders of George Washington. In his book *Washington's Crossing*, which covers a pivotal nine days during the Revolutionary War, historian David Fischer devotes a section to "Policy of Humanity." In that section, he quotes from a letter Adams wrote to his wife Abigail concerning a "policy of humanity" and from General Washington's orders concerning the treatment of prisoners. Several passages of the section merit quotation. To begin with, Fischer writes,

> In 1776, American leaders believed that it was not enough to win the war. They also had to win in a way that was consistent with the values of their society and the principles of their cause. One of their greatest achievements in the winter campaign of 1776–77 was to manage the war in a manner that was true to the expanding humanitarian ideals of the American Revolution. It happened in a way that was different from the ordinary course of wars in general. In Congress and the army, American leaders resolved that the War of Independence would be conducted with a respect for human rights, even of the enemy. This idea grew stronger during the campaign of 1776–77, not weaker as is commonly the case in war. In Congress, John Adams took the lead. . . . [He] resolved that the guiding principles of the

American Republic would always be what he called the policy of humanity. (Fischer 2004, 375–76)

The policy was extended to Hessian prisoners, who, given the cruel abuse and starvation of American prisoners at the hands of the British, expected quite different treatment from the Americans. Moreover after the battle of Princeton, the policy was extended to British prisoners as well. Washington wrote expressly of these prisoners to Lieutenant Colonel Samuel Blachley Webb: "'Treat them with humanity, and Let them have no reason to Complain of our Copying the brutal example of the British army in their Treatment of our unfortunate brethren. . . . Provide everything necessary for them on the road'" (379).

Adams's "policy of humanity" is fundamentally a policy of not harming. War is obviously a breach of the policy, but respect must nevertheless prevail for those against whom one fights.[29] The policy thus recalls Huizinga's concept of an agon discussed in Chapter 3. A true battle is one in which adversaries are equals; the humanness of the other—"the enemy"—is neither diminished nor transmogrified. Whatever the differences in the name of which a battle is fought—territorial claims, beliefs, resources, or whatever—they are honored as variations on an all-embracing human theme. Accordingly, from the perspective of a policy of humanity, the challenge of human existence is not simply to be human but to be part of an all-embracing humanity. To rise to the occasion of the latter, however, is clearly not simply to cooperate rather than compete. The challenge is rather to refrain from action in the form of not harming, and to refrain not by dint of rules and laws but in virtue of a sense of humanity, a particular sense of interconnectedness that gives rise to the attitudinal affect of caring. When Fischer writes that Hessian captives "were amazed to be treated with decency and even kindness" (378), he attests to actions motivated by just such an attitudinal affect. Caring is thus distinct from cooperating, but the distinction warrants further clarification precisely because cooperation is often given as an answer to the challenge of human existence, perhaps most notably by Konrad Lorenz in his emphasis on various outlets for "team spirit" and on a "feeling of togetherness," which "is greatly enhanced by the presence of a definite, threatening enemy whom it is possible to hate" (Lorenz 1966, 272, 276; see also E. O. Wilson's hedged remarks in Wilson 1998, 252–53). A brief review of caring will be helpful in preface.

As described in the previous section, awakening aptly captures the vibrant living nature of caring. The temporal dimension of that distinctive existential attitude toward and experience of other living beings and the world is not being-toward-death but being-toward-life, toward the ongoing being of living forms, the earth, the cosmos. When ideologies, acquisitiveness, and identifications gain sufficient motivational power to turn into shibboleths for destruction, they turn humans away from caring and any sense of interconnectedness. Indeed, they override if not destroy the very possibility of the sense-makings that underlie the experience: greed takes over, war takes over, raping takes over, ravaging the land takes over, killing, starving, and mutilating other beings takes over. It is hardly surprising that in such circumstances being-toward-life dissolves, interconnectedness dissolves, caring dissolves. All such possible existential dimensions of being are swept away in acts of violence and by a living fear of one's own death. Becker's observation cited earlier and in Chapter 1, "if we don't have the power of gods, we can at least destroy like gods" (Becker 1973, 85), eloquently epitomizes the barbaric mentality of the moral dissolution. Whatever its driving force—nationalism, religion, ethnicity, territoriality—Nature is left behind. Whatever the ensuing internecine onslaught, individual humans become war machines in pursuit of meaning, glory, salvation, eternal life, or whatever defines and maintains the ideology, the identity, or the resources in support of which they fight to the death in endless destruction—Athenians against Spartans, Hutus against Tutsis, Christendom against Muslims, Muslims against Hindus, Nazis against Jews, Rome against Carthage, Mongols against China, Israelis against Palestinians, Palestinians against Israelis, Serbs against Bosnians, and so on, and so on, in century after century of cruelties and killings. In brief, humans are estranged from the oneness of all being by the oneness of a self whose life, like that of Hobbes's man in a state of nature, is "solitary, poor, nasty, brutish, and short."

The rationality of caring transcends Hobbes's solitary state of nature; sense-makings give rise to insights leading to caring. The precept to refrain from harming, that is, to honor the intricate connections that bind all in a common Nature, is an active expression of both the insights and the attitudinal affect of caring, *a valuing of things for their own sake*. Not harming is thus a deterrent quite unlike that commonly pictured under the aegis of cooperation, the latter being frequently put forward as the solution to the human practice of harming and killing. Cooperation promotes *helping*, a bonding together for the common good, as in harvesting a crop; it does not promote *not harming*, or if it does, it does so only as a by-product. As we have seen, it in fact promotes harming and killing in war by cementing male bonding. It is indeed a central facet of the amity that sustains the amity/enmity complex. Moreover while cooperation certainly has rational components, they are not grounded in the specific kinds of sense-makings of analogical apperception and comsigns highlighted in this chapter—and certainly not in the sense-makings of Nature described here.

Cooperation in fact has its own distinctive rational ties, diverse ones that may be, and often are, readily reduced to a selfish motif. Philosopher John Troyer, for example, in offering a possible answer to the seeming antithesis between biology and morality—"evolutionary theory shows people are inherently selfish" while "morality often requires sacrifice"—writes that "good behaviour often makes good selfish sense. Cooperation often pays, favours are often returned, non-violent methods of resolving conflict often work to everyone's advantage, etc." (Troyer 2000, 65). (See also, for example, Keeton and Gould 1986, 599: "The realization that much of what we recognize as altruistic behavior is ultimately selfish underscores the point that innate behavior . . . enhances the fitness of the genes coding for it"—though oddly enough, these same biologists in the same book earlier affirm that "it is extremely unlikely that any behavior can be classified as strictly innate or strictly learned" [554]). Whether the allegation is true that cooperation is basically selfish—and it is highly unlikely that it is since cooperation can bring about something greater than the sum of its parts, e.g., on a small scale, the delight of children playing together; on a global scale, the camaraderie of working together as in Carter's Habitats for Humanity program—or whether the allegation is merely an argumentative ploy against the purported purity of cooperation, there is no doubt but that cooperation is consistently taken as antithetical to competition, and in turn construed a palliative to aggression and violence. The cliché conception, however, is far from viable, especially as offering a foundation for morality. We can readily see its shortcomings in psychologist Dennis Krebs's thesis, for example. To begin with, Krebs writes, "I believe the benefits of cooperation contain the key that will unlock the door to an explanation of the evolution of morality" (Krebs 2000, 142). He later states, "We are evolved to behave morally, that is to say to cooperate, when it is in our genetic interests, but we also are evolved to behave immorally when it is not." He concludes, "We are moral, but only as moral as we need to be" (143). What Krebs overlooks in this rather glib and simplistic reductionist notion of morality is the fact that to cooperate is not only not equivalent to not harming but, as indicated above, does not preclude harming. Indeed, Krebs overlooks the inherent vulnerability of humans, their fear of death, the history of human warfare that knows neither cultural nor temporal bounds, the human quest for *more*, whether in pursuit of territory, power, glory, or whatever, and so on. His focused reliance on cooperation is misplaced, deflecting attention from, if not precluding, a recognition of the central moral significance of not harming. In a word, cooperation falls short of addressing the fundamental problem of human morality: the infliction of untold sufferings upon other humans and the outright killing of them. Indeed, just as a focus on aggression prevents a recognition and keen understanding of the primary moral significance of male-male competition, so a focus on cooperation prevents a recognition and keen understanding of the primary moral significance of not harming. In each instance the non-recognition—and even conflation of terms—prevents a genuine evolutionary ethics from coming into view. To put the point in the broadest of perspectives, a genuine evolutionary ethics requires recognition of a fundamental evolutionary truth: humans constitute an infinitesimally puny part of the whole of Nature but are powerful beyond measure. The capacity of humans for rational thought—for sense-making—carries with it the possibility not only of an awareness of the fundamental evolutionary truth, but of its primary implication: in its recognition of the inherent value of all forms of being, the act of not harming preserves the intricate integrity of the whole.

The central import of *not harming* to a genuine evolutionary ethics is dramatically exemplified in Sartre's last published thoughts on fraternity. Surprising as it may seem in light of his earlier strongly individual ontological concerns, a conception of humanity comes to the fore that is anchored in a striking evolutionary realization of the interconnectedness of humans. Indeed, there is less a *"policy* of humanity" than a natural way of being toward fellow humans motivated by what is essentially evolutionary sense-making. Sartre's notion of fraternity is, in other words, not a political principle but a "primary relationship": "If . . . I take society as being the result of a bond among people that's more basic than politics, then I take it that people should, can, or do entertain a certain primary relationship, which is that of fraternity" (Sartre and Levy 1996, 86). While his injection of "should" clearly makes the primary relationship a moral obligation, "can" suggests rather that the relationship is a human capacity, and "do" suggests that it is a spontaneous practice. The capacity and practice in fact coincide more exactly with the society Sartre envisions: his idea of a bond "more basic than politics" is a bond that conjoins humans in "a single family" (87):

> For every person, birth is the same phenomenon as it is for his neighbor to such a degree that, in a certain way, two men talking to each other have the same mother. Not the same mother, empirically, of course, but a mother without eyes, without a face. It's a certain idea, but the two of us share it, as we all do, for that matter. To belong to the same species is, in a way, to have the same parents. In that sense, we are brothers. Besides, this is how people define the human species—not so much in terms of certain biological characteristics as a certain relationship that obtains among us, the relationship of fraternity. It's the relationship of being born of the same mother. (87)

A page later, Sartre states succinctly and unequivocally: "Fraternity is the relationship members of the species have with one another" (88).

The foundational human bond that Sartre envisions, however, has yet to be achieved. That "there is an ethics," as Sartre affirms, testifies to a future time when humans will realize "that they are all bound to each other in feeling and in action" (91). At that future time, humans will realize their common origin and end, i.e., experience their fraternity: "I think that the total, truly conceivable experience will exist when the goal that all men have within them—Humanity—is achieved. At that moment it will be possible to say that men are all the products of a common origin, derived not from their father's seed or their mother's womb but from a total series of measures taken over thousands of years that finally result in Humanity. Then there will be true fraternity" (90).

What intercedes and blocks true fraternity is scarcity, violence, "fraternity-terror" (80, 91), what Sartre characterizes generally as "the colonized against the colonizer" (93). Yet he looks hopefully toward the ultimate realization of fraternity: "We must try to explain why the world of today, which is horrible, is only one moment in a long historical development, that hope has always been one of the dominant forces of revolutions and insurrections" (110). When he formulates the realization of fraternity in terms of hope—"I know I shall die in hope . . . hope is my conception of the future" (110)—he epitomizes the perennial individual challenge of human existence: to apprehend the evolutionary relationship by which humans are bound together in a common nature and to a common natural world. The relationship is empirical through and through, as Darwin meticulously demonstrated, but its meaning extends to the metaphysical or meta-empirical, precisely as Sartre indicates when he says, "Not the same mother, empirically, of course," and as Donne and Lawrence indicate in their writings. To write "No man is an *Island* entire of it self" or "That I am part of the earth, my feet know perfectly" is not just a poetic flourish but a metaphysical truth. The relationship in each instance goes beyond mere physical dependency of one individual being on another individual being to an interconnectedness of the whole, an interconnectedness greater than the sum of its individual parts. Sartre's humanity as an expression of fraternity is similarly a metaphysical truth. We are all descended from the same source; we are all related, morphologically, kinetically, affectively, cognitively, existentially, evolutionarily. We may not speak the same language but we are humanly of a piece. Caring enunciates that humanity.

## NOTES

1. The concept of a philosophical zoology has its origin in Jean Baptiste Lamarck's *Zoological Philosophy* (*Philosophie zoologique*). See Lamarck 1960 and 1963. For a discussion of Lamarque's writings in relation to Darwin, see Sheets-Johnstone 1982. (Note: the title of the latter article was changed without the author's permission. The author's title was: "Why Lamarck Could Be 'Observed in the Act of Not Discovering the Principle of Natural Selection,'" the quoted material being taken from an article by noted biology historian J. S. Wilkie in reference to his discussion of eighteenth century biologist Georges Buffon, i.e., Buffon could be "observed in the act of not discovering the principle of natural selection" [Wilkie 1959, p. 278]. The quotation was intended as a springboard for the author's critical examination of the common view that Lamarck, like Buffon, could be similarly caught in the act.)

2. An indirectly present, verbally described body of another, a body that, it should be noted, might actually be thousands of miles away or a fictional body altogether, might also be apperceived, but on the basis of an imaginative rather than sensuously present presence.

3. For more on the body as a semantic template, see Sheets-Johnstone 1990.

4. For both an empirical and phenomenological account of intuition, see Sheets-Johnstone 1999b, chap. 4, on Husserl and von Helmholtz; see also Sheets-Johnstone 1990, 19.

5. Bower, corroborating observations of Piaget concerning "inside," writes: "Piaget's son was surely typical in finding the relation 'inside' fascinating. . . . One of my own daughters spent the best part of one night placing small objects in my hand, closing my hand on them, moving my hand to a new location, and then opening it up to see if the object were still there. This kept her happy and busy till nearly 4 a.m." (Bower 1979, 238).

6. Precisely because the tactile-kinesthetic body is the foundation of such experience—any noted change in the visual body is parasitic on the latter—the transfer may also be rightly described as a new "I can" in the infant's repertoire. In other words, the power to move brings a dynamic visual world to life and not the reverse.

7. Because the experience of ownness elaborated in the transfer is not other-dependent, parasitism claims about the constitution of others, as in Sallis's account (Sallis 1971), are mistaken.

8. At a feeling level, this intercorporeal sense-making is reflected in the fact that, as psychoanalysts Anni Bergman and Arnold Wilson point out, "One must know how it feels to be hurt before one can realize that one is capable of hurting another person." They go on to say, "This is a selective identification, in which the child does not become the other, but imagines the pain of the other by imagining the other's experience" (Bergman and Wilson 1984, 72).

9. The curiosity of young children about the bodies of others testifies to this transfer of sense: what is "like me and unlike me," whether culturally exaggerated or not, is a basic concern of growing children.

10. It is of special interest to note that the same act may be common to different species, but its communicative value may not be the same. Yawning, for example, is common to baboons and humans, but the communicative meaning of the act is species-specific: what is threat to the former is boredom or fatigue to the latter.

11. However, Schaller notes too that occultation is not employed stereotypically even though when it is not so employed, stalking frequently fails. Since Schaller writes that lionesses know the value that cover confers, but that occultation is not employed stereotypically, one might judge that a lioness who does not employ occultation in stalking is simply not very smart. But several factors may explain the seeming "perversity." First of all, everyone makes mistakes, humans included—e.g., killing a hunting mate by accident, cutting oneself with a knife, burning oneself, "forgetting" to duck, and so on. Second, lionesses behave differently when they know that some of the animals they are hunting are alert to their presence. Third, an observer of a hunt—or a reader reading about a hunt—is in a far different position from the actual individuals engaged in the hunt. If all hunters, human ones included, were privy to the outside eye and vantage point of an uninvolved observer, they too might behave differently and thereby improve their strategy. Fourth, more firsthand information might be gathered to corroborate the initial evidence.

12. Though Darwin does not speak specifically of humankind in this context, his observations on the interconnectedness of life are in fact implicitly relevant to war and strife among humans. "The dependency of one organic being on another, as of a parasite on its prey, lies generally between beings remote in the scale of nature. . . . But the struggle almost invariably will be most severe between the individuals of the same species, for they frequent the same districts, require the same food, and are exposed to the same dangers" (Darwin 1859, 126). Indeed, a paragraph later, he observes, "As species of the same genus have usually, though by no means invariably, some similarity in habits and constitution, and always in structure, the struggle will generally be more severe between species of the same genus, when they come into competition with each other, than between species of distinct genera" (127).

13. Psychiatrist René Spitz, for example, labels its smile a "response" (Spitz 1983).

14. Science writer David Quammen's observation in his *National Geographic* article on evolution is topical to the point. In the process of specifying different morphological ways in which evolution is confirmed, he writes, "Vestigial characteristics are still another form of morphological evidence, illuminating to contemplate because they show that the living world is full of small, tolerable imperfections" (Quammen 2004, 20).

15. It is pertinent in this context to note that recent publications by biologists have

begun to call sociobiological thought into question. In his book, *Why Men Won't Ask for Directions: The Seductions of Sociobiology*, biologist Richard Francis, for example, calls both the adaptationism and the atomistic reductionism of sociobiology into question (Francis 2004). Biologist H. Allen Orr, in the course of his review of several new books in biology, warns that "[s]ociobiological claims of an almost unbelievably unnuanced sort run throughout *Adam's Curse* [a book by Brian Sykes, a professor of genetics at Oxford]" (Orr 2005, 20).

16. Indeed, however "mindlessly" genes "advance their own interests" (Nesse 2000, 228) by creating and designing "their kind of organism," they cannot get off the moral hook. Genetic competition is the bottom line (230), and the driving task of scientists is to understand how, through genetic competition, genes create brains that induce behavior that increases their representation in future generations. If this reductionist scenario is true, then the fact that moral issues are experienced at the level of individual beings is beside the point. *Life* does not enter into the picture at all; it plays no part. People are totally manipulated by their genes, and nurture counts for nought. Most important too, education counts for nought—unless the truth be that some people's genes seduce them into thinking that it does.

17. The ready analogue of music to describe the flow of Nature is intriguing. Husserl's seminal use of the term "harmonious" to describe the process of pairing in the constitution of intersubjectivity is a further topical example. But far earlier uses testify to the immediate cogency of music. In the fourth volume of *Handful of Leaves*, Buddhist monk Thanissaro Bhikkhu (2003, 205–6) comments at some length on a line in the Sutta Nipata that describes a wandering solitary sage as "[p]ondering what is on-pitch and off." He writes:

> On-pitch and off (*sama* and *visama*): Throughout ancient cultures, the terminology of music was used to describe the moral quality of people and acts. Discordant intervals or poorly-tuned musical instruments were metaphors for evil; harmonious intervals and well-tuned instruments were metaphors for good. In Pali, the term sama—"even"—described an instrument tuned on-pitch: In a famous passage (AN VI:55) [i.e., Anguttara Nikaya, anthologized in volume 3 of *Handful of Leaves*], the Buddha reminds Sona Kolivisa—who had been over-exerting himself in the practice—that a lute sounds appealing only if the strings are neither too taut nor too lax, but "evenly" tuned. This image would have special resonances with the Buddha's teaching on the middle way. It also adds meaning to the term *samana*—monk or contemplative—which the texts frequently mention as being derived from *sama*. The word *samañña*—"evenness," the quality of being in tune—also means the quality of being a contemplative. The true contemplative is always in tune with what is proper and good.

18. Hutton's notion of change and the interconnectedness of Nature—in particular, the relationship of the dissolution of rocks and solid strata to plant life and to food for animals—is in fact remarkable, its intimate ties to explaining the wisdom of a "divine Creator" notwithstanding. See Hutton [1795] 1960, 2:219–37.

19. However much Heidegger attempts to bring past and present within the temporal compass of care—not as a progression of moments, but as ontological dimensions of Dasein (Heidegger 1962, 373–76)—care remains essentially directed toward the not-yet.

20. The issue is present from the very start of *Being and Time*: "Dasein is an entity . . . ontologically distinguished by the fact that, in its very Being, that Being is an *issue* for it" (Heidegger 1962, 32). See also 236 for a specification of the term.

21. The "house of Being . . . enjoins the essence of man to dwell in the truth of Being" (Heidegger 1977a, 236).

22. Being-guilty is "the existential condition for the possibility of the 'morally' good and for that of the 'morally' evil—that is, for morality in general and for the possible forms which this may take factically" (Heidegger 1962, 332). Heidegger adds that morality "already presupposes" being-guilty.

23. The moral tone is apparent too in the "musts" that appear in the course of Heidegger's exposition of Dasein. For example, he writes that the existential analytic of Dasein "must seek for one of the *most far-reaching* and *most primordial* possibilities of disclosure," that "[t]he way of disclosure in which Dasein brings itself before itself must be such that in it Dasein becomes accessible as *simplified*," and that "the structural totality of the Being we seek must then come to light in an elemental way" (Heidegger 1962, 226).

24. Heidegger cannot either escape from a conception of language as a *deus ex machina* phenomenon. In other words, the question of how language could ever have arisen, *how it ever came to be invented, shaped, elaborated, and so on, by the genus* Homo, never itself arises. Language is simply taken for granted as being "already there," fully and completely "already there."

25. As Marjorie Grene points out, Heidegger's "world" is not "the immense, indefinitely extended cosmos of astrophysics," but specifies "a common sphere of activity or interest"—as in speaking of a "'world of sports'"—or "the time and the society which affects and is affected by a personality"—as in speaking of the "world of Shakespeare"—or "the mental universe, the perspective through which one's physical, geographical, and historical environment becomes one's very own"—as in speaking of two people being "worlds apart" (Grene 1967, 459).

26. Because the relationship of Being-with "is one which, with Dasein's Being, already is" (Heidegger 1962, 162), that is, because others are ontologically "already there," others are never constituted in a Husserlian sense. Heidegger hedges his ontological assertion that others are already there, however, when he affirms, for example, "Of course it is indisputable that a lively mutual acquaintanceship on the basis of Being-with, often depends upon how far one's own Dasein has understood itself at the time" (162). He also states, oddly enough, that empathy becomes possible "only on the basis of Being-with," and that "it gets its motivation from the unsociability of the dominant modes of Being-with" (162).

27. It would be easy to invoke the eminently meritorious Buddhist principle of not harming. What I would like to show in what follows, however, is how the principle is latent in Western thought, and on that account, how it is indeed latent in pan-cultural human experience, i.e., in the experience of interconnectedness and in the sense-makings underlying the experience of interconnectedness. The experiential foundation is in fact intimately related to the eightfold path in Buddhist teachings: what is skillful or "right"—"right action," "right speech," "right effort," and so on—is always a skillfulness or "rightness" to be experientially validated by the meditator, not a rule from on high.

28. It might be added that what Bullough terms a "concordance" (Bullough 1959, 650) must obtain between an artwork and the intellectual and emotional acumen of the spectator. Both the spectator of the work and the artist in creating the work must in this sense be prepared for appreciation and production, respectively. But beyond this, the personal feelings of spectator and artist cannot intrude without destroying the aesthetic distance of the work and thereby obviating the possibility of the aesthetic qualities of the work from appearing or from being created in the first place.

29. Social psychologist Robert Folger's account of "the Churchill effect" aptly illustrates the point. Folger documents both the principle of respect in describing Churchill's notification of the Japanese ambassador in London on the day following the bombing of Pearl Harbor that Britain had declared war on Japan and the public's outrage at the

civility of his letter to the Japanese ambassador. After noting "the very proper British letter" that Churchill wrote, Folger then quotes its closing statement: "I have the honour to be, with high consideration, Sir, Your obedient servant, Winston S. Churchill." He subsequently cites Churchill's answer to the public's outrage—"When you have to kill a man, it costs nothing to be polite"—and then proceeds to describe "the Churchill effect": "The public's response, consistent with avoidance, distancing, and derogating the enemy's status of (future) victim, contrasts with Churchill's use of politeness and consideration even for one's enemy or those one would harm. We call interpersonal distancing by harmdoers the *Churchill effect* in reference to the effect of Churchill's letter on the public. . . . A Churchill effect involves denying the need for, or legitimacy of, any politeness or considerateness toward those one would harm or has harmed. We identify the Churchill effect as a special case of an avoidance orientation consistent with victim derogation" (Folger and Pugh 2003, 170).

# Epilogue

## Re-Naturing the De-Natured Species: An Interdisciplinary Perspective

It is so easy to be immature. If I have a book to serve as my understanding, a pastor to serve as my conscience, a physician to determine my diet for me, and so on, I need not exert myself at all. I need not think, if only I can pay: others will readily undertake the irksome work for me.
—IMMANUEL KANT, "An Answer to the Question: What Is Enlightenment?"

Wonder dislodges man from the prejudice of everyday, publicly pregiven, traditional and worn out familiarity. . . . [It] drives him from the already authorized and expressly explicated interpretation of the sense of the world and into the creative poverty of not yet knowing.
—EUGEN FINK, "The Problem of the Phenomenology of Edmund Husserl"

Man continues to create and re-create God as a place to put that which is good in himself, and which he might spoil if he kept it in himself along with all the hate and destructiveness which is also to be found there.
—D. W. WINNICOTT, *The Maturational Processes and the Facilitating Environment*

One does not become enlightened by imagining figures of light but by making the darkness conscious. The latter procedure, however, is disagreeable and therefore not popular.
—C. G. JUNG, *Alchemical Studies*

## I. INTRODUCTION

The aim of this Epilogue is to bring the essentially opposing themes of the previous chapters into unified perspective by a return to the question of what it is to be human and, in turn, by deepened reflections on the nature of human nature. The opposing themes—life/death, mortality/immortality, attunement/aggression, male/female, infant/adult, trust/mistrust, competition/play, human/nonhuman—are embedded in human history. They are emblematic of those elemental binary oppositions that extend across all human cultures. In a broad sense, they are variations on the common human theme of good and evil. In a finer sense, they are variations on basic oppositional human feelings—love and hate, serenity and fear, security and insecurity. However cognitively tethered any such feelings might be, it is the feelings that motivate specific movement dynamics. Cognitive dimensions of life are, in other words, permeated through and through with affects that motivate behaviors.

Mid-twentieth-century psychiatrist Carl Jung set forth a unified perspective on basic binary oppositions, speaking, for example, of the conjunction of spirit and instinct, fundamental oppositional energies of the psyche (Jung 1969, see especially 117), and of the syzygy of male and female elements (Jung 1968b, 11–22). Though elucidating oppositions primarily by way of symbols and archetypes, i.e., cognitively rather than affectively, Jung's writings consistently illuminate the unity of opposites that through and through defines human nature.[1] Centuries before Jung's penetrating psychoanalytic, Socrates's injunction to "know thyself" and the Buddha's call to "awaken" directed humans to attend to the truths of their nature. Whether in the form of questioning or of developing mindfulness, these earlier teachings riveted attention on the importance of noticing and acknowledging fundamental aspects of oneself, aspects commonly suppressed, overlooked, or otherwise neglected. Attending to the truths of human nature clearly means being "at the pains of a little thought," in this instance a literally appropriate descriptive borrowing from eighteenth-century philosopher George Berkeley (Berkeley 1709)[2] since discovered truths about oneself can indeed be painful. In particular, being at the pains of a little thought can enlighten one with respect not only to one's motivations, habits of thought, beliefs, and so on, but to both the vagaries of one's mind, which may be surprisingly and even appallingly erratic and vacuous to one who has heretofore conceived his or her mind to be an orderly abode, and the darker recesses of one's mind, which may be profoundly disturbing and even harrowingly dreadful to one who has never before looked.

Given the pellucid insights of Jung, of Socrates, and of the Buddha, the present chapter might appear redundant. We twenty-first-century humans already have sufficient resources and food for thought, even an overabundance. If the roots of morality lie in human nature, however, and if humans in any great and influential numbers have yet to discover and acknowledge that nature, then further perspectives and elucidations may not be amiss. In particular, if humans on the whole perceive themselves as good and righteous while human history and cultural practices unequivocally testify to foul and deadly deeds, then clearly, humans have yet—even in this twenty-first century—much to learn about their own human nature.

In what follows, a global and even planetary net will first be cast over the whole in the hope that, in however a preliminary and unfinished way, it will open a new vista that has sufficient scope ultimately to encompass the rich insights of the past. On the basis of this opening move, we will turn to human ontogeny and to an elucidation of the earliest natural signs having moral import, signs that are foundationally social, that are affectively oppositional in nature, that persist throughout life as well as across species, and that thus engender both existential and evolutionary continuities (for more on such continuities, see Sheets-Johnstone 1986a). Elucidating one of these natural signs at both a finer and broader level, a sign widely recognized as problematic and substantively challenging, will allow us to examine the moral import of xenophobia and in turn the socialization of fear and its aggressive and acquisitive complexities in depth. Finally, having identified the foundational affective social oppositions inherent in human nature, we will attempt to pinpoint the moral imperative inherent in a unified perspective, namely, the imperative to provide an education that, from its very beginnings, enlightens humans about themselves, turning them toward an awakening to and understandings of the nature of their own psyches rather than near exclusively toward the world about them and what they must learn to be able to navigate successfully in it.

II. ENDANGERED SPECIES

Present-day concerns with endangered species focus attention on a vast range of imperiled creatures in the animal kingdom and on the concomitant ecological hazards of a diminished biological diversity. The diminished biological diversity may be described in twentieth- and twenty-first-century terms as a lack of biological pluralism. Just as a belief in and valuing of pluralistic societies demands respect for others, so also does a belief in and valuing of biological diversity. From a moral standpoint, biodiversity and sociological pluralism are indeed sister concepts. The "other" is in each instance commonly recognized as morphologically different in some way from oneself, but not so different as to be ranked inferior, deemed expendable, and so on. Indeed, in a Darwinian sense, i.e., in the sense of a conjoint evolutionary history, morphological difference is a matter of degree, not of kind. Conceptions and valuations of others thus logically reflect natural gradient differences rather than egoistically inflected "Us against Them" categorical differences. The former kinds of differences propel us toward thoughtful, equitably negotiated decisions concerning Nature and other living beings, the latter toward peremptory and myopic acts that sever relational bonds.[3] Moreover from a moral standpoint, whatever the morphology of other living forms, they are sentient beings of one kind or another—flora included[4]—whose hallmark is responsivity. Sociological pluralism and biological diversity are from this perspective equal markers of our respect for others, a respect not for their "right to life" in the sense of a legalistic ruling, but a respect for their sheer living presence in the world. In effect, whether a matter of biodiversity or sociological pluralism, the key determining factor is an individual's sense of the inherent existential worth of others, a sense that is clearly not a ready-made but contingent on an individual's experiential acuity and reflective powers, and ultimately on an individual's motivation to develop such acuity and powers. Indeed, an individual's awareness of the origin or basis of his or her feelings and beliefs concerning others, an awareness of the motivations that impel him or her to initiate certain courses of action with respect to others—to do or not do certain things with reference to them—is imperative to a bona fide appreciation and promotion of biodiversity and sociological pluralism. Equally critical is an individual's capacity to probe and question his or her motivations to begin with. The capacity to reflect, as Arendt emphasizes, is basic to human morality, but here in the added essential sense of reflecting on the *affective* why of a proposed course of action or lack of action. In short, what affectively motivates one to act or not to act can be brought to light through reflection and thereby become open to investigation.

Present-day calls for biodiversity—and pluralism—attempt to awaken people to just such reflection, hence to a wider frame of reference that extends both spatially and temporally beyond a person's immediate life. Clearly, however, it is not enough to urge people to consider the plight of other species or to conserve and protect earthly resources, and even to offer them rewards for doing so. Neither is it enough to try to reason with them toward such ends. As indicated above, what is essential is another kind of awakening that itself demands a quite particular motivation and even considerable effort since it centers on self-knowledge. In fact, essential to any sustained awakening to a wider frame of reference is a foundational awakening to a deep self-knowledge of the nature of human nature, hence of the nature of one's own human being. Obviously, one must be motivated toward this end, that is, motivated toward self-knowledge to begin with.

Put in this epistemological perspective, understandings of the source of threats to biodiversity—and by extension, to pluralism—shift radically. In particular, one readily sees that endangered species are not simply species that have failed to come to human attention because the proper human awarenesses are and have been lacking or because the compass of human thought and feeling is and has been constricted. By definition, what is endangered is endangered because a danger is present: nonhuman species are at risk because humans have the capacity to put them at risk. If endangered species exist, it is because humans exist. Indeed, it can hardly be denied that humans have become *the* most dangerous species ever spawned by Nature. Moreover they are *the* most dangerous species not just with respect to other species. Their *intra-*species danger is in fact unique: no nonhuman animal species decimates its own kind as humans do and have done for millennia. And no nonhuman animal species decimates its environmental resources, fouls its own air and water, or puts the global planet itself at risk as humans do and have done over the last century in particular.

A unified perspective on elementary binary oppositions requires just such epistemological insights into and acknowledgments of human nature. The dual antithetical powers at the heart of humans—to exploit and destroy or to nurture and protect—are not abstract formulations. Neither are they theoretical or rarified possibilities. They are real-life human realities. Moreover the distinct powers are not powers proper only to certain individual humans—for example, exploitative powers to males on the one hand, nurturing ones to females on the other—or to certain so-defined individuals—for example, aggressive individuals on the one hand and docile ones on the other, or domineering ones on the one hand and meek ones on the other, and so on. The dual antithetical powers are endemic to all. They are pan-human "action potentials."[5] We witness them in everyday human interactions—in acts of kindness and generosity, and in acts of greed and abuse; we witness them in myriad types of human situations—in homes, communal celebrations, and hospitals, and in stock market dealings, criminal assaults, political manoeuverings, and war. The very existence of endangered species testifies to kindred inter-species action potentials, humans in like fashion either exploiting and destroying other species or nurturing and protecting them.

A common but striking human practice illustrates the basic oppositional ways in which nonhuman animals are valued and in turn treated, and the motivational source of the valuation and treatment. Some nonhuman animals are explicitly—even munificently—accorded privileged status, as one can readily see in the long and often multiple aisles given over in supermarkets to cat and dog food and paraphernalia in the United States. The differential valuing and treatment of household animals—"pets"—over wild and laboratory animals, or more pointedly, of animals humans cultivate and treasure as part of their immediate lives over those untamed and in various ways remote, is indeed remarkable. Those not personally favored are in comparative terms hardly cared for, much less privileged. Laws, not personal motivation, afford them protection. The analogy to the wholly human world is transparent: those who are related by family ties, by religion, race, ethnicity, or citizenship are commonly and consistently favored; those who are unrelated in at least one of these "domesticated" ways are not. Laws, in turn, are needed to protect undomesticated others, i.e., outsiders.

Surely, given the commonness and consistency of these categorical valuations and practices, we should be motivated to inquire into the nature of human nature. In particular, we should ask what is foundationally brooding in the darkness of human nature that prevents a genuine biodiversified and pluralistic respect and even reverencing of undomesticated others to come to light. Before launching that inquiry by inquiring into ontogenetical matters of fact, thereby identifying the earliest natural signs in infancy that are at once social and affective, it will be instructive to put the antithetical powers of humans to exploit and to protect other species in broader psychological perspective and thus demonstrate in further ways what endangered species teach us about ourselves.

In his phenomenology of the self—and in a small aside in his *Answer to Job* where he calls the notion a "nonsensical doctrine" (Jung 1971, 547)—Jung stresses that evil is not a *privatio boni*, a privation of good or love. In other words, evil is not, as medieval ecclesiastics conceived it, 'the accidental lack of perfection' (Jung 1968b, 41); it is rather one aspect of "a totality of inner opposites," both of which are equally powerful (Jung 1971, 531). Jung dramatically illustrates the equality of their power when, in writing about the shadow side of the self, "which ought not to be judged too optimistically," he states: "So far as we can judge from experience, light and shadow are so evenly distributed in man's nature that his psychic totality appears, to say the least of it, in a somewhat murky light" (Jung 1968b, 42). The psychic totality of humans does indeed appear murky when we observe ourselves closely, all the more so when we look closely into the relationship of humans to nonhumans and to Nature generally. Concomitantly, there is psychological work to do if the whole of human nature is to be fully acknowledged and literally clarified. The work is necessary because the dark side is not immediately conscious. Only by being "at the pains of a little thought" does the possibility of opening to the shadow side of human nature arise. Whatever the effort, individuals of a species having the power to reflect have the power to attend to motivations, to become familiar with difficult feelings, to recognize malevolent proclivities and urgings, to deliberate, to weigh actions, and to choose wisely, indeed, *sapiently*, among possible courses of action. In turn, *wisdom* rather than power becomes the preeminent human character. *Wisdom* is in fact the biological character by which humans single themselves out as a species in the world. What the shadow side thus requires[6] is the living realization of what is otherwise a biological pretension. Short of consistent and patient efforts to illumine the *terra incognita* of the human psyche and in particular the *terra incognita* of one's own human psyche, the species that emerges is *Homo nescius et barbarus:* the dangerous species.[7]

Jung's observations pertaining to an analysis of the God of the Old Testament—a "divine unconsciousness"—are notably pertinent to humans in this context, all the more so if, as Jung comments, "We cannot tell whether God and the unconscious are two different entities" (Jung 1971, 647–48). With respect to the Old Testament God, Jung points out that "[d]ivine unconsciousness and lack of reflection . . . enable us to form a conception of God which puts his actions beyond moral judgment and allows no conflict to arise between goodness and beastliness" (547), but he also subsequently observes that a God knowing neither reflection nor morality "would be [psychologically] described as *non compos mentis*" (571). Surely the same observations hold true for humans. Those who are unaware of the motivational source of their actions and incapable of self-reflection are both morally and psychologically disabled. The diagnosis of a moral and psychological self-opacity in fact coincides analytically with Arendt's assessment of Eichmann, who may readily be psychologically described *"non compos mentis."*

Unless a human applies himself or herself reflectively to his or her motivations, he or she, like the Old Testament God, "is too unconscious to be moral" (534).

Now if Eichmann exemplifies just this incapacity and thus how the dangerous species can so readily and easily inflict mortal wounds on its own kind, then *mutatis mutandis*, it is immediately apparent how nonhuman animal species come to be endangered and how a foundational awakening to a deep self-knowledge is as essential to preserving biodiversity as it is to ensuring a pluralistic respect for human others. Mortal woundings of other species such as the now extinct dodo and moa, and mortal threats to untold other species such as the mountain gorilla, testify unequivocally to the dark side of human nature. Endangered species and the "beastliness" of humans go hand in hand, though of course the defining pejorative epithet is inappropriate since it is not beasts who are "beastly" but humans. Moreover it is not the dark side itself that precludes moral awakening and attunement, but the opacity of individual humans to their dark side. Achievement of a veritable moral society—and world—in fact proceeds individual by individual. To become morally awakened and attuned, individuals must recognize "goodness and beastliness" as their own dual antithetical human possibilities.[8] They can do so, however, only if the possibilities are experienced as actual proclivities of their own being, that is, as oppositional forms of feeling and action that define the full compass of their own human nature. Hence the quintessential significance of bringing the shadow side of human nature into the light and the need for each individual human to look within both deeply and with probity, acknowledging and reflecting on what is psychically there. The dangerous species will otherwise prevail, a species that, by thoughtlessly and persistently posing the dangers it does, actually de-natures itself as a species. It destroys not only the source of its creation, but the resources that sustain it along with all other living forms. *Homo nescius et barbarus* is indeed a thoroughly unnatural species, an antagonist of Nature through and through, a contender that has no natural forebears, no phyletic link to any distant progenitor, no familial resemblance to any close primate relative. The unnatural species is in reality a pompous but utterly vacuous blockhead, a blight on the face of Nature. It endangers other species precisely because it fails to comprehend Nature and is epistemologically opaque to itself.

III. ONTOGENY AND NATURAL SIGNS

Humans are clearly not born with a moral sense any more than they are born "good" or "bad," e.g., generous or greedy, kind or mean, protective or rapacious, and so on. They are, however, naturally disposed toward acquiring a moral sense and in turn naturally endowed with the capacity to be "good" or "bad." The concern here is to spell out natural human dispositions, and in turn to identify the origin of a moral sense. Certain phenomena in ontogeny point toward that origin; that is, certain developmental phenomena are natural signs encapsulating dispositions and constitute the grounds of a moral sense.[9] Accordingly, if the quest is to elucidate the roots of human morality, one cannot start out at an adult level. An ontogenetic perspective is essential. So also in preface is a brief clarification of natural signs.

When Merleau-Ponty writes that "in man there is no natural sign," and that "[i]t would be legitimate to speak of 'natural signs' only if the anatomical organization of our body produced a correspondence between specific gestures and given 'states of mind'" (Merleau-Ponty 1962, 188–89), he is surprisingly oblivious of the dynamic congruity that binds movement and emotions (Sheets-Johnstone 1999a)—or in his terms, that binds "specific gestures and given 'states of mind'." Foucault is similarly wide of the mark when he writes, "Nothing in man—not even his body—is sufficiently stable to serve as the basis for self-recognition or for understanding other men" (Foucault 1977, 153; also in Dreyfus and Rabinow 1983, 110). When such adultist views by seemingly infant-remote males become part of received wisdom, insights into elemental aspects of human nature are effectively muffled. While Foucault's declaration might be less surprising than Merleau-Ponty's in that Foucault did not write on infants and children and did not teach child psychology at the Sorbonne as did Merleau-Ponty (Spiegelberg 1971, 529), his repudiation of the natural is no less lamentable and misleading. As with any other species, where would humans be without a species-specific intercorporeal semantics anchoring interpersonal meanings and understandings? However disparate their cultural groomings, smiling, hitting, embracing, and kicking are kinetic staples of human sociality. Further, we might ask how hominids could possibly have devised verbal language(s) short of species-specific tactile-kinesthetic invariants; and how, short of the absence of one's tactile-kinesthetic body—or alternatively, short of the presence of pathological conditions—one could possibly fail to recognize oneself? As for the dynamic congruity binding movement and emotion, one has only to examine the dynamics of any feeling and the dynamics of the movement to which the feeling gives rise: a particular kinetic form unfolds coincident with the form of the feeling, its waxings and wanings, its urgencies and attenuations, and so on. The affective and kinetic clearly share a common qualitative structure (Sheets-Johnstone 1999a), as when one folds inward in grieving and expands outward in joy, or when one soothes another in soft tones and gestures and explodes angrily toward another in hard ones. The dynamic congruency of movement and feeling—of the kinetic and the affective—is a natural congruency. One does not learn how to express one's feelings kinetically except in the sense of being taught, over and above one's natural kinetic dispositions, what is culturally or familially acceptable and what is not. The basic concordance is natural through and through. Hence the "sign," i.e., any affectively charged movement, is fundamentally a natural sign. Such natural signs are part of a species' kinetic semantics, and, in a larger sense, part of an evolutionary semantics (Sheets-Johnstone 1990, 1999b, 1999d; see also the discussion of Peircean-based biosemiotics in Hoffmeyer 1996, Hoffmeyer and Emmeche 1991, and Emmeche 1991 and 1994).

A smile is just such a natural sign. It is no wonder, then, that it is a pan-cultural human phenomenon, a sign of openness toward another, a sign of friendliness and warmth. Being a natural sign, it is no wonder either that it is part of an evolutionary semantics: a human's smile is partially homologous to the silent bared-teeth face of chimpanzees and of some species of monkey such as mandrills. A human's smile furthermore functionally resembles chimpanzee lip-smacking (van Hooff 1969, 75, 83). Finally, it is no wonder that *infants smile* and that their directed smile at approximately three months of age is precisely a culturally unadulterated natural sign, one that might be described as inviting an "affect attunement" (Stern 1985) by way of a correlative gesture on the part of the adult at whom they are smiling. What is of wonder, and in fact, of considerable wonder, is the young age at which an infant directs its smile toward another, thus engaging in a full-fledged social interaction. Psychiatrist René Spitz, in his carefully detailed and well-known experimental study of "the smiling response," attempts to identify the conditions for the appearance of a smile by analyzing the disposition of three-month old infants to smile (Spitz 1983). In the process, he comments pointedly on the extraordinary nature of the phenomenon, first calling attention to the fact that the infant's smile is "an essentially social manifestation, the manifestation of pleasure experienced when beholding the presence of a human partner" (100), then remarking that no other behavior in the third or fourth month of life "shows as much perceptive discrimination or specificity." Indeed, Spitz states, "It is as if the infant had suddenly developed a behavior pattern far in advance of the rest of its behavior" (101).

Spitz qualifies his attribution of pleasure to the smiling infant, saying, "We have no way of knowing whether the infant really experiences pleasure when it smiles" (98). On the basis of both evolutionary homologies and of tactile-kinesthetic invariants, however, we do of course have ways of knowing, ways whose validity counts all the more in that three-month-old infants do not and cannot deceive us, pretending to smile, for example, and to feel pleasure when they do not. Neither do or can infants do the socially, morally, or politically correct thing by smiling in certain circumstances, as they might in later years as an older child or grown-up. Moreover, when an infant smiles, it does not simply make a mouth gesture, as an adult might; its whole body smiles in kinetically apparent open and pleasurable "feelings toward" someone. It may concurrently kick its legs and wave its arms, for example, and may not only smile, but break into "laugh[ter], gurgling[s], or crowing[s]," as in experiments carried out by Spitz (115). In short, an infant is as pleasurably and wholly engaged in its smile as its smile is pleasurably and wholly engaging. In turn, there is no mistaking the positive sociality of its smile any more than there is any mistaking the smile as a natural sign of amiable openness toward another.

It is of considerable interest in this regard to recall (from Chapter 8) what Darwin wrote in one of his notebooks—"Seeing a Baby (like Hensleigh's) smile & frown, who can doubt these are instinctive—child does not sneer" (Darwin 1987, Notebook M, no. 96, p. 542). The point is actually brought home in a striking way by one of Spitz's own experiments in which the experimenter wore a mask that approximated "to certain Japanese theatrical masks used in the No-plays, a species of *rictus* or *risus sardonicus*," the expression of the masked experimenter being "perhaps best described as that of a savage animal baring its fangs." Spitz in fact remarks, "No grown-up would be inclined, even for a moment, to mistake this expression for one of friendliness, or of pleasure. Its savagery is unmistakable" (Spitz 1983, 112). In spite of the mask and its "bared fangs," infants smiled in this instance too. Moreover in another experiment in which the experimenter wore a mask allowing only the tongue to protrude and to move about, infants smiled. As Spitz observed, the usual smiling movements of the experimenter's mouth could be "effectively replaced" by a moving tongue (114). In fact, the dual conditions for eliciting a smile, Spitz found, are an *en face* appearance and movement. If the experimenter turned to a profile visage, the infant stopped smiling or lost interest. In contrast, and as indicated, a relatively broad array of movement on the part of the experimenter was possible: infants would continue to smile if the experimenter were smiling, nodding, or talking, if the experimenter was "sticking his tongue rhythmically through the mouth-slit of the mask," or if the experimenter was "rhythmically widening and narrowing [his] mouth" as in "baring fangs" (113). Spitz's conclusion, that "the *emotion* expressed in the human face has no significance for the smiling reaction of the child between its third and sixth month" (113), is further validation that an infant's smile is basically an initiatory rather than a responsive act.

In sum, an infant's social smile is a spontaneous expression of its human nature. It is the first natural sign of recognition of another that, in its gesture of amiability, carries with it a natural moral tone: to be open and friendly toward others. It warrants emphasis that such a sociality is a spontaneous individual kinetic act, and precisely not legislated or taught. It furthermore bears emphasis that this first affectively charged social kinetic act has no aim beyond itself: it is not a means to any end and has no other kind of ulterior motive, but is meaningful in and of itself. In other words, an infant's smile is not performed out of immediate "self-interest," for example, or to assure future gain, or to repay a past kindness. On the contrary, its meaning is uncluttered. It is a purely affective social gesture, the first one of its kind, and the first one that is morally weighted. It is remarkable that prominent psychoanalytic theorists omit this ontogenetically significant marker of human life in their theories of infancy: Freud's theory of infant sexuality and Lacan's theory of infant aggressivity and his theory of the mirror stage of infancy are all blind to a fundamental ontogenetical social reality.

The roots of morality, however, have a double strand. The second strand, equally anchored in ontogeny, contrasts markedly with the first in a number of senses, each of which is fundamental. What warrants attention first, however, is a seeming conflation of reflexes.

Were it glossed as an inchoate fear response, the Moro reflex could be described as the affective antithesis of an infant's later social smile.

All the more so since the Moro reflex is sometimes either undifferentiated from the startle reflex—e.g., "This [the Moro reflex] is also called the *startle reflex*" (Bee 1989, 92)—or spoken of in terms of startle—"The infant startles, arches its back, and throws its head back. At the same time, it throws out its arms and legs and then brings them abruptly back toward its body. The infant cries, then startles, and then cries because of the startle" (Larson 1990, 35; see also Young 1973). Each reflex is tied to a sudden loud noise or loss of support. But a conflation of the two easily leads to confusion since the bodily kinetics of the two reflexes are virtually mirror opposites of each other. In the Moro reflex, the infant "throws both arms backward and arches her back" (Bee 1989, 92), whereas in the startle reflex, the infant moves into a contractive posture: there is a "forward movement of the head, . . . [a] raising and drawing forward of the shoulders, abduction and pronation of the upper arms, flexion of the fingers, forward movement of the trunk, contraction of the abdomen, and bending of the knees" (Young 1973, 221).[10] A radically *extended* bodily kinetic clearly defines the Moro reflex; a radically *flexed* bodily kinetic clearly defines the startle reflex. As psychologist Paul Young explicitly points out, "the startle pattern and the Moro reflex are distinguishable organic patterns." But he also suggests, on the basis of the rapidity of the startle reflex and the "slower, grosser, more obvious Moro reflex," that though "[b]oth are evoked by the stimulation of a loud noise, . . . it is not the *kind* of stimulation but rather the *age* of the subject . . . which determines whether the Moro reflex or the startle pattern will be more obvious to an observer" (225). He adds, "This fact in itself is interesting from the standpoint of emotional development" (225).

We will presently attempt to flesh out Young's additional remark, specifying the nature of the "emotional development" from Moro reflex to startle pattern and thus attempt to de-conflate the two. Our initial concern, however, is to contrast the similar affective nature of both reflexes with the affective nature of "the smiling response."

As is evident, the reflexes are an *environmental response* and are thus doubly distinct from the smile: they constitute an impersonal relationship to something that is either there—loud noise—or not there—support—in an infant's surrounding world, and they are non-initiatory kinetic acts, i.e., they are genuinely responsive acts, indeed, *reflexive* ones. Furthermore, while infants smile periodically, evanescently, and in half-formed ways in the first weeks of life—at eight days of age and even earlier, which of course is prior to the time they direct a smile to a moving human face—the Moro and startle reflexes are not periodically evident in any way prior to their first manifestation. Thus, unlike nonsocial smiling, the reflexes are not "one of numerous expressive movements of the face observed in the baby, such as frowning, opening and closing of the mouth, protruding of the tongue, and facial distortion" (Spitz 1983, 99). Spitz labels such "expressive movements of the face," movements that are unconnected to any particular situation, "pathognomic activity" (98, 99). Though certainly expressive to an observer, neither reflex is such an expressive movement, nor is it an expressive movement of the face to begin with. The movement pattern identified as the Moro reflex is a whole-body response that other researchers have described as follows: "First the infant thrusts her arms outward, opens her hands, arches her back, and stretches her legs outward. Then she brings her arms inward in an embracing motion with fingers formed into fists" (Vasta et al. 1992, 169; see also Robeck 1978, 127). Ernst Moro, the scientist who first described the reflex, attempted an evolutionary explanation, "argu[ing] that it was a relic of an adaptive reaction by primates to grab for support while falling" (Vasta et al. 1992, 169), or as psychologist Mildred Robeck states, "[the reflex is] a remnant of primate behavior, exhibited when the newborn had to clasp and cling to the mother to stay with the troop" (Robeck 1978, 127).

It is worth noting that any hypothesized "adaptive function" is of far less import than the existential meaning of the Moro reflex and its triggering event, i.e., a sudden noise or loss of support. The plausibility of the hypothesized "adaptive function" is in fact conceptually parasitic on the existential meaning of the reflexive response. This meaning is suggestively limned by Robeck when she explains why the infant responds as it does: "The infant is startled because the flow of sensations to which she or he has habituated are [sic] disrupted" (127; see also Tomkins 1991, 62, and Sroufe 1996, 62, on "the fear system": "Any event that stops the flow of behavior will cause the [distress] reaction . . . [that is] a precursor of and prototype for fear"). However possibly confusing her use of the word *startled* in conjunction with the Moro reflex, Robeck's explanation of the reflex is of critical significance. Her explanation properly grounds the understanding of the Moro reflex—and the startle reflex as well—in an experiential understanding of the lived character of the reflexive reaction. A sudden noise or loss of support disturbs a familiar world with a suddenness that, for an infant, is unsettling if not frightening. From this vantage point, one readily sees that the Moro reflex is an inchoate natural sign of fear. It is the harbinger of fear in face of the unknown, a fear that in later years, for older children and adults, may be anywhere from minimally unnerving to terrifying or life-threatening, depending on both the individual and the situation. This fleshed-out affective understanding of the Moro reflex—of the unfamiliar suddenly intruding on the familiar—explains why an infant's reaction is an *environmental* and not a social response. Whether a matter of a loud noise or loss of support, an infant is jarred by something that suddenly changes a familiar environment into an unfamiliar one, "jarred" having a specifically kinetic meaning, i.e., the infant moves into a radical hyperextension that, by its very nature, makes the infant hypertense throughout its body to the point of being quasi-rigid.

As Young notes, the contractive "organic pattern" of the startle reflex is the contrary of the Moro reflex: whatever the age of the individual, he or she moves into flexion rather than extension. The organic pattern of the startle reflex is nonetheless a developmental sequel to the earlier organic pattern of the Moro reflex, being similarly a spontaneous and environmental whole-body response. It is a full-fledged rather than inchoate natural sign of fear, specifically, fear of the unknown. Whether one is an infant or an adult, when one is startled, one immediately stops what one is doing, hence puts a stop to whatever has been to that moment a familiar "flow of sensations." From this existential perspective, Robeck's use of the word *startled* in conjunction with the Moro reflex appears to make sense. But unlike the *exposed* body that the first phase of the Moro reflex presents, the startle reflex presents a *protected* body. There is indeed a developmental change in the nervous system; with the disappearance of the Moro reflex at three months, "a stage in the normal development of the nervous system has passed" (Robeck 1978, 127), opening the way to a different but intimately related reflex. In particular, what is existentially evident in the first phase of the inchoate fear response of the Moro reflex is *sheer vulnerability* in face of the unknown. It is as if an electric charge disperses throughout the body, rigidifying it, yes, but most important, laying open its utter defenselessness. In contrast, what is existentially evident in the full-fledged fear response of the startle reflex is a complex of moves to protect oneself, to defend oneself against what is unknown. The existential meaning of the two responses is palpably different but developmentally of an affective-kinetic piece: vulnerability is at the heart of fear. Without it, there would be no fear because there would be nothing to fear: one would be precisely invulnerable to any disturbance or threat from the environment. In the startle reflex, vulnerability is suppressed; that is, the first phase of the Moro is eclipsed. The body no longer kinetically embodies its vulnerability by being fully exposed but rushes, as it were, to protect itself in face of the unknown. The rapidity of the startle reflex is indeed significant.

In sum, the age of a subject may well determine which organic pattern is the more obvious to an observer, extension or flexion, as Young suggests. In turn, the age of a subject may well be thought to determine whether an observer sees a totally vulnerable body or a body moving to protect itself. The matter cannot be left there, however, because the two kinetic patterns are in and of themselves not just distinct but uniquely meaningful. In other words, a kinetic semantics is clearly in evidence with respect to the two kinetic patterns. The movement response of the infant that culminates in total exposure culminates in total vulnerability and is expressive of that vulnerability. The developmental sequel to total vulnerability is kinetically embodied in the later startle reflex: the closing-in movements of the body are protective and expressive of that self-protection. With the latter movements, fear of something unfamiliar is palpably at the forefront of the experience and stays at the forefront of the experience. In terms of emotional development, the bodily kinetics of older infants, young children, and adults is no longer an articulation of vulnerability, the elemental human condition prompting fear, but an articulation of fear itself, a direct expression of feelings from apprehension to terror of the unknown. Moreover the later protective fear response is elicited not only by an unexpected loud noise or loss of support, but by a broad and varied range of sudden environmental changes. In effect, the natural sign of fear is an evolving sign that does not disappear.

A third natural sign originating in ontogeny is developmentally of a piece with the previous two and in two distinct ways. Before proceeding to a delineation of this third and final sign to be considered, a critical topic merits attention, one that, as may be evident, is intimately related to natural signs and to a determination of the roots of morality: existential continuities.

The importance of an ongoing-life perspective, in essence, a recognition of *existential continuities*, is strikingly demonstrated by the conceptual hazards encountered in its lack. The lack is notably apparent in a common view of the self that has approached the status of received wisdom, namely, if one has a "self," one can recognize oneself in a mirror. Using as evidence the failure of babies to pass "the mirror test," a psychology text affirms, "Babies are not born with a sense of self" (Roediger et al. 1987, 349), as if human babies were a different species of animal from human adults because they do not recognize themselves in a mirror.[11] Indeed, a mysterious Rubicon divides selfless babies from the selfhood of adults in that the process by which children and adults come to procure a self that they can recognize in a mirror is nowhere detailed. The textbook, for example, merely implicitly affirms that when there is a subject and an object, a separation of "I" from "other-than-I," there is a self.[12] In effect, adults simply have what infants do not have—a self. By reverse analogy, infants have what adults do not have—a Moro reflex. Since no existential continuities obtain, the worlds of infants and adult are discontinuous: never the twain shall meet. Language, of course, can figure prominently in support of claims of discontinuity (e.g., Dennett 1983),[13] but in a comparative sense, no more prominently than mirrors that mysteriously separate human selves from human nonselves or than affective barriers that categorically separate the Moro reflex of infants from the later startle reactions of older infants, children, and adults.

The reverse analogy between a mirror notion of the self and what commonly amounts to no more than a footnote notion of the Moro reflex is additionally instructive with respect to existential continuities. While mirrors have nothing to do in a foundational way with a sense of self (see Stern 1985 on the emergent and core self; for a critique of the mirror notion, see Sheets-Johnstone 1990, 370–73), the Moro and startle reflexes have everything to do in a foundational way with the human and in fact pan-animate emotion of fear. In broad terms, natural phenomena have natural import. As indicated earlier, the Moro reflex is a kinetic embodiment of vulnerability, hence an inchoate form of fear, the harbinger of later feelings of fear from apprehension to terror. Like the startle reflex, these later feelings of fear—like all forms of feeling—are involuntary: they simply arise. In a critically important passage in which Jung introduces the concept of the shadow, he points out that emotion "is not an activity of the individual but something that happens to him" (Jung 1968b, 8–9). The truth of Jung's observation is often missed, and with it, veridical understandings of motion and emotion, that is, of what is and is not in our control, not just in infancy, but throughout our lives (Sheets-Johnstone 1999a). The involuntary nature of emotions is in fact not unlike the involuntary nature of reflex movements. Just as we were involuntarily moved affectively and kinetically when jarred and later startled as infants,[14] so we are involuntarily moved affectively and kinetically when startled as adults, and more generally, when we are initially overcome by fear or any other emotion. No matter our age, in each instance, what comes, comes unbidden, kinetically sculpting our bodies along the way. Fear initially grips us, for example. We may stiffen in a way not unlike the initial stiffening evident in the arched extension of the Moro reflex. The stiffening is involuntary. What is voluntary is what we do in face of the fear or any other emotion. Accordingly, and as Jung's observation implicitly indicates, we are not responsible for our feelings but for the actions we take in light of our feelings. In short, adulthood does not confer privileged status. However much we may kinetically dissemble, suppress, exaggerate, or otherwise re-form our natural emotional "expressions" as adults, i.e., however much we may now control our affective feelings and movements, emotions happen to us just as they happened to us in infancy and as we matured as children and adolescents into adulthood. If we examine the matter carefully, we see that existential continuities obtain.

Evolutionary continuities obtain equally and are equally apparent, as various chapters of this book have shown (see also Sheets-Johnstone 1986a). Jung's insight thus applies equally to nonhuman animals: emotions come unbidden across the animal kingdom. It is in turn hardly surprising that Darwin implicitly remarked on the fact when he observed, "[T]hat the lower animals are excited by the same emotions as ourselves is so well established, that it will not be necessary to weary the reader by many details. Terror acts in the same manner on them as on us, causing the muscles to tremble, the heart to palpitate, the sphincters to be relaxed, and the hair to stand on end" (Darwin 1871, 39). Neither is it surprising that evolutionary biologist John Alcock discusses the startle response in invertebrates as well as vertebrates in the context of discussing antipredator behavior. For example, in the course of his study of a species of *Automeris* moth possessing false eyes, he discovered that "in the chilly dawn" when the moth was "sluggish" he could pick it up gently, but that the moth immediately exposed its false eyes if suddenly jostled or poked (Alcock 1989, 2; see also 344–46). In a way closer to human home, the example of Mike, the male chimpanzee whose noisy hooting and clashing kerosene-can tactics dispersed a group of grooming males (as cited in Chapter 3), documents how a sudden intrusion into an ongoing activity is similarly startling, initially provoking fear and protective movement. Mike initially alarmed the males by suddenly disrupting their "flow of grooming sensations." As Goodall observed, Mike "made the most appalling racket: no wonder the erstwhile peaceful males rushed out of [his] way" (Goodall 1971, 113). Not only were the males duly startled by the sudden intrusion, but their subsequent submissive gestures toward Mike were a further validation of their fear. It is of interest to note too that in her discussion of flight and avoidance as expressive movements, Goodall specifically describes the "startled reaction," identifying it as a reflex:

> When a chimpanzee is alarmed by a sudden noise or movement nearby—from a low-flying bird, large insect, snake, or the like—the immediate response is to duck its head and fling one or both arms across its face or to throw both hands up in the air. A reaction similar to the first is observed in the gorilla and in man, and one similar to the second is observed in the baboon. Occasionally these reflex actions were followed up by a hitting-away movement with the back of the hand toward the object. This movement, probably defensive in origin, has been incorporated into the repertoire of threat gestures. (Goodall 1972, 38)

Clearly, the potential to be startled and in turn beset with fear has both existential and evolutionary continuities. The potential is an indication of the built-in vulnerability of animate creatures in face of the unknown. Indeed, it is not too much to say that the potential to be startled and fearful informs animate life throughout, both existentially and evolutionarily. Something unfamiliar may happen at any moment to any animal, human or nonhuman, precipitating an immediate, correlative, emotional "happening." The involuntary nature of the happening is justly captured in dictionary definitions of startle: "to give a sudden involuntary jerk, jump, or twitch, as from a shock of surprise, alarm, or pain"; "to start, to undergo a sudden involuntary movement of the body, caused by surprise, alarm, acute pain, etc." (OED, Webster's 1996 New Universal Unabridged). The definitions in fact justly capture the sudden "happening" of startle at both ends, so to speak, i.e., both "the shock" and "the start." In effect, the total situation is "involuntary."

What is voluntary is what happens afterward. The grooming males' rush from Mike, for example, may or may not have begun with an involuntary jerk, a jump, or a twitch, or for that matter with a reflex pattern related to the initial extension phase of a Moro reflex or the flexion movements of a human startle reflex. Their response was described only as "rushing out of the way." But their reaction to the *sudden* onset of Mike's clamorous charge was clearly to desist *suddenly* in doing what they were to that moment doing. Though distanced from such close experiential understandings (but see too below in this text), psychologist Silvan Tomkins's neuro-functional definition of startle enunciates the same truth: startle "serves as an interruptor of ongoing neural firing in the central assembly" (Tomkins 1991, 495), its "main function" being "to disassemble the central assembly and force a *change in consciousness* as an interruptor of whatever the individual was consciously attending" (63–64; italics in original).

In sum, the potential to be involuntarily "interrupted," to have one's flow of sensations suddenly changed, to be shocked and to move involuntarily in twitches, jerks, and so on, is a lifelong developmentally primed and evolutionarily primed vulnerability persisting throughout both the whole of any particular animate life in which it exists and the whole of any particular species in which it exists. The potential is, in brief, both existentially and evolutionarily embedded.

The third natural sign—stranger anxiety—testifies in further ways to these dual continuities. It signals a pivotal development in the ontogeny of fear, specifically, a development from an environmental response in general to a social response in particular. Fear of strangers is a well-documented if still interpretively debated social infant fear that, though unrelated to suddenness of any kind, is obviously—by definition—anchored in the experience of the unfamiliar. Stranger anxiety[15] thus builds on the earlier environmental fear responses: it is a further elaboration of fear in face of the unknown. Though psychologist L. Alan Sroufe does not mention the Moro reflex or startle reflex as foundational signs of fear and in fact dismisses the startle reflex as an "emotion" (Sroufe 1996, 60), he forcefully underscores developmental understandings of emotion to begin with, i.e., earlier forms of an emotion do not disappear but remain "precursors" (102) even as they are replaced by "more mature reactions" (116), and attempts specifically to spell out the precursor of fear in an infant's feeling of "wariness" in face of the unknown (102), a feeling that precedes the full-blown *"categorical negative reaction*" that is fear (102; see also 104ff.). As Sroufe explains, "Prototype and mature form are related developmentally, not morphologically. While the physiological prototype is embodied in the mature emotion . . . it has become part of a transformed psychological process. Emotions do not appear; rather, they develop, and developmental changes continue even after the emergence of the mature expression" (65). Indeed, as he later points out, "negative reactions to the unknown continue throughout life" (102). Throughout his study of emotion, he emphasizes a developmental continuity rather than a discontinuous process of infant stages. Debate about "stranger anxiety" and its onset is thus of far less value for him than recognition of the phenomenon of fear itself: "[T]he 'age of fear' is not critical. What is far more important is an appreciation of the developmental process" (108). In particular, the fear that emerges as a "categorical response at 9 months is qualitatively different from the emotional reaction at 4 months" (108). The former is evidenced in "negative reactions to intruding strangers" (105), the latter is evidenced, for example, in experimental studies of "distress reactions in response to the still and unresponsive face of the mother" (104).

But formal discontinuities are nevertheless apparent, and precisely from a developmental perspective. In particular, kinetic-morphological differences merit attention. Sroufe's specification of wariness as a precursor of infant fear notwithstanding, neither the Moro reflex (which, as noted, Sroufe does not mention) nor the startle reflex can be discounted on the grounds of being merely "a reflex" and "not best thought of as emotions themselves" (60). As is evident from earlier descriptions, the Moro reflex has first what one might call a shock phase and then a recovery phase: a radical extension, then a flexion or "slow return to the normal position" (Young 1973, 224). The first phase awakens the body wholly and intensely, in a way akin to the initial grip of fear; the second phase is a recovery phase, which, as noted, some have seen as adaptive in its suggestive "clasping" movement (e.g., Robeck 1978, 127; but see also Young 1973, 224). The first phase in fact accords with neuropsychiatrist Nina Bull's corporeally rooted distinction between startle and fear and her identification of the initial kinetic pattern in the biphasic form of fear, namely, "the primary start or shock of surprise," "tonic rigidity," or "prolonged startled state" (Bull 1951, 100). This "startle pattern," she observes, "changes into the fear pattern through a more specific association of the stimulus with danger, and a concomitant attitude of preparation for escape. . . . The typical uneasiness resulting from this opposition of functions [total bodily riveted attention toward the stimulus to determine what it is and movement away from it as a source of danger] is the outstanding characteristic of fear" (105).

Stranger anxiety, while sometimes written of in terms of conflicting tendencies (see, for example, Sroufe 1996, 110–11, 113–14), does not have the kinetic precision of the Moro reflex, or of the startle reflex for that matter. Furthermore, stranger anxiety is not evident in all infants, nor, as psychologist T. G. R. Bower notes in accord with Sroufe's later evaluation, does it have a definitive beginning, "emerg[ing] suddenly at around eight months of age" (Bower 1979, 310). The phenomenon, however, is common enough to have a classic description: "The term 'stranger fear' as classically used refers to a complex of behaviors, central to which is prolonged loud crying on approach by a stranger, with turning away or movement away if the baby is mobile." It also has classic chronological contours: "This severe type of behavior is rarely seen before eight months of age; thereafter it gradually increases in intensity, reaching a peak in the second year of life and then gradually diminishing" (312).

The classic description and chronological contours may be kinetically glossed as follows: Apart from "prolonged loud crying," an infant in essence moves in such a way as to make the stranger disappear; it avoids the possibility of contact, it withdraws by putting itself out of touch and sight. In effect, the infant flees in its own kinetic way. In time, its "severe" reaction to an unfamiliar other diminishes, but there is no indication that the elemental fear of strangers disappears altogether. On the contrary, and as we shall presently see, from an existential perspective xenophobia is an altogether perduring human reaction sturdily anchored in phylogeny.

Though Rochat views stranger anxiety through the prism of attachment, his concept of exclusivity—cited earlier in Chapter 7—and his concept of social selectivity are relevant to the glossed description. "[J]ust prior to infants' entry into the people/object stage (nine to twelve months)," Rochat states, "[infants] start manifesting a novel sense of exclusivity with their primary caretakers, reacting with marked anxiety when encountering or left alone with a stranger ('eighth-month' or 'stranger anxiety')" (Rochat 2001, 162). As noted in the earlier chapter, his term "social selectivity" specifies "the growing attachment and selective attention of infants toward certain individuals in their environment" (166). While his focal emphasis is clearly on attachment, "exclusivity" and "social selectivity" can be and perhaps even should be also explicitly defined negatively with respect to strangers;[16] that is, for a period of time in infant life, a stranger is an unfamiliar intrusion into an exclusively select social world of familiar others, a stranger "markedly" disrupting an infant's "flow of familiar, exclusively select sensations," just as a sudden loud noise or loss of support earlier disrupted its flow of familiar sensations, and as other sudden environmental changes disrupted its flow of familiar sensations. In short, what is unfamiliar is now specifically social rather than environmental in general. Suddenness is not a factor, but the unfamiliar continues to intrude and fear of the unfamiliar persists but in a new form. In effect, what is unfamiliar remains an affectively disturbing and kinetically unsettling experience.

Rochat's reading of stranger anxiety as social selectivity is significant in a further respect. It points toward perhaps the most ominous social division that can appear in childhood and in later life, namely, xenophobia, which can blossom into an "Us against Them" mentality, and from there into an active social selectivity with respect to a range of others, others defined by their social standing, religious affiliations, ethnic practices, financial holdings, national allegiances, and so on. The active social selectivity may surface in multiple circumstances, in schools, businesses, along racial and ethnic lines, and so on, but it is most notable historically with respect to religion and nationalism. Fear of strangers translates into hatred of others whose beliefs and values—and at times whose language—are different from one's own. In this respect, attachment theory that describes positive infant relations is on par with stranger anxiety; that is, attachment theory too has far-reaching social relevance: we become attached to others whose beliefs and values match our own and whose national boundaries we share, for example; we socially select those with whom we affiliate and to whom we attach ourselves. Yet in spite of their parity, in contrast to attachment theory, xenophobia remains notably unexamined as a developmental character and enduring human affect. It appears to be taken seriously and investigated only in Europe, where studies by the Council of Europe (1995; Oakley 1996, 1997), Human Rights Watch/Helsinki (1995), and European Studies in Education (Dieckmann et al. 1997) have contributed case studies, practical guidance, analyses of violence, and so on.[17] It is of interest to note in this context that the word *xenophobia* literally specifies *fear* of strangers (from Greek *xenos,* alien, foreign, strange + *phobos,* fear, panic), but that Webster's 1996 New Universal Unabridged Dictionary defines xenophobia as "an unreasonable fear *or hatred* of foreigners or strangers or of that which is foreign or strange" (italics added), dating the definition from 1900–1905. Indeed, fear of strangers not only may be unreasonable, but may be motivated by hatred and aggressively acted out in violence. Xenophobia in adulthood in fact has its own kinetic pattern: it does not *withdraw*, avoiding contact by putting out of touch and sight in the manner of an infant; it assaults and attacks, avoiding contact by killing and annihilating.

Given the paucity of attention to xenophobia, it is not surprising that, like "the smiling response," the Moro reflex, and the early startle reflex, stranger anxiety is duly mentioned as a phenomenon in infant development, but is commonly treated as if it had precisely *no* relevance to later life. Indeed, it is as if xenophobia were a foreign feeling as well as foreign word, as if adults were impervious to fear—or hatred—of strangers, except perhaps in the vapid sense of the buzzword "adaptation" or in the specialized context of the cultural practice of war. With respect to the former, adaptation is a one-size-fits-all survival explanation that fails to shed edifying light on anything in particular. In the end, it simply explains life itself as a means to self-preservation. As for the cultural practice of war, it is notable that while the topic goes unmentioned in standard psychology texts, statements about wartime fear can be found in textbooks on *abnormal* psychology, such as James C. Coleman and colleagues' *Abnormal Psychology and Modern Life*. In a discussion titled "Causal Factors in Combat Exhaustion," Coleman and colleagues write, "Strangeness and unpredictability can be a source of severe threat and stress. When the soldier knows what to expect and what to do, the chances are much better of coming through with a minimum of psychological disorganization. But even the best training cannot fully prepare a soldier for all the conditions of actual battle" (Coleman et al. 1980, 177).

One might paraphrase the end sentence by saying that even the best upbringing and finest culture cannot fully prepare a developing child for all the conditions of actual life. Its familiar everyday lifeworld, like the familiar everyday lifeworlds of all animate creatures, is perpetually at the edge of the unfamiliar; the unknown is a permanent horizon of the known. Indeed, "adaptation" to that horizon requires acknowledgment of the fact that one cannot predict and control it any more than one can control and predict what literally lies ahead. *Real* adaptation requires unreserved acknowledgment of one's own vulnerability.

Accordingly, to view a soldier's fear of the unknown or his "psychological disorganization" as in any way an abnormal response to his situation elides foundational truths. It not only fails to acknowledge the fact that expectations, however solidly grounded in past experience and training, may be foiled, and that, like a stranger, the future is an unknown quantity, it says nothing of the affective import of putatively "knowing what to expect and what to do"; namely, that such putative knowledge putatively works virtually to efface underlying and at times overpowering feelings of vulnerability. The foundational vulnerability of being a body is muffled in such a view; the vulnerability that fuels feelings of fear—feelings of "severe threat and stress" in face of "strangeness and unpredictability"—is suppressed.

The point, of course, is that fear is not an unnatural, *abnormal* response to the unfamiliar or unknown, but a natural affect of animate life. In a specifically social sense, it is no less an affective attunement than smiling, but an attunement to one's own vulnerability in face of a stranger or of unpredictable others. In the beginning, it motivates one to care for oneself by putting the stranger out of touch and sight, that is, by fleeing in one's own kinetic way. Stranger anxiety is thus the earliest social marker of the normal disposition to protect oneself from possible danger from others, the earliest expression of one's own felt vulnerability in face of unknown others. Though not so named and specified, fear of the unfamiliar or unknown is indeed a phylogenetic primate character. Primatologist Jane Goodall, for example, describes at length how chimpanzees afflicted with polio are shunned by other chimpanzees, who find their strange ways of moving frightening (Goodall 1971, 219–24): "When Pepe, for instance, shuffled up the slope to the feeding area, squatting on his haunches with his useless arm trailing behind him, the group of chimps already in camp stared for a moment and then, with wide grins of fear, rushed for reassurance to embrace and pat each other while staring at the unfortunate cripple" (221). Goodall furthermore relates an episode in which chimpanzees actually attacked the afflicted member of their group (221–22). In a broader sense, xenophobia is territorially expressed by chimpanzees (Goodall 1990, 98–111) and by a few other primate species as well. Primatologist Thelma Rowell, in her review of territoriality in monkeys, provides an informatively precise definition of territory, noting first of all that the concept "was first developed by ornithologists, describing the defence of a small area by a cock bird, or by a pair of birds, during the breeding season." Given this notion of a defended terrain, Rowell states, "A territory, then, is a defended area . . . recognized by the sharp change of behaviour of its owner at its border—within the territory the owner is confident and aggressive, outside it he is timid and defensive towards strangers" (Rowell 1972, 164–65). Though she goes on to say, as do other primatologists, that territorial behavior so defined is not common among primates (168; see also Fedigan 1982, 75), her definition itself is keenly descriptive to the point of concern. Fear of strangers is a biologically driven disposition; it is phylogenetically as well as ontogenetically rooted. In reviewing studies showing a fundamental difference in behavior toward strangers as contrasted with behavior toward familiar group conspecifics, primate anthropologist Linda Fedigan succinctly underscores the evolutionary ties: "In general, [primate] individuals direct the most aggression toward adults of their own sex who are strangers to them" (Fedigan 1982, 77).[18] In its human form, with its home- and culture-grown escalations, fear of strangers can develop into virulent forms of xenophobia that attest not just to the strength of the fear and the felt vulnerability, but to the sizable impact that human differences can embody: individuals with a different skin color, with different beliefs and values, different ethnic origins and practices, and so on—become threats to one's own life and to the meaning of that life. Indeed, on the basis of home and cultural groomings, unreasonable hatreds of others flourish at times with a vengeance in humans.

Human escalations aside, fear of strangers is a natural sign that, unlike the Moro reflex and the startle reflex, is a natural *social* sign, and that, like directed smiling, is a natural *affective* social sign, in this instance a sign signaling alarm, apprehension, uneasiness, and so on, in face of an unknown other. It is, in other words, the first step in the socialization of fear. In first-person terms, feelings of fear in the presence of a stranger are the antithesis of feelings of friendliness; their appearance in infancy heralds a felt disposition to turn away from rather than to open toward. Viewed from this ontogenetic perspective, smiling and fear are the primary forms of human sociality, the antithetical strands that define human interactions at their most elemental level and that continue to be the basic modes in which human relate to each other throughout their lives. These primary forms of sociality require us to take infancy seriously. Quite specifically, they require us to recognize that we were all once *those infants*, little ones who were jarred by a sudden noise or loss of support, who were startled by other environmental happenings, who smiled at other humans, and who were anxious or fearful of strangers. Moreover it requires us to acknowledge that, however forgotten and however minimal any one of those early experiences might have been in any particular individual life, the experiences were hardly foreign experiences as we developed and aged, and are hardly foreign to us as adults. On the contrary, smiling and fear define the social extremes of our human nature and endure as elemental affective forms throughout the whole of our lives. Because the dangerous species remains blind to its fundamental human nature, especially to its own fears, it is requisite to explore those basically fearful facets of its nature and attempt to unravel how it comes to be what it is.

IV. AGGRESSIVE COMPLEXITIES IN THE SOCIALIZATION OF FEAR

It is a psychological truism that underneath anger is fear or hurt, or both. That is, rather than feeling fear or hurt, one feels anger toward the feared person or the one who inflicts—or has the potential to inflict—harm. Typically, one resents the person and feels aggressive toward him or her. Anger can thus camouflage the affective realities of fear and hurt, all the more so through entrenched habits of feeling and reacting. In what follows, attention is concentrated mainly on underlying realities of fear, though *mutatis mutandis*, in many instances a similar relationship may be spelled out with respect to hurt, not least because whoever harms one or can potentially harm one is—or becomes—an object of fear.

Feelings of fear—dread, apprehension, terror, uneasiness—are uncomfortable, even traumatic. The anger that rises up in their stead is akin to a desire to do away with the person or persons feared. Indeed, if one's anger were magical, it would likely destroy such persons and thereby destroy the agonizing feelings of threat, wariness, or terror prompted by them. By doing away with them, one would be free of fear and thus free of those oppressively disturbing experiences that arise coincident with such persons. One would, in effect, no longer be vulnerable. Anger might thus be seen by some people as functioning "adaptively" in the service of self-preservation.

Magical scripts aside, from the perspective of actual affective energies, a dynamically inverse relationship obtains between fear and anger. The more suppressed one's actual fears, the more intense, immediate, and reactive one's anger, the energy of an otherwise consuming or near consuming fear converting into the energy of a violent or near violent anger. Indeed, with respect to each other, fear and anger are experientially different bodily feelings; the affective dynamics of the one necessarily recede in a bodily felt sense as the affective dynamics of the other inflate and intensify. Moreover fear and anger are incompatible *kinetic* feelings: they move us to move in dynamically distinct patterns. They in fact move us to move in dynamically *oppositional* kinetic patterns. Classic descriptions attempt to capture their dynamic oppositionality in the words *away* and *against*, i.e., fear propels us away from, anger propels us against. Psychologist Joseph de Rivera's "geometry" of emotions brings the classic verbal descriptions to life, concretizing what we may designate their respective *kinetic forms*, that is, their basically contractive or extensive patterns of movement.[19] His geometry begins as follows: "If the arms are held out in a circle so that the fingertips almost touch, they may either be brought toward the body (a movement of contraction) or moved out in extension. The entire trunk may follow these movements." De Rivera points out that in this movement, the palms may be turned either toward the body or turned outward. After describing the corresponding feelings if the palms are facing toward the body, he describes the corresponding feelings if the palms are facing outward: "If the palms are rotated out, the extension movement corresponds to the thrusting against of anger, while the contraction intimates the withdrawal away of fear. . . . If one allows oneself to become involved in the movement and imagines an object, one may experience the corresponding emotion" (de Rivera 1977, 40; for a discussion of de Rivera's analysis and a fuller analysis of movement with respect to emotion, see Sheets-Johnstone 1999a; see also Bull 1951).

Moving through these kinetic forms, one can verify by one's own experience the oppositional dynamics of fear and anger, their kinetic contrariety in the flesh. In turn, one can begin to appreciate how the aggressive complexities of fear can run along a dynamic gradient from mild to extreme, i.e., from a benign aggressively charged anger that is transient and relatively trivial to a violent, unappeasable aggressively charged anger, the underlying fear being in any and all instances consistently proportional to the experienced anger's gradient value. As anger waxes and fear wanes, actual aggressive acts against others effectively dispel feelings of fear of them. Indeed, it is notable that in *moving against* in anger, one defends oneself *against* feelings of fear at the same time that one strikes out *against* another. What one would normally call "aggressive acts" develop at a relatively early age: "[h]itting, biting, scratching, pulling, kicking" appear "after the eighth month" (Spitz 1965, 285) or sometime "[i]n the second half of the first year" (Spitz 1983, 324). But as Spitz points out, such acts "[have] nothing to do with the popular meaning of the word 'aggressive'." The aggressive drive, he goes on to say, "designates one of the two fundamental instinctual drives operating in the psyche, as postulated by Freud" (324). He has in fact clarified the Freudian meaning of aggression at an earlier point, writing that the aggressive drive "indicates pressure as well as direction in relation to the object," and that it serves "to approach, to seize, to hold, to overpower, or to destroy the object." Quoting Freud, he states that aggression is expressed or carried out "through the instrumentality of a special organ. This special organ would seem to be the muscular apparatus" (Spitz 1965, 8–9).

Spitz's Freudian specification of "aggressive drive" and of the term "aggression" are echoed by psychiatrist Donald Winnicott, who first states, "at the start aggressive drives are associated with muscle erotism and not with anger or hate." Winnicott later points out more finely that "[i]n this vitally important early stage the 'destructive'. . . aliveness of the individual is simply a symptom of being alive, and has nothing to do with an individual's anger at the frustrations that belong to meeting the reality principle" (Winnicott 1989, 239). In short, psychoanalytic assessments of early hitting, biting, and other such acts affirm that early "aggressive acts" are not fear-driven; they are not the result of subversions of feelings of fear. However, it bears note that the "progressively destructive activities" of infants (Spitz 1983, 324), precisely because they are movement-driven, are precisely the kinds of activities that can be put in the service of later experiences of fear. In other words, ample time exists for the "muscular apparatus" and "muscle erotism" to be honed and for the aggressive complexities of fear to develop, and in being honed and in developing, for the specifically social "thrusting against" movements of anger to overpower the "withdrawal" movements of fear.

Indeed, many societies provide ample time for male indoctrination into the brotherhood of fearlessness, with its thematic that to be a man is to be unafraid and to be unafraid is to be powerful. The fraternal maxim is indeed quite simple: real men do not feel fear; they feel anger. Similarly, they do not cry. The epitome of a real man is a macho-male in whom the aggressive complexities of fear reach their zenith. The socialization of fear is thus of moment. Tomkins's extensive writings on fear and in particular on a cultivated maleness—machismo—warrant extended citation in this context.

Tomkins specifies the macho personality as made of three basic elements: virility (expressed in callous sexual relations with women), masculinity (expressed in violent acts), and physicality (expressed in finding excitement in danger). In part quoting from an article written with psychologist D. L. Mosher on macho males (Tomkins and Mosher 1987), Tomkins states, "The ideological script of the macho man is socially inherited within a macho culture by virtue of being a male. It 'exalts male dominance by assuming masculinity, virility, and physicality to be the ideal essence of real men who are adversarial warriors competing for scarce resources (including women as chattel) in a dangerous world'" (Tomkins 1991, 267). Embedded in this description are themes met with in previous chapters of the present text: the prominencing of warriors and the heroic honing of males, dominant male hierarchies, sheer physicality, and excitement. Indeed, Tomkins contrasts the fearlessness of the warrior with the shame the warrior wants to bring on his enemy (Tomkins 1995, 162–63). In the context of this analysis, he writes, "Fear is a deadly affect for successful warfare, being the most serious enemy within. It is assigned to the enemies to be defeated. One should try to terrorize one's enemy." In contrast, "[d]istress must be born manfully. A man must not weep, but rather make his enemy cry out in surrender. . . . [T]he warrior must above all be proud. . . . Shame is what the proud warrior should inflict on his enemy. He as warrior should rather die than surrender in shame" (162–63).

In his book-length treatment of anger and fear, Tomkins aptly describes the warrior's fear of shame and his shame of fear:

> Warrior cultures bind fear and shame together so that fear as such evokes shame because cowardice in battle violates pride. This bind is further magnified by its inverse: the ever-present possibility of defeat in any contest, with its necessary consequence of shame, makes the warrior ever alert and fearful of any scene which might evoke shame. He becomes just as afraid of shame as he is ashamed of fear. . . . Paradoxically, under such mutual magnification the enemy within becomes as dangerous and terrifying as the enemy without. (Tomkins 1991, 538–39)

Tomkins's insights into fear and its devolution into anger, and his subsequent insights into fear and shame are clearly powerful and trenchant. Moreover they dovetail at certain points with Rank's and Becker's insights into the importance of winning over an enemy, not just in warfare but in everyday life. When Tomkins observes that "[p]olemic within a profession or within a business or within a sport can be as severe in shame and in fear as in any war or honor culture" (Tomkins 1991, 539), he gives voice from a different perspective to the same elements of human nature as Rank and Becker do, elements cited in Chapter 1 in Rank's observation that "[e]very conflict over truth is in the last analysis just the same old struggle over . . . immortality," and in Becker's amplification of Rank's observation to the effect that "[i]f anyone doubts this [that conflict over truth is a struggle over immortality], let him try to explain in any other way the life-and-death-viciousness of all ideological disputes . . . if your adversary wins the argument about truth, *you die."* Of considerable further significance are the social dynamics that Tomkins itemizes as the developmental script necessary to the "magnification" of affects proper to machodom. The required dynamics succinctly specify the complex progressive relationship between anger and fear and the devolution of fear into anger. His summary itemization of the devolution warrants quotation in full:

> First, distress is intensified by the socializer until it is transformed into anger. Second, fear expression and fear avoidance are inhibited through parental dominance and contempt until habituation partially reduces them and activates excitement. Third, shame over residual distress and fear reverses polarity through counteraction into exciting manly pride over aggression and daring. Fourth, pride over aggressive and daring counteraction instigates disgust and contempt for shameful inferiors. Fifth, successful reversal of interpersonal control through angry and daring dominance activates excitement. Sixth, surprise becomes an interpersonal strategy to achieve dominance by evoking fear and uncertainty in others. Seventh, excitement becomes differentially magnified as a more acceptable affect than relaxed enjoyment, which becomes acceptable only during victory celebration. (267–68; see also Tomkins 1995, 162–63)

Aggressive complexities of fear can take different forms according to the way or ways in which fear is socialized. But as the fraternal maxim suggests and as the macho-male's acculturation straightforwardly demonstrates, the socialization easily runs developmentally along a male/female divide. We can begin to appreciate the import of the divide by asking what happens when the natural sign of fear is subverted, that is, what happens when spontaneously arising feelings of fear—whether of others, of death, of injury, or of pain—are denied, ignored, or suppressed and the natural affect *fear* is quashed. The body in question is no longer open to alarm, to the grip of fear, to apprehension, dread, and so on. A vulnerable body is denied, ignored, or suppressed along with fear. The kinetic reality of the Moro reflex—long gone as a neurological phenomenon in a faraway infancy, but enduring as the affective harbinger of fear in the form of a consummately vulnerable body exposed to the world—and the kinetic reality of the startle reflex are both experientially extirpated. Fear of strangers metamorphoses into the excitement of power and the cultivation of macho displays. In brief, feelings of vulnerability are no longer acknowledged or even a possibility. Palms turn outward and move outward, the body aggrandizing itself and its surrounding space as it thrusts against in aggressively charged anger.

It is instructive to consider the dynamic relationship of anger and fear when the latter is not quashed but is vibrantly alive in a body that, in the beginning, at the first sense of being in danger, feels "*sealed* into the 'situation'. Scared" (Cataldi 1993, 14). Philosopher Sue Cataldi's personal narrative of a mugging is a dramatically unembellished account of such a relationship, an account that, in its phenomenological acuity and candor, cannily illuminates the complex progression of feeling from "Scared" to "FURIOUS" to "*Sheer* terror" (11–16). Her aim is to elucidate the meaning of emotional depth, not simply through her personal narrative of a mugging, but through a diversity of descriptive accounts of emotion. She in fact describes her own experience of emotional depth amid a broad range of examples drawn from everyday language and from literature—Camus, Huxley, Orwell, Sophocles, Styron.

With respect to her own experience, she writes in the beginning that in "a fuzzy, inchoate way . . . something is 'wrong' "; she feels "vaguely threatened—like 'something funny is going on' "( 13). She writes of her confusion about being "so abruptly 'thrown off track'," and in her "Hindsight Reflections" notes, "I am momentarily dumb-founded, as though I do not understand what he is saying; and I have no inclination whatsoever to give him my purse. I continue to marvel at this—at why I felt no inclination to simply hand over my purse." She later adds, "I had no *time* to think about what was going on or what might happen" (14). When the mugger tries to yank the strap of her purse from her shoulder, Cataldi's fear and confusion over her "sealed situation" give way to anger: "I become FURIOUS," she writes, and "[b]efore I 'know' what I am doing, I'm beating him back with all my might, tearing at wool and wildly vacuous (drugged?) eyes. The 'strongest' obscenities I know are hurling from my mouth. I hear myself calling him a motherfucker. I cannot believe my mouth, his mouth. All I see are teeth: squared, spaced" (15). When she feels "the blunt of a blow coming down hard" on her head and sees a skinny silver knife," she is "slackened out of my righteous rage, and in the next sliver of a second, skewered to the ground beneath my feet by a profound feeling lasering its way down the length of my body.... I experience this crystalized hair's breadth of a feeling as ... *Sheer* terror" (15).

Cataldi later limns the experience of sheer terror, beginning with its initial felt sense when, she says, "Our body's first and instinctual response to the life threatening is, so to speak, to 'flash forward' and to 'play dead'. In terror, our flesh freezes, immediately.... Our heart slows down; and the blood drains from our face. Terror is also skin depthful. For terror is also a 'chilling' experience. We freeze in it. Even afterwards, we may shudder or tremble—even to think of it. This makes sense. The emotion has a 'finality.' Corpses are, after all, cold" (168–69). She goes on to describe in kaleidoscopic fashion the multiple facets of terror. What makes her affective narrative of moment here is that it lays bare elemental dynamics operative in aggressive complexities of fear. When one allows the complexities to come to light, when one actually attends to them and perhaps even attempts to describe them as Cataldi has, one readily sees that fear and anger are as inextricably woven feelings as they are incompatible feelings. Cataldi's narrative makes their inverse dynamic relationship palpably evident. Indeed, as the excerpts from her narrative show, feelings of fear and anger present a profoundly inverse flow of felt affective energies. Fathoming these inverse energies at deeper experiential levels, we correlatively begin to fathom what happens when fear is suppressed: not only is a sizable domain of natural human feeling lost, but in virtue of its loss, sizable misunderstandings arise as to what constitutes courage, bravery, valor, heroism, and "manliness." It is important to illustrate the import of these misunderstandings to morality.

Aggressive habits of feeling and action that mushroom into macho-male aggressive habits of response typically grow in proportion to the cultivation of a fearless soul. But a fearless soul is *not* to be mistaken for courage, valor, manliness, and the like. Courage is present only in relation to fear that is real, lived, palpable, where danger is imminently present and actively faced, and where either intense social feelings and concerns or intense self-feelings and concerns motivate actions that override fear, precisely as in Cataldi's becoming "FURIOUS" and beating on the male who is attacking her. Her striking out against in such circumstances was courageous. The very *machismo* of macho males prevents them from being correspondingly courageous: it prevents them from feeling the feeling essential to courageous acts. To use de Rivera's kinetically graphic paradigm, it prevents them from ever turning palms inward and withdrawing. Of course, not all courageous acts are anger-driven, as in Cataldi's experience, but when they are, and however prompted by immediate feelings of outrage, intrusion, affront, or abuse, they are acts underwritten by fear. One might even say that acts of courage are by definition acts in defiance of felt fear. In a courageous act, courage supervenes on fear, overriding it. Cataldi's move from being sealed into the situation, constricted, scared, to being furious and striking out exemplifies just such supervenience. Fear and anger indeed move in different ways through the body and move us in ways dynamically opposite to each other. By denying fear, macho males deny themselves the experience of the oppositional dynamics. Thrusting against in anger and denying the contractions of fear, they are incapable of courage.

Studies of fear and aggression in young boys are illuminating in ways that ultimately connect with psychological assessments of machismo, of male violence, and of wartime military experience. In their classic study *The Psychology of Sex Differences,* psychologists Eleanor Maccoby and Carol Jacklin present exhaustive reviews of developmental studies of aggression and other social behaviors together with critical appraisals of current theories and conclusions drawn therefrom. With respect to studies primarily of childhood aggression, they write that "males are consistently found to be more aggressive than females," and that "[t]he behavioral sex difference is found in a variety of cultures" (Maccoby and Jacklin 1974, 228). They note, "The aggressiveness of the male has been thought to express itself in a number of ways other than in interpersonal hostility," and in consequence they examine studies of competition and dominance, both of which are "thought to have an aggressive element." They point out with respect to the latter relationship that aggression in nonhuman animal research studies is carried out in "the context of the establishment and maintenance of dominance hierarchies" (247). With respect to the former relationship, they find that among young boys, dominance "is largely achieved by fighting or threats" (263), i.e., through competition, noting in a later discussion that "during childhood a boy's aggressiveness has a considerable bearing upon his ability to dominate other boys" (274). They open their summary of studies of aggression with the statement, "The evidence is strong that males are the more aggressive sex," and emphasize their having found weak support for "the widely held view that the two sexes are actually equivalent in aggressive motivation," girls being "conditioned to be afraid of displaying their aggressive tendencies openly, showing them instead in attenuated forms." They say the view "is inconsistent with much that is known about the nature and development of aggression in the two sexes" (274), and turn instead toward a biological explanation, namely, that males are biologically disposed toward "a greater state of readiness to learn and display aggressive behavior," and this on the basis of "the relationship between sex hormones and aggression" (274). They conclude, as noted in Chapter 4, "The evidence for greater male aggressiveness is unequivocal" (see also, for example, Bramblett 1976, 99: "Aggressive displays and postures are a conspicuous part of adult male roles in anthropoids"; and Fedigan 1982, 87: "Almost all reviews of sex differences in aggression begin with the statement that males are more aggressive than females"").

It should be noted, however, that in concluding that the evidence for greater male aggressiveness is unequivocal, Maccoby and Jacklin also point out that "[m]ale competition in real-life settings frequently takes the form of groups competing against groups . . . an activity that involves within-group cooperation as well as between-group competition, so that cooperative behavior is frequently not the antithesis of competitiveness." They point out further, again, as noted in Chapter 4, that "[m]ost research on competition has been conducted in contrived situations that fail to take account of this fact [within-group cooperation] and that do not correspond well with the naturalistic conditions under which competitiveness is most intense" (Maccoby and Jacklin 1974, 274). Compelling instances of cooperation are of course found most readily in wartime. The term "cooperation," however, fails to do justice to the caring concern of one male comrade for another. Eloquent testimonial to this concern is given by Brian Keenan in his book detailing horrifyingly punitive incarcerations he experienced over a four-and-a-half-year period as a hostage of jihadists in Lebanon (Keenan 1992). Statistical testimonial is given in psychiatrist David Marlowe's ratings of events linked to high levels of stress in the Gulf War: "Buddy killed in action" generated by far the greatest stress, "Buddy wounded in action" was rated second, but both events generated less stress than "Attacked by enemy artillery" (Marlowe 2001, 142). Prior to combat, the amount of worry or stress connected with the thought of a buddy being killed or wounded in action was recorded as even higher (137). Clearly, it is not only a matter of not taking "cooperation" into proper account, as Maccoby and Jacklin point out, but a matter of realizing that "cooperation" falls far short of capturing the capacity of men to care not only *for* each other, but *about* each other, and in so caring, be motivated to act courageously on behalf of others. Cooperation may be purely pragmatic or it may be affective—or it may be both.

In the opening paragraph of their succeeding chapter, "On the Origins of Psychological Sex Differences," Maccoby and Jacklin temper their biological explanation: while the acquisition of certain sex-typical behaviors is "related to certain sex-linked biological predispositions," it is nonetheless socially shaped. In other words, biological predispositions do not "deny the importance of social learning" (Maccoby and Jacklin 1974, 275). In effect, biology is destiny only if social shaping moves it in that direction. Maccoby and Jacklin point out, for example, that a study involving children in six cultures "found that boys who had been involved in caring for younger siblings were less aggressive in their daily encounters with age-mates than boys who had not had such responsibilities." They comment, "It would appear, then, that aggression is largely incompatible with child care, and that the process of caring for children moderates aggressive tendencies" (372). They are not thereby saying that mothers are free of aggression. On the contrary, they state, "Studies of battered children indicate that mothers are at least as likely as fathers to brutalize their children" (372). What they are saying is that having the responsibility of caring for others and taking that responsibility seriously in the sense of caring about others promotes nuturant behavior.

Young boys who are acculturated psychologically and socially to be macho males are not encouraged to care responsibly for and about others and thereby not only fail to experience a natural range of human feeling, but magnify the feelings that quash fear. They thus develop a quite specific range of social affective proclivities. It is instructive to consider these social affective proclivities in terms of what Tomkins terms "scripts"—"*sets of ordering rules* for the interpretation, evaluation, prediction, production, or control of scenes" ["scenes" being, in a very loose sense, "real-life situations" that may be transient or habitual] (Tomkins 1991, 84). Scripts are driven by specific affects and ideologies, and result in the enactment of what may be described as a certain social dynamics constituting relatively set but modifiable social behaviors. Tomkins's analysis of the socialization of fear and anger clearly validates their inverse affective energies at the same time that it delineates the affective social consequences of the suppression of male fear. Moreover the socialization dynamics of fear and anger harbor a male/female divide that Tomkins recognizes and aptly describes without simplifying the complexity of the emotions. On the contrary, he demonstrates in detail the various ways in which fear and anger may be *developmentally* scripted in the course of growing up and how the scripting is in each instance tied to ideological principles. In this context, he points out specifically how ideological principles condition affect stratification and how affect stratification conditions male/female stratification: e.g., men are strong, women are weak; if a man is not strong, he is not a man; women are "loving, timid, distressed, shy, and humble"; a woman not characterizable as such, i.e., a woman who takes on warrior characteristics, is a "masculine female [and] becomes as repellent as an effeminate male" (Tomkins 1995, 163; see also 383). It is notable that Tomkins considers the affective stratification that emotionally segregates males and females to be the result of competition for resources: "Social stratification rests upon the affect stratification inherent in adversarial contests" (Tomkins 1991, 163). Though he does not mention male-male competition as a biological matrix in this context or allude to evolutionary continuities—except to observe that "[m]any animals begin stratification in contests between males for exclusive *possession* of females," and to remark that "[t]he paradox in this is that the prize of the contest, the female, is diminished to a position of lower status"—it is abundantly clear that human male-male competition sharply stratifies emotions along a male/female divide. In particular, human male-male competition critically specifies which emotions are of merit and which are not, and axiologically separates males and females in the process.

In sum, in adversarial and warring cultures (Tomkins 1991, e.g., 162,

163, 356), scripting indoctrinates children affectively toward certain feelings and away from others, which is to say that, from a developmental perspective, any particular emotion within the natural range and flow of human emotions may be suppressed, distorted, elaborated, or exaggerated by parents just as it may be by the home culture itself. Indeed, parental groomings exist alongside cultural groomings (for illustrations and analyses of the latter, see Sheets-Johnstone 1994b), reinforcing or resisting them; parents may suppress what they deem affectively and ideologically repugnant or undesirable, exaggerate what they deem affectively and ideologically worthy and positive, and so on, supporting or opposing cultural values in the course of doing so. With respect to affects in particular, parental groomings, like cultural groomings, rework what is evolutionarily given, i.e., they rework what is natural to the human range of emotions and hence what is innate and dispositionally present.

A final point regarding the aggressive complexities of fear and their socialization warrants explicit attention. In particular, it is important to acknowledge and underscore the fact that human females are indirectly part of human male-male competition, not only applauding and being attracted to the hero along the biological lines of female choice, but being equally caught up ideologically and emotionally in the pursuit of power, glory, resources, and so on. Human females are indeed caught up in the glories and fruits of competition and in the ignominy and destitution of defeat, identifying alike with the victories and grievances in battles won and lost. They are furthermore not infrequently a direct and sizable part of the competition, their bodies being literally up for grabs: rape is considered not only part of the booty of victors, but a not incidental perquisite of being a warrior in the first place. As Tomkins points out, virility is proved by callous sex. Moreover human females can be part of the competition in the form of the military itself, some of them exemplifying Tomkins's depiction of the masculine female, the female who, like a true warrior, enacts shaming behaviors that demean and humiliate the enemy.[20]

In sum, human individuals may certainly be opaque to themselves, but the dark side of human nature is surely not socially invisible.

## V. ACQUISITIVE COMPLEXITIES IN THE SOCIALIZATION OF FEAR

The previous section underscores the fear-fueled, life-destroying proclivities and habits of the dangerous species within the confines of its own members. The present section underscores the same proclivities and habits but from a different perspective. It is not fear of strangers directly, but fear of loss and want that in various guises looms threateningly and in turn drives the dangerous species to appropriate and to consume beyond measure. The framework in which the destructive proclivities and habits are evident is accordingly wider in that what is preyed on and consequently at risk is not simply human lives, but the life of the planet itself and the flora and fauna that that life supports. As described in the first section of this chapter, by plundering resources, *Homo nescius et barbarus* not only decimates its own kind and fouls its own nest, but decimates other species, and destroys and depletes Nature. This unnatural species is thus aptly described along Hobbesian lines as engaging in two forms of nastiness: it harms its own kind, and it harms other species and the earth. Moreover in light of its predacious behaviors toward others and following further along the lines of Hobbes, the species is aptly described as solitary and poor; its acquisitive practices are indeed tied to its being essentially solitary, poor, and nasty. From this perspective, it is not "the *life* of man" that is first of all solitary, poor, and nasty, but *man himself* who is. The priority is ironically and readily apparent in contemporary environmental struggles, that is, in the fact that multiple organizations are formed to protect and preserve endangered species and endangered resources, to save the earth itself by moving to sustainable ways of living. At its base, the priority resides in man's seemingly endless pursuit of *more*. A greedy and gluttonous "taking, taking, taking" turns his life into a relentless rampaging of nature, into acts in which he is heedless or uncaring of the natural costs, often giving back nothing but toxins that are self- as well as other-destructive. His greed and gluttony are driven on the surface by the pursuit of pleasure and a desire for dominance in the power and wealth hierarchy, but at base they are driven by a fear of death, loss, and want, all of which are transformed into a relentless pursuit of *more*.[21]

Kingdon's thesis of hominid evolution intersects with and corroborates this picture of the dangerous species. Niche-stealing is not a practice in a dim hominid past; it has been alive and well for centuries, and is robustly alive and well in the present global world. At its core, niche-stealing entails wanton desecrations and annihilations that signal a stunting if not dissolution of sense-making, since what was once naturally abundant is depleted and cannot be regenerated, what was once alive is killed off and cannot be reborn. In such circumstances, the rationality of caring has no ground on which to root itself and flourish, and is in fact nowhere to be found. Acquisitiveness rules out its possibility. A persistent and remorseless rapacity geared wholly and exclusively to one's wants precludes a recognition, let alone valuing, of virtually any other being.

Present-day Western science similarly intersects with and corroborates this picture of the dangerous species. Present-day Western science is pivotally addicted to technology in the form of war and medicine, the former in the service of doing away selectively with human life, the latter in the service of selectively prolonging it. Robotic soldiers are envisioned along with not just an extended human life span, but one free of all disease.[22] In mobilizing humans toward the expectation of *more*, present-day Western science underwrites more than is either natural or necessary to humans, a *more* in which precisely robots will fight their wars and they will live to be "Methuselahs."[23] Interestingly enough, early Greeks had a word for this excess: *pleonazein*, to be or have more than enough, a word which derives from the Greek *pleion*, more. The English word *pleonasm*, meaning "the use of more words than are necessary to express an idea" (e.g., a free gift), derives from the Greek. Lexical pleonasms, however, are paltry and benign compared with living pleonasms, whose effects can be lethal; avaricious, edacious, dissolute humans are not "airy nothing[s]" conjured into being by a "poet's pen" (Shakespeare, *A Midsummer Nights Dream*, Act 5, scene 1). Their relentless support of a pleonastic culture is motivated not simply by the immediate pleasures it brings, but by the fears it suppresses. Their pursuit of *more* is in other words of a piece with size, power, and death. The fear of death and its corollary, the desire for more life—not more life in general, but more life *for me*—go hand in hand. Size and power are thus solidly and unshrinkingly on the side of *more*; they effectively keep the fear of death at bay.

From the perspective of the socialization of fear, the relentless pursuit of more is the sign of an ever-gnawing but largely suppressed lack, in Hobbesian terms, a poorness and solitariness that hover silently but threateningly at the core of one's existence and that are indirectly ministered to and catered to, indirectly in that the threatening existential condition is acted out in the pursuit of more. In effect, the pursuit of more signifies an anxious emptiness covered over with never-ending fulfillments.[24] Philosopher David Loy has written of *lack* not along the different channels in which the socialization of fear is enacted, but in the context of a missing self as it is treated in psychotherapy, existentialism, and Buddhism. Loy draws converging lines from all three perspectives and anchors them predominantly in Buddhist thought. His analysis of lack centers on a groundless sense of self, or as he more dramatically puts it, on "the quite valid suspicion that 'I' *am not real*" (Loy 2000, xi). In this context, he discusses a broad range of topics—anxiety, love, meaning, Heidegger on death and time, Sartre on freedom and the dual nature of being, and more—in each instance relating the particular discussion to "a sense-of-self" that is felt as a lack never to be fulfilled" (36). His point is that once we let go of the need to be "real," we are transformed into a connection with everything: "The sense-of-self is not self-existing but a mental construction which experiences its groundlessness as a *lack*" (101). When we realize that the self is nothing but a mental construction, we liberate ourselves from our own chains: "[D]riven by *lack*, desire becomes a sticky attachment that tries to fill up a bottomless pit. Without *lack,* the serenity of our no-thing-ness, that is, the absence of any fixed nature, grants the freedom to become anything" (101).[25]

A tenuous resonance obtains between *lack* and the pursuit of more that is spelled out in Loy's later exemplification of ways in which humans attempt to cope with their sense of *lack*. When they liberate themselves, he states, "the seriousness of adult preoccupations reveals itself to be—nothing but childish games" (132), childish games of "trying to become real." In the subsequent chapter that bears that title ("Trying to Become Real"), he itemizes and discusses four such games or "projects" (152): "The pursuit of fame and money are attempts to realize oneself through symbols; romantic love tries to fill in one's *lack* with the beloved; technological progress has become our collective attempt to ground ourselves by 'developing' the environment into our ground, until the whole earth testifies to our reality" (134). As Loy describes them, and as might be apparent, the projects coincide with the pursuit of *more*, not only insofar as *more*, in the sense of becoming added to or plentiful, is a close conceptual contrary of *lack*, but insofar as *the pursuit of more* is what one might call the "natural attitude" of humans toward their "lapsed" condition; it is the unnamed but common, i.e., unenlightened, ontological answer to "the quite valid suspicion that 'I' *am not real*'." That Loy should choose the pursuit of fame and money as central aspects of that "natural condition" is indeed notable: fame and money are, respectively, the precise opposites of "solitary" and "poor"; they are human *answers* to what Hobbes describes as "the life of man." One could in fact say that, as seen from opposite ends of the human spectrum, fame is another name for solitary and money another name for poor; each is an answer to the underlying human condition that is "the life of man." Further still, and again, from opposite ends of the human spectrum, just as solitary and poor are anchored in fear as Hobbes observes, so also are fame and money. The anchorage is only marginally recognized in Loy's account because ontological matters are his primary concern. While the projects are at times specified at their motivational core, i.e., as driven by fear, their analysis remains at a preeminently symbolic level. For example, Loy quotes at length from philosopher Donald Verene's discussion of Hegel's analysis of the master/slave relationship (Verene 1984) to the effect that "[w]hat rides the back of the servant-self is the fear that it is nothing" (Loy 2000, 151). He ties the fear to the delusive sense-of-self, but focuses no further on fear itself. Similarly, when he writes of "our economic system"—capitalism—as "requir[ing] continual growth if it is not to collapse" (148), he writes forthrightly of fear, but only in passing and without elaboration: "What motivates it [continual growth] is not need but fear, for it feeds on and feeds our sense of *lack*" (148). In short, what is pursued is seen not as *more*, but as *realness*.[26]

The point is that, however much affects recede in the distance, they remain at the core of our being. *Their* realities cannot be denied no matter how much a "self" is nothing more than a mental construction. Affective realities can be suppressed, willfully orchestrated, neglected, or ignored in myriad other ways, but the energies generating and fueling them are not diminished. As with the pursuit of more, the energies can only be transformed. So transformed, the fear of death, loss, and want—or in Hobbesian terms, the fear of death, solitude, and poverty—becomes all the more locked in for it is robbed of its force and debarred from showing itself. Similarly with what Loy describes as *lack* and the projects that attempt to answer to it. The "quite valid suspicion that 'I' am not real" would count for nothing were it not saturated in fear, for it is the bodily trepidations and spasms of fear and not mere suspicion, however valid, that infuses us with anxious, quivering tensions and drives us to acts that dispel them. *More* is a bulwark against such disquieting human realities, but it does not and cannot alter them; it can only suppress them. It is thus not only that fame and money—whether as Loy symbolically conceives them or as actually pursued and experienced—cannot provide what is not there to begin with, but that fame and money can only cover over a fear of meaninglessness or of a future that is not there. Loy indirectly suggests just this when he writes of the letting-go of the ego and moreover implicitly recognizes in just this context the reality of such fears and the need to awaken experientially to their reality:

> *In terms of life and death,* the ego is that which believes itself to be alive and fears death; hence the ego, although only a mental construction, will face its imminent disappearance with horror. Uncovering that repression, recovering the denial of death for consciousness requires the courage to suffer. Our struggle against death is usually redirected into symbolic games of competition, as the urge to defeat our opponent or at least be a little better than our neighbor. To free us from the paralysis of death-in-life, the energy which is distorted into such symptomatic activities must be translated back into its more original form, the terror of death, and that terror endured. (57)

In sum, however much existential fears are suppressed, and however much their energies are converted into something else, they remain at the core of our being. In effect, however much humans aggrandize themselves in the pursuit of more to protect themselves from the terrors of suffering and oblivion, they remain fundamentally ignorant of themselves. Rather than awakening to the nature of human nature and the nature of life itself, they subvert fundamental affective realities, identifying instead with the entitlements and abundance of their wealth, the feats that have made them heroes and the glory that has come their way, the splendor and newness of their possessions, and so on.[27] Their identifications turn them away from the basic affect that actually motivates them and propel them instead toward affects that transmute them into the dangerous species.

We might note that what was formerly seen under the rubric of scarcity, i.e., the competitive pursuit of resources for mere subsistence—to allay famine or starvation, for instance, or to provide adequate shelter—is more than offset today by the competitive pursuit of more simply for the sake of more. *More* is the antithesis, the reverse, of scarcity. Like scarcity, it can propel individuals to plunder, kill, consume, devour, and so on, not for the sake of life itself, but for the sake of whatever maximizes and embellishes, whatever guarantees a life overflowing with riches of one kind or another, all such riches armoring one against any threat of loss or want, and even against death. Living in the moment intensifies the competitive pursuit of more. One ensures one's immediate life by surrounding oneself with an excess of life-sustaining commodities, engorging oneself with food and fineries beyond measure, glutting and stuffing more and more into one's life. In this context of scarcity and *more*, a final observation is warranted. When the power to alleviate suffering in the pursuit of happiness is more important than the power to inflict suffering in the pursuit of more, then humans will have achieved the self-insight necessary to a life-enhancing rather than life-destroying way of life. To arrive at this self-insight is to discover that one has more than enough, and indeed has had enough of *more*.

## VI. ON PSYCHOLOGICAL IGNORANCE

The inverse energies and consequences of the suppression of fear are indirectly corroborated in psychological studies of men in everyday life and in wartime service. In confronting the question, "why are men so violent?" psychiatrist Anthony Clare recalls the words of a forensic psychiatrist who, in preface to answering the question, identifies "the usual, fashionable suspects—testosterone, head injury, poor nutrition, crime, poverty, unemployment and youth," but who goes on instead to conclude that the key factor is psychology (Clare 2000, 67). As Clare himself later urges, "What is needed is a proper, systematic and co-ordinated introduction to human psychology—the psychology of personality, the psychology of behaviour, the psychology of feelings, the psychology of individuals and groups, the psychology of memory and will and impulse control, the psychology of sexuality." He points out that "[w]e teach our children the history of war, but little of its psychology. . . . We teach our children the intricacies of the human body, but little of the functioning (and malfunctioning) of the human mind" (218). In short, as Clare intimates, the violence of men is at the most elemental level a matter of psychological ignorance. He himself declares, "There is nothing intrinsically, innately, biologically incorrigible about male aggression and violence" (217).

Bringing psychological ignorance to light, however, is not simply a matter of acknowledging the falsity of biological determinism. Neither is it simply a matter of male violence or of males pure and simple.

Females support war, "cheering on the troops," for example, as psychologist Lawrence LeShan observes (LeShan 1992, 91). LeShan even affirms, "There is ... no real evidence that women are less attracted to war than are men" (90). Though LeShan's observation and affirmation are breezy and lack bio-socio-political substance, there is no doubt but that females are no less psychologically ignorant than males. In his article "The Indiscreet Charm of Tyranny," socio-cultural historian Ian Buruma substantiates the point from a different perspective: "The terrifying thing about dictatorship is people's willingness to believe in the divine aspirations of dictators. The hundreds of thousands of screaming, crying, praying, book-waving, flag-waving men and women in Beijing, Berlin, Moscow, or Pyongyang, worshiping their leaders, are not only doing so because they are forced to; many, perhaps even most, really are caught up in the hysteria. This is partly a matter of crowd psychology. Collective emotion can spread like a brush fire" (Buruma 2005, 36). The psychological ignorance of females, however, is most commonly played out in domains other than war. Maladroit mothers who play favorites with their children, for example, or who do not allow or encourage their infants to develop their own autonomy, who rush them into action, swooping them up in their own aims and desires, their own thoughts and affects, and so on, deprive their children—male or female—of growing up into and creating a life of their own. In Spitz's terms, there is no reciprocity or dialogue; in Stern's terms, there is no attunement; in Winnicott's terms, there is not a "good-enough" mother. However described, a maladroit mother is a soul-destroying mother, who, through preferential treatment, or through lack of tactile softness or comforting tones, lack of creative energies or a sense of play, stunts an infant in one way or another, passing on variations of her own dysfunctionality to her infant or encouraging new dysfunctionalities to emerge in answer to her own.

Psychological ignorance takes its toll wherever it is present and in whomever it is present. It is at bottom not a delimited ignorance of psychology, but more broadly, an ignorance of the nature of human nature, hence an interdisciplinary ignorance, whose malevolent effects are unconfined with respect to sex, race, class, religion, or nation. Clare himself suggests as much when he speaks of what we teach and do not teach our children. Psychology alone is thus not the answer to aggression, violence, and machismo, to brutalizing or maladroit mothers, or to any other form of human behavior that harms other beings. Education about human nature is the answer, and this answer is unmistakably multidisciplinary. It embraces philosophy, history, art, literature, sociology, psychology, and biology equally. Until ignorance of the nature of human nature is directly acknowledged and in turn investigated, however, and with the same intensity, the same fervor, the same funding, and the same institutional and societal support as *the brain*, for example, or the human genome, there is hardly reason for hope that education will or even can rise to the occasion and that harmful and malevolent behaviors will change. Further still, until human nature is specifically investigated phenomenologically, there is little reason for hope that education can supply the answer and that harmful or malevolent behaviors will change. Experiential analyses are crucial because they speak from the heart of life. Phenomenological analyses concretize human nature in its living flesh, precisely as Cataldi's narrative demonstrates. Moreover phenomenological studies are foundationally concerned with origins, answering to the question of what Husserl called "constitution" or how we come to have the meanings and values we have. What is needed is, as Husserl put it, *"a radical clarification"* of meaning and origin—for him specifically, *"a radical clarification of the sense and origin* (or of the sense in consequence of the origin) *of the concepts: world, Nature, space time, psychophysical being, man, psyche, animate organism, social community, culture,* and so forth" (Husserl 1973, 154), his "and so forth" clearly embodying the need of *"a radical clarification"* of death, stranger, Other, difference, and evil.[28] These latter concepts are saturated in affects on the dark side of human nature. They require elucidation if human nature is to be understood. Indeed, the psychological studies that Clare proposes need phenomenological clarification, and this because existential dimensions of human life can be fathomed in depth only if examined experientially in depth, which is to say that questions concerning humans come to life only in the realities of life itself.

The dark side of human nature exists equally in males and females. Males offer the more ready exemplification, however, not only in terms of an abundant literature on male violence and aggression and of an amply public expression of their dark side in war, massacres, murder, rape, and multiple kinds of other criminal assaults, but in terms of the conventional "schism" between emotions and males in the first place: males are rational, not emotional. Psychological studies of males affirm quite otherwise, both indirectly and directly. Initial steps can in fact be taken toward a radical clarification of received wisdom by consulting key studies. While connected with the earlier discussion of how machismo is cultivated, the considerations that follow have a different aim, namely, to bring the dark side of human nature into the light and thereby show the need for self-knowledge, and correlatively, the need to develop a capacity to reflect and awaken to the motivation to harm. Freud's noble but psychologically short-sighted, even arrogant rationalized attempt to explain World War I provides a notable if indirect example of these needs.

In his 1915 essay "Thoughts for the Times on War and Death," in the section titled "The Disillusionment of the War," Freud writes that in spite of differing living conditions and values, in spite of animosities, and so on, "[w]e had expected the great ruling powers among the white nations upon whom the leadership of the human species has fallen, who were known to have cultivated world-wide interests, to whose creative powers were due our technical advances in the direction of dominating nature, as well as the artistic and scientific acquisitions of the mind— peoples such as these we had expected to succeed in discovering another way of settling misunderstandings and conflicts of interest" (Freud 1958, 207). He goes on to speak of how the "fellowship in civilization was from time to time disturbed by warning voices" (209), of how a "mutual comprehension" between civilized nations is "so slight that the one can turn with hate and loathing upon the other" (211), of how "the brutality in behaviour shown by individuals" is at odds with "partakers in the highest form of human civilization" (213), of how "the inmost essence of human nature consists of elemental instincts, which are common to all men" and how the instincts themselves "are neither good nor evil" (213). He explains on the basis of these and other observations "that our mortification and our grievous disillusionment regarding the uncivilized behaviour of our world-compatriots in this war are shown to be unjustified. They were based on an illusion to which we had abandoned ourselves. *In reality our fellow-citizens have not sunk so low as we feared, because they had never risen so high as we believed*" (218; italics added).

Freud glosses his explanation with the idea that war is based on regressive behavior, behavior typical of earlier emotional life. Thus, just as there may be regressive behavior in the individual, so "the transformations of instinct on which our cultural adaptability is based, may also be permanently or temporarily undone by the experiences of life" (220). His concluding statement on the subject is astonishingly naive:

"Undoubtedly," he writes, "the influences of war are among the forces that can bring about such regression; therefore we need not deny adaptability for culture to all who are at the present time displaying uncivilized behaviour, and we may anticipate that the refinement of their instincts will be restored in times of peace" (220).

Freud's sanguine thoughts about war and peace, together with the racial, technological, and theoretical allegiances they articulate, are emblematic of a psychological ignorance tethered to an elite society and to psychoanalytic doctrines that preclude insight into basic human affective social dispositions and their motivating force. In short, rather than to instincts and to regression, we must look to what is there from the beginning in the affective social nature of humans and honor those elemental affective social proclivities for what they are: defining features of human social life that motivate actual movements toward, away, and against others. Morality is clearly tied to our bodies first and foremost. As we have seen, affects move us to move in both life-enhancing and life-destroying ways. The less we acknowledge the full range of our basic social affects, the less we know ourselves, the less awakened we are to our dark side, and the more likely we are to compromise the possibility of a morally enlightened life. Surely enough has been written by male as well as female writers on the "schism" between emotions and males for societies to rise to the educational occasion.

The need is all the more pressing in light of Freud's thoughts about death that follow upon his thoughts about war. Several of the former are perceptive but at the same time at odds with what he has written of war. For example, in relation to "[p]ious souls, who cherish the thought of our remoteness from whatever is evil and base," he comments. "What no human soul desires there is no need to prohibit. . . . The very emphasis of the commandment *Thou shalt not kill* makes it certain that we spring from an endless ancestry of murderers, with whom the lust for killing was in the blood, as possibly it is to this day with ourselves" (230). While hyperbolic in terms of a "lust for killing being in the blood," the basic thought of an ancestry of war is certainly justified by even the most casual reading of human history; it is furthermore supported by Keeley's detailed archaeological research studies of war, as we saw in Chapter 1. The same basic thought, however, is plainly at odds with the idea that "the refinement" of instincts of "all who are at the present time displaying uncivilized behaviour . . . will be restored in times of peace" (220). Moreover Freud's further comment on the unconscious, that it "will murder even for trifles" (232), is equally at odds. He equates the unconscious with primitive man: "[I]f we are to be judged by the wishes in our unconscious, we are, like primitive man, simply a gang of murderers" (232). He later declares that the unconscious is "as murderously minded towards the stranger, as divided or ambivalent towards the loved, as was man in earliest antiquity" (234). With respect to the ambivalence, he affirms that love and hate are "twin opposites" of human nature, and declares, "Nature, by making use of these twin opposites, contrives to keep love ever vigilant and fresh, so as to guard it against the hate which lurks behind it" (234). However, when he states, "War is not to be abolished; so long as the conditions of existence among the nations are so varied, and the repulsions between peoples so intense, there will be, must be, wars" (235), he all but nullifies his previous thoughts that war is something of an aberration of civilized society and nullifies his comments concerning love and hate as well since "repulsions between peoples" must likewise be Nature's way of keeping their love of each other "vigilant and fresh."

In such mixed theoretical circumstances, a lucid and rigorous clarification of the "twin opposites" at the "instinctive" heart of human nature becomes impossible: at one moment Freud indicates that in general, i.e., whether a matter of hate or war, evil is a *privatio bono,* that man is basically loving and that Nature has so provided to keep love "vigilant and fresh" through evil; at the next moment, he indicates that, whatever Nature has provided in the way of "vigilant and fresh" love, that love will be, and "must be" overridden by war. In effect, a form of biological determinism is set in place that appears unalterable. Any appeal to education would seem in vain.

Freud's suggestion that humans recognize the finality of their lives is nonetheless compelling. In particular, he asks if it would not be better "to give death the place in actuality and in our thoughts which properly belongs to it, and to yield a little more prominence to that unconscious attitude toward death which we have hitherto so carefully suppressed," since "in the unconscious every one of us is convinced of his own immortality" (223). Without naming it, his question crystallizes the human fear of death. What eludes him, however, is the tight connection between the human fear of death and the doing of evil. Rank's and Becker's perspicuous grasp of the connection is decisive. So long as one remains in the dark by clinging to immortality ideologies or otherwise denying death, one remains psychologically ignorant. So long as one does not fathom that psychological ignorance, the fear of death heightens its power to express itself in life-destroying ways, perpetuating evil.

Marlowe's study of "the nature and power of combat stress" further substantiates the reality of psychological ignorance and the need to bring the dark side of human nature into the light. In his book *The Psychological and Psychosocial Consequences of Combat and Deployment*, Marlowe demonstrates the ignorance and the need not from the viewpoint of an "instinct" to harm, as in Freud, but from the viewpoint of the feelings of soldiers actually involved in killing and being killed in war. In his Foreword, he points out that "[t]hroughout history, persistent cultural biases have attempted to deny various aspects of human psychological vulnerability, labeling them as not applicable or demeaning if stated about 'people like us', for example" (Marlowe 2001, xiii–xiv). He describes in the course of his finely detailed study how a polarized notion of men as either cowards or courageous prevailed in World War I. Indeed, in World War I, soldiers were shot for cowardice when they were actually suffering from shell shock: "Men whom we would today classify as combat-stress casualties were shot for 'cowardice'" (41). By the time of World War II, military thinking changed: "[I]t became clear that while some men were more vulnerable to the development of psychological symptoms and syndromes, all men, no matter how brave or courageous, were vulnerable. . . . 'every man has his breaking point'" (47).

Marlowe quotes several psychiatrists who treated soldiers who fought at Guadalcanal. In his attempt to describe factors contributing to "the tremendous psychiatric casualty levels of this prolonged battle," one of the psychiatrists points to multiple forms of fear:

> [T]he tension of suspense in one form or another; waiting to be killed, for death had begun to seem inevitable to many, and some walked out to meet it rather than continue to endure the unbearable waiting; waiting for the next air raid and the minutes of trembling after the final warning; waiting for the relief ships. . . . The fears were numerous; of death, of permanent crippling, of capture and torture, of ultimate defeat in a war that was starting so badly . . . as well as fear of cowardice . . . and of madness. (50)

Though each war presents its own complex of factors, feelings of vulnerability and fear remain basic. For example, "the experience of Vietnam taught us to see the veteran as part of a vulnerable population affected by a myriad of environmental stressors that generated various classes of psychological and psychophysiological symptoms," part of them produced by an unreceptive, stigmatizing American society (113). By the time of the Gulf War, further complexities became evident, in part through the fact "that psychological components of illness . . . bear a stigma in our society—a stigma of moral and mental weakness" such that, to admit "a psychological component in a physical illness means to admit that something 'is wrong' with the physical and chemical structure of one's brain" (160). "Such beliefs and concerns," Marlowe believes, "are part of the context through which we should approach the patterns of illness presented by a number of Gulf War veterans." But he also states that they are "the outer shell only": they define "terms of reference underlining and legitimating a threat to life and happiness from dark and arcane sources" (161). Psychological components are subjective, of course, rather than objective, but it is clear that they are coincident with the fact that "psychological pain" is transferred to the body in the form of a physical symptom and that "[t]he major psychological correlates" of somatic symptoms are depression and/or anxiety (162). In short, feelings of vulnerability, anxiety, fear, and stress are feelings that society views as unmanly: real men have no such experiences and certainly no background knowledge of such experiences.

What Marlowe writes of "the nature and power of combat stress" implicitly shows the costs of that view, the costs of cultivating "scripts," as Tomkins calls them, that instantiate and support the view. Correlatively, and more broadly, what he writes implicitly shows the wisdom of opening to the nature of human nature and the value of developing powers of self-reflection and self-knowledge, thereby gaining insight into the full spectrum of human feeling and the core motivational significance of affects. Moreover it is not just that "all men, no matter how brave or courageous, [are] vulnerable" and have their "breaking point"; all humans, no matter how brave or courageous, are essentially and inescapably vulnerable and can collapse at certain critical moments in fear, the very fear that in fact essentially if covertly fuels their bravery or courageousness.

Freud's and Marlowe's writings testify to the fact that, as William Tecumseh Sherman said, "War is hell." But if "War is hell," and "Hell is—other people!" as a character in one of Sartre's plays affirms (Garcin, in *No Exit*), then is it not time humans put two and two together? Is it not time, in other words, that humans realize not simply that greed and killing, for example, go hand in hand, just as the pursuit of power and violence go hand in hand, but that *Homo sapiens sapiens* is a self-inflated fantasy and that, to borrow a phrase from Husserl, "the dream is over" (Husserl 1970a, 315). The dream was in fact historically over and has been consistently over even before it began with taxonomists' doubly honorific christening of humans as sapient: *Homo nescius et barbarus* has attested unequivocally to the shadow side of human nature for centuries. The species is transparent in its endless wars, in its tyrannical cruelties, in its rapacious depredations of other forms of life and of earthly resources, and in the dark motivations that Hobbes so long ago recognized and aptly described as a proclivity toward execrable deeds motivated by competition, fear, and self-preservation. To achieve the dream, truly sapiential humans would have to work not only to awaken to their dark side, but to cultivate their gift for wisdom. Jung's *Answer to Job* casts an illuminating light on this double task. His answer recognizes both the power to do evil and the power to cultivate wisdom through the power to reflect, and through reflection, to become aware of the moral significance of one's actions. Indeed, if one is unconscious in the sense of being asleep to one's motivations and the moral character of one's actions, one remains outside the bounds of morality altogether. *Homo nescius et barbarus* is asleep in just this sense, the human species equivalent of what Jung pictures as the Old Testament God who is angry and vengeful, whose violence is untempered, who wants unending praise and glory, and who is essentially *non compos mentis*. Ignorance and barbarity go hand in hand.

## VII. A MORAL EDUCATION

A possibility ensconced within evolutionary biology leads directly to an appeal to education to mitigate if not counteract or even neutralize the dangers posed by *Homo nescius et barbarus*. However paradoxical a conjunction of intelligence with ignorance and barbarity might at first appear, one could theoretically sustain the sapiential status of an ignorant, i.e., self-opaque, and barbaric *Homo sapiens sapiens* on evolutionary grounds. In particular, as intelligent *Homo* species evolve, a distinctly channeled variant of the species might appear on the evolutionary scene, a species using its intelligence to wholly malevolent ends not only against individuals of its own kind, but against individuals of any kind that get in the way of its reaping all the bounties Nature has to offer, including the open-ended, morally unrestricted bounties of its own intelligence. The evolutionary scenario is not only perfectly conceivable, but to a point, coincident with the struggle for existence. Given basic survival constraints in the way of food and shelter, for example, and the basic biological matrix of male-male competition, natural selection could work to favor individuals geared to using their intelligence to destroy anyone or anything that stands in their way. More individuals would in turn be born who are temperamentally and physically geared to the high-pitched enjoyment of sheer physicality and excitement, for example, to violence and the competitive use of force, to a belligerent disposition fueling an insatiable quest for *more* in the form of power or resources, to a combatively channeled imagination readily fixated on the production of weaponry and the build-up of technological arsenals of greater and greater complexity, and so on. In so using its intelligence, the species could ultimately—though quite by chance—destroy itself in a cataclysmic distillation of the earth: through unexpected leakages of radioactive wastes, accidental detonations of some kind, or any one—or many—of a number of such possibilities.

Clearly, intelligence, like empathy, is not of necessity constructive, promising, or sunny. Like empathy, it can be directed toward malevolent ends, and those ends can conceivably gain ascendancy. *The scenario thus lies within the range of possibilities in the evolution of intelligence;* it lies in the nature of the evolution of an intelligent species.[29] Whether understood as a caveat or as words of wisdom, the scenario carries with it an essential message: the direction in which intelligence—and empathy—is cultivated determines the vigor of the root branches and in turn the direction in which the roots of morality grow or do not grow. The message has a moral with a decisively Socratic ring. The self-proclaimed sapient species of the genus *Homo* would be wise to turn its flaunted intelligence inward, answering to the challenge of knowing itself, for in default of a bona fide and deep self-knowledge, its sapiential capacities run loose, untempered by moral concerns or questionings. Untold mortifications of others are in turn not only possible but actively realized, and this because the sapiential possibilities of *Homo sapiens sapiens* become progressively the sapiential possibilities of the variant strain. In the latter's hands, the capacity for evil waxes unconstrained, extending far beyond the decimation of its own kind.

Research techniques that aim at the enhancement of the "human good" under the banner of "medical advancements" are striking cases in point. They involve the mortification and transmogrification of other forms of life. "Chimeric experimentation"[30] involving the transplantation of human brain cells into mice carries just such a banner (Rifkin 2005). The experimentation is more properly described as a form of "biological alchemy" (Kevin Sheets, pers. comm.).[31] Morally as well as substantively, the latter alchemy exceeds the alchemy of the Middle Ages, which, experimenting with minerals rather than living beings, attempted to transmute baser metals into gold and to prolong human life through the discovery of an elixir. Biological alchemy attempts to transmute what it considers baser forms of life into what it considers the most lofty form of life and thereby provide medical science with humanlike experimental animals, medical science in turn being able to inject the humanlike animals with all forms of human disease to the end that human ills are cured and human life prolonged. Biological alchemy manifestly operates with ethical blinders; it is written all over with self-serving aims replete with human conceit and glory.[32] Moreover given that the possible biological effects of chimeric experimentation are totally unknown—the proliferation or escape of chimeric animals, for example, the introduction of new viruses and diseases, the breakdown of existing life-supporting ecological relationships, and so on, not to mention the lives and livability of humanly contrived chimeras—the moral insouciance of biological alchemists is not only blatantly evident but testifies unequivocally to the dangers of *Homo nescius et barbarus*.

An appeal to education to answer to the dangers is not only reasonable but urgent. The appeal is neither a vague gesture toward education nor does it signal a notion of education as panacea. It is a petition for the development of an education rooted in understandings of the nature of human nature, thus in bona fide *self*-understandings, understandings of oneself as a human being. Such an education is clearly not caught up in the formulation of moral principles, imperatives, or rights, for example. Its concern is with fundamental understandings of the vulnerabilities inherent in being a body and the moral valences that go with those understandings—the moral valences of size, power, and death, for example, and the way in which those valences color the meaning of one's life and the lives of all those about one. When Becker affirms that "the reality of death" is the primary problem and in light of that primary problem that what the world needs in the way of leaders is "well-analyzed men," he tempers the remark, saying that even the best analysis does not guarantee to produce [the desired] level of self-conscious, tragic sophistication" (Becker 1975, 167). Indeed, the desired level of sophistication demands more than psychoanalysis or psychology because neither can, by themselves, do justice to the nature of human nature. They are not equivalent to an interdisciplinary education. Moreover "what the world needs" is not simply leaders wise in the ways of human nature. It needs a populace—a global populace—wise in the ways of human nature, thus a populace individually capable of self-knowledge. It needs awakened communities and societies in which each individual is attuned to the range and complexities of human feeling and capable of thinking rationally for him/herself. Education in this sense is the key to the realization of morally enlightened humans.

But just how, one might ask, does education carry out such a mission? How does it go about educating humans about their own human nature? It does so by educating them about ontogenetical matters of fact: about smiling, about the startle reflex, about stranger anxiety, about fundamental human social feelings, and the potency of fear and of feelings of vulnerability over smiling and feelings of openness. It does so by educating them about ontogenetical matters of fact from a phylogenetic perspective: about xenophobia in nonhuman primate societies, for example, and about the relationship between human smiling and laughter and kindred facial expressions and sounds in nonhuman primates. It does so by educating them about evolutionary matters of fact: about phylogenetic relationships and the origin of species, thus about worms and the interconnectedness of living forms, for example, and about comsigns and the natural history of sense-making. In educating them about such matters, education educates humans in the deepest sense about human nature and about the fact that human nature is a product of *Nature*. Indeed, there could be no human *nature*—not to mention humans pure and simple—without *Nature*.[33] Because humans originated and evolved through the workings of Nature, they live not in a meta-natural vacuum—of whatever ideological persuasion—but amidst other equally natural life forms, some of whom they resemble because they share a common line of descent. It is thus not surprising that humans share certain feelings, dispositions, and social behaviors with their closest evolutionary relatives in addition to having distinctive feelings, dispositions, and social behaviors of their own. Understandings of human ontogeny and phylogeny are central to a moral education precisely because they bring to light foundational aspects of human nature and the relationship of those foundational aspects to the larger natural world in which humans live and in which they evolved.

A moral education rooted in understandings of human nature is rooted not only in the ontogenetic and phylogenetic histories of humans but in human history, that is, in cultural histories over centuries of human existence. These latter roots are not tethered to names and dates, but to what might be termed human historical invariants having moral relevance: the pursuit of power, territorial conflict and expansion, immortality ideologies of leaders and their followers, environmental degradation. All such invariants carry with them correlative historical invariants having moral relevance: the invariants of oppression, poverty, dispersion, depletion, and so on. The challenge of a moral education is to show not simply how these linked invariants are thematically reiterated across human history, but how they are rooted in human nature, the dark side of human nature that Hobbes perspicuously described and valiantly exposed, but a side that has yet to see the light in an educational system geared toward enlightening humans about themselves. In this respect, one might profitably recall mid-second-century B.C. historian Polybius's insistence that true history has a mission, which is not to entertain but to teach: "The tragic poet seeks to thrill and charm his audience for the moment by expressing through his characters the most plausible words possible, but the historian's task is to instruct and persuade serious students by means of the truth of the words and actions he presents, and the effect must be permanent, not temporary" (Polybius 1979, 168). Polybius implicitly specifies the basis of the effect's permanence when he later points out that "if we remove from history the analysis of why, how and for what purpose each thing was done and whether the result was what we should reasonably have expected, what is left is a mere display of descriptive virtuosity, but not a lesson, and this, though it may please for the moment, is of no enduring value for the future" (207). In the present context, the lesson that has enduring value is less practical, as in Polybius's history of the Punic Wars, than it is straightforwardly epistemological: history provides insights into invariants of human nature, possibilities or propensities of feeling and acting that we would find in ourselves if we but looked. Indeed, a history devoid of insights into human nature is no more than a series of events, most commonly a mere recounting of socio-economic-political exploits and their consequences, one after the next across centuries of human history, together with a listing of the men who led the exploits and descriptions of the armies that carried them out. History has indeed more to offer than such recountings. It is replete with lessons of enduring value with respect to human nature.[34]

Human history as taught in public schools typically concerns itself with exploits, deeds and events that could in fact readily introduce and illuminate invariants on the dark side of human nature. Not only this, but an equally invincible and exceptional human history exists that is not ordinarily taught in public schools. It is no less a part of the cultural history of humans but is typically separated categorically from the commonly taught socio-political-economic history of humans. Indeed, it is generally ensconced in art departments of higher education under the heading "art history," in music departments of higher education under the heading "music history," in dance departments of higher education under the heading "dance history," in language departments of higher education under the heading "seventeenth-century French literature" or "nineteenth-century Russian literature," and so on. However categorically separated, these histories have the potential to illuminate foundational invariants of human nature no less decisively and emphatically than the socio-economic-political histories of humans. Indeed, these histories could readily introduce and illuminate invariants on the other side of human nature, the side that is creative rather than destructive. As noted in Chapter 5, the two most salient historical features of human civilizations are war and art: the remains of the one are treasured and prominently housed in museums or performed on stages and in concert halls; the remains of the other are treasured and prominently housed in cemeteries or have monuments and memorials erected in their honor. Through public education and the active cultivation of a populace awakened to the histories of art and literature, it is possible to highlight and accentuate real-life values emerging from creativity—perhaps in time even the real-life values of cultivating creativity directly in public schools—and in so doing, encourage a balancing of the historical ledger and an appreciation of the oppositional tendencies at the heart of human nature. Concentrated attention on works of art and literature—a Bach fugue, a short novel by Dostoyevsky—develops formal sensitivities and awarenesses, insights into the range and complexity of forms that can emerge from creative labors and into the intricacies of a completed aesthetic creation. Through such attention, the value of creative efforts becomes apparent: a coherent whole is attainable and attained. What is present is complex but all of a piece, and its formal integrity is grasped and understood. In heightening an awareness of the value of creativity—not in theoretical terms, but in experiential terms—public education in the history of art and literature has the possibility of actively developing the creative side of human nature, perhaps even making it ascendant.

Play and creativity—two essential dimensions of human nature—would in fact emerge from a balancing of the historical ledger, their commonly marginalized and often trivialized roles proportionately redressed, their intrinsic worth brought to the fore and set in relief. Play and creativity are activities natural to humans, as they are to many species of mammalian life—species of nonhuman primates, cetacea, and carnivora. As with other forms of animate life, they lead humans into unfamiliar territory, to new possible ways of being and living, to an expansion of their repertoire of "I cans," to discoveries fresh to their senses and understanding. In Chapter 2, the call to creativity was linked to living without illusions, to an ontological dimension of Being no less foundational than Heidegger's 'call to conscience'. Like the latter, creativity calls us to explore paths divergent from the mainstream—from "the they." It calls us to something that arises spontaneously from within, something we ourselves not only do not control, but something we cannot predict, something we attentively and assiduously follow to conclusions unknown in advance. In composing a dance, for example, we are not simply doing this movement and then that movement; we are listening to a form that is moving through us and taking shape—*its* shape—in the process of moving through us and being created. Creativity keeps us tethered to *"Being toward the possibility"* of bringing forth something of value in and of itself. At the center of this creative 'being toward' is play, the capacity to be actively in the present of whatever presents itself and to let that immediate present flow into whatever future reveals itself and challenges us anew. Play is the biological ground on which the disposition to create arises. In play, we are totally immersed in an unfolding dynamic created in the course of, and by dint of, our kinetic inclinations and actions. In both play and creativity, we are focused wholly on something other than ourselves, answering to whatever exigencies and explorations play and creativity demand. Play and creativity are thus neither a self-indulgent ego trip nor a simple amusement. They require knowledge in just the sense that child's play requires knowledge, an ever-expanding knowledge of one's body and one's possibilities of movement, as shown in Chapter 6. Indeed, since play, like creativity, never repeats itself, it is always fresh. Being fresh, it awakens a natural spontaneity that feeds into the development of discriminatory powers and an abiding acuity, and itself becomes rooted in those powers and acuity. Play and creativity are sense-making activities precisely in the double sense described in Chapter 5: making intelligible and creating meaning.

Biologist Eibl-Eibesfeldt's observations of a male badger playing and inventing something new in the process of playing capture the basic relationship of play to creativity. In locomotor play, Eibl-Eibesfeldt writes, a badger commonly "runs in curves, suddenly changes direction and rolls over" (Eibl-Eibesfeldt 1978, 142). The badger he observed, however, "showed a peculiar preference for real 'somersaults'," that is, a preference not just for rolling over, but for rolling forward. In particular, the badger "forced himself between wall and desk, put his head between his forelegs, curled himself up and made a real *somersault*" (142). The somersault at first appeared to Eibl-Eibesfeldt "a product of chance: the badger wanted to scratch his belly with his teeth, he toppled over forward, the two walls preventing a lateral tipping over" (142). But the somersault was clearly marked as an intentional act when the badger did not force himself into the gap, but crawled into the gap between wall and desk from the front. Moreover he later did somersaults approaching from the other direction, and even learned to do somersaults outdoors, "where [not having side supports] he first fell to the side," and then later "learned all by himself to roll down a gently sloping meadow in a whole series of somersaults" (143).

Clearly, creativity and play are a natural arena for learning. They call us to life and to as yet unrealized possibilities. An education that allows room for, that in fact inspires and promotes creativity and play makes space for the innocence of the child, an innocence precisely in the sense of not knowing it all and of not making anything routine, but of *playing*. Playing brings smiles and a receptivity to exploration, a capacity to be alive in the present. In cognitive terms, it brings discovery. Psychiatrist D. W. Winnicott succinctly if implicitly captures this aspect of play and creativity when, in speaking of mathematical learning, he upholds the creative value of conceptually informed guessing over formulaic answers. "When you teach sums, you have to teach children as they come," he writes, pointing out that there are three types of children, the last of whom "manipulate concepts" but "are held back by banal considerations of pounds, shillings and pence." He comments, "You will feel like starting these last children off on the slide-rule and differential calculus. Why not ask them to *guess* rather than to *calculate*, thus using their personal computers. I don't see why, in arithmetic, there is so much emphasis *on the accurate answer*. What about the fun of guessing? Or of playing around with ingenious methods?" (Winnicott 1986, 61). He later states pointedly that "in the teaching of mathematics, *one can catch on to the creative impulse*, perhaps the play gesture of a child, and then use this and the child's reaching out, giving all that the child can take by way of teaching until the child comes to the end, for the time being, of the creative reaching out" (64). Clearly, discovery is at the heart of the mathematical education Winnicott envisions; it comes naturally in the context of play and creativity. When Winnicott declares, "Creativity is inherent in playing" (64), he substantiates from a reverse perspective the foundational biological relationship between the two.

A moral education grounded in creative discoveries taps into depths not only untouched by, but beyond the reach of, information, perfunctory answers, and foregone conclusions. It involves active rather than passive learning; it requires a full engagement in something that is livingly present, whether the mysteries of summing, the experience of a painting or a piece of sculpture, or whatever. It enraptures precisely because it is not routine, not a compendium of facts or statements about an X of one kind or another, but a challenge to sense-making that is progressively answered to, answered to precisely in a way akin to the call to creativity itself. Obviously, this kind of moral education can flourish only in a society that values a sense-making intelligence and the motivating sense of wonder that necessarily goes with it. A brain crammed full of information is morally blind. Eugen Fink, a long-time assistant to Edmund Husserl and dedicated phenomenologist in his own right (see Bruzina 2004), aptly characterized wonder when he linked it to "the creative poverty of not yet knowing." When wonder is allowed space, when it is in fact cultivated, it propels individuals toward discovery, opening new horizons for thought. In wonder, one actively seeks answers for oneself, and makes sense of the world in the process. Not only this, but when directed toward oneself, wonder opens the possibility of self-insights and more. One is precisely awakened philosophically to the task of knowing oneself and of understanding the human nature of which one is a part. A society beholden to information, a society that supports educational systems pledged to the production of information and to the drenching of students in information, is and remains creatively impoverished. It does not and cannot give rise to or eventuate in sense-making or wonder for the simple reason that it does not encourage sense-making or wonder; it encourages factual ingestion, uncritical factual ingestion. Such an education can all too quickly produce a robotic sapience that can itself all too quickly take humanity on a further turn for the worse, spawning societies of technological drones in the service of *Homo nescius et barbarus*.

Being essential dimensions of human nature, play and creativity have a genuine place within a moral education, and not only on phylogenetic, ontogenetic, historical, and cognitive grounds, but on sociological grounds. They bring communal health, encouraging open, positively meaningful relationships with others and this because they provide everyday arenas in which humans come together openly and constructively, whether to play or take part in a communal creative project of some kind—municipal, neighborly, theatrical, environmental, artistic. They come together openly and constructively because a reciprocal relationship of trust exists. Whatever the form of play or creative endeavor, if one breaches the kinetic rules of play that define the base line of a social morality—the "I cans" and "I cannots," as described in Chapter 6—then one is no longer played with because one is not trusted. It is thus not simply a matter of one's trusting others, but of being trusted oneself. Yet play and creativity can also be sociologically diverted. Torture, for example, is a form of play and creativity gone mad. One can readily see the madness not only in graphics of the twentieth- and twenty-first century human world, but in museums such as the Castle of the Counts in Ghent, Belgium, for example, where instruments for inflicting pain and suffering, some of them ingeniously designed, are startlingly evident. Play and creativity, like empathy and intelligence, can indeed be used for life-destroying ends. When they emerge, on the contrary, as life-enhancing activities, the open and constructive engagements they foster with others are the antithesis of an amity forged by a common enmity toward others. As life-enhancing activities, they are equally the antithesis of posturing calls by vainglorious leaders for a heroics, and equally the antithesis of a cultural elaboration of male-male competition in which dominance and power are at stake. Of moment in this sociological context are searches for "a moral equivalent of war," an equivalence which in actuality is a search for the fervid equal of human male-male competition but without its violence.

The connection with male-male competition is apparent from the beginning, that is, in philosopher William James's original call for a moral equivalent of war and in his concretized idea of what would constitute an equivalent, namely, "a conscription of the whole youthful population to form for a certain number of years a part of the army enlisted against *Nature*" (James [1910] 1987, 223). What James means by being "enlisted against *Nature*" is that human life is forthrightly challenging, hard, and that the unequal toiling and pain endured by some simply to keep alive should be experienced by those who, "by mere accidents of birth and opportunity," live a life of ease and luxury, enduring no such miseries (223). In short, those who live by "unmanly ease" should be subjected to the "military ideals of hardihood and discipline" (223). That "the whole youthful population" is exclusively a population of males is clearly not in doubt, for James's concern is precisely with instilling an "army discipline" (222) into males: the "manly virtues"—"toughness" among them—would be realized in the conscription, for "[t]he martial type of character," James affirms, "can be bred without war" (224). Specifying the moral equivalent of war more finely, James writes that "our gilded youths [would] be drafted off, according to their choice, to get the childishness knocked out of them, and to come back into society with healthier sympathies and soberer ideas. They would have paid their blood tax, done their own part in the immemorial human warfare against nature; they would tread the earth more proudly, the women would value them more highly, they would be better fathers and teachers of the following generation" (223–24). Where the cultivation of "manliness" (222) is the driving social priority, the social values of play and creativity fall by the wayside. Play and creativity are in fact hardly considered. They resonate with effeminate, sissy auras. Certainly they would not "preserve . . . the manly virtues which the military party is so afraid of seeing disappear in peace"; they would not preserve what James calls "manliness of type" (224).

Though he does not speak of "the moral equivalent of war," ethologist Konrad Lorenz voices equal concerns about war and "manliness" toward the end of his book *On Aggression*: "Virtues such as heroism and courage are regarded as being 'manly' and are traditionally associated with waging war. Conversely, the avoidance of war or the pursuit of peace are generally regarded as 'effeminate,' passive, cowardly, weak, dishonorable or subversive" (Lorenz 1966, 275). His central focus is on "militant enthusiasm," which he specifies as both "a specialized form of communal aggression, clearly distinct from and yet functionally related to the more primitive forms of petty individual aggression" (259), and "[the] most dangerous form of aggression" (272). His urgings toward a redirection of militant enthusiasm are akin to James's urgings toward a moral equivalent of war. Moreover his prominencing of males is of a piece with James's central attention on manliness, and his neglect of play and creativity as natural palliatives to violence—genuine alternatives to the honing of heroes and cultivation of war—is akin to James's neglect. Proposing counters to "the danger of war," he focuses on international sporting contests as exemplified by the Olympics (273). Like James's "youthful conscription," international sporting contests are fundamentally conceived as taming "the masculine spirit" to more peaceful ends—"get[ting] toughness without callousness," as James puts it at one point (James 1910, 224). Lorenz thoughtfully justifies the contests in terms not only of providing "an outlet for the collective militant enthusiasm of nations," but of promoting personal relationships among people of different nations and of uniting otherwise distant people in a common cause (Lorenz 1966, 273). The redirected enthusiasm, however, spotlights precisely that male "spirit" that is basically the biological matrix of male-male competition, and not an "instinct of aggression" as Lorenz affirms. When that biological matrix is overlooked, the psychological dark side of humans that fuels the social cultivation of "true" militant enthusiasm in quests for power, glory, resources, excitement, and so on, is concomitantly overlooked.

It is in fact significant that *competitive* sports enter the picture; that is, it is as if Lorenz recognizes that competition drives aggression, and not the reverse. The competitive source of aggression is indeed apparent in the very way Lorenz describes the redirection of aggression toward nonviolent ends: "[as] in the ritualized fighting of many vertebrates," he writes, "all human sport" has the aim of ascertaining "which partner is stronger, without hurting the weaker" (105). Obviously, competition determines who is the "stronger" partner, in effect, who is the more powerful, who has more options, and so on. Moreover when Lorenz later affirms that "the main function of sport today lies in the cathartic discharge of aggressive urge," he adds that the value of sport "is much greater than that of a simple outlet of aggression." In particular, he states, "It educates man to a conscious and responsible control of his own fighting behavior" (271). If we ask where this "fighting behavior" comes from, we can hardly avoid acknowledging the evolutionary phenomenon of male-male competition, and we can hardly avoid recognizing its social expression in "manliness" and its cultural elaboration in war.

Lorenz's error is in fact to posit a single driving energy at the base of human action, and in consequence, to overlook the oppositional tendencies at the heart of human nature and to transliterate the power of those tendencies into superficial distinctions between the "manly" and the "effeminate." He not only reduces "fighting behavior" to the instinct of aggression in the form of "militant enthusiasm," which propels members of one group to defend their "social norms and rites against another group not possessing them" (250), but projects the compass of militant enthusiasm far more broadly. Militant enthusiasm, he affirms, is pivotal to those endeavors through which the great works of humanity are realized and is thus exercised in ways utterly outside the need for defense. "Without the concentrated dedication of militant enthusiasm," he writes, "neither art, nor science, nor indeed any of the great endeavors of humanity would have come into being." Lorenz thus adduces Beethoven's symphonies, Chaucer's tales, and so on to a redirection of militant enthusiasm, and attributes the humanistic or warring direction militant enthusiasm takes to crucial developmental periods: "Whether enthusiasm is made to serve these endeavors ["these great endeavors of humanity"], or whether man's most powerfully motivating instinct makes him go to war in some abjectly silly cause, depends almost entirely on the conditioning and/or imprinting he has undergone during certain susceptible periods of his life" (262).

In sum, in Lorenz as in James, there is a notable concentration on redirecting "manly" energies without any thought of there being other *natural* human proclivities. Yet play is a natural disposition of *all* humans, indeed, a biological matrix among young mammals. Play and the potential for creativity with which it is bound have their roots in human nature. Play begins with the individual. While it might produce heroes—individuals whom others want to emulate, individuals who risk themselves to protect others, and so on—it does not foster heroics or heroic posturings. That is not its mission. Moreover it does not provide a moral equivalent of war in either James's original sense or that of Lorenz. There is in fact no moral equivalent of war in either sense: the moral equivalent of war is neither a war against Nature as a substitute for "the manliness to which the military mind so faithfully clings" (James 1910, 222)—or to show that "[t]he martial type of character can be bred without war" (224)—as James so strongly recommends, nor a redirection of militant enthusiasm toward international sporting contests to quell the "instinct of aggression" as Lorenz recommends. A moral education thus consists not in the redirection of some innate or latent energy, but in a sapiential response to the realities of *Homo nescius et barbarus*, a response that entails a deep and personal knowledge of the oppositional dispositions at the heart of human nature and the wisdom to cultivate those that are life-enhancing rather than life-destroying. A good part of this cultivation lies in the hands of males because males control socio-political-economic life in virtually all nations, tribes, and human groupings. All the same, re-naturing the de-natured species means the awakening of *all* humans to the challenge of living up to their sapiential billing. It requires that one turns inward, toward one's own nature, reflecting deeply on one's own motivations to harm others in pursuit of power, immortality, money, excitement, fame, and so on, and to reflect equally deeply on one's capacities for attunement, reciprocity, a sense of interconnectedness, play, and creativity, and in turn, to reflect on one's motivations toward caring that spring from the exercise of those capacities, motivations that are otherwise trampled in vainglorious pursuits. A moral education is in this sense the only genuine moral equivalent of war. It is an interdisciplinary education that educates humans about their own human nature.

VIII. CONCLUDING THOUGHT

Human nature has been the central theme of this book. With the rise first of sociobiology, and then of the cognitive sciences, interest in and investigations of human nature have given way to interest in and investigations of *the* brain and the human genome. It is urgent now that humans get back on track and attempt to understand themselves, both as part of Nature and as having a distinct nature within that global phenomenon. What I once described as "the tag-end of a fractious and fractionating twentieth century" (Sheets-Johnstone 1994b, 2) is now the beginning of a roiled and raging twenty-first century. Surely it is time for *Homo sapiens sapiens* to demonstrate its upward ratcheted wisdom by sensitively and compassionately acknowledging its ignorant and barbarous Other and the fear-driven brawn and might that drive it to mutilate, ravage, and kill in a rage for power and meaning. Surely it is time for

*Homo sapiens sapiens* to turn away from the pursuit of dominion over all and to begin cultivating and developing its sapiential wisdom in the pursuit of caring, nurturing and strengthening that most precious muscle which is its heart.

NOTES

1. The possibility of a unified perspective is also adumbrated in recent writings, some of them already cited and discussed in the course of this text: Chris Hedges in the context of war, Martha Nussbaum in the context of desire (Nussbaum 1994), Carol Gilligan and Grant Wiggins in the context of sexual differences in early conceptions of morality (Gilligan and Wiggins 1987), Adam Phillips in the context of Darwin's and Freud's conjunction of thought about their own deaths, Jonathan Kingdon in the context of an encompassing evolutionary view of humans. Each writer brings to the fore elusive but perduring aspects of a basic opposition within human nature, examining its many facets and enlightening us—at times eloquently—in the process.

2. For example: "This [the incommensurability of visual and tangible distance], perhaps, will not find an easy admission into all men's understanding. However, I should gladly be informed whether it be not true, by any one who will be at the pains to reflect a little, and apply it home to his thoughts" (Berkeley 1709, 72–73); "As for those that will not be at the pains of a little thought, no multiplication of words will ever suffice to make them understand the truth, or rightly conceive my meaning" (85).

3. The point is thus not to decide where a putatively rational deciding line should be drawn in a situation where "one of us must go," but rather to insist on the moral sense of others, precisely as described in the previous chapter.

4. See Sinnott 1963 on the recovery of trees after their limbs have been cut, and on their sensitivity to sunlight and water.

5. The neurological analogy is not without interest. What one cultivates becomes second nature in the form of habit.

6. What the shadow side requires is, in a Jungian sense, what the unconscious requires as "the unknown of the inner world" (see Jung 1969, 3): it needs to be brought to light.

7. It is even barbarous in the sense of being an unnatural element within the whole of Nature, something foreign to the whole of Nature, since, as already noted, no other species decimates its own kind, much less members of other species just for sport, or recreation, or excitement, or out of anger.

8. The term "beastliness" is, of course, ironic in the extreme in view of the esteem in which many if not most humans hold themselves, namely, quite apart from "the beasts."

9. In the same way, certain later affective tendencies and inclinations may be psychologically judged natural signs pointing in the direction of "good" or "bad."

10. Psychologist Silvan Tomkins's earlier description, based on psychologists Carney Landis and William A. Hunt's original and well-known analysis of the "startle pattern" (Landis and Hunt 1968), is coincident with Young's: i.e., "There is a raising and drawing forward of the shoulders, abduction of the upper arms, bending of the elbows, pronation ... of the lower arms, flexion of the fingers, forward movement of the trunk, contraction of the abdomen and bending of the knees" (Tomkins 1962, 509).

11. According to the psychology text, researchers studied the question of when infants recognize the "'self' ... by putting a spot of rouge on infants' noses and placing them in front of mirrors." Their purpose was "to determine when infants would recog-

nize themselves enough to try to rub the rouge off their noses." They found that "[a] few of the 15-month-old infants rubbed off the rouge, and nearly all the 18-to-24-month-olds did" (Roediger et al. 1987, 349).

When psychiatrist Daniel Stern describes in his 1985 book how, "[s]everal years ago," he and his colleagues ran an experiment on four-month old Siamese twins prior to an operation that would separate them, he shows incontrovertibly that infants have a "sense of self" quite independent of mirrors (see Stern 1985, 78–79).

12. Lacan's psychoanalytic, with its structural dependence on the mirror-stage when an infant sees its idealized self, affirms virtually the same received wisdom. (For a critical discussion of his psychoanalytic, particularly as it relates to infants, see Sheets-Johnstone 1994b.)

13. In answer to his own question, what is it like to be a human infant? Dennett declares: "My killjoy answer would be that it isn't like very much. How do I know? I don't 'know,' of course, but my even more killjoy answer is that on my view of consciousness, it arises when there is work for it to do, and the preeminent work of consciousness is dependent on sophisticated language-using activities" (1983, 384).

14. The affective experience of infants is not simply a matter of inference; particular movement dynamics articulate particular affects. See further in text for a discussion of the relationship between affect and movement (see also Sheets-Johnstone 1999a).

15. The terms *fear* and *anxiety* are used interchangeably. Infant psychologist Thérèse Décarie points out that "[w]hether they speak of fear or anxiety, all investigators stress the complexity of the negative reaction to strangers and seek to determine the principal factors involved" (1974, 27). Psychologist L. Alan Sroufe, however, states, "It may be even more reasonable to drop both the terms *stranger fear* and *stranger anxiety*, substituting instead *stranger reactions*." His explanation is based on the fact that the response of infants is sometimes similar to anxiety and sometimes similar to fear: "Anxiety aspects of the reaction . . . include the fact that it is greatly reduced when there are response options open to the infant . . . and that it generally occurs only when the stranger intrudes on the infant's space." Alternatively, "the response can be immediate" on the order of "'I do not like this' or 'I do not like what is happening here'" (Sroufe 1996, 109). Sroufe's concern is that, while "[i]t is clear that negative stranger reactions are common in infancy" (111), a "milestone" (112) approach to infant social development (referring to Spitz's notion of "eight-month infant anxiety" [111]) fails to contextualize fear in the developing social world of the infant, i.e., "the organization of wariness/fear with the attachment, affiliative, and exploratory behavioral systems" (112).

16. From this broader perspective, Rochat's observations offer ontogenetical support of the amity/enmity complex. Indeed, the oppositional feelings and their kinetic dispositions—toward and away—are emblematic of the complex.

17. For an in-depth study of a nation's societal practices in relation to "alien others," see Kidd 1999.

18. It is of interest to note too Fedigan's comment that unlike strange or intruding adults, "[i]nfants and juveniles, as strangers or intruders, are generally accepted into social groups with little aggression" (Fedigan 1982, 77).

19. The terms "contractive" and "extensive" derive from a phenomenological analysis of movement. They specify spatial aspects of the body and body movement; in particular, they specify in each instance one of the two extremes inherent in the *areal quality* of the body and bodily movement, respectively. See Sheets-Johnstone 1966 and 1999b for a phenomenological analysis of movement.

20. Female contractors and female soldiers are in the employ of the United States military in Iraq, for example. Some of them, through their sexual tauntings and affronts, shamed male prisoners.

21. Economist Robert H. Frank's *Luxury Fever: Why Money Fails to Satisfy in an Era of*

*Excess* (1999) offers dramatic testimony to this pursuit. While pointing out that alternative, simpler lifestyles are urged by some—"All we need do is control our appetites" (7)—Frank also points out that "the more we have, the more we seem to feel we need" (74). A major thesis is that "both the things we feel we need and the things available for us to buy depend largely—beyond some point, almost entirely—on the things that others choose to buy. When people at the top spend more, others just below them will inevitably spend more also, and so on all the way down the economic ladder. And as this happens, simpler versions of products that once served perfectly well often fall by the wayside" (11). Frank proposes a progressive consumption tax to stem the tide of waste in current economic practices and policies.

22. "If biologist Steven Austad is correct, some children alive today will live to the age of 150—thanks to scientific advances in the field of aging, such as cloning and stem cell research. 'Many of my colleagues in the field think that my prediction is far too conservative,' Austad says" (*AARP Bulletin*, 2004, 4). Consider too chemist and biomedical engineer Robert Langer's statement: "While perhaps optimistic, I believe that by the end of the next century disease as we know it today will no longer pose a major threat to human life and that highly effective methods to diagnose disease, prolong life, and relieve suffering will have been created" (Langer 1999, 92).

23. *Time Magazine*, October 8, 1979, unpaginated advertisement by Champion International Corporation that in the beginning reads (in large bold print): "In the future, incredibly expensive technology could enable a few people to live for 200 years or more. Who will be chosen? And, who will choose?"

Across from the text is a picture of an old, gray, and wrinkled but smiling couple in jogging suits who are admirably slim and fit looking. The advertisement goes on to say that "If life-extension becomes a national priority like the space program, if high-technology countries like America, Russia, Germany and Japan could work together, if there were a multi-billion dollar, multi-discipline assault on aging and death, we could produce dramatic results within the foreseeable future. . . . Within the next few decades, a lifespan of 100, 200, 400 years and up may become a part of Homo Sapiens' on-going evolutionary destiny."

But the ad also goes on to ask, "If life extension becomes commonplace, what will we do with all those great-great-great-great-great-great grandparents? Will they hold onto their jobs forever? If they don't who'll support them? On the other hand, what if the first technology to prevent aging is incredibly expensive? Will that mean that only the wealthy will be able to turn back the clock, or that the government will select the future 'Methuselahs,' based on its own criteria—intelligence, race, talent, or perhaps, even political affiliation?" After terming the latter "an untenable solution," the ad goes on to ask, "How can the people have a say in the matter? We have a lot of things to think about."

We do indeed have a lot of things to think about.

24. It is notable that close to twenty-five years ago, psychiatrist Anthony Stevens commented on the pursuit of more in terms of the imbalance between the innovations and material richness of Western culture and the lack of happiness and creativity in its people:

> In the West, our technological triumphs, economic miracles, redistributed wealth, planned cities and welfare states have not noticeably coincided with greater personal happiness or any apparent flowering of the human spirit. Indeed, those indices of flourishing civilization, music, the arts, costume, philosophy, religion and architecture, all in their present forms would seem diagnostic of an imminent descent into barbarism. Delight in the glory of human existence is not what strikes one first on contemplating our materially pam-

pered contemporaries; rather disenchantment, resentment, an obsession with material possessions, and an insatiable appetite for *more*. (Stevens 1983, 279)

25. Interesting theoretical similarities and differences obtain between Lacan's notion of lack and Loy's analysis of lack, though in contrast to Loy, in Lacan's psychoanalytic, lack has virtually no affective character whatsoever. Lacan's notion of lack is a matter of filling holes, and these holes too are ontologically analyzed, be they literal holes in the body or metaphorical holes in being. The Lacanian subject is in fact a subject riddled with holes, he/she is *le sujet troué*, the pawn of an unconscious expressed by way of language and duped into thinking he/she exists all of a piece in the mirror stage of his/her infancy (for a fuller discussion of Lacan's psychoanalytic, see Sheets-Johnstone 1994b).

According to Lacan, to see that lack, and that desire to which lack is tied is the true mark of my being. It is to see something quite opposite to and at the same time something quite coincident with what Loy is trying to show. On the one hand, Loy is saying that the self is simply a mental construction, an ontological *un*reality, and Lacan is saying that the subject is a symbolic construction, again, an ontological *un*reality. Whether self or subject, an ontological *un*reality pervades. On the other hand, Loy is saying that "the cure" is to realize the mental construction as such, and Lacan is saying that "the cure" is to realize the symbolic construction as such. In each instance, "the cure" is to realize the unreal, but for Loy such an insight would have broad ontological significance: it would liberate us, connecting us to the world, freeing us from our rooted condition in an illusory separate *I*. For Lacan, in contrast, such an insight would have a constricting significance, binding us tightly to the linguistic subjects we are and to a trivializing sexualized significance in terms of telling us that at bottom, or at heart, or at whatever level of the body we care to focus, we have gaps that reduce us to nothing. We don't measure up and can never measure up because lack defines our being.

26. Verene's analysis of technology as desire in fact provides deeper understandings of the fear that one is nothing, and this because his analysis focuses finely on domination in the master-slave relationship, on differences in domination between the slave in relation to his work and the master in relation to his pleasure, and on the foiled nature of domination in each instance.

His analysis is furthermore enriched at the end by comments on luxury in relation to technology, comments that draw on the writings of eighteenth-century philosophers Giambattista Vico and Jean-Jacques Rousseau. Interestingly enough, the comments and quotations from Vico and Rousseau complement Frank's analysis of luxury (see note 21). Verene's essential theme is that technology supports the pursuit of luxury and that the pursuit of luxury supports technology. A provocative and unexplored extension of his theme is that technology is a *doppelgänger* of the self, that *the double* exists in the form of machines—cars, computers, planes, and so on—in a way far beyond McLuhan's "the medium is the message." The techno-*doppelgänger* self takes form in fMRI imagings, clonings, virtual realities, personal websites, and so on.

27. Religionists are not immune to the pursuit of *more*. Size, for example, figured centrally in the building of cathedrals in France in the Middle Ages. Beauvais is a well-known example: "C'est ici que la témérité des architectes a reçu sa punition." As the *Encyclopédie par L'Image: Les Cathédrales* (1925, 28) explains, rival communities vied to have "la plus grande cathédrale," but in attempting to outdo all others, "leur ambition passa leurs moyens et jamais il ne fut possible de bâtir la nef, dont les voûtes s'écroulèrent deux fois" (see also the illustrations on pages 79 and 80 in *Cathédrales de France* 1950).

28. Correlatively, a radical clarification of creativity is needed. The final section will address this need.

29. I owe this trenchant and challenging line of thought and questioning to my polymathic son, Kevin Sheets.

30. The label "chimeric" is of particular interest since it aptly if unwittingly describes the experimentation from two points of view. On the one hand, chimeric means "unreal, imaginary, visionary," and certainly the experimentation does not fulfill this meaning since what is done to nonhuman animals is, on the contrary, quite real. On the other hand, chimeric means "wildly fanciful, highly unrealistic," and certainly the experimentation fulfills this meaning since what is created, while quite real, is from the viewpoint of life and viable living forms "wildly fanciful" and "highly unrealistic." What is produced is produced not to live but to serve human purposes.

31. Science writer Jeremy Rifkin reports, "The experiments are designed to advance medical research. Indeed, a growing number of genetic engineers argue that human-animal hybrids will usher in a golden era of medicine. Researchers say that the more humanized they can make research animals, the better able they will be to model the progression of human diseases, test new drugs, and harvest tissues and organs for transplantation." But he also notes that what genetic engineers "fail to mention is that there are equally promising and less invasive alternatives to these bizarre experiments, including computer modeling, in vitro tissue culture, nanotechnology, and prostheses to substitute for human tissue and organs" (Rifkin 2005).

32. For example, asked what the ecological consequences might be "of mice who think like human beings, . . . [experimental biologist] Weissman says that he would keep a tight rein on the mice, and if they showed any signs of humanness he would kill them." Rifkin finds Weissman's answer "[h]ardly reassuring," and goes on to comment, "Experiments like the one that produced a partially humanized mouse stretch the limits of human tinkering with nature to the realm of the pathological" (Rifkin 2005).

It is worthwhile quoting Rifkin's discussion of the issue more fully, for chimeric experimentation is further along than perhaps most people realize. Rifkin reports:

> Some researchers are speculating about human-chimpanzee chimeras—creating a humanzee. This would be the ideal laboratory research animal because chimpanzees are so closely related to us. . . . Fusing a human and chimpanzee embryo—which researchers say is feasible—could produce a creature so human that questions regarding its moral and legal status would throw 4,000 years of ethics into chaos. Would such a creature enjoy human rights? Would it have to pass some kind of "humanness" test to win its freedom? Would it be forced into doing menial labor or be used to perform dangerous activities?

Rifkin notes in answer:

> The possibilities are mind-boggling. For example, what if human stem cells—the primordial cells that turn into the body's 200 or so cell types—were to be injected into an animal embryo and spread throughout the animal's body into every organ? Some human cells could migrate to the testes and ovaries where they could grow into human sperm and eggs. If two of the chimeric mice were to mate, they could potentially conceive a human embryo. If the human embryo were to be removed and implanted in a human womb, the resulting human baby's biological parents would have been mice.

What is finally of moment and worth quoting in full are Rifkin's startling end comments. He writes:

> Please understand that none of this is science fiction. The National Academy of Sciences, America's most august scientific body, is expected to issue guidelines for chimeric research some time next month, anticipating a flurry of new experiments in the burgeoning field of human-animal chimeric experimentation.
>
> Bioethicists are already clearing the moral path for human-animal chimeric experiments, arguing that once society gets past the revulsion factor, the prospect of new, partially human creatures has much to offer the human race. And, of course, this is exactly the kind of reasoning that has been put forth to justify what is fast becoming a journey into a brave new world in which all of nature can be ruthlessly manipulated. But now, with human-animal chimeric experiments, we risk even undermining our own species' biological integrity in the name of human progress.
>
> With chimeric technology, scientists have the power to rewrite the evolutionary saga—to sprinkle parts of our species into the rest of the animal kingdom as well as fuse parts of other species with our own genome and even to create new human sub-species and super-species. Are we on the cusp of a biological renaissance, or sowing the seeds of our destruction?

(All quotations are from Rifkin 2005.)

33. It is of interest to point out that, in his article on the philosophy of education in *The Encyclopedia of Philosophy*, Kingsley Price attributes the introduction of the term "human nature" to Augustine; that is, in earlier Greek philosophy, though education was of moment, no mention was made of human nature. With Augustine, "new philosophy" emerges: "Human nature, according to [Augustine's] view, must be described in terms of substance and faculties influenced by historical forces," a "historical force always determin[ing] how these faculties operate." In short, "from original sin, of which the Fall was a natural consequence, flows the force which determines their descendants [the descendants of Adam and Eve] to act sinfully." Thus, "Human nature must be painted in terms of substance and faculties corrupted by early events in human history" (Price 1972, 232).

What is oxymoronic in this account is the very notion of nature. If humans were created by an all-powerful, always beneficent God, but if "[t]he ultimate objective of education grows out of the corruption of human nature and God's concern over it" (232), then an error must have occurred in the original theological selection, so to speak, of human nature, which is a contradiction in theological terms.

34. For example, "in some cases where a given course of action has failed, we are impelled to take precautions so as to avoid a recurrence, while in others we can deal more confidently with the problems that confront us by repeating a solution which has previously succeeded" (Polybius 1979, 440).

# References

AARP Bulletin. 2004. "Bulletin Board." December, 3–8.
Alcock, John. 1989. *Animal Behavior: An Evolutionary Approach.* 4th ed. Sunderland, Mass.: Sinauer Associates.
Alexander, Richard D. 1987. *The Biology of Moral Systems.* New York: Aldine de Gruyter.
Allen, Reginald, ed. 1991. *Greek Philosophy: Thales to Aristotle.* 3rd ed. New York: The Free Press.
Altmann, Stuart A. 1967. "The Structure of Primate Social Communication." In *Social Communication Among Primates,* ed. Stuart A. Altmann, 325–62. Chicago: University of Chicago Press.
Ambrose, Anthony. 1963. "The Age of Onset of Ambivalence in Early Infancy: Indications from the Study of Laughing." *Journal of Child Psychology and Psychiatry* 4:167–81.
Andersson, Malte. 1994. *Sexual Selection.* Princeton: Princeton University Press.
Andreski, Stanislav. 1964. "Origins of War." In *The Natural History of Aggression,* ed. J. D. Carthy and F. J. Ebling, 129–36. New York: Academic Press.
Applebaum, Anne. 2000. "Inside the Gulag." *New York Review of Books,* June 15, 33–35.
Ardrey, Robert. 1961. *African Genesis.* New York: Dell.
———. 1966. *The Territorial Imperative.* New York: Dell.
Arendt, Hannah. 1958. *The Origins of Totalitarianism.* New York: Meridian Books.
———. 1977. *Eichmann in Jerusalem: A Report on the Banality of Evil.* New York: Penguin Books.
Aristotle. 1984a. *Parts of Animals.* Trans. W. Ogle. In *The Complete Works of Aristotle,* ed. Jonathan Barnes, vol. 1, 994–1086. Bollingen Series LXXI.2. Princeton: Princeton University Press.
———. 1984b. *Physics.* Trans. R. P. Hardie and R. K. Gaye. In *The Complete Works of Aristotle,* ed. Jonathan Barnes, vol. 1, 315–446. Bollingen Series LXXI.2. Princeton: Princeton University Press.
Arnhart, Larry. 1998. *Darwinian Natural Right: The Biological Ethics of Human Nature.* Albany: State University of New York Press.
Attenborough, David. 1979. *Life on Earth.* Boston: Little, Brown.
———. 1990. *The Trials of Life: A Natural History of Animal Behavior.* Boston: Little, Brown.
Austin, J. L. 1962. *How to Do Things with Words.* Oxford: Clarendon Press of Oxford University Press.
Bacon, Francis. 1883. *Works.* Vol. 4. Ed. James Spedding, Robert Ellis, and Douglas Heath. London: Longmans.

Baldwin, Dare A., and Jodie A. Baird. 1999. "Action Analysis: A Gateway to Intentional Inference." In *Early Social Cognition: Understanding Others in the First Months of Life*, ed. Philippe Rochat. Mahwah, N.J.: Lawrence Erlbaum Associates.

Barash, David. 1979. *The Whisperings Within: Evolution and the Origin of Human Nature*. Harmondsworth, U.K.: Penguin Books.

———. 1982. *Sociobiology and Behavior*. New York: Elsevier.

Barkow, Jerome H., Leda Cosmides, and John Tooby, eds. 1992. *The Adapted Mind: Evolutionary Psychology and the Generation of Culture*. New York: Oxford University Press.

Baron-Cohen, Simon. 1995. *Mindblindness: An Essay on Autism and Theory of Mind*. Cambridge, Mass.: MIT Press.

Bataille, Georges. 1989. *The Tears of Eros*. Trans. Peter Connor. San Francisco: City Lights Books.

Batson, C. Daniel. 2000. "*Unto Others*: A Service . . . and a Disservice." *Journal of Consciousness Studies* 7, no. 1/2: 207–10.

Beach, Frank A. 1978. "Current Concepts of Play in Animals." In *Evolution of Play Behavior*, ed. Dietland Müller-Schwarze, 225–43. Stroudsburg, Pa.: Dowden, Hutchinson & Ross.

Becker, Ernest. 1973. *The Denial of Death*. New York: The Free Press.

———. 1974. "Toward the Merger of Animal and Human Studies." *Philosophy of the Social Sciences* 4:235–54.

———. 1975. *Escape from Evil*. New York: The Free Press.

Bee, Helen. 1989. *The Developing Child*. 5th ed. New York: Harper & Row.

Bekoff, Marc. 1995. "Play Signals as Punctuation: The Structure of Social Play in Canids." *Behaviour* 132:419–29.

———. 2000. *Strolling with Our Kin*. New York: Lantern Books.

Bell, Jeffrey A. 1998. *The Problem of Difference*. Toronto: University of Toronto Press.

Bell, Sir Charles. 1844. *The Anatomy and Philosophy of Expression*. London: John Murray.

Bergman, Anni, and Arnold Wilson. 1984. "Thoughts About Stages on the Way to Empathy and the Capacity for Concern." In *Empathy II*, ed. Joseph Lichtenberg, Melvin Bornstein, and Donald Silver, 59–80. Hillsdale, N.J.: The Analytic Press.

Berkeley, George. 1709. *An Essay Towards a New Theory of Vision*. In *Berkeley: Essay, Principles, Dialogues, with Selections from Other Writings*, ed. Mary Whiton Calkins, 3–98. New York: Charles Scribner's Sons, 1929.

Bertenthal, Bennett I., D. R. Proffitt, and J. E. Cutting. 1984. "Infant Sensitivity to Figural Coherence in Biomechanical Motions." *Journal of Experimental Child Psychology* 37:214–30.

Bertenthal, Bennett I., and Jeannine Pinto. 1993. "Complementary Processes in the Perception and Production of Human Movements." In *A Dynamic Systems Approach to Development*, ed. Linda B. Smith and Esther Thelen, 209–39. Cambridge: Bradford Books/MIT Press.

Bethe, Hans A. 1999. "The Treaty Betrayed." *New York Review of Books*, November 18, 6.

Biben, Maxeen. 1998. "Squirrel Monkey Playfighting: Making the Case for a Cognitive Training Function for Play." In *Animal Play: Evolutionary, Comparative, and Ecological Perspectives*, ed. Marc Bekoff and John A. Byers, 161–82. Cambridge: Cambridge University Press.

Birkhead, T. R. 2000. *Promiscuity: An Evolutionary History of Sperm Competition*. Cambridge: Harvard University Press.

Birkhead, T. R., and A. P. Moller. 1998. *Sperm Competition and Sexual Selection*. San Diego: Academic Press.

Blass, Thomas. 2000. "The Milgram Paradigm after 35 Years: Some Things We Now Know About Obedience to Authority." In *Obedience to Authority: Current Perspectives on the Milgram Paradigm*, ed. Thomas Blass, 35–59. Mahwah, N.J.: Lawrence Erlbaum Associates.

Blazina, Chris. 2003. *The Cultural Myth of Masculinity*. Westport, Conn.: Praeger.

Bloom, Lois. 1993. *The Transition from Infancy to Language*. Cambridge: Cambridge University Press.

Blurton Jones, N. G. 1969. "An Ethological Study of Some Aspects of Social Behaviour of Children in Nursery School." In *Primate Ethology*, ed. Desmond Morris, 437–63. Garden City, N.Y.: Anchor Books.

———. 1972. "Non-Verbal Communication in Children." In *Non-Verbal Communication*, ed. R. A. Hinde, 271–96. Cambridge: Cambridge University Press.

Boehm, Christopher. 1992. "Segmentary 'Warfare' and the Management of Conflict: Comparison of East African Chimpanzees and Patrilineal-Patrilocal Humans." In *Coalitions and Alliances in Humans and Other Animals*, ed. Alexander H. Harcourt and Frans B. M. de Waal, 137–73. New York: Oxford University Press.

———. 2000a. "Conflict and the Evolution of Social Control." In "Evolutionary Origins of Morality: Cross Disciplinary Perspectives," ed. Leonard D. Katz. Special issue, *Journal of Consciousness Studies* 7, no. 1/2: 79–101.

———. 2000b. "Group Selection in the Upper Palaeolithic." In "Evolutionary Origins of Morality: Cross Disciplinary Perspectives," ed. Leonard D. Katz. Special issue, *Journal of Consciousness Studies* 7, no. 1/2: 211–15.

———. 2000c. "The Origin of Morality as Social Control." In "Evolutionary Origins of Morality: Cross Disciplinary Perspectives," ed. Leonard D. Katz. Special issue, *Journal of Consciousness Studies* 7, no. 1/2: 149–83.

Bolwig, N. 1963. "Facial Expression in Primates." *Behaviour* 22:167–92.

Bower, Bruce. 2001. "Rumble in the Jungle." *Science News*, January 27, 58–60.

———. 2004. "To Err Is Human." *Science News*, August 14, 106–8.

Bower, T. G. R. 1971. "The Object in the World of the Infant." *Scientific American*, October 1971, 30–38.

———. 1979. *Human Development*. San Francisco: W. H. Freeman.

Bowlby, John. 1973. *Attachment and Loss*. Vol. 2, *Separation*. London: Hogarth Press.

Bramblett, Claud A. 1976. *Patterns of Primate Behavior*. Palo Alto, Calif.: Mayfield.

Braudy, Leo. 2003. *From Chivalry to Terrorism: War and the Changing Nature of Masculinity*. New York: Alfred A. Knopf.

Brown, Stuart. 1998. "Play as an Organizing Principle: Clinical Evidence and Personal Observations." In *Animal Play: Evolutionary, Comparative, and Ecological Perspectives*, ed. Marc Bekoff and John A. Byers, 243–59. Cambridge: Cambridge University Press.

———. "Play Maxims." National Institute for Play, Carmel Valley, Calif.

Bruner, Jerome. 1990. *Acts of Meaning*. Cambridge: Harvard University Press.

Bruzina, Ronald. 2004. *Edmund Husserl and Eugen Fink: Beginnings and Ends in Phenomenology, 1928–1938*. New Haven, Yale University Press.

Bugental, Daphne Blunt, Hal Kopeikin, and Linda Lazowski. 1991. "Children's Responses to Authentic Versus Polite Smiles." In *Children's Interpersonal Trust*, ed. Ken J. Rotenberg, 58–79. New York: Springer Verlag.

Bull, Nina. 1951. *The Attitude Theory of Emotion*. New York: Nervous and Mental Disease Monographs, Coolidge Foundation.

Bullock, Alan. 1992. *Hitler and Stalin: Parallel Lives*. New York: Alfred A. Knopf.

Bullough, Edward. 1959. "'Psychical Distance' as a Factor in Art and an Aesthetic Principle." In *Problems in Aesthetics*, ed. Morris Weitz, 646–56. New York: Macmillan.

Buruma, Ian. 2000. "Divine Killer." *New York Review of Books*, February 24, 20–25.

———. 2005. "The Indiscreet Charm of Tyranny." *New York Review of Books*, May 12, 35–37.

Butler, Judith. 1989. "Gendering the Body: Beauvoir's Philosophical Contribution." In *Women, Knowledge, and Reality: Explorations in Feminist Philosophy*, ed. Ann Garry and Marilyn Pearsall, 253–73. Boston: Unwin Hyman.

Butterworth, George. 1983. "Structure of the Mind in Human Infancy." In *Advances in Infancy Research*, vol. 2, ed. Lewis P. Lipsitt and Carolyn K. Rovee-Collier, 1–29. Norwood, N.J.: Ablex.

Byers, John A. 1984. "Play in Ungulates." In *Play in Animals and Humans*, ed. Peter K. Smith, 43–65. Oxford: Basil Blackwell.

Caputo, John D. 1997. *The Prayers and Tears of Jacques Derrida*. Bloomington: Indiana University Press.

Carling, Alan. 2000. "Boehm's Golden Age: Equality and Consciousness in Early Human Society." *Journal of Consciousness Studies* 7, no. 1/2: 119–23.

Carpenter, C. R. 1963. "Societies of Monkeys and Apes." In *Primate Social Behavior*, ed. Charles H. Southwick, 24–51. New York: Van Nostrand Reinhold.

Carthy, J. D., and F. J. Ebling, eds. 1964. *The Natural History of Aggression*. New York: Academic Press.

Cataldi, Sue L. 1993. *Emotion, Depth, and Flesh: A Study of Sensitive Space*. Albany: State University of New York Press.

*Cathédrales de France*. 1950. Paris: Éditions des Deux Mondes.

Chance, M.R.A. 1980. "An Ethological Assessment of Emotion." In *Emotion: Theory, Research, and Experience*, ed. R. Plutchik and H. Kellerman. New York: Academic Press.

Ciompi, Luc. 1997. "The Concept of Affect Logic: An Integrative Psycho-Socio-Biological Approach to Understanding and Treatment of Schizophrenia." *Psychiatry* 60:158–70.

Clare, Anthony. 2000. *On Men: Masculinity in Crisis*. London: Chatto and Windus.

Coleman, James C., James N. Butcher, and Robert C. Carson. 1980. *Abnormal Psychology and Modern Life*. 6th ed. Glenview, Ill.: Scott, Foresman.

Council of Europe/Conseil de l'Europe. 1995. *Tackling Racism and Xenophobia: Practical Action at the Local Level*. Strasbourg: Council of Europe Press.

Crick, Francis, and Christof Koch. 1992. "The Problem of Consciousness." *Scientific American*, September 1992, 153–59.

Csibra, Gergely. 2007. "Mirror Neurons and Action Observation: Is Simulation Involved?" *Interdisciplines*, May 19, http://www.interdisciplines.org/mirror/papers/4.

Cunningham, Merce. 1968. *Changes: Notes on Choreography*. New York: Something Else Press.

Curtis, Helena. 1975. *Biology*. 2nd ed. New York: Worth Publishers.

Cushing, F. H. 1892. "Manual Concepts: A Study of the Influence of Hand-Usage on Culture-Growth." *American Anthropologist* 5:289–317.

Daly, Martin, and Margo Wilson. 1983. *Sex, Evolution, and Behavior*. 2nd ed. Belmont, Calif.: Wadsworth.

Damasio, Antonio. 2003. *Looking for Spinoza*. New York: Harcourt.

Darwin, Charles. 1859. *The Origin of Species*. Ed. J. W. Burrow. Harmondsworth, U.K.: Penguin Books, 1968.

———. 1871. *The Descent of Man, and Selection in Relation to Sex*. 2 vols. Princeton: Princeton University Press, 1981.

———. 1872. *The Expression of the Emotions in Man and Animals*. Chicago: University of Chicago Press, 1965.

———. 1881. *Darwin on Earthworms: The Formation of Vegetable Mould Through the Action of Worms with Observations on Their Habits*. Ontario, Calif.: Bookworm, 1976.

———. 1987. *Charles Darwin's Notebooks, 1836–1844*. Ed. Paul H. Barrett, Peter J. Gautrey, Sandra Herbert, David Kohn, and Sydney Smith. Ithaca: Cornell University Press.

Dawkins, Richard. 1989. *The Selfish Gene*. New York: Oxford University Press.

———. 1998. *Unweaving the Rainbow*. Boston: Houghton Mifflin.

Décarie, Thérèse Gouin. 1974. *The Infant's Reaction to Strangers*. Trans. Joyce Diamanti. New York: International Universities Press.

Dennett, Daniel. 1983. "Intentional Systems in Cognitive Ethology: The 'Panglossian Paradigm' Defended." *Behavioral and Brain Sciences* 6:343–90.

Depraz, Natalie. 2001. "The Husserlian Theory of Intersubjectivity as Alterology." *Journal of Consciousness Studies* 8, no. 5–7: 169–78.

de Rivera, Joseph. 1977. *A Structural Theory of the Emotions*. New York: International Universities Press.

Derrida, Jacques. 1973. *Speech and Phenomena*. Trans. Newton Garver. Evanston: Northwestern University Press.

———. 1976. *Of Grammatology*. Trans. Gayatri Spivak. Baltimore: Johns Hopkins University Press.

———. 1978. "La Parole Soufflée." In *Writing and Difference*, trans. Alan Bass, 169–95. Chicago: University of Chicago Press.

Derrida, Jacques, and John Caputo. 1997. *Deconstruction in a Nutshell*. Ed. John Caputo. New York: Fordham University Press.
Descartes, René. 1984. *Meditations on First Philosophy*. In *The Philosophical Writings of Descartes*, vol. 2, trans. John Cottingham, Robert Stoothoff, and Dugald Murdoch, 1–62. Cambridge: Cambridge University Press.
———. 1985a. *The Passions of the Soul*. In *The Philosophical Writings of Descartes*, vol. 1, trans. John Cottingham, Robert Stoothoff, and Dugald Murdoch, 325–404. Cambridge: Cambridge University Press.
———. 1985b. *Principles of Philosophy*. In *The Philosophical Writings of Descartes*, vol. 1, trans. John Cottingham, Robert Stoothoff, and Dugald Murdoch, 177–291. Cambridge: Cambridge University Press.
de Waal, Frans. 1982. *Chimpanzee Politics*. New York: Harper Colophon Books.
de Waal, Frans, and Frans Lanting. 1997. *Bonobo: The Forgotten Ape*. Berkeley and Los Angeles: University of California Press.
Diamond, Jared. 2004. "Twilight at Easter." *New York Review of Books*, March 25, 6–10.
Dieckmann, Bernhard, Christoph Wulf, and Michael Wimmer, eds. 1997. *Violence: Nationalism, Racism, Xenophobia*. European Studies in Education. New York: Waxmann Münster.
Dolhinow, Phyllis Jay. 1972. "The North Indian Langur." In *Primate Patterns*, ed. Phyllis Dolhinow, 181–238. New York: Holt, Rinehart and Winston.
Donaldson, O. Fred. 1995. "Belonging: That Bargain Struck in Child's Play." In "Evolution and Play." Special issue, *ReVision: A Journal of Consciousness and Transformation* 17, no. 4:25–34.
Donne, John. 1624. *Devotions upon Emergent Occasions Together with Death's Duell*. Boston: Small, Maynard, 1926.
Dreyfus, Hubert L., and Paul Rabinow. 1983. *Michel Foucault: Beyond Structuralism and Hermeneutics*. 2nd ed. Chicago: University of Chicago Press.
Dundes, Alan, ed. 1992. *The Evil Eye: A Casebook*. Madison: University of Wisconsin Press.
Eberhard, William G. 1985. *Sexual Selection and Animal Genitalia*. Cambridge: Harvard University Press.
Eibl-Eibesfeldt, Irenäus. 1978. "On the Ontogeny of Behavior of a Male Badger (*Meles Meles* L.) with Particular Reference to Play Behavior." Trans. Christine Müller-Schwarze. In *The Evolution of Play Behavior*, ed. Dietland Müller-Schwarze, 142–48. Stroudsburg, Pa.: Dowden, Hutchinson, and Ross.
———. 1979. *The Biology of Peace and War: Men, Animals, and Aggression*. Trans. Eric Mosbacher. New York: Viking Press.
———. 1980. "Strategies of Social Interaction." In *Emotion: Theory, Research, and Experience*, vol. 1, ed. Robert Plutchik and Henry Kellerman, 57–80. New York, Academic Press.
Eimas, Peter D. 1975. "Speech Perception in Early Infancy." In *Infant Perception*, ed. L. B. Cohen and P. Salapatek, 193–231. New York: Academic Press.
Eimerl, Sarel, and Irven DeVore. 1965. *The Primates*. New York: Times.
Einarsen, A. S. 1948. *The Pronghorn Antelope and Its Management*. Washington, D.C.: The Wildlife Management Institute.

Ekman, Paul. 1989. "The Argument and Evidence About Universals in Facial Expressions of Emotion." In *Handbook of Social Psychophysiology*, ed. H. Wagner and A. Manstead, 143–64. New York: John Wiley and Sons.

———. 1992. "Facial Expressions of Emotion: An Old Controversy and New Findings." *Philosophical Transactions of the Royal Society of London*, series b, 335:1–7.

Elgee, Neil. 2002. "Non-Violent Anger, Soul and Will." *Ernest Becker Foundation Newsletter* 9, no. 1: 2.

Eliot, T. S. 1943. *Four Quartets*. New York: Harcourt, Brace.

Elon, Amos. 2004. "War Without End." *New York Review of Books*, July 15, 26–29.

Emmeche, Claus. 1991. "A Semiotical Reflection on Biology, Living Signs and Artificial Life." *Biology and Philosophy* 6:325–40.

———. 1994. "The Computational Notion of Life." *Theoria* 9, no. 21: 1–30.

*Encyclopédie par L'Image: Les Cathédrales*. 1925. Librairie Hachette, Paris.

Epstein, Jason. 1999. "Always Time to Kill." *New York Review of Books*, November 4, 57–64.

Epstein, Mark. 1995. *Thoughts Without a Thinker*. New York: Basic Books.

Erikson, Erik. 1950. *Childhood and Society*. New York: W. W. Norton.

Evans, J. Claude. 1991. *Strategies of Deconstruction*. Minneapolis: University of Minnesota Press.

Fagen, Robert. 1981. *Animal Play Behavior*. New York: Oxford University Press.

Fedigan, Linda Marie. 1982. *Primate Paradigms: Sex Roles and Social Bonds*. Montreal: Eden Press.

Fink, Eugen. 1939. "The Problem of the Phenomenology of Edmund Husserl." Trans. Robert M. Harlan. In *Apriori and World: European Contributions to Husserlian Phenomenology*, ed. William McKenna, Robert M. Harlan, and Laurence E. Winters, 21–55. The Hague: Martinus Nijhoff, 1981.

———. 1995. *Sixth Cartesian Meditation: The Idea of a Transcendental Theory of Method*. Trans. Ronald Bruzina. Bloomington: Indiana University Press.

Finzsch, Norbert, and Dietmar Schirmer. 1998. *Identity and Intolerance: Nationalism, Racism, and Xenophobia in Germany and the United States*. Cambridge: Cambridge University Press; Washington, D.C.: German Historical Institute.

Firth, Raymond. 1978. "Postures and Gestures of Respect." In *The Body Reader*, ed. Ted Polhemus, 88–108. New York: Pantheon Books.

Fischer, David Hackett. 2004. *Washington's Crossing*. New York: Oxford University Press.

Flew, Anthony. 1964. *Body, Mind, and Death*. New York: Macmillan.

———. 1967. "Immortality." In *The Encyclopedia of Philosophy*, ed. Paul Edwards, 3:139–50. New York: Macmillan.

Folger, Robert, and S. D. Pugh. 2003. "The Just World and Winston Churchill: An Approach/Avoidance Conflict About Psychological Distance When Harming Victims." In *The Justice Motive in Everyday Life: Essays in Honor of Melvin Lerner*, ed. M. Ross and D. T. Miller, 168–86. Cambridge: Cambridge University Press.

Foster, Mary LeCron. 1978. "The Symbolic Structure of Primordial Language."

In *Human Evolution: Biosocial Perspectives*, ed. Sherwood L. Washburn and Elizabeth R. McCown, 77–121. Menlo Park, Calif.: Benjamin/Cummings.
———. 1990. "Symbolic Origins and Transitions in the Paleolithic." In *The Emergence of Modern Humans: An Archaeological Perspective*, ed. Paul Mellars, 517–39. Edinburgh: Edinburgh University Press.
———. 1992. "Body Process in the Evolution of Language." In *Giving the Body Its Due*, ed. Maxine Sheets-Johnstone, 208–30. Albany: State University of New York Press.
———. 1996. "Reconstruction of the Evolution of Human Spoken Language." In *Handbook of Symbolic Evolution*, ed. Andrew Lock and Charles Peters, 747–72. Oxford: Oxford University Press.
Foucault, Michel. 1977. "Nietzsche, Genealogy, History." In *Language, Counter-Memory, and Practice*, ed. Donald F. Bouchard, trans. Donald F. Bouchard and Sherry Simon, 139–64. Ithaca: Cornell University Press.
Fraiberg, Selma. 1987. *Selected Writings of Selma Fraiberg*. Ed. Louis Fraiberg. Columbus: Ohio State University Press.
Francis, Richard. 2004. *Why Men Won't Ask for Directions: The Seductions of Sociobiology*. Princeton: Princeton University Press.
Frank, Robert H. 1999. *Luxury Fever: Why Money Fails to Satisfy in an Era of Excess*. New York: The Free Press.
Freedberg, David, and Vittorio Gallese. 2007. "Motion, Emotion and Empathy in Esthetic Experience." *Trends in Cognitive Sciences* 11, no. 5: 197–203.
French, Peter A., and Howard K. Wettstein, eds. 2000. *Life and Death: Metaphysics and Ethics. Midwest Studies in Philosophy XXIV*. Boston: Blackwell Publishers.
Freud, Sigmund. 1915. "Thoughts for the Times on War and Death." Trans. E. Colburn Mayne. In *On Creativity and the Unconscious*, 206–35. New York: Harper Colophon Books, 1958.
———. 1955. "The Ego and the Id." *The Standard Edition of the Works of Sigmund Freud*, vol. 19, ed. and trans. James Strachey, 19–27. London: Hogarth Press.
———. 1957. "The Acquisition of Power over Fire." In *Collected Papers*, vol. 5, *Miscellaneous Papers 1888–1938*, ed. James Strachey, 288–94. London: The Hogarth Press.
———. 1962. *Civilization and Its Discontents*. Trans. James Strachey. New York: W. W. Norton.
———. 1963. *A General Introduction to Psychoanalysis*. New York: Liveright.
Furuhjelm, Mirjam, Axel Ingelman-Sundbert, and Claes Wirsén. 1976. *A Child Is Born*. Rev. ed. New York: Delacourte Press.
Gallagher, Shaun. 2000. "Phenomenological and Experimental Research on Embodied Experience." Paper presented at Atelier phénoménologie et cognition, CREA, Paris.
———. 2001. "The Practice of Mind." *Journal of Consciousness Studies* 8, no. 5–7: 83–108.
Gallagher, Shaun, and Andrew Meltzoff. 1996. "The Earliest Sense of Self and Others: Merleau-Ponty and Recent Developmental Studies." *Philosophical Psychology* 9:213–36.

Gallese, Vittorio. 2005. "Embodied Simulation: From Neurons to Phenomenal Experience." *Phenomenology and the Cognitive Sciences* 4:23–48.

———. 2007a. "The 'Conscious' Dorsal Stream: Embodied Simulation and Its Role in Space and Action Conscious Awareness." *Psyche* 13, no. 1: 1–20.

———. 2007b. "Intentional Attunement. The Mirror Neuron System and Its Role in Interpersonal Relations." *Interdisciplines*, May 17, http://www.interdisciplines.org/mirror/papers/1.

Gallese, Vittorio, Morris N. Eagle, and Paolo Migone. 2007. "Intentional Attunement: Mirror Neurons and the Neural Underpinnings of Interpersonal Relations." *Journal of the American Psychoanalytic Association* 55:131–76.

Gallese, Vittorio, Luciano Fadiga, Leonardo Fogassi, and Giacomo Rizzolatti. 1996. "Action Recognition in the Premotor Cortex." *Brain* 119:593–609.

Gallese, Vittorio, Christian Keysers, and Giacomo Rizzolatti. 2004. "A Unifying View of the Basis of Social Cognition." *Trends in Cognitive Science* 8, no. 9: 396–403.

Gallese, Vittorio, and George Lakoff. 2005. "The Brain's Concepts: The Role of the Sensory-Motor System in Conceptual Knowledge." *Cognitive Neuropsychology* 21:1–25.

Gardner, Robert, and Karl G. Heider. 1968. *Gardens of War: Life and Death in the New Guinea Stone Age.* New York: Random House.

Garver, Newton. 1973. "Preface" to Jacques Derrida's *Speech and Phenomena*, trans. David B. Allison, ix–xxix. Evanston: Northwestern University Press.

Geertz, Clifford. 1973. *The Interpretation of Cultures.* New York: Basic Books.

Gibbs, Raymond W., Jr. 2006. *Embodiment and Cognitive Science.* New York: Cambridge University Press.

Gilligan, Carol, and Grant Wiggins. 1987. "The Origins of Morality in Early Childhood Relationships." In *The Emergence of Morality in Young Children*, ed. Jerome Kagan and Sharon Lamb, 277–305. Chicago: University of Chicago Press.

Glover, Jonathan. 2000. *Humanity: A Moral History of the Twentieth Century.* New Haven: Yale University Press.

Godolphin, Francis R.B. 1942. *The Greek Historians.* Vol. 1. New York: Random House.

Goins, Major Morris T. 2003. "Quotation of the Day." *New York Times*, April 13. http://www.nytimes.com/2003/04/13/international/worldspecial/13INFA.html?t.

Goldman, Alvin. 2007. "Mirror Systems, Social Understanding and Social Cognition." *Interdisciplines*, May 19, http://www.interdisciplines.org/mirror/papers/3.

Goodall, Jane van Lawick-. 1968. "The Behaviour of Free-Living Chimpanzees in the Gombe Stream Reserve." *Animal Behavioral Monographs*, ed. J. M. Cullen and C. G. Baer, vol. 1, pt. 3.

———. 1971. *In the Shadow of Man.* New York: Dell.

———. 1972. "A Preliminary Report on Expressive Movements and Communication in the Gombe Stream Chimpanzees." In *Primate Patterns*, ed. Phyllis Dolhinow, 25–84. New York: Holt, Rinehart and Winston.

———. 1973. "Cultural Elements in a Chimpanzee Community." In *Precultural Primate Behavior*, ed. Emil W. Menzel Jr., 144–84. Basel: S. Karger.
———. 1990. *Through a Window: My Thirty Years with the Chimpanzees of Gombe*. Boston: Houghton Mifflin.
Goodwin, Brian. 2001. *How the Leopard Changed Its Spots*. Princeton: Princeton University Press.
Gould, Stephen Jay, and Richard Lewontin. 1979. "The Spandrels of San Marco and the Panglossian Paradigm: A Critique of the Adaptationist Programme." *Proceedings of the Royal Society of London*, series b, *Biological Science* 205:581–98.
Gould, Stephen J., and Elisabeth S. Vrba. 1982. "Exaptation—A Missing Term in the Science of Form." *Paleobiology* 8:4–15.
Gowitzke, Barbara A., and Morris Milner. 1988. *Scientific Bases of Human Movement*. 3rd ed. Baltimore: Williams and Wilkins.
Graves, Robert. 1960. *The Greek Myths*. 2 vols. Harmondsworth, U.K.: Penguin Books.
Grene, Marjorie. 1967. "Martin Heidegger." In *The Encyclopedia of Philosophy*, ed. Paul Edwards, 3:459–65. New York: Macmillan.
Groos, Karl 1901. *The Play of Man*. London: William Heinemann.
Hall, K.R.L. 1967. "Social Interactions of the Adult Male and Adult Females of a Patas Monkey Group." In *Social Communication among Primates*, ed. Stuart A. Altmann, 261–80. Chicago: University of Chicago Press.
———. 1968. "Aggression in Monkey and Ape Societies." In *Primates: Studies in Adaptation and Variability*, ed. Phyllis C. Jay, 149–71. New York: Holt, Rinehart and Winston.
Haraway, Donna. 1985. "A Manifesto for Cyborgs: Science, Technology, and Socialist Feminism in the 1980s." *Socialist Review* 15, no. 2: 65–107.
Hardin, Russell. 2002. *Trust and Trustworthiness*. New York: Russell Sage Foundation.
Hedges, Chris. 2002. *War Is a Force That Gives Us Meaning*. New York: Public Affairs.
Heidegger, Martin. 1962. *Being and Time*. Trans. John Macquarrie and Edward Robinson. New York: Harper & Row.
———. 1977a. "Letter on Humanism." Trans. Frank A. Capuzzi amd J. Glenn Gray. In *Basic Writings*, ed. David Farrell Krell, 193–242. New York: Harper & Row.
———. 1977b. "The Origin of the Work of Art." Trans. Albert Hofstadter. In *Basic Writings*, edited and abridged by David Farrell Krell, 149–87. New York: Harper & Row.
Heider, Karl. 1979. *Grand Valley Dani: Peaceful Warriors*. New York: Holt, Rinehart and Winston.
Hertz, Robert. 1973. "The Pre-eminence of the Right Hand: A Study in Religious Polarity." In *Right & Left: Essays on Dual Symbolic Classification*, ed. Rodney Needham, 3–31. Chicago: University of Chicago Press.
Hobbes, Thomas. 1651. *Hobbes: Selections*, Ed. Frederick J. E. Woodbridge. New York: Charles Scribner's Sons, 1930.
Hockett, Charles F. 1960. "The Origin of Speech." *Scientific American*, September, 89–96.

Hoffmeyer, Jesper. 1996. *Signs of Meaning in the Universe*. Trans. Barbara J. Haveland. Bloomington: Indiana University Press.

Hoffmeyer, Jesper, and Claus Emmeche. 1991. "Code-Duality and the Semiotics of Nature." In *On Semiotic Modeling*, ed. Myrdene Anderson and Floyd Merrell. New York: Mouton de Gruyter.

Höglund, Jacob, and Rauno V. Alatalo. 1995. *Leks*. Princeton: Princeton University Press.

Holloway, Ralph L. 1974. *Primate Aggression, Territoriality, and Xenophobia: A Comparative Perspective*. New York: Academic Press.

Hughes, Robert. 2003. *Goya*. New York: Alfred A. Knopf.

Huizinga, Johan. 1955. *Homo ludens: A Study of the Play-Element in Culture*. Boston: Beacon Press.

Human Rights Watch/Helsinki. 1995. *"Germany for Germans": Xenophobia and Racist Violence in Germany*. New York: Human Rights Watch.

Hume, David. 1739. *A Treatise of Human Nature: Being an Attempt to Introduce the Experimental Method of Reasoning into Moral Subjects*. Ed. L. A. Selby-Bigge. Oxford: Clarendon Press, 1888.

Humphrey, Nicholas. 2000. *How to Solve the Mind-Body Problem*. Thorverton, U.K.: Imprint Academic.

Humphreys, Anne P., and Peter K. Smith. 1984. "Rough-and-Tumble in Preschool and Playground." In *Play in Animals and Humans*, ed. Peter K. Smith, 241–69. Oxford: Basil Blackwell.

Hurley, Susan L. 2007. "The Shared Circuits Model: How Control, Mirroring, and Simulation Can Enable Imitation and Mind Reading." *Interdisciplines*, May 19, http://www.interdisciplines.org/mirror/papers/5.

Husserl, Edmund. 1970a. *The Crisis of European Sciences and Transcendental Phenomenology: An Introduction to Phenomenological Philosophy*. Trans. David Carr. Evanston: Northwestern University Press.

———. 1970b. "The Origin of Geometry." In *The Crisis of European Sciences and Transcendental Phenomenology*, trans. David Carr, 353–78. Evanston: Northwestern University Press.

———. 1973. *Cartesian Meditations*. Trans. Dorion Cairns. The Hague: Martinus Nijhoff.

———. 1977. *Phenomenological Psychology*. Trans. John Scanlon. The Hague: Martinus Nijhoff.

———. 1980. *Ideas Pertaining to a Pure Phenomenology and to a Phenomenological Philosophy: Third Book (Ideas III)*. Trans. Ted E. Klein and William E. Pohl. The Hague: Martinus Nijhoff.

———. 1983. *Ideas Pertaining to a Pure Phenomenology and to a Phenomenological Philosophy, First Book (Ideas I)*. Trans. Fred Kersten. The Hague: Martinus Nijhoff.

———. 1989. *Ideas Pertaining to a Pure Phenomenology and to a Phenomenological Philosophy, Second Book (Ideas II)*. Trans. Richard Rojcewicz and André Schuwer. Dordrecht: Kluwer Academic.

Hutton, James. 1795. *Theory of the Earth*. Vols. 1 and 2. Weinheim: H. R. Engelmann, 1960.

Hyland, Drew A. 1984. *The Question of Play*. Lanham, Md.: University Press of America.

Iacobnoi, Marco, Istvan Molnar-Szakacs, Vittorio Gallese, Giovanni Buccino, John C. Mazzlotta, and Giacomo Rizzolatti. 2005. "Grasping the Intentions of Others with One's Own Mirror Neuron System." *PLoS Biology* 3, no. 3: 1–7, http://www.plosbiology.org.
Ignatieff, Michael. 1999. "Human Rights: The Midlife Crisis." *New York Review of Books*, May 20, 58–62.
Jacob, Pierre, and Marc Jeannerod. 2007. "The Motor Theory of Social Cognition: A Critique." *Interdisciplines*, May 19, http://www.interdisciplines.org/mirror/papers/2.
James, William. 1890. *The Principles of Psychology*. Vol. 2. New York: Dover, 1950.
———. 1910. "The Moral Equivalent of War." In *Philosophical Perspectives on Peace: An Anthology of Classical and Modern Sources*, ed. Howard P. Kainz, 213–25. Athens: Ohio University Press, 1987.
Johnsgard, Paul. A. 1994. *Arena Birds: Sexual Selection and Behavior*. Washington, D.C.: Smithsonian Institution Press.
Jolly, Clifford. 1970. "The Seed Eaters: A New Model of Hominid Differentiation Based on Baboon Analogy." *Man* 5:5–26.
Jung, Carl G. 1960. *On the Nature of the Psyche*. Trans. R. F. C. Hull. Ed. Sir Herbert Read, Michael Fordham, Gerhard Adler, and William McGuire. In *Collected Works*, vol. 8. Bollingen Series XX. Princeton: Princeton University Press.
———. 1967. *Alchemical Studies*. Trans. R. F. C. Hull. Ed. Sir Herbert Read, Michael Fordham, Gerhard Adler, and William McGuire. *Collected Works*, vol. 13. Bollingen Series XX. Princeton: Princeton University Press.
———. 1968a. *The Archetypes and the Collective Unconscious*. 2nd ed. Trans. R. F. C. Hull. Ed. Sir Herbert Read, Michael Fordham, Gerhard Adler, and William McGuire. *Collected Works*, vol. 9, pt. 1. Bollingen Series XX. Princeton: Princeton University Press.
———. 1968b. *Aion: Researches into the Phenomenology of the Self*. 2nd ed. Trans. R. F. C. Hull. Ed. Sir Herbert Read, Michael Fordham, Gerhard Adler, and William McGuire. *Collected Works*, vol. 9, pt. 2. Bollingen Series XX. Princeton: Princeton University Press.
———. 1969. *On the Nature of the Psyche*. Trans. R. F. C. Hull. Ed. Sir Herbert Read, Michael Fordham, Gerhard Adler, and William McGuire. *Collected Works*, vol. 8. Bollingen Series XX. Princeton: Princeton University Press.
———. 1971. "Answer to Job." In *The Portable Jung*, ed. Joseph Campbell, trans. R. F. C. Hull, 519–650. New York: Viking Press.
Kainz, Howard P., ed. 1987. *Philosophical Perspectives on Peace: An Anthology of Classical and Modern Sources*. Athens: Ohio University Press.
Kant, Immanuel. 1784. "An Answer to the Question: What Is Enlightenment?" In *Perpetual Peace and Other Essays*, trans. Ted Humphrey, 41–48. Indianapolis: Hackett, 1983.
Katz, Leonard D., ed. 2000. "Evolutionary Origins of Morality: Cross Disciplinary Perspectives." Special issue, *Journal of Consciousness Studies* 7, no. 1/2.
Keeley, Lawrence H. 1996. *War Before Civilization*. New York: Oxford University Press.

Keen, Sam. 1991a. "To Create an Enemy." In *Faces of the Enemy: Reflections of the Hostile Imagination*. New York: HarperCollins.
———. 1991b. *Fire in the Belly: On Being a Man*. New York: Bantam Books.
———. N.d. "Conversation with Ernest Becker." Manuscript.
Keenan, Brian. 1992. *An Evil Cradling*. New York: Viking.
Keeton, William T., and James L. Gould. 1986. *Biological Science*. 4th ed. New York: W. W. Norton.
Keith, Sir Arthur. 1946. *Essays on Human Evolution*. London: Watts.
———. 1968. *A New Theory of Human Evolution*. Gloucester, Mass.: Peter Smith.
Kelso, J. A. Scott. 1995. *Dynamic Patterns: The Self-Organization of Brain and Behavior*. Cambridge: Bradford Books/MIT Press.
Kidd, José E. Ramírez. 1999. *Alterity and Identity in Israel*. Berlin: Walter de Gruyter.
Kingdon, Jonathan. 2003. *Lowly Origin: Where, When, and Why Our Ancestors First Stood Up*. Princeton: Princeton University Press.
Kinsley, David R. 1993. *Hinduism: A Cultural Perspective*. 2nd ed. Englewood Cliffs, N.J.: Prentice Hall.
Koestler, Arthur. 1964. *The Act of Creation*. New York: Macmillan.
Krebs, Dennis. 2000. "As Moral as We Need to Be." In "Commentary Discussion of Christopher Boehm's Paper." In "Evolutionary Origins of Morality: Cross Disciplinary Perspectives," ed. Leonard D. Katz. Special issue, *Journal of Consciousness Studies* 7, no. 1/2: 139–43.
Kummer, Hans. 1968. "Two Variations in the Social Organization of Baboons." In *Primates: Studies in Adaptation and Variability*, ed. Phyllis C. Jay, 293–312. New York: Holt, Rinehart and Winston.
Lamarck, Jean Baptiste. 1960. *Philosophie zoologique*. Weinheim: H. R. Engelmann.
———. 1963. *Zoological Philosophy*. Trans. Hugh Eliot. New York: Hafner.
Landis, Carney, and William A. Hunt. 1968. *The Startle Pattern*. New York: Johnson Reprint.
Langer, Robert. 1999. "Millennial Musings." *Chemical and Engineering News*, December 6, 92.
Larson, David E., ed. 1990. *Mayo Clinic Family Health Book*. New York: William Morrow.
Lawrence, D. H. 1980. *Apocalypse and the Writings on Revelation*. Ed. Mara Kalnins. Cambridge: Cambridge University Press.
Leach, Edmund. 1967. "The Bible as Myth." In *Myth and Cosmos*, ed. John Middleton, 1–13. Austin: University of Texas Press.
LeShan, Lawrence. 1992. *The Psychology of War: Comprehending Its Mystique and Its Madness*. Chicago: Noble Press
Liberman, Alvin M., and Ignatius G. Mattingly. 1985. "The Motor Theory of Speech Perception Revised." *Cognition* 21, no. 1: 1–36.
Lieberman, Philip. 1983. "On the Nature and Evolution of the Biological Bases of Language." In *Glossogenetics*, ed. E. de Grolier, 91–114. New York: Harwood.
Lill, Alan. 1976. *Lek Behavior in the Golden-Headed Manakin, Pipra erythrocephala in Trinidad*. Berlin: Verlag Paul Parey.

Lloyd, G. E. R. 1966. *Polarity and Analogy: Two Types of Argumentation in Early Greek Thought*. Cambridge: Cambridge University Press.
Lorenz, Konrad. 1966. *On Aggression*. Trans. Marjorie Kerr Wilson. New York: Bantam Books/Harcourt, Brace & World.
Love, Glen A. 2003. *Practical Ecocriticism: Literature, Biology, and the Environment*. Charlottesville: University of Virginia Press.
Loy, David. 1992. "The Deconstruction of Buddhism." In *Derrida and Negative Theology*, ed. Harold Coward and Toby Foshay, 227–53. Albany: State University of New York Press.
———. 2000. *Lack and Transcendence*. Amherst, N.Y.: Humanity Books.
Ludwig, Theodore M. 1994. *The Sacred Paths of the West*. New York: Macmillan.
Luhmann, Niklas. 1979. *Trust and Power*. Trans. Howard Davis, John Raffan, and Kathryn Rooney. Ed. Toms Burns and Gianfranco Poggi. New York: John Wiley & Sons.
Luria, Alexander. 1973. *The Working Brain*. Trans. Basil Haigh. Harmondsworth, U.K.: Penguin Books.
Maccoby, Eleanor Emmons, and Carol Nagy Jacklin. 1974. *The Psychology of Sex Differences*. Stanford: Stanford University Press.
Malinowski, Bronislaw. 1948. *Magic, Science and Religion and Other Essays*. Glencoe, Ill.: The Free Press.
Malnes, Raino. 1993. *The Hobbesian Theory of International Conflict*. Oslo: Scandinavian University Press.
Marler, Peter. 1968."Aggregation and Dispersal: Two Functions in Primate Communication." In *Primates: Studies in Adaptation and Variability*, ed. Phyllis C. Jay, 420–38. New York: Holt, Rinehart and Winston.
Marlowe, David H. 2001. *Psychological and Psychosocial Consequences of Combat and Deployment*. Santa Monica, Calif.: Rand.
Mayr, Ernst. 1988. *Toward a New Philosophy of Biology*. Cambridge: Harvard University Press.
McCullough, David. 1992. *Brave Companions: Portraits in History*. New York: Simon and Schuster/Touchstone.
McCully, Marilyn. 2002. "The Surreal Life of Dora Maar." *New York Review of Books*, April 25, 25–28, 37.
McWhorter, Ladelle. 1989. "Culture or Nature? The Function of the Term 'Body' in the Work of Michel Foucault." *Journal of Philosophy* 86, no. 11: 608–14.
Mead, Margaret. 1968. "Introduction." *Gardens of War: Life and Death in the New Guinea Stone Age*. New York: Random House.
Meeker, Joseph W. 1995. "Comedy and a Play Ethic." In "Evolution and Play." Special issue, *ReVision: A Journal of Consciousness and Transformation* 17, no. 4:21–24.
Mehler, Jacques, Peter Jusczyk, Ghislaine Lambertz, Nilfar Halsted, Hosiane Bertoncini, and Claudine Amiel-Tison. N.d. "A Precursor of Language Acquisition in Young Infants." Laboratoire de Sciences Cognitives et Psycholinguistique, CNRS and EHESS, Paris.
Meltzoff, Andrew N. 1990. "Foundations for Developing a Concept of Self: The Role of Imitation in Relating Self to Other and the Value of Social Mirror-

ing, Social Modeling, and Self Practice in Infancy." In *The Self in Transition: Infancy to Childhood*, ed. D. Cicchetti and M. Beeghly, 139–64. Chicago: University of Chicago Press.

———. 1993. "The Centrality of Motor Coordination and Proprioception in Social and Cognitive Development: From Shared Actions to Shared Minds." In *The Development of Coordination in Infancy*, ed. G. J. P. Savelsberghin, 463–96. New York: Elsevier Science Publishers.

———. 1995. "Understanding the Intentions of Others: Re-Enactment of Intended Acts by 18-Month Old Children." *Developmental Psychology* 31, no. 5: 838–50.

Meltzoff, Andrew N., and M. Keith Moore. 1977. "Imitation of Facial and Manual Gestures by Human Neonates." *Science* 198:75–78.

———. 1983. "Newborn Infants Imitate Adult Facial Gestures." *Child Development* 54:702–9.

———. 1994. "Imitation, Memory, and the Representation of Persons." *Infant Behavior and Development* 17:83–99.

———. 1995. "Infants' Understanding of People and Things: From Body Imitation to Folk Psychology." In *The Body and the Self*, ed. J. L. Bermúdez, A. Marcel, and N. Eilan, 43–69. Cambridge: MIT Press.

Menaker, Esther. 1982. *Otto Rank: A Rediscovered Legacy*. New York: Columbia University Press.

Menzel, Emil. 1973. "Leadership and Communication in Young Chimpanzees." In *Precultural Primate Behavior*, ed. Emil Menzel, 192–225. Basel: Karger.

Merchant, Carolyn. 1980. *The Death of Nature*. New York: Harper and Row.

Merleau-Ponty, Maurice. 1962. *Phenomenology of Perception*. Trans. Colin Smith. New York: Routledge and Kegan Paul.

———. 1964. *Le visible et l'invisible*. Paris: Éditions Gallimard.

———. 1968. *The Visible and the Invisible*. Ed. Claude Lefort. Trans. Alphonso Lingis. Evanston: Northwestern University Press.

Milgram, Stanley. 1973. *Obedience to Authority: An Experimental View*. New York: Harper and Row.

Milius, Susan. 2001. "First Gene-Altered Primate Beats the Odds." *Science News*, January 20, 38.

Mishra, Pankaj. 2000. "Death in Kashmir." *New York Review of Books*, September 21, 36–42.

Monick, Eugene. 1987. *Phallos: Sacred Image of the Masculine*. Toronto: Inner City Books.

Moran, Dermot. 2000. *Introduction to Phenomenology*. New York: Routledge.

Morris, Desmond. 1967. *The Naked Ape*. New York: Dell.

Morton, Eugene S., and Bridget J.M. Stutchbury. 1998. "Editor's Preface." In Martin Moynihan, *The Social Regulation of Competition and Aggression in Animals*. Washington, D.C.: Smithsonian Institution Press.

Mysterud, Iver. 2000. "Group Selection, Morality, and Environmental Problems." *Journal of Consciousness Studies* 7, no. 1/2: 225–27.

Nagel, Ueli, and Hans Kummer. 1974. "Variation in Cercopithecoid Aggressive Behavior." In *Primate Aggression, Territoriality, and Xenophobia*, ed. Ralph L. Holloway. New York: Academic Press.

Needham, Rodney, ed. 1973. *Right & Left: Essays on Dual Symbolic Classification*. Chicago: University of Chicago Press.
———. 1987. *Counterpoints*. Berkeley and Los Angeles: University of California Press.
Nesse, Randolph. 2000. "How Selfish Genes Shape Moral Passions." In "Commentary Discussion of Sober and Wilson's 'Unto Others.'" In "Evolutionary Origins of Morality: Cross Disciplinary Perspectives," ed. Leonard D. Katz. Special issue, *Journal of Consciousness Studies* 7, no. 1/2: 227–31.
Neumann, Erich. 1963. *The Great Mother: An Analysis of the Archetype*. Trans. Ralph Manheim. Bollingen Series XLVII. Princeton: Princeton University Press.
Nooteboom, Bart. 2002. *Trust: Forms, Foundations, Functions, Failures, and Figures*. Cheltenham, U.K.: Edward Elgar.
Norton-Taylor, Duncan. 1974. *The Celts*. New York: Time-Life Books.
Nuland, Sherwin B. 1994. *How We Die*. New York: Knopf.
———. 2005. "Killing Cures." *New York Review of Books*, August 11, 23–25.
Nussbaum, Martha C. 1994. *The Therapy of Desire*. Princeton: Princeton University Press.
———. 2003. "Emotions as Judgments of Value and Importance." In *What Is an Emotion?* ed. Robert C. Solomon, 271–83. New York: Oxford University Press.
Oakley, Robin. 1996. *Tackling Racist and Xenophobic Violence in Europe: Review and Practical Guidance*. Strasbourg: Council of Europe Publications.
———, consultant. 1997. *Tackling Racist and Xenophobic Violence in Europe: Case Studies*. Strasbourg: Council of Europe Publications.
O'Donald, Peter. 1980. *Genetic Models of Sexual Selection*. Cambridge: Cambridge University Press.
Orr, H. Allen. 2005. "Vive la Différence!" *New York Review of Books*, May 12, 18–20.
Overgaard, Søren. 2003. "The Importance of Bodily Movement to Husserl's Theory of *Fremderfahrung*." *Recherches Husserliennes* 19:55–65.
Panksepp, Jaak. 2000. "The Neuro-Evolutionary Cusp Between Emotions and Cognitions: Implications for Understanding Consciousness and the Emergence of a Unified Mind Science." *Consciousness and Emotion* 1, no. 1: 15–54.
Parker, Geoff. 1998. "Sperm Competition and the 'Evolution of Ejaculates': Towards a Theory Base." In *Sperm Competition and Sexual Selection*, ed. T. R. Birkhead and A. P. Moller. San Diego: Academic Press.
Pellis, Sergio M., and Vivien C. Pellis. 1996. "On Knowing It's Only Play: The Role of Play Signals in Play Fighting." *Aggression and Violent Behavior* 1, no. 3: 249–68.
———. 1998. "The Structure-Function Interface in the Analysis of Play Fighting." In *Animal Play: Evolutionary, Comparative, and Ecological Perspectives*, ed. Marc Bekoff and John A. Byers, 115–40. Cambridge: Cambridge University Press.
Perutz, M. F. 2000. "The Threat of Biological Warfare." *New York Review of Books*, April 13, 44–49.

Peters, Roger, and L. David Mech. 1975. "Behavioral and Intellectual Adaptations of Selected Mammalian Predators to the Problem of Hunting Large Animals." In *Sociology and Psychology of Primates*, ed. Russell H. Tuttle. The Hague: Mouton.

Peterson, Jordan. 1999. *Maps of Meaning*. New York: Routledge.

Petitot, Jean, Francisco J. Varela, Bernard Pachoud, and Jean-Michel Roy, eds. 1999. *Naturalizing Phenomenology: Issues in Contemporary Phenomenology and Cognitive Science*. Stanford: Stanford University Press.

Phillips, Adam. 2000. *Darwin's Worms*. New York: Basic Books.

Piaget, Jean. 1968, 6th ed. *La naissance de l'intelligence chez l'enfant*. Neucháftel, Switzerland: Delachaux et Niestlé.

Pinker, Steven. 1997. *How the Mind Works*. New York: W. W. Norton.

Polanyi, Michael. 1969. *Knowing and Being*. Chicago: University of Chicago Press.

Polybius. 1979. *The Rise of the Roman Empire*. Trans. Ian Scott-Kilvert. Harmondsworth, U.K.: Penguin Books.

Poulin-Dubois, Diane. 1999. "Infants' Distinction Between Animate and Inanimate Objects: The Origins of Naive Psychology." In *Early Social Cognition: Understanding Others in the First Months of Life*, ed. Philippe Rochat. Mahwah, N.J.: Lawrence Erlbaum Associates.

Price, Kingsley. 1972. "Philosophy of Education, History of." In *Encyclopedia of Philosophy*, ed. Paul Edwards, 6:230–43. New York: Macmillan.

Prinz, Wolfgang, and Andrew N. Meltzoff, eds. 2002. *The Imitative Mind: Development, Evolution, and Brain Bases*. Cambridge: Cambridge University Press.

Pycraft, W. P. 1912. *The Infancy of Animals*. London: Hutchinson.

Quammen, David. 2004. "Was Darwin Wrong?" *National Geographic*, November 2004, 2–35.

Rank, Otto. 1936. *Will Therapy and Truth and Reality*. New York: Knopf.

———. 1950. *Psychology and the Soul*. Trans. William D. Turner. Philadelphia: University of Pennsylvania Press.

———. 1958. *Beyond Psychology*. New York: Dover.

———. 1968. *Will Therapy and Truth and Reality*. Trans. Jessie Taft. New York: Alfred A. Knopf.

———. 1971. *The Double*. Ed. and trans. Harry Tucker Jr. Chapel Hill: University of North Carolina Press.

———. 1998. *Psychology and the Soul: A Study of the Origin, Conceptual Evolution, and Nature of the Soul*. Trans. Gregory C. Richter and E. James Lieberman. Baltimore: Johns Hopkins University Press.

Relethford, John. 1990. *The Human Species: An Introduction to Biological Anthropology*. Mountain View, Calif.: Mayfield Publishing.

Reynaud, Emmanuel. 1983. *Holy Virility: The Social Construction of Masculinity*. Trans. Ros Schwartz. London: Pluto Press.

Richardson, Lewis Fry. 1960. *Statistics of Deadly Quarrels*. Ed. Quincy Wright and C. C. Lienau. Philadelphia: Boxwood Press; Chicago: Quadrangle Books.

Ridley, Matt. 1996. *The Origins of Virtue*. Harmondsworth, U.K.: Penguin Books.

Rifkin, Jeremy. 2005. "Are You a Man or a Mouse? *Guardian Unlimited* (U.K.), March 15, http://www.guardian.co.uk/comment/story/0,,1437701,00 .html.
Rizzolatti, Giacomo, and Laila Craighero. 2004. "The Mirror Neuron System." *Annual Review of Neuroscience* 27:169–92.
Rizzolatti, Giacomo, Luciano Fadiga, Vittorio Gallese, and Leonardo Fogassi. 1996. "Premotor Cortex and the Recognition of Motor Actions." *Cognitive Brain Research* 3:131–41.
Rizzolatti, Giacomo, and Vittorio Gallese. 1997. "From Action to Meaning: A Neurophysiological Perspective." In *Les Neurosciences et la philosophie de l'action,* ed. Jean-Luc Petit, 217–29. Paris: Librairie Philosophique J. Vrin.
Robeck, Mildred C. 1978. *Infants and Children: Their Development and Learning.* New York: McGraw-Hill.
Robinson, John. 1962. "The Australopithecines and Their Bearing on the Origin of Man and of Stone Tool-Making." In *Ideas on Human Evolution: Selected Essays, 1949–1961,* ed. William Howells, 279–94. New York: Atheneum.
Robinson, Mary. 2000. "Chechnya: Mary Robinson's Report." *New York Review of Books,* May 25, 12–13.
Rochat, Philippe. 2001. *The Infant's World.* Cambridge: Harvard University Press.
Roediger, Henry L. III, J. Philippe Rushton, Elizabeth Deutsch Capaldi, and Scott G. Paris. 1987. *Psychology.* 2nd ed. Boston: Little, Brown.
Rowell, Thelma. 1972. *The Social Behaviour of Monkeys.* Harmondsworth, U.K.: Penguin Books.
Roy, M. Aaron, ed. 1980. *Species Identity and Attachment: A Phylogenetic Evaluation.* New York: Garland STPM Press.
Rudofsky, Bernard. 1971. "The Fashionable Body." *Horizon* 13, no. 4: 56–65.
Ruse, Michael, and E. O. Wilson. "The Evolution of Ethics." *New Scientist* 17: 50–52.
Sagi, Abraham, and Martin L. Hoffman. 1976. "Empathic Distress in the Newborn." *Developmental Psychology* 12, no. 2: 175–76.
Sallis, John. 1971. "On the Limitation of Transcendental Reflection or Is Intersubjectivity Transcendental?" *Monist,* 312–33.
Sartre, Jean-Paul. 1947. *Huit-Clos.* Paris: Editions Gallimard.
———. 1955. *No Exit.* New York: Vintage Books.
———. 1956. *Being and Nothingness.* Trans. Hazel E. Barnes. New York: Philosophical Library.
Sartre, Jean-Paul, and Benny Levy. 1996. *Hope Now: The 1980 Interviews.* Trans. Adrian van den Hoven. Chicago: University of Chicago Press.
Savage-Rumbaugh, Sue. 1993. "Data Base to Accompany *Bonobo People."* Atlanta: Language Research Center, Georgia State University. Video tape.
Schaller, George. 1972. *The Serengeti Lion.* Chicago: University of Chicago Press.
Scheler, Max. 1954. *The Nature of Sympathy.* Trans. Peter Heath. New Haven: Yale University Press.
Schopenhauer, Arthur. 1915. *The Basis of Morality.* Trans. Arthur Brodrick Bullock. New York: Macmillan.

Schulz, Walter. 2000. "On the Problem of Death." Trans. Chad Albers. *Continental Philosophy Review* 33, no. 4: 467–86.
Schutz, Alfred. 1966. "The Problem of Transcendental Intersubjectivity in Husserl." In *Collected Papers III: Studies in Phenomenological Philosophy*, ed. I. Schutz, 51–91. The Hague: Martinus Nijhoff.
Schwartz, Hillel. 1996. *The Culture of the Copy*. New York: Zone Books.
Seabright, Paul. 2004. *The Company of Strangers: A Natural History of Economic Life*. Princeton: Princeton University Press.
Searle, John. 1969. *Speech Acts*. Cambridge: Cambridge University Press.
———. 1983. *Intentionality*. Cambridge: Cambridge University Press.
Seidler, Victor Jeleniewski. 1997. *Man Enough: Embodying Masculinities*. London: Sage Publications.
Sheets-Johnstone, Maxine. 1966. *The Phenomenology of Dance*. Madison: University of Wisconsin Press. 2nd ed. London: Dance Books, 1979; New York: Arno Press, 1980.
———. 1982. "Why Lamarck Did Not Discover the Principle of Natural Selection." *Journal of the History of Biology* 15, no. 3: 443–65.
———. 1986a. "Existential Fit and Evolutionary Continuities." *Synthese* 66:219–48.
———. 1986b. "On the Conceptual Origin of Death." *Philosophy and Phenomenological Research* 47, no. 1: 31–58.
———. 1990. *The Roots of Thinking*. Philadelphia: Temple University Press.
———. 1992. "Taking Evolution Seriously." *American Philosophical Quarterly* 29, no. 4: 343–52.
———. 1994a. "The Body as Cultural Object/The Body as Pan-Cultural Universal." In *Phenomenology of the Cultural Disciplines*, ed. Mano Daniel and Lester Embree, 85–114. Dordrecht: Kluwer Academic.
———. 1994b. *The Roots of Power: Animate Form and Gendered Bodies*. Chicago: Open Court.
———. 1996. "Taking Evolution Seriously: A Matter of Primate Intelligence." *Etica & Animali* 8:115–30.
———. 1999a. "Emotions and Movement: A Beginning Empirical-Phenomenological Analysis of Their Relationship." *Journal of Consciousness Studies* 6, no. 11–12: 259–77.
———. 1999b. *The Primacy of Movement*. Amsterdam/Philadelphia: John Benjamins.
———. 1999c. "Re-Thinking Husserl's Fifth Meditation." *Philosophy Today* 43: Suppl. 99–106.
———. 1999d. "Sensory-Kinetic Understandings of Language: An Inquiry into Origins." *Evolution of Communication* 3, no. 2: 149–83.
———. 2000. "Binary Opposition as an Ordering Principle of (Male?) Human Thought." In *Feminist Phenomenology*, ed. Linda Fisher and Lester Embree, 173–94. Dordrecht: Kluwer Academic.
———. 2002a. "Descriptive Foundations." *Interdisciplinary Studies in Literature and Environment* 9, no. 1: 165–79.
———. 2002b. "Size, Power, Death: Constituents in the Making of Human Morality." *Journal of Consciousness Studies* 9, no. 2: 49–67.

---. 2003a. "Child's Play: A Multidisciplinary Perspective." (Keynote Address at Society for the Philosophy of Sport, Pennsylvania State University, October 2002.) *Human Studies* 26:409–30.
---. 2003b. "Kinesthetic Memory." *Theoria et Historia Scientiarum* (Nicolas Copernicus University) 7, no. 1: 69–92.
---. 2003c. "Death and Immortality Ideologies in Western Philosophy." *Continental Philosophy Review* 36: 235–262.
---. 2004. "Preserving Integrity Against Colonization." *Phenomenology and the Cognitive Sciences* 3:249–61.
---. 2005. "What Are We Naming?" (Keynote Address, International Workshop, "Body Image and Body Schema: (Neuro)phenomenological, (Neuro)psychoanalytical and Neuroscientific Perspectives," University of Ghent, 30 March–1 April 2003.) In *Body Image and Body Schema: Interdisciplinary Perspectives on the Body*, ed. Helena De Preester and Veroniek Knockaert, 211–31. Amsterdam/Philadelphia: John Benjamins.
---. 2006a. "Essential Clarifications of 'Self-Affection' and Husserl's 'Sphere of Ownness': First Steps Toward a Pure Phenomenology of (Human) Nature." *Continental Philosophy Review* 39:361–91.
---. 2006b. "Sur la nature de la confiance." Trans. Albert Ogien. In *Les moments de la confiance*, ed. Albert Ogien and Louis Quéré, 23–41. Paris: Economica.
---. 2007. "Finding Common Ground Between Evolutionary Biology and Continental Philosophy." *Phenomenology and the Cognitive Sciences* 6, no. 3: 327–48.
Sherrard, Philip. 1966. *Byzantium*. New York: Time-Life Books.
Simic, Charles. 2000. "Anatomy of a Murderer." *New York Review of Books*, January 20, 26–29.
Simmons, Leigh W. 2001. *Sperm Competition and Its Evolutionary Consequences in the Insects*. Princeton: Princeton University Press.
Sinnott, Edmund Ware. 1963. *The Problem of Organic Form*. New Haven: Yale University Press.
Sober, Elliott, and David Sloan Wilson. 2000a. "Morality and 'Unto Others': Response to Commentary Discussion." In "Evolutionary Origins of Morality: Cross Disciplinary Perspectives," ed. Leonard D. Katz. Special issue, *Journal of Consciousness Studies* 7, no. 1/2: 257–68.
---. 2000b. "Summary of Unto Others: The Evolution and Psychology of Unselfish Behavior." In "Evolutionary Origins of Morality: Cross Disciplinary Perspectives," ed. Leonard D. Katz. Special issue, *Journal of Consciousness Studies* 7, no. 1/2: 185–206.
Socrates. *Apology*. 1937. *The Dialogues of Plato*. Trans. B. Jowett. Vol. 1. New York: Random House.
Southwick, Charles H. 1963. *Primate Social Behavior*. New York: Van Nostrand Reinhold.
Spencer, Herbert. 1892. *The Principles of Ethics*. Vol. 1. Indianapolis: Liberty Classics, 1978.
Sperry, Roger. 1952. "Neurology and the Mind-Brain Problem." *American Scientist* 40: 291–312.

Spiegelberg, Herbert. 1971. *The Phenomenological Movement: A Historical Introduction.* 2nd ed. Vol. 2. The Hague: Martinus Nijhoff.
Spitz, René. 1965. *The First Year of Life: A Psychoanalytic Study of Normal and Deviant Object Relations.* New York: International Universities Press.
———. 1983. *Dialogues from Infancy.* Ed. Robert N. Emde. New York: International Universities Press.
Sroufe, L. Alan. 1996. *Emotional Development: The Organization of Emotional Life in the Early Years.* Cambridge: Cambridge University Press.
Stearns, Frederic R. 1972. *Laughing: Physiology, Pathophysiology, Psychology, Pathopsychology and Development.* Springfield, Ill.: Charles C. Thomas.
Stern, Daniel. 1977. *The First Relationship: Mother and Infant.* Cambridge: Harvard University Press.
———. 1985. *The Interpersonal World of the Infant: A View from Psychoanalysis and Developmental Psychology.* New York: Basic Books.
———. 1990. *Diary of a Baby.* New York: Basic Books.
Stevens, Anthony. 1983. *Archetypes: A Natural History of the Self.* New York: Quill.
Strum, Shirley C. 1987. *Almost Human: A Journey into the World of Baboons.* New York: W. W. Norton.
Sully, James. 1907. *An Essay on Laughter: Its Forms, Its Causes, Its Development and Its Value.* New York: Longmans, Green.
Symons, Donald. 1978. *Play and Aggression: A Study of Rhesus Monkeys.* New York: Columbia University Press.
Takooshian, Harold. 2000. "How Stanley Milgram Taught About Obedience and Social Influence." In *Obedience to Authority: Current Perspectives on the Milgram Paradigm,* ed. Thomas Blass, 9–24. Mahway, N.J.: Lawrence Erlbaum Associates.
Thanissaro Bhikkhu, trans. 2003. *Handful of Leaves.* Vol. 4, *An Anthology from the Khuddaka Nikkaya.* Valley Center, Calif.: Sati Center for Buddhist Studies and Metta Forest Monastery.
Thera, Nyanaponika. 1965. *The Heart of Buddhist Meditation.* York Beach, Maine: Samuel Weiser.
Thompson, Evan. 2007. *Mind in Life: Biology, Phenomenology, and the Sciences of Mind.* Cambridge: Belknap Press of Harvard University Press.
Thucydides. 1942. *The Peloponnesian War.* Trans. Benjamin Jowett. In *The Greek Historians,* ed. Francis R. B. Godolphin, 1:567–1001. New York: Random House.
Tiger, Lionel, and Robin Fox. 1971. *The Imperial Animal.* New York: Holt, Rinehart and Winston.
Tinkelpaugh, O. L. 1942. "Social Behavior of Animals." In *Comparative Psychology,* 2nd ed., ed. F. A. Moss. New York: Prentice Hall.
Tomasello, Michael, and Josep Call. 1997. *Primate Cognition.* New York: Oxford University Press.
Tomkins, Silvan S. 1962. *Affect, Imagery, Consciousness.* Vol. 1, *The Positive Aspects.* New York: Springer.
———. 1991. *Affect, Imagery, Consciousness.* Vol. 3, *The Negative Affects: Anger and Fear.* New York: Springer.

———. 1995. *Exploring Affect: The Selected Writings of Silvan S. Tomkins*. Ed. Virginia E. Demos. Cambridge: Cambridge University Press; Paris: Editions de la Maison des Sciences de l'Homme.
Tomkins, Silvan S., and Donald L. Mosher. 1987. "Scripting the Macho Man: Hypermasculine Socialization and Enculturation." *Journal of Sex Research* 25, no. 1: 60–84.
Tooby, J., and L. Cosmides. 1992. "Psychological Foundations of Culture." In *The Adapted Mind: Evolutionary Psychology and the Generation of Culture*, ed. J. H. Barkow, L. Cosmides, and J. Tooby. New York: Oxford University Press.
Toynbee, Arnold J. 1957. *A Study of History*. Vol. 2. Authorized abridgement of vols. 7–10 by D. C. Somervell. New York: Dell.
Traub, James. 2000. "The Worst Place on Earth." *New York Review of Books*, June 29, 61–66.
Trevarthen, Colwyn. 1977. "Descriptive Analyses of Infant Communicative Behaviour." In *Studies in Mother-Infant Interaction*, ed. H. R. Schaffer, 227–70. London: Academic Press.
Trivers, Robert. 1972. "Parental Investment and Sexual Selection." In *Sexual Selection and the Descent of Man, 1871–1971*, ed. Bernard Campbell, 136–79. Chicago: Aldine.
Troyer, John. 2000. "Human and Other Natures." In "Commentary Discussion of [Jessica C.] Flack and [Frans B. M.] de Waal's Paper." In "Evolutionary Origins of Morality: Cross Disciplinary Perspectives," ed. Leonard D. Katz. Special issue, *Journal of Consciousness Studies* 7, no. 1/2: 62–65.
Urquhart, Brian. 2000. "In the Name of Humanity." *New York Review of Books*, April 27, 19–22.
van Buren, John. 1994. "Martin Heidegger, Martin Luther." In *Reading Heidegger from the Start*, ed. Theodore Kisiel and John van Buren, 159–74. New York: State University of New York Press.
Van den Assem, J. 1967. *Territory in the Three-Spined Stickleback Gasterosteus aculeatus L.: An Experimental Study in Intra-Specific Competition*. Leiden: E. J. Brill.
van Hooff, J. A. R. A. M. 1969. "The Facial Displays of the Catarrhine Monkeys and Apes." In *Primate Ethology*, ed. Desmond Morris, 9–88. Garden City, N.Y.: Anchor Books.
———. 1972. "A Comparative Approach to the Phylogeny of Laughter and Smiling." In *Non-Verbal Communication*, ed. R. A. Hinde, 209–41. Cambridge: Cambridge University Press.
Vasta, Ross, Marshall M. Haith, and Scott A. Miller. 1992. *Child Psychology: The Modern Science*. New York: John Wiley & Sons.
Verene, Donald Phillip. 1984. "Technological Desire." In *Research in Philosophy and Technology*, ed. Paul T. Durbin and Carl Mitcham, 7:99–112. Greenwich, Conn.: JAI Press.
Vetlesen, Arne. 1994. *Perception, Empathy, and Judgment: An Inquiry into the Preconditions for Moral Performance*. University Park: Pennsylvania State University Press.
von Uexküll, Jakob. 1934. "A Stroll Through the Worlds of Animals and Men."

Trans. Claire H. Schiller. In *Instinctive Behavior*, ed. Claire H. Schiller, 5–80. New York: International Universities Press, 1957.

Washburn, S. L., and D. A. Hamburg. 1968. "Aggressive Behavior in Old World Monkeys and Apes." In *Primates: Studies in Adaptation and Variability*, ed. Phyllis C. Jay, 458–78. New York: Holt, Rinehart and Winston.

Whiten, Andrew. 1977. "Assessing the Effects of Perinatal Events on the Success of the Mother-Infant Relationship." In *Studies in Mother-Infant Interaction*, ed. H. R. Schaffer, 403–25. New York: Academic Press.

Whiten, A., and R. W. Byrne. 1988. "Tactical Deception in Primates." *Behavioral and Brain Sciences* 11:233–73.

Wilbur, J. B., and H. J. Allen, eds. 1979. *The Worlds of the Early Greek Philosophers*. Buffalo: Prometheus Books.

Wilkie, J. S. 1959. "Buffon, Lamarck, and Darwin: The Originality of Darwin's Theory of Evolution." In *Darwin's Biological Work*, ed. Peter Robert Bell. Cambridge: Cambridge University Press.

Wilkinson, David. 1980. *Deadly Quarrels: Lewis F. Richardson and the Statistical Study of War*. Berkeley and Los Angeles: University of California Press.

Williams, Bernard. 1967. "René Descartes." *The Encyclopedia of Philosophy*, ed. Paul Edwards, 1:344–54. New York: Macmillan.

———. 1978. *Descartes: The Project of Pure Enquiry*. New Jersey: Humanities Press.

Williams, George C. 1989. "A Sociobiological Expansion of *Evolution and Ethics*." In *T. H. Huxley's "Evolution and Ethics" with New Essays on Its Victorian and Sociobiological Context by James Paradis and George C. Williams*. Princeton: Princeton University Press. 179–214.

———. 1993. "Mother Nature Is a Wicked Old Witch." In *Evolutionary Ethics*, ed. Matthew H. Nitecki and Doris V. Nitecki, 217–31. Albany: State University of New York Press.

Wilson, E. O. 1998. *Consilience: The Unity of Knowledge*. New York: Alfred A. Knopf.

Wimmer, Manfred. 1995. "Evolutionary Roots of Emotions." *Evolution and Cognition* 1, no. 1: 38–50.

Wimmer, Manfred, and Luc Ciompi. 1996. "Evolutionary Aspects of Affective-Cognitive Interactions in the Light of Ciompi's Concept of 'Affect-Logic.'" *Evolution and Cognition* 2, no. 1: 37–58.

Winnicott, Donald Woods. 1965. *The Maturational Processes and the Facilitating Environment: Studies in the Theory of Emotional Development*. New York: International Universities Press.

———. 1971. *Playing and Reality*. London: Tavistock.

———. 1986. *Home Is Where We Start From: Essays by a Psychoanalyst*. Ed. Clare Winnicott, Ray Shepherd, and Madeleine Davis. New York: W. W. Norton.

———. 1989. *Psycho-analytic Explorations*. Ed. Clare Winnicott, Ray Shepherd, and Madeleine Davis. Cambridge: Harvard University Press.

Wolpoff, Milford. 1980. *Paleo-Anthropology*. New York: Alfred A. Knopf.

Wrangham, Richard, and Dale Peterson. 1996. *Demonic Males: Apes and the Origins of Human Violence*. Boston: Houghton Mifflin.

Wright, Esmond. 1985. *History of the World: Prehistory to the Renaissance.* Feltham, U.K.: Bonanza Books.
Wright, Robert. 1994. *The Moral Animal: Evolutionary Psychology and Everyday Life.* New York: Pantheon Books.
Yoshiba, Kenji. 1968. "Local and Intertroop Variability in Ecology and Social Behavior of Common Indian Langurs." In *Primates: Studies in Adaptation and Variability,* ed. Phyllis C. Jay, 217–42. New York: Holt, Rinehart and Winston.
Young, Paul Thomas. 1973. *Emotion in Man and Animal: Its Nature and Dynamic Basis.* 2nd rev. ed. Huntington, N.Y.: Robert E. Krieger.
Zeki, Semir. 1992. "The Visual Image in Mind and Brain." *Scientific American,* September, 69–76.
Zilboorg, Gregory. 1943. "Fear of Death." *Psychoanalytic Quarterly* 12:465–75.
Zimbardo, Philip G., Christina Maslach, and Craig Haney. 2000. "Reflections on the Stanford Prison Experiment: Genesis, Transformations, Consequences." In *Obedience to Authority: Current Perspectives on the Milgram Paradigm,* ed. Thomas Blass, 193–237. Mahwah, N.J.: Lawrence Erlbaum Associates.
Zimmermann, Warren. 1999. "Milosevic's Final Solution." *New York Review of Books,* June 10, 41–43.

# Index of Names

*AARP Bulletin*, 408, n. 22
Adams, John, 330, 331
Adler, Alfred, 75
Adorno, Theodor, 135
Alatalo, Rauno V., 101, 123, n. 3
Alcock, John, 358
Alexander, Richard D., 50, 58, n. 15
Allen, H. J., 263, n. 15
Allen, Reginald E., 9
Allison, David B., 91, n. 21
Altmann, Stuart A., 222, 223, 237, n. 24, 246, 295–96
Ambrose, Anthony, 254–56, 262, nn. 9–10, 262–63, n. 11
Andersson, Malte, 99, 123, n. 1
Andreski, Stanislav, 128
Ardrey, Robert, 51, 161–62, 165–66, 169–70, 187, n. 21, 188, nn. 23–24
Arendt, Hannah, 129–34, 137, 139, 158–9, 175, 185, n. 2, 344, 347–8
Aristotle, 68, 199, 200, 285
Artaud, Antonin, 90, n. 18
Attenborough, David, 37, 101, 123, n. 4
Augustine, 411, n. 33
Austin, J. L., 238, n. 32

Bacon, Francis, 21, 50
Baird, Jodie A., 213, 236, n. 14
Baldwin, Dare A., 213, 236, n. 14
Barash, David, 58, n. 13, 248
Baron-Cohen, Simon, 231
Bataille, Georges, 19, 31, n. 12
Batson, C. Daniel, 54
Beach, Frank A., 262, n. 4
Becker, Ernest, 9, 44, 46–52, 59, n. 17, 64, 73–74, 76–78, 87, 89, n. 10, 110–14, 119–22, 154, 159, 312–13, 332, 371, 389, 394–95
Bee, Helen, 353
Bekoff, Marc, 185, n. 5, 253
Bell, Sir Charles, 255, 263, n. 12
Bell, Jeffrey A., 73
Benhabib, Seyla, 136

Bentham, Jeremy, 2
Bergman, Anni, 337, n. 8
Berkeley, George, 238, n. 35, 314, 342, 406, n. 2
Bertenthal, Bennett I., 213, 237, n. 23
Biben, Maxeen, 245
Birkhead, T. R., 97
Blass, Thomas, 175–76, 188, n. 29
Blazina, Chris, 116–17
Bloom, Lois, 210, 213, 217
Blurton Jones, N. G., 243, 245, 254
Boehm, Christopher, 37–38, 42–45, 56, n. 2, 58, n. 16, 94
Bolwig, N., 262, n. 4
Bowditch, Lowell, 31, n. 14
Bower, Bruce, 185, n. 7, 188, n. 31
Bower, T. G. R., 210, 213, 274, 288, 305, 336, n. 5, 362
Bowlby, John, 274
Bramblett, Claud A., 375
Braudy, Leo, 148, 155–56, 188, n. 20
Brown, Stuart, 111, 242, 260, n. 1
Bruner, Jerome, 213
Bruzina, Ronald, 30, n. 1, 400
Buddha, 342
Buechner, Helmut, 187, n. 20
Bugental, Daphne Blunt, 266
Bull, Nina, 132, 361–62, 368
Bullock, Alan, 56, n. 5
Bullough, Edward, 328–29, 339, n. 28
Buruma, Ian, 24, 60, n. 17, 138, 385
Butler, Judith, 95
Butterworth, George, 282, n. 8
Byers, John A., 249, 252
Byrne, R. W., 297

Call, Josep, 219, 221
Caputo, John D., 86, 89, n. 9
Carling, Alan, 58, n. 16
Carpenter, C. R., 162–66
Carthy, J. D., 119
Cataldi, Sue L., 372–73, 374, 386
*Cathédrales de France*, 409, n. 27

Index of Names 437

Catton, Bruce, 173
Chagnon, Napoleon, 185, n. 7
Chamisso, Adalbert, 82
Chance, M. R. A., 263, n. 13
Churchill, Winston, 44, 154, 173, 339–40, n. 29
Ciompi, Luc, 205–7, 235, n. 10, 236, n. 13
Clare, Anthony, 384, 385, 386
Coleman, James C., 364–65
Comte, Auguste, 311
Cosmides, L., 282, n. 4, 313
Council of Europe/Conseil de l'Europe, 363
Craighero, Laila, 60, n. 18
Crick, Francis, 235, n. 12
Csibra, Gergely, 231, 239, n. 37
Cunningham, Merce, 91, n. 24
Curtis, Helena, 215, 217
Cushing, F. H., 30, n. 5, 31, n. 7
Cutting, J. E., 213

Daly, Martin, 58, n. 14, 99
Damasio, Antonio, 206–7
Darwin, Charles, 7, 24, 30, n. 2, 36–37, 57, n. 7, 61–62, n. 18, 93–94, 96–97, 99–102, 111, 113, 120, 123, n. 1, 223–24, 238, n. 28, 251, 255, 262, n. 9, 263, nn. 12–13, 286, 300, 301, 305, 306, 308, 309, 311–12, 315–18, 324, 336, 337, n. 12, 343, 351, 358, 406, n. 1
Dawkins, Richard, 57, n. 10, 59, n. 16, 89, n. 11, 311
Décarie, Thérèse Gouin, 407, n. 15
Dennett, Daniel, 357, 407, n. 13
Depraz, Natalie, 230
de Rivera, Joseph, 368
Derrida, Jacques, 63–64, 78–82, 84–87, 89, n. 12, 89–90, n. 13, 90, nn. 14–16, 18, 20, 91, n. 21, 151, 257
Descartes, René, 63, 65–69, 81, 86–87, 88, nn. 3–4, 151
DeVore, Irven, 35, 260, n. 2
de Waal, Frans, 37, 38, 40, 186, n. 8
Diamond, Jared, 189, n. 36
Dieckmann, Bernhard, 363
Dolhinow, Phyllis Jay, 266
Donaldson, O. Fred, 241
Donne, John, 285, 301, 306, 308, 309, 315, 324, 336
Dostoyevsky, Fyodor, 81–82, 86
Dreyfus, Hubert L., 349
Dundes, Alan, 39

Eagle, Morris N., 60, n. 18
Eberhard, William G., 113, 123, n. 2
Ebling, F. J., 119
Eddington, Sir Arthur Stanley, 65, 77, 88, n. 2
Eibl-Eibesfeldt, Irenäus, 125, n. 13, 128–29, 399
Eichmann, Adolph, 130, 132
Eimas, Peter D., 238, n. 30
Eimerl, Sarel, 35
Einarsen, A. S., 249
Ekman, Paul, 238, n. 31
Eliot, T. S., 88, n. 2
Elon, Amos, 166
Emmeche, Claus, 350
Encyclopédie par L'Image: Les Cathédrales, 409, n. 27
Epicurus, 277–78
Epstein, Jason, 138
Epstein, Mark, 89, n. 5
Erikson, Erik, 259
Evans, J. Claude, 91, n. 21

Fagen, Robert, 244–45, 247, 248, 249–50
Faulkner, William, 204
Fedigan, Linda Marie, 366, 375, 407, n. 18
Fink, Eugen, 30, n. 1, 257, 341, 400
Firth, Raymond, 40
Fischer, David Hackett, 330–31
Flew, Anthony, 66
Fogassi, Leonardo, 60, n. 18
Folger, Robert, 339–40, n. 29
Foster, Mary LeCron, 237, n. 27
Foucault, Michel, 257, 349
Fox, Robin, 110–12, 119, 121–22
Fraiberg, Selma, 305
Francis, Richard, 337–38, n. 15
Frank, Robert H., 407–8, n. 21, 409, n. 26
Franklin, Benjamin, 127
Fraser, Sir James, 83
Freedberg, David, 236, n. 12
French, Peter A., 82
Freud, Sigmund, 19–20, 75, 173, 198, 238, n. 29, 352, 369, 387–89, 390, 391, 406, n. 1
Fromm, Erich, 135
Furuhjelm, Mirjam, 290

Gadamer, Hans, 257
Gallagher, Shaun, 229, 230
Gallese, Vittorio, 60, n. 18, 231, 235–36, n. 12, 239, n. 37
Gardner, Robert, 143–46, 149–52, 184

Garver, Newton, 91, n. 21
Geertz, Clifford, 20, 22
Gibbs, Raymond, 60–61, n. 18, 236, n. 12
Gilligan, Carol, 136, 406, n. 1
Glover, Jonathan, 185, n. 4
Godolphin, Francis R. B., 178
Goins, Major Morris T., 63
Goldman, Alvin, 231, 239, n. 37
Goodall, Jane van Lawick, 8, 38, 70–74, 105–7, 266, 298, 359, 365
Goodwin, Brian, 59, n. 16, 62, n. 19, 99
Gould, James L., 333
Gould, Stephen Jay, 94, 188, n. 22, 237, n. 27
Gowitzke, Barbara A., 197
Goya, Francisco, 184
Graves, Robert, 18, 31, n. 11
Grene, Marjorie, 339, n. 25
Groos, Kurt, 245

Habermas, Jürgen, 136
Hall, K. R. L., 260–61, n. 2
Hamburg, D. A., 260, n. 2
Haney, Craig, 179, 189, nn. 32–34
Haraway, Donna, 95
Hardin, Russell, 266
Harlow, Harry, 243
Harlow, Margaret, 243
Hedges, Chris, 153, 155, 159, 187, n. 19, 406, n. 1
Heidegger, Martin, 63, 70, 77–78, 181–82, 85–88, 89, nn. 6, 8, 91, nn. 21–23, 185, n. 2, 257, 300, 310, 318–24, 325, 330, 338, nn. 19–21, 339, nn. 22–26, 381, 398
Heider, Karl G., 31, n. 13, 141–51, 184, 186, nn. 12–13, 15
Heraclitus, 258
Herodotus, 124, n. 5, 173
Hertz, Robert, 9–10
Hobbes, Thomas, 2, 6, 15, 23–25, 302–7, 325–26, 332, 379, 380, 381, 382, 392, 396
Hockett, Charles F., 237, nn. 25–27, 295
Hoffman, Martin L., 325
Hoffmeyer, Jesper, 209, 218, 350
Höglund, Jacob, 101, 123, n. 3
Horkheimer, Max, 135
Hughes, Robert, 184
Huizinga, Johan, 103–5, 107–8, 124, n. 5, 141–42, 186, n. 10, 246, 260–61, n. 2, 331

Human Rights Watch/Helsinki, 363
Hume, David, 2–8, 13–14, 22, 25, 59, n. 17, 69, 193, 262, n. 7
Humphrey, Nicholas, 38
Humphreys, Anne P., 245, 263, n. 17
Hunt, William A., 406, n. 10
Hurley, Susan L., 231, 239, n. 37
Husserl, Edmund, 5, 30, n. 1, 78–81, 85, 89, n. 12, 185, n. 6, 193–96, 197–99, 200–201, 213, 214–15, 217, 218, 228–29, 230–33, 234, nn. 3–4, 235, n. 8, n. 12, 236, n. 18, 239, n. 37, 262, n. 6, 265, 286, 289, 294, 336, n. 4, 338, n. 17, 386, 392, 400
Hutton, James, 318, 338, n. 18
Hyland, Drew A., 257, 258–59, 262, n. 8

Iacoboni, Marco, 231
Ignatieff, Michael, 185, n. 4
Ingelman-Sundbert, Axel, 290

Jacob, Pierre, 231, 239, n. 37
Jacklin, Carol Nagy, 174, 177, 180–81, 374–76
James, William, 243–44, 261, n. 2, 402–5
Jaspers, Karl, 185, n. 2
Jeannerod, 231, 239, n. 37
Johnsgard, Paul. A., 101
Jolly, Clifford, 167
Jung, Carl G., 1, 47, 75, 291, 341, 342, 346–47, 357, 358, 392, 406, n. 6

Kant, Immanuel, 130–31, 341
Katz, Leonard D., 42
Keeley, Lawrence H., 26–27, 45, 56, n. 4, 138, 261, n. 2, 388
Keen, Sam, 112–13, 127
Keenan, Brian, 376
Keeton, William T., 333
Keith, Sir Arthur, 50, 62
Kelso, J. A. Scott, 235, n. 12, 289–90
Keysers, Christian, 60, n. 18
Kidd, José E. Ramírez, 407, n. 17
Kingdon, Jonathan, 166–69, 170–73, 188, n. 26, 379, 406, n. 1
Kinsley, David R., 31, n. 9
Koch, Christof, 235, n. 12
Koestler, Arthur, 241
Kohlberg, Lawrence, 136
Krebs, Dennis, 333–34
Kummer, Hans, 93, 188, n. 23, 220

Index of Names    439

Lacan, Jacques, 21, 352, 407, n. 12, 409, n. 25
Lakoff, George, 236, n. 12
Lamarck, Jean Baptiste, 336, n. 1
Landis, Carney, 406, n. 10
Langer, Robert, 22, 408, n. 22
Lanting, Frans, 186, n. 8
Larson, David E., 353
Laski, Harold J., 187, n. 17
Lawrence, D. H., 285, 301, 306, 308, 309, 324, 329–30, 336
Leach, Edmund, 16–17
LeShan, Lawrence, 152–53, 159, 188, n. 21, 385
Lewontin, Richard, 237, n. 27
Liberman, Alvin M., 237, n. 23
Lifton, Robert J., 111
Lill, Alan, 101, 123, nn. 3–4
Linnaeus, 281, n. 3
Lloyd, G. E. R., 10, 30, n. 7
Lorenz, Konrad, 110–11, 119, 121–22, 204, 224, 260, n. 2, 331, 402–5
Love, Glen A., 1
Loy, David, 90, n. 15, 380–83, 409, n. 25
Ludwig, Theodore M., 31, n. 10
Luhmann, Niklas, 265–83
Luria, Alexander, 62, n. 18

Maccoby, Eleanor Emmons, 174, 177, 180–81, 374–76
Malinowski, Bronislaw, 17, 31, n. 8
Malnes, Raino, 326
Marler, Peter, 260, n. 2
Marlowe, David H., 114, 178, 376, 390–91
Maslach, Christina, 179–82, 189, nn. 32–34
Matthew, 21
Mattingly, Ignatius G., 237, n. 23
Mayr, Ernst, 99
McLuhan, Marshall, 409, n. 26
McWhorter, Ladelle, 95
Mead, Margaret, 143
Mech, L. David, 296
Meeker, Joseph W., 241
Mehler, Jacques, 238, n. 30
Meltzoff, Andrew N., 213, 215, 230, 231, 235, n. 6, 282, n. 8, 289, 290, 291, 305
Menaker, Esther, 87
Menzel, Emil, 220, 236, n. 19
Merleau-Ponty, Maurice, 38, 59, n. 17, 349
Migone, Paolo, 60, n. 18
Milgram, Stanley, 174–77, 180, 187, n. 17, 188, nn. 28–31

Milius, Susan, 185, n. 5
Mill, John S., 2
Milner, Morris, 197
Mishra, Pankaj, 138
Moffatt, C. B., 187, n. 20
Monick, Eugene, 19
Moore, M. Keith, 215, 230, 282, n. 8, 289, 290, 291, 305
Moran, Dermot, 90–91, n. 20
Moro, Ernst, 354
Morris, Desmond, 188, nn. 23–24
Morton, Eugene S., 100
Mosher, Donald L., 370
Mysterud, Iver, 58, n. 16

Nagel, Ueli, 93, 188, n. 23
Nesse, Randolph, 58, n. 16, 311, 313–14, 338, n. 16
Needham, Rodney, 9–12, 30, n. 4
Neumann, Erich, 18
Nietzsche, Friedrich, 81, 91, n. 23, 257
Nooteboom, Bart, 265
Norton-Taylor, Duncan, 154
Nuland, Sherwin B., 39, 88, n. 1
Nussbaum, Martha C., 236, n. 13, 406, n. 1

Oakley, Robin, 363
O'Donald, Peter, 123, n. 1
Orr, H. Allen, 338, n. 15
Overgaard, Soren, 194, 195–96, 197, 228

Panksepp, Jaak, 214
Parker, Geoff, 97–98
Pellis, Sergio M., 253
Pellis, Vivien C., 253
Perutz, M. F., 185, n. 4
Peters, Roger, 296
Peterson, Dale, 38, 44, 57, nn. 7–8, 139–41, 185, n. 7, 186, n. 9, 261, n. 2
Peterson, Jordan, 17, 46–50
Petitot, Jean, 236, n. 12
Phillips, Adam, 316–17, 406, n. 1
Piaget, Jean, 235, 288, 336, n. 5
Pinker, Steven, 313
Pinto, Jeannine, 213, 237, n. 23
Poe, Edgar Allan, 82
Polanyi, Michael, 252
Polybius, 396, 411, n. 34
Poulin-Dubois, Diane, 213
Price, Kingsley, 411, n. 33
Proffitt, D. R., 213
Pugh, S. D., 339–40, n. 29
Pycraft, W. P., 262, n. 4

## Index of Names

Quammen, David, 337, n. 14

Rabinow, Paul, 349
Rank, Otto, 9, 16, 51, 59, n. 17, 63–65, 73–78, 82–87, 89, n. 10, 90, n. 16, 111, 159, 312, 371, 389
Rawls, John, 136
Relethford, John, 314
Reynaud, Emmanuel, 93
Richardson, Lewis Fry, 124, n. 9
Rifkin, Jeremy, 394, 410, n. 31, 410–11, n. 32
Rizzolatti, Giacomo, 60, n. 18, 231, 235, n. 12, 239, n. 37
Robeck, Mildred C., 354, 355, 361
Robinson, John, 188, n. 24
Robinson, Mary, 185, n. 4
Rochat, Phillipe, 274, 282–83, n. 13, 362, 363, 407, n. 16
Rousseau, Jean-Jacques, 2, 6, 15, 409, n. 26
Rowell, Thelma, 211, 218, 224, 365–66
Roy, M. Aaron, 282, n. 7
Rudofsky, Bernard, 37
Rumsfeld, Donald, 107
Ruse, Michael, 59, n. 16

Sagi, Abraham, 325
Sallis, John, 286, 337, n. 7
Sartre, Jean-Paul, 38, 73, 89, n. 7, 285, 334–36, 381, 391
Savage-Rumbaugh, Sue, 38
Schaller, George, 296–97, 337, n. 11
Scheler, Max, 56, n. 3, 229, 238, n. 34
Schopenhauer, Arthur, 285–86, 302, 307–10, 326–27
Schulz, Walter, 88–89, n. 4
Schutz, Alfred, 229, 286
Schwartz, Hillel, 90, n. 16
Seabright, Paul, 57, n. 7
Searle, John, 213–14, 236, n. 14, 238, n. 32
Seidler, Victor Jeleniewski, 117, 124, n. 12
Shakespeare, William, 127, 140, 380
Sheets, Kevin, 394, 410, n. 29
Sheets-Johnstone, Maxine, 7, 8, 12, 19, 21, 29, 30, n. 6, 35, 38, 40, 54, 56, n. 3, 60–62, n. 18, 102, 109, 113, 122, 132, 168, 193–94, 201, 202, 203, 208, 209, 210, 211, 212, 213, 214, 215, 217, 230, 234, 235, n. 7, 235–36, n. 12, 236, n. 15, 237, n. 22, 238, n. 26, 239, n. 29, 246, 251, 262, n. 6, 282, n. 5, 283, n. 16, 288, 289, 294, 297, 298, 323, 336, nn. 3–4, 343, 349, 350, 357, 358, 368, 378, 405, 407, nn. 12, 14, 19
Sherman, William Tecumseh, 391
Sherrard, Philip, 138
Simic, Charles, 185, n. 4
Simmons, Leigh W., 97–98
Sinnott, Edmund Ware, 406, n. 4
Smith, Peter K., 245, 263, n. 17
Sober, Elliott, 54, 58, n. 16, 310–11, 313, 325
Socrates, 63, 342, 393
Southwick, Charles H., 163
Spencer, Herbert, 26, 50, 56, n. 4, 154, 156, 161–63, 185, n. 14, 187, n. 20, 188, n. 21
Sperry, Roger, 62, n. 18
Spiegelberg, Herbert, 349
Spitz, René, 9, 30, n. 3, 210, 213, 290, 305, 337, n. 13, 350–51, 354, 369, 385, 407, n. 15
Sroufe, L. Alan, 354, 360–61, 362, 407, n. 15
Stearns, Frederic R., 262, n. 9
Stern, Daniel, 7, 194, 199, 200–203, 207, 208, 209, 211, 214, 215, 217, 227, 236, n. 16, 266, 282, n. 8, 350, 357, 385, 407, n. 11
Stevens, Anthony, 120, 125, n. 14, 408–9, n. 24
Stevenson, Robert Louis, 81
Strum, Shirley C., 261, n. 2, 266
Stutchbury, Bridget J. M., 100
Sully, James, 262, n. 9
Symons, Donald, 244, 247

Takooshian, Harold, 188, n. 30
Thanissaro Bhikkhu, 338, n. 17
Thera, Nyanaponika, 57, n. 12
Thompson, Evan, 60–61, n. 18, 236, n. 12
Thucydides, 35, 173
Tiger, Lionel, 110–12, 119, 121–22
Tillich, Paul, 113
*Time*, 408, n. 23
Tinkelpaugh, O. L., 262, n. 4
Tomasello, Michael, 219, 221
Tomkins, Silvan S., 117–19, 354, 360, 370–71, 377–78, 391, 406, n. 10
Tooby, John, 282, n. 4, 313
Toynbee, Arnold J., 155, 159–60, 173
Traub, James, 138
Trevarthen, Colwyn, 266
Trivers, Robert, 99
Troyer, John, 333
Turney-High, Harry Holbert, 44–45, 154

Urquhart, Brian, 185, n. 4

van Buren, John, 91, n. 23
Van den Assem, J., 99–100, 124, nn. 6, 8
van Hooff, J. A. R. A. M., 236, n. 15, 253–54, 255–56, 350
Vasta, Ross, 354
Verene, Donald Phillip, 382, 409, n. 26
Vetlesen, Arne, 133–37, 175, 184, 236, n. 13
Vico, Giambattista, 409, n. 26
von Helmholtz, Hermann, 336, n. 4
von Uexküll, Jakob, 12
Vrba, Elisabeth S., 94, 188, n. 22

Washburn, S. L., 261, n. 2
Washington, George, 330, 331
Weismann, August, 59, n. 16
Wettstein, Howard K., 82
Whiten, Andrew, 210, 297
Wiggins, Grant, 406, n. 1
Wilbur, J. B., 263, n. 15
Wilde, Oscar, 82
Wilkie, J. S., 336, n. 1
Wilkinson, David, 124, n. 9
Williams, Bernard, 65–66
Williams, George C., 49–50
Wilson, Arnold, 337, n. 8
Wilson, David Sloan, 54, 58, n. 16, 310–11, 313, 325
Wilson, E. O., 59, n. 16, 331
Wilson, Margo, 58, n. 14, 99
Wimmer, Manfred, 205, 206, 235, n. 9, n. 10
Winnicott, Donald Woods, 114–16, 124, n. 11, 262, n. 10, 263, nn. 16, 18, 341, 369, 385, 399–400
Wirsén, Claes, 290
Wolpoff, Milford, 168–70, 188, n. 23
Wrangham, Richard, 38, 44, 57, nn. 7–8, 139–41, 185, n. 7, 186, n. 9, 261, n. 2
Wright, Robert, 59, n. 16, 138

Yoshiba, Kenji, 260, n. 2
Young, Paul Thomas, 353, 355, 361, 406, n. 10

Zeki, Semir, 235, n. 12
Zilboorg, Gregory, 35
Zimbardo, Philip G., 179–84, 188, n. 13, 189, nn. 32–34
Zimmermann, Warren, 138

# Index of Terms

acquisitiveness, tied not to "the life of man," but to man himself, 379. See also *more*
adaptation, and unreserved acknowledgement of one's own vulnerability, 364–65
adultery, and homicide, 43
adultist problem of other minds, 213, 282, n. 5
adultist theoretical claims, 268–69, 282, n. 5
affect attunement, 7, 199, 208–10, 211–12, 350
 and empathy, 203
 and Husserl's concept of harmoniousness, 200–201
 and kinetic dynamics, 200
 rooted in movement as a dynamic happening, 200
 and turn-taking, 210–11
affect-logic, 205–6
 affect-logic-kinetic, 206, 208, 211
 *See also* bodily logos; emotions
affect stratification, 117–18
affective dynamics. *See* dynamic congruency; kinetic dynamics
affective realities, 382–83
*agon*, 103, 104, 141, 331
 and non-agonistic combat, 104–5, 107, 108
aggression, 119, 121, 129, 185, n. 1
 a biological variable, 120
 cultural honing of, in males, 121
 devolves from competition, not the reverse, 171, 403
 instinct theory of, 111, 121, 170, 171
 and male–male competition, 120
 psychoanalytic assessments of, 369
 studies of, and fear in young boys, 374–76
 and women, 125, n. 14
alpha male, 37
alpha male societies, 42

altruism, 312–13, 324–25
 and caring, 315
 dependent on intercorporeal sense-makings, 314–15
 evolutionary altruism, 2, 310–11, 324, 325
 and selfish genes, 313–15
Amazons, 108
amity/enmity code, 50–51, 161–62, 326
 and territoriality, 165–66
 *See also* Spencer; Ardrey
analogical apperception, 195, 227–28, 292, 293–94, 327–38
anger. *See* fear, livingly experienced rather than quashed; fear, oppositional dynamics of, and anger
animation, 195, 225
 and intersubjectivity, 199, 212
 *See also* movement, our mother tongue and matchpoint
animate form, 12
antinomy of distance, 329
auto-affection, 80, 81, 85, 89, n. 13

baboons, 216, 220, 296, 315
battles and raids, 141, 148
 distinction between, 143–44
 relationship between, 142–43
 *See also* chimpanzee raids, distinct from human battles
beasts, 129
 differentiating man from, 128
being alive, wonder(s) of, 330
being alive among other humans, 40, 43, 146–47, 148, 151, 256, 278, 304
 power of life and death over other humans, 154
 *See also* vulnerability/vulnerabilities
"Being-towards-death," 70–72, 85
 and anxiety, 73
 and Dasein, 71–73
 and the life of the text, 81
 "my," 78, 79
 and the "they," 70–72

Index of Terms    443

being-toward-life, 331
binary oppositions, 8, 12, 13, 16, 341–42
   embedded in bodily experience, 11–12
   and insights into human nature, 345
   light/dark, 9, 10, 11, 16
   male/female, 9, 10, 11, 16
   naturalness of in question, 9–13
   and pan-human "action potentials," 345
   right/left, 9, 10–11, 16
   unevenly valorized, 8, 9, 12–13
   *See also* unevenly valorized binary oppositions
"biological alchemy," 394. *See also* twenty-first-century technology; Western science (present–day)
biological marker(s), 36, 40
biological matrix, and male–male competition, 119. *See also* lek behavior
biological determinism, 384, 389
biological diversity, 343, 345
   biological pluralism, 343
   and sociological pluralism, 343, 344
body
   and fear of death, 52–53
   as pan-cultural universal, 12
   as semantic template, 12, 287
   and size as measure of power, 40–41
   and thinking, 12
bodily logos, 208–9, 211, 218, 248. *See also* affect-logic–kinetic
bonding among males, 173–74, 178. *See also* war
bonobos (*Pan paniscus*), 42, 185, n. 8
Buddhism, 48, 57, n. 12, 342

care-giving, naturalness of, 15
caring, 36
   attitudinal affect of, and sense of interconnectedness, 331
   and awakening, 330, 331–32
   differs radically from Heideggerian care, 318–19
   distinct from cooperating, 331, 332–33
   a valuing of things for their own sake, 332
   *See also* difference removed; "Do harm to no one"; fraternity
Cartesianism, 49
CEOs (*c*hemically *e*ngineered *o*rganisms), 22
challenge of languaging experience, 230. *See also* language

child's play and fragment from Heraclitus, 258–59
chimpanzees (*Pan troglodytes*), 38, 42, 56, n. 2, 219, 296
   chimpanzee raids, 139–40, 141
   chimpanzee raids distinct from human battles, 143
   and humans as competitors, 172
   lip-smacking resembles human smiling, 350
   responses to startle and fear, 358–59
   *See also* bonobos
Christianity, 17, 18, 48
"Churchill effect," 339–40, n. 29
cloning. *See* twenty-first-century technology
cognitive neuroscience, "embodied," 236, n. 12. *See also* embodiment
common creaturehood/common humanity, 299, 300, 309–10, 328
compassion, Schopenhauer's conception of, 308–9. *See also* "Do harm to no one"; difference removed
competition, and perversion of child's play, 242, 257
competitive sports, 403–4
comsigns, 222–25, 246, 295–99, 395
   and analogical apperception, 296
   at the core of intercorporeal intelligibility, 297
   corporeal-kinetic underpinnings of, 222–23
   and an intercorporeal semantics, 299
   kinetic basis of intercorporeal sense-makings, 297
   phenomenological import of, 222
   rationality of, 295, 297–98
   *See also* kinetic/tactile–kinesthetic invariants
conceptual complementarities, between first and third person methodologies and knowledge, 235, n. 12
consistent bipedality, 167–71
   and the development of weaponry, 169
   and the opening of movement possibilities, 168–69
   and "squat-feeding," 167, 168, 169
   *See also* "niche-stealing"; "squat-feeding"
cooperation, 174, 332–34, 375–76. *See also* bonding among males; male–male competition

444   Index of Terms

corporeal concepts, 247. *See also* thinking in movement
corporeal matters of fact, 96
creativity, 87–88, 398–99, 405
  affinities with Heidegger's concept of conscience, 87–88
  and the hero-artist, 87
  and living without illusions, 398
  moral educational value of, 397–401
  an ontological dimension of Being, 87
  and play, 253
  a sense-making activity, 399
  sociological value of, 401
  *See also* moral education; play
cross-modal matching. *See* transfers of cultural artifacts. *See* unevenly valorized binary oppositions
culture/nature opposition, 15–28
  cultural reworkings of what is evolutionarily given, 122, 166
  and mythologies and religion, 16–19
  relationship to illusions, 16
  *See also* evolutionary biology, and sociopsychoanalytic / cultural analyses of humans

Dani ghosts, 145–46, 149, 150
  akin to Derrida's texts, 151
  akin to Descartes's soul, 151
Dasein, 323–24
  care structure of, 318–22, 324, 325
Daseinanalysis, 321–22
death, 6, 7–8, 9, 143, 144–45
  adultist rendition of, 323
  awareness and fear of, 55
  and birth, 8–9
  Freud's thoughts about, 388–39
  Heidegger's adultist rendition of, 322–23
  and illusions, 9
  and the "little death," 19
  no more than "a wink of the eyelids," 309
  no-moreness of death, 8, 36, 41
  rage against, 52
  a uniquely human concept, 8, 36, 38, 45, 54
  *See also* culture/nature opposition; fear of death; subjective phenomena
dedicated brain modules, 2
*Der Doppelgänger. See* the Double
descriptive foundations, 61–62, n. 18. *See also* challenge of languaging experience
difference removed, 308, 309, 319, 327–28
  experiences of interconnectedness, 323–24
  and the principle of not harming, 310
  and "psychical distance," 328–29
  *See also* caring; "Do harm to no one"; fraternity
"Do harm to no one" (Schopenhauer), 308, 326–27
  and a genuine evolutionary ethics, 327
  and the non-act of not harming, 327
  preserves intricate integrity of the whole of Nature, 334
  *See also* caring; difference removed; fraternity
dominance, 105, 109, 110, 119, 182
  as displays of power, 106–7
  primate male dominance hierarchies, 105–6
  social dynamics of, in Stanford Prison Experiment, 181–82
dynamics, nonlinear, 205–6. *See also* emotions; intercorporeal dynamics; kinetic dynamics
dynamic congruency, 199, 207–8, 212–13, 236, n. 12, 349
  common qualitative structure of kinetic and affective, 350
dynamics of pairing, 198. *See also* analogical apperception; intercorporeal dynamics; intercorporeal harmonious pairings; intercorporeal meaning; intercorporeal pairing

egoism, Schopenhauer's conception of, 307–8
Eichmann, 130, 132, 133–34, 158, 347–48
embodiment, 60–62, n. 18, 199
emotion(s)
  emotional-kinetic resonance, 207
  evolutionary studies of, 205
  involuntary nature of, 357–58
  as motivating, as responsive, 207
  "motivating and mobilizing" energies of, 205, 207
  move us to move, 204–5, 207, 208, 388
empathic understandings, 252–53
empathy, 7, 36, 133, 134, 175
  as anchored in ontogeny, 135–36
  common understanding of, 198

empathy (continued)
  directed toward malevolent ends, 393
  as distinct from attunement, 203
  a dynamically and affectively intuitive sense of another, 287
  harmonious pairing movements of, 207–8
  origin in kinetic dynamics, 225–27
  as outgrowth of affect attunement and turn-taking, 202
  and "seeing deeply into another," 225–26
  seeing others as human beings, 135
  and transfers of sense, 294
(the) enemy, 145, 148, 149
  as less than human, 156–57, 179
  in Stanford Prison Experiment, 179
ethics, 2
  genuine evolutionary ethics, 324–25, 327, 334
  *See also* foundationalist morality; fraternity
evil, 121
  dissociated from religion, 129–30
  evolutionary clues to pan-cultural human motivation to, 139
  human power to do, 392
  killing, death, and fear in banality of, 143
  not a contained adult preserve, 186, n. 15
  a paradigmatic portrayal of, 139
  is a *privatio boni*, 389
  not a *privatio boni*, 346–47
  pan-cultural human capacity for, 137
  roots of indifference fostering, 134–35
  in the Third Reich, 130–31
evil eye, 39
evolutionary biology, 61–62, n. 18, 94
  and culture, 166
  and socio-psychoanalytic/cultural analyses of humans, 110–22
  and variation, 95, 96, 120
evolutionary continuities, 287, 358–60. *See also* existential continuities
evolutionary matters of fact/facts of life, 122, 141, 160, 217, 288, 395
evolutionary semantics, 209, 211–12, 215, 217, 218, 219
exaptation(s), 94, 102, 103–4, 108, 169
excitement. *See* sheer physicality and excitement; wanton brutality
existential continuities, 356–60

fear, 357–58
  and being a man, 369
  and breathing, 255
  evolutionary continuities and, 358–60
  as livingly experienced rather than quashed, 372–74
  a natural affect of animate life, 365–66, 372
  ontogeny of, 360
  oppositional dynamics of, and anger, 367–69, 372–74
  phenomenological description of, 204
  socialization of, and anger, 377–78
  *See also* macho male
fear of death, 35–36, 139, 147–48, 151, 303
  motivating source of evil, 47–48
  and nonhuman animals, 36, 38
  psycho-cultural analyses of, 46–48
  and a rage against Nature, 41–42, 48
  tied to body, 52–53
  *See also* punctuated existence
fear of strangers. *See* natural signs; stranger anxiety; xenophobia
fear of the feminine, 114, 116–17
  Tomkins's analysis, 117–19
  Winnicott's analysis, 114–16
feelings, distinction between sensations and, 198. *See also* movement; sensation and perception
female choice, 98, 100, 113
females, 112, 113–14
  and Dani funeral rites, 151–52
  not experimentally in a position of authority, 188, n. 28
  not trained as warriors, 186, n. 15
  omission of, in traditional studies of humans, 114
  psychological ignorance of, 385–86
  the question of what it is to be a woman, 112, 113
  *See also* fear of the feminine
Fifth Cartesian Meditation (Husserl), 193, 195, 199, 201, 286
first moral principle. *See* "Do harm to no one"; difference removed; "policy of humanity"
foundationalist morality, 1, 5, 53, 55
  and human nature, 1–2
  and pan-cultural human realities, 1, 2, 53
  and phenomenology, 2–3, 5
  and reductionism, 58–59, n. 16

446    Index of Terms

and universal morality, 53
  See also Hobbes; Hume; Rousseau
fraternity (Sartre), 334–36
freedom, 265, 280, 281
  and affective experience, 265
  freedom of others, 265, 275
  freedom to act, 277, 279
fundamental human concepts, 11–12

gene therapy. See twenty-first-century
  technology
God/gods, 17, 19, 312–13, 332
  Old Testament God, 347–48, 392
  Shiva, 315
  gorillas, 219–20

hand-clapping, 219–20
harmoniousness, 195, 199, 237, n. 21, 294
  flow of Nature and analogy to music,
    338, n. 17
  rootedness in movement as dynamic
    happening, 200
  See also intercorporeal harmonies; inter-
    corporeal pairing; pairing
Hero/Heroics, 47, 49, 57, n. 11, 75, 114
  the drive to be a hero, 113
  fundamental character of, 116–17
  the hero-artist, 87
  heroic transcendence, 76, 110, 111, 114,
    121
  "the 'real' man," 48
  war as a "hero-game," 111
  See also heroic honing of males; male–
    male competition; warriors
heroic honing of males, 153, 154, 155–57.
  See also Hero/Heroics; male–male
  competition; warriors
Hinduism, 18
*Homo erectus*, 95, 169
*Homo habilis*, 95
*Homo nescius et barbarus*, 28, 347, 348, 392,
  394, 401, 405
  ignorance and barbarity go hand in
    hand, 392
*Homo sapiens*, 169
*Homo sapiens sapiens*, 26, 27, 28, 122, 128,
  154, 300, 301, 325, 392, 393, 405–6
human condition, converted into male
  condition, 113, 119–20
human infirmities in comparison with
  other animals, 4

human history, 137–38, 231
  educationally neglected dimensions of,
    397–401
  integral worth of, 178
  and science, 178–79
  and war, 173
  See also "pacified [human] past"
human intelligence, 25
  directed toward malevolent ends, 393
  See also *Homo nescius et barbarus*, *Homo
    sapiens sapiens*
human morality
  linkage with human mortality, 53
  tied to our bodies first and foremost, 388
  See also "Do harm to no one";
    emotion(s); war
human nature
  dark side of, 378, 386–87, 390, 392, 397,
    403
  dichotomous tendencies of, 2, 3–5, 8
  and foundationalist morality, 1
  "inconveniences" of, 4, 14, 25
  and innovatively designed experimental
    studies, 183
  "kind affection" and "possessiveness,"
    3–4, 5, 6
  "natural temper," 3, 5
  nature of, 1, 137
  shaped by ontogeny and phylogeny,
    178–79
  understandings of, 183–84
humans, 348
  beastliness of, 348
  puny but powerful beyond measure
    part of Nature, 334
  shadow side of, 347, 348, 378
  *the* most dangerous species, 345, 348,
    378–80
  an unnatural species, 22, 348
  and wisdom, 347

"I cans," 217, 220, 221, 281, n. 2, 296, 398,
  401
  and infant transfer of sense, 337, n. 6
  lexical origin and significance of, 262,
    n.6
  repertoire of, 252–53, 259
"I cannots," 401
  lexical origin and significance of, 262,
    n.6
  repertoire of, 252–53, 259
if/then relationships, 217

illusion(s), 65, 75–78, 87–88
  psychologically justified, 74
  of the "they," 72
  *See also* creativity
imitation, 281, 289–90
immortality
  and Derrida's reading of Husserl, 78–80, 81
  historical, 159–60
  rational grounds for belief in, 65–66
  and "the sign," 79–81
immortality ideologies, 16, 22, 46–53, 55, 139
  as answers to the fear of death, 150–51
  Descartes's immortality ideology, 65–66
  history as a succession of ideologies, 76
  and the honing of heroes, 93
  and human rituals, 46, 77
  and ideological disputes, 51–52
  as ideology, 64–65
  nationalist, 23, 108
  and psychological ignorance, 389–90
  religious, 18–19, 108
  Schopenhauer's immortality ideology, 309
  and risk-taking in sports, 258
  and selfish genes, 59, n. 16, 313–14
  and "the sign," 79–81
  societies "as structures of immortality power," 77
  weaning oneself from, 55
  *See also* Becker; Peterson; Rank
infants, human, 6, 13, 217–18, 366–67
  attentiveness to movement, 30, n. 3., 227, 250
  unlike other infant animals, 6–7
  *See also* affect attunement; empathy; Moro reflex; natural signs; ontogeny; sense-making; startle reflex; reflex; stranger anxiety; turn-taking
interconnectedness of Nature, 300–302, 308, 309–10, 315, 316, 318, 324–30
  and comsigns, 405
  and Dasein, 322, 324
  epistemological foundations of, 323, 332–33
  experiences of, *see* difference removed of living forms, 395
  and living the rationality of one's own being, 300, 302, 323, 330, 405
  and a moral education, 395–96

and natural history of sense-making, 405
and worms, 315–18, 324, 405
intercorporeal dynamics, 201
  and "the highest sphere," 213
intercorporeal harmonies, 201, 208
intercorporeal meaning(s), 220–22, 286–87, 315, 322
  and an intercorporeal semantics, 349
intercorporeal sense-making. *See* sense-making, intercorporeal
intercorporeal harmonious pairings, 208, 209, 211
intercorporeal logos, 296, 297, 315, 316
intersubjectivity, 208, 210, 212, 215, 269
  in actuality, an intercorporeality, 294
  and a communally intelligible world, 194
  constitution of, 197
  development of, 203
  history of, 231
  and interanimate meanings, 223
  and intercorporeal meaning, 224–25, 294
  origin of, and origin of geometry, 231–34
  passage from "I" to "You," 281, n. 1, 282, n. 3
  problem of, and species identity and attachment, 269
  wrongly conceived as problem of translation, 229
intrinsic dynamics, 289–90
introspection, 54–55
  and self-examination, 55
  *See also* moral education
Islam, 18

joint attention, 281
Judaism, 18

Kantian ethics, 2, 130
"the keys of the kingdom," 21, 28. *See also* Nature, control of and domination by Western Science
killing, 45, 110, 144–45, 388–89
  and the awareness and fear of death, 45
  and being killed, 143
  and fear of being killed, 390–91
  and feelings of soldiers involved in, 390
  and greed go hand in hand, 392
  to increase one's power, 43–44
  and "man" (males), 49

one's own kind, 128
success in, brings admiration, 26
a uniquely human act, 44, 57, n. 7, 140
kinesthesia, 60–61, n. 18
"kinetic/kinaesthetic melodies," 62, n. 18
kinetic dynamics, 195, 201, 212–13, 214, 215, 227
and affective dynamics, 207–8, 287
of attunement, 208
congruency with affective dynamics, 212–13
of empathy, 208
and a kinetic semantics, 356
mediates across sensory modalities, 199
not a matter of "body language," 215
and spontaneity, 208–9
and topological specificity in imitation, 290
*See also* dynamic congruency; intercorporeal dynamics
kinetic-semantic relationship, 212, 217, 218, 222–23, 228
and intersubjectivity, 230
kinetic/tactile–kinesthetic bodies, 194–95
kinetic/tactile–kinesthetic invariants
and iconicity, 224–25
and interchangeability, 222, 292
*See also* comsigns; sense-making, intercorporeal
language, 228–30, 231, 237, n. 27
as *deus ex machina* phenomenon, 339, n. 24
and learning of vulnerabilities, 248–48
and an original kinetic semantics, 226–27, 356
is post-kinetic, 214
"seduction of," 230
as short-cut to sense-making, 214
and tactile–kinesthetic/affective meanings, 292–93
*See also* challenge of languaging experience

language and experience, 80, 252. *See also* immortality, and the sign; language
laughter
of infants, 254–55
phylogenetic commonalities, 253–54, 255–56
"law of battle." *See* male–male competition

lek behavior/competitions, 101
an archetype of male–male competition, 103–4
lek(s), 25, 101, 103
"life of man" (Hobbes), 302–7, 379, 381
life/death polarity, 9, 12, 15, 16
*Ur* polarity, 13
lions/lionesses, 296–97
"living dead." *See* Dani ghosts
linguistic legerdemain/sleight of hand, 112, 113, 119–20
locomotor-rotational play, movements of, 249–50. *See also* rough and tumble play; play; play sport

macho males, 369–72, 376–77
and the quashing of fear, 372
males, 111–12
and emotions, 116–18, 124–25, n.12, 386, 388, 390–91
male-hunting biogram, 110, 111–12, 121
the need "to be a man among men," 112
"obvious focus of power and excitement," 151
psychological ignorance of, 384
and redirection of "manly" energies, 404
and unmanly feelings, 390–91
what it means to be a man, 113, 114, 369–70
male–male competition, 127, 173, 174
avian and mammalian, 101–2
a biological matrix, 114, 119, 120–21, 170
a culturally supported biological phenomenon, 93, 122
distinction between fighting and killing, 44
exapted in the service of agonistic or non-agonistic combat, 108
as exemplifying lek behavior, 103
historical exemplifications of, 102–5
human, *not* a predetermined biological program, 183
lack of empirical studies of, 99–101
"the law of battle," 108, 157
and the moral equivalent of war, 401–5
and nationalist immortality ideologies, 24
*real*, a biological archetype, 109
and size and power, 25
and the Stanford Prison Experiment, 181–84

male–male competition (continued)
  transformation of individual, into group form, 24–25, 127–28
  and war, 260–61, n. 2
  *See also* leks; Nature, gives us other options; sperm competition; war; warriors; masculinity, masculine condition contrasted with human condition, 112, 113
meaning(s)
  of Being, 73
  of (one's) life, 14, 94, 108, 153
  intercorporeal, 40, 220–22
  and war, 129, 159
  and writing, 80–81
"militant enthusiasm," 110, 111–12. *See also* war; warriors
mind
  as non-material substance, 66–67
  non-temporal nature of, 68–70
mirror neurons, 60–62, n. 18, 235, n. 12, 239, n. 37
moral education, 2, 306–7
  appeal to, for understandings of human nature, 394–97
  an interdisciplinary undertaking, 395, 405
  and human history, 396–98
  and the need for radical clarifications of the dark side of human nature, 386–87
  the only genuine moral equivalent of war, 405
  and ontogenetical matters of fact, 395–96
  and psychological ignorance, 385–86
  and phylogenetic matters of fact, 395–96
  *See also* creativity; human history; introspection; play
"moral equivalent of war." *See* war, "moral equivalent of war"
moral judgments, 133, 134, 135
  emotional component of, 134
  'male' picture of moral reasoning, 136–37
  philosophers' preoccupation with converting an *is* into an *ought*, 158, 187, n. 18
moral imperatives
  "musts," 339, n. 23
  "ought," 327
*more*, 8, 16, 19, 379, 380, 393

  the crowning touch of immortality, 160
  insatiable desire for, 4–5, 158–59, 306
  and lack, 380–83
  life for *me*, 380
  and scarcity, 383–84
Moro reflex, 352–56, 357–58, 361, 366, 372
  corporeally distinct from startle reflex, 353, 354–56
  developmental concordance of with startle reflex, 355–56
  as disruption in the "flow of sensations," 354, 355, 369
  an inchoate fear response, 352–53, 354, 355–56
  and sheer vulnerability, 355
  *See also* emotion(s), involuntary nature of
mothers, maladroit, 385. *See also* females, and psychological ignorance
motives, and human morality, 132–33, 186, n. 16
motivation(s), 133, 137, 138, 140–41, 148, 208
  and affectivity, 342, 344
  complexity of, in warriors, 158–60
  to engage in war, 152–53
  to harm and kill, 156–57
movement
  experience of, and language, 252
  as "external" and "internal," 195
  "indicates somatically," 228
  "kinesthetic movement," 196, 197
  as matchpoint, 194
  as motivator or attractor, 250–52
  not sensational, 198–99, 238, n. 34
  our mother tongue and matchpoint, 210, 213, 216, 227–28
  perceptions and feelings of, 198–99
  phenomenological analysis of, 202–3
  qualitative dynamics of, 196–97, 212
  a *sensu communis*, 228, 290

narcissism. *See* the Double, as narcissistic creation
Native American narrative. *See* Nature, gives us options
natural history
  cultural elaborations of, 161, 166
  and national histories, 166–67
  *See also* territory
natural opposition and the male sexual organ, 19–21

natural selection, 36, 94
natural signs, 349–67
  environmental and social responses distinguished, 355
  fear of strangers, 366–67
  smile, 305, 350–52, 353–54
  See also Moro reflex; startle reflex; stranger anxiety
Nature, 67, 122
  as challenge to phenomenology, 232
  control of and domination by Western science, 21–22, 283, n. 19
  death-giving power of, 16
  as evil, 49–51
  and females, 20
  gives us options, 109, 122
  and male/female bodies, 95–97
  and mind, 68–69
  Mother as "wicked old witch," 49–50
  Nature's "values," 47
  *non facit saltus*, 281, n. 3, 300
  timeless plenum of, 318
  the want of absolute perfection in, 311–12
Neandertals, 45, 57, n. 9
neurophenomenology. See embodiment
"niche-stealing," 171–73, 379–80
  distinct from scavenging, 171–72
  and territorialism, 172–73
  See also consistent bipedality; "squat-feeding"; territory
nonhuman animals, 185, n. 5
  differential human evaluations of, 346
nonhuman animal behaviors, 55–56, n. 1
  male badger play and creativity, 399
nonhuman animal societies, 37–38, 57, n. 7

obedience to authority, 130, 135, 158
  and human history, 178
  Milgram's classic experimental study of, 174–78
  and war, 173–74
ontogeny, 137, 179, 211, 213, 265
  and learning to trust, 268–69
  and play, 258
  See also infants, human
Other, Others, Otherness, and difference, 72–73, 343–44
  as undercurrent thematic of death, 72–73

"pacified [human] past," 26–27, 56, n. 4, 105

Paleolithic/Late Paleolithic, 42, 45
pairing, 195, 293
  harmonious, 203
  as problem of *my* body rather than that of *the other*, 195
pan-cultural human realities, 2
  the banality of evil, 137
  pan-cultural similarities and differences, 53
"Parma group," 60–62, n. 18
"Pass on your genes," 58, n. 16, 99
patriarchal values, 49
"patriarchal kingdom of human culture," 49
phallus, power of, 19–21
phenomenology, of feelings underlying human morality, 5. See also fear; fear of death; foundationalist morality
philosophical zoology, 336
phylogeny, 137, 179, 211, 254
physical bodies *as such*, 38–39, 40, 298–99
play, 36, 102, 398–99, 404, 405
  adult perversion of, 242–43
  adultist conceptions of, 257
  "child playing at draughts" and playing with death, 258–59
  child's, the original sport, 257–58
  creativity inherent in, 400
  distinction between competition and, 242, 245, 247
  kinetic markers of, 243, 245, 247
  and learning of vulnerabilities in being a body, 246, 247–49, 252–53
  as motor training or practice for adult behavior, 246, 252
  moral educational value of, 398–401
  motivation to and import of, 247
  of nonhuman animals, 244–45
  from ontogenetic, phylogenetic, and philosophical perspective, 247
  as purposeless and irrational, 246
  rule-*un*governed as opposed to rule-governed games, 258–59
  a sense-making activity, 399
  sociological value of, 401
  See also child's play and fragment from Heraclitus; creativity; locomotor-rotational play; moral education; play sport; rough and tumble play
play sport, 253, 259
  principles of, learned kinetically and not game-specific, 259

playing with death, 258
"policy of humanity," 330–31, 334. *See also* "Churchill effect"
power
   "common power," need for, 24
   conversion of size-is-power equation, 40–41
   cultural, 46–47
   expertise as conferring, 171
   fantasies of, 121
   and immortality ideologies, 46–47
   of the phallus, 19–21
   "situational," 179, 182–83
   size as a biological marker of, 36–40
   and size keep fear of death at bay, 380
   and violence go hand in hand, 392
   *See also* Stanford Prison Experiment
practicing philosophy close-up, 109
priapic totemism, 19. *See also* macho males
primal animation, 289
prisoner's dilemma, 2
psychological egoism, 2
punctuated existence, 36, 70

rationality, 297, 299, 300–302
   of the animate, 297–98
   of comsigns, 295–96, 297–98
   condition of possibility of caring, 302
   constancies of tactile–kinesthetic/affective life and, 294–95
   and cooperation, 333–34
   human, 277
   infant's developing, 290–91
   metaphysical readings of rationality of universe, 309
   rational readings of the universe, 306, 329–30
   and sense-making, 334
   thinking in movement, bedrock of infant's developing, 290–91
   transfers of sense fundamental to, 291
   *See also* sense-making
removed difference. *See* difference removed
responsivity, 215
   distinction between environmental and social, 360
   responding individual and meaning, 211–12
rough and tumble play
   attack and defense movements of, 244, 245
   movement patterns of, 243–44
   play with vulnerabilities of being a body, 248–49
   winners and losers in, 244, 245, 247
   *See also* locomotor-rotational play; play; play sport

science and religion, ideational conjunction of, 58, n. 16
seeing deeply into depths of another, 214, 215
   and seeing deeply into oneself, 234
self-knowledge, 342, 344–45
   mirror notion of the self, 357, 407–8, n. 11
self-movement, 196
   dynamic reality of, 198
   phenomenological analysis of, 198
selfish genes, 2
   immortality ideology of selfish gene theory, 52, 59, n. 16
   reductionism and the moral hook, 338, n. 16
selfishness, 3
   cultural and natural ties of, 4, 14–15
   origins of, 6–8
"semiotic freedom," 218
sensations and perceptions, distinction between, 198–99
sense-making, 194, 208–9, 379, 399
   and being first and foremost a physical body, 299
   challenge to, 400–401
   and cross-modal matchings/transfers of sense, 290–91
   and developing concepts, 323
   double sense of, 209
   and a Heideggerian ontology, 322–23
   in infancy, 288–89, 290
   interanimate, 215–16, 219, 298
   intercorporeal, 291–95, 297, 314–15
   natural history of, 395
   and rationality, 334
   and the rationality of caring, 300
   *sine qua non* of the concept of death, 322
   spontaneous, 209–10
   and transfers of sense, 288–95
   and wonder, 400
   *See also* comsigns
sexual selection, 36, 58, n. 16, 94
sheer physicality and excitement, 141, 142–43, 153, 171

the essential realities of raids and
    battles, 142
  of fighting and killing, 154–55
  and motivation of warriors, 157–58
  *See also* male–male competition; wanton
    brutality; warriors
size. *See* power; see also *more*
smile. *See* natural signs, smile
"smiling response," 350–52, 353
"sphere of ownness," 194, 198, 199, 289
  and feelings, 198
"squat-feeding," 167–69
  and build-up of technological prowess,
    171
  *See also* consistent bipedality; "niche-
    stealing"
societies
  nonhuman, egalitarian, hunter-gath-
    erer, hierarchical, 42–44
  "as structures of immortality power,"
    46
soul, 75
  immortality of, 65–67, 69
  and "primitive monism," 83–84
  and psychology, 75–76
  soul-belief, 64–65, 75–76
  *See also* mind, as non-material
    substance; mind, non-temporal
    nature of
sperm competition, 97–99, 108, 122. *See
  also* male–male competition
Stanford Prison Experiment, 179–84
  and aggression, 189, n. 34
  an all-male experiment, 181
startle reflex, 354–55, 361–62, 364, 366, 372
  in chimpanzees, 359
  corporeally distinct from Moro reflex,
    353, 355
  developmental concordance with Moro
    reflex, 355–56
  as disruption in "flow of sensations,"
    354, 355, 360
  and vulnerability, 356, 357, 359
  *See also* emotion(s), involuntary nature
    of; natural signs
stranger anxiety
  as an attunement to one's own vulnera-
    bility, 365
  classic description and temporal
    contours of, 360–61, 362
  disruption in "flow of sensations," 363
  and social selectivity, 362–63, 282–83, n.
    13

and xenophobia, 362, 363–64
  *See also* fear; emotion(s); natural signs
strangers. *See* xenophobia
style (and conduct), 194, 199
subjective phenomena, 53
  as methodological problem, 54–55,
    61–62, n. 18
  necessity of recognizing, 54
  and neurological happenings in primate
    brains, 60, n. 18
sympathy, 3
  based on resemblance and contiguity, 7,
    13–14
  cultural and natural ties of, 13–15
  origins of, 6–8
  *See also* Hume

tactile–kinesthetic/affective experience,
    292–3
  and sensory–kinetic descriptive anal-
    yses, 294
tactile–kinesthetic invariants, 349
  and transfers of sense, 286–7
  *See also* affect attunement; dynamic
    congruency; kinetic dynamics
territory, 161–62
  centrality of in human affairs, 165
  evolutionary nature of territorialism,
    165
  "territorial imperative," 161, 165–66
  territorial interpretation of the Jew,
    165–66
  territorial practices of monkeys and
    apes, 163–65
  *See also* amity/enmity code; xenophobia
terror. *See* fear
the Double (*Der Doppelgänger*), 64, 81–86
  and Derridean texts, 81, 84–86, 90, n. 18
  and irrational aspects of the self, 86–87
  and literature, 81, 82–83, 86–87
  as narcissistic creation, 83–84
  and present-day science, 90, n. 16
  and self-love ("primitive monism"),
    83–84, 85
  and the shadow, 83
  and technology, 409, n. 26
  as text in relation to author, 82
  *See also* immortality ideologies, and "the
    sign"
thinking in movement, 217
  and infancy, 217–18, 290–91
  *See also* movement; rationality

time and draughts-playing child. *See* child's play and fragment from Heraclitus
transcendental clue(s), 193–95, 231–32
transfers of sense, and cross-modal matchings, 290–91. *See also* sense-making; thinking in movement
trust, 36
  affective experiences in learning to, 266–67
  affective foundations of, 281
  affective vulnerability of, 280
  continuity in maturational development of trust, 268–70
  and distrust, 267, 271, 275, 279–80, 283, n. 18
  and familiarity, 270, 271, 272, 275
  and fear, 266, 275–78, 280
  lack of study of, 266
  learning to, 265, 266–67
  motivation to, 271–72
  move from psychological to sociological understanding of, 269–71
  ontogenetic basis of learning to, 266
  "readiness to," 271, 272–75
  as "reduction of complexity," 271, 272, 277, 279
  and strangers, 270–71, 279
  *See also* intersubjectivity; uncertainty; xenophobia
turn-taking, 210–11, 281
twenty-first century technology, 408, nn. 23–24, 410, n. 30, 410–11, n. 31
  and cloning, gene therapy, and virtual realities, 21
  and human disease, 22

uncertainty, 270, 271–72, 274–76, 277, 278, 280
  existential meaning of, 265
unevenly valorized binary oppositions, 47, 49, 50, 52, 53–54
  cultural artifacts and Nature, 20
  emblematic of the fear of death, 139
  and Freud's essay, 19–21
  as indicative of felt safety/danger, 16
  *See also* binary oppositions

violence, 109, 110, 119, 121, 143
  chimpanzee, 139–40
virtual realities. *See* twenty-first century technology
vitality affects, 227–28

vulnerability/vulnerabilities, 36, 43, 55
  of being a body, 246, 299
  built-in of animate creatures in face of unknown, 359
  learning of, 247–49
  nonlinguistic awareness and corporeal concepts of, 247
  in relation to others, 265
  rules and, 259
  and sense-makings, 299
  and size and power, 39–40
  and trust, risk-taking, 259
  *See also* physical bodies *as such*; play, and learning of vulnerabilities in being a body

wanton brutality, physical disposition toward, 140. *See also* male–male competition; sheer physicality and excitement; violence; war; warriors
war, 143–44, 147–48, 387–88
  an attitudinal disposition toward, 23–24
  as a beastly practice, 128
  at the center of life and death, 144
  as cultural elaboration of what is evolutionarily given, 24, 105, 128
  a cultural form of human male–male competition, 108
  a cultural function, 104–5
  Dani ritual and secular warfare, 141–51, 149, 152
  detailed causes and aspects of, 124, n. 9
  as an emotional outlet, 152–53
  and evolutionary history, 24
  as giving meaning to one's life, 129
  a "hero-game," 111
  "is hell," 391
  and "militant enthusiasm," 402–5
  "moral equivalent of," 401–3, 404–5
  mythical and sensory perceptions of, 152–53
  as non-agonistic combat, 104
  and nonhuman primate aggressive interactions, 260–61, n. 2
  and territoriality, 166–67
  victories and grievances of, passed on generationally, 153–54
  war games, 143
  *See also agon*; male–male competition; moral education, the only genuine equivalent to war; violence

454   Index of Terms

warrior(s), 24, 26, 27, 28, 114
　cultural/pan-cultural cultivation of, 28, 121, 141, 143, 144
　as keeper of "the keys of the kingdom," 28
　and the mythic hero, 27, 148
　as public heroes, 153
　"plumed" as a bird, 150
　and sheer physicality and excitement, 141
　*See also* Hero/Heroics; heroic honing of males; male–male competition; war
weaponry, 128
　weapons as distinct from tools, 169
　*See also* consistent bipedality; "squat-feeding," and build up of technological prowess
Western science (present-day), 380, 394
　mobilizing humans toward expectation of *more*, 380
　*See also* "biological alchemy"; twenty-first-century technology
wonder, 400. *See also* sense-making, and
worms, 300, 395. *See also* interconnectedness of Nature, and worms

xenophobia, 166, 326, 363–64, 365, 366, 379, 395
　and predatory intolerance of competitors, 171
　*See also* stranger anxiety; trust

www.ingramcontent.com/pod-product-compliance
Lightning Source LLC
Chambersburg PA
CBHW020300010526
44108CB00037B/181